DISCARD

An

Anthology

of

German Literature

800 - 1750

PRENTICE-HALL GERMAN SERIES

Karl S. Weimar, Editor

edited by

PETER DEMETZ, *Yale University*

and

W. T. H. JACKSON, *Columbia University*

An

𝔄nthology

of

𝔊erman 𝔏iterature

800 ~ 1750

PRENTICE-HALL, INC. *Englewood Cliffs, New Jersey*

Prentice-Hall International, Inc. *London*
Prentice-Hall of Australia, Pty. Ltd., *Sydney*
Prentice-Hall of Canada, Ltd., *Toronto*
Prentice-Hall of India Private Ltd., *New Delhi*
Prentice-Hall of Japan, Inc., *Tokyo*

Library of Congress Card No.: 68-10014

Current printing (last digit)

10   9   8   7   6   5   4   3   2   1

Printed in the United States of America

Preface

The present anthology is planned to introduce students to German literature from c. 800, or the first extant Old High German text, to the middle of the eighteenth century when the inherited literary norms dissolved and were replaced by forms of art and thought later predominant in romanticism, nationalism, and a literature of highly personal expression.

The editors intend to strike a useful compromise between historical documentation and aesthetic relevance and hope to combine texts representative of successive stages of historical developments with those of intrinsic interest. Confronted with the literary treasures of almost a thousand years, they have decided to present a few groups of meaningful, related, and compact units which may serve prolonged and detailed class discussion, rather than many disconnected excerpts.

The editors have seen little reason either to continue the *Kulturpropaganda* explicitly or implicitly inherent in many collections coming from German-speaking countries or to isolate the most excellent achievements of *German* literature. Their aim is different: German developments are viewed as part of a growing world literature, and German literature is presented with a constant awareness of the shifts of European sensibility and imagination.

The excerpts (with the exception of those coming from the mid-eighteenth century) are "translations" or "modernizations" of the texts which, in their original form, would cause considerable difficulties to American readers; only on occasion have the editors thought it best to present an original text with appropriate glossing. But to "translate" or "modernize" older texts does not imply new procedures; in German-speaking countries also, educated readers enjoy older poetry in modernized versions and leave the finer philological points of original spelling, etc., to the specialist. Thus it happens that our selections are derived from a variety of sources; for example, the *Iwein* appears in a nineteenth-century verse translation while the *Gregorius* is in an original modern prose version. Similarly, all Baroque selections have been "modernized" (some for the first time here) and come from a variety of editions, old and more recent: the poem by Quirinus Kuhlmann, for example, comes from the first printing of his *Kühlpsalter,* to be found in the Baroque collection at the Beinecke Rare Book and Manuscript Library (Yale University); the selections from *Landstörzerin Courage* of von Grimmelshausen, from a recent useful edition of the text ([East]-Berlin, 1961). Our first aim has been to present a readable text to be enjoyed by students who, for the first time in their academic career, are to encounter the German literary tradition; and although we are aware of the many important questions which we had to neglect, we do hope to serve the student as well as the cause of German studies by putting a regard for the attractive and the occasionally exciting above the inevitable concern with the philological original.

The first part of the anthology is necessarily somewhat different from the second inasmuch as most of its selections are from long narrative poems. In order to enable the reader to follow the plot and to understand the full scope of the work, short summaries have been inserted to connect the German selections. A few lyric poems have been left in the original Middle High German, with appropriate glossing. Considerations of sentence rhythm made it important to keep the original form of the selection from the *Ackermann aus Böhmen*; and here too the difficult words and expressions have been footnoted.

Where nineteenth-century translations have been used, the translation and occasionally other, more recent versions are listed in the Bibliography. Where no translator is mentioned, it may be assumed that the editor of the first part of the anthology is responsible. He would like to express his gratitude to his wife, Erika, and son, Thomas, for long stretches of typing.

The editor of the latter part of the present anthology (Reformation/Baroque/ Enlightenment) would like to convey his gratitude to many publishers (including Reclam, Propyläen, and the Carl Hanser Verlag), colleagues, and students who have made his task less burdensome in many ways. Heinz S. Bluhm and Jeffrey L. Sammons have been extremely generous with bibliographical advice; the late Curt von Faber du Faur, unforgettable teacher and connoisseur of the arts, and Professor Werner Vordtriede (Munich) have offered welcome advice concerning the intractable Kuhlmann excerpt; Gisela Brude, Volker Schmeissner, Cyrus Hamlin, Janis Gellinek, and, above all, Heidi von Löffelholz have loyally helped with interpreting mythological allusions and annotating *realia*. Last but not least I should like to thank Miss Mary Kitson (London) and Mrs. Margaret Broekhuysen who have demonstrated unusual patience in typing and careful checking, and I would feel amply rewarded if future readers would equal their meticulous dedication and literary interest.

P. D.

W. T. H. J.

Table of Contents

The Medieval Period 1

INTRODUCTION 3

HILDEBRANDSLIED 19

INTRODUCTION 19

Hildebrandslied 21

NINTH-CENTURY GOSPEL HARMONIES 25

INTRODUCTION 25

Heliand 27

Otfried's Evangelienbuch 30

LUDWIGSLIED 35

INTRODUCTION 35

Ludwigslied 37

HARTMANN VON AUE 39

INTRODUCTION 39

Iwein 41

Gregorius 49

WOLFRAM VON ESCHENBACH 55

INTRODUCTION 55

Parzival 59

GOTTFRIED VON STRASSBURG 73

INTRODUCTION 73

Tristan und Isot 75

EARLY LYRIC POETRY 85

INTRODUCTION 85

Friedrich von Hausen 89
Kreuzlied 89
Heinrich von Morungen 89
Liebesleiden 89
Spiegel der Liebe 90
Süsse Töterin 90
Tagelied mit Variationen 91

WALTHER VON DER VOGELWEIDE 93

INTRODUCTION 93

Wahlstreit 97
An die Welt 98
Unter Krone 98
Der Leitstern 98
Saladin und Richard 99
Der Hof zu Eisenach 99
Kirchensammlungen 99
Milde und Länge 100
Das Reichslehen 100
Die Traumdeuterin 101
Tanzweiſe 101
Unter der Linde 102
Frühling und Frauen 103
Güte gibt Tugend 103
Maienwonne 104
Anerlässlichkeit der Gegenliebe 104
Auf Reinmar des Alten Tod 105
Heimkehr 105

NEIDHART VON REUENTHAL 107

INTRODUCTION 107

Minneparodie 109
Sommerlied 109

NIBELUNGENLIED   111

INTRODUCTION   111

Nibelungenlied   115

KONRAD VON WÜRZBURG   137

INTRODUCTION   137

Herzmaere   139

WERNHER DER GARTENAERE   141

INTRODUCTION   141

Meier Helmbrecht   143

JOHANNES VON TEPL   149

INTRODUCTION   149

Ackermann aus Böhmen   151

DONAUESCHINGER PASSION PLAY   157

INTRODUCTION   157

The Judas Scenes   159

REINEKE FUCHS   161

INTRODUCTION   161

Reineke Fuchs   163

The Age of the Reformation   167

INTRODUCTION   169

MARTIN LUTHER   173

INTRODUCTION   173

Aus tiefer Not (Der 130. Psalm)   175
Ein' feste Burg (Der 46. Psalm)   175
Ein Sendbrief vom Dolmetschen   176
Aus dem Neuen Testament   180

DAS VOLKSBUCH VON DOCTOR FAUSTUS 183

INTRODUCTION 183

Doctor Faustus 185

HANS SACHS 197

INTRODUCTION 197

Der Bauer im Fegefeuer 199

𝕿he Age of the Baroque 207

INTRODUCTION 209

ANGELUS SILESIUS 217

INTRODUCTION 217

Der cherubinische Wandersmann 219

ANDREAS GRYPHIUS 223

INTRODUCTION 223

Tränen des Vaterlandes 225
Es ist alles eitel 225
Menschliches Elende 225
Abend 226
Grösse und Elend der Sprache 226
Grabschrift Marianae Gryphiae, seines Brudern Pauli Töchterlein 227
Über Nicolai Copernici Bild 227
Grabschrift, die er ihm selbst in tödlicher Leibesschwachheit aufgesetzet 227
Über den Untergang der Stadt Freistadt 227
Gott verlässt uns nicht 229
Grossmütiger Rechtsgelehrter, oder Sterbender Papinianus 230

HANS CHRISTOFFEL VON GRIMMELSHAUSEN 247

INTRODUCTION 247

Die Landstörtzerin Courasche 249

PAUL FLEMING 261

INTRODUCTION 261

Gedanken über der Zeit 263

Widerstreit in sich selbst 263

Was bin ich doch bemüht 263

Wie er wolle geküsset sein 264

Nachwehen 264

Bekenntnis 265

An sich 265

Er verwundert sich seiner Glückseligkeit 265

Paul Flemings Grabschrift 266

CHRISTIAN HOFMANN
VON HOFMANNSWALDAU 267

INTRODUCTION 267

Auf den Mund 269

Vergänglichkeit der Schönheit 269

*An Amaranthen, über sein an sie geschicktes
Bildnis* 269

Grabschrift General Wallensteins 270

*Streit der schwarzen Augen, roten Lippen
und weissen Brüste* 271

DANIEL CASPER VON LOHENSTEIN 275

INTRODUCTION 275

Venus **277**

QUIRINUS KUHLMANN 281

INTRODUCTION 281

Der 4 (*64*) Kühlpsalm **283**

The Age of Enlightenment 291

INTRODUCTION 293

JOHANN CHRISTOPH GOTTSCHED 301

INTRODUCTION 301

Versuch einer critischen Dichtkunst:
Von dem Charaktere eines Poeten 305

J. J. BODMER AND J. J. BREITINGER 315

INTRODUCTION 315

Von dem Wunderbaren und dem
Wahrscheinlichen 317

ANACREONTIC POETRY 321

INTRODUCTION 321

Friedrich von Hagedorn 323
An die Dichtkunst 323
Der Wunsch 323
Johann Wilhelm Ludwig Gleim 323
Anakreon 323
Geschäfte 323
Gotthold Ephraim Lessing 324
Die Namen 324
Lob der Faulheit 324
Johann Peter Uz 324
Die Nacht 324

FRIEDRICH GOTTLIEB KLOPSTOCK 325

INTRODUCTION 325

Der Zürchersee 327
Die Genesung 328
Weihtrunk an die toten Freunde 329
An Gott 329

GOTTHOLD EPHRAIM LESSING 333

INTRODUCTION 333

Aus den Briefen, die neuste Literatur
betreffend 337
Aus den Abhandlungen von dem weinerlichen oder
rührenden Lustspiele 338
Philotas 342

Selected Bibliography 355

An

Anthology

of

German Literature

800 - 1750

The Medieval Period

It can be said that the literature of any nation begins with its first extant work; for Germany this is the ninth century to which the earliest manuscripts of works written in German belong. Yet we cannot ignore the fact that a great many works, some of them of a high degree of literary skill, were circulating in oral form before this time. We can be sure of this because there exist in other languages, notably Old English and Old Norse, works that clearly belong to a common Germanic tradition. The events they recount, so far as they are historical, took place during the *Völkerwanderungen* of the fifth and sixth centuries, that is, before the Germanic tribes split into the groups we now designate as German, Scandinavian, and Anglo-Saxon. There can be no doubt that these troubled times gave a great impulse to literary creation and that poets of ability were available to give them artistic form. The historical events were interwoven with mythological elements and motifs from other cultures, but there is a great deal of material common to all the Germanic literatures. It was during this period also that there was developed the peculiar poetical form known as *Stabreimdichtung,* whose characteristics are the use of regular alliteration of stressed syllables and a four-beat line, associated with the poetical device of kennings, descriptive periphrases of nouns.

Although we are aware of the existence of this body of poetry and can trace its influence on works that are extant, it is pointless to attempt to reconstruct Germanic works or to set up a "Germanic hero" type, in the sense that such heroes are endowed with qualities not found in other literatures. In fact, the heroes of Germanic works, so far as we can determine, share most of their characteristics with early heroes of many cultures. Nevertheless, there are some important moral and social values which will be considered later.

Medieval literature in Germany is traditionally divided into Old High German, early Middle High German, the classical period of Middle

High German literature, and Later Middle High German literature. The first of these divisions, which covers the period from about 800 to about 1050, is a linguistic rather than a literary division. It actually includes works written in several dialects, and one of the most important poems of the period is the Old Saxon *Heliand*. The second period encompasses the numerous but widely different literary monuments of the late eleventh and early twelfth centuries. The classical period, during which almost all the really important works of medieval German literature were written, extends from about 1170 to 1230. Its cultural and literary characteristics are clearly defined. The long period from 1230 to 1450 produced a great deal of poetry and an increasing amount of prose, but works of value are rare.

Early Influences

Most of the works of the Old High German period that have come down to us are Christian didactic works. Actually, they cannot be considered works of literature but translations of works basic to the conversion of the Germanic tribes, such as forms of creed and confession. More important from the literary point of view are the translations of Gospel harmonies, such as the translation of the Gospel harmony of Tatianus, and those of the harmonies written by the early fathers of the Church. Such works made known the Christian and through it the Latin tradition of learning. They widened the vocabulary of the Germanic languages by direct borrowing or loan translation of technical religious and later philosophical terms and, perhaps more important, they introduced Christian morality and ways of thought. Thus the Old High German period is in one important respect a time of change, of the absorbing of material from a foreign culture. At first the number of people directly affected by these changes was small, for only the monasteries and those connected with them had the opportunity to come into contact with the literary aspects of Christianity. Gradually the new ideas affected a wider circle, but it is unlikely that the effect on the population as a whole was very great.

The older Germanic literature continued to exert a strong force on literature. The clergy not only despised but feared it, and hence its works were seldom written down. But the *scops* or *Spielleute,* the professional performers of poetry, continued to be honored, and the strength of the tradition is shown by the fact that a poem like *Beowulf* could be composed in Christian times and presumably by a Christian author and yet use a pagan form and to a large degree incorporate a pagan spirit. The *Hildebrandslied,* in spite of the linguistic distortions it has undergone in transmission, is the only representative we have of a type that must have been very common—the heroic lay. It tells in a terse and effective style a simple story of conflict of duties, to kinsman and to liege lord, which was one of the staple subjects of national poetry (not only in German). It thus exemplifies one of the most important features of the poetry of this early culture, its effort to influence the conduct of its audience by the representation of the actions of noble ancestors. This function was to continue long after the "heroic" style of poetry had become sophisticated and modified by other influences.

There can be no doubt that the so-called "comitatus" ideal, that is, the bond between liege man and liege lord, remained a powerful influence even after the introduction of Christianity. So did the concept of honor which thought of a man's reputation as his most precious possession and the preservation of this reputation—his honor—as the principal factor determining his conduct. Honor in one form or another is in fact the most important motivating feature in the majority of medieval narrative works. The Christian concept of honor as a reconciliation of a man's conduct with his conscience is not often present in medieval literature, except, of course, in hagiographic works.

It might be expected that we would find traces of Germanic religion and mythology in early German literature, but unless we interpret religion in a very broad sense, this is not so. The "Merseburger Zaubersprüche" name some gods, but they can hardly be called literature. Otherwise we can say only that many of the figures in later works, such as the *Nibelungenlied,* have obvious mythological antecedents, as, for example, the god of light (Siegfried). Yet the connection cannot really be said to have any significance for the interpretation of these works as literature.

Although there is little evidence of their influence on the earliest literature written in German, it may be well to mention here the material derived from Greek romances and from Latin literature other than that of Christian origin. Naturally, the Germanic peoples knew nothing at any period of the Middle Ages of Greek prose romances in the original form. Yet they had access to the Alexander romance through Latin and French translations, and much of the more exotic romance material came to them in orally transmitted stories which were told by wandering performers. Often the names of characters and milieu were changed, but the stories themselves and particularly motifs are clearly recognizable. It is scarcely necessary to note that the influence of such authors as Vergil, Ovid, Statius, and Cicero increased as medieval culture developed, and works once accessible only to the learned few became the property of an increasing literate minority. More important still was the influence of Latin rhetoric. By this we mean not merely the rules of rhetorical composition propounded by the writers of Greece and adapted by such writers as Cicero and Quintilian but the training in what we would now call literary appreciation and style. The schools practiced their students in various types of ornament and in particular in the use of standard treatments of such commonplaces as the ideal landscape, the war of love, female beauty, and heroic battle. E. R. Curtius has given the name *topos* to this kind of formalized commonplace. The use of *topoi*—not merely as descriptive ornament but as themes on which variations could be played—is an important part of medieval literature, more important probably than the direct influence of individual classical authors. Indeed, so far as vernacular literature is concerned, it may well be questioned how far we are able to determine direct influence, since the impact of classical literature came through training in the part of the trivium called rhetoric rather than through the reading of classical authors in their entirety.

Needless to say, this indirect influence also came to German authors through works written in German and French. The works of the twelfth century and later owe a great deal to the writers in French and Provençal. The themes of both epic and lyric poetry and even the details of the stories are largely derived from French models, and the style and treatment, the lyric meters, and the imagery are of Romance origin. These matters will be mentioned in more detail later.

Although the great works of the German Middle Ages are often lacking in specific Christian references, the impact of religion is always present. The Augustinian contrast between the eternal real world and the transitory secular world is as implicit in the Arthurian romance as it is in *The City of God*. Christian concepts of virtue and vice are behind much of what we call the "courtly code," and the highly developed use of allegorization, that is, the interpretation of individual events and actions in terms of general concepts, influenced secular as well as religious works. Secular love can be thought of in the terms of mystical love for God, the pursuit of the Holy Grail in terms of the Christian search for Heaven. It is a mistake to overestimate the formal aspects of Christianity in medieval literature or to think of any works not obviously moral or didactic in tone as departing from normal medieval ways of thinking. But it is equally false to imagine that any work, however secular in conception, could be written without being permeated by the prevailing intellectual climate, which was Christian.

The Old High German Period.

It has already been pointed out that there is little in the Old High German period which can be classed as literature. In this anthology the period is represented by the *Hildebrandslied* and scenes from the *Heliand* and the *Evangelienbuch* of Otfried von Weißenburg. The various creeds, Pater nosters, and confessions are linguistic and cultural but not literary monuments. The "Wessobrunner Gebet" (*c.* 800) does contain some fine descriptions, and the "Muspilli" (early ninth century) has an account of the Day of Judgment that has provided generations of scholars with the opportunity of speculating about its immediate and ultimate origins.

The end of the century is marked by the appearance of some shorter poems of a religious nature, most of which are really vernacular versions of Latin poems, the "Georgslied," "Christus und die Samariterin," and the "Galluslied." Although didactic in purpose, their style is simple and largely narrative. The best of these short poems is the "Ludwigslied," which appears in this anthology.

It is hardly necessary to state that throughout the period in which these German works were being written there was also a flourishing Latin literature of much greater sophistication. Both poetry and prose experienced a revival under Charlemagne and his immediate successors which has sometimes been dignified with the description "Carolingian Renaissance." The term is misleading, for there was little of real moment produced. The most important feature of the period is that it made sure that the classical heritage did not perish and that it made it available to a wider public. During the tenth and early eleventh centuries the impetus to writing in the vernacular seems to have weakened, and little of significance was produced that was not written in Latin. This was at least in part due to the chaotic state of society, which ensured that any literary works produced were written in monasteries or at least by persons close to the church. One or two of the Latin works are significant, not because they were written by Germans but because they very probably incorporated material from native Germanic sources. The *Waltharius,* an account of the escape of Walther of Aquitaine from the court of Attila and his fight with Gunther and Hagen near Worms, belongs in this category. Some scholars have claimed that the poem is little more than a cento of scenes from Vergil and Statius, but this is not true. It is essentially a Germanic poem written in Latin and is of great value in showing that there already existed in western Germany a tradition of a weak King Gunther and a strong and noble Hagen. Unfortunately arguments about its date and authorship (ninth or tenth century; Geraldus or Ekkehard of St. Gallen) have distracted attention from its literary importance. *Ruodlieb,* a fragmentary poem about a young man who finds wisdom and fortune abroad and brings them home, is also from about the mid-tenth century.

The only author who wrote in German during this period who is of any importance is Notker der Deutsche, or Notker Labeo (950–1022). He was a schoolmaster and commentator at St. Gallen whose work is of more significance for the development of the language and for education than for literature.

Early Middle High German

When works in the vernacular start to appear again, they are largely religious but are more original and more enterprising than the Old High German works. They are no longer translations or even adaptations but new works of religious devotion. Certainly they are influenced by current theological and mystical concepts, but they are independent of any direct model. They show the authors searching for ways to use the language to express pathos, exaltation, and fear of the consequences of sin. Such works as Williram's reworking of the *Song of Songs* (*c.* 1060), the "Annolied" (*c.* 1105), which tells of the saintly life of a bishop, Anno of Köln, "Ezzos Lied" (*c.* 1060), a brief account of the history of salvation, and the "Memento mori" (*c.* 1070) are of promise rather than performance. Frau Ava's "Leben Jesu" (*c.* 1120) is much closer to true poetry with its genuine feeling for the Virgin.

We may pass over other minor works to reach some of major importance. The first important influence of French literature is to be seen in the adaptations of two works, the Alexander romance of Alberich de Briançon by Pfaffe Lamprecht (*c.* 1150), of which we possess several versions, and the Roland epic by Pfaffe Konrad (*c.* 1170?). These works are remarkable for their use of essentially secular material for religious didactic purposes and for the somewhat pedestrian way in which the adaptation is handled. Yet they are important, for here for the first time we see those elements of conduct, display, polish, and nobility of character that were later to be associated with the courtly epic. With them German literature may be said to join the mainstream of European literature in the Middle Ages that derived its materials and style largely from classical and French sources. The German contributions remained distinct in their treatment and often produced the best example of a particular type, but they are dependent on Romance impulses.

It is unfortunate that the literature which would have been of greatest interest to students of this early Middle High German period has reached us in a fragmentary form. There were extant at this time a large number of narrative works whose main stress was on action and exotic adventure and whose central theme was very often the winning of a bride for a nobleman against the opposition of her father. Such works are known by the rather misleading term *Spielmannsepos,* because it was believed that they were composed and performed by wandering professional actors who passed them on orally within their own fraternity. There is little doubt that such performers existed, and they may have recited as part of their repertoire the works we call *Spielmannepen*. If they did, the performance must have spread over several days. It is less likely that such men composed them in the rather haphazard fashion just described. The works of this class have a very clear bipartite structure in which the first winning of the bride or the first "quest" goes off smoothly. Then there is a sudden reversal of fortune, and the second quest is much more difficult. The hero comes close to destruction and is saved only by some fortunate intervention. The resemblance to the situations in the Greek romances is probably not accidental, for it seems likely that much of the material was transmitted orally from the works of late classical antiquity.

Oswald, the story of an Anglo-Saxon king's search for a bride, and *Orendel,* a bride-quest that centers around the gray cloak of Christ, both exist only in late medieval versions, although the originals undoubtedly date from the later twelfth century. They both show a mixture of secular adventure and religious enthusiasm. *Salman und Markolf* is a good example of a type of literature in which formal wisdom is shown to be less important than practical common sense. The bride in this story is not truly faithful; for this she is punished. Two other works also exist only in later versions. There are fragments of *Herzog Ernst* dating to the period about 1170. It is an adventure story about characters of the Ottonian period, but the history is extremely confused, and the interest centers rather on tales reminiscent of the *Arabian Nights.* Much the same can be said of *Graf Rudolf* (before 1173). Both owe much to the "revolted barons" cycle of the French *chansons de geste.* The best work of this type by far is *König Rother.* It also is a bridequest poem and stresses adventure; it has great vigor and humor, and the author knows how to keep his story moving.

In addition to the works mentioned, we know of the existence of several Germanic poems, which unfortunately have not come down to us: an early *Nibelungenlied,* a *Waltharilied,* and early Dietrich poems. There was also some versified history in the *Kaiserchronik* (*c.* 1150), which gives a history of the Empire from Julius Caesar to Konrad III, with special emphasis on its conversion to Christianity under Constantine.

The Classical Period

The period from about 1170 to 1230 was one of the most productive in the whole history of German literature. The rule of the Hohenstaufen, the impetus of the crusading idea, relative prosperity and tranquillity, and an interest in secular literature combined with cultural influences from abroad to produce a climate extremely favorable to literature. Most important of all, there appeared several writers of a stature that was not to be equaled for several hundred years. It is no exaggeration to say that for this short time German literature dominated the European scene.

Two literary genres are of outstanding importance, the romance and the lyric, both of which owe their form and much of their content to

French influence. The period also saw the appearance of the *Nibelungenlied* and the *Gudrun,* the finest examples of the *Volksepos,* or national epic. It is usual in German literary histories to call the romance "das höfische Epos," since its background, attitudes, stories, and ethic are dependent on French models which influenced the aristocratic members of society, in contradistinction to the "popular" *Volksepos.* The distinction is not quite so valid as appears at first sight, but it is well established and will be observed in the present discussion. It may be remarked that the term "romance" is derived from Romance languages, since the earliest romances were all thought of as French in inspiration.

The term "höfisch," or "courtly," needs definition. It was used during the Middle Ages to designate an attitude and a type of behavior conditioned by training and upbringing. Many attempts have been made to show that there was actually a code of courtly behavior in the sense that there can be a philosophical system. Gustav Ehrismann sought to demonstrate that the knightly code was based on moral philosophy derived from Aristotle and transmitted into German literature through the translation into verse by Wernher von Elmendorf (*c.* 1170–80) of the *Moralium dogma philosophorum.* The Latin work, ascribed without valid reasons to Guillaume de Conches, is a collection of moral sayings from numerous ancient authors, and E. R. Curtius is probably right in his contention that it could not have formed the basis for a courtly code.

There is a real question whether such a code actually existed. The twelfth century certainly sought higher standards of morality among laymen and, among the upper classes, higher standards of social behavior. It is certainly possible to point to certain qualities that were regarded as essential for courtly conduct—generosity (*milte*), loyalty (*triuwe*), courage (*tapferheit*), good bearing (*zuht*), self-restraint (*maze*). Yet most of these qualities would have been expected of a hero in the Norse *Edda* or the Anglo-Saxon *Beowulf.* The courtly knight's concern with his honor (*ere*) or reputation would also have been characteristic of earlier works. The difference lies in the stress on what would later be called polite behavior—the ability to converse, to play instruments, to honor women and those weaker than oneself, to show humility to one's superiors and to the aged, and above all in the self-restraint which meant that a man must control sensuality and greed, grant mercy to a defeated enemy, and allow no quality (*tugend*), not even a good one, to dominate his actions. If the knight observed all these, he would reach that state of exaltation that was called *joi* in France and *hoher muot* in Germany.

This state was also characteristic of true love—*hohe Minne,* which the poets of southern France called *fin amors.* The love for a good woman was an important part of the life and courtliness of the hero of the romance. A great deal of nonsense has been written about "courtly love," which is a nineteenth-century term coined by the French critic Gaston

Paris. Much of what has been written is based on the assumption that the information given in the *De amore* or *De arte honesti amandi* ("on loving like a gentleman") of Andreas Capellanus, written about 1180, is directly applicable to all literary works in the courtly tradition. This is not so. The frequently heard statement that courtly love was adulterous, which is based on the statement by Andreas that there could be no true love between married people, is clearly disproved by the fact that Iwein, Erec, and Parzival all find true love in marriage. In fact, in *narrative* works only those in the Tristan and some of those in the Lancelot tradition show adulterous love and how it results in disaster.

In the lyrics the situation is different. The lady is shown as unattainable, and in the works of the classical period we may assume that, as a *frouwe,* she is married, but the fact is nowhere stated, nor is it of importance, for the jealous husband has little or no significance in the best German, as distinct from much of the Provençal lyric. He would be important in the *Tagelied,* or Dawn-song (see p. 91), but few of these were were written in the period we are discussing.

It cannot be said that love was a simple phenomenon in either the lyrics or the romances. After years of research it is still far from clear what influences caused the writers of Provençal lyrics, of narrative poetry in northern France, and their imitators in other countries to present a view of women and love that contrasted so sharply with the attitudes of the medieval church and even with the classical treatment of love between the sexes. From the earliest times, the Church had regarded celibacy as the ideal state and marriage as second best for those who lacked the spiritual discipline necessary for celibacy. A good marriage was characterized by calm companionship rather than by sensual attraction. To this the writers opposed an idea of love that glorified woman as a being not only of beauty but also of nobility of character, spiritual sensitivity, and, unfortunately, complete aloofness. Naturally she is also of noble birth and she has the same position vis-à-vis the poet as a liege lord has to his liege man. He adores her, obeys her every command, never expecting a reward but always hoping that a miracle will occur and that she will accept him as her lover. Yet even this he does not really desire, for if she yielded, the very quality that makes her so desirable would be lost. He is thus in a state suspended between sorrow and joy which cannot be resolved. It should be emphasized that this state is to be found only in lyric poetry. In the great narrative works, the problem is not the winning of the lady's love, which usually proves reasonably easy, but the recognition that love is not a purely sensual emotion. It must be combined with the other duties of a knight's life so that his life is a harmonious whole. When love becomes obsessive, as it does with Lancelot and Tristan, it becomes a destructive force, not only destructive of the lovers but of the very society of which they form a part. They may

obey the rules, the lover may carry out every whim of his mistress, even
when she demands the unreal and ridiculous, their love may in itself
be a fine thing infinitely superior to the passion of normal men and even
to the refined love of the court, but if it is the sole preoccupation of
man and woman, it will destroy them.

The romances are entertainment but, like all medieval literary works,
they are also didactic. For they show us men and women very conscious
of their environment struggling with a difficult problem. How could
a man reconcile his Christian duty to God and his desire to save his immortal soul with his duties to an earthly secular society? St. Augustine
had said that the city of this world is unimportant. Our eyes must be
fixed on the City of God. Subsequent historians had modified this view
without denying its validity. They had seen in the Roman Empire the
divinely ordained body politic that allowed the Christian Church to
develop, and sometimes they had extended this divine purpose to include
their own country, as the French did with Charlemagne. The romances
are concerned with a nonhistorical society and it behaves according
to an ideal set of values. The knights do not fight in wars, and the individual who has been trained at the court leaves it to test his own prowess in a series of independent adventures. He finds these in the un-
civilized areas away from the court, he makes mistakes, undergoes a
complete change that amounts almost to a rebirth at one point in the
narrative (so that the structure of the romance is always bipartite), and
finally recognizes that his life must be a series of purposeful adventures
to help those to whom the enlightenment of the court has not yet come,
even though they may sometimes be members of it. The emphasis is
always on the individual and his struggle to attain a moral and spiritual
state which will enable him to function in the ideal society of which he
forms a part. We have already pointed out that in some of the romances
there is tragic failure to attain this state although the knights who seek
it are in every way as good as those who do attain it—except for the one
important quality of *maze*.

The ideal court of Arthur is Christian only in a formal sense. It has
its own values, and we hear little of a struggle for the soul. It is probably
for this reason that Wolfram and even Chrétien in France rejected it in
their Parzival romances and that later romances place more and more
stress on the Grail story. For whatever its origins, the Grail is a Christian
symbol, a symbol of yearning for a spiritual state the courtly world could
not offer, a higher spiritual ecstasy that surpassed even *hohe Minne*.

Christianity is inevitably present even in the most secular of the romances. The courtly qualities are largely Christian too, although their
application may be different. Gottfried von Straßburg can think of no
better terminology for his love between two *"edele herzen"* than that of
mysticism. The more serious a poet was, the more immediate seemed

to him the problem of reconciling the highest secular achievement with Christianity. From these attempts emerge his famous "three goods": the material, the honorable, and the spiritual. They are clearly a trinity, equally clearly though indirectly connected with the Platonic division of the human being into the body, the spirit, and the soul. Critics have seen here the *utile* (practical life), the *honestum* (honor), and the *summum bonum* (highest spiritual good). Ideas from many sources have affected the treatment of the problem, but it remained difficult for the twelfth-century men of the Hohenstaufen culture to see how they could reconcile their spiritual with their worldly duties. To Walther von der Vogelweide, as to many others, it seemed that the Crusade was the only solution. This seemed especially true when the brightness faded from the courtly scene, and it was ridiculed or used for base purposes.

It was essential for any one who believed in courtly society also to believe in a divine order. The values of courtliness were basically aristocratic, not so much because they believed that noble birth alone would ensure good qualities and make a man fit to be a knight but because their civilization was that of an élite. Knighthood was the highest quality, not royal birth, but the existence of a court, whether it was Arthur's at Camelot, Priam's at Troy, or Alexander's in Greece, was an essential focal point for their culture. They believed in the *ordo mundi*, that everyone was in the place that God thought he should be, and they believed too that while each person fulfilled his function, the secular world could be thought of as part of the divine order. This belief, often called gradualism, offered a partial solution to the question of the purpose of the secular world, for it implied that the secular society in which they lived was as much part of God's purpose as the divine city in Heaven. Such a belief could be held, however, only when the order was stable and not subverted. It is typical that the complaints of Walther are almost all directed against those who would change the order.

The ideal evolved in the twelfth century continued to dominate men's minds for centuries, even though they often understood only its externals —its exaggerated love scenes and its formal jousts and not its spirit. The attitude toward woman has remained the ideal of Western culture to this day.

The individual authors of the classical Middle High German period are discussed in the introductions preceding their selections. Here it will suffice to state that Heinrich von Veldeke, a poet of the northwestern area of Germany was the first to introduce the form of the French romance to Germany in his *Eneit* (finished *c.* 1189). It is an adaptation of the French *Roman d'Enée*. Hartmann von Aue began his work with a brief didactic treatise, the *Büchlein*. About 1180 he wrote a free adaptation of the *Erec* of Chrétien de Troyes, followed by two works with Christian emphasis, the *Gregorius* about 1187–89 and *Der arme Heinrich* about 1195.

His last work, *Iwein,* again taken from Chrétien, is dated about 1200. Hartmann is thus the earliest of the great writers of romance. He is mentioned by his successors with admiration—he affected them profoundly. Wolfram's *Parzival* and Gottfried's *Tristan* were written in the first decade of the thirteenth century. It is impossible to determine exactly which came before the other, and probably the authors knew parts of each other's work before it was completed. Wolfram worked on his *Willehalm* in the second decade of the thirteenth century and on his *Titurel* at approximately the same time.

Other romances appeared during this period. The Troy story was presented by Herbort von Fritzlar (*c.* 1195), the Lancelot story by Ulrich von Zazikhoven (*c.* 1194), although the loosely connected episodes of his *Lanzelet* have little in common with the well-known version of Chrétien de Troyes.

Lyric poetry, as we have seen, shared many of the characteristics of courtliness. Its development is sketched in the introduction to the selections from early lyric poetry.

The somewhat misnamed "popular epic" (*Volksepos*) was affected only tangentially by the rise of the courtly epic. A brief account of its main features is given in the introductions to the *Nibelungenlied.* The only other work of any significance was the *Kudrun,* preserved in the *Ambraser Heldenbuch,* a strange mixture of motifs from various threads of the heroic tradition and of Christian virtues.

Literary activity in the Middle High German classical period was concentrated in the fields of romance and lyric. There is no drama in German extant, very little prose indeed, and hardly any didactic poetry. One special type, the beast epic, is represented by the work of Heinrich der Glichezaere (1180), but his work is a mere anticipation of the developments that were to come later.

Later Medieval Literature

The number of literary works written during the thirteenth, fourteenth, and fifteenth centuries exceeds that of the classical period by far. In addition to works of the kind that had flourished at the end of the twelfth century, there were others, such as the drama, short narrative poems, and didactic works. Although many of these can be considered important, it cannot be said in all honesty that any of the literary works of these centuries is remotely comparable with the great achievements of the classical period. The romances become longer, the stress is shifted from the development of the individual to the more superficial aspects of description and action, and there is an increasing tendency to stress formal religion and morality. Rudolf von Ems (*fl.* 1220–54) is an excellent example of these developments. His output is vast, his themes are largely taken from French literature, and he is a conscientious but utterly uninspired writer. Konrad von Würzburg, part of whose *Herzmaere* appears in this anthology, was roughly a contemporary (*fl.* 1220–87) and presents the same genres with greater talent and technical skill. The Arthurian tradition appears at its best in this period in the *Jüngerer Titurel* (1272) of Albrecht (von Scharfenburg?).

The heroic material is best represented by the Dietrich epics, but the extant versions of these are usually very late reworkings. Although the *Nibelungenlied* continued to be popular, the only original work in the tradition was the *Gedicht vom Hürnen Seyfried,* a thirteenth-century work extant only in a sixteenth-century printed version.

Lyric poetry continued to be composed in the *Minnesang* tradition, and much of it is nothing more than variation on the clichés of this type of poetry. The more interesting poets—Steinmar (*c.* 1250–1300), Gottfried von Neifen (*c.* 1234–55) follow the tradition of Neidhart von Reuenthal in parodying the *Minnesang* by giving it a peasant background. Other poets, particularly Frauenlob (*c.* 1250–1318), stress the didactic and religious elements, whereas Ulrich von Lichtenstein (*fl.* 1250–75) and Johans Hadlaub (*c.* 1300–1340) introduce a biographical element, which, whether accurate or not, makes their poetry more personal. The poetry of Oswald von Wolkenstein (1377–1445) encompasses all these elements, for his poetry is in turn formal, religious, personal, coarse, and realistic. The lyric poetry of the period is never far from didacticism, and several poets wrote both love lyrics and the *Spruch.* Longer didactic works are *Der Renner* of Hugo von Trimberg (*c.* 1300) and Freidank's *Von der Bescheidenheit* (*c.* 1230).

Although the old types of courtly literature continued to be written, the audience for them changed completely. The courts of the great nobles ceased to be the centers of literary culture—their place was taken by the towns. Here the patrons were naturally the wealthy merchants, and their tastes are reflected in the development of literature. They mistrusted the idealism of the courtly literature of the twelfth century and probably did not understand the unofficial code of virtues it celebrated. They felt literature should have an obvious purpose, such as entertainment or moral instruction. Thus they not only caused the existing types to be modified but they also encouraged new types, particularly those concerned with moral behavior. Perhaps the best examples of these are the works of Der Stricker (*c.* 1215) and the moral verse *Novellen.* The latter are short stories with an obvious moral, of which by far the most effective is *Meier Helmbrecht* of Wernher der Gartenaere (before 1282), a large part of which is included in this selection. This work also reflects another new aspect of literature, concern with the peasant. Many of the works in which peasants appear are far from sympathetic to them, and we should beware of thinking in terms of "realism." The yokels are often stereotyped characters in stereotyped situations, but this does not prevent the scenes presented from being very amusing and vividly drawn. The two favorites were the peasant wedding and the drunken brawl, which appear at their most comic in Heinrich Wittenweiler's *Ring* (*c.* 1426).

Much the same can be said about the short poems on the relations between man and wife. Occasionally a virtuous woman is depicted, but far more frequently there are scenes of quarreling, violence, or sheer eroticism. Such works provided a great deal of the source material for Hans Sachs.

As might be expected, the later Middle Ages saw a great advance in prose writing. In theology in particular a distinctive style was developed and the technical vocabulary enlarged by the vernacular works of Meister Eckehard (*c.* 1260–1328), Johannes Tauler (*c.* 1300–1361), and Heinrich Suso (*c* 1293–1366), who virtually created a new means of expression for mystical theology. On a more mundane level, the great poetical works of earlier ages were put into popular prose form. Short stories, such as those about Till Eulenspiegel, were also very popular. By far the most distinguished prose work of the later Middle Ages is the *Ackermann aus Böhmen* (*c.* 1400), a debate between Death and the Ploughman of which a part is given on pp. 153–157.

There is a considerable amount of drama from the later Middle Ages. The Easter plays were originally short scenes at the sepulcher of Christ and were presented before the main altar or in a side chapel. The dialogue was in Latin and the plays' chief interest for the lay audience probably lay in their music. Later the Easter plays were gradually expanded so that they took in not only the Passion, Crucifixion, and Resurrection but often the whole life of Christ and the events of the Old Testament which prefigured it. Comic scenes were also introduced, of which the best known are the Unguentarius, or Quacksalber, scene, in which the selling of the ointment to the three Marys is accompanied by slapstick comedy, and the boasting of the soldiers who guard the sepulcher. Before their full development the plays must have moved outside the church, since it was important for those who produced the plays that they be presented to a large audience.

The Passion plays consist in fact of a series of scenes whose unity is provided by the Christian doctrine they illustrate and which are best understood when interpreted allegorically. They are often called cycles, and the best known are the *Alsfelder* (*c.* 1500), the *Donaueschinger* (*c.* 1500), already mentioned, the *Luzern* (*c.* 1476), and the *Frankfurt* (1493). It should be remembered that the growth of such cycles was a long process of addition and modification. There are also shorter plays on one theme, such as the *Zehnjungfrauspiel* (1321), the only play in which the intervention of the Virgin does not save a sinner, and the play of Theophilus about a priest who sold his soul to the Devil but repented and was saved by the Virgin.

Some of the most effective writing of the later Middle Ages is in Low German. The Theophilus play is extant in a Low German version and there are several other plays in various dialects. By far the best known type, however, is the beast epic, which is concerned with the struggle between the cunning and amoral fox Reynard (Reinhart, Reineke) and the equally amoral but stupid wolf Isengrim. These epics developed entirely in the Low Countries, and versions are extant in Latin, French, Dutch, and German. The various stories in verse, which are known collectively as the *Roman de Renart,* appeared in France in the late twelfth and in the first part of the thirteenth century, but there was a parallel, if less well documented development in Holland which resulted in the production of several very similar versions of the story, in prose at Gouda (1479) and Delft (1485), and in verse at Antwerp in 1487. The earliest Low German version appeared in verse in Lübeck in 1498. It was frequently reprinted. The beast epic was a very effective form of social and political satire and was used by both sides in the Reformation struggle.

Das Hildebrandslied

The *Hildebrandslied* has had a most eventful existence. The sixty-seven-line fragment was found on the flyleaves of a religious work preserved at Cassel. During World War II the leaves were stolen and only one has been recovered —in the United States. It is now back in Kassel. Fortunately the work had been copied, and many facsimiles are available. The poem is important because it is the only known example of what must have been a common type in the Germanic period—the short heroic lay. It should be emphasized that such lays were complete poetic works, transmitted orally, and their style is such that merely tacking them together would never have produced an epic such as *Beowulf* or the *Nibelungenlied*. Although part of the beginning and the last parts of the *Hildebrandslied* are missing, it clearly could not have been much more than a hundred lines long. It tells in this short space the whole story of the meeting between the father Hildebrand and his son Hadubrand, of the father's discovery that he is facing his son, of his attempt to avoid the impending conflict without telling his son who he is, and of the final outcome. The narration is economical and terse. There is relatively little descriptive ornament and no digression.

The story itself is widespread in Indo-European literature, and its dramatic possibilities are fully exploited in the poem. The father can easily recognize his son but he cannot reveal himself without compromising the army for which he is fighting. Loyalty to his lord decrees that he should win even though his opponent is his own son. The son, on the other hand, wishes to defeat the celebrated Hildebrand and will not listen to his father's offer to exchange gifts, that is, call off the battle. Unfortunately it is clear that the version we possess was copied by a scribe who did not understand the dialect in which his original was written, and there is great confusion of dialects within the poem, and some lines are incomprehensible. The efforts to determine the original dialect and the conditions under which the poem was written down have sometimes verged on the ridiculous, but it is now generally believed that the poem as we have it may well have been Langobardic and that its present form may be due to its having been copied at or near Fulda.

The verse form of the poem is *Stabreim*, that is, a line of two distinct halves, each of which has two main stresses. The number of unstressed syllables is indefinite. The sound that begins the syllable on which the third main stress falls is the *Hauptstab* and must appear at the beginning of at least one other stressed syllable in the first half-line. Usually there is triple alliteration of this sort in the full line. Most modern critics, following the theory of Andreas Heusler, believe that each half line contained two full beats of musical time, not counting those unstressed syllables that occur before the first stress. In making this count, a

normal stressed syllable is regarded as a quarter-beat but it may be lengthened
to a half-beat. Unstressed syllables represent either a quarter-beat or an eighth-
beat. The meter of the *Hildebrandslied* is thus the same as that found in the
Anglo-Saxon *Beowulf* and the Old Saxon *Heliand*, but the vicissitudes of transmission have produced considerable irregularities, so that some lines cannot be
scanned according to the rules.

The version here presented attempts to keep the metrical form of the original.
It is taken from Bötticher and Kinzel's *Denkmäler der älteren deutschen Literatur*,
with some modifications. How closely it follows the original may be judged
from a comparison with the following, which corresponds to lines 12 to 25 of
the translation.

> *Hadubrant gimahalta,   Hiltibrantes sunu:*
> *dat sagetun mi   usere liuti,*
> *alte anti frote,   dea erhina warun,*
> *dat Hiltibrant hætti min fater: ih heittu*
>   *Hadubrant.*
> *forn her ostar giweit,   floh her Otachres nid,*
> *hina miti Theotrihhe   enti sinero degano filu.*
> *her furlæt in lante   luttila sitten*
> *prut in bure   barn unwahsan,*
> *arbeo laosa: her raet ostar hina.*
> *sid Detrihhe   darba gistuontun*
> *fateres mines: dat was so friuntlaos man.*
> *her was Otachre   ummet tirri,*
> *degano dechisto   miti Deotrichhe.*
> *her was eo folches at ente: imo was eo fehta ti*
>   *leop . . . .'*

DAS HILDEBRANDSLIED

$\mathfrak{J}$ch hörte sagen   sich heischten zum Kampf
Hildebrand und Hadubrand   unter Heeren zwein,
Des Sohns und des Vaters.[1]   Sie sahn nach der Rüstung,
Die Schlachtgewänder suchten sie,   gürteten die Schwerter an,
5 Die Recken, über die Ringe,   und ritten hin zum Kampfe.
Hildebrand erhob das Wort: er war der hehrere[2] Mann,
Erfahrener und weiser;   zu fragen begann er
Mit wenigen Worten,   wer sein Vater wäre
Der Helden im Volke   „oder welcher Herkunft du seist.
10 Sagst du mir nur einen,   die andern weiß ich mir:
Kind im Königreiche   kund ist mir an Männiglich.“[3]
Hadubrand erhob das Wort,   Hildebrands Erzeugter:
„Das sagten vor Alters   mir unsere Leute,
Alte und weise,   die eher dahin sind,
15 Daß Hildebrand hieße mein Vater;   ich heiße Hadubrand.
Früh zog er gen Osten,   floh vor Otackers Zorn
Hin mit Dietrichen   und seiner Degen viel.[4]

Er ließ im Lande   der Hilfe ledig sitzen
Das Weib in der Wohnung   und unerwachsenen Sohn,
Erblos das Volk,   da er otswärts hintritt. 20
Aber darben mußte   Dietrich seitdem
Meines Vaters,   der freundlose Mann.
Dem Otacker war er   eifrigst erzürnt;
Aber dem Dietrich   der teuerste Degen,
Immer an des Volkes Spitze: fechten war 25 ihm stets zu lieb.
Kund war er allen   kühnen Mannen:
Ich glaube nicht,   daß er noch lebt . . . .“
„Weiß es Allvater   oben im Himmel,
Daß du nie hinfort   mehr fährst zum Kampfe
Mit so gesipptem Mann . . . .“ 30
Da wand er vom Arme   gewundene Ringe
Aus Kaisermünzen,   wie der König sie ihm gab,
Der Herrscher der Heunen: „daß ich mit Huld dirs gebe.“
Hadubrand erhob das Wort,   Hildebrands Erzeugter:
„Mit Geren[5] soll man   Gabe empfahen, 35
Schärfe wider Schärfe.   Du scheinst dir, alter Heune,
Doch allzulose,   lockest mich
Mit deinen Worten,   willst mich mit deinem Speere werfen.
Bist so zum Alter kommen,   daß du immer trogst.
Mir aber sagten   Seefahrende 40
Westlich über den Wendelsee,   hinwegnahm ihn der Krieg.
Tot ist Hildebrand,   Heribrands Erzeugter.“
Hildebrand erhob das Wort,   Heribrands Erzeugter;
„Wohl hör ich das und sehe   an deinem Harnische,
Du habest daheim noch   einen guten 45 Herrn,
Mußtest nicht entrinnen   noch aus diesem Reiche.

---

[1] The formal opening "Ich hörte sagen" is intended to show the historical and hence authentic nature of the happenings. Even though some part of the poem is missing, it probably began with those words.

[2] **hehrer:** older; more distinguished.

[3] Hildebrand's inquiry was normal in a combat of this sort. He wishes to know whether he is fighting a worthy opponent.

[4] Ottaker is probably to be identified with Odoacer or Ottovacar who deposed the last Roman emperor in the West in 476 and made himself viceroy of the Byzantine emperor and ruler of Italy. He became increasingly independent and between 489 and 493 his power was destroyed by Theodorich the Ostrogoth (Dietrich), himself acting as the representative of Byzantium. It will be observed that the situation in the *Hildebrandslied,* and indeed in all the poems in which Dietrich is involved, is the exact reverse of history. Neither Odoacer nor Theodoric was ever connected with Attila, who died in 453. The Ostrogoths were, however, subject to the Huns from 370 to 453, and thus a tradition could have grown up. Theodoric was in fact a hostage at Byzantium as a boy—a far cry from the court of the Huns.

[5] **Ger:** spear.

Die erste Seite des *Hilde-*
brandsliedes. (Nach der Handschrift 8–9. Jahrhundert) *Landes-*
bibliothek Kassel.

Weh nun, waltender Gott,[6]   Wehgeschick
  erfüllt sich!
Ich wallte der Sommer   und Winter
  sechzig,
Daß man stets mich scharte   zu der
  schießenden Volk;
50 Vor keiner der Städte   doch kam ich zu
  sterben;
Nun soll mich mit dem Schwerte   das
  eigne Kind erschlagen,
Mit der Waffe treffen,   oder ich sein
  Töter werden.
Doch magst du nun leichtlich,   wenn dir
  langt die Kraft,
Von so ehrwürdigem Mann   die Rüstung
  gewinnen,
55 Den Raub erbeuten,   hast du irgend
  Recht dazu.

Denn der sei doch der ärgste   der Ostleute,
Der dir den Kampf nun weigre   nun dich
  so wohl des lüstet.
In handgemeiner Schlacht   entscheide
  die Begegnung,
Wer von uns heute   die Harnische
  räumen müsse,
Oder dieser Brünnen[7]   beider walten." 60
Da ließen sie zum Ersten   die Eschen
  schmettern
In scharfen Schauern, daß   es in den
  Schilden stand;
Dann stapften zusammen   die Steinrand-
  klaren,[8]
Hieben harmlich   die hellen Schilde,
Bis ihnen die Linden   nicht mehr langten, 65
Zermalmt mit den Waffen . . . .

---

[6] **Waltender Gott** (*OHG* **waltant got**): "powerful god," which is certainly not, as some critics think, a proof of Christian influence.

[7] **Brünnen**: body armor.

[8] **Steinrandklaren** (*OHG* **stainbort**): shields with precious stones on the edges(?).

Ninth-Century Gospel Harmonies

The *Diatessaron,* or Gospel harmony, of Tatianus was probably the literary form in which the life of Christ was best known to the men of the ninth century, and it is not surprising, therefore, that there were several versions of it: a prose rendering in Old High German and two epics, the Old Saxon *Heliand*, and the High German *Evangelienbuch* of Otfried of Weißenburg. The date of the *Heliand* is disputed but it can hardly be far removed from 850. Otfried wrote his poem between 863 and 871. Although both works are epics on the life of Christ, based on the same source material, they differ fundamentally in form and treatment. The *Heliand* is written in the Germanic epic *Stabreimdichtung* tradition and owes a great deal to the Anglo-Saxon epics. Its style and vocabulary are those of heroic poetry, and Christ is described in the terms appropriate to such poetry. This has led many critics to suppose that the poem is a "Germanization" of the life of Christ, intended to win over the recently converted tribes to accepting Christ as a hero. Such an interpretation is probably inaccurate, because the poet simply wrote in his customary style, and the epithets he used to describe Christ belong to this style. The work follows its source closely, its attitudes and doctrine are altogether orthodox. It is not unlikely that it was a kind of *tour de force,* an exercise to show that the life of Christ could be expressed in terms of heroic poetry.

Otfried's work is easier to interpret. He was a monk, writing for a learned audience, and his work shows this. His poem, written in the South Rhenish Franconian dialect, is longer than the *Heliand* (roughly 8000 lines against 7000) because he inserts in his narrative interpretations of the events of the life of Christ which he has taken from the standard commentaries. Such interpretations are introduced by the words *mystice* (allegorically), *moraliter* (morally, interpreted according to conduct), *spiritualiter* (spiritually, interpreted according to Christian doctrine). It is sometimes difficult to see the distinction between these categories. The work is written in rhymed couplets which Otfried imitated from hymns. He was quite possibly the first to use this type of poetry in German. Although his attempts at rhyme are often not much better than assonance, his skill improves as the work proceeds. As a narrative poem the *Evangelienbuch* is not as successful as the *Heliand*, but it is a pioneering effort, whereas the *Heliand* is a late representative of a style of poetry that was dying out.

In order to show the different approaches of the two poets, we give here the same incident, the coming of the Magi to the birthplace of Christ. Otfried's prologue is of interest in that it shows his ambition for an independent German culture. The translation of the *Heliand* by K. Simrock reproduces the alliteration and four-stressed line of the original.

Bötticher and Kinzel's translation of Otfried shows the internal rhyme and four-beat line of the original. The rhymes of the translation are in fact better and more consistent than those of Otfried.

HELIAND

Die Mär erscholl
In der Welt nicht weiter,   als sein Wille ging,
Des Himmelsherrn Gedanke.   Ob heilige Männer schon
Den Christ erkannten,   doch ward es am Königshof
5 Nicht den Mannen gemeldet,   die im Gemüte
Ihm Huld nicht hegten.   Verhohlen blieb es ihnen
Mit Worten und Werken,   bis westwärts von Osten her
Hochbegabte   gegangen kamen,
Schneller Degen[1]   drein zu dem Volke
10 Auf langem Wege   über das Land dahin.
Sie folgten glänzendem Zeichen   und suchten Gottes Kind
Mit lauterm Herzen,   hinzuknien vor ihm,
Seine Jüngerschaft bekennend.   Sie trieb Gottes Kraft
Dahin, wo sie Herodes,   den Herrscher, fanden
15 In seinem Saale sitzen,   auf Arges sinnend,
Hochmütig bei den Mannen,   den Mordgierigen Mann.
Sie grüßten ihn höflich,   wie dem Herrscher gebührte,
In seinem Saal nach Sitte.   Da fragte er sie schnell,
Welche Absicht   sie nach außen brächte,
20 Die Wege zu wandern.   „Führt ihr gewunden Gold
Zur Gabe der Gönner,[2]   zu dem ihr gegangen kommt,
Gefahren zu Fuße?   Von ferne kommt ihr doch,
Andrer Völker Fürsten: denn vornehm scheint ihr geboren,
Gutem Stamm entsprossen;   nie kamen uns noch solche

Boten von andern Völkern,   seit ich hier 25 gewalte
Dieses weiten Reichs.   Drum sagt mir in Wahrheit
Vor diesen Leuten,   warum ihr zu diesem Lande kamt."
Da gaben ihm zur Antwort   die östlichen Männer,
Weise von Worten: „Der Wahrheit nach mögen wir
Unser Gewerbe   dir wohl berichten,   30
Frei bekennen   warum wir gefahren kommen
Von Osten der Erde.   Edle lebten einst,
Seligsprechende,   die uns Segen viel,
Hilfe verhießen   vom Himmelskönig
Mit wahren Worten.   Ein Wissender 35 darunter,
Erfahren und weise,   war in früher Zeit
Unser Ahn im Osten;   kein anderer seitdem
War der Sprachen so kündig: er kannte Gottes Wort,
Denn verliehen hat ihm   der Leute Herr,
Daß er von der Erde   aufwärts vernahm 40
Des Waltenden Wort: drum war das Wissen groß
In des Degens Gedanken.   Dann, als er sollte
Diese Wohnungen räumen,   der Verwandten Genossenschaft,
Der Leute Traum verlassen,   andres Licht zu suchen,
Und nun die Jünger   sich näher gehen 45 hieß,
Die Erbwarte   und die Angehörigen:
Da sagte er für sicher,   was seither geschah
Und ward in dieser Welt.   Ein weiser König,
Sagte der Seher,   sollte kommen
Ruhmvoll und mächtig   zu diesem 50 Mittelkreis,
Von bester Geburt,   aus Gott geboren:
Der werde walten   in dieser Welt
Bis zu ewigen Tagen   der Erd und des Himmels
Und am selben Tage,   wo ihn, den Seligen,
An diesem Mittelkreis   die Mutter 55 gebäre,
Da sollte scheinen,   sagt' er, von Osten her
Ein heller Himmelsstern,   wie wir hier nicht sahen

---

[1] The three wise men would hardly have been "schnelle Degen." It is a specific example of the frequent use of the clichés of heroic poetry.
[2] One of the commonest gifts in heroic poetry was that of golden bracelets.

Zwischen Erd und Himmel   noch irgend anderswo
Solch Kind noch solch Zeichen.   Es zu verehren sollten dann
60 Dort aus dem Volke   drei Männer fahren:
Im Augenblick, da sie im Osten   aufsteigen sähen
Das Gotteszeichen,   sollten sie gegürtet sein
Und wir ihm dann folgen,   wie es fürder ginge
Westlich über die Welt.   Das ist nun wahr geworden,
65 Durch Gottes Kraft gekommen.   Der König ist geboren
Stark und schön: wir sahn sein Zeichen scheinen
Hell unter den Himmelssternen,   wie der Herr uns selber,
Der Mächtige, melden ließ.   Jeden Morgen sahen wir
Des Sternes Strahlenglanz: wir folgten ihm stets
70 Auf waldigen Wegen;   unser Wunsch war nur,
Daß wir ihn selber sähen,   ihn zu suchen wüßten,
Den König, in diesem Kaisertum.   Nun künd' uns, wo das Kind entsproß."
Da ward dem Herodes   inwendig der Brust
Das Herz voll Harm,   ihm wallte heiß der Mut,
75 Die Seele mit Sorgen,   da er sagen hörte,
Daß er ein Oberhaupt   sollt über sich haben,
Einen kräftigern König,   von edler Abkunft,
Einen seligern unter dem Gesinde.   Versammeln hieß er da,
Was weiser Männer   wär in Jerusalem,
80 Die klügsten und kundigsten   Kenner in Sprachen,
Die in der Brust auch bärgen   der heiligen Bücher
Wahrhaftes Wissen.   Zu diesen gewendet fragte
Nun aufs genauste   der neidherzge Mann,
Der König des Landes,   wo Christ geboren
85 Werden sollte   im Weltreiche,
Der beste Friedenswart.   Der Frage antworten

Die Weisen nach Wahrheit: sie wüßten, er werde
In Bethlem geboren: „so ist in den Büchern
Weislich verzeichnet,   wie die Wahrsager
Durch Gottes Kraft,   begabte Männer,   90
Hochweise Leute,   weiland sprachen,
In Bethlehem solle   der Burgen Hirte,
Der liebe Landeswart   ans Licht gelangen,
Der reiche Berater,   der da richten soll
Über der Juden Volk   und seine Gabe   95 teilen
Mild über den Mittelkreis   der Menge der Völker."
Nun erfuhr ich, daß sofort   der falsche König
Der Wahrsager Worte   den Wallern sagte,
Die dahin aus der Heimat   als Herolde waren
So fernher gefahren.   Er fragte sie dann,   100
Wann sie im Ostenland   zuerst gesehen
Den Königsstern strahlen,   die Standarte leuchten
So hell am Himmel.   Nichts hehlen wollten sie,
Gaben redlich Bericht.   Da hieß er sie reisen,
Bis sie alles aufgefunden,   ihrem Auftrag   105 gemäß,
Von des Kindes Kunst.   Der König gebot auch
Und erheischt' es hart,   der Herrscher der Juden,
Den weisen Männern,   eh sie von Westen führen,
Ihm kundzutun,   wo er den König sollte
In seinem Sitze suchen: mit dem Gesinde   110 dächt er dann
Den Gebornen anzubeten.   Alsbald ertöten wollt er ihn
Mit der Waffen Schärfe.   Aber der waltende Gott
Dachte anders zu dem Ding   und mochte mehr gedenken
Und leisten an diesem Licht: das blieb noch lang ersichtlich,
Gottes Kraft ward kund.   115
              Strahlend klommen die Zeichen
Weiter zwischen Wolken.   Die Weisen waren
Fertig zu ihrer Fahrt: da fuhren sie hin sofort,

Die Botschaft zu vollbringen,   den
Geborenen Gottes
120 Selber aufzusuchen.   Des Gesindes war
nicht mehr,
Die dreie nur; der Dinge   wußten sie
doch Bescheid,
Die gottbegabten Männer, die   die
Gaben brachten.
Weislich sahen sie wohl   unter der
Wolken Wölbung
Auf zu dem hohen Himmel,   wie die
hellen Sterne fuhren:
125 Da erkannten sie Gottes Zeichen,   die
dem Christ zu Liebe waren
Dieser Welt gewirkt: ihnen wanderten
sie nach,
Folgten in Ehrfurcht.   Sie förderte der
Mächtige
Weiter, bis sie gewahrten,   die wegmüden
Männer,
Hell am Himmel   das hehre Gotteszeichen
130 Stillestehen.   Der Stern leuchtete
Hell über dem Hause,   wo das heilige Kind
Willig wohnte,   bewacht von der Jung-
frau,
Die ihm demütig diente: da ward der
Degen Herz
Erquickt in ihrer Brust,   sie erkannten an
dem Zeichen,
135 Daß sie des Friedenskind Gottes   ge-
funden hatten,
Den heiligen Himmelskönig.   Da in das
Haus sie nun
Mit ihren Gaben gingen,   die Gäste von
Osten,
Die fahrtmüden Fürsten,   sofort erkannten
sie
Wohl den waltenden Christ.   Die Wand-
erer fielen
140 Vor ihm ins Kniegebet,   und in Königs-
weise
Grüßten sie den guten,   brachten die
Gaben dar,
Gold und Weihrauch   nach den göttlichen
Zeichen,
Und Myrrhen zumal.   Die Mannen
standen bereit,

Hold vor ihrem Herren,   die mit Händen
alles
Fröhlich empfingen.   Dann schieden die 145
frommen
Recken zu ihrer Ruhe: die reisemüden
Männer
Gingen in den Gastsaal,   wo Gottes
Engel
Den Schlafenden bei Nacht   ein Gesicht
zeigte,
Ein Scheinbild im Schlummer,   wie es der
Schöpfer selber,
Der Waltende, wollte,   als würd ihnen 150
geboten,
Daß sie auf anderm Wege   gen Osten
führen,
Zu Lande gelangten   und zu dem leiden
Mann,
Herodes, nicht wieder   zurückkehrten,
Dem meinrätgen König.   Da nun der
Morgen kam
Wonnig zu dieser Welt,   begannen die 155
Weisen sich
Ihre Gesichte zu sagen   und erkannten
selber
Des Waltenden Wort,   da sie Weisheit
viel
Bargen in ihrer Brust.   Sie baten den
Allwaltenden,
Den hehren Himmelkönig,   daß sie um
seine Huld auch ferner
Seinen Willen dürften wirken,   denn zu 160
ihm gewandt sei Herz
Und Mut allmorgenlich.   Da fuhren die
Männer hin,
Die Gesandten von Osten,   wie der
Engel Gottes
Sie mit Worten gewiesen,   einen andern
Weg nehmend
Und Gottes Lehre folgend.   Dem Juden-
könig wollten
Von des Neugebornen Geburt   die Boten 165
von Osten,
Die gangmüden Gäste,   gar nichts
melden, und heim
Wenden nach eigenem Willen.

DAS EVANGELIENBUCH

Otfried von Weißenburg (800?–?880)

Prologue

Es hat viel Leute schon gegeben,   die
  waren stark in dem Bestreben,
Durch Bücherschreiben zu bereiten   sich
  gut Gerücht für alle Zeiten;[1]
Und darauf auch gerichtet war   ihr starkes
  Sehnen immerdar,
Daß man in Büchern es erzählte,   wie
  ihnen Tatenlust nicht fehlte.
5 Dazu verlangte ihre Ehre,   daß auch ihr
  Scharfsinn sichtbar wäre,
So wie der Anmut schöne Feinheit   in ihres
  Dichtens klarer Reinheit.
Sie haben alles, wie's sich schickt,   sorg-
  sam und kunstvoll ausgedrückt,
Und haben's gut herausgefunden—   zwar
  dunkel scheint's, doch wohl verbunden—
Wodurch es dann auch dazu kam,   daß
  jedermann sie gern vernahm,
10 Und wer daran Gefallen fand,   des Witz
  sich übte und Verstand.
Wie leicht wohl könnte man dafür   gar
  vieler Leute Namen hier
Aufzählen und besonders nennen,   von
  denen wir die Bücher kennen.
Griechen und Römer, hochberühmt,   die
  machen's, wie es sich geziemt,
Und haben's also hergestellt,   wie es dir
  immer wohlgefällt.
15 Sie machen's nach dem rechten Maß   und
  schlecht und recht ohn' Unterlaß;
So muß es denn ein Ganzes sein,   grad' so,
  als wär's aus Elfenbein.
Wenn man die Taten so erzählt,   die Lust
  zum Leben keinem fehlt.
Und willst du dich zur Dichtung kehren,
  so wirst du deine Einsicht mehren.
So wohl der Prosa schlichtes Wesen   wirst
  mit Genuß du immer lesen,
20 Als auch des Metrums feine Zier   ist eine
  reine Freude dir.

Sie machen es mit vieler Süße   und messen
  gut der Verse Füße,
Ob kurz, ob lang sie müssen sein,[2]   auf
  daß es würde glatt und fein.
Auch darauf stets ihr Trachten geht,   daß
  jede Silbe sicher steht,
Und daß ein jeder Vers so klingt,   wie
  jeder Versfuß es bedingt.
Sie zählen mit Genauigkeit   die Läng' 25
  und Kürze jeder Zeit,
Und sichre Grenzen sind gezogen,   wo-
  nach das Silbenmaß gewogen.
Auch säubern sie's mit rechter Reinheit
  und auch mit ausgesuchter Fein-
  heit,
So wie ein Mann mit Fleiß und Treu'   die
  Körner sondert von der Spreu.
Ja, selbst den heil'gen Büchern geben   sie
  eine Versform rein und eben,[3]
Kein Fehler findet sich darin,   so liest du 30
  es mit frohem Sinn. —
Nun, da so viele es betreiben,   daß sie in
  eigner Zunge schreiben,
Und da sie eifrig danach streben,   sich
  selber rühmend zu erheben,
Wie sollten da die Franken zagen,   auch
  selber den Versuch zu wagen,
Daß sie's mit Eifer dahin bringen,   auf
  Fränkisch Gottes Lob zu singen?
Zwar ist der Sprache nicht bekannt   der 35
  Regeln festgefügtes Band,
Doch fehlt der grade Ausdruck nicht,
  noch auch die Einfalt schön und schlicht.

Sie sind genau so unverzagt,   wie man
  es von den Römern sagt.[4]
Auch darf man nicht zu sagen wagen,   daß
  kühnern Mut die Griechen tragen.
Ganz ebenso ist es bewandt   mit ihrem
  Wissen und Verstand.
Sie sind voll Mut und Tapferkeit   an 40
  jedem Ort, zu jeder Zeit,
Viel Macht und Ansehn haben sie,   und
  Kühnheit fehlet ihnen nie.
Zum Schwerte greifen sie verwegen,   das
  ist die Art der wackern Degen.

---

[1] The whole passage is Otfried's variation on the theme that poets ensure immortality for their subjects.

[2] It should be remembered that such verse was strange to the Germans of this time.
[3] He is alluding to biblical epics such as that of Juvencus.
[4] Otfried's praise of the Franks follows the formal rules of rhetoric for the praise of a people or city.

Vollauf versehn und wohl im Stande,   so
   wohnen sie in reichem Lande.
Von alters her ihr Gut sich mehrt,   derhalben sind sie hochgeehrt.
45 Gar schön und fruchtbar ist ihr Land;
   wem wäre dies nicht wohlbekannt?
Es gibt dort vielerlei Gewinnst—   es
   es ist nicht eigenes Verdienst—
Dort kann man Erz und Kupfer haben,
   das zum Gebrauche wir gegraben.
Und denket nur, wie wunderbar!   Eis-
   steine gibt es dort sogar.
Und von Metallen man noch füge   dazu
   das Silber zur Genüge:
50 Auch lesen sie daselbst im Land   Gold,
   das sie finden in dem Sand.

Es ist ihr Sinnen fest und stet,   das immer
   nur aufs Gute geht,
Und ist zum Nutzen hingewandt,   so wie
   sie's lehret ihr Verstand.
Sie sind zu jeder Zeit bereit,   zu schützen
   sich vor Feindes Neid;
Der mag nichts gegen diese wagen,   zu
   Boden wird er stets geschlagen.
Kein Volk gibt's, das ihr Land berührt,   55
   das ihre Gegenwart nicht spürt;
Sie dienen ihnen notgedrungen,   von
   ihrer Tüchtigkeit bezwungen.
Sie haben alles Volk besiegt,   wo nicht
   die See dazwischen liegt.
Nach Gottes Willen und Gedanken   hat
   jedermann Furcht vor den Franken,

Eine Seite aus Otfrieds *Evangelienbuch*. (Nach einer Handschrift des 9. Jahrhunderts) *Nationalbibliothek Wien*.

Da nirgendwo ein Volk wohl lebt,   das da
     nach Kampf mit jenen strebt.
60 Den Feinden haben sie mit Waffen   Be-
     weise oft genug geschaffen
Und haben gründlich sie belehrt   nicht
     mit dem Wort, nein, mit dem Schwert,
Mit Speeren scharf und spitz geschliffen,
     deshalb hat alle Furcht ergriffen.
Kein Volk gibt's das nicht deutlich wüßte:
     trägt es nach Frankenkrieg Gelüste,
Dann sinken sie dahin geschwind,   wenn's
     Meder auch und Perser sind!
65 Ich las dereinst in einem Buch   und weiß
     es drum genau genug:
Ganz eng verwandt sind mit einander   das
     Frankenvolk und Alexander,
Der aller Welt ein Schrecknis war,   die er
     besiegte ganz und gar,
Die er darnieder zwang und band   mit
     seiner allgewalt'gen Hand

Da kamen Leute in das Land   von
     Osten, denen war bekannt
70 Der Sonne und der Sterne Lauf;   denn
     all ihr Sinnen ging darauf.
Nun fragten diese nach dem Kind   bei der
     Gelegenheit geschwind
Und kündeten zugleich die Märe,   daß
     dieses Kind der König wäre,
Und forschten eifrig immerfort   nach
     dieses Knaben Heimatort
Mit stetem Bitten und mit Fragen,   man
     möcht' es ihnen doch ja sagen
75 Und auch die Wegfahrt zeigen an,   auf
     der zum Kind man kommen kann.
Nun sprachen sie auch von dem Zeichen,
     das seltsam war und ohnegleichen.
Daß hier von einer Jungfrau zart   jemals
     ein Mensch geboren ward,
Und daß ein Zeichen schön und klar   im
     Himmelraum erschienen war.
Sie sagten, daß sie hoch und fern   plötz-
     lich erblickten einen Stern,
80 Und machten ruchbar laut und frei,   daß
     dies der Stern des Herren sei:
„Sein Stern sich uns gezeiget hat,   wenn
     wir auch irrten in der Stadt,
Wir sind gekommen anzubeten,   daß
     seine Gnade wir anflehten.
So ist uns denn im Osten fern   daheim
     erschienen dieser Stern.

Lebt nun wohl einer hier im Land,   dem
     davon etwas ist bekannt?
So viel wir Sterne auch gezählt,   der hat   85
     bis jetzt uns stets gefehlt;
Derhalben glauben alle wir,   ein neuer
     König zeigt sich hier.
Das haben Greise uns gelehrt   zu Hause,
     klug und hochgeehrt;
Nun bitten wir euch vorzutragen,   was
     eure Bücher davon sagen."
Als nun zum König selbst sofort   die
     Kunde drang von diesem Wort,
Ward durch die Nachricht er sogleich   90
     von Angst erfüllt und schreckensbleich,
Und auch so mancher andre Mann   daraus
     viel Traurigkeit gewann.
Die hörten ungern und mit Schmerzen,
     was uns mit Freude füllt die Herzen.
Die weisen Schriftgelehrten dort   ver-
     sammelten sich dann sofort
Und forschten, wo auf dieser Erde   wohl
     Christ der Herr geboren werde,
Und wandten sich in diesen Tagen   auch   95
     an die Priester mit den Fragen.
Doch mocht' er arm sein oder reich,   stets
     lautete die Antwort gleich.
Sie nannten ihm sogleich die Stadt,   wie's
     früher schon bezeuget hat
Vom alten Bunde manch Prophet,   so
     wie es aufgeschrieben steht.
Als es ihm so ward offenbar,   wo Christ
     der Herr geboren war,
Ersann er schnell und fürchterlich   nun   100
     eine große Bosheit sich.
Er ließ die Weisen zu sich kommen   von
     denen ihr durch mich vernommen,
Die fing er heimlich an zu fragen   und
     ohne andern es zu sagen
Und forschte dann mit Emsigkeit   nach
     dieses Sternes Ankunftszeit
Und bat sie selber zu ergründen,   wo
     wohl das Kindlein sei zu finden:
„Vergeßt nicht, mir zu offenbaren   den   105
     Weg, den dieser Stern wird fahren,
Und reiset dann an jenen Ort   und fraget
     nach dem Kindlein dort.
Wenn ihr dort angekommen seid,   dann
     forscht nach ihm mit Emsigkeit
Und tut es schleunig mir zu wissen,   der
     Arbeit seid nur recht beflissen;
Ich bete ihn dann selber an,   dazu riet
     mir gar mancher Mann,

110 Auf daß ich selber danach strebe, daß
ich dem Kind Geschenke gebe."

Wie kläglich jener Mann da log und
gegen Recht und Wahrheit trog!

Er wünschte, daß der Heiland stürbe, daß
unser Segen so verdürbe!

Als sie gehört des Königs Wort und
nach dem Ziele eilten fort,

Da zeigte ihnen sich von fern sogleich
der wunderbare Stern!

115 Wie waren sie da hochentzückt, als sie
ihn alsobald erblickt!

Erfreut versäumten sie es nicht, ihn zu
behalten im Gesicht,

Er führte sie auch dorthin klar, wo Gottes Kind zu finden war.

Und da, wo ging des Sternes Bogen, sind
sie ihm willing nachgezogen;

Da haben sie das Haus gesehn und nicht
gezögert hinzugehn.

120 Da fanden sie denn auch geschwind die
Mutter mit dem guten Kind

Und fielen eilig vor ihm nieder, die
guten Männer, treu und bieder;

Sie beteten das Kindlein an und baten
es um Gnade dann.

Daran ermahnt uns diese Reise, daß
auch wir selbst in gleicher Weise

Mit Eifer dafür Sorge tragen, das Land
der Heimat zu erfragen.

125 Doch ist dies, glaub' ich, nicht bekannt:
das Paradies wird es genannt.

Hoch rühmen ich es kann und muß, doch
fehlet mir der Rede Fluß.

Und wenn auch jedes meiner Glieder
Rede und Sprache gäbe wieder,

So hätt' ich's niemals unternommen, mit
seinem Lob zu End' zu kommen.

Doch siehst du's nicht mit eignen Augen,
was können meine Worte taugen?

130 Und selbst dann wird sehr viel dran fehlen,
daß du es könntest her erzählen.

Dort gibt es Leben ohne Tod, Licht
ohne Finsternis und Not,

Dazu der Engel schöne Schar und sel'ge
Minne immerdar

Das haben selbst wir aufgegeben, des
müssen wir in Trauer leben,

Und innen muß uns heimatwärts sich
klagend sehnen unser Herz.

Sind wir doch selbst herausgegangen, in 135
unserm Übermut befangen,

Denn uns verlockte leis' und stille des
Herzens eigner böser Wille.

Wir haben Schuld auf uns geladen, das
ist jetzt klar zu unserm Schaden.

Nun weinen wir im fremden Land, von
Gott verstoßen und verbannt.

Ja, unbenutzt liegt und verloren das
Erbgut, das für uns erkoren.

Nichts nützt uns dieses große Gut, das 140
macht nur unser Übermut.

So wird denn, ach! von uns entbehrt das
Schöne, das uns war beschert,

Wir müssen bittre Zeiten dulden von
nun an nur durch unsre Schulden.

Viel Leid ist uns und Not bekannt mit
Schmerzen hier in diesem Land,

Voll Wunden sind wir und voll Pein um
unsre Missetat allein,

Viel Elend und Mühseligkeit, das ist 145
hier stets für uns bereit.

Zur Heimat können wir nicht reisen, wir
jammervollen, armen Waisen.

O weh, du fremdes Schreckensland, wie
hab' ich dich als hart erkannt!

Ach wie, so schwer ertrag' ich dich, das
sage ich dir sicherlich!

Nur Müh' und Not wird dem gegeben,
der nicht kann in der Heimat leben.

Ich hab's erfahren ja an mir, nichts 150
Liebes fand ich je an dir.

Ich fand an dir kein ander Gut als Jammer
und betrübten Mut,

Ein tief verwundet, wehes Herz und
mannigfaches Leid und Schmerz!

Doch kommt uns einmal in den Sinn, daß
uns verlangt zur Heimat hin,

Und hat sich unser Herz gewandt voll
Sehnsucht nach dem Vaterland,

Dann fahren wir, wie jene Mannen, 155
auf andrer Straße gleich von dannen,

Auf den Weg, welcher führt allein in
unser Vaterland hinein.

Das Ludwigslied

The *Ludwigslied* is one of the very few medieval poems that can be dated with almost complete accuracy. It describes the victory of the Frankish king Ludwig III over the invading Northmen at Saucourt, in northern France. The battle took place on August 3, 881. Ludwig died the following year, and since he is spoken of as still alive in the poem, it must have been written in late 881 or early 882.

The object of the poem is clearly to put Ludwig in the same tradition of Christian kingship as that which was growing up at this time around the figure of Charlemagne. The work has many of the characteristics of the formal panegyric —the reference to the childhood of its subject, to God's favor, to the corresponding piety of Ludwig and his complete dedication to Christian ideals. The description of his victory is markedly reminiscent of the legend of Constantine's success at the Milvian bridge, the prototype of the victory in Christ's name. At the same time there is evidence of the belief of Christians that the Northmen were a pagan scourge sent to punish the sins of the Christians.

The poem is written in a form very like that of Otfried's *Evangelienbuch*. The long lines are divided into two parts, each of which has two main and two secondary stresses, with little regard to the number of unstressed syllables. There is rhyme or at least assonance between the last words in each half-line. The four lines of Old High German given here will illustrate the form.

> *Einan kuning uueiz ih,*   *Heizsit her Hluduig,*
> *Ther gerno gode thionot:*   *Ih uueiz her imos lonot.*
> *Kind uuarth her faterlos.*   *Thes uuarth imo sar buoz*
> *Holoda inan truhtin,*   *Magaczogo uuarth her sin.*

DAS LUDWIGSLIED

Einen König kenne ich   er heißt Herr
  Ludwig,
Er dient Gott gerne: ich weiß, der lohnt
  es ihm.
Als Kind war er vaterlos;   dafür bekam
  er bald Ersatz:
Der Herr berief ihn,   sein Erzieher ward
  er.
5 Er gab ihm Tüchtigkeit,   herrliche
  Degenschaft,
Den Thron hier in Franken;   so brauch'
  er ihn lange!
Das teilte er dann   sofort mit Karlmann,
Seinem Bruder,   die Fülle der Wonnen.
Als das alles geendet ward,   wollte Gott
  ihn prüfen,
10 Ob er Mühsal   so jung erdulden könnte.
Er ließ heidnische Männer   über See
  kommen,
Das Volk der Franken   ihrer Sünden zu
  mahnen.
Einige wurden bald verloren,   einige
  ausgewählt.
Züchtigung leidete   wer früher misgelebet
  hatte.
15 Wer dann ein Dieb war   und mit dem
  Leben davon kam,
Nahm seine Fasten;   danach ward er ein
  guter Mann.
Mancher war Lügner,   mancher Raub-
  mörder,
Mancher voll Zuchtlosigkeit,   und be-
  freite sich davon.
Der König war entfernt,   das Reich
  ganz zerrüttet,
20 Christus war entzürnt,   dafür mußte das
  Reich Not leiden.
Doch Gott erbarmte sich dessen,   er
  wußte all die Sorgen.
Er ließ Ludwig   sofort dahin reiten:
„Ludwig, mein König,   hilf meinen
  Leuten!
Die Normannen haben sie   hart be-
  drängt."
25 Da sprach Ludwig: „Herr, so tue ich
Wenn mich der Tode nicht hindert,   alles,
  was du gebietest."
Da nahm er Gottes Urlaub,   er hob die
  Kriegsfahne auf,

Er ritt dahin in Frankreich   gegen die
  Normannen.
Gott sagten Dank,   die auf ihn warteten.
Sie sagten alle: Mein Herr, wie lange 30
  warten wir!
Da sprach laut   Ludwig der gute:
„Tröstet euch, Gesellen,   meine Not-
  gefährten,
Her sandte mich Gott   und mir selber
  gebot,
Wenn es euch gefiele,   daß ich hier kämpfte.
Nun will ich,   daß mir folgen alle Gottes 35
  Holden.
Auf Erde weilen wir   so lange Christus
  will.
Will er unsere Hinfahrt,   deren hat er
  Gewalt
Wer hier mit Kraft   Gottes Willen tut,
Kommt er gesund davon,   ich lohne es
  ihm;
Bleibt er darin,   seinem Geschlechte." 40
Da nahm er Schild und Speer,   kraftvoll
  ritt er,
Er wollte die Wahrheit darlegen   seinen
  Widersachern;
Da war es nicht sehr lang,   er fand die
  Normannen,
Gott sagte er Lob,   er sieht, was er
  begehrte.
Der König ritt kühn,   sang ein heiliges 45
  Lied,
Und alle sangen zusammen: „Kyrie
  eleison!"
Der Sang war gesungen,   der Kampf war
  begonnen.
Blut schien auf den Wangen,   froh
  kämpften die Franken.
Da focht der Degen   keiner so wie Lud-
  wig,
Tapfer und kühn: das war ihm angeboren. 50
Manchen durchschlag   er,   manchen
  durchstach er.
Seinen Feinden schenkte er   ein Getrank
Bitteren Leides.   Weh ihnen und immer
  weh!
Gelobt sei Gottes Kraft!   Ludwig war
  sieghaft.
Und allen Heiligen Dank!   Sein war der 55
  Siegkampf.
Heil aber Ludwig,   König kampfselig!
So bereit wie er stets war,   wo irgend
  Not war,
Erhalte ihn der Herr   bei seiner Herrlich-
  keit!

Hartmann von Aue

(fl. c. 1170–1215)

There are several families whose name could correspond with that of the poet, but it is not definitely known to which family he belonged or which family he served. It is likely that he was a Swabian. One thing seems certain; he was closely attached to his liege lord, whoever he was, for it is generally agreed that his abandonment of secular epics was due to his sorrow over his lord's death. His earliest works were lyric poems, including love poetry and crusading songs. His *Büchlein* is a dialogue between the heart and the body on the hardheartedness of love. The remainder of his works consists of narrative poems, two of them based on Arthurian romances of the French poet Chrétien de Troyes. *Erek,* written about 1190-95, is the story of a knight who married a beautiful woman but became so uxorious that he neglected adventurous pursuits. He hears his wife lamenting the criticisms of his attitude made by some of his knights. Thinking that she shares their opinion of him, he takes her on a series of exploits. Although he has forbidden her to warn him of impending dangers, she disobeys and saves his life several times. He is at last convinced that she is loyal and comes to learn the full meaning of *Minne*. Hartmann follows Chrétien fairly closely but does use some material not in his source.

On the death of his patron, Hartmann appears to have undergone a profound revulsion of feeling, and his next two works are exemplary legends. *Gregorius,* probably written first, shows that even the most terrible sinner can be saved if his repentance is sincere. The story is based on a widespread, though nonhistorical, story of a child of incest, who later unknowingly commits the same sin, but by the most rigid penance so purges himself that God directs that he is to be elected pope. Hartmann's immediate source was probably the French *Histoire de la vie du pape Grégoire.* We know nothing of the source of Hartmann's best known poem, *Der Arme Heinrich.* A plausible suggestion is that it may have been a family legend of Hartmann's patron explaining why a forebear married a peasant girl. The main motif, the cure of leprosy by the use of the blood of an innocent is very common, as is the idea of the outward corruption of the disease indicating the inward corruption of the soul. Heinrich is a good man in the worldly sense, but he fails to recognize his debt to God, becomes leprous, and fails to see his responsibility for his plight. He reluctantly accepts the offer of the young daughter of one of his peasants to let her heart's blood be used to cure him but in the end he cannot allow her sacrifice, although she protests strongly, feeling herself deprived of becoming a martyr. Heinrich's recognition of his true state brings about a cure for both body and soul.

Iwein is a very close adaptation of the *Yvains* of Chrétien. It is structurally Hartmann's best poem and shows that by this time, about 1204, he was a master of

the narrative form, as many contemporaries agree. Iwein neglects his wife for
personal adventure and is brought back to true knighthood by a series of exploits, in all of which he rescues women from the forces of evil. Here, as elsewhere, Hartmann treats the courtly ethic very seriously, as a way of attaining
secular glory that is not merely empty adventure. But in the *Iwein* he seems less
pompous, and certainly his technique is equal to that of any medieval poet with
the possible exception of Gottfried. Hartmann's works, like all courtly epics,
are written in four-beat rhyming couplets. The last beat may fall on a stressed
syllable at the very end of the line (*volle Kadenz*), on a normally unstressed syllable immediately following a stressed syllable (*klingende Kadenz*), or on a stressed syllable followed by an unstressed syllable (*weiblich volle Kadenz*). Very rarely
there is no syllable for the last stress and it has to be assumed to fall on a
pause (*stumpfe Kadenz*).

The *Gregorius* lends itself well to the almost literal prose translation given
here.

IWEIN

Wer an rechte Güte*
  Wendet sein Gemüte,
Dem folgen Heil und Ehre.
Dess gibt gewisse Lehre
5 König Artus der Gute,
Der mit Rittermute
Ruhmwürdig konnte streiten.
Ihm ward bei seinen Zeiten
So herrlich Lob zum Lohne,
10 Daß er der Ehren Krone
Da trug, und trägt sie noch zur Stund.
Dess ward die Wahrheit kund,
Denn seine Landesleute
Sagen, er lebe noch heute.
15 Er hat den Kranz erworben:
Ist ihm der Leib gestorben,
Lebt doch sein Name fort und fort;
Kein Schimpf, kein lästernd Wort
Hat jemahls den versehrt,
20 Der noch auf seinen Wegen fährt.[1]
  Ein Ritter der die Kunst verstand
Zu lesen, was er in Büchern fand,[2]
Daß wenn er nach den Waffen
Sich Muße konnte schaffen,
25 Er oftmals auch der Dichtung pflag
Wie man gern sie hören mag,
Und Luft und Fleiß daran gewandt:—
Hartmann war er genannt,
Als Dienstmann auf der Au verpflichtet:—
30 Der hat diese Märe gedichtet.

Arthur's court is assembled at Caridol at Whitsun, and there is clearly bad blood between Kei, the crude seneschal of the court, and Kalogreant, Iwein's cousin. Only the intervention of Queen

Guinevere allows Kalogreant to tell of an adventure that happened to him almost ten years before. He rode into the wood of Bresilian seeking adventure and spent the night as the guest of a nobleman and his daughter. The next day he met a huge and ugly herdsman in charge of fierce animals. After being assured that the animals will not hurt him, Kalogreant asks the herdsman where he can find adventure.

  Also sprach er drauf zu mir;*
„Steht es so beschaffen mit Dir,
Daß Du nach Ungemache strebest,
Und nicht gern in Frieden lebest—
(Ich hörte noch in meinen Tagen   5
Von solchem Dinge nimmer sagen,
Was Abenteuer wäre)[3]—
So künd' ich Dir die Märe:
Willst Du den Leib dran wagen,
Brauchst Du nicht lang zu fragen.   10
Hier ist ein Bronnen nahe bei,
Etwa kurzer Meilen drei;
Getraust Du Dirs den zu erspähn
Und läßest ihm sein Recht geschehn,
Und findest hernach die Wiederkehr   15
Ohne große Schmach und Unehr,
So bist Du in Treu'n ein tapfer Mann,
Und zweifeln will ich nicht daran.
Was hilft Dir's, wollt ich mehr Dir sagen?
Ich weiß, Du pflegst nicht zu versagen: 20
So siehst Du denn in kurzer Frist
Selber, wovon die Rede ist.
Noch höre, was sein Recht denn sei:
Eine Kapelle steht nahe bei,
Die ist schön und zierlich, aber klein.   25
Kalt und viel rein
Ist derselbe Bronne;
Ihn treffen nicht Regen noch Sonne,
Noch trüben ihn die Winde:
Dess schirmt ihn die schönste Linde.   30
Ihre grünen Zweige, breit und flach,
Sind sein Schatten und sein Dach:
Sie ist mächtig hoch, und also dick,
Daß nicht Regen noch Sonnenblick
Nimmer je hindurch sich drängt;   35
Ihr schadet der Winter nicht, noch kränkt
An ihrer Schönheit er ein Haar,
Sie grünt und blüht das ganze Jahr.

---

* The following are lines 1–30 of the Middle High German version.
[1] This prologue is a clear statement of the "Arthurian values," and corresponds to the prologue in a religious poem in which the praise would be given to God. The belief in the survival of Arthur was widespread among the Celtic peoples and is mentioned, for example, in Malory's *Morte d'Arthur*.
[2] Hartmann's claim to be a literate knight, made here and in the prologue to *Der arme Heinrich*, is an amusing contrast with Wolfram's statement that he himself is not a learned man. It is conceivable that Wolfram knew of Hartmann's claim and deliberately put himself in the opposite camp.

---

* The following are lines 534–662 of the Middle High German version.
[3] The herdsman, a child of nature, shows more sense than the sophisticated Arthurian knight.

Über dem Bronnen steht ein
40 Wunderzierlicher Stein,
Unterstellt mit vieren
Marmelgehauenen Tieren,
Durchlöchert hin und wieder.
Von einem Ast hernieder
45 Hängt ein Becken von lauterm Gold;
Ich traue daß niemand haben sollt
Gold so fein geprägt.
Die Kette so die Schaale trägt,
Die ist aus Silber geschlagen.
50 Willst Du nun nicht verzagen,
So tu dem Becken nicht mehr als dies:
Auf den Stein, der da stehet, gieß
Von des Bronnens Wasser ein Teil;
Und wahrhaftig, Du hast Glück und Heil,
55 Ziehst Du mit Ehren von der Stelle.“
Da wies mir der riesige Waldgeselle
Einen Steig zur linken Hand:
Ich zog des Weges und fand
Seine Rede genau und klar.
60 Was er mir sagte, verhielt sich wahr,
Und große Pracht erblickt’ ich dort.
Man hört wohl nimmer an keinem Ort,
Die Welt steh’ kurz oder lang,
So wonniglichen Vogelgesang,
65 Als ich aus jener Linde vernahm,
Da ich herangeritten kam.
      Und wär’ ein Mann bis in den Tod
Betrübt gewesen durch Gram und Not,
Dess Herze hätte sich erfreut.
70 Mit Vöglein war der Baum bestreut,
Daß ich die Äste kaum noch sah,
Und selbst das Laub verschwand beinah.
Da waren nicht zwei einander gleich.
Ihr Chorgesang verteilte sich reich,
75 Die Melodie bald hoch, bald nieder;
Anmutig klangen die süßen Lieder,
Und wiedertönend aus dem Wald
Das Echo zu den Stimmen schallt.
Den Bronnen fand ich auch sofort,
80 Wie mir der Riese beschrieb den Ort:
Der Stein darauf war ein Rubin,
Und aus jeglicher Ecke schien
Ein also leuchtender Smaragd,
Daß selbst des Morgensternes Pracht
85 Nicht schöner glänzt, wenn er aufsteigt,
Und die trübe Nacht vor ihm entweicht.
      Als ich das Becken hangen sah,
In meinem Sinn gedacht ich da,
Wollt’ ich als Ritter Ruhm erreiten,
90 So müss’ ich mir’s als Feigheit deuten,
Wenn ich des Wagestücks entbehre,
Und nicht versüche, was da wäre.

So riet mir mein unweiser Mut,
Der mir so häufig Schaden tut,
Daß ich Wasser goß auf den Rubin.   95
Da erlosch die Sonne die eben schien,
Rings verstummte der Vögelgesang,
Ein schwarzes Gewitter zog entlang.
Sturmeswolken flogen
An den Himmels Bogen   100
Von vier Enden finster und schwer,
Es schien der lichte Tag nicht mehr,
So daß ich die Linde kaum ersah:
Große Trübsal mir da geschah.
Es zückten nun viel balde   105
Rings um mich her im Walde
Viel tausend Blitze zumal;
Und neben mir zu Tal
Fiel so heftig ein Donnerschlag,
Daß ich entsetzt am Boden lag.   110
Es erhob sich Sturm, Hagel und Regen,
Und hätte nicht Gottes Segen
Mich geschirmt vor des Wetters Not,
Läg ich derweile zehnmal tot.
Der Sturm ward also ungemach,   115
Daß der Wald zusammenbrach.
Jeglicher Baum wie breit und groß,
Stand nun verwüstet, kahl und bloß,
Und alles Schmuckes leer,
Als ob er versenget wär.   120

*The weather quickly clears, and a knight charges
out, accusing Kalogreant of laying waste his property. In spite of his denials, Kalogreant is attacked
and unhorsed. He walks back to his host of the
previous night, who again receives him well. Iwein
proclaims his determination to avenge the insult
to the family but is mocked by Kei. King Arthur
declares that the whole court will go to the fountain
to try the adventure, but Iwein leaves the court
secretly and sets out alone. He repeats his cousin’s
actions exactly, however, he is not unhorsed. The
two knights begin to fight with their swords, and
Iwein succeeds in inflicting a serious wound on his
opponent, who turns and flees. Iwein pursues him,
but the manner in which he strikes at his enemy
calls forth a rebuke from Hartmann. As the knight
approaches his castle, Iwein is hard on his heels:*

So fuhren sie in der Enge*
Beide durch Gedränge
Bis an die Halle: da war davor
Gehängt ein Eisentor
Da mußte man hindurch fahren,   5

\-\-\-\-\-\-\-\-\-\-
* The following are lines 1077–1117 of the Middle
High German version.

Und sich viel wohl bewahren
Vor jenem selbigen fallenden Tor,
Daß man das Leben da nicht verlor.
Wenn Roß und Reiter nicht unverwandt
10 Des Weges rechte Mitte fand —
So wie ein Tritt den Knauf berührte
Der all' die schwere Wucht regierte,
Und das gewaltige Eisentor
Vom Boden aufwärts hob empor,
15 So nahm es plötzlich seinen Fall,
Und schlug so jäh zu Tal,
Daß ihm niemand entrann:
So war geblieben mancher Mann.
Der Wirt ritt vorn, der kannte den Bau
20 Und sein Getriebe ganz genau.
Weil's von ihm selbst geordnet war,
Mocht's er entgehn der schlimmen Gefahr.
Das Eisen war schwer und scharf also,
Daß es im Niederfall wie Stroh
25 Unfehlbar durchschnitt Stahl und Bein.
Nun konnte sich Herr Iwein
Nicht behüten davor,
Und fällte das Tor:
Da schoß hernieder das Gitter:
30 Er aber traf zugleich den Ritter,
Und kam davon, wie ich's Euch sage.
Er hatte nach seinem Schlage
Sich vorwärts über das Roß gebogen
So ward er noch dem Tod' entzogen
35 Daß wie das Tor hernieder schoß,
Er selber genaß, doch nicht das Roß.
Den armen Hengst, erzählt die Mär,
Traf's hinterm Sattel den Rücken quer,
Und schnitt des Schwertes Scheide
40 Und die Sporen beide
Hinter den Fersen ab wie Zunder
Daß er davon kam wie ein Wunder.

*Iwein is trapped; fortunately the first person to
find him is a lady-in-waiting, Lunete, to whom
he had been kind at Arthur's court. She gives
him a ring to make him invisible. At court, he
sees a lady overcome by grief; she is clearly the
wife of the knight he has killed. Even though the
corpse begins to bleed when Iwein draws near, the
soldiers in the castle are unable to see him. When
Lunete returns, he tells her that he is deeply in love
with the lady he has seen, Laudine. Lunete decides
to attempt to win over her mistress for him.*

Da sie beide schweigen, da sprach die
Magd:*

---

* The following are lines 2255–2339 of the Middle
High German version.

„Herr Iwein wie seid Ihr so verzagt?
Lebt Ihr? — verschloß sich Euer Mund?
Ihr war't noch eben frisch und gesund,
Seit wann denn wurdet Ihr stumm?   5
Sagt mir um Gott, warum
Fürchtet Ihr ein so schönes Weib?
Gott tröste nimmer dessen Leib,
Der ohne Dank einen tapfern Mann,
Und der sonst selber wohl reden kann, 10
Zu schöner Fraue führte her,
Daß er sie fliehe so sehr?
Ihr dürft nicht so gar verzagen,
Mögt gern Euch näher wagen.
Meine Fraue, Herr Ritter, beißt Euch nicht. 15
Wem von jemand geschieht
So leid als sie erfuhr durch Euch,
Soll der dann Gnade finden sogleich,
Dazu gehört mehr Dank und Lohn.
Ihr habt den König Ascalon   20
Ihren lieben Mann erschlagen:
Soll man Euch dafür Gnade sagen?
Ihr habt viel schwere Schuld,
Nun sucht auch ihre Huld.
Laßt uns sie anflehn beide,   25
Daß sie ihr Leide
Geruhe zu vergessen!"—
Da ward nicht länger gesessen:
Auf sprang er, warf sich ihr zu Füßen,
Und sucht' ihre Huld und ihr Grüßen   30
Als ein schuldiger Mann.
Er sprach: „Ich weiß nicht noch kann
Ich Euch darbieten mehre
Vergütung oder Ehre,
Als, richtet selber über mich: 35
Wie Ihr wollt, also will ich."
    „Wollt Ihr Alles was ich will?"
„Ja, mich dünket nichts zu viel."
„So möcht' ich vielleicht Euch nehmen den
    Leib!"
„Wie Ihr's gebietet, selig Weib."   40
„Nun, was frommt da Reden lang?
Da Ihr einmal Euch ohne Zwang
In meine Gewalt gegeben,
Nähm' ich Euch das Leben,
Unweiblich wäre das viel sehr.   45
Herr Iwein, denkt auch nimmermehr,
Es sei durch treulosen Unbestand,
Wenn ich geneigt mich fand
So bald Euch zu begnaden.
Ihr tatet mir solchen Schaden,   50
Daß stünde so frei mein Hab und Gut,
Wie es andern Frauen tut,
Nimmer hätt' ich gewollt
So eilig, noch gesollt

55 Euch Gnade lassen geschehn.
    Nun muß ich leider gestehn,
    Es ist mit mir also bewandt,
    Ich möchte leicht verlieren mein Land
    Heute oder auch morgen.
60 Deshalb muß ich's versorgen
    Mit einem Mann zu Schutz und Wehr:
    Ein solcher fehlt in meinem Heer,
    Seit der König war erschlagen;
    Drum muß ich in den nächsten Tagen
65 Mir einen Herren küren,[4]
    Oder das Land verlieren.
        Ich bitt' Euch, wollt noch nichts mir
        sagen.
    Weil Ihr meinen Gemahl erschlagen
    Seid Ihr wohl ein so tapfer Mann,
70 Daß wenn mir Gott Euch gann,[5]
    Ich wäre wohl in sichrer Hut
    Vor allem fremden Übermut;
    Und glaubet mir die Märe —
    Eh ich Euer entbehre,
75 Verletzt' ich lieber des Weibes Sitte:
    Wie selten ein Weib sich den Mann erbitte,
    Euch erbät ich mir ehr: —
    Eure tödliche Feindin bin ich nicht mehr;
    Ich will Euch gerne: wollt Ihr mich?" —
80 „Frau, spräch ich nein jetzt, ewiglich
    Wär' ich dann ein unselger Mann.
    Der liebste Tag, den ich je gewann
    Der ist mir heute widerfahren
    Gott wolle mir das Heil bewahren,
85 Daß ich gesellt Euch bleibe forthin!"[6]

*Iwein and Laudine are married, and Iwein is able
to defend the fountain when Arthur's court arrives.
He gains his revenge on Kei by unhorsing him in
disgraceful fashion. There is a great celebration,
in the course of which Gawain reminds Iwein of
how Erek, another knight of Arthur's court,
nearly forfeited his honor because excessive devotion
to his wife kept him from engaging in adventurous
exploits. Iwein obtains leave from his wife to seek
adventures for one year. However, he inadvertently
overstays his leave, and Lunete arrives to denounce
Iwein before King Arthur.*

        Die Härte, mit der Lunete*

---

[4] **küren** is a modern German equivalent of **kiesen**
(*MHG*): choose.
[5] **gann: gönnte.**
[6] The whole of this scene is a play, not without
ironical touches, on the convention of the complete
submission of the knight to his lady.
* The following are lines 3201–3238 of the Middle
High German version.

Den guten Ritter schmähte,
Ihr rasches Zurückekehren,
Der jähe Sturz all' seiner Ehren,
Dann daß sie also von ihm schied,   5
Und weder ihn tröstet' noch ihm riet;
Die grimme Kränkung und Schmach,
Als sie ihm die Treu' absprach —
Die verspätete Reue,
Und die große Treue   10
Seines festen Mutes;
Der Verlust des Gutes,
Die Sehnsucht nach dem Weibe,
Die nahmen seinem Leibe
Beides, die Freude und den Sinn.   15
Nach dem Einen treibt und drängt's ihn hin,
Er möchte von aller Welt getrennt
Hinausziehn wo ihn keiner kennt,
Und niemand hörte Märe
Wohin er kommen wäre.   20
    Da ward er sich selber verhaßt,
Denn seines Vergehens Last
Mochte kein Andrer für ihn tragen;
Sein eignes Schwert hatt' ihn erschlagen.
Von allem Außern abgelenkt   25
Brütet' er ganz in sich versenkt,
Und als ihn niemand ersah,
Schweigend stahl er sich da
Bis fern vom Lager und Gezelt
Er hatt' erreicht das freie Feld. —   30
Da wurden die Schmerzen ihm so groß
Daß in das Hirn ihm schoß
Ein Rasen und tobende Sucht;
Da brach er alle Sitt' und Zucht,
Abzerrt' er sein Gewand,   35
Daß er bloß ward wie eine Hand.
So lief er übers Gefilde
Nacht hinaus und suchte die Wilde.[7]

*He lives like an animal for some time until he is
brought back to sanity by the ministrations of the
lady of Narison. When completely cured, he rids
her of an importunate suitor, Graf Aliers, but
does not accede to her request to stay. As he rides
on he sees a battle between a lion and a serpent.
He helps the lion, and it follows him in gratitude,
provides him with food, and, incidentally, gives
him the title* Löwenritter. *Iwein finds his way
back to the fountain and is overcome by emotion.
The lion thinks him dead and attempts suicide!
Nearby he finds a lady locked in a chapel. She tells*

---

[7] This is a scene that marks the "death" of the old
Iwein, his descent to a subhuman level. Later,
rebirth will bring him a new awareness of his
responsibilities.

*him that she has been imprisoned because of her
alleged betrayal of her mistress. She proves to be
Lunete, who has been condemned by the seneschal
of Laudine's castle. The only way in which she
can be saved is for a knight to fight the seneschal
and his two brothers at once. She has failed to get
Gawain to aid her. Iwein reveals his identity and
promises her assistance. The lord of the castle in
which he spends the night also needs his help.
A giant, Harpin, has captured his six sons and
has already hanged two of them. The next day
Harpin will hang the other four unless their sister
is given to him as his wife. Furthermore, he threatens
that if he has to capture the castle by force, he will
hand her over to a common soldier. The knights
at Arthur's court were absent because of the
abduction of Queen Guinevere and could not be
called upon to help. The next day Iwein kills the
giant, though not without some help from his
faithful lion, and hastens to the aid of Lunete,
who is to be burned at noon if no champion appears.*

   Ihm waren die Wege wohl bekannt,*
So daß er bald die Stätte fand,
Und erreichte Bronnen und Kapelle.
Die Magd war von der Stelle
5 Geführt, wo sie gefangen lag,
(Denn es war grad' um mitten Tag)
Und schon die Händ' ihr mit Stricken
Gebunden auf den Rücken,
Abgestreift ihr Kleid und Gewand,
10 Daß sie im Hemde stand.
Der Scheiterhaufen war schon geschichtet,
Und von Flammen gelichtet:
Da fiel in heißem Gebete
Auf ihre Knie Frau Lunete,
15 Befahl sich Gott in ihrer Not,
Und war gefaßt auf ihren Tod.
   Also hatte sie eben
Alles irdischen Trostes sich begeben;
Da kam ihr Retter daher,
20 Und war ihm viel leid und schwer
Die Qual die sie erduldet,
Und die er selbst an ihr verschuldet.
Doch hatte mein Herr Iwein
Große Hoffnung zu den Zwein,
25 Zu ihrer Unschuld und Gottes Macht,
Der über die Frommen wacht,
Und beisteht dem Gerechten:
Auch hofft' er, es solle für ihn fechten
Der Leu sein guter Geselle,

Daß er die Feinde fälle.   30
   Nun jagt' er mit scharfen Sporen,
Denn sie war schier verloren,
Hätt' er ein wenig noch gesäumt.
Da rief er: „Übles Gesindel, räumt
Das Feld für diese Magd.   35
Wess man sie hier anklagt,
Dess will ich Bürge stehn:
Und braucht sie dann zum Kämpfen wen,
Bin ich für sie zu fechten bereit."
Das hörten die Drei mit Leid,   40
Und waren sehr betroffen;
Doch ließen sie das Feld ihm offen,
Und wichen vor ihm zurück.
Nun spähte rings sein Blick,
Und suchte die mit Schmerzen,   45
Die er heimlich im Herzen
All'zeit sah, und trug sie im Sinn
Als seine Frau und Gebieterin:
Bald hatt' er sie da erkannt,
Und wär' um Sinn und Verstand   50
Schier gekommen wie ehe:
Denn man sagt, nichts tu' so wehe
Als seine Herzgeliebte sehn,
Und wie ein Fremder ihr ferne stehn.

*   *   *

   Das erhöht' ihm Kraft und Mut,*
Zu fechten stark und gut.
Da ritt er zur Stelle wo er sie [Lunete] sah,
Hieß sie aufstehn und sprach allda:
„Fraue, zeiget mir die,   5
Die Euch hier kränken, sind sie hie;
Und heißt sie gleich Euch lassen gehn,
Oder sie müssen mich bestehn,
Und proben, was ich im Kampf vermag."
Der Löwe, der allzeit seiner pflag,   10
Der spürte seinen heft'gen Zorn,
Und drängte sich an den Ritter vorn.
   Nun war die reine gute Magd
Von Ängsten also gar verzagt,
Daß sie kaum aufzublicken wagt.   15
Jetzt fühlt sie wieder Mut und sagt:
„Ritter, das vergelt' Euch Gott,
Der weiß wohl, daß ich diesen Spott
Und diese Schmach muß dulden
Ganz ohne mein Verschulden;   20
Nun hoff' ich, daß Eu'r gutes Schwert
Sich ihrer also leicht erwehrt,
Als ich hier stehe von Schulden frei";
Und zeigt ihm ihre Gegner drei.

---

* The following are lines 5145–5199 of the Middle
High German version.

* The following are lines 5217–5281 of the Middle
High German version.

25 Da ritt der Truchseß vor,
    Und rief: „Der ist ein Tor,
    Und verrückt, bei Gott! der sich
    In den Tod hier wagt für Dich.
    Nun ist billig, wenn Einer zu sterben begehrt,
30 Daß man dem willfährt;
    Er mag sich versuchen im Gefecht
    Für eine Sache so falsch und schlecht:
    Denn es hat unser ganzes Land
    Ihre Untreu gar wohl erkannt,
35 Und wie sie ihre Frau erriet,
    Und sie von ihrer Ehre schied.
    Fürwahr, ich rat' Euch gut,
    Überlegt's Euch erst mit kälterm Blut.
    Ich warn' Euch dess viel sehre,
40 Daß wir Euch Eure Ehre
    Müssen nehmen und den Leib
    Für ein so ungetreues Weib.
    Nun seht, daß wir zu dreien sind:
    Und wärt Ihr was anders als ein Kind,
45 Ihr möchtet wohl von der Red' abstehn,
    Die Euch muß ans Leben gehn."
    Da sprach der Ritter mit dem Leu'n:
    „Ihr mögt viel heftig dräu'n[8]
    Jetzt müßt Ihr mich bestehn,
50 Oder die Jungfrau lassen gehn.
    Mir hat die tugendliche Magd
    Mit teurem Eide gesagt,
    Daß sie an ihrer Frauen sei
    Alles Verrates frei,
55 Und daß sie weder in Wort noch Tat
    Sie je verlockt durch bösen Rat.
    Was hilft Euch das, daß Euer Drei?
    Wähnt Ihr, daß ich allein hier sei?
    Gott und die Wahrheit schieden sich nie,
60 Mit den Beiden steh' ich hie.
    Ich vertraue wohl, sie halten zu mir;
    So bin ich selb drei so gut als Ihr;
    Und bringt mir's, wähn' ich, größre Kraft,
    Als Euch Eure Gesellenschaft."

The seneschal is not willing to permit the lion to take part in the battle. Iwein will not tie the lion, but he is compelled to remove it from the scene or else forfeit the contest. One of his opponents is speedily put out of action when the fight begins, but the others press him hard.

Da kämpfte tapfer und wohl bewahrt*

---

[8] **dräu'n**: drohen.
* The following are lines 5366–5411 of the Middle High German version.

    Der fechtenden Brüder Paar,
    Und bracht' ihn in große Gefahr
    Und manche sorgliche Not.
    Ja, fast bis an den Tod   5
    Drängten sie ihm viel sehre,
    Doch ohne von seiner Ehre
    Ein Quintlein[9] zu gewinnen.
    Nun aber kam zu Sinnen
    Ihr Bruder, der Truchseß wieder,   10
    Und lag nicht länger darnieder.
    Er griff zu Schild und Schwert,
    Und ging zu seinen Brüdern wert.
    Da däuchte dem Leun die höchste Zeit
    Teil zu nehmen am Streit,   15
    Und rannt' alsbald den schreitenden Mann
    Viel unsänftlich an,
    Und zerrt' am Eisengewand:
    Die Ringe fielen zuhand
    Als wär' das Panzerhemd von Stroh: 20
    Da ward er fertig mit ihm also;
    Denn wo er ihn trifft, gewiß und wahr,
    Zerreißt er ihn ganz und gar.
    So gewannen des Leun Gebete
    Frieden für Frau Lunete;   25
    Sein Beten ging auf Blut und Tod,
    Sie aber freut sich, es tat ihr Not.
    So ward's mit dem Truchseßen.
    Nun wollte der Leu sich messen
    Mit seinen Kampfgenossen,   30
    Die manchen schweren und großen
    Schlag empfingen und teilten aus.
    Hielten sie nun sich gut im Strauß.
    So wehrt' ihnen das den Tod;
    Denn jetzt bedrängt sie schlimme Not. 35
    Jetzt standen Zwei entgegen Zwein,
    Denn es wollte mein Herr Iwein
    Den Löwen nicht vertreiben,
    Und ließ es dabei auch bleiben;[10]
    Er mochte sein entbehren,   40
    Doch ließ er ihn ohne Zorn gewähren,
    Und als er ihm zu Hilfe sprang,
    Schalt er ihn weder, noch sagt' ihm Dank.
    Sie faßten von beiden Seiten sie an,
    Hier der Löwe und da der Mann.   45

*   *   *

---

[9] **Quintlein**: a very small quantity; a scruple.
[10] Strictly speaking, Iwein was at fault in allowing the lion to take part in the combat, but the fight had been unfair from the start. It will be noted that in the fight with Gawain the lion is kept out of the way. The seneschal, like all those of his class in the romances, belongs to courtly society but fails to live according to its spirit.

So waren sie überwunden,*
Doch hatten sie grimmer Wunden
Herrn Iwein vier geschlagen.
Dess hört ihn da niemand klagen,
5 Noch fragt er anderm nach,
Als seines Löwen Ungemach.
  Nun war in jenem Land
Also zu Recht erkannt,
Daß der schuldige Mann
10 Denselben Tod gewann
Den der Beklagte sollte leiden;[11]
Er mußte vom Leben scheiden
Wenn er erlag im Gottesgericht.
Das erließ man auch diesen nicht,
15 Sie wurden zum Holzstoß hingeführt.
Die Mägdlein froh und gerührt
Drängten herzu sich alle,
Mit brünstigem Fußfalle
Dankten sie ihm sehre,
20 Und boten ihm all' die Ehre,
Die er empfangen mochte da;
Mehr als er wünscht' ihm dess geschah.
  Frau Lunete war hoch erfreut,
Ihr Leben und Hoffen erneut:
25 Sie gewann ihrer Frauen Huld,
Und hatte frei von Schuld
Erlitten Kummer und Not:
Das macht' ihrs wett[12] bis an den Tod.

Laudine, who is present, does not recognize him and offers to help him recover the favor of his lady. Iwein's next task is to act as the champion of the younger daughter of the Graf von dem schwarzen Dorne. She claims that she is being deprived by her older sister of part of her inheritance. Gawain is the champion of the older sister. Before the battle is fought, however, Iwein releases a company of noble maidens who have been kept at hard labor by two brother giants. Again the lion is of great help. The culminating battle between Iwein and Gawain follows the usual course. They are unknown to one another, fight a long, indecisive struggle and finally reveal their identity. The quarrel is settled by King Arthur. We next see Lunete again pleading with her mistress to find a defender for the fountain. Lunete offers a suggestion, but this time she first takes the precaution of making Laudine swear that she will not punish her if things do not work out well.

  „Wenn der Ritter kommt auf mein Gebot,*
Und rettet mich aus meiner Not,
Mit dem der Löwe fahrend ist:
Schwör' ich ohne Falsch und List,
5 Daß ich mit ganzem Willen und Sinn
Ihm verpflichtet bin,
Seiner Frauen Minnen
Ihm wieder zu gewinnen.
Ich bitte Gott, er helfe mir so,
10 Daß ich ewig werde froh,
Und diese lieben Heiligen hier."[13]
Also verschweigt sie nicht vor ihr,
Was dem frommen sollte
Den sie bringen wollte:
15 Dann rüstet sich die Magd
Zur Fahrt, die sie mit Freuden wagt.
  Urlaub nahm die Gute
Mit fröhlichem Mute;
Sie hatte da zur Stunde
20 Wenig davon noch Kunde
Als sie die Fahrt begann,
Wo sie fände den Mann,
Und ward gar bald ihr kund
Ihr viel seliger Fund,
25 Als sie ihn bei dem Bronnen fand.
Er ward ihr an dem Leu'n erkannt:
Und auch die Magd von ihrem Herrn
Ward erkannt von fern.
  Mit gutem Willen grüßt' er sie.
30 Sie sprach: „Daß ich so bald Euch hie
Funden habe, dess lob' Gott."
„Jungfrau, das ist Euer Spott:
Oder suchtet Ihr mich im Feld?"
„Ja lieber Herr, wenn's Euch gefällt!"
35 „Was führt Euch hierher zu mir?"
„Nun seht, Ihr tilgtet schier
Einen Teil von Eu'rer Schuld,
Und seid nicht fern mehr ihrer Huld,
Die Euch befahl dies Land,
40 Und heut mich ausgesandt
Zu langer Unmüßigkeit:
Bricht sie nicht geschwornen Eid,
Die mich zu Euch gesendet,

---

* The following are lines 5428–5456 of the Middle High German version.

[11] This was in fact the law in some countries.

[12] **Das . . . wett: Das machte sie ihr wieder gut.**

---

* The following are lines 7924–7972 of the Middle High German version.

[13] With the oath, taken on holy relics, Lunete has tricked Laudine into taking back Iwein and at the same time protected herself against any consequences.

So hab' ich auch vollendet
45 Die Rede also fern,
Daß ich Euch als meinen Herrn
Begrüßen werd' in kurzer Frist;
Gleich wie sie meine Fraue ist."

Thus Iwein is taken to Laudine as the Löwenritter.
Lunete makes known his real identity.

Die Rede däucht sie wunderlich.*
Viel schnell entfärbt sie sich,
Und sprach: „Wenn das Wahrheit ist,
Dann hat mich Deine List
5 Wundersam dahin gegeben.
Soll ich für den fürder leben,
Der mich so gar verachtet hat?
Wahrlich, dess hätt' ich gerne Rat!
Das Wetter träfe mich nie so schwer,
10 Ich hätt' es lieber gelitten ehr,
Als daß ich auf Lebenszeit
Wäre zum Bund bereit
Mit einem so gemuten Mann,
Der nie ein Herz für mich gewann:
15 Und sag' ich Dir's in Wahrheit
Zwänge mich nicht der Eid
So wär's nicht so ergangen.
Der Eid hat mich gefangen;
Sei denn der Zorn meinthalb dahin.
20 Ich seh', ich muß noch dienen um ihn,
Daß er mich lieber wolle ha'n,

Als er bisher noch hat getan."
Herr Iwein fröhlich da sprach,
Als er hörte und sach,
Daß alles wohl ausschlug,   25
Und der Kummer den er trug,
Daß er ein Ende sollte ha'n:
„Fraue, ich habe mißgetan,
Und Gott weiß, das schmerzt mich sehr.
Nun aber ist Sitte von jeher   30
Daß man dem schuldigen Mann,
Wie schwere Schuld er auch gewann,
Wenn er bereut, vergebe,
Und er in der Buße lebe,
Nicht mehr zu sündigen fortan.   35
Nun sei es abgetan,
Und find' ich wieder Eure Huld,
Wird sie durch meine Schuld
Nie und nimmer verloren."
Sie sprach: „Ich hab' es geschworen,   40
Und sei mir's lieb oder leid,
Einmahl gesprochnen Eid
Muß ich halten mit Herz und Munde."
Er sprach: „Dies ist die Stunde
Die ich wohl immer nennen mag   45
Meiner Freuden Ostertag!"

*Thus the two are finally reconciled and we are told
that Lunete, who had served them so faithfully,
stayed with them. Of the rest of their lives, says
Hartmann, he knows no more.*

---

* The following are lines 8075–8120 of the Middle
   High German version.

GREGORIUS

Hartmann begins his poem with an apology for his own "wasted youth." He feels that he has devoted himself to trivia and should repent before it is too late. This leads to awareness of the omnipresence of death and the need not to depend on last-minute repentance. On the other hand, no one should consider his sins too great for God's forgiveness, for this belief leads to the sin of despair. Hartmann then uses the parable of the Good Samaritan to show that such forgiveness may be bestowed upon the "hopeless sinner."

The story of Gregorius is as follows. A king of Aquitaine has a son and daughter of surpassing beauty. Their mother dies shortly after their birth; their father when they are ten years old. His death draws them closer together, and the boy, tempted by the devil, succeeds in seducing his sister in spite of her resistance. When she becomes pregnant, he seeks the advice of a wise man whose name his dying father had given him. The wise man suggests that the boy make a pilgrimage to the Holy Land and that his sister rule in his absence. Meanwhile the adviser arranges for her to bear the child in secret.

They decide that the best thing would be to put the child in God's hands; they wrap it carefully and place it in a chest with twenty gold pieces and an ivory tablet explaining the circumstances of its birth, without divulging the names of its parents. The chest is put on a boat, which is then set adrift. The brother dies on his journey; the sister refuses all suitors, devoting herself to the service of God.

Meanwhile a poor fisherman has found the boat and taken the chest ashore to the abbot of a nearby cloister. The abbot gives the child to the fisherman and, handing over some of the gold pieces for its support, says that it must henceforth be accepted as the fisherman's brother's son.

The fisherman's wife demands an explanation of the gold pieces and finally wheedles the true story out of him. She keeps it to herself until the child Gregorius is fifteen. He has been educated by the abbot and is in all respects superior to the children with whom he plays. One day he inadvertently hurts one of the fisherman's own children, and the mother is so incensed that she lets slip, in Gregorius' hearing, that he is a foundling.

In his misery he goes to the abbot and says that he must leave his home and find a new place to live.

Dann sagte der Abt: „Liebes Kind, höre nun, ich will Dir raten, wie ich meinem geliebten Sohn raten sollte, den ich von Kindheit an erzogen habe.* Gott hat Dir sehr viel Gutes getan. In seiner Liebe hat er Dir an Leib und Geist freie Wahl gegeben. So kannst Du selbst Dein Leben verdienen und Dir daraus Leben oder Schande schaffen. Nun mußt Du selber gerade in diesem Lebensalter entscheiden, ob Du Heil oder Verderben haben willst und wie Du anfangen sollst. Mein Sohn, sei Dir selber treu und folge meiner Lehre. Dann hast Du anstatt Laster und Schande Ehre und Aufrichtigkeit erwählt. Laß Deinen jugendlichen Zorn Dich nicht zwingen, voreilig zu tun, was Du später bereuen wirst. Du bist ein begnadeter Junge, Deine Gaben sind ausgezeichnet, Du hast einen sehr guten Anfang gemacht, die Leute in diesem Land sind Dir freundlich geneigt. Nun höre zu, mein liebes Kind. Du bist an das geistliche Leben gewöhnt. Gebe es nicht auf. Du wirst in den Büchern gelehrt. Ich bin schon alt geworden, mein Leben neigt zu seinem Ende. Jetzt versichere ich Dir, daß nach meinem Tode die Jungen und die Alten in unserem Konvent Dich zum Abt ernennen. Laß das Schwätzen einer Törin Dich nicht stören. Ich kann auch dafür bürgen, daß solche Worte ihr nie wieder über die Lippen kommen."

Gregorius sagte: „Herr, Ihr habt Gott sehr an mich gelobt und Euer Heil vermehrt. Das Vorteilhafteste habt Ihr mir vorgeschlagen. Meine Unerfahrenheit aber ist so groß, daß ich Euch nicht folgen kann. Drei Dinge treiben mich zu meinem Unglück aus diesem Lande. Das erste ist die Schande, die infolge dieses Vorwurfs über mich geht; das zweite, das mich herausjagt, ist, daß ich jetzt weiß, daß ich kein Fischerskind bin. Wie wäre es denn, wenn meine Verwandten von solcher Herkunft wären, daß ich Ritter werden könnte, wenn ich den Willen und die Ausrüstung dazu hätte? Ich habe eigent-

---

* The following are lines 1432–1598 of the Middle High German version.

49

lich immer begehrt, Ritter zu werden, wenn ich nur die richtige Abstammung und entsprechendes Gut hätte. Süßer Honig ist

50 bitter für den, der ihn nicht genießen kann. Glücklich ist der Mann, der sich so ein Leben mit Recht ausgesucht hat. Ich würde vielleicht hier immer bleiben, wenn ich den Willen dazu hätte, den ich leider nicht habe.

55 Mein ganzes Begehren steht auf Ritterschaft."

„Mein Sohn, was Du sagst ist nicht gut. In Gottes Namen, bekehre Dich. Der Mann, den Gott vom geistlichen Stand entfremdet, und der Ritterschaft verfolgt, muß durch

60 seine viele Missetaten seine Seele und sein Leben verwirken. Jeder, sei es Mann oder Frau, der sich von Gott abwendet, wird dafür gestraft und der Hölle überliefert. Mein Sohn, ich wollte Dich als Diener Got-

65 tes erwählen und wenn ich so einen in Dir finden würde, wäre ich immer froh."

Da antwortete Gregorius: „Das Ritterleben bringt einen Mann am besten zu seinem Heil, wenn er es nur mit Vernunft zu führen

70 versteht. Viel besser Gottes Ritter zu werden als ein unberufener Mönch."

„Mein Sohn, Du machst mir Sorgen. Du hast überhaupt keine Erfahrungen in Ritterschaft gemacht. Sobald sie Dich so

75 unbeholfen reiten sehen, machen sich die anderen Ritter über Dich lustig. In Gottes Namen, lieber Sohn, laß diese Absicht."

„Herr, ich bin ein junger Mann und kann noch lernen, was mir jetzt fehlt. Ich lerne

80 schnell alles, wonach mein Sinn strebt."

„Mein Sohn, viele, denen das ritterliche Leben gut bekannt ist, haben mir gesagt, daß jeder, der vor seinem zwölften Jahr nicht geritten hat und so lange in der Schule

85 geblieben ist, sich immer wie ein Klosterbruder benehmen muß. Du bist für den Chor als Gotteskind sehr geeignet. Nie hat die Kutte einem Mann so gut gestanden wie Dir."

90 „Herr, versucht es doch und gebt mir die Kleidung eines Ritters und wenn sie mir nicht steht, gebe ich sie gerne einem anderen Mann und lege mir wieder die Kutte an. Herr, man hat Euch die Wahrheit gesagt.

95 Von Kindheit an muß ein Mann sich streng üben, um ein guter Ritter zu werden. Ich habe es von Kindheit an gut gelernt—hier in meinem Herzen. Es wollte

mir nie aus dem Sinne gehen. Ich sage Euch, von der Stunde, da ich zwischen Gut 100 und Böse unterscheiden konnte, stand mein Begehren nach Ritterschaft. In meinen Gedanken war ich weder Bayer noch Franke. Im Geiste saß ich besser auf meinem Roß als ein Ritter von Hennegau, von Brabant 105 und von Haspengau. Herr Abt, ich bereue nie die Kenntnisse, die ich erworben habe und ich würde gerne noch mehr lernen. Aber auch wenn man mich bisher zum Bücherlernen zwang, ritten meine Gedanken 110 immer im Tournier. Wenn man mich zu den Büchern führte, wie sehnte sich mein Herz, wie spielten meine Gedanken um einen Schild. Ich begehrte immer einen Speer anstatt eines Griffels, ein Schwert 115 anstatt einer Feder. Das war mein steter Wunsch. Ich fühlte mich niemals so glücklich als wenn ich im Geiste auf dem Roß saß, den Schild um den Hals hängte, den Speer kunstgerecht unter den Arm stellte und auf 120 meinem Roß im Galopp davongetragen wurde."

Gregorius then pictures his "riding skill" in such technical terms that the abbot cannot understand him. He yields to the boy's pleas and provides him with knight's clothing, but makes one last attempt to retain him by offering to arrange a rich marriage. The boy refuses and leaves, taking the ivory tablet the abbot has given him. After a sea voyage, Gregorius arrives at a castle under siege by a suitor unwelcome to its mistress. Gregorius and the lady are attracted to one another—the silk of his garb reminds her of her lost son. (Thus we hear who the lady is.) He practices in tournaments and, with skill and cunning, defeats the unwelcome suitor. Although the lady has sworn never to marry, her vassals advise her that unless she does, her land might again be in jeopardy. She marries Gregorius. As Hartmann remarks: Thus does the devil work his will.

In spite of his success, Gregorius in not happy. He frequently reads the tablet and weeps. A maid reports this to her mistress; she has observed that his unhappiness is apparently connected with this object, which he hides in an aperture. While Gregorius is on a hunt, she secures the tablet for her mistress who immediately recognizes its significance. She sends a messenger for him. She tells Gregorius that she is his mother. Both lament—

she feels she is clearly destined for Hell, and that her only hope to make his suffering more tolerable is by her repentance.

„Mutter", sagte Gregorius, „Ihr sollt nie wieder so sprechen.* Es ist gegen das Gebot. Gebt die Hoffnung auf Gott nicht auf. Ich habe ein tröstliches Wort gelesen, daß Gott
5 die wahre Reue als Buße für alle Sünden annimmt. Glaubt mir, Eure Seele ist nie so verdorben, daß Ihr nicht sofort gerettet seid, wenn in Euren Augen nur einmal die Tränen wahrer Reue stehen. Bleibt hier in
10 Eurem Lande. Verzichtet nur auf Essen und Kleider, bleibt aller Bequemlichkeit und Freude fern. Ihr müßt das Land aber nicht behalten, um durch dessen Verwaltung weltliche Ehre zu erlangen, sondern nur mit
15 der Absicht, Gott dadurch besser dienen zu können. Wer die Möglichkeit hat, ein gemütliches Leben zu führen, leidet viel mehr unter solcher Entbehrung als der, dem das gute Leben fremd ist. Ihr seid eine
20 sündbeladene Frau. Das sollt Ihr durch tägliche Mühsal büßen, da Ihr Eurem Leib alles absagt, was er am meisten begehrt. Haltet ihn so, bis er in den Banden der Reue liegt. Das Einkommen von Eurem Land
25 sollt Ihr den Armen schenken. So muß Euch Gott seine Barmherzigkeit zeigen. Stiftet reiche Klöster, wie sich ziehmt, auf den Gütern, wo die Weisesten es Euch angeben. So lindert Ihr den Zorn, den wir mit
30 Recht auf uns gebracht haben. Ich will auch vor ihm Buße tun. Meine Herrin, meine geliebte Mutter, ich spreche mit Euch jetzt zum allerletzten Mal. Wir wollen es so einrichten, daß Gott uns beide in sein
35 Reich wieder zusammenbringt. Ich sehe Euch nie wieder. Es wäre besser gewesen, wenn wir früher uns getrennt hätten. Von nun an sage ich dem Land, dem Gut, dem weltlichen Leben ab."
40 Er legte seine reichen Gewänder ab und zog, ärmlich gekleidet, aus dem Land hinaus.

In his wanderings Gregorius comes to a fisherman's cottage, but the fisherman turns him away, telling him that since he is of stout frame he will

eat all their food, and then murder them. Gregorius endures this abuse as part of his penance. The fisherman's wife takes pity and calls him back. Gregorius eats only a crust, but the fisherman continues his abuse and finally asks who he is.

Er sagte: „Herr, ich bin ein Mann, der seine unermäßlichen Sünden selbst nicht erfassen kann.* Um Gottes Gnade zu gewinnen suche ich mir einen Ort in dieser Wüste, wo ich bis zu meinem Tod Buße tun und am
5 Körper Not leiden kann. Heute ist schon der dritte Tag, daß ich mich von der Welt abkehre und in der Wilde wandere. Ich hatte nicht geahnt, daß ich hier Gebäude oder Leute finden würde. Aber da mein Weg mich
10 heute zu Euch geführt hat, bitte ich Euch um Gnade und Rat. Wenn ihr hier in der Nähe eine geeignete Stätte, eine einsame Klippe oder eine Höhle kennt, zeigt sie mir bitte."
Der Fischer erwiderte also: „Mein Freund,
15 da Du es so willst, mach Dir keine Sorgen. Ich bringe Dich bald zu einer Ruhestatt. Mir ist hier in der Nähe ein Felsen bekannt, der sich ein Stück über dem See befindet. Da kannst Du Dich wohl peinigen. Wenn es
20 uns gelingt, hinüber zu kommen, kannst Du wohl dort viele schwere Tage lang über Deinen Kummer klagen. Dieser Felsen ist Dir einsam genug. Wenn das nicht nur Einbildung war, daß du Buße tun wolltest,
25 weiß ich für Dich den richtigen Rat. Schon seit langer Zeit habe ich eiserne Ketten bei mir; die gebe ich Dir gerne zu Hilfe, daß Du auf jenem Stein Dein Leben unentwegt verbringen kannst. Schließ diese Kette Dir
30 um die Beine. Falls Du es vielleicht später bereuen magst, mußt Du dann doch auf dem Felsen bleiben, auch wenn es Dir nicht mehr gefällt. Die Klippe ist so geformt, daß auch ein Mann mit ungehinderten
35 Füßen nur mit großer Schwierigkeit herunterklettern könnte. Wenn es wirklich Dein Ernst ist, geh jetzt schlafen und stehe früh auf. Nimm die Kette mit und setze Dich zu mir in meinem Boot, wenn ich vor Tageslicht
40 zum Fischen fahre. Dir zuliebe begebe ich mich dahin, helfe Dir auf den Felsen hinauf und befestige Dir die Beine mit der Eisenket-

---

* The following are lines 2695–2750 of the Middle High German version.

* The following are lines 2955–3018 of the Middle High German version.

te. So mußt Du da alt werden, und auf dieser
45 Erde kannst Du mich bestimmt nicht mehr
belästigen, davon bin ich ganz sicher."

Er sprach mit bitterem Hohn, aber Gregorius gefiel sein Vorschlag sehr. Es war völlig
wie er es sich selber gewünscht hatte.

Gregorius sleeps so soundly that the fisherman's half-hearted attempts to wake him fail, and he sets out without him. But the fisherman's wife wakes him in time to run after the fisherman to be taken to the rock. There he is chained, and the key to his shackles thrown into the sea.

Der arme Gregorius blieb nun also ohne
alle Hilfe dort auf dem einsamen Felsen.*
Das war seine einzige Behausung. Als Dach
hatte er bloß den Himmel. Gegen Frost und
5 Schnee, gegen Wind und Regen hatte er
nur Gottes Gnade zum Schutz. Kleider
besaß er keine, abgesehen von einem Buß-
hemd. Seine Arme und Beine waren nackt.
Von der Nahrung, die er dort fand, hätte er
10 bestimmt keine fünfzehn Tage leben können,
hätte ihm nicht Christus den Heiligen Geist
geschickt, um ihn vorm Verhungern zu
schützen und am Leben zu erhalten. Ich
kann euch sagen, was er zu sich genommen
15 hat. Aus dem Stein tropfte ein ganz wenig
Wasser. Darunter grub er eine Höhle, wo
Wasser zum Trinken sich sammelte, aber so
wenig, wie die Erzählung berichtet, daß in
einem Tag sie nur ein Mal voll wurde. Dies
20 trank der erbärmliche Mann und lebte davon
siebzehn Jahre. Vielen scheint es, daß dies
nicht die Wahrheit sein kann. Ich sage aber,
daß sie irren. Denn Gott kann alles machen,
was er will. Kein Wunder ist ihm zu groß.

Seventeen years pass. The pope dies and rivalry is so great that it proves virtually impossible to name a successor. The convocation finally agrees to leave the choice to God and await a sign. Two of the most upright men have the same dream, that in Aquitania a man has been chained to a rock for seventeen years, that his name is Gregorius, and that he is to be pope. The two men are sent to find him. After much wandering they come to the hut of the fisherman, and he receives them well—since they have their own food and drink. However, they agree to buy a fish, just caught

by the fisherman. As he cuts it up, he finds in its belly the key he himself had thrown into the sea, with the sarcastic remark that when it were found, Gregorius would be free from sin. Overcome by remorse, he tells his visitors the whole story, and they at once recognize that this must be the man they are seeking. He offers to take them to Gregorius, but adds that it will be useless, since he must long be dead. They know better, and on the following morning arrive at the rock and find Gregorius naked and appallingly emaciated. They ask him whether he is indeed Gregorius and then tell him of the dream. He cannot accept the fact that God does not expect more penance from him, for he is still thinking in terms of justice rather than mercy. He begs them to leave him.

Dann stand er auf und wollte weg.* Aber
die beiden Männer beschworen ihn bei Gott
und seinem furchtsamen Gebot bis er endlich
wieder still saß und ihrem Bericht weiter
zuhörte. Dann versicherten sie ihm mit Eid   5
und Beteuerung, was sie ihm schon berichtet
hatten, daß er es ihnen endlich wohl glaubte.
Er sagte: „Ich war ein Gefäß von Sünde und
Schande, als ich mit diesen Fesseln, die ihr
jetzt an meinen Beinen seht, auf diesen Felsen   10
gebracht wurde. Wie groß eine Sünde auch
sein mag, die Gnade dessen, der die Hölle
aufschloß, ist noch größer. Aber wenn Gott
der Herr mir wirklich in seiner Gnade die
Sünden vergeben hat und ich nun rein   15
geworden bin, dann muß er uns dreien ein
klares Zeichen geben. Sonst bleibe ich bis
zu meinem Lebensende auf diesem Felsen.
Gott muß mir wieder den Schlüssel schicken,
mit dem ich hier so fest angeschlossen bin.   20
Sonst verlasse ich nie diese Stelle." Dann fiel
der Fischer in Tränen vor ihm auf die Knie
nieder und sagte: „Herr, ich bin der sündige
Mann, der dies alles verbrochen hat. Arm
und verloren wie ich bin, habe ich Euch mit   25
Zorn empfangen. Anstatt Brot habe ich
Euch böse Worte gegeben—das war die
Bewirtung, die Ihr von mir bekommen habt.
Mit Eifer habe ich Euch Schmähungen
geschenkt. So habe ich Euch mit Schmach   30
und großem Lärm unterhalten. Nun bin ich
alt geworden und habe für die Sünde keine
Buße geleistet. Sie liegt mir noch immer auf
der Seele. Wenn die Fahrt, die ich heute mit

---

* The following are lines 3101–3136 of the Middle
High German version.

* The following are lines 3585–3652 of the Middle
High German version.

35 Aufrichtigkeit gemacht habe, mir nicht
zu Nutze kommt, dann muß ich alles am
Ende büßen. Ich habe Eurer Bitte gefolgt,
obgleich ich es mit Hohn gemacht habe.
Ich führte Euch auf diesen Felsen, befestigte
40 Eure Beine und warf den Schlüssel in den
See. Ich dachte nie mehr an Euch, bis meine
sündige Hand gestern den Schlüssel in einem
Fisch fand. Das haben diese Herren gesehen,
wenn Zeugen nötig sind."

*The fisherman unchains Gregorius, the delegates
share their clothes with him, and he spends the
night in the penitent fisherman's hut. Gregorius
is most reluctant to leave without the tablet,
which he has lost. The hut in which he had first
stayed had meanwhile been destroyed, but a search
of the ground soon yields the tablet, undamaged.
Gregorius is taken to Rome, where the bells ring
spontaneously three days before his arrival. As
pope, he soon establishes a reputation for justice
and mercy. His mother hears of this and, without
knowing that the pope is her son, goes to him for
help. He does not recognize her, for she too has
done penance, until she tells him the story of both
their lives.*

"Edle Frau, sagt mir, in Gottes Namen,
habt Ihr seitdem Nachricht von Eurem
Sohn, wohin er gekommen ist?* Lebt er oder
ist er tot?" Da seufzte sie in ihrer Trauer und
5 sagte: "Nein, Herr. Ich bin überzeugt, er
hat aus Reue sich so gepeinigt, daß ich es
für sicher halte, daß er nicht mehr lebt."
Er erwiderte: "Wenn durch Gottes Gnade
es geschehen könnte, daß Ihr ihn wiedersehen
10 dürftet, glaubt Ihr, ihn wieder erkennen zu
können?"
Sie sprach: "Wenn meine Sinne nicht
gestört wären, würde ich ihn sicher erkennen."
15 Er sagte: "Nun, sagt mir, bitte, wenn
Ihr ihn wieder sehen dürftet, würde es Euch
Freude oder Leid tun?"
Sie sprach: "Ihr wißt, daß ich meinen
Leib, meinen weltlichen Besitz, alle Freude
20 und alle Begehr aufgegeben habe und wie
ein armes Weib lebe. In diesem Leben ist
mir nun nur eine Freude noch möglich—daß
ich ihn wiedersehe."

Da sprach er: "Seid getrost. Ich kann
Euch etwas Frohes mitteilen. Es ist nicht 25
lange her, ich habe ihn gesehen, und er
versicherte mir, niemand wäre ihm so teuer
und innig verbunden wie ihr."
"O lieber Herr, lebt er noch?"
"Gewiß." 30
"Und wie geht es ihm?"
"Er ist gesund und ist hier."
"Darf ich ihn sehen?"
"Ja, edle Frau, er ist nicht weit von hier."
"Herr, laßt mich ihn anschauen." 35
"Edle Frau, das kann leicht geschehen.
Wenn Ihr ihn sehen wollt, braucht Ihr nicht
länger zu warten. Liebe Mutter, seht mich an.
Ich bin Euer Sohn und Euer Mann. So groß
und schwer meine Sünden auch waren, Gott 40
hat sie vergeben und von ihm bekam ich
dieses hohe Amt. Es war sein Wille, daß ich
erwählt wurde. Deswegen habe ich ihm
Seel' und Leib übergeben."

*The two live together for the rest of their days,
devoting their lives to God, and Gregorius also
ensures that his father, too, will enter eternal joy.
An epilogue follows.*

Von diesen guten Geschichten, die von
Sündern erzählen, wie sie trotz großer
Sünden Gottes Gnade gefunden haben,
darf kein sündiger Mensch sich ein Vorbild
zum Bösen machen und von Gott verfremdet 5
sich denken: Nun sei unerschrocken und
lustig.* Wie kannst du verdammt werden?
Diese Leute sind nach einer unerhörten
Schandtat doch gerettet, und so kannst
du auch Erlösung finden. Wenn ich über- 10
haupt gerettet werden soll, bin ich gerettet.
Wen der Teufel so überreden kann, daß er
in der Hoffnung sündigt, den hat er erobert
und in seine Gewalt geführt. Auch wenn seine
Sünde am Anfang unbedeutend ist, kommt 15
ihm immer derselbe Gedanke, wenn er
tausendfache Sünden begeht. So kann er
nicht mehr gerettet werden. Nein, ein sündiger Mensch sollte sich vielmehr ein Vorbild
zum Heile machen und daraus verstehen, 20
daß er trotz seiner vielen Sünden erlöst
werden kann, wenn er nur Reue empfindet
und wahre Buße tut.

---

* The following are lines 3880–3935 of the Middle
High German version.

* The following are lines 3959–3988 of the Middle
High German version.

Wolfram von Eschenbach
(fl. c. 1170–1220)

Wolfram's *Parzival* is rightly regarded as one of the great works of Western literature. It presents a search for the noblest goals in a society which is idealized without sentiment and religious without dogmatism. The work contains much humor and adventure, bright description of courtly life, as well as serious discussion of the destiny of man. Its overall structure is brilliantly conceived and executed, yet individual scenes and motifs often seem to be loosely narrated or left in suspense. It is a work full of mysteries and contradictions.

Of its author we know little except what he tells us himself. It is now regarded as certain that he was born at "Wolfram's Eschenbach," a small village near Ansbach, in Bavaria. He prides himself on being a true knight, primarily concerned with the bearing of arms—not with writing of poetry. He, like Hartmann von Aue, was of the service nobility, that is, he had no land of his own and was forced to rely on patronage or employment from greater nobles. One of these was Hermann von Thüringen, the patron of Walther von der Vogelweide, whose court he is believed to have visited. In spite of his protestations in *Parzival* that he "does not know a single letter," it is hard to believe that he was uneducated. In all probability he wished to poke fun at Hartmann and Gottfried, who call attention to their learning. Certainly he has a mass of information at his disposal, sometimes ill-digested and quite possibly acquired by hearing rather than reading. His style departs quite deliberately from the clarity of Hartmann and Gottfried, both in vocabulary and structure, and succeeds in thoroughly mystifying the reader.

Parzival is a Grail romance, the earliest complete Grail romance in European literature. The etymology of the word "grail" is still violently disputed. In Christian tradition the Grail was the cup used to drink the wine at the Last Supper and, in some versions, the cup used to catch the blood that flowed from Christ's side. It was preserved by Joseph of Arimathea, who was imprisoned by the Jews and miraculously kept alive by the vessel. According to the account given in a poem of Robert de Boron, the *History of the Romance of the Grail,* written about 1200, and later prose versions of the story, Joseph collected a band of followers, some of whom were exposed as sinners by their inability to see the vessel and ousted from the group. The band finally came to Britain, where Joseph was buried; he was succeeded by Alan and ultimately by Perceval. It is basically this Christian tradition of the Grail that appears, naturally with many variations, in the French prose versions of the Grail romances and in Malory's *Morte d'Arthur.*

There is, however, very little reference to this tradition in Wolfram's work or in that of his source, Chrétien de Troyes. Some critics believe that many of the features of the Grail, for example, its ability to feed people with all the food they desire is derived from Celtic mythology. The vessel is not a chalice in the work of either Chrétien or Wolfram but a large dish and a stone, respectively. Thus it seems unlikely that either author drew only on the Christian tradition. Chrétien's poem is unfinished; he does not at any time definitely associate the Grail with Christianity, although he does mention that the vessel contained a holy wafer. For Wolfram, the Grail is definitely Christian. It receives its powers from a wafer brought down from Heaven by a dove every Good Friday. Yet nowhere in the poem are there the strong Christian features found in the French prose tradition.

Careful comparisons have shown that Chrétien de Troyes' *Perceval* or *Li Contes del Graal* (date uncertain; perhaps 1194) was the main source of Wolfram's work. Although Wolfram adds a long prologue about the double marriage of Gahmuret, Parzival's father, which is of great importance for the later development of the story and for which there is not even the remotest basis in Chrétien's poem, the ensuing incidents described are those of the French work. We hear of Parzival's childhood in the wilderness, his meeting with the knights, his departure for Arthur's court, his killing of the Red Knight, education by Gurnemanz, rescue of Condwiramurs (called Blancheflur by Chrétien) and marriage with her, and unsuccessful visit to the Grail castle. Both poems tell of his return to Arthur's court and the denunciation by the Ugly Damsel (Wolfram's Kundrie) which causes him to leave without being admitted to the Round Table. Perhaps most significant is that Wolfram has taken from Chrétien the long account of the adventures of Gawain, which takes up most of the latter part of the French poem. There is only one more incident involving Perceval before the French poem breaks off.

There can be no doubt that the main structure and almost all the incidents have been borrowed from Chrétien. Yet Wolfram denies this specifically near the end of his work. One can only ascribe this to his desire to mystify, and probably it was humorous fantasy that led him to state that the true source of the poem was a work by "Kyot." If Kyot stands for "Guiot," as seems probable, and if, in turn, "Guiot" was a familiar diminutive for Gui de Provence (an historical personage none of whose extant works could have been a source for *Parzival*,) then Kyot could not have been the "true source" of the poem. But Guiot could also stand for "Guillaume"— a common enough name — and we cannot be certain that there was no such person who wrote a poem that contributed something to Wolfram's work, for there are many features in which *Parzival* is far removed from *Perceval*. The introduction of Belakane, the heathen queen by whom Gahmuret has a son (Feirefiz), means that the end of the work, where the two brothers meet and where Feirefiz marries one of the virgin attendants on the Grail, must necessarily have departed from the French source. Moreover, the scene in which Parzival appears during the recital of the adventures of Gawain is very different in the two works. Chrétien shows us a humble and repentant Perceval visiting the hermit's cave and taking part in a normal church service there. Wolfram, in a scene nine times as long, describes in detail how Parzival, still proud and unrepentant, even though he knows he is in a state of sin, is told by the brother of the Fisher King Amfortas, of the dangers of pride and the need for humility and submission to God's will.

It is possible, of course, that Wolfram may have found some of these ideas in other sources, but most likely they are mainly his own. Even in scenes closely modeled on those in Chrétien's poem, he makes significant changes. The first meeting with Condwiramurs, as rendered by Wolfram, is free of any sexual elements, whereas the corresponding French scene is quite the reverse. The role of Sigune, Parzival's cousin, whose lover has been killed and who mourns him throughout the work, is given more significance in *Parzival* than in *Perceval* and she, like many other characters, is named by Wolfram but not by Chrétien.

The real difference between the two works, however, lies in their purpose. Chrétien is concerned entirely with the education of a crude young knight. Whether he would have turned into a Christian knight we can only speculate. Certainly some contrast with the courtly Gawain must have been intended. Parzival also starts out as untutored, but he is innocent, not stupid. He must learn that true knighthood involves not only prowess (Gawain has that) but purpose and, particularly, humility and submission to God's will. There is little evidence of a Grail company in Chrétien's poem, but in *Parzival* the attainment of the office of Grail king means the opportunity to use knighthood for good ends. In other words, the Grail company is a special order, oriented toward religion. It stands higher than the court of Arthur.

Thus the structure of *Parzival*, with all its complications of detail, is really simple. In one series of episodes it tells of the slow and stumbling progress of an outstanding man to the highest of earthly reponsibilities. In parallel incidents, it tells of a knight's adventures that have already been recognized by his peers as unmatched. These exploits follow the courtly tradition and lead to a great deal of personal satisfaction for Gawain — they have no higher purpose than this. The introduction of Feirefiz gives Wolfram the opportunity to show that pagans too, as soon as they are baptized, are capable of the highest attainments.

Wolfram's style, as we have already remarked, is often tortured and obscure, and he has a penchant for flying off at tangents even in the middle of a serious scene in order to produce humorous effects. There are also some long battle scenes where the technical interest of the man of arms seems to get the better of the writer of romances. His versification, too, is less smooth than that of either Hartmann or Gottfried, but what he lacks in polish he amply makes up for in vigor. The work contains 24 ,810 lines and is written in the usual form for narrative works—rhyming couplets with four stresses to the line, although in many cases the final stress falls on a syllable normally unaccented.

PARZIVAL

The work begins with a prologue that reflects upon all earthly life—there is much that is black and much that is white, and a man is not lost eternally if he doubts but only if he despairs. Much of the prologue is in language so obscure that we can only guess at Wolfram's meaning. It is possible that he is replying to critics (among them perhaps Gottfried von Straßburg), who had read parts of the poem published earlier, by claiming "authority" and "purpose" in high-flown metaphors not intended to be taken seriously. He makes it clear, however, that it is his intention to portray his idea of a noble man and noble women. The first two books are devoted to the exploits of Gahmuret, Parzival's father. He is a younger son of the house of Anjou and seeks his fortune in the East. He finds Belakane, queen of Zazamanc, besieged in her capital Patelamunt by an army seeking revenge for Isenhart, who had died of love for her. Gahmuret defeats the besiegers and marries Belakane according to the rites of her country. He grows restless and leaves her before the birth of her son, Feirefiz. He returns to Europe and takes part in jousting where Herzeloyde of Waleis is the prize. Although he tells her of his previous marriage and of his commitment to the queen of France, Herzeloyde insists on her rights when he is proclaimed the best of the warriors. Their marriage is happy, but Gahmuret returns to the East and is treacherously killed. Parzival is born in sorrow.

Ach, wie so mancher mir zum Grame*
Wird doch des Weibes schöner Name!
Die Stimme wohl klingt allen hell:
Doch viele sind zur Falschheit schnell
5 Und wenige von Falschheit rein:
Die sollten doch geschieden sein.
Wie oft mein Herz mit Scham empfand,
Das alle diese gleich benannt!
Dein echter Brauch, o Weiblichkeit,
10 Hat immer Treue zum Geleit.
  Man sagt, der Hölle Glut vermeidet,
Wer Armut wegen Treue leidet.
Das tat ein Weib, und ewge Gaben

Wird es dafür im Himmel haben.
Frau Herzeloyd, die reiche, ließ   15
Drei Lande, wo sie Herrin hieß.
Nie hat an ihr zu keinen Stunden
Aug' und Ohr ein Falsch gefunden.
Zum Nebelgrau ward ihr die Sonne;[1]
Sie floh von aller Erdenwonne,   20
Und gleich war ihr so Nacht wie Tag.
Ihr Herz nur noch des Jammers pflag.
  So zog die jammervolle Frau
Hinweg nach einer Waldesau,
In wilder Einsamkeit gelegen,   25
Doch wahrlich nicht der Blumen wegen:
Was galt ein Kranz in ihrer Qual,
Ob er nun rot war oder fahl?
Sie flüchtet aus der Welt Getriebe
Den Sohn, den Erben ihrer Liebe,   30
Und sie befahl dort ihren Leuten,
Das Feld zu baun, den Wald zu reuten.[2]
Doch allen unter strengstem Drohn
Verbot sie, daß vor ihrem Sohn
Der Name Ritter würde laut: 35
„Denn hörte das mein Herzenstraut,
Sollt' er von Rittern wissen,
Würd' er mir auch entrissen.
Drum haltet klug die Zung' in Haft
Und schweiget ihm von Ritterschaft!"—   40
  Das blieb mit Ängstlichkeit gewahrt.
So in der stillen Wildnis ward
Der junge Königssohn erzogen,
Um königliches Tun betrogen,
Nur daß er einen Bogen schnitzte   45
Und Schäfte sich zu Bölzlein spitzte,
Im Wald die Vögel zu bekriegen.
Doch sah er tot nun vor sich liegen
Den Sänger, der so lustig war,
So rauft er weinend sich das Haar.   50

Parzival's sorrow over the dead bird reflects the essential tenderness of his nature which is inhibited later by the knightly instruction he receives. The boy of ten hunts with the short hunting-spear and one day while roaming he encounters a knight. Because his mother has told him that God is "brighter than the day, with the appearance of a man," he thinks the knight is God. Even when he is disabused of this idea, he can think of no greater

---

* The following are lines 3442–3507 of the Middle High German version.

[1] Wolfram does not by any means share the "courtly" attitude toward women. Chastity, purity, and fidelity are his ideals and love should be married love.

[2] **reuten: roden.**

*happiness than to be dressed in armor and to ride
on a horse.*

    Das einzige, was er begehrt*
Und immer wieder, ist ein Pferd.
Sie dacht' in Herzensklagen:
„Ich will's ihm nicht versagen;
5 Doch soll es ein gar schlechtes sein,
Da doch die Menschen insgemein
Schnell bereit zum Spotte sind,
Und Narrenkleider soll mein Kind
An seinem lichten Leibe tragen:
10 Wird er gerauft dann und geschlagen,
So kehrt er mir wohl bald zurück."
Aus Sacktuch schnitt aus einem Stück
Sie Hos' und Hemd: das hüllt ihn ein
Bis mitten auf sein blankes Bein,
15 Mit einer Gugel obendran.
Zwei Bauernstiefel wurden dann
Aus rauher Kalbshaut ihm gemacht.
    Sie bat ihn: „Bleib noch diese Nacht!
Du sollst dich nicht von hinnen kehren,
20 Eh Du vernahmst der Mutter Lehren:
Ziehst pfadlos Du durch Wald und Heiden,
Sollst Du die dunkeln Furten meiden;
Sind sie aber seicht und rein,
So reite nur getrost hinein.
25 Du mußt mit Anstand Dich betragen
Und niemand Deinen Gruß versagen.
Wenn Dich ein grauer weiser Mann
Zucht will lehren, wie er's kann,
So folg ihm allerwegen
30 Und murre nicht dagegen.
Eins achte ferner nicht gering:
Wo eines guten Weibes Ring
Du kannst erwerben und ihr Grüßen,
So nimm's; es wird Dir Leid versüßen.
35 Küsse keck das holde Weib
Und drück es fest an Deinen Leib.
Denn das gibt Glück und hohen Mut,
Sofern sie züchtig ist und gut.
Und endlich, Sohn, sollst Du noch wissen:
40 Zwei Lande wurden Dir entrissen
Von Lähelins, des stolzen, Hand,
Der Deine Fürsten überrann.
Ein Fürst von ihm den Tod empfing,
Indes Dein Volk er schlug und fing."[3]

„Das soll er wahrlich nicht genießen: 45
Ich werd' ihn mit dem Pfeile spießen."[4]
    Dann in der frühsten Morgenzeit
War schon der Knabe fahrtbereit,
Der nur von König Artus sprach.
Sie küßt' ihn noch und lief ihm nach. 50
O Welt von Leid, was da geschah!
Als ihren Sohn sie nicht mehr sah—
Dort ritt er hin, wann kehrt er wieder?—
Fiel Herzeloyd zur Erde nieder.
Ihr schnitt ins Herz der Trennung Schlag, 55
Daß ihrem Jammer sie erlag.

*Parzival does not turn around and hence does not
see his mother's plight (as he does in Chrétien's
version). He rides for a whole day and night and
on the following morning comes upon a tent in
which is lying Jeschute, wife of Orilus.*

    Doch als der wilde Knabe da*
An ihrer Hand ein Ringlein sah,
Sprang er ans Bett, den Reif zu holen,
Wie's ihm die Mutter anbefohlen.
Das reine Weib in Scham erschrak, 5
Als ihr der Knab' im Arme lag.
Sie, die man keusche Zucht gelehrt,
Sprach: „Wer hat mein Gemach entehrt?
Jungherr, Ihr waget allzuviel.
Geht, suchet Euch ein andres Ziel!" 10
Doch er, wie laut die Schöne klagt,
Ihn kümmert's nicht, was sie auch sagt.
Er drückt' an sich die Herzogin,
Zwang ihren Mund an seinen hin
Und nahm den Ring. Auch brach der Range 15
Von ihrem Hemd die goldne Spange.
Sie wehrt sich, doch mit Weibes Wehr:
Ihr war sein Arm ein ganzes Heer.[5]
„Mich hungert," klagt er, „gib mir Essen!"
Sie sprach: „Ihr wollt doch mich nicht fres- 20
    sen?
Wärt Ihr zu Nutzen weise,
Ihr nähmt Euch andre Speise.
Seht, dort beiseit steht Brot und Wein

---

  * The following are lines 3756–3820 of the Middle
   High German version.
  [3] The advice given is significant only in part. The
   caution against muddy fords seems almost a joke,
   but Parzival takes the advice about women very

seriously without understanding it at all. Parzival
accuses the Red Knight (Ither) of "perhaps" being
Lähelin, again revealing his ignorance.
[4] Parzival shows that he is very unsophisticated.
  It was unknightly to use a javelin against a man,
  but Parzival keeps his word and kills Ither with it.
* The following are lines 3883–3941 of the Middle
  High German version.
[5] Jeschute belongs to the class of courtly ladies
  whom Wolfram despises.

Und zwei Rebhühnchen obendrein.
25 Das hat ein Mägdlein hergebracht,
Die's Euch doch wenig zugedacht."
   Er ließ von ihr, indem er saß
Und einen guten Kropf sich aß,
Wo nach er schwere Trünke schlang.
30 Ihr währt sein Wesen hier zu lang:
Sie deucht, dem Jungen fehlt's im Hirne;
Der Angstschweiß stand ihr auf der Stirne.
Drum sprach sie: „Jungherr, lasset mir
Das Ringlein und die Spange hier
35 Und hebt Euch fort! Denn kommt mein
      Mann
Und trifft Euch hier im Zelte an,
So müßt Ihr Zorn erleiden,
Den Ihr gern möchtet meiden."
Er sprach mit trotzigem Gesicht:
40 „Er komme nur! Ich fürcht' ihn nicht.
Doch schadet's Dir an Ehren,
Will ich von hinnen kehren."
Aufs neu' kam er ans Bett gegangen,
Die Schöne küssend zu umfangen;
45 Ungerne litt's die Herzogin.
Denn ohne Abschied ritt er hin;
Doch sprach er noch: „Gott hüte Dein!
So lehrte mich's die Mutter mein."

The wretched Jeschute pays the penalty of Parzival's crudity. When Orilus returns, he thinks a lover has visited her and makes her ride in tattered clothes on slashed harness before him until he can avenge his honor.

Parzival's next encounter is with his cousin Sigune. Her lover, Schionatulander, had fought for Parzival's side against Lähelin and had been killed by the same Orilus who is now seeking his revenge on Parzival. Sigune recognizes who Parzival is when she hears that all he has been called up to now is "bon fils, cher fils, beau fils." She addresses him by his real name which we now hear for the first time. Parzival promises to avenge her and rides on. He is guided to Arthur's court by a fisherman and outside meets Ither, the Red Knight, who asks him to deliver a challenge. The boy agrees and enters the court. He asks for Ither's armor, and although Arthur likes him, he refuses. The malicious Kei twists Arthur's reply to Parzival's request to make him think the king consents. Two other persons suffer from Kei's cruelty— Kunneware, who was not to laugh until she saw the best knight in the world, and Antenor, who could not speak until she laughed and now tells

Kei he will suffer for his ill-treatment of her. Parzival goes back to Ither and tells him that Arthur has granted him the armor.

„Gewähr' mir's, bist Du bei Verstand!"*
„Hat Artus Dir mein Kleid gegeben,
Fürwahr, er gibt Dir auch mein Leben,
Wenn Deine Kraft mir's abgewinnt.
So ist er Freunden wohlgesinnt. 5
Er war Dir wohl von früher hold?
Dein Dienst erwirbt je schnellen Sold."
„Mein Dienst mag haben, was er soll.
Des Herrn Geschenk war ehrenvoll.
Gib her und laß Dein Rechten! 10
Ich bleib' nicht bei den Knechten;
Ich will mich zu den Rittern scharen."—
Er kam ihm in den Zaum gefahren:
„Du magst der Lähelin wohl sein,
Von dem mir klagt die Mutter mein." 15
Da stieß ihn mit verkehrtem Schaft
Der Held, daß von des Stoßes Kraft
Er samt dem Gäulchen, das ihn trug,
Sich in den Blumen überschlug.
Im Grimme hieb der Held ihn wieder; 20
Ihm spritze Blut vom Haupte nieder.
Da sprang er voller Zorn empor,
Zog seinen Wurfpfeil rasch hervor,
Und wo durch Helm und durch Visier
Man auslugt ob dem Hersenier, 25
Da schnitt durchs Aug' der Pfeil im Saus
Und fuhr zum Nacken ihm heraus,
Daß tot der Held zur Erde fiel.
Da gibt's zerrissener Herzen viel,
Als Ithers Tod von Gahevies 30
Manch liebend Weib in Tränen ließ.

Parzival is unmoved by what he has done. With the help of a squire, Iwanet, he takes Ither's armor and puts it on over his fool's clothing. His next encounter is with Gurnemanz, an elderly knight who has lost three sons. Gurnemanz instructs Parzival in courtly manners and the bearing of arms. He learns quickly.

„. . . Gebt jedem Ding sein rechtes Maß.†
Ich kann nicht leugnen, denn ich sah's,
Daß Ihr des Rats bedürftig seid.
Was sich nicht ziemt, das laßt beiseit.

* The following are lines 4583–4615 of the Middle
  High German version.
† The following are lines 5094–5123 of the Middle
  High German version.

5   Vor allem sollt Ihr nicht viel fragen,
    Doch wohlbedächtig Antwort sagen,
    Daß, was der Frager ihr entnimmt,
    Auch recht zu seiner Frage stimmt.
    Gebrauchet aller Euer Sinne,
10 Daß Ihr des Wahren werdet inne.
    Folgt meinem Wort und übt im Streit
    Bei kühnem Mut Barmherzigkeit.
    Sofern Ihr nicht im Lanzenbrechen
    Habt schweres Herzeleid zu rächen,
15 Will der Besiegte sich ergeben,
    So nehmt sein Wort und laßt ihn leben.
    Ihr sollt nun oft die Waffen tragen;
    Da wird Euch Eisenruß beschlagen.
    Legt Ihr sie ab, so säumet nicht
20 Und wascht Euch Hand und Angesicht;
    Laßt wieder Euch in Armut schaun;
    Denn darauf achten edle Fraun.
    Seid männlich stets und wohlgemut;
    So lobt man Euch und wird Euch gut.
25 Denkt, daß Ihr Frauen liebt und ehrt;
    Denn das erhöht des Jünglings Wert.
    Bleibt ihnen treu ergeben;
    Das edelt Mannes Leben.
    Verlegt Ihr Euch auf Lügen,
30 Ist manche zu betrügen."[6]

Parzival stays two weeks with Gurnemanz, who would much like him to remain and marry his daughter Liasse. Although he is attracted by her innocence and beauty, Parzival decides he needs more experience in chivalric exploits. He rides on and arrives in the town of Belrapeire, which is under strict siege and whose inhabitants are starving. He is well received by its princess, Condwiramurs, who is the niece of Gurnemanz. During the night she determines to visit his room to ask for his help against the besiegers.

    Ich will Euch sagen, wie das kam:*
    Nicht gegen Weibes Zucht und Scham,
    O nein, die junge Fürstin war
    In keuschem Sinn unwandelbar.
5   Sie zwang des wilden Krieges Not

---

[6] Gurnemanz represents all that is best in the chivalric word, and his advice is sound, but for a man with Parzival's mission, insufficient. After the meeting with Gurnemanz, Parzival does not mention his mother's advice again.
* The following are lines 5691–5755 of the Middle High German version.

Und lieber Helfer blutger Tod;
So lag in ihrer Kammer
Sie wach im Herzensjammer.
Da glitt sie aus dem Bette leis
Im Seidenhemd wie Schnee so weiß,   10
Worüber sie zum nächtgen Gang
Den langen Sammetmantel schwang.
Sie ließ im Schlaf, wer um sie war,
Die Kämmrer und der Mägdlein Schar,
Und ging, auf Minne nicht bedacht,   15
Die zum Weib die Jungfrau macht;
Sie suchte Hilf' und Freundesrat.
So schlich sie nach der Kemenat,
Wo Parzival lag ganz allein;
Taghell war's von Kerzenschein.   20
Zum Bette ging die Königin
Und kniete auf den Teppich hin,
Und ihres Jammers Tränen flossen,
Daß seine Wangen sie begossen.
Er hört ihr Weinen und erwacht   25
Und sieht sie bei sich in der Nacht.
Indem's ihn wohl und weh durchrinnt,
Setzt er sich aufrecht und beginnt:
„Frau, treibt Ihr mit mir Euren Spott?
Knien sollt Ihr nur vor Gott."   30
Dann war sein Bitten und Begehr:
„Geruht und setzt Euch zu mir her
Oder legt Euch, wo ich lag,
Und laßt mich bleiben, wo ich mag!"
Sie sprach: „Wollt Ihr Euch ehren   35
Und Mäßigung bewähren,
Daß Ihr nicht ringen wollt mit mir,
Leg' ich mich Euch zur Seite hier."
Er gab ihr Frieden feierlich,
Und in das Bette schmiegt sie sich.   40

The night is passed in complete innocence (a fact Wolfram emphasizes); the next day Parzival defeats Kingrun, one of the besiegers and sends him, as a mark of honor, to Kunneware to make his surrender. Parzival marries Condwiramurs and defeats other besiegers, among them Klamide. After about a year of happiness, Parzival asks leave to seek out his mother. The first day he arrives at a lake where he sees a nobleman fishing and is invited by him to his castle. There he is well received. A rich cloak is given him by Repanse de Schoye, the guardian of the Grail. He sees his host sitting before a great fire. A bleeding lance is borne around amid great lamenting. Then a procession of maidens enters.

Doch sieh, noch sechse treten ein,*
Den letzten sechs in Anzug gleich:
An ihnen schimmert bunt und reich
Zwiefarbig halbgeteilte Tracht
5   Aus Goldgewirk und Seidenpracht.
Dann kam die Königin herein;
Ihr Antlitz gab so lichten Schein:
Sie meinten all, es wolle tagen.
Als Kleid sah man die Jungfrau tragen
10   Arabiens schönste Weberei.[7]
     Auf einem grünen Achmardei[8]
Trug sie des Paradieses Preis,
Des Heiles Wurzel, Stamm und Reis.
Das war ein Ding, das hieß der Gral,
15   Ein Hort von Wundern ohne Zahl.
Repanse de Schoye sie hieß,[9]
Durch die der Gral sich tragen ließ.
Die hehre Art des Grales wollte,
Daß, die sein würdig pflegen sollte,
20   Die mußte keuschen Herzens sein,
Von aller Falschheit frei und rein.
Die Jungfraun tragen vor dem Gral
Sechs Glasgefäße lang und schmal,
Aus denen Balsamfeuer flammt.
25   Sie wandeln züchtig insgesamt
Mit abgemessnem Schritte
Bis in des Saales Mitte.
Die Königin verneigte sich
Mit ihren Jungfraun feierlich
30   Und setzte vor den Herrn den Gral.
Gedankenvoll saß Parzival
Und blickte nach ihr unverwandt,
Die ihren Mantel ihm gesandt.
Drauf teilt sich all das Gralgeleite;
35   Zwölf Jungfraun stehn auf jeder Seite,
Und in der Mitte steht allein
Die Magd in ihrer Krone Schein.

*   *   *

Denn wie ich selber sie vernommen,†

Soll auch zu Euch die Märe kommen:
Was einer je vom Gral begehrt,
Das ward ihm in die Hand gewährt,
Speise warm und Speise kalt,   5
Ob sie frisch sei oder alt,
Ob sie wild sei oder zahm.[10]
Wer meint, daß dies zu wundersam
Und ohne Beispiel wäre,
Der schelte nicht die Märe.   10
Dem Gral entquoll ein Strom von Segen,
Vom Glück der Welt ein vollster Regen,
Er galt fast all dem Höchsten gleich,
Wie man's erzählt vom Himmelreich.

*   *   *

     Wohl sah mit Staunen Parzival*
Die Pracht der Wunder sich bezeigen;
Jedoch aus Anstand wollt' er schweigen.
Er dachte: „Der getreue Mann
Gurnemanz befahl mir an,   5
Vieles Fragen zu vermeiden.
Drum will ich höflich mich bescheiden
Und warten, bis man ungefragt
Von diesem Haus mir alles sagt,
Wie man bei Gurnemanz getan."   10
Drauf sah er einen Knappen nahn
Mit einem Schwerte schön und stark;
Die Scheide galt wohl tausend Mark,
Der Griff ein einziger Rubin.
Das ward vom Wirt dem Gast verliehn: 15
„Ich hab' es oft im Kampf getragen,
Bis Gott am Leibe mich geschlagen.
Herr, nehmt es als Ersatz entgegen,
Sollt' man Euch hier nicht wohl verpflegen."
     Ach, daß auch jetzt er nicht gefragt! 20
Um seinetwillen sei's geklagt,
Da mit dem Schwert, das er empfing,
Die Mahnung doch an ihn erging.
Auch jammert mich sein Wirt zumal;
Denn von der ungenannten Qual   25
Würd' er durch seine Frage frei.
Damit war nun das Mahl vorbei.

Parzival sees an old man who is later identified as Titurel, the grandfather of Amfortas the Fisher King. Parzival spends a disturbed night

---

* The following are lines 6987–7031 of the Middle High German version.
[7] The procession of women is much more elaborate than in the same scene in Chrétien's poem. It may be reminiscent of Eastern or Mozarabic rites.
[8] **Achmardei**: a kind of rich silk.
[9] Repanse de Schoye is a name invented by Wolfram. It will be noted that at this point we are told little more about the Grail than Parzival himself could observe, in fact less. We do not yet know that it is a stone.
† The following are lines 7077–7039 of the Middle High German version.

[10] The "cornucopia" motif is very common in association with the Grail, but it is not mentioned by Chrétien.
* The following are lines 7107–7139 of the Middle High German version.

*and the next morning he finds the castle deserted—
there is no one to help him don his armor. He
departs grumbling, and, to add to his perplexity,
the drawbridge is pulled up when he is barely
across, and he hears a voice from the battlements
reproaching him for not asking the question.
Shortly afterward he again meets Sigune, her
appearance so changed by grief over her lover's
death that he does not recognize her. She tells
him a few details of the Grail castle, but curses
him when she too hears that he has not asked the
question.*

*Only a short distance away Parzival finds
Jeschute in all her misery. She tells him her story
and warns him to flee from Orilus' wrath, but he
refuses; when the knight appears, Parzival attacks
him. The combat is indecisive.*

  Herr Orilus stritt kunstgerecht,*
Und wie so manchmal im Gefecht,
Dacht' er, soll's ihm auch heut gelingen.
Er faßte Parzival im Ringen,
5 Um ihn von seinem Roß zu ziehn;
Doch der griff zu, indem er ihn
Vom Sattel hob in e i n e m Ruck
Und unterm Arm mit kräftigem Druck
Wie eine Hafergarbe schwang
10 Und so mit ihm vom Rosse sprang.
Da lag ein Stamm vom Wind gefällt;
Darüber drückte ihn der Held:
„Nun zahlst Du, was in blindem Wahn
Du diesem armen Weib getan.
15 Fürwahr, Dein Leben steht zu Kauf,
Nimmst Du sie nicht in Gnaden auf."
„So schnell wird Sühne nicht gefunden;
Denn noch bin ich nicht überwunden."
  Da preßt ihn der gewaltge Degen
20 So mächtig an sich, daß ein Regen
Von Blut aus dem Visier ihm sprang.
Da ward ihm vor dem Sterben bang:
Er rief den Sieger schmerzlich an:
„Weh", sprach er, „kühner starker Mann,
25 Womit verdient' ich diese Not,
Daß ich vor Dir soll liegen tot?"
„Ich lasse Dich ja gerne leben,
Willst dieser Frau Du wiedergeben
In Treuen Deine alte Huld."
30 „Nein, Herr, zu groß ist ihre Schuld.
Ich leiste sonst, was Du begehrst,

---

* The following are lines 7884–7928 of the Middle
  High German version.

Wenn Du das Leben mir gewährst.
Das ward mir erst durch Gottes Kraft;
Nun dank' ich's Deiner Ritterschaft."

*Orilus is finally compelled by Parzival to forgive
Jeschute, who is glad to be reconciled with him,
and he is sent back to render service to Kunneware.*

*Parzival also moves toward Arthur's court
and is spellbound by three drops of blood in the
snow, for the red-on-white reminds him of Condwiramurs. He is attacked by Segramors and Kei,
both of whom he unhorses with ease. (In these
events he atones for what may be called his chivalric
"sins," the sorrow he had caused Jeschute, Kunneware, and Antenor.) Gawain breaks the spell
and leads Parzival to the court. He is held in great
honor and about to become a member of the Round
Table, when the hideous but learned Kundrie
arrives and denounces him; she declares that the
Round Table would be disgraced by his presence.*

  Dann ritt sie hin vor Parzival:*
„Daß meinen Gruß an diesem Tage
Ich Artus und dem Hof versage,
Davon habt Ihr die Schuld allein.
Schmach über Euren lichten Schein   5
Und Eurer Glieder Kraft und Kühne!
Geböt' ich über Fried' und Sühne,
Euch würde beides teuer.
Dünk' ich Euch ungeheuer,
Ich bin geheurer doch als Ihr.   10
Herr Parzival, steht Rede mir!
Wie kam's doch, als vor Euch im Saal
Der Fischer saß in seiner Qual
Ungefreut und ungetröstet,
Wie kam's, daß Ihr ihn nicht erlöstet?   15
Er wies Euch, ungetreuer Gast,
Seines schweren Jammers Last;
Doch Euch ward kein Erbarmen kund.
Der Zunge leer sei Euer Mund,
Wie Euer Herz des Mitleids bar!   20
Unter der verdammten Schar
Wird Euer Name mit genannt

Im Himmel vor der höchsten Hand:
So sollt Ihr auch schon hier auf Erden
Verdammt von allen Guten werden.   25
Vom Glück verflucht, vom Heil verbannt,
Nur mit Verachtung noch genannt,

---

* The following are lines 9397–9428; 9462–9464 of
  the Middle High German version.

Seid Ihr an Ehren todeskrank,
Wofür kein Arzt weiß einen Trank.
30 Euch gab der Burgherr doch sein Schwert,
Wart Ihr auch dessen wenig wert:
Da ward zur Sünde Euer Schweigen.
Nun schlingt Euch ein der Hölle Reigen.
Verworfner Ihr, Herr Parzival,
35 Ihr saht doch, wie man trug den Gral,
Saht schneidend Silber, blutgen Speer.
Ach, das verwind' ich nimmermehr,
Daß er, den Herzeloyd geboren,
In Schmach und Schande ging verloren!"

*Kundrie also announces that ladies imprisoned
in the Castle of Wonders are in need of a brave
knight to rescue them. The knights disperse from
Arthur's court, some to seek the Castle of Wonders,
and Gawain to prepare for his duel with Kingrimursel, who has challenged him. Parzival departs
in sorrow.*

*From now on most of the action is concerned
with Gawain, probably as a kind of secular coun-
terpart to the adventures of Parzival. The two
streams join up toward the end of the story. In his
first adventure Gawain charmingly acts as the
champion of a little maid, Obilot.*

Das sprach in seinem Herzen laut*
Für Obilot und ihre Klagen;
Er konnt' ihr's länger nicht versagen:
„In Euren Händen sei mein Schwert.
5 Wenn einer Tjost mit mir begehrt,
Müßt Ihr den Anlauf reiten
Und hilfreich für mich streiten.
Ich selber kämpfe nur zum Schein;
Denn, wer da kämpft, seid Ihr allein."
10   Das Kind sprach: „Ich bin treugewillt
Euer Schirm und Euer Schild.
Ich tröst' Euch, wie Ihr mich getröstet,
Da Ihr von Sorgen mich erlöstet.
Ich steh' Euch als Geleite
15 In aller Not zur Seite.
Mein Minnen bringt Euch Kraft und Heil."
„Ja, beides will ich als mein Teil,
Euern Trost und Eure Minne."
Er hielt dabei von Anbeginne
20 Ihr Händchen zwischen seinen Händen.
Sie sprach: „Nun gilt's, mich heimzuwenden.
Sonst bleibt Ihr ohne meinen Sold;

Dazu bin ich Euch allzu hold.
Drum muß ich nun beizeiten
Mein Kleinod Euch bereiten.   25
Tragt Ihr's, Ihr werdet freudenreich,
Und Eurem Preis kommt keiner gleich."

*The next encounter is quite different. At the castle
of Vergulaht Gawain meets the full-blooded and
sensuous Antikonie and loses no time in making
love to her.*

Ihr Mund war schwellend heiß und rot,*
Dem Gawan seine Lippen bot;
Sie küssen sich wie längst vertraut.
Er, der verlangend auf sie schaut,
Setzt nah sich zu der Holden nieder.   5
In süßem Plaudern hin und wieder
Wechseln sie manch freundlich Wort.
Dabei erneun sie fort und fort
Er sein Flehn, sie ihr Versagen.
Drob hebt er innig an zu klagen   10
Und ruft ihr Herz um Gnade an.
Die junge Königsmaid begann:
„Herr Ritter, seid Ihr anders klug,
So dünk' es Euch hiemit genug.
Da mich mein Bruder drum gebeten,   15
Nahm ich Euch auf, daß Gachmureten,
Meinem Oheim, von Anpflisen
Ward niemals schönre Huld erwiesen.
Doch hat sie je im Leben
Sich ihm als Weib ergeben?   20
Ja, wollte unsre Gunst man wägen,
Die größre bracht' ich Euch entgegen
Und weiß doch nicht, Herr, wer Ihr seid,
Daß Ihr schon in so kurzer Zeit
Anspruch macht auf meine Minne."   25

*Gawain is gaining ground in his pursuit of love
love when the lady's brother appears and attacks
him. There is a ludicrous battle in which Gawain
defends himself with a door bolt and chessboard
until his opponent Kingrimursel appears and
stops the fighting. Gawain leaves to find the Grail.*

*Parzival has been mentioned occasionally in the
preceding narrative. Now, however, he becomes the
main figure. He meets Sigune again; she has been
walled into a cell with the body of her lover, Schionatulander. She tells him a little more about the
Grail and how it sends her food. She is no longer*

---

* The following are lines 11052–11090 of the Middle
High German version.

* The following are lines 12097–12119 of the Middle
High German version.

angry with Parzival, and hopes for his success in finding the Grail, although she herself doubts that he will. Parzival sets out on his quest and meets some pilgrims, who reproach him for riding armed on Good Friday—a fact of which he is unaware. Almost in despair, he throws the reins over his horse's neck and more or less challenges God to lead him to the Grail.

Wolfram now interjects an "account" as to his source of the Grail story—a wild tale of the heathen Flegetanis, later baptized, who told how angels left the Grail on earth and how the story was translated into Latin by "Kyot."

The story continues: Parzival meets Trevrizent, a hermit, whose cave is in the same place where he had defeated Orilus four and a half years ago, and tells the hermit at once that he needs help, for he has sinned.

„Nun weiß ich erst", rief Parzival*
„Wie lang ich irrte dort und da
Und Glückes Trost mich übersah!
Ach, Freud' und Glück ist mir ein Traum.
5 Herr, hört' noch mehr! Ich mied den Raum,
Wo man von Gottes Ehren spricht.
In Kirch' und Münster ward ich nicht
Gesehn in all' den Zeiten;
Ich suchte nichts als streiten
10 Gott hegt' ich Haß im Herzensgrund:
Denn ist mein Herz im Tiefsten wund,
Setzt Trauer ihren Dornenkranz
Auf alles, was im Waffenglanz
Von Siegesehren ich gewann,
15 So rechn' ich's ihm zu Schanden an,
Der so gewaltig helfen könnte,
Mir aber keine Hilfe gönnte."[11]

The hermit does not reply directly to Parzival's complaint but tells him the story of the fall of Lucifer and of man, so that he may realize that he shares the common fate of the human race and that only God in His wisdom and mercy can solve his problem. Parzival then tells him that his greatest concerns are for the Grail and for his wife. The hermit is perturbed by this, for he knows that only the chosen can attain the Grail, and Parzival

does not relate his experience at the castle. The hermit then reveals a great deal more about the Grail than Parzival has learned up till now. He tells of the knightly band who live at the castle, whom he calls Templars; they are sustained by the power of the Grail stone, which also has the power to rejuvenate men and which causes the phoenix to rise from its own ashes.

„ . . . Zu ihm kommt eine Sendung heut,*
Die seine höchste Kraft ihm beut;
Denn am Karfreitag jenes Jahr
Zeigt sich ein Anblick wunderbar:
Weiß aus blauen Himmelshöhn   5
Fliegt eine Taube leuchtend schön
Und bringt herab zu diesem Stein
Eine Oblat weiß und fein;[12]
Die legt sie auf dem Steine nieder
Und schwingt sich auf zum Himmel wieder.   10
Davon ist ihm die Macht gegeben,
Mit paradiesisch reichem Leben
In Speisen und Getränken
Die Seinen zu beschenken,
Daß alles frei den Wunsch genießt,   15
Was duftiges von Früchten sprießt
Und was von Wild auf Erden lebt,
Läuft, schwimmt und in den Lüften schwebt,
Die Pfründe gibt des Grales Kraft
Der ritterlichen Bruderschaft."   20

The men chosen to serve the Grail are named by the stone itself—their names will appear on it. The angels who took sides neither with God nor Lucifer were the original guardians of the Grail (it is not known whether God forgave them or not), but now the chosen men guard it.[13]

„Wenn Ritterschaft", sprach Parzival,†
„Zugleich der Seele Seligkeit

---

* The following are lines 13751–13779 of the Middle High German version.

[11] Parzival is, of course, referring to God, and his remarks are blasphemous. He is guilty of pride in his belief that his deeds must induce God to consider him favorably.

---

* The following are lines 14020–14041 of the Middle High German version.

[12] The idea of the Grail's being revivified by the bringing of a wafer on Good Friday by a dove (the resemblance to the coming of the Holy Spirit at Pentecost is obvious) is found only in Wolfram's poem. He lays great stress on the Grail's power to sustain life on earth but as a result of heavenly power.

[13] Although the neutral angels are mentioned by Dante, little was written about them in the Middle Ages, and certainly no source is known for what Wolfram says about them here.

† The following are lines 14082–14130 of the Middle High German version.

Szenen aus dem *Parzival* Wolframs von Eschenbach. (Aus einer Handschrift des 13. Jahrhunderts) *Staatsbibliothek München.*

Sich samt des Leibes Ruhm im Streit
Erjagen kann mit Schild und Schwert,
5   Stets hab' ich Ritterschaft begehrt.
Ich stritt, wo ich zu Streiten fand;
Auch sind die Taten meiner Hand
Vom Ruhme nicht mehr allzu weit.
Versteht sich Gott auf rechten Streit,
10   So soll er mich zum Gral ernennen.
Fürwahr, sie sollen bald mich kennen:
Wer Kampf sucht, findet ihn bei mir."
„Herr", sprach der Wirt, „dort müßtet Ihr
Vor zu hochfahrendem Gebaren
15   Mit sanftem Willen Euch bewahren.
In Demut still Euch zu bescheiden,
Möcht' Eurer Jugend leicht entleiden.
Doch Hoffart kam zu Fall von je."—
Sein Auge überquoll vom Weh,
20   Das ihm die Märe brachte,
Die er zu künden dachte.
Dann sprach er noch von Tränen naß:
„Es war ein König Amfortas
Und ist noch heut'. Mich Armen
25   Und Euch muß stets erbarmen
Die herzergreifend grimme Not,
Die Hoffart ihm zum Lohne bot.
So hat die Jugend und die Macht
An ihm die Welt viel Leid gebracht
30   Und daß er warb um Minne,
Doch nicht mit keuschem Sinne.
Der Brauch verletzt des Grales Recht;
Da muß der Ritter und der Knecht
Der Sünde Lockung sich entziehen,
35   Muß Hoffart vor der Demut fliehen.
Bis heut' verwehrt mit Heldenkraft
Den Gral die werte Bruderschaft
Dem Volk aus allen Gauen,
Und keiner durft' ihn schauen,
40   Der nicht des Grales Ruf vernahm.
Ein einzger Unberufner kam;
Das war ein töricht junger Gast.
Der trug mit fort der Sünde Last,
Daß er kein Wort des Mitleids sprach
45   Bei seines Wirtes Ungemach.
Traun, ich will niemand schelten
Doch mög' er's noch entgelten,
Daß er den Wirt nicht mochte fragen,
Den Gottes Hand so schwer geschlagen. . . ."

*The hermit now asks Parzival directly about his
identity and when he hears it, tells him that Ither
was his relation; that his mother is dead, that he is
also related to Siguné, that he himself is Amfortas'*

*brother, and that Repanse de Schoye is his sister.
He speaks of Amfortas' wound—how the
intensity of the pain varies with the positions of
the planets and how the pain can be relieved only
by laying on the lance that Parzival had seen. He
also explains that it was Repanse de Schoye
who had given him her cloak and Amfortas who
had given him the sword at the Grail castle. Parzival
stays for fifteen days before resuming his journey.*

*The Gawain narrative now resumes. The knight
becomes devoted to a proud lady, Orgeluse, who
sets him difficult and dangerous tasks to test the
love he professes for her.*

*The most amazing adventures are those in the
Castle of Wonders, where Wolfram seems to be
parodying some of the clichés of Arthurian romance.*

Der Held ging in die Kemenat.*
Der Estrich glich, darauf er trat
Dem Glas an Glanz und Glätte.
Hier war das Wunderbette.
Windschnell unter seinen Stollen   5
Liefen eingelassne Rollen
Aus lichten Scheiben von Rubin.
Von Jaspis, Chrysolith, Sardin
Strahlt der Estrich in der Runde.
Das alles war mit Zauberkunde   10
Von Klinschor, der den Bau erdacht,
Aus manchen Landen hergebracht.
So schlüpfrig war's, wohin er schritt,
Daß Gawans Fuß bei jedem Tritt
Ausgleitend fast den Halt verlor.   15
Auf gut Glück drang er mutig vor.
Doch naht er sich dem Bette,
So fährt es von der Stätte
Und flieht behende vor dem Gast.
Ihn aber hemmt des Schildes Last,   20
Den er am Arme mit sich trägt,
Wie's ihm sein Wirt ans Herz gelegt.
Er dachte: „Fliehst du so von mir?
Wie alle Welt komm' ich zu dir?
Sieh zu, willst du dem Schritt entweichen,   25
Ob ich im Sprung dich mag erreichen?"
Und wie es wieder vor ihm stand,
Schnellt er sich auf und springt gewandt
Mitten in das Bett hinein
Nun aber fuhr's erst drauf und drein,   30
Stieß hin und wieder lauten Krachs
An alle Wände des Gemachs;

---

* The following are lines 16810–17121 of the Middle
High German version.

Die ganze Burg erdröhnte mit.
So tat er manchen tollen Ritt.
35 Wie stark auch tost des Donners Schall,
Und wären die Posauner all
Beisammen aus der ganzen Welt
Und bliesen drauf um gutes Geld,
Nicht ärger könnt' es krachen.
40 Traun, Gawan mußte wachen;
In diesem Bett gab's keine Ruh.
Er deckte sich mit dem Schilde zu
Vor all dem Graus und rief ihn an,
Der helfen will und helfen kann
45 Daß er in seiner mächtgen Güte
Auch ihn in dieser Not behüte.
Da, wie der Lärm sich endlich legt,
Bleibt das Bette unbewegt
Mitten in der Kammer stehen.
50 Doch nun soll schlimmres ihm geschehen:
Fünfhundert Schleudern aus den Wänden
Beschossen ihn von allen Enden
Mit runden Kieseln hart genug,
Daß mancher ihm den Schild durchschlug.
55 Gleich kamen noch von Armbrustbogen
Fünfhundert Pfeile nachgeflogen;
Die zielten all auf einen Schlag
Nach dem Bette, wo er lag.
Hat einer seine Ruhe gern,
60 Der bleibe diesem Bette fern!
Wohl manchem möcht' in jungen Tagen
Das Haar ergraun bei dem Behagen,
Das Gawan auf dem Bette fand.
Doch unverzagt von Herz und Hand
65 Blieb er in diesem Hagelguß,
Wenn auch nicht jeder Wurf und Schuß
Ihn verfehlt zu dieser Stunde;
Mit mancher Quetschung, mancher Wunde
War er durchs Ringelhemd getroffen.
70 Doch nun nach alldem darf er hoffen,
Zu Ende seien Not und Qual.
Da trat zu ihm mit einem Mal
Erschrecklich dem Beschauer
Herein ein starker Bauer;
75 Dem hüllte Scheitel, Rumpf und Bein
Ein Anzug ganz aus Fischhaut ein.
Der Knüttel, den er mit sich trug,
War oben dicker als ein Krug.
Damit ging er zu Gawan her;
80 Der hatte seiner kein Begehr.
Doch dacht' er sich: „Der Kerl da kann
So ohne Rüstung mir nicht an."
Vom Bett erhob sich der Beherzte
Und saß, als ob kein Glied ihm schmerzte.

85 Da trat der Mann zurück im Nu
Und rief ihm grimmen Blickes zu:
„Vor mir braucht Ihr Euch nicht zu bangen;
Doch weiß ich's wohl noch anzufangen,
Daß Ihr den Leib zu Pfande gebt.
90 Der Teufel macht's, daß Ihr noch lebt!
Doch hat er Euch bis jetzt bewahrt,
Der Tod ist Euch nur aufgespart,
Dem sollt Ihr nicht entrinnen;
Laßt mich nur erst von hinnen!"
95 Er ging; doch Gawan schlug in Eile
Von dem bespickten Schild die Pfeile;
Die waren alle durchgedrungen,
Daß in der Rüstung sie erklungen.
Ein grollend Brülle scholl herein,
100 Als hörte man zu Tanz und Reihn
Zwanzig dumpfe Trommeln schlagen.
Er, unberührt von Furcht und Zagen,
Sprach zu sich: „Wie soll's nun ergehn?
Ist mir nicht Leids genug geschehn?
105 Soll sich das Leid noch mehren?
Nun gilt es, sich zu wehren."
Er blickt gespannt dem Bauern nach
Als ins Gemach ein Löwe brach,
Groß wie ein Roß. Am Riemen faßt
110 Gawan den Schild, indem in Hast
Er auf den Estrich niederspringt.
Der Löwe, den der Hunger zwingt,
Stürzt wütend gegen ihn heran;
Doch stand zur Wehr der kühne Mann.
115 Beim ersten Griff war von den Klaun
Des Ungetüms sein Schild durchhaun
Und ward ihm fast vom Arm gerissen.
Doch wollte den der Held nicht missen;
Vom Bein er ihm die Tatze hieb,
120 Daß sie im Schilde haften blieb.
Vom Blute starrt der Estrich bald,
Und Gawans Fuß fand festern Halt.
Da hinkt mit zornersträubter Mähne
Der wunde Löwe, fletscht die Zähne,
125 Und sein ergrimmtes Schnauben dröhnt.
War er an solche Kost gewöhnt,
Wackre Leute aufzufressen,
Wär' ich nicht gern bie ihm gesessen.
Auch Herrn Gawan war er verhaßt;
130 Ums Leben stritt der edle Gast.
Und wieder sprang da aus dem Blut
Auf ihn das wilde Tier in Wut
Und wollte ihn zücken unter sich.
Doch Gawan bohrt ihm seinen Stich
135 Durch die Brust bis an die Hand,
Davon des Löwen Zorn entschwand;

Denn auf den Boden fiel er tot.
So ging der Held aus all der Not
Hervor als Sieger. Doch, was nun?
140 In diesem Blut mag er nicht ruhn;
Das Bett auch muß er klüglich scheun:
Er möchte seine Fahrt erneun.
Nun war ihm von der Würfe Prall
Der Kopf betäubt; die Wunden all
145 Fingen stark zu bluten an,
Daß schwindelnd ihm die Kraft zerrann.
So sank er nieder sinnberaubt,
Und auf dem Löwen lag sein Haupt.
Der Schild war seinem Arm entglitten;
150 Zu Schweres hat er hier erlitten.

*Gawain is brought before Arnive, King Arthur's
mother, who cures his wounds. She as well as
Sangive, Gawain's mother, and his sisters, Kundrie
and Itonje, are held captive in a castle belonging
to the magician Klinschor. Itonje is in love with
Gramoflanz, whom Gawain has to fight for the
honor of Orgeluse. After returning Arthur's
relations to him when the court comes near to the
Castle of Wonders, Gawain practices for his
forthcoming joust with Gramoflanz.*

So sprengt allein mein Herr Gawan*
Vom Heere ferne auf dem Plan
Da sah er—möge Glück nun walten!—
Am Flusse einen Ritter halten.
5 Das war ein Fels der Manneskraft
Ein Hagelschlag der Ritterschaft;
Sein Herz kennt keinen falschen Rat,
Und niemals von der Ehre Pfad
Wich sein Tritt um eine Spanne.
10 Ihr hörtet wohl schon von dem Manne.
Und endlich mögen unsre Mären
Zu ihrem rechten Stamme kehren.
Wird von dem werten Herrn Gawan
Hier wehrhaft eine Tjost getan,
15 So war ich nie wie diesen Morgen
Um seinen Ruhm in solchen Sorgen,
Wie? Nicht auch um den andern? Nein,
Um den braucht mir nicht bang zu sein:
Der war im Streit ein ganzes Heer.
20 Kamfzier, die fernher übers Meer
Von Helden kam, umschimmert ihn;
Es glänzt noch röter als Rubin
Sein Rock und seines Rosses Kleid.

Er suchte ritterlichen Streit.
Sein Schild war ganz durchstochen;   25
Ein Reis, das er gebrochen
Vom Baum des Königs Gramoflanz
Schmückt seinen Helm als lichter Kranz.
Gawan erkannte gleich den Zweig:
Dort hält der König! Wär's nicht feig   30
Käm' ich nicht eilends ihm entgegen?
Und harrt er mein des Streites wegen,
So mag sofort der Streit ergehen,
Wenn uns auch keine Frauen sehen.—
Sie spornten drauf, den Speer zur Hand,   35
Betauter Klee, nicht staubger Sand
War's wo sich der Kampf entspann.
Mich jammert, daß er je begann.

*Meanwhile Gramoflanz has arrived at Arthur's
court and messengers are sent for Gawain.*

Die Boten kehrten heim sofort*
Und nahten unterwegs dem Ort,
Wo mit dem Fremden stritt Gawan.
Laut schrien sie auf, da sie ihn sahn:
Des Gegners übermächtgen Schlägen   5
War er beinahe schon erlegen.
Da riefen, wie sie näher kamen,
Die Jungherrn klagend seinen Namen.
Doch wer so sieghaft vorwärts drang,
Hielt ein bei dieses Namens Klang;   10
Weit aus der Hand warf er das Schwert:
„Unselig bin ich und entehrt",
Rief weinend aus der edle Gast,
„Allem Glück bin ich verhaßt,
Daß meiner frevlerischen Hand   15
Dieser Streit je ward bekannt.
Hier kommt es wieder recht zu Tage,
Daß ich des Unglücks Wappen trage.
Wenn ich dem trefflichen Gawan
Mit Feindschaft hier Gewalt getan,   20
Hab' ich mich selber überwunden
Und nichts als Herzeleid gefunden.
Weh, da der Streit begann war schon
Glück und Stern von mir geflohn."

*Parzival now reveals his identity. Gawain is not
yet well enough to fight Gramoflanz, and Parzival
decides to fight in his stead. Again he is on the
point of defeating him when Gawain himself
arrives. Gawain and Gramoflanz are reconciled,*

---

* The following are lines 20268–20313 of the Middle
High German version.

* The following are lines 20558–20583 of the Middle
High German version.

*Gawain has Orgeluse and there is general happiness.
Only the wretched Parzival steals away in loneliness.*

*Parzival encounters Feirefiz, Gahmuret's son,
and fights with him. Neither is victorious, but
Feirefiz has the advantage when Parzival's sword
breaks. They make a truce and recognize one
another. The two return to Arthur's court, where
they are well received. There Kundrie tells Parzival
that his name has appeared on the Grail and that
he is to be Grail king.*

Zurück zum Bruder kehrt sie sich:*
„Doch Du in Demut freue dich
Wohl Dir des hohen Teiles,
Du Krone Menschenheiles!
5 Die Wunderschrift erschien am Stein
Du sollst des Grales König sein.
Kondwiramurs soll mit Dir ziehen
Und auch Dein Sohn, Loherangrin:
Sie hat, eh Du von ihr gegangen,
10 Ein Zwillingspaar von Dir empfangen.
Dem anderen Söhnlein, das sie trug,
Kardeis, bleibt Land und Macht genug.
Und wurde Dir im ganzen Leben
Die eine Freude nur gegeben,
15 Daß Du den Werten, Süßen,
Nun sollst mit Rede grüßen,
Sollst Amfortas von seinen Leiden
Mit Deines Mundes Frage scheiden,
Wer möcht' in allen Reichen
20 Sich Dir an Glück vergleichen?“

*The two brothers are conducted to the Grail
castle by Kundrie, and Amfortas begs Parzival
either to say the words that will cure him or withdraw the Grail from his sight for a week so that
he may die.*

Doch Parzival begann mit Weinen:†
„Wo liegt der Gral? Belehret mich!
Vor aller Augen zeige sich,
Ob ich von Gott begnadigt bin.“
5 Dreimal nach jener Seite hin
Warf er sich nun der Trinität
Zu Ehren nieder im Gebet,
Daß sie den Mann von Qualen rette.
Dann trat er an des Kranken Bette

Und sprach ihn an: „Was fehlt dir, Ohm?“   10
Und der Silvesters Stier in Rom,
Den toten, hieß von dannen gehn,
Der Lazarus hieß auferstehen,[14]
Der half auch Amfortas zur Stund,
Daß er ward heil und ganz gesund.   15

*Parzival again meets his wife and sees his children
for the first time; Kardeis is crowned lord of
Parzival's fiefs. While riding they pass by the
hermitage in which Sigune lived and find her dead
upon her lover's coffin. The Grail is borne in
before Parzival.*

Der Heide staunt wie hier dem Zecher*
Von selbst sich füllt der leere Becher
Ein Wunder, das ihm wohl behagte,
Und Amfortas, den er befragte,
Wies nach dem Gral: „Seht Ihr ihn nicht?“   5
Doch Feirefiz der bunte spricht:
„Ich sehe nur ein Achmardei,
Das jene Jungfrau trug herbei,
Die dort mit Krone vor uns steht
Und deren Schein ins Herz mir geht.   10
Ich glaubte mich so stark von je,
Nie sollt' ein Weib mit Liebesweh
Vom frohen Mut mich scheiden . . . .“

*It is made clear by Titurel that Feirefiz cannot
see the Grail because he is a heathen; the hero
himself is more concerned about Repanse de Schoye.
Feirefiz agrees to baptism:*

Der Heide sprach: „Nun, wenn mir's
        frommt,†
Im Ungemach zugute kommt,
So glaub' ich alles, was ihr wollt.
Lohnt mich dafür ihr Minnesold,
So folg' ich, Bruder, ohne Spott.   5
Hat deine Muhme einen Gott,
An diesen glaub' ich und an sie.
In solcher Not war ich noch nie.
All meine Götter sind verschworen;

---

[14] A Jew killed a bull by whispering into its ear the
name of his God. St. Sylvester revived it by whis-
pering the name of Christ. The story of the raising
of Lazarus is in John 11.
* The following are lines 24211–24225 of the Middle
High German version.
† The following are lines 24448–24459 of the Middle
High German version.

---

* The following are lines 23351–23369 of the Middle
High German version.
† The following are lines 23780–23792 of the Middle
High German version.

10 Für Sekundille[15] sei verloren,
Was sie mir tat zu ihrem Ruhme.
So tauft mich auf den Gott der Muhme!"

The baptism is performed; Feirefiz can now see
the Grail. He departs with Repanse de Schoye
for "India," where they have a son, Prester John.
Many details are cleared up in the last scene at the
Grail castle. Amfortas declares his intention of
pursuing a life of chastity and humility, even though
he has been rejuvenated. Trevrizent, who joins the
company, tells Parzival that the neutral angels
were in fact damned; he had left the matter in
doubt only to encourage Parzival.

A brief account of the future adventures of
Parzival's son, Loherangrin, follows. Wolfram
then concludes his story. He denies that Chrétien
de Troyes told the Grail story correctly and again
affirms that his source was Kyot.

Durch Abenteuer mannigfach*
Hab' ich Wolfram von Eschenbach
Herrn Parzival zum Ziel begleitet,
Das ihm vom Glücke war bereitet.
Was Leben so sich endet,   5
Daß er Gott nicht entwendet
Die Seel' durch des Leibes Schuld
Und er daneben doch die Huld
Der Welt mit Ehren sich erhält,
Der hat sein Leben wohl bestellt.   10
Mich dünkt, daß Frauen von echtem Sinn
Ich fortan um so werter bin,
Wenn eine gütig zu mir spricht,
Weil ich vollendet dies Gedicht.
Geschah das einer Frau zu Ehren,   15
Soll sie mir holden Dank gewähren.

---

[15] Sekundille was the pagan wife of Feirifiz and was
    queen of "India."

---

* The following are lines 24730–24745 of the Middle
High German version.

Gottfried von Straßburg

(fl. 1210)

We have no factual data on the life of Gottfried. The geographical designation could mean that he was a burgher of the city of Straßburg, but there is no evidence to prove or disprove this. The Heidelberg manuscript of lyric poetry speaks of him as "Meister," which indicates that he was not a nobleman. (Several poems in this collection are inaccurately ascribed to him.) In all probability he was educated as a cleric to the standard of a "Master"; in other words, he had received the best available formal education of his time. His works testify to the degree of his formal education. He had a far greater knowledge of the classics and of French than any of his German contemporaries, and his style reflects his deep acquaintance with the rules of classical rhetoric.

Although he was fully conversant with the chivalric poetry of his time, he clearly stood apart from it and felt none of the need expressed by Wolfram to justify the life of the knight. On the contrary, he deliberately showed its weaknesses by making his hero a cultured man rather than a knight.

The Tristan story had already been treated many times before Gottfried took it up. Of the extant versions, the most primitive is that by Eilhart von Oberg. This work, which may date from as early as 1170 or as late as 1190, shows Tristan as a great knight whose powers are ruined by a fatal love. There is no attempt here to make love the great and wonderful force whose commands transcend all other earthly matters. The French version ascribed to Béroul, of which only fragments exist, seems to follow the same tradition. Thomas of Britain, on the other hand, about 1175, wrote a work in which he attempted to display the power of love to weld two people into full union, a union not only of the senses but of the spirit. His stress is on the social aspects of this love, which he sets in the world of courtly romance. Thus Tristan enters the Arthurian world and in many respects his career is similar to that of Lancelot. The great difference lies in the fact that the two lovers are completely inseparable and that the element of love service, so important in all the Lancelot stories, is absent from the *Tristan.*

Gottfried openly states that he regards Thomas' version as the right one, and he pays it the supreme compliment of following its story closely. Our ability to compare the two versions is severely restricted because Gottfried's unfinished version breaks off almost where the extant manuscripts of Thomas' work begin —there is very little overlap. Fortunately, a Norwegian monk, Brother Robert, prepared a Norse version of Thomas' work in 1226, and we can at least compare this with Gottfried's poem. The story itself hardly differs, but there are significant changes in detail. The most important changes occur in the insertion of the passage of literary criticism instead of a description of Tristan's knighting ceremonies and in the allegorical portrayal of the grotto of love.

In the very elaborate prologue to his poem, Gottfried tells his readers that for the good of the world, but in particular for the group he calls *edele Herzen*, he wants to tell the story of two lovers who suffered for love but also found great joy. He wants his story to encourage lovers to persist in their love, although it may bring them sorrow as well as joy. Thus we conclude that Gottfried's *Tristan* is written for a select company and that it is intended to do for them what a legend of a saint's life would do for a religious man. The poet senses this, and the religious nature of the love experience is stressed throughout the poem. He uses the terminology of mystical love—his allegory of the love grotto could be that used by a theologian to symbolize the Church. And throughout Gottfried emphasizes the dual nature of love, at once spiritual and sensual. As one might expect from a man of his attainments, he sees that this love can best be won by the senses, when properly directed, and by the intellect through the arts. All through the poem the hero's cultural abilities are stressed, and it is through them that he wins Isolde.

Gottfried's style has a classical limpidity and purity, yet it is deliberately charged with double meanings. He strives with great success to represent in words the doubts and struggles of his hero and heroine. To this end he makes use of all his classical learning as well as his training in theology. He considers himself a learned man — he writes for the cultivated men who can appreciate him. In this regard we should not omit to mention the obvious rivalry between Gottfried and Wolfram von Eschenbach. Gottfried clearly despised Wolfram's style, which he thought muddy and confused. He also scorned Wolfram's deep morality, which in *Parzival* seems to belong only to the knightly class. Though neither poet alludes to the other by name, Gottfried's references to Wolfram as a purveyor of wild tales whose style "hops like a hare over the field of words" is unmistakable. In Wolfram's poem, too, there are references to "overlearned" writers who are artists first and knights second.

Wolfram has, until very recently, enjoyed a much higher reputation in Germany than Gottfried because of his deep moral earnestness. Yet aesthetically it cannot be denied that Gottfried is the better artist. His style is both subtle and brilliant; he appeals very strongly to those educated in the classical tradition.

Gottfried's *Tristan* was continued by Ulrich von Türheim (*c.* 1240) and Heinrich von Freiberg (*c.* 1285). Neither appreciated Gottfried's intentions, and their continuations are much more like the work of Eilhart von Oberg than that of Gottfried.

TRISTAN UND ISOT

Prologue

The work begins with a prologue which falls into two parts. The first is a brief statement of the position of the author. His audience should judge him by his intentions, even if they do not fully agree with him. He then tells how he will approach the problem of love:

*   *   *

Ich hab' mir ein Werk ausersehen;*
  Der Welt zu Liebe soll's geschehen
Und edlen Herzen zum Behagen,
Den Herzen, die wie meines schlagen,
5 Der Welt, wie sie ins Herz mir scheint.
Hier ist nicht aller Welt gemeint,
Nicht die, von der ich höre sagen,
Daß sie den Schmerz nicht könne tragen
Und nur in Freuden wolle schweben:[1]
10 Die lass' auch Gott mit Freuden leben!
  Nein, dieser Welt und ihrem Drang
Hat meine Rede fremden Klang;
Ihr Weg und meiner scheiden sich:
Zu einer andern wend' ich mich,
15 Die willig trägt in e i n e m Herzen
Die süße Qual, die lieben Schmerzen,
Die Herzenslust und Sehnensnot,
Liebes Leben, leiden Tod,
Lieben Tod und leides Leben.[2]
20 Dem Leben will ich meins ergeben,
Der Welt mich als ein Weltkind weihen,
Mit ihr verderben und gedeihn.
Ihr zugesellt mit treuem Sinn
Bracht' ich die jungen Tage hin,
25 Die mir für alles Leid im Leben
Lehr' und Leitung sollten geben,
Und ihr zur Kurzweil soll geschehn
Das Werk, das ich mir ausersehen.

*   *   *

Nur heißer liebt ein echter Mut,

---

* The following are lines 45–130 of the Middle High German version.
[1] The allusion is to "normal" courtly romance.
[2] The exchange of adjectives and nouns is a characteristic feature of Gottfried's style, intended to show the inextricable mixture of human emotions.

Je mehr er brennt in Schmerzens Glut.
Dies Leid ist so an Freuden reich
Und seine Last so sanft und weich,
Daß, übt es seinen Herzensbann,   5
Kein edles Herz es missen kann.
Ich weiß es sicher wie den Tod
Und hab's erkannt in eigner Not:
Wer minnt mit edlem Sinne,
Liebt Mären von der Minne.   10
Drum wer nach solchem trägt Begier,
Der hat nicht weiter als zu mir.
Ich künd' ihm süße Schmerzen
Von zweien edlen Herzen,
Die Liebe trugen echt und wahr,   15
Ein sehnend junges Menschenpaar,
Ein Mann, ein Weib, ein Weib, ein Mann,
Tristan, Isold, Isold, Tristan.

The prologue concludes with a statement by Gottfried that he regards the version of Tristan written by Thomas of Britain as the only authentic one, and that he will follow it. Thus Gottfried's poem is to be to the edele Herzen *the very bread of life.*
  The work proper begins with a long account of Tristan's origins. His father, Riwalin, after a successful campaign against his enemy Morgan of Britanny, comes to visit King Mark of Cornwall. He is well received and impresses everyone by his fine physical presence and prowess in the tournament. He and Blancheflor, Mark's sister, fall in love. When Riwalin is wounded in fighting for Mark and brought back, apparently dying, Blancheflor revives him with her embrace, and Tristan is conceived. Riwalin takes Blancheflor to his lands in Parmenie. Shortly after his marriage to her he is killed in battle with Morgan. Blancheflor dies as Tristan is born (note the connection with the French "triste"). Morgan takes over his lands, and only the loyalty of Rual, seneschal of the kingdom, saves the infant. Tristan is brought up as Rual's son and trained in chivalric and courtly arts, horsemanship and fencing.

Und gab ihm einem weisen Mann;*
Mit diesen sandt' er ihn sodann
Nach Landen, fremden, fernen,
Die Sprachen dort zu lernen.
Auch sollte Lesen er und Schreiben,   5
Der Bücher Kunst mit Fleiß betreiben

---

* The following are lines 2061–2092 of the Middle High German version.

Und ihr sich ganz ergeben.
Aus seinem freien Leben
Tat Tristan so den ersten Schritt:
10 Wo er nun ging, da gingen mit
Die auferzwungnen Sorgen,
Die ihm zuvor verborgen
Und noch erlassen waren.
In den aufblühnden Jahren,
15 Da seine Wonne sollt' erstehen,
Da er mit Freuden sollte gehen
In seines Lebens Anbeginn,
War schon sein bestes Leben hin.
Als freudig er zu blühn begann,
20 Da fiel der Sorgen Reif ihn an,
Der mancher Jugend Schaden tut,
Und knickt' ihm seinen blühnden Mut.
Und doch, wie er damit begann,
Er wandte seinen Sinn daran
25 Und seinen jungen Fleiß so sehr,
Daß er der Bücher lernte mehr
Und schneller, als uns bis zur Frist
Von einem Kind berichtet ist.

*Tristan's education is largely intellectual and
musical, but he also becomes a fine warrior. When
merchants visit Rual's lands, he plays chess with
them and is kidnapped. Later he is put ashore,
makes friends with a master of the hunt whom he
impresses by his knowledge of hunt ceremonial,
and finds his way to the court of Mark, his uncle.
Neither Mark nor Tristan is aware of their
relationship, but the fourteen-year-old boy so
attracts the king by his skill in music and languages
that they become firm friends.*

Ihm [Tristan] fielen liebe Weisen ein*
Die Lieder vom Bretonenland.
Da nahm den Schlüssel er zur Hand,
Stimmte die Harfe für die Lieder
5 Die Wirbel drehend auf und nieder.
Dann schlug er seltsam süße
Klangvolle Saitengrüße,
Daß alles Volk zusammenlief
Und einer nach dem andern rief.
10 Das Hofgesinde, Mann für Mann,
Die kamen meist im Lauf heran,
Und keiner kam sich früh genug.
    Da Tristan so die Saiten schlug,
Saß Marke still auf alles achtend,

Erstaunt den jungen Freund betrachtend,   15
Der zu verhehlen sich beflissen
Solch schöne Kunst, solch edeles Wissen.

*   *   *

   Der König sprach: „Dir ist beschert*
Alles, was mein Herz begehrt.
Du kannst, was mir von je gefiel:
Jagen, Sprachen, Saitenspiel.
Drum wollen wir Gesellen sein,   5
Ich der deine, du sei mein!"

*This close friendship, which is to be a source of
misery to Tristan, continues even more strongly
after Mark hears from Rual who Tristan really is.
He knights his nephew, who sets out to avenge
his father's death on Morgan of Britanny. On his
return he discovers that Morold, a powerful Irish
knight, is claiming the tribute due from Cornwall
—thirty boys to be sent into servitude. The only
solution is to defeat Morold. An impassioned
speech by Tristan fails to stir the knights of Cornwall, and Tristan therefore undertakes the task
himself, young and inexperienced though he is.*

„Doch nimmt sich kein beherzter Mann†
Eurer und des Landes an,
So stellet es an Gott und mich
Ja, edle Herren, so will ich
Meine Jugend und mein Leben   5
Mit Gott ans Abenteur geben
Und will für euch den Kampf bestehen.

*   *   *

Er, den ich soll alleine bestehen
Der ist ja, wie die Sagen gehen
An Heldenmut und Leibeskraft
Im Kampfesernst der Ritterschaft
Ein lange her bewährter Mann.   5
Dagegen ich fang' eben an,
Von Mut und Kraft noch ungestählt,
Als Kämpe nicht so auserwählt
Und reich an Heldenehre,
Wie's jetzt uns nötig wäre.   10
Doch Gott und unser gutes Recht,
Die beiden stehen im Gefecht

---

* The following are lines 3556–3581 of the Middle
   High German version.

* The following are lines 3721–3726 of the Middle
   High German version.
† The following are lines 6147–6187 of the Middle
   High German version.

Tristans und Morolts Zweikampf. (Aus einer Handschrift des *Tristan* Gottfrieds von Straßburg (13. Jahrhundert) *Staatsbibliothek München*.

Als Siegeshelfer mir zur Seite;
Auch bring' ich freudgen Mut zum
    Streite."

*The two combatants embark for the island where
the fight takes place, a form of duel that is probably derived from the Scandinavian Holmgangr,
or island fight. Their encounter is far from chiv-
alrous. Tristan is wounded, and Morold tells him
that the wound contains poison and that he can be
cured only by the queen, sister to Morold. Instead
of making him yield, the revelation arouses Tristan
to fury, and he hacks his opponent down, leaving
in his skull a chip of his sword blade. He returns
to Mark's court amid great rejoicing, but his
wound will not heal and festers; its stench is so
sickening that he is shunned by everyone. He decides
to go to Ireland and after completing most of the
journey in a ship, he is set adrift in a small boat
with only his harp for company.*

Tristan indessen trieb umher*
Einsam auf dem öden Meer
Mit Jammer und mit Sorgen
Bis an den lichten Morgen.
5   Als die von Develin den Kahn
Unferne draußen schwimmen sahn
Führerlos im Wellen braus,
Da schickten Leute sie hinaus,
Um zu erkunden, was das sei;
10 Die ruderten sofort herbei.
Da hörten sie beim nahen,
Obgleich sie niemand sahen,
Von jenem fremden Schifflein her
Herzentzücken übers Meer
15 Eine süße Harfe klingen
Und einen Mann zur Harfe singen
Mit solcher Wundersüße:
Es war, als ob sie grüße
Ein holdes Abenteuer.
20 Sie rührten nicht das Steuer,
So lang der Schall herüber drang.
Doch währte diese Lust nicht lang:
Denn klang's ihm auch von Hand und Mund,
Es kam doch nicht vom Herzensgrund.
25 Die Jugend nur, sie war's allein,
Die Kurzweil suchend trotz der Pein,
Des Dulders Mund und Hände zwang,
Daß er ihr harfte und ihr sang:

---
* The following are lines 7503–7542 of the Middle
  High German version.

Ihm aber brachte beides
Nur Mehrung seines Leides.   30

*Tristan's first contact with the people of Ireland
is thus made through his music, even though it is
the music of a dying man. The news of his playing
reaches the ears of the tutor of Isolde, daughter
of the king of Ireland, and he brings the minstrel,
who calls himself Tantris, before the queen, also
named Isolde. He plays with renewed spirit.*

Die Herrin sprach, als er geendet:*
„Tantris, wenn sich dein Übel wendet
Und wird der Giftgeruch gestillt,
Der noch aus deiner Wunde quillt,
So daß man bei dir bleiben kann,   5
. . . Dann nimm dich als Berater an
Isoldens hier, der jungen Maid!
Die wendet auch schon Fleiß und Zeit
Auf Bücher und auf Saitenspiel
Und hat auch dessen ziemlich viel   10
Gelernt für diese kurze Frist,
Die sie dabei gewesen ist.
Lebt etwas Schönes nur in dir,
Das ihrem Meister und auch mir
Bis heute noch verborgen blieb,   15
So lehre sie das mir zulieb.
Ich will dir Leib und Leben
Dafür zum Lohne geben;
Die beiden sind in meiner Hand."
„Traun, ist es so mit mir bewandt",   20
Sprach da der Spielmann freudenvoll,
„Daß ich mit Spiel genesen soll,
So hoff' ich sicher zu genesen.³
Auch habe ich Bücher viel gelesen,
Und was von seltnem Wissen mein,   25
Das soll ihr ganz zu Diensten sein."

*The queen succeeds in curing Tristan, and in twenty
days the wound's odor is no longer offensive. He can
begin to instruct Isolde.*

Nun kam zu ihm als Schülerin†
Isot die junge Königin;
Sein ganzer Fleiß und seine Zeit

---
* The following are lines 7840–7873 of the Middle
  High German version.
³ There is much play in this scene on the various
  possible meanings of "Leben," "genesen," and
  "Spiel."
† The following are lines 7962–8131 of the Middle
  High German version.

War ihrer Pflege nur geweiht.
5 Zur freien Wahl legt er ihr dar
Das Beste, was sein eigen war
Von Wissenschaft und Saitenspiel:
Sie wählte draus, was ihr gefiel;
Das Allerschönste, das ihm kund,
10 Das lernte sie mit Hand und Mund.
Auch half ihr, daß sie früher schon
So viel gelernt in Wort und Ton,
In mancher edlen Kunde:
Sie sprach mit holdem Munde
15 Des Landes Sprache schön und rein,
Dazu Französisch und Latein.[4]
Sie strich mit Händen weiß und zart
Die Fiedel nach Waliser Art,
Verstand die Leier wohl zu rühren
20 Und mit Gewalt den Ton zu führen
Hin durch der Harfe Saiten;
Sie ließ die Finger gleiten
Auf und ab in einem Nu
Und sang manch süßes Lied dazu.
25 Doch was von Kunst in ihrer Macht,
Das war der Spielmann nun bedacht
Zu bessern und zu mehren.
Er tat mit andern Lehren
Ihr eine neue nun bekannt;
30 Die wird moraliteit[5] genannt:
Das ist die Kunst der schönen Sitten.
Wir sollten jede Jungfrau bitten,
Daß ihren Fleiß sie daran Kehre.
Moralität, die süße Lehre,
35 Wie selig ist sie und wie rein!
In ihre Pflege schließt sie ein
Erd' und Himmel, Gott und Welt:
Wer sich an ihre Vorschrift hält,
Wird Gott und Welt gefallen.
40 Den edlen Herzen allen
Ist zur Amme sie gegeben,
Daß sie Nahrungssaft und Leben
Suchen in ihrer Lehre.
Es findet Glück und Ehre
45 Nur der, dem sie die Wege weist.
Darin mühte sie zumeist

Isot die junge Königin;
Mit Freude übte sie darin
Geist und Sinne immerdar,
50 Bis all ihr Tun veredelt war,
Ihr Herz geklärt und schöngemut
Und ihr Gebaren süß und gut.
So war die junge Königin,
Bevor ein halbes Jahr dahin,
55 Mit allem, was den Sinn entzückt,
Mit Geist und Huld so reich geschmückt,
Daß man sie rühmte weit und breit
Und sich an ihrer Herrlichkeit
Die Eltern freuten inniglich.
60 Und manches Mal begab es sich,
Wenn Gurmun froher Laune war[6]
Oder fremde Ritterschar
An seinem Hofe war zu Gast,
Daß dann Isot in den Palast
65 Vor ihren Vater ward gesandt,
Und was der Holden war bekannt
Von schönem Tun und edler Kunde,
Damit verkürzte sie die Stunde
Ihm und all den Leuten,
70 Und mit dem Vater freuten
Sich ihrer in der Halle
Die edlen Gäste alle.
Hoch und nieder hatten beide
Eine selge Augenweide;
75 Die Ohren füllte sie mit Lust
Und mit Verlangen manche Brust.
Wer ist, dem ich vergleiche
Die schöne, freudenreiche?
Das sollen die Sirenen sein,
80 Die mit dem Magnetenstein[7]
Die Kiele ziehn in ihren Bann:
So zog Isot viel Herzen an,
Die sich schon vor der Sehnsucht Leid
Sicher wähnten und gefreit.
85 Gleicht doch das Menschenherz gar sehr
Dem ankerlosen Schiff im Meer:
Ach wie selten vor den Winden
Die beiden ihre Straßen finden!
Pfadlos hin und her gerissen
90 Irren sie im Ungewissen
Schwankend vor der Wellen Stoß:
So treibt Begierde führerlos,
Treibt Liebessehnsucht ohne Ziel
Recht wie ein ankerloser Kiel.

---

[4] French and Latin were the principal languages of culture, but the recognition of Breton and Welsh (Waliser) skill in music is frequent in the poem.

[5] **moraliteit:** This word appears nowhere else in Middle High German literature. Obviously Gottfried did not mean "morality" and doubtless intended something other than courtliness. Quite probably he is thinking of the special intellectual and moral qualities required for the *edele Herzen*. Cf. Moralität, line 34.

[6] Gurmun was Isolde's father, the king of Ireland.

[7] The Sirens, unlike those in Greek mythology, are here associated with magnetic rocks, frequently mentioned in medieval romances and stories.

95   Ja sie, die junge Königin,
     Zog die Gedanken zu sich hin
     Aus manches Herzens Schiffe,
     Wie der Magnet zum Riffe
     Die Barke beim Sirenensang.
100 Ihr Sang, der in die Herzen drang,
     Ging durch die Ohren hell und rein
     Und lautlos durch die Augen ein.
     Der Laute war ihr süßes Singen
     Und ihrer Saiten lieblich Klingen,
105 Das durch das Ohr zum Herzen klang.
     Doch der unhörbare Gesang
     War ihre wundersame Schöne,
     Die mit berauschendem Getöne
     Sich so süß und sänftiglich
110 Durch der Augen Fester schlich
     In manches Herz geheim und sacht
     Und dort mit ihrer Zaubermacht
     Die Gedanken fing und band
     Und sie mit Sehnsuchtsqual umwand.

Upon their first meeting, Tristan and Isolde are drawn to each other by a common bond—their intellect and their music. As yet there is no evidence that they are in love. Tristan pleads that he has a wife at home waiting for him—a lie whose purpose is not at all clear, unless he thinks that this is the surest way of winning the sympathy of the queen and hence of obtaining leave to go. (To the court of Dublin he is a simple minstrel; there could be no question of a royal marriage.) Tristan returns to Cornwall and finds that Mark's desire to make him heir has aroused considerable opposition among the barons. They urge Mark to marry Isolde, and Mark, thinking that a marriage with the niece of the dead Morold would be impossible to arrange, swears that he will marry no one else and thus hopes to ensure the succession for Tristan. But Tristan, to Mark's consternation, insists on attempting to win Isolde for his uncle. He knows, as the others do not, that the king of Ireland has sworn to give his daughter in marriage to any man of noble birth who can rid his country of a ravaging dragon. He hopes that by killing the dragon he can win Isolde. Setting out with a hundred men, including some of the barons who have attacked him, he leaves them in hiding upon reaching Ireland and sets out alone. He does succeed in killing the dragon and cuts out its tongue as proof of his conquest. Foolishly, he thrusts the tongue inside his shirt, and its venom causes him to faint. Meanwhile a seneschal finds the dead beast, cuts off its head, and claims Isolde as his reward. Isolde and her mother do not believe him and are led by a dream to search in the area in which the fight took place. They find Tristan, remove the tongue, take him home, and cure him. They naturally recognize him as the minstrel, Tantris, and he gives a fictional account of his being forced to return to their shores. Since they regard him as a minstrel, they have no fear that he will claim Isolde's hand. One day, while Tristan is in the bath, Isolde, for no particular reason, examines his armor and wonders why so brave a man is not a nobleman. She idly draws his sword, sees the notch in the blade, and hastens to compare it with the fragment taken from Morold's skull. It matches, and she rushes to kill Tristan. His appeals to her feminine sense of propriety and perhaps her own feelings prevent her from carrying out her intention until the arrival of her mother. Tristan's appeal and his reminder that they are dependent on him for help against the seneschal restore peace. He now reveals his mission for Mark, and it is agreed that the marriage shall take place. With great sorrow Isolde sets out with Tristan and his retinue, and there is marked tension between the two. Brangaene, Isolde's lady-in-waiting, has been entrusted by the queen Isolde with a draught which her daughter and Mark are to drink on their wedding night and which will ensure everlasting love between them. This potion Brangaene keeps in her cabin.

Tristan, der Schiffer Herr, gebot,*
Am Lande anzulegen,
Um dort der Ruh zu pflegen.
Man hielt an eines Hafens Strand
Zur Kurzweil ging das Volk ans Land,   5
Und still und einsam ward's an Bord.
Tristan aber kam sofort
Ins Kämmerlein der Frauen
Um nach Isot zu schauen,
Und als er bei der Lichten saß   10
Und plauderte bald dies, bald das
Von ihrer beiden Dingen,
Hieß er zu trinken bringen.
Nun war da bei der Königin
Niemand in der Kammer drin   15
Als einge kleine Mägdelein;
Von denen rief eins: „Hier steht Wein.

---

* The following are lines 11654–11706 of the Middle
  High German version.

Ein Glas voll, seht, in diesem Schrank."
Wohl glich dem Weine dieser Trank:
20 Ach, leider nein, es war kein Wein,
Es war die ungestillte Pein,
Die endlos heiße Herzensnot,
Von der einst beide lagen tot.
Doch arglos sprang das Kind empor,
25 Zog den verborgnen Trank hervor
Und reicht' ihn seinem Meister hin;
Der bot ihn erst der Königin.
Ungern und nur auf sein Begehr
Trank sie und danach trank auch er,
30 Und beide wähnten, es sei Wein.
Inzwischen trat Brangaene ein;
Die hatte kaum das Glas gesehn
So wußte sie, was hier geschehn.
Da fuhr ihr durch die Glieder
35 Der Schrecken lähmend nieder,
Und ihr Gesicht ward totenbleich.
Mit totem Herzen ging sie gleich,
Nahm das unselge Glas zur Hand
Und warf es von des Schiffes Rand
40 Ins Toben der empörten See.[8]
„O weh mir Armen", rief sie, „weh,
Daß ich zur Welt je ward geboren!
Wie hab' ich Ehr' und Treu' verloren!
Weh immerdar mir Armen!
45 Das möge Gott erbarmen,
Daß ich zu dieser Reise kam,
Daß mich der Tod nicht mit sich nahm,
Als ich zu dieser Unglücksfahrt
Hier mit Isot beschieden ward!
50 O weh Tristan, o weh Isot,
Der Trank ist euer beider Tod!"

Although the lovers are irresistibly attracted to each other after drinking the love-potion, they do not yield to its effect immediately. Isolde still thinks of her uncle and is ashamed of her feelings; Tristan is deeply concerned about his relation to his uncle and the loss of honor he will incur if he is unfaithful to his trust. He hears Isolde say that "Lamer" is causing her misery. At first he thinks that she is referring to the sea (la mer) or bitterness (amer), but then he hears from her own lips that it is love (l'amour).

Als er des Wortes Deutung fand*
Und Minne klar darin erkannt,
Sprach, heiß und heimlich er zu ihr:
„Traun, schöne Maid, so ist auch mir;
Lamer und Ihr seid meine Not.   5
Ja, Herzenskönigin Isot,
Nur Ihr und Eure Minne,
Ihr habt mir meine Sinne
Verkehret und benommen.
Ich bin vom Weg gekommen   10
Und irre pfadlos nun umher,
Und keinen Ausweg find' ich mehr.
Die ganze Welt ist mir zur Qual,
Und alles dünkt mich arm und schal,
Was immer mir ins Auge fällt,   15
Und nichts in dieser weiten Welt
Ist meinem Herzen lieb als Ihr."
Isot sprach: „Herr, so seid Ihr mir."

The emotion of joy mixed with sorrow persists. In an attempt to keep their love secret, Tristan and Isolde persuade Brangaene to substitute for Isolde on the bridal night. Mark is thoroughly deceived. Later, in panic, Isolde contrives to have Brangaene killed by some huntsmen. She repents, however, and is relieved when she finds out that the men failed to accomplish the deed. Tristan rescues the queen from an Irish minstrel called Gandin, who has claimed her as a boon for his singing and then follows a series of assignations with Isolde, arranged by Brangaene. These meetings, which lead to growing suspicion, are thwarted by Mark's courtiers. Finally the dwarf Melot strews flour between the beds of the two lovers after Mark has announced that he will be away. Tristan leaps the flour but he has recently been bled and leaves traces of blood. He flees the court, and Isolde is forced to defend her honor by undergoing the ordeal of the hot iron. She arranges that Tristan, disguised as a pilgrim, shall carry her from the ship and fall with her on the sand. Thus she can swear with truth that she has lain in the arms of no man but those of the king and the "pilgrim."

Apparent harmony is restored. Tristan, still in exile, sends Isolde the little dog Petitcriu, won from the giant Urgan, to delight her with the music of the magic bell tied around its neck. She tears off the bell, refusing to be happy while Tristan is not. Tristan comes back to court, but soon

---

[8] In Gottfried's source, Brangaene does not throw away the remainder of the potion, and it is later drunk by Mark. Gottfried refuses to put Mark in the same situation toward Isolde as that in which Tristan is depicted.

---

* The following are lines 12011–12028 of the Middle High German version.

suspicions arise again, and this time the lovers
are banished. They go to a cave of love which Tristan
had discovered, a place of great beauty but cut off
from civilization by grim mountains. Here they
reach the high point of their love. The grotto
symbolizes the perfection of their mystical and
sensual passion and Gottfried describes it in
allegorical terms:

Nun laßt euch aber nicht verdrießen,*
Wenn ich den Sinn euch will erschließen,
Mit welchem, wie ich meine,
Die Grotte im Gesteine
5   Entworfen war nach weisem Plan.
Sie war, wie ich euch kund getan,
Weit und rund nach allen Enden,
Schneeweiß mit hohen, glatten Wänden.
Der Wände Rundung innen
10 Ist Einfalt in dem Minnen:
Die Einfalt ist der Minne eigen;
Die soll ja keinen Winkel zeigen.
Der Winkel der im Minnen ist,
Das ist Verrat und Hinterlist.
15 Die Weite ist der Minne Kraft,
Die ohne Schranken wirkt und schafft.
Die Höhe ist der hohe Mut,
Der aufwärts strebt und nimmer ruht,
Bis wo der Tugenden Verein
20 Sich schließt und wölbt wie Stein an Stein.[9]
Nie fehlt dort Schmuck und Schimmer:
Die Tugenden sind immer
Verherrlicht mit des Ruhmes Kranz
Und leuchten mit Juwelenglanz.
25 Weiß, glatt und eben war die Wand:
Daran wird Redlichkeit erkannt.
Ihr schlichtes Weiß, ihr gleicher Schein
Soll niemals bunt noch schillernd sein:
Auch soll Verdacht trotz allem Spähn
30 Daran nicht Tal noch Hügel sehn.
Der Estrich, der von Marmor war,
Der gleicht der Treue ganz und gar
An Grüne und an Feste;
So deut' ich ihn aufs beste:
35 Die sei von Farbe grün wie Gras,
Von Fläche glatt und blank wie Glas.
Und der kristallnen Minne

Prachtbette mitten inne
War so mit Recht und Fug genannt.
Dem war ihr Recht gar wohl bekannt,   4(
Der ihr aus lauterem Kristalle
Ihr Lager schnitt in dieser Halle:
Denn Minne soll kristallenrein,
Durchsichtig und durchlauter sein.

The entrance is guarded by a door that can be
opened only by a key made of soft tin—physical
force will not avail to open it. Gottfried explains
the significance of the fact that the grotto was
surrounded by a wilderness and then adds:

„Das weiß ich wohl; denn ich war dort,*
Hab' auch durch wildes Waldrevier
Gespürt nach Vogel und Getier
Und Hirsch und Hinde nachgejagt,
Blieb mir auch Weidmannsheil versagt.   5
Ich kam zur Grotte, fand den Knauf
Und hob die goldne Klinke auf,
Trat zum kristallnen Bette hin;
Doch ruht' ich leider nie darin.
Oft haben mir ins Herz hinein   10(
Die sonnigen drei Fensterlein
Ihren reinen Glanz gesandt.
Mir ist die Grotte wohlbekannt,
Und schon seit meinem elften Jahr,
Wenn ich auch nie in Kornwall war."[10]   15

In the grotto the two lovers pass their time in
storytelling and musical pursuits. One of Mark's
huntsmen finally discovers them by looking through
one of the openings of the cave. He calls Mark,
and the king sees them lying separated by Tristan's
sword. He is deeply moved by the sight, and his
passion for Isolde flares anew. The lovers are
recalled to court, but before very long the king
finds them in a garden, sleeping together. Tristan
flees and after a visit to his father's territories he
joins Kaerdin in Arundel. There Isolde of the
White Hands is attracted to him, and Tristan, in
his loneliness, feels some affection for her.

At this point Gottfried's poem breaks off.
We know from Thomas of Britain that Tristan
marries Isolde of the White Hands, that he does

---

* The following are lines 16923–16984 of the Middle
   High German version.
[9] The allegorical explanation of the characteristics
   of the grotto deliberately parallels the standard
   allegorization of the parts of the church building
   which is found in many of the Christian fathers.

* The following are lines 17100–17138 of the Middle
   High German version.
[10] Thus the experience of love is not confined to the
   lovers in the poem. Their story is to be interpreted
   in allegorical fashion and their cave exists in the
   hearts of all true lovers.

not consummate the marriage for a long time, and that he takes Kaerdin to see the first Isolde to explain his feelings. Subsequently Tristan receives a wound that only Isolde can cure. She is sent for, but Isolde of the White Hands, prompted by jealousy, tells Tristan that the returning ship carries a black sail—the prearranged sign that Isolde has refused to come. Tristan dies, and Isolde, arriving too late to save him, falls dead upon his body.

Early Lyric Poetry

Although many critics have postulated the existence of lyric poetry in Germany in the early Middle Ages by pointing out that all cultures have some forms of song transmitted in oral form, the fact remains that there are no true lyrics in German now extant that can be dated before the middle of the twelfth century. The earliest works we possess belong to the "Danubian" school, that is, they were written by authors who lived in the southeast of the German-speaking area. They seem to be very little influenced by the poetry of France. Of their authors nothing is known. Der von Kürenberg is mentioned in one of the poems attributed to a knight of that name, and it was assumed by the compilers of the great medieval collections of lyric poetry that all the strophes written in the *Nibelungenstrophe* were composed by the same author, since the verse form is not elsewhere used in lyric poetry and the strophes do have a similar style. They are forceful and direct and express little of the yearning found in the *Minnesang*. We know nothing of another poet, Dietmar von Aist, to whom many strophes in the manuscripts are attributed.

In the last thirty years of the twelfth century the centers of lyric activity were in the west, near the Rhine, and the influence of French and Provençal poetry is unmistakable. The verse forms and themes are the same as those in French poetry, and it is probable that the tunes were also borrowed. Yet no German poet mentions that he has copied French originals, and, although there are a few German lyrics that seem to be dependent on extant French or Provençal poems, there are no examples of actual translation. The early German *Minnesänger* wrote in meters taken from the Romance languages, and it may well be that they borrowed melodies (we have no extant music for the early *Minnesang*); they also used French imagery, yet their treatment of love is different. There is a more serious tone, and the poet seeks to analyze the phenomenon of love rather than praise an individual lady. The poet's own emotions are stressed. The lady is not only anonymous, as she is in Romance lyric, but also shadowy. It is very hard to tell whether the ladies really existed, but the poet's interest in love is real, and, if he did not suffer, it must be admitted that he convinces his hearers that he did.

The commonest type of lyric in the early period is the *Minnelied*, a formal love poem based on the Provençal *canzon*. Although the earliest examples in all languages have a flexible strophic and metrical form, one type of strophe soon became customary for this type of poem. The *Aufgesang*, or first part, fell into two halves, each of which showed exact correspondence with the other in length of lines and rhyme scheme. These two parts were called *Stollen*. The third part or *Abgesang* was completely independent of the form of the first two. It could be very short, only two or three lines, or longer than the other two combined. There was usually a division of subject as well as of form. Thus the metrical and rhyme scheme of a *Minnelied* might appear as follows, with number representing stresses, and letters rhymes:

4a, 3b, 4a, 3b	*Stollen*
3c, 3c, 3c,	*Abgesang*

It is not uncommon to find between the *Stollen* and the *Abgesang* an unrhymed line a called a *Waise,* which sometimes rhymes with the corresponding line in the other strophes. The technical terms are those used by the Meistersinger, not, so far as we know, by the *Minnesänger* themselves.

The translations of the early *Minnesänger* that appear here do not reflect these forms, since no attempt has been made to retain the rhymes. The typical *Minnelied* form may be seen in many of the translations of poems of Walther von der Vogelweide, for example, "Tanzweise," "Unter der Linde," "Frühling und Frauen," and "Güte gibt Tugend."

The formal love song is the most common type among the *Minnesänger* at all periods, but there were others. The *Botenlied* shows the lady or the man revealing to a messenger emotions that, by convention, could not be expressed directly to the beloved. The *Kreuzlied*, or crusading song, does not usually tell of a Crusade and its hardships but rather of the pain caused by leaving the beloved behind. The *Wechsel* is an actual conversation between the two lovers, but often convention is served by making the conversation take place in a dream. In all these types of poems the rules of formal love poetry are preserved, and the formal aspects of the *Minnelied* appear. The *Tagelied*, also, has usually the same formal aspects, but its attitudes are quite different. It shows the parting of two lovers at dawn after a night of illicit love. A watchman cries that dawn has come; the lovers are in danger from spies sent by a jealous husband or perhaps from a less successful wooer. The stress is on the feelings of the woman rather than those of the man, and there is no attempt to idealize the situation. German poets clearly did not like the *Tagelied*, since there are few examples of it in early German lyric. Nor are there any of the *pastourelle,* a type in which a knight accosts a peasant girl and either persuades or forces her to accept his love.

In Provençal poetry there were several types of poetry that were not concerned with love; they were not imitated to any degree by German authors except Walther von der Vogelweide in his political and moral poems. Even these are related only distantly to their Romance counterparts. Their forms are those of the *Minnelied*, but most of them are single strophe poems.

A little more is known of the Rhineland poets who introduced Romance forms into German than of their Danubian predecessors. Friedrich von Hausen was a knight of some importance. He was killed at the battle of Philomelium while on a Crusade with Frederick Barbarossa (1190). He had a deep sense of the *hoher muot* considered an attribute characteristic of a lover, and also of the sorrow that love brings.

Heinrich von Morungen is also attested in contemporary documents. He too served with Frederick Barbarossa and went to the Middle East. He came of Thuringian family and was given a property near Leipzig by Dietrich von Meißen, later the patron of Walther von der Vogelweide. This property he willed to the Convent of St. Thomas. He died in 1222. The work of Heinrich von

Morungen is remarkable for its brilliant imagery, its formal beauty, its spirit of independence, and its ability to handle the themes of the *Minnesang* according to the rules, yet with complete individuality.

To his contemporaries Reinmar der Alte, or Reinmar von Hagenau (*fl. c.* 1180–1210), was the greatest of the *Minnesänger*. Much of the superiority ascribed to him seems to have rested on his melodies, but he was also much admired for his skill in exploring the recognized themes of *Minnesang*, particularly the tension between the desire for and the fear of fulfillment. Indeed, his treatment of these very limited subjects was so detailed and copious that it left little for his successors to do. They could either imitate from afar or break new ground as Walther von der Vogelweide did.

Friedrich von Hausen
(d. 1190)

Heinrich von Morungen
(d. c. 1220)

KREUZLIED

LIEBESLEIDEN

*This crusading song is probably based on a work
of Conon de Bethune, a French trouvère. By using
the theme of a knight's separation from his lady
while on a Crusade, the author sets up a series of
clever paradoxes. A Crusader should have his heart
set wholly on God. But he has given it to his lady
—he now fights for God with his body. Thus his
immortal soul is endangered by his love.*

*This poem shows brilliant treatment of a con-
ventional theme: the pain of love. Notice the lover's
tension—created by his desire to keep his feelings
to himself for fear of ridicule. He longs for recognition from the lady, but knows that it is unattainable. He realizes it would be foolish to continue
to love her, yet he cannot help it—she is so very
beautiful.*

Mein Herz und mein Leib wollen sich tren-
nen,
die so lange miteinander gezogen sind.
Der Leib will gerne gegen die Heiden
kämpfen,
aber mein Herz hat sich eine Frau ausgesucht
5   vor der ganzen Welt. Seitdem quält es mich,
daß sie nicht mehr mit einander gehen wollen.
Mir haben meine Augen sehr weh getan
Gott allein kann diesen Streit schlichten.

Ich glaubte frei zu sein von solchem Kummer,
10 als ich das Kreuz zu Gottes Ehre nahm.
Es wäre auch richtig, daß das Herz dabei
wäre,
wenn es ihm seine Treue nicht verbieten
würde.
Ich wäre zu Recht ein lebendiger Mann,
wenn es nur seine törichte Absicht aufgeben
würde.
15 Nun sehe ich, daß es ihm ganz gleichgültig
ist,
was mir am Ende geschehen mag.

Da ich, dich mein Herz, nicht davon abbringen
kann,
daß du mich nicht ganz unglücklich verläßt,
bitte ich Gott, daß er dich schickt
20 an einen Ort, wo man dich gut empfängt.
O weh, wie soll es dir Armen gehen
wie wagst du, eine solche Gefahr auf dich
zu nehmen?
Wer kann dir helfen, diese Sorgen zu beenden,
mit gleicher Treue, wie ich es getan habe?

Schmerzliche Blicke und gewaltiger Kummer
haben mir das Herz und das Leben fast
zerstört.
Meine alte Not klagte ich immer wieder,
wenn ich nicht Angst hätte vor der Spötter
Zorn.
Ich singe aber von ihr, die mich früher froh   5
machte.
So wird niemand meine Treue bezweifeln,
denn ich bin zum Singen auf die Welt gekommen.

Viele sagen, „Nun seht, wie der singt.
Wenn er wirklich litte, täte er anders."
Sie können nicht wissen, was für Leid mich 10
peinigt.
Nun tue ich aber recht als ich damals tat;
da ich von Leide ergriffen war, habe ich sie
wenig geehrt.
Das ist eine Not, die mich zum Singen treibt.
Kummer ist nicht würdig, wo die Leute
fröhlich sind.

Die Wonne und Krone meines Herzens, 15
von allen Frauen, die ich je gesehen habe,
schön und schön und von allen die schönste
ist sie, meine Herrin, das muß ich ihr erklären.
Die ganze Welt muß sie um ihre Schönheit
anbeten.
Es wäre Zeit, meine Herrin, daß du mich 20
belohntest.
Sonst wäre das Lob, das ich ausgesprochen,
nur töricht gewesen.

Wenn ich vor ihr stehe und das Wunder
   anschaue
die Schönheit, die Gott an ihr geschaffen
   hat,
so gibt es für mich so vieles zu betrachten,
25 daß ich sehr gerne immer da stehen wollte.
O weh, da muß ich sehr traurig von ihr
   scheiden.
Eine so dunkle Wolke zieht heran,
daß ich von ihrem Glanze nichts mehr habe.

SPIEGEL DER LIEBE

*The poem consists of a series of images each de-
signed to show the difference between love in the
poet's mind and its actuality. The mirror is broken
when the child tries to snatch the beauty it sees—
Narcissus is deluded by an image of perfect beauty
that is unattainable because he himself has created it.
The figures are probably borrowed from a poem
of the Provençal troubadour Bernard de Ven-
tadorn.*

Mir ist geschehen wie einem Kindelein,
das sein schönes Bild in einem Spiegel sah.
Es griff hinein nach seinem eigenen Schein,
so stark, daß es den Spiegel ganz zerbrach.
5 So wurde all seine Freude ein schmerzliches
   Leid.
So glaubte ich, immer fröhlich zu sein,
als ich meine liebe Herrin sah,
von der ich so viel Glück und Leid bekomme.

Minne, die der Welt Freude bereitet,
10 seht, die brachte mir im Traum die Herrin
   mein,
als ich im Schlafe lag,
und bei dem Anblick verlor ich mich in
   Freude.
Da sah ich ihren edlen Wert, ihren klaren
   Glanz,
schön und über alle Frauen erhöht,
15 Nur daß ihr roter, kleiner, freudenreicher
   Mund
ein klein wenig versehrt war.
Davon hatte ich große Angst,

daß ihr so roter, kleiner Mund so verbleichen
   mußte.
So habe ich von neuem meine Klage begonnen,
nachdem mein Herz so sehr gelitten hat, 20
daß ich mit meinen Augen solche Not erblicke,
wie ein Kind, das noch nicht klug genug
in einer Quelle seinen Schein erblickte
und bis an den Tod ihn lieben mußte.

Frauen von größerem Wert und edelerem 25
   Sinn
kann man unter dem Himmel nicht entdecken,
als die Edle, der ich zu meinem Unglück
fern bleiben und doch immer anhangen
   muß.
O weh, und Not, ich glaubte schon am Ziel
   zu sein
ihrer wunderschönen, hohen Liebe. 30
Nun bin ich kaum erst am Anfang.
So ist meine Freude hin und auch mein
   sehnender Wahn.

SÜSSE TÖTERIN

*One of the principal conventions of the Minnesang
is that of the cruel lady whom the poet nevertheless cannot put out of his mind or cease to love.
In this poem Heinrich von Morungen plays with
this convention in a series of paradoxes and oxymora, of which the first line is a good example,
and threatens even to haunt his lady in the next
life if she rejects him in this one.*

O süße, sanfte Töterin,
warum wollt ihr mir den Leib töten,
wenn ich euch so vom Herzen liebe,
wirklich, Herrin, über alle Frauen?
Glaubt ihr, wenn ihr mich tötet, 5
daß ich euch nimmer mehr ansehe?
Nein, eure Minne hat mich dazu gezwungen,
daß eure Seele meiner Seele Herrin ist.
Wenn ihr hier kein Glück passiert
von eurem edlen Leib, 10
so muß meine Seele euch behaupten,
daß sie eurer Seele dort dienen wird als
einer reinen Frau.

Tagelied mit Variationen

Tagelieder *are rare in the works of the early*
German Minnesänger. *This example is clearly*
an ironical treatment of this type of poetry.

O weh, soll mir nie mehr
leuchten durch die Nacht
noch weißer als der Schnee
ihr Leib so schön gestaltet.
5 Der hat mir die Augen betrogen.
Ich glaubte, es müßte sein
des hellen Morgens Schein.
   Da wurde es Tag.

„O weh, soll er denn nicht mehr
10 hier bei mir bis zum Morgen bleiben.
So könnte die Nacht vergehen,
daß wir nicht zu klagen brauchten:
‚O weh, nun ist es Tag.‘
Wie er es klagend tat,
15 als er das letzte Mal bei mir lag.
   Da wurde es Tag.“

O weh, sie küßte ohne Zahl
Im Schlafe mich.
Da fielen herrunter
Die Tränen dahin.   20
Doch tröste ich sie,
daß sie ihr Weinen ließ
und mich umfing.
   Da wurde es Tag.

„O weh, daß er so oft   25
sich in meinem Anblick verlor,
als er mir die Decke nahm
wollte er ohne Kleider
mich Arme sehen bloß.
Es war ein großes Wunder,   30
daß es ihm nicht verdrießlich wurde
   Da wurde es Tag.“

𝔚alther von der Vogelweide

(c. 1170–c. 1230)

Walther is undoubtedly the greatest of the lyric poets of the Middle High German period and has a good claim to be considered the greatest lyric poet of the Middle Ages. His claim rests not so much on his supremacy in any one lyric type—Heinrich von Morungen and Reinmar der Alte are both better poets of true *Minnesang*—but on his great range, profound humanity, and mastery of love poetry, political poetry, and religious verse. His deep concern with questions which troubled not only the Germans of the Hohenstaufen period but which are the universal concern of thinking men at all times gives him a timelessness rare in medieval poets. His love poetry moves into a freer treatment of spontaneous love between two human beings, not a study of the inner conflicts arising from courtly love service. Love for Walther is, in his best poems, natural in the sense that it is part of nature's plan. Moreover, Walther can find it possible to treat the phenomenon of love with irony and humor. He was deeply involved in the politics of his time, and it would be sentimental to say that his support of one or other candidate for the imperial throne was always based on his sense of what was best for Germany and that personal considerations played no part. There is direct evidence to the contrary in his poetry. Yet Walther had strong feelings about the role of secular and in particular imperial government in the world order which, according to medieval political thinking, was the ideal that all rulers must seek. His call for strong government and for the exclusion of papal influence from German affairs is based on a real concern for the welfare of the German state. He knew that outside interference could lead only to disunity among the German princes and the collapse of orderly government. How correct his judgment was can be appreciated if one reads the history of Germany in the thirteenth century.

Although he attacked papal interference in secular affairs, Walther was far from being an irreligious man. Throughout his work he reveals his belief in the overriding importance of God's mercy and in the necessity of living one's life on earth in accordance with Christian concepts. His last poems are deeply concerned with the need for a new Crusade, not only to defeat the Saracen but primarily to rehabilitate the souls of Christian men.

Walther's birthplace is uncertain. Many towns claim him—even more perhaps than claimed Homer—but such evidence as there is points to the region of Bolzano. He was a *ministerialis*, that is, a member of the "service nobility," who had no land and was dependent for his livelihood on the whim of greater nobles. This fact was to cause Walther much anguish, for he made his living by singing, that is, composing lyric poetry for patrons. For a man of his independent temperament this was a hard lot, and we can sense his anger and frustration and guess at the sudden termination of some of his relationships. He learned his trade at the court of the duke of Austria in Vienna and his teacher was the great *Minnesänger* Reinmar der Alte. A change of regime in 1198 forced him to leave— the new ruler Leopold VI did not care for poetry—and for many years he served different patrons, among them two very slippery politicians, Hermann von Thüringen and Dietrich von Meißen. Walther spent considerable time at one or the other of their courts and mentions Hermann's court in very uncomplimentary fashion. Their self-seeking political maneuvers certainly must have disgusted him even as he tried to praise them in his poetry. We know also that in 1203 the poet was in the service of Wolfger von Passau, Patriarch of Ravenna, for his name appears in the bishop's account books as the recipient of money for the purchase of a fur coat.

Much more important than any of these connections were his relations with three imperial candidates: Philip II, Otto IV, and Frederick II. The emperor Henry VI died on a Crusade on September 28, 1197. Although the German nobles had agreed prior to his departure that they would accept his infant son Frederick as emperor in the case of his death, the boy's age (he was not quite three) soon forced the regent, Henry's brother Philip of Swabia, to abandon the pretense of regency and declare himself emperor. He was supported by some of the nobles and crowned with the imperial insignia but in Mainz, not Cologne, and by the Archbishop of Tarentaise. This September, 1198, coronation had been anticipated by a rival claimant to the throne, Otto of Brunswick or Poitou, a member of the Welf family, who had the support of Richard I of England and the newly elected pope, the able and ambitious Innocent III. Otto's coronation took place in Aachen and was conducted by the right ecclesiastic, the Archbishop of Cologne. Thus each candidate had some claim to legitimacy. The struggle between the two lasted until 1208. Walther took service under Philip and wrote some of his best poetry in the form of one-strophe calls to the princes of Germany to rally to the support of Philip and to Philip to assert his divinely given rights. Walther almost certainly supported Philip because he saw in him the emperor who was independent of foreign, and particularly papal influences. The struggle was going against Otto when Philip was murdered by Otto of Wittelsbach in 1208. There seems to have been no suspicion of any complicity in the murder by Otto of Poitou. Indeed he tracked down and punished the assassin.

Otto was elected as Otto IV without opposition. Although crowned by Innocent in Rome, he soon showed that imperial policy changed little according to person of the emperor. His expeditions to Italy caused him to attack papal territory and in 1210 he was excommunicated. Many of the German nobles plotted against him, and he had to return north in great haste to prevent the crown from slipping from his grasp.

Walther now supported him eagerly, since he was no longer under papal influence, but his poems show that he had little personal liking for the crude and stingy Otto, and he does not hesitate to compare him unfavorably with his generous predecessor. Meanwhile the pope had thrown his support to Frederick II, seventeen years old and brilliantly talented. Frederick attracted support among the nobles, but the decisive blow was struck in northern France when Philip Augustus completely defeated Otto at Bouvines. Thus in 1214 Frederick became undisputed emperor and remained so for the rest of Walther's life.

Although Walther had not been among his supporters, Frederick proved more generous than either Philip or Otto. He presented the poet with a small fief near Würzburg, calling forth in return one of Walther's most heartfelt poems.

It may be presumed that from 1220, when he received the fief, until about 1230, when he died, the poet lived on this fief. His last years were materially more prosperous, but his later poems reflect his deep concern over the decline in the courtly spirit and the disinclination of his fellow countrymen to serve either God or the emperor. It is easy to attribute such an attitude to the discontent of an old man, but events were to prove that Walther was right. The continued absence of the emperor in Sicily and the lack of central authority did bring about a decline in the Hohenstaufen culture which had raised German-speaking lands to a level as high as that in France. It was to be centuries before such a period returned. The last datable reference in Walther's work is to the excommunication of Frederick II by Gregory IX for his failure to leave on the Crusade as he had promised.

Many attempts have been made to produce an accurate chronology of Walther's poetry, but there is no real agreement. Certainly his first efforts were love poems in the style of Reinmar der Alte, but he abandoned this style at a relatively early stage in his career, and about the time that he left the Viennese court he engaged in a poetic controversy with the older poet which touches on the very nature of love poetry. Out of the new view of love poetry came some of Walther's best known works, the so-called *Mädchenlieder*, poems addressed to girls, not courtly ladies. These probably belong to the midpoint of his career, but they are naturally hard to date exactly. Later in life Walther returned to the poems of *hohe Minne*, but with emphasis rather on the moral aspects than the forms of love.

Much easier to date and in some ways more significant are the poems Walther wrote about specific political events of his day. They reflect his own views not only of the event in question but also of its importance in the survival of the Germany (in a very broad linguistic sense) that he loved. Such political poetry as was written during the Middle Ages was usually concerned with the activities of a liege lord and was for or against a specific person. Walther alone sees the wider issues involved in the struggle. His political poems are one-strophe works but they can be grouped together by the melody (*Ton*) used, as reflected in the strophic pattern of lines of varying length. Thus a group of poems on Otto IV contains poems all of which are written in the "*Ottenton*" and all of which presumably were sung to the same melody. It is unnecessary to stress how effective this grouping would be in emphasizing the continuity—or in calling attention to changes—of policy.

Coupled with the strophes on specific events are the longer poems on political and moral subjects. These extend throughout Walther's active career, from his poem "Wahlstreit" of about 1198 to the poem "Heimkehr," which clearly belongs to the last years of the poet's life. Their tone changes from the firm but optimistic note of the earlier years to the deep melancholy of his last works, but in all poems there is a profound sense of the divine order of the world.

Walther displays the linguistic and stylistic ability of a true poet—the ability to write poetry of great profundity and power in language whose apparent simplicity conceals its art. His versification is at least as highly wrought as that of Reinmar, he is a master of variety in strophic pattern and hence of melody. But his greater attribute as a poet remains his simplicity and wide humanity.

WAHLSTREIT

This is Walther's most famous political-moral poem. Although some critics regard the stanzas as separate entities, we have assumed that it is to be read as one. The author shows himself in a formal attitude of contemplation to give authority to his words. He then discusses the problem of combining Christian ethics with worldly honor (Ehre) and material goods. The trinity he mentions, besides the obvious reference to the Holy Trinity, has often been interpreted as the moral trio of values, discussed on p. 13. Walther wishes to show that without protection from a secular authority, the chance of achieving a union is remote. The second strophe refers to the universal struggle Walther observes in nature—the urge of all living creatures to appoint a strong ruler. This "natural law" he uses as a basis to call on Philip to assert his rights against the petty kings. He is undoubtedly referring to Richard I of England and Philip Augustus of France, who supported the opponents of Philip II, and he emphasizes their lower estate by his reference to their coronets (cirkel in the original, here translated "Fürsten Ehre") as compared with the emperor's crown with its "Waise," a large precious stone, set in the back. Thus any prince who stepped back would see the sign of imperial supremacy.

The third strophe refers directly to the struggle with Pope Innocent III and accuses Rome of using excommunication as a political weapon. Very effective is the introduction of the hermit, representing simple Christian faith, who complains about the Pope's conduct.

Ich saß auf einem Steine:
Da deckt' ich Bein mit Beine,
Darauf der Ellenbogen stand;
Es schmiegte sich in meine Hand
5   Das Kinn und eine Wange.
Da dacht' ich sorglich lange
Dem Weltlauf nach und irdschem Heil;
Doch wurde mir kein Rat zu Teil,
Wie man drei Ding erwürbe,
10 Daß keins davon verdürbe.
Die zwei sind Ehr und zeitlich Gut,
Das oft einander Schaden tut,
Das dritte Gottes Segen,
An dem ist mehr gelegen:
15 Die hätt' ich gern in e i n e n Schrein.

Ja leider mag es nimmer sein,
Daß Gottes Gnade kehre
Mit Reichtum und mit Ehre
Je wieder in dasselbe Herz.
Sie finden Hemmung allerwärts: 20
Untreu hält Hof und Leute,
Gewalt fährt aus auf Beute.
  So Fried als Recht sind Todeswund:
Die dreie haben kein Geleit, die zwei werden
    erst gesund.
  Ich hört ein Wasser rauschen   25
Und ging den Fischen lauschen,
Ich sah die Dinge dieser Welt,
Wald, Laub und Rohr und Gras und Feld,
Was kriechet oder flieget,
Was Bein zur Erde bieget,   30
Das sah ich und ich sag euch das:
Da lebt nicht Eines ohne Haß.
Das Wild und das Gewürme,
Die streiten starke Stürme,
So auch die Vögel unter sich;   35
Doch tun sie eins einmütiglich:
Sie schaffen stark Gerichte,
Sonst würden sie zunichte;
Sie wählen Könige, ordnen Recht
Und unterscheiden Herrn und Knecht.   40
So weh dir, deutschem Lande,
Wie ziemet dir die Schande,
Daß nun die Mücke hat ihr Haupt,
Und du der Ehren bist beraubt!
Bekehre dich! Vermehre   45
Nicht noch der Fürsten Ehre.
  Die armen Könge drängen dich:
Philippen setz den W a i s e n auf, so wei-
    chen sie und beugen sich.
  Ich ließ die Augen schauen
Auf Männer und auf Frauen: 50
Was Einer tat, was Einer sprach,
Vernahm ich wohl und sann ihm nach.
Zu Rom hört' ich lügen,
Zwei Könige betrügen:
Das gab den allergrößten Streit,   55
Der jemals ward in aller Zeit;
Da sah man sich entzwein
Die Pfaffen und die Laien.
Die Not war über alle Not;
Da lagen Leib und Seele tot.   60
Die Pfaffen wurden Krieger;
Die Laien blieben Sieger:
Das Schwert sie legten aus der Hand:
Und griffen zu der Stola Band:
Sie bannten wen sie wollten,   65

Den sie nicht bannen sollten;
Zerstört ward manches Gotteshaus.
Ich hörte fern in einer Klaus
Ein Jammern ohne Ende:
70 Ein Klausner rang die Hände;
   Er klagte Gott sein bittres Leid:
„O weh, der Papst ist allzujung, Herr Gott,
   hilf deiner Christenheit!"

AN DIE WELT

*Walther here expresses many of the sentiments
of his later poem "Heimkehr."*

  O weh dir Welt, wie schlimm du stehst!
Was du für Dinge jetzt begehst,
Die ohne Schmerz kein Edler mag betragen!
   Vergessen hast du Zucht und Scham;
5 Weiß es Gott, ich bin dir gram:
Bist du nicht völlig aus der Art geschlagen?
   Ist uns wohl Ehre noch geblieben?
Niemand sieht dich Freude lieben,
Wie man weiland Freude pflag.
10 Wes mussen milde Herzen nun entgelten?
Man lobt jetzt nur die reichen Kargen.
Welt, du liegst so sehr im Argen,
Daß ichs nicht beschreiben mag:
Treu und Wahrheit sieht man beschelten,
15 Und alle Ehre trifft ein Schlag.

UNTER KRONE

(19, 5)

*This poem refers to the marriage of Philip on
Christmas Day, 1199, to Irene, daughter of the
Byzantine emperor. She took the name Mary on
her marriage, and the poet makes a play on words
with the name of the town (Magdeburg), the
birth of Christ from the Virgin (Magd), and,
tangentially, the trinity of power represented by
the emperor. He deliberately applies to the queen
imagery usually associated with the Virgin.
Note that he works in a reference to his patrons,
the lords of Meißen and Thüringen. This poem,*

*like the next one, is written in a strophic form
and its accompanying melody came to be called the
"Erster Philippston," since it is always connected
with poetry about Philip II.*

  Zu Magdeburg ging an dem Tag, da Gott
   geboren
Ward von der Magd, die er zur Mutter sich
   erkoren,
Der König Philipp schön und tadelsohne:
   Da gingen König, Kaisersbruder, Kaisers-
   kind
In e i n e m Kleid, ob auch der Namen dreie   5
   sind:
Er trug des Reiches Zepter und die Krone.
   Gemessnen Schritts ging er dahin,
Ihm folgte sacht die hochgeborne Königin,
Ros' ohne Dorn, ein Täublein sonder Gallen.
Solch Fest noch sah man nirgendwo,   10
Es dienten ihm die Thüringer und Sachsen so,
Daß es den Weisen mußte wohlgefallen.

DER LEITSTERN

(18, 29)

*Philip was crowned on September 8, 1199, in
Mainz, with the authentic imperial regalia but
by the wrong bishop and in the wrong place (see
p. 000). Walther therefore stresses how well the
crown suits the king and the significance of the
"Waise," the precious stone already mentioned.*

  Die Kron' ist älter als der König Philipp
   ist:
Drum scheints ein Wunder jedem Auge, das
   ermißt,
Wie ihr der Schmied das rechte Maß ver-
   liehen.
   Sein kaiserliches Haupt geziemt ihr also
   gut,
Daß wer sie scheiden will, als ein Verräter tut;   5
Keins mag dem andern Schein und Glanz
   entziehen:
   Sie leuchten sich einander an,
Die edeln Steine mit dem jungen süßen
   Mann:
Der Anblick muß den Fürsten wohlgefallen.
Wen nun nach anderm Herrn verlangt,   10

Der schaue, wem der W a i s e überm Scheitel
  prangt:
Der mag ein Leitstern sein den Fürsten allen.

SALADIN UND RICHARD

(19, 17)

*This poem shows Walther at his worst. He is
begging shamelessly and deliberately, comparing
Philip with two opponents, Richard I and Saladin,
a Muslim. Although the later was renowned as
a noble opponent (he died in 1193), the comparisons
are nevertheless decidedly odious. Walther was no
longer at Philip's court at this time. He intention-
ally uses the* Erster Philippston *to remind the
emperor of his earlier poems in his praise.*

Herr Philipp, die ich nah besehen, zeihen
  dich,
Du gebest nicht mit freier Lust: nun dünket
  mich,
Du werdest so viel größer Gut verlieren.
  Es nutzt dir mehr, gibst du mit Freuden
    tausend Pfund,
5 Als dreißigtausend mit Verdruß: dir ist nicht
  kund,
Wie Gabe mag mit Preis und Ehre zieren.
  Fällt dir denn Saladin nicht ein?
Der sprach, durchlöchert müßten Königs-
  hände sein,
So würden sie gefürchtet und geminnet;
10 Und Richard nicht von Engeland,
Den man so schwer gelöst ob seiner milden
  Hand?
Ein Schad' ist gut, wenn doppelt man ge-
  winnet.

DER HOF ZU EISENACH

(20, 4)

*The poet here shows another side of the patronage
system. He had to live at a court, that of Landgraf
Hermann von Thüringen at Eisenach, where too
much time and money was given over to riotous*

living. *The criticism is tempered but undoubtedly
intended to be serious. Wolfram von Eschenbach
complains about the same excesses in* Parzival.

Wer in den Ohren siech ist oder Krank
  im Haupt,
Der meide ja Thüringens Hof, wenn er mir
  glaubt:
Käm' er dahin, er würde ganz betöret.
  Ich drang so lange zu, daß ich nicht vermag,
Ein Zug fährt ein, ein andrer aus, so Nacht   5
  als Tag:
Ein Wunder ists, daß da noch Jemand
  höret.
  Der Landgraf hat so milden Mut,
Daß er mit stolzen Helden, was er hat, vertut,
Davon ein jeder wohl als Kämpe stände.
Mir ist sein hohes Tun wohl kund: 10
Und gält ein Fuder guten Weines tausend
  Pfund,
Doch niemand leer der Ritter Becher fände.

KIRCHENSAMMLUNGEN

(34, 4)

*This is Walther's most vicious antipapal satire.
Unlike the anticlerical satire of the Latin poets,
it is directed against the person of the pope and
blames him for the misconduct it alleges. At
Easter in 1213, collection boxes for financial
contributions for a new Crusade were placed in the
churches. Walther assumes, without any evidence
that we know of, that the funds were to be diverted
to the personal treasury of the pope. The poem is
clearly chauvinistic, attacking the pope because he
was attempting the overthrow of Otto IV, whom
Walther was now supporting. The only criterion
Walther uses is whether German unity and independence will be helped or hindered by the pope's
actions. The poem is thus pure propaganda, intended to persuade the German people not to
contribute money to the papal see, even for a good
cause. Apparently it was effective, as we know
from the remarks of Thomasin von Cerclaere.
In his poem, written in 1215, he says that many
Germans had been misled by Walther's attacks.
These attacks are made more deadly by the device
of making the pope reveal his own plans.*

*The language of the poem presents few difficulties
if it is read aloud.*

Ahî wie kristenlîche nû der bâbest lachet,
swenne er sînen Walhen[1] seit „ich hânz[2]
   alsô gemachet!"
daz er dâ seit,[3] des solt er niemer hân gedâht.
er giht[4] „ich hân zwên Allamân undr eine
   krône brâht,
5   daz siz[5] rîche sulen stœren unde wasten.
ie darunder füllen wir die kasten:
ich hâns[6] an mînen stoc[7] gement, ir guot ist
   allez mîn.
ir tiuschez silber vert in mînen welschen
   schrîn.
ir pfaffen, ezzet hüener und trinket wîn,
10 unde lât die tiutschen [leien magern unde][8]
   vasten.

MILDE UND LÄNGE

(26, 3)

*The exact meaning of this poem has been greatly
disputed, but the general sense is clear. Philip II
was a short man but long on generosity. Otto IV
was a tall man, but his gifts were in inverse proportion to his height.*

Herrn Otto M i l d e wollt ich nach der
   L ä n g e messen;
Vergriffen hatt ich mich an diesem Maß
   indessen:
Wär' er so mild als lang, viel Tugend hätt
   er dann besessen.
Nun mäß' ich aber seinen Leib nach seiner
   Ehre,
5 Da ward er plötzlich viel zu kurz, wie ein
   zerbrochen Schwert,

---

[1] **Walhen (Welschen):** southern Europeans; here,
Italians:
[2] **hânz: habe es.**
[3] **seit: sagt.**
[4] **giht: behauptet, sagt.**
[5] **siz: sie das.**
[6] **hâns: habe sie.**
[7] **stoc (Opferstock):** alms chest.
[8] The words in brackets are supplied by editors.
They simply elaborate the meaning, but disrupt
the line's metrical pattern for this *Ton.*

An mildem Sinn zum winzig kleinsten Zwerg
   verkehrt;
Ja wenn er, noch zu wachsen, nicht zu alt
   an Jahren wäre!
Dem König bracht ich nun das Maß: der
   schoß empor!
Sein junger Leib ward stark und groß wie
   nie zuvor;
Er wächst wohl noch und ragt schon riesig 10
   über ihn hervor.

Walther von der Vogelweide.
(Bild aus der großen Heidel-
berger Liederhandschrift „C"
des 14. Jahrhunderts.) *Heidel-
berger Universitätsbibliothek.*

DAS REICHSLEHEN

(28, 31)

*This poem is not only an outburst of joy over the
small fief near Würzburg, granted to the poet
by Frederick II in 1220, but also an admission*

that his miseries had caused him to be crude and
bitter in his relations with others and in his writings.

Ich hab' ein Lehen, alle Welt, ich hab
　ein Lehen!
Nun fürcht' ich länger nicht den Hornung
　an den Zehen,
Will auch alle kargen Herrn desto minder
　flehen.
Der edle Herr, der milde Herr hat mich
　beraten,
5　Daß ich im Sommer freie Luft und Winters
　　Glut gewann.
Die Nachbarn sehn mich jetzt um so viel
　lieber an:
Nicht mehr als Kobold fliehn sie mich, wie sie
　vor diesem taten.
Zu lange lag ich an der Armut übel krank,
Ich war so voller Scheltens, daß mein Atem
　stank:
10　Den hat der König rein gemacht, dazu auch
　　meinen Sang.

DIE TRAUMDEUTERIN
(94, 11)

Here the poet ridicules dream-interpreters and super-
stitious people in general. Crows were prophets
of doom, old women experts at interpreting dreams.

Als der Frühling wiederkam,
Da man Blumen wonnesam
Bei der Vöglein Singen
Sah aus dem Grase dringen,
5　Kam ich einem langen
Gefilde zugegangen,
　Wo ein lauter Bronn entsprang:
Vor dem Walde war sein Gang
Bei der Nachtigall Gesang.

10　Auf dem Felde stand ein Baum,
Da entspann sich mir ein Traum.
Ich war zu dem Bronnen
Gegangen aus der Sonnen,
Bei der breiten Linden
15　Ein Schattendach zu finden.
　An den Bronnen setzt ich mich.
Alle Sorge bald entwich:
So entschlief ich wonniglich.

Da bedauchte mich zuhand,　　　　　　20
Wie mir diene Meer und Land,
Wie der Geist vor Sorgen
Im Himmel sei geborgen
Und dem Leib gegeben
Ein neues freies Leben.
　Alles Leids vergaß ich da.　　　　　　25
Weiß der wie's geschah,
Schönern Traum ich nimmer sah.

Daß ich dort nicht länger schlief!
Aber eine Krähe rief
Mit unselgem Schalle.　　　　　　30
Ihr Krähen, wärt ihr alle,
Wo ichs möchte leiden!
Mich so von Glück zu scheiden!
　Ich erschrak von ihrem Schrein:
Fänd' ich da nur einen Stein,　　　　　　35
Traun, es müßt' ihr Ende sein.

Doch ein Weib zum Wundern alt
Tröstete mich Armen bald:
Was die Gute sagte,
　(Als ich mein Leid ihr klagte)　　　　　　40
Was der Traum bedeute,
Vernehmt es, liebe Leute:
　Zwei und Einer, das sind drei.
Ferner sagte sie dabei,
Daß mein Daum ein Finger sei.　　　　　　45

TANZWEISE
(74, 20)

This poem is considered one of the best of the
Mädchenlieder. *The young lady is not the hard-*
hearted "frouwe" *of the courtly love poems but*
a modest girl—for the poet she is part of spring.
A pity that she proves to be a dream. Note the
symbolism of the falling blossoms and the reference
to the Tagelied *in the fourth strophe.*

„Nehmt, Herrin, diesen Kranz",
Sprach ich jüngst zu einem Mägdlein
　wunderhold,
　„So zieret ihr den Tanz
Mit den schönen Blumen, die ihr tragen
　sollt.
　Hätt' ich viel Gold und Edelsteine,　　　　5

Sie müßten euch gehören
Kann ich redlich schwören
Vertraut mir, daß ichs ernstlich meine.

Ihr seid so wohlgetan,
10 Daß ich euch ein Kränzlein gönnte herzlich
        gern,
    So gut ichs winden kann
    Noch viele Blumen stehen, rot– und weiße,
        fern,
    Die weiß ich dort in jener Haide,
    Wo sie gar hold entspringen
15 Bei der Vöglein Singen:
    Da sollten wir sie brechen beide.“

    Sie nahm, was ich ihr bot,
    Einem Kinde gleich, dem Freundliches
        geschieht;
    Ihr Wänglein wurde rot
20 Wie die Rose, da man sie bei Lilien sieht.
    Ihr Auge schämt sich, das lichte:
    Ein holdes Gegengrüßen
    Ward mir von der Süßen
    Und bald noch was ich nicht berichte.

25 Ich glaubte niemals mehr
    Freude zu gewinnen, als ich da besaß:
    Die Blüten fielen schwer
    Von den Bäumen bei uns nieder in das Gras.
    Ich war so fröhlich, daß ich lachte.
30 Als mich der Traum umsponnen
    Hielt mit solchen Wonnen,
    Da ward es Tag, und ich erwachte.

    Mir ist von ihr geschehn,
    Daß ich allen Mägdlein jetzt zur Sommerzeit
35   Muß in die Augen sehn;
    Fänd’ ich meine wieder: o der Seligkeit!
    Wär’ sie bei diesem Ringeltanze?
    Ihr Frauen habt die Güte,
    Rücket auf die Hüte:
40 Säh’ ich sie wieder unterm Kranze!

UNTER DER LINDE

(39, 11)

*This charming lyric poem, given here in the original
Middle High German, is a fine example of art*
*concealing art. It is ironical in its treatment of
a love affair recounted by a peasant girl, who is
clearly overwhelmed because she has found favor
with a person of higher status. Technically, this is
one of the few "Frauenstrophen" in early
Minnesang and it has distinct overtones of the
pastourelle, where a knight meets a peasant girl
and makes violent love to her.*

*If the poem is read aloud it is easily understood.
Read ie as two separate vowels.*

„Under der linden
an der heide,
dâ unser zweier bette was,
dâ muget ir vinden
schône beide   5
gebrochen bluomen unde gras.
vor dem walde in einem tal,
    tandaradei
schône sanc diu nahtegal.

Ich kam gegangen   10
zuo der ouwe:
dô was mîn friedel[1] kommen ê
dâ wart ich enpfangen,
hêre frouwe,[2]
daz ich bin saelic iemer mê.   15
kuster[3] mich? wol tûsentstunt:[4]
    tandaradei,
seht wie rôt ist mir der munt.

Dô het er gemachet
alsô rîche   20
von bluomen eine bettestat.
des wirt noch gelachet
inneclîche,
kumt iemen an daz selbe pfat.
bî den rôsen er wol mac,   25
    tandaradei,
merken wâ mirz houbet[5] lac.

Daz er bî mir laege
wessez iemen

---

[1] **Friedel: Liebling.**
[2] **Hêre frouwe,** believed by many editors to be an
    exclamation, **gnädige Jungfrau:** Holy Virgin.
    Were it not set off with commas, it could mean
    "I was received like a great lady," a sentiment in
    harmony with the ironical mood of the poem.
[3] **Kuster: küsste er.**
[4] **tûsentstunt: tausendmal.**
[5] **houbet: Haupt.**

30 (nu enwelle[6] got!), sô schamt ich mich.
wes er mit mir pflaege,[7]
niemer niemen
bevinde daz, wan[8] er und ich,
unt ein kleinez vogellîn
35   tandaradei,
daz mac wol getriuwe[9] sîn."

Frühling und Frauen

*In this lyric Walther shows his ability to make
the "Spring-topos" come alive. Again the girl
is seen as a part of nature.*

Wenn die Blumen aus dem Grase dringen,
Gleich als lachten sie hinauf zur Sonne,
Des Morgens früh an einem Maientag,
Und die kleinen Vöglein lieblich singen
5 Ihre schönsten Weisen: welche Wonne
Hat wohl die Welt, die so erfreuen mag?
    Man glaubt sich halb im Himmelreiche.
Wollt ihr hören, was sich dem vergleiche.
So sag ich, was mir wohler doch
10 Schon öfter an den Augen tat und immer
    tut, erschau ichs noch.
    Denkt, ein edles, schönes Fräulein schreite
Wohlbekleidet, wohlbekränzt hernieder,
Sich unter Leuten fröhlich zu ergehn,
Hochgemut im fürstlichen Geleite,
15 Etwas um sich blickend hin und wieder,
Wie Sonne neben Sternen anzusehn:
    Der Mai mit allen Wundergaben
Kann doch nichts so Wonnigliches haben
Als ihr viel minniglicher Leib;
20 Wir lassen alle Blumen stehn und blicken
    nach dem werten Weib.
    Nun, wohlan, wollt ihr Beweise schauen:
Gehn wir zu des Maien Lustbereiche,
Der ist mit seinem ganzen Heere da.
    Schauet ihn und schauet edle Frauen,
25 Was dem Andern wohl an Schönheit weiche,
Ob ich mir nicht das beßre Teil ersah.
    Ja, wenn mich Einer Wählen hieße,
Daß ich Eines für das Andre ließe,

---

[6] **enwelle got**: verhüte Gott.
[7] **pflaege**: machte.
[8] **wan**: als.
[9] **getriuwe**: treu (in the sense of keeping a secret).

Ach, wie so bald entschied' ich mich:
Herr Mai, ihr müßtet Jenner[1] sein, eh ich 30
    von meiner Herrin wich.

Güte gibt Tugend

*A Botenlied, in which the lady talks about her
lover to a messenger.*

Bote

Herrin, hört euch neue Kunde senden:
Ich bin ein Bot und soll euch sagen,
    Eines Ritters Trauer sollt ihr wenden,
Die er lange mußte tragen.
    Dies erbitten soll ich so: 5
Gebt ihr Freuden ihm zum Lohne,
Zweifelsohne
Wird dann manches Herz noch froh.

    Laßt euch dessen, Herrin, nicht verdrießen,
Gebt ihm willig hohen Mut: 10
    Ihr und alle mögens noch genießen,
Denen sanft die Freude tut.
Davon wird sein Sinn bereit,
Daß er findet
Eure Ehr und Würdigkeit.   15

Herrin

Noch vertrau ich ihm nicht solchermaßen,
Daß er wohl behüte sich:
    Krumme Wege gehn bei allen Straßen,
Davor, Gott, behüte mich.
Ich will des rechten Weges fahren,   20
Wer mich auch ein andres lehre:
Wohin ich kehre,
Der Himmel müsse mich bewahren.

Bote

Herrin, sendet ihm ein Hochgemüte,
Ihr nur macht ihn freudenreich.   25
    Laßt ihr ihn genießen eurer Güte,
Hat er Ehr und Tugend gleich.
    Herrin, gebt ihm hohen Mut,
Daß ihn Gram nicht mehr beschweret,

---

[1] **Jenner**: Januar

30 Und Freud ihn lehret,
    Daß er gern das Beste tut.

MAIENWONNE

*The personification of the forces of nature and the
ironical treatment of "love-in-spring" combine to
make this the most successful of Walther's spring
poems. The poet mocks at the convention of the
"cruel lady" by calling upon her to be just a little
less unrelenting.*

    Wollt ihr schauen, was im Maien
Wunder man gewahrt?
    Seht die Pfaffen, seht die Laien,
Wie das stolz gebart.
5   Ja, er hat Gewalt!
Ob er Zauberlist ersonnen?
Wo er naht mit seinen Wonnen,
Da ist niemand alt.

    Uns wird alles wohl gelingen:
10 Laßt uns diese Zeit
    Lustig tanzen, lachen, singen,
Nur mit Höflichkeit.
    Ei, wer wär nicht froh?
Da die Vöglein nun alle
15 Singen mit dem schönsten Schalle,
Täten wir nicht so?

    Wohl dir, Mai, wie du beglücktest
Alles weit und breit:
    Wie du schön die Bäume schmücktest,
20 Gabst der Haid' ein Kleid.
    War sie bunter je?
„Du bist kürzer, ich bin langer,"
Also streiten auf dem Anger
Blumen mit dem Klee.

25 Roter Mund, wie dichs entehret!
Laß' dein Lachen sein:
    Schäm dich, da du mich beschweret,
Noch zu lachen mein.
    Ist das wohlgetan?
30 Weh der unheilvollen Stunde,
Soll von minniglichem Munde
Mir Unminne nahn!

    Was mir raubte Glück und Segen,
Frau, seid ihr allein,

    Immer müßt ihr mir entgegen,   35
Gnadenlose, sein.
    Wißt ihr, was ihr tut?
Gnädig hört man doch euch preisen:
Wollt ihr mir nicht Gnad' erweisen,
Seid ihr ja nicht gut.   40

    Laßt es, Herrin, mich zu quälen,
Gönnt mir frohe Zeit,
    Oder mir muß Freude fehlen,
Daß ihr fröhlich seid!
    Herrin, blickt umher: 45
Alles freut sich im Vereine,
Sendet mir auch endlich eine
Kleine Freude her!

ANERLÄßLICHKEIT DER GEGENLIEBE

*As in the previous poem, Walther takes a con-
ventional topic, "Was ist Minne," and treats
it in his own, inimitable way.*

    Sag mir einer, was ist Minne?
Weil ich halb es weiß, so wüßt ich gerne mehr:
    Hat es jemand besser inne,
So belehr er mich, warum sie schmerzt so
    sehr.
    Minn' ist Minne, wenn sie freut: 5
Macht sie traurig, ist es nicht die rechte
    Minne,
    Und ich weiß nicht, was man ihr für Namen
    beut.

    Sollt ich jetzt es nicht verfehlen,
Was die Minne sei, so sprechet alle Ja!
    Minn' ist Wonne zweier Seelen: 10
Teilen beide gleich, so ist die Minne da.
    Kann jedoch nicht Teilung sein,
So vermags e i n Herz alleine nicht zu tragen;
    Darum solltest D u mir helfen, Herrin
    mein!

    Frau, zu schwer hab ich zu tragen;   15
Willst du helfen mir, so tu' es noch bei Zeit:
    Bist du taub für meine Klagen,
Sprich es endlich aus, so fass' ich mich im
    Leib,
    Bin hinfort ein freier Mann.
Aber Eines, dächt' ich, solltest du bedenken: 20

daß dich schwerlich einer besser loben
kann.

Darf sie Haß für Lieb erweisen?
Soll ich Freud ihr geben für mein bittres
Leid?
Hab' ich Grund ihr Lob zu preisen,
25 Wenn sie's kehren will zu meiner Niedrigkeit?
So tät ich übel, ihr zu traun:
Doch was sprech ich Ohrenloser, Augen-
ohner?
Den die Liebe blendete, wie mag er schaun?

Auf Reinmar des Alten Tod
(82, 24)

*This poem is an elegy for the poet Reinmar der
Alte. There can be little doubt that Reinmar was
Walther's teacher, formally or informally, at the
Viennese court. A group of poems shows that
there was sharp rivalry between them—rivalry
that was rekindled when Walther was more or
less forced to leave Vienna and Reinmar was
retained. The date of the elegy is uncertain—
perhaps 1208 to 1210. Its first strophe is largely
formal, its second more personal, a tribute to an
artist and friend. As Wapnewski remarks, we
cannot exclude the possibility that Walther hoped
to succeed Reinmar as court poet in Vienna. If he
did, he was disappointed. The poem is written in
the "Leopoldston," a melody used in poems to
the duke of Austria.*

O weh, daß Weisheit doch und Jugend,
Daß Mannesschönheit, Mannestugend
Sich nicht vererbt, geht ihm der Leib zu
Grabe!
Mit Recht beklagts ein weiser Mann,
5 Der den Verlust vermessen kann,
Reinmar, was Kunst an dir verloren habe.
Nun solltest du's im Tode noch genießen:
Du ließest dich nicht einen Tag verdrießen
Der Frauen Preis und Lobgesang . . . .
10 Sie sollten immer danken deiner Jungen;
Und hättest du nichts als das Lied gesungen
„So wohl dir, Weib, dein Name rein", du
hättest so gestritten
Zu ihrem Ruhm, daß jede Frau dir Gnade
sollt erbitten.

Gewiß Reinmar, du schmerzt mich
Gar viel härter als ich dich,   15
Wenn du lebtest und ich wär gestorben.
Ich will aufrichtig sein und sagen,
Dich selber wollt ich minder klagen
Als deine edele Kunst, daß die verdorben.
Du konntest neue Luft der Erde spenden,   20
Wenn du dein Lied zum Guten wolltest
wenden.
Mich schmerzt dein wohlberedter Mund,
dein süßer Liedersang,
Daß sie zu meiner Zeit von dannen fliehen.
Was möchtest du ein Weilchen nicht ver-
ziehen?
So hätt ich deine Fahrt geteilt: mein Singen   25
wahrt nicht lang.
Nun habe deine Seele Heil und deine Zunge
Dank.

Heimkehr

*Walther's songs usually are written in forms
borrowed ultimately from French and Provençal,
but this poem is in a metrical form whose lines
closely approximate those of the Nibelungenlied.
Walther probably intended to impart a heroic and
archaic tone to this particular work and also, of
course, a purely German one. This work is frequently called "Walther's Elegy," because of its
general tone of sadness and remembrance of things
past. Certainly it incorporates many formal expressions of the decay of nobility and the emptiness
of life—the laudatio temporis acti, or praise
of life as it used to be when the poet was young,
the "life is a dream" motif, the degeneracy of
modern youth, the bitterness of life even in its
sweetest moments. But the poem is far from being
a mere collection of commonplaces. It is a deeply
felt statement that the world as the poet had
known it in his youth was gone forever, and with
it, ideals of behavior and conduct which graced life
at court. He was right. The world of Hohenstaufen
chivalry was gone. Walther's imagery is very appropriate. Water, usually the image of change
and transitoriness, is the one stable thing left.
The woods and fields (which appear in so many
of his love poems as figures of ideal beauty) are
devastated. Most of all, however, he is horrified
at the behavior of young men who act like peasants;*

*this, in all probability, is a barb aimed at his
younger contemporary, Neidhart von Reuental.*

O weh, wohin verschwunden ist so man-
    ches Jahr?
Träumte mir mein Leben, oder ist es wahr?
Was stets mich wirklich dauchte, wars ein
    trüglich Spiel?
Ich habe lang geschlafen, daß es mir entfiel.
5   Nun bin ich erwacht und ist mir unbekannt,
Was mir so kund einst war wie diese jener
    Hand.
Leut und Land, die meine Kinderjahre sahn,
Sind mir so fremde jetzt, als wär es Lug und
    Wahn.
Die mir Gespielen waren, sind nun träg und
    alt,
10 Umbrochen ist das Feld, verhauen ist der
    Wald;
Nur das Wasser fließet, wie es weiland floß:
Ja gewiß, ich bin des Unglücks Spielgenoß.
Mich grüßet mancher lau, der mich einst
    wohl gekannt.
Die Welt fiel allenthalben aus der Gnade
    Stand.
15   Weh, gedenk' ich jetzt an manchen
    Wonnetag,
Der mir nun zerronnen ist wie in das Meer
    ein Schlag:
Immer mehr, o weh!

    O weh, wie sind versagt die jungen Leute
    nun,
Vor Kummer, der sie nagt, wie jämmerlich
    sie tun!
20 Sie wissen nur von Sorgen, weh, wie tun sie
    so?
Wohin ich blick und schaue, find ich niemand
    froh.
Tanzen, Singen, das vergeht vor Sorgen gar:
Nie sah man unter Christen solche Jammer-
    schar.

Geht nur der Frauen Schmuck, der einst so
    zierlich stand;
25 Die stolzen Ritter tragen baurisches Gewand.
Uns sind ungnädge Briefe[1] jüngst von Rom
    gekommen:

Uns ist erlaubt zu trauern, Freude gar
    benommen;
Nun schmerzt mich sehr (wir lebten ehmals
    wonnevoll),
Daß ich mein Lachen jetzt für Weinen tau-
    schen soll.
Die Vögel in den Lüften dauert unsre Not: 30
Was Wunder, wenn es mich betrübt bis in
    den Tod?
    Was sprech ich, dummer Mann, in Schmerz
    manch unnütz Wort?
Wer diese Wonne folgen will, der misset
    jene dort
Immer mehr o weh!

    O weh, wie hat man uns mit Süßigkeit   35
    vergeben!
Ich seh' die Galle mitten in dem Honig
    schweben;
Die Welt ist außen lieblich, weiß und grün
    und rot,
Doch innen schwarzer Farbe, finster wie
    der Tod;
Wen sie verleitet hat, der suche Trost und
    Heil,
Für kleine Buße wird ihm Gnade noch zu   40
    Teil.
Daran gedenket, Ritter, es ist euer Ding:
Ihr tragt die lichten Helme und manch harten
    Ring,
Dazu den festen Schild und das geweihte
    Schwert.
Wollte Gott, ich wär für ihn zu streiten wert,
So wollt ich armer Mann verdienen reichen   45
    Sold;
Nicht mein ich Haufen Landes, noch der
    Fürsten Gold:
Ich trüge Krone selber in der Engel Heer;
Die mag ein Soldner[2] wohl erwerben mit dem
    Sper.
    Dürft ich die liebe Reise fahren über See,
So wollt ich ewig singen Heil und nimmer-   50
    mehr O weh!
Nimmermehr O weh!

Walther is alluding when he expresses his wish to
go on the "liebe Reise" (line 49). Only such dedication, he believes, can restore the moral fiber of the
nation.

[2] **Soldner:** may be simply "a soldier" or may refer
to the centurion, traditionally called Longinus,
who pierced Christ's side with a spear and, according to some legends, was thereby miraculously
cured of blindness, both physical and spiritual.

---

[1] **ungnädge Briefe:** refer to the bull of excommunication issued against Frederick II by Pope
Gregory IX in 1227 because of his failure to carry
out a promised Crusade. It is to this Crusade that

𝕹eidhart von Reuenthal

(c. 1190–c. 1246)

Neidhart, a Bavarian by birth, spent much of his life traveling, once as far as Italy. He divulges a great deal about himself in his poems, but it is hard to determine whether he is really talking about himself or about a "persona" of Neidhart who takes part in the action of his lyrics. These poems are among the most interesting and puzzling in medieval German literature. Almost all of them deal with the peasant class and can be divided into those that describe the peasants' summer amusements in the open fields and the winter dances indoors. Their activities, especially in the *Winterlieder,* are described in language and poetic form that is deliberately reminiscent of the high *Minnesang.* Many poems begin with lines about spring and a love lament that could easily be taken seriously, but then the illusion is suddenly shattered by a peasant girl's name, a description of some rural activity, or a crude peasant expression. It is quite clear that Neidhart's main purpose was satire, both of the peasants and of the conventions of the *Minnesang,* and that his method, in general, is to make his lowborn and ill-behaved characters attempt to ape the more extreme conventions of courtly love. It is certain that there are some realistic touches in his work, but the object is not realistic portrayal but caricature. Unquestionably the results are brilliant, even though Neidhart's language is often obscure, and there can be little doubt that a good deal of the *double-entendre* escapes the modern reader.

Neidhart's influence on later poetry was profound and much of the lyric poetry of the next two centuries follows his example in coupling peasants with the conventions of the *Minnesang.* The picture of himself that he presents in his poetry—a nobleman who contends with the peasants on their own ground for the love of peasant girls and is constantly worsted in the encounters—became the foundation upon which the later Middle Ages built a series of "Neidhart Plays," of which he is the hero and in which he continues his conflict with the peasants.

The poems are difficult to render into modern German. Not only are there many words whose meaning is obscure or unknown, but the whole point of the satire rests on the parody of the *Minnesang,* which is naturally lost in modern idiom. The two poems here given are rendered as closely as possible in the words of the original, even at some sacrifice of clarity.

MINNEPARODIE

*The first two strophes of this poem sound exactly
like a conventional* Minnelied. *The break comes
in line 32, where the poet suddenly interjects the
names of "rivals" who are clearly peasants. The
crude behavior described in the rest of the strophe
needs no comment. The exact meaning of the
reference to the pear tree is not clear but it is
worth noting that the pear was a symbol of sexual
license.*

O weh, Sommerfreude,
daß ich dich entbehren muß.
Wer dich mir entrissen hat,
möge nie Heilung finden
5 von seelischem Leide.
Und der schönen,
nach der mein Herz strebt,
soll ich ihrer beraubt sein?
Das wäre wider meinen Willen.
10 Wenn ich mich von ihr trenne,
fällt es mir schwerer als nie von einer Frau.
Lieber wäre mir der Tod
als schmerzliche Not,
die zu lange bei mir verharrt.

15 Wenn ich über alles klage,
was ich je gelitten habe,
halte ich es für ein Wunder,
daß mir mancher nicht davon läuft.
Wenn mir nur Liebe zuteil würde
20 von der besten Frau,
die ich je mit meinen Augen gesehen habe.
An ihr
Ist alles Schöne zu finden.
Wie sie mich auch verschmäht,
25 glaube ich nicht, daß sie es vom Herzen meint.
Ich traue ihr, wie ich soll,
daß sie Lohn und Gnade schenkt,
und doch hilft es mir wenig.

Ich bin ihnen mit Recht
30 immer neidisch und ärgerlich,
die mich von ihrer Gnade
verjagen. Das sind Berchtran
und der junge Goze
und der ungenannte
35 den ich nicht nennen darf,

der gerne glaubte,
sie hätte mich bemerkt.
Von seinen Spießgesellen
schwang sich einer von dem höchsten Birn-
    baum:
als er um ihre Liebe bat,   40
trat er ihr auf das Röcklein
unten bei dem Saume.

SOMMERLIED

*The poem begins with variations on the "ideal
spring" theme, but the last few lines again shatter
the illusion.*

Schauet den Wald an, wie reich er mit neuem
    Laube steht,
wie fein ihm seine grünen Kleider stehen.
Davon hat der Mai ihm
viele geschickt.
Mädchen, wenn wir tanzen,
vergeßt nicht
alle,
daß wir die Rosenkränze
brechen
wenn der Tau darauf uns nur gefällt.   10

O Sommer, wie viele Herzen bei deiner
    Ankunft lachen!
Die Vögel, die der Winter traurig gemacht
    hat,
sie singen wunderbar
ihren Gesang.
Das wollen sie aber treiben   15
den Sommer lang.
Singen
üben sie am Morgen;
gegen Abend
spielen wir Kinder Ball.   20

In diesem Jahre wollen wir Freude und
    Vergnügen suchen.
Gott soll es allen jungen Mädchen gebieten,
daß sie mit bunten Kleidern
seien bereit
und den Sommer lang   25
höfische Sitten nie vergessen.

Winter
ist vergangen.
Die Alten
30 soll er als seine Kinder haben.

Die Sommerfreude habe ich an dem Vogel-
   sang erkannt.

Die Blumen, die der Mai aus dem Bande des
   Reifes erlöste,
mit seinem hellen Schein
so herrlich,
hätte ich nur Juteline,   35
würde ich anschauen gehen.

𝕹ibelungenlied

The exact date of the poem cannot be determined, but the traditional 1203 is a reasonably close approximation. The author's accurate geographical knowledge of the southeastern part of the German-speaking area obviously places him in this region; his knowledge of the northwest is vague. Attempts to show that the lyric poet Der von Kürenberg, Walther von der Vogelweide, or Wolfger von Passau may have been the author have little solid substance behind them.

It is perhaps unfortunate that the *Nibelungenlied* was rediscovered at just the right time to be designated the German national epic, for criticism of it has undoubtedly suffered from the constant attempts to compare it with the *Iliad* and other "national epics." The efforts to show that it has something very specifically "Germanic," that it is virtually uninfluenced by non-Germanic sources or motifs, and that it describes the Germanic hero and heroine resulted in excessive concentration of scholarly effort on determining the sources of the poem and its connections with stories about heroes of the same names in the verse *Edda*, the prose *Edda*, and the *Völsungasaga* in Old Norse and in the Scandinavian *Thidrekssaga*. More recent scholarship has fortunately moved away from these obsessions and has begun to treat the poem as a literary work.

There are clearly two distinct stories in the poem, that of Siegfried and Kriemhilde and that of the fall of the Burgundians. The former is found in Scandinavian literature in a rather different form—familiar to many readers through Wagner's operas. In the Norse versions, Sigurd frees Brunhilde from an enchantment, represented by a ring of fire. By the very act he is declared worthy of her love and is indeed betrothed to her. The various versions differ in details, but in all he marries another lady, Guthrun (who corresponds to Kriemhilde), after being given a draught of forgetfulness by her mother. He secures Brunhilde for Gunnar, and the two queens later quarrel as they do in the *Nibelungenlied*. Brunhilde has Sigurd killed, not by Högni (Hagen), who refuses to do so on the grounds of friendship, but by Guthorm, Gunnar's brother. Ostensibly, the reason for the murder is the insult, when in fact it is jealousy because Guthrun has married Sigurd. Brunhilde herself sets fire to her house and dies in it after the death of Sigurd. This Norse version contains many mythological elements that are not found in the *Nibelungenlied*, and many motifs, for example, the invulnerability of Siegfried found in the German versions, are absent in it. There are numerous hints and indications that the German author was familiar with these other versions, but he has deliberately made Siegfried and Kriemhilde a pair of courtly lovers, and the jealousy motif has been eliminated. Brunhilde is a far less important character in the German poem; in the second part she

an rehten triwen. daz er vch selben habt erslagn. Die blům allenthal
ben von blvte warn naz. do ringet mit dem tode: vnlange tet er daz.
wande in des todes wafen. al rerete snert. do mohte reden nihte mere. d'rehe
chůn vñ gemeit. Do die herren sahen. daz d' helt was tot. si leiten in vf
einen schilt. d' was von golde rot. vñ wrden des zerate: wie daz solde er
gan. daz man ir vhele. daz ir her Hagene getan. Do sprchen ir genů
ge: vns ist vbele geschehn. ir sult ez heln alle. vñ sult geliche iehn. da er
rite iagn eine. d' Chriemh man. in slugen schachere: da er fúre durch den
Tan. Do sprch d' ungetriwe. ich fvren in daz lant. mir ist vil vnmære. vñ
wirt er ir bechant. diu so hat getrûbet. miner frowen můt. ez ahtet mih
vil ringe. swaz si weinens getůt. Von dem selben brunnen. da Svrit
ward erslagn. sult ir diu rehten mære: von mir hoen sagn. vor dem Otin
walde. ein dorf lit Otenhaim. da vliuzet noch d' brunne. des ist zwifel
dehein. Sument wie Chr ir man klagte vñ wie man in begr.
Oerbuten si d'nahte: vñ füren vb' Rin. von helden chunde
nimmi. wirs getaget sin. ein iter daz si da slugen. daz wein
ten edeliv kint. ia můsin sin engelten. vñ gute wigande
sint. Von grozer vbirmůte. mugt ir nv horen sagn. vñ
von starch' rache. do hiez Jagen tragn. Svride den herren. von Nibelun
ge lant. fvr eine kemenaten. da man Chriemh vant. Er hiez in also
toten. legn an die tvr: daz si in da solde vinden. so si d' gienge fvr: hin
ter mettine. e daz ez wrde tac. d' diu frowe Chriemh. dehein sleffen ver
lac. Man lute da zem munster: nach gewonheit. do wachte diu frowe.
vor ir manige mett. si bat ir balde bringen. lieht vñ ir gewant. do chom
ein kamerere. da er Svriden vant. Er sach in blvtes roten. sin wat
was elliv naz. daz er sin herre wære. nihte enwesser daz. hin ter kemena
ten daz lieht trvg an d' hant. von dem vil leid mære. Kv vrŏ Chriemhilt
ervant. Do si mit ir frowen. zem munst' wolde gan. do sprch d' kamer
re. ia sult ir stille stan. ez lit vor dem gademe. ein ritter tot erslagn. da
begunde Chriemh. harte vnmæliche klagn. E daz si reht erfunde.
daz ez were ir man. an die Hagene vrage: denchen si begun. wie in wol
de vristen. do ward ir erst leit. ir was alle ir freuden. mit sime tode
wiis leit. Do seich si zv d' erden. daz si niht ensprch. die schonen frev

disappears from the scene and becomes a subordinate, shadowy figure. Nevertheless, it is clear that the Norse and the German versions are ultimately derived from the same sources—a Siegfried–Brunhilde story, perhaps of Merovingian origin, with a principal theme of the rivalry of two women for a hero's love.

The second part has an historical basis—the destruction of the Burgundians by the Huns in 435. Yet in all the extant versions this catastrophe is secondary to the revenge motif, which is the core of the story. In all the Norse works Guthrun marries Atli (Attila), and when he invites her brothers and Högni, she warns them not to come. They do not heed the warning because their pride will not allow them to refuse. All are killed after a heroic struggle, and Guthrun avenges her brothers by first killing Atli's children and making him unwittingly eat their flesh and then by murdering the king himself. In these versions Atli is a cruel tyrant, and the whole stress is on the revenging of kinsmen by blood. Guthrun does not mourn for the dead Sigurd and apparently has no hostile feelings toward her brothers because of his murder. This version is the "northwestern," in which the Burgundians are noble and the Huns treacherous and cruel. In the German *Nibelungenlied* what is substantially the same story is treated from a completely different point of view. Etzel is a gentle, even weak ruler, who is completely dominated by Kriemhilde. The greatest of all the heroes is Dietrich, who is introduced into this version because he was the outstanding man among the Goths. Here it is the Burgundians who are cruel (although not in the way that Atli is portrayed in the Norse versions), and the whole emphasis is on the continuing mourning for Siegfried by Kriemhilde and her determination to avenge him. It cannot be claimed that the earlier versions have been changed to produce this result. It is perfectly possible that among the southeastern peoples there was always the tradition that the Burgundians met their deserts.

Thus, although we do not know the immediate sources of the poem, we can be fairly sure that it derives ultimately from two lays of the *Völkerwanderung* period, one on the ill-starred love of Siegfried and Brunhilde, the other on the fall of the Burgundians. Yet this does not exclude the possibility that many of the minor incidents and some of the modifications may be due to influence from such sources as the French *chansons de geste*. Even more important is the fact that the author knew the courtly romance and was at some pains to incorporate its conventions in his work. Siegfried is knighted at a great feast, his love for Kriemhilde is deliberately made to appear like the love of the knight for his lady, and even the conventional terms of the courtly works are used. It is hard to say whether the author seriously intended to make Siegfried a courtly hero. If he did so intend, he was not very successful, But if his purpose was to point to the inadequacy of some of the courtly views of life, especially in regard to war and the conflict of peoples, he makes a good case. Siegfried is a fine warrior but he is astonishingly naïve in his handling of people. This is not to say that the author of the *Nibelungenlied* was writing an anticourtly poem (as some critics contend), but rather that his limited understanding of the courtly ethic made him feel that it was inadequate for depicting the serious business of actual life at court and in battle.

In other aspects too the author shows modifications of the old "heroic tradition." One of the finest features of the work is his introduction of Rüdiger, a Christian gentleman, who is unselfish, not swayed by empty notions of honor, but deeply concerned with doing right as he sees it. His chivalry and mercy are in contrast with the traits of most of the major characters. It is he who most clearly shows Christian influence. For most of the others, Christianity is something demanding little more than lip service.

Although Kriemhilde is a weak character in the first part of the poem, the whole work is really devoted to a struggle between Hagen and Siegfried/Kriemhilde in the first part, and Hagen and Kriemhilde in the second. Hagen is the important man at court, and his prestige is weakened by Siegfried's successes. His resentment shows itself in his readiness to avenge Brunhilde, but even at this point we have to recognize the driving force of Hagen's behavior in the second part—his determination to preserve the king's honor at all costs—even if it means the king's death. To this end he employs methods that are utterly ruthless but entirely logical. The author's sympathy, which appears to be with Kriemhilde when Siegfried is killed, definitely shifts to Hagen. Gunther fights bravely enough, but he is of feeble moral fiber. Without Siegfried and Hagen he would be a miserable failure.

In spite of the introduction of the courtly clichés already metioned, the style of the *Nibelungenlied* is still largely that of heroic poetry. The vocabulary is relatively small, the recital of events factual, with a great deal of repetition of standard descriptive phrases. There is very little attempt to show the motivation of actions, still less to give abstract discussions of them. Much use is made of the "comment by the author," in which he calls the attention of his audience to the dire effects a particular action will have. The actual descriptions of persons are highly conventional; it is through their actions that we gain deeper insight into their characters.

The poem is written in the four-line *Nibelungenstrophe*, which is reproduced quite accurately in the translation. Note that the last half-line of each strophe is longer by one or two syllables than the others. The strophic form tends to stop the action every four lines, and this often gives a sententious effect, particularly when the last line is one of the author's "foreboding comments."

Simrock's translation, itself a minor classic, is made from the C version of the poem, which is a slightly revised version of the B text used in most modern editions. Consequently it will sometimes show minor variations from the standard MHG texts of the poem.

NIBELUNGENLIED

1   Viel Wunderdinge melden   die Mären
    alter Zeit
Von preiswerten Helden,   von großer
    Kühnheit,
Von Freud' und Festlichkeiten,   von
    Weinen und von Klagen,
Von kühner Recken Streiten   mögt ihr
    nun Wunder hören sagen.

2   Es wuchs in Burgunden   solch edel
    Mägdelein,[1]
Daß in allen Landen   nichts Schöners
    mochte sein.
Kriemhild war sie geheißen   und ward
    ein schönes Weib.
Um die viel Degen mußten   verlieren
    Leben und Leib.[2]

3   Die Minnigliche lieben   brachte nimmer
    Scham;
Ihr dienten kühne Recken,   niemand war
    ihr gram.
Schön war ohne Maßen   die edle Maid zu
    schaun;
Die Tugenden der Jungfrau   zierten wohl
    alle Fraun.

4   Es pflegten sie drei Könige   edel und
    reich,
Gunther und Gernot,   die Recken ohne-
    gleich,
Und Geiselher der junge,   ein weidlicher
    Degen;
Sie war ihre Schwester,   die Fürsten
    hatten sie zu pflegen.

5   Die Herren waren milde,[3]   von hohem
    Stamm geboren,

---

[1] The Burgundian tribe was in fact destroyed by the
Huns, although not under Attila's leadership, in
435. Their territory did not correspond to modern
Burgundy but centered, as the poem says, on
Worms on the Rhine.
[2] This line is typical of hundreds in the poem which
cast an air of foreboding over the work.
[3] **milde:** "generous with gifts," as becomes a medieval ruler.

Unmaßen Kühn aus Kräften,   die Recken
    auserkoren.
Nach den Burgunden   war ihr Land
    genannt;
Sie schufen starke Wunder   noch seitdem
    in Etzels Land.

      *   *   *

In ihren hohen Ehren   träumte Kriem- 13
    hilden,
Sie zög' einen Falken,   stark–, schön–,
    und wilden.
Den griffen ihr zwei Aare,   daß sie es
    mochte sehn:
Ihr konnt auf dieser Erde   größer Leid
    nicht geschehn.

Sie sagt' ihrer Mutter   den Traum, Frau 14
    Uten:
Die wußt' ihn nicht zu deuten   als so der
    Guten:
„Der Falke, den du ziehest,   das ist ein
    edler Mann:
Ihn wolle Gott behüten,   sonst ist es bald
    um ihn getan."

„Was sagt ihr mir vom Manne,   vielliebe 15
    Mutter mein?
Ohne Reckenminne   will ich nimmer
    sein;
So schön will ich verbleiben   bis an meinen
    Tod,
Daß ich von Reckenminne   nie gewinnen
    möge Not."

„Verred' es nicht so völlig,"   die Mutter 16
    sprach da so,
„Sollst du je von Herzen   auf Erde werden
    froh,
Das geschieht von Mannesminne: du
    wirst ein schönes Weib,
Will Gott dir noch vergönnen   eines
    guten Ritters Leib."

„Die Rede lasset bleiben,   vielliebe Mut- 17
    ter mein.
Es hat an manchen Weibern   gelehrt der
    Augenschein,
Wie Liebe mit Leide   am Ende gerne
    lohnt:
Ich will sie meiden beide,   so bleib' ich
    sicher verschont."

18 Kriemhild in ihrem Mute   hielt sich von Minne frei.
So ging noch der Guten   manch lieber Tag vorbei,
Daß sie niemand wußte,   der ihr gefiel zum Mann,
Bis sie doch mit Ehren   einen werten Recken gewann.

19 Das war derselbe Falke,   den jener Traum ihr bot,
Den ihr beschied die Mutter.   Ob seinem frühen Tod
Den nächsten Anverwandten   wie gab sie blut'gen Lohn!
Durch dieses einen Sterben   starb noch mancher Mutter Sohn.

20 Da wuchs im Niederlande   eines edeln Königs Kind:
Siegmund hieß sein Vater,   seine Mutter Siegelind,
In einer reichen Feste,   weithin wohl-bekannt.
Unten an dem Rheine;   Xanten[4] war sie genannt.

21 Ich sag' euch von dem Degen,   wie so schön er ward.
Er war vor allen Schanden   immer wohl bewahrt.
Stark und hohen Namens   ward bald der kühne Mann:
Hei! was er großer Ehren   auf dieser Erde gewann!

22 Siegfried war geheißen   der schnelle Degen gut.
Er erprobte viel der Recken   in hochbe-herztem Mut.
Seine Stärke führt' ihn   in manches fremde Land:
Hei! was er schneller Degen   bei den Burgunden fand!

23 Bevor der kühne Degen   ganz erwuchs zum Mann,

----

[4] **Xanten**: capital of Siegmund's kingdom, a small town on the Rhine north of the Ruhr and not far from the Dutch border.

Da hatt' er solche Wunder   mit seiner Hand getan,
Davon man immer wieder   singen mag und sagen;
Wir müssen viel verschweigen   von ihm in heutigen Tagen.

In seinen besten Zeiten,   bei seinen jungen Tagen
Mochte man viel Wunder   von Siegfrie-den sagen,
Was Ehren an ihm blühten   und wie er schön zu schaun:
Drum dachten sein in Minne   viel der weidlichen Fraun.

* * *

Da dacht' auf hohe Minne   Sieglindens Kind:
All der andern Werbern war   wider seins wie Wind.
Er mochte wohl verdienen   ein Weib so auserwählt:
Bald war die edle Kriemhild   dem starken Siegfried vermählt.

Ihm rieten seine Freunde   und die in seinem Lehn,
Hab er stete Minne   sich zum Ziel ersehn,
So soll' er werben, daß sich   der Wahl nicht müßte schämen.
Da sprach der kühne Siegfried: „So will ich Kriemhilden nehmen.

Die edle Königstochter   von Burgunden-land
Um ihre große Schöne.   Es ist mir wohl bekannt.
Kein Kaiser sei so mächtig,   hätt' er zu freien im Sinn,
Dem nicht zu minnen ziemte   diese junge Königin."

Diese Märe hörte   der König Siegmund.
Es sprachen seine Leute: also ward ihm kund
Seines Kindes Wille.   Es war ihm grimmig leid,
Daß er werben wolle   um diese herrlich Maid.

7 Es erfuhr es auch die Königin,   die edle Siegelind:
Die mußte große Sorge   tragen um ihr Kind.
Sie sorgt' es zu verlieren   von König Gunthers Heer;
Die Werbung dem Degen   zu verleiden fliß man sich sehr.

8 Da sprach der kühne Siegfried: „Viellieber Vater mein,
Ohn' edler Frauen Minne   wollt's ich immer sein,
Wenn ich nicht werben dürfte   nach Herzensliebe frei."
Was jemand reden mochte,   so blieb er immer dabei.

9 „Ist dir nicht abzuraten",   der König sprach da so,
„So bin ich deines Willens   von ganzem Herzen froh
Und will dir's fügen helfen,   so gut ich immer kann;
Doch hat der König Gunther   manchen hochfärt'gen Mann.

10 „Und wär' es anders niemand   als Hagen der Degen,
Der kann in Übermute   wohl der Hochfahrt pflegen,
So daß ich sehr befürchte,   es mög' uns werden leid,
Wenn wir werben wollen   um diese herrliche Maid."

11 „Wie mag uns das gefährden?"   hub da Siegfried an:
„Was ich mir im Guten   da nicht erbitten kann,
Mag ich schon sonst erwerben   mit meiner starken Hand:
Ich will von ihm erzwingen   so die Leute wie das Land."

12 „Leid ist mir deine Rede",   sprach König Siegmund,
„Denn würde diese Märe   dort am Rheine kund,

Du dürftest nimmer reiten   in König Gunthers Land.
Gunther und Gernot,   die sind mir lange bekannt.

13 Mit Gewalt erwerben   kann niemand die Magd",
Sprach der König Siegmund,   „das ist mir wohl gesagt;
Willst du jedoch mit Recken   reiten in das Land,
Die Freunde, die wir haben,   die werden eilends besandt."

Siegfried sets out for Burgundy with a large entourage. On his arrival, during his first meeting with Gunther, Siegfried displays arrogance and hostility—traits that are atypical of his character.

37 Zur Antwort gab ein Recke   mit Namen Ortewein;
Stark und kühnes Mutes   mocht' er wohl sein:
„Da wir sie nicht erkennen,   so heißet jemand gehn
Nach meinem Oheim Hagen;   dem sollt ihr sie lassen sehn.

38 Ihm sind wohl kund die Reiche   und alles fremde Land;
Erkennt er die Herren,   das macht er uns bekannt."
Der König ließ ihn holen   und sie in seinem Lehn:
Man sah ihn stolzen Schrittes   mit Recken hin zu Hofe gehn.

39 Warum nach ihm der König,   frug Hagen da, geschickt.
„Es werden fremde Degen   in meinem Haus erblickt,
Die niemand mag erkennen: habt ihr in fernem Land
Sie wohl schon gesehen?   Das macht mir, Hagen, bekannt."[5]

[5] Hagen is the source of all information at Gunther's court; as the poem progresses he becomes the person who determines all policy. His account of Siegfried's acquisition of the treasure and indeed of all his actions differs markedly from the accounts in the Norse versions of Siegfried's youth.

40 „Das will ich", sprach Hagen.   Zum Fenster schritt er drauf,
Da ließ er nach den Gästen   den Augen freien Lauf.
Wohl gefiel ihm ihr Geräte   und auch ihr Gewand;
Sie waren ihm gar fremde   in der Burgunden Land.

41 Er sprach, woher die Recken   auch kämen an den Rhein,
Es möchten selber Fürsten   oder Fürstenboten sein.
„Schön sind ihre Rosse   und ihr Gewand ist gut;
Von wannen sie auch ritten,   es sind Helden hochgemut."

42 Also sprach da Hagen: „Soviel ich mag verstehn,
Hab' ich gleich im Leben   Siegfried nie gesehn,
So will ich doch wohl glauben,   wie es damit auch steht,
Daß er es sei, der Degen,   der so herrlich dorten geht.

43 Er bringt neue Mären   her in dieses Land:
Die kühnen Nibelungen[6]   schlug des Helden Hand,
Die reichen Königssöhne   Schilbung und Nibelung;
Er wirkte große Wunder   mit des starken Armes Schwung.

44 Als der Held alleine   ritt aller Hilfe bar,
Fand er an einem Berge,   so hört' ich immerdar,
Bei König Niblungs Horte   gar manchen kühnen Mann;
Sie waren ihm gar fremde,   bis er hier die Kunde gewann.

45 Der Hort König Niblungs   war hervorgetragen
Aus einem hohlen Berge: nun höret Wunder sagen,

Wie ihn teilen wollten,   die Niblung untertan.
Das sah der Degen Siegfried,   den es zu wundern begann.

46 So nahe kam er ihnen,   daß er die Helden sah
Und ihn die Degen wieder.   Der eine sagte da:
‚Hier kommt der starke Siegfried,   der Held aus Niederland.'
Seltsame Abenteuer   er bei den Nibelungen fand.

47 Den Recken wohl empfingen   Schilbung und Nibelung.
Einhellig baten   die edlen Fürsten jung,
Daß ihnen teilen möchte   den Schatz der kühne Mann:
Das begehrten sie, bis endlich   er's zu geloben begann.

48 Er sah so viel Gesteines,   wie wir hören sagen,
Hundert Leiterwagen,   die möchten es nicht tragen;
Noch mehr des roten Goldes   von Nibelungland:
Das alles sollte teilen   des kühnen Siegfriedes Hand.

49 Sie gaben ihm zum Lohne   König Niblungs Schwert:
Da wurden sie des Dienstes   gar übel gewährt,
Den ihnen leisten sollte   Siegfried der Degen gut.
Er konnt' es nicht vollbringen: sie hatten zornig Mut.

50 So mußt' er ungeteilt   die Schätze lassen stehn.
Da bestanden die Degen   in der zwei Kön'ge Lehn:
Mit ihres Vaters Schwerte,   das Balmung war genannt,
Stritt ihnen ab der Kühne   den Hort und Nibelungenland.

51 Da hatten sie zu Freunden   kühne zwölf Mann,

---

[6] The word "Nibelungen" is puzzling. Here it applies to the original owners of the treasure. When Siegfried acquires it, he takes the name. After Hagen has sunk it in the Rhine, the Burgundians take over the name.

Die starke Riesen waren: was konnt'
   es sie verfahn?
Die erschlug im Zorne Siegfriedens Hand
Und siebenhundert Recken zwang er
   vom Nibelungenland

52 Mit dem guten Schwerte, geheißen
   Balmung.
Vom Schrecken überwältigt war mancher
   Degen jung
Zumal vor dem Schwerte und vor dem
   kühnen Mann:
Das Land mit den Burgen machten sie
   ihm untertan.

53 Dazu die reichen Könige, die schlug er
   beide tot.
Er kam durch Albrichen darauf in große
   Not:
Der wollte seine Herren rächen allzuhand,
Eh' er die große Stärke noch an Siegfrie-
   den fand.

54 Da war ihm nicht gewachsen der
   gewalt'ge Zwerg.
Wie die wilden Leuen liefen sie an den
   Berg,
Wo er die Tarnkappe Albrichen abge-
   wann.
Da war des Hortes Meister Siegfried, der
   schreckliche Mann.

55 Die sich getraut zu fechten, die lagen all'
   erschlagen.
Den Schatz ließ er wieder nach dem Berge
   tragen,
Dem ihn entnommen hatten die Niblung-
   untertan.
Alberich der starke das Amt des Kämm-
   rers gewann.

56 Er mußt' ihm Eide schwören, er dien'
   ihm als sein Knecht;
Zu aller Art Diensten ward er ihm
   gerecht."
So sprach von Tronje Hagen: „Das hat
   der Held getan;
Also große Kräfte nie mehr ein Recke
   gewann.

Hagen now tells of Siegfried's invulnerability,
brought about by his bathing in the dragon's blood.

Siegfried then delivers to Gunther a challenge to
fight him for his kingdom—a totally unmotivated
action—and very nearly precipitates a general fight.
However, he is calmed by the tactful behavior of
Gernot, Gunther's brother, and agrees to stay
at the Burgundian court. He performs numerous
feats of strength and soon becomes a general favorite.
He wins further acclaim for helping Gunther
defeat the Saxons in a great battle.

Siegfried is known to be "in love" with Kriem-
hilde, Gunther's sister, even though he has yet to see
her. Finally they meet, but not until a great feast
is arranged at the court. But even after the meeting,
he progresses so slowly in his guest for Kriemhilde
that he is on the point of returning home. Giselher,
Kriemhilde's younger brother, persuades him to
stay. Gunther now hears of the beauty of Brunhilde,
who is a queen "across the sea," but Siegfried tells
him that she treats her suitors cruelly and advises
him against the expedition. Hagen suggests that
Siegfried help Gunther to win her, since he already
knows so much about her.

Er sprach: „Viel edler Siegfried, willst VI, 12
   du mein Helfer sein
Zu werben um die Schöne? Tu' nach der
   Bitte mein;
Und gewinn' ich mir zur Trauten das
   herrliche Weib,
So vermag' ich deinetwillen Ehre, Leben
   und Leib."

Zur Antwort gab ihm Siegfried, König 13
   Siegmunds Sohn:
„Gibst du mir deine Schwester, so tu'
   ich es schon,
Kriemhild die Schöne, eine Königin
   hehr:
So begehr' ich keines Lohnes nach meinen
   Arbeiten mehr."

„Ich gelob' es", sprach Gunther, „Sieg- 14
   fried, an die Hand.
Und kommt die schöne Brunhild her
   in dieses Land,
So will ich dir zum Weibe meine Schwe-
   ster geben:
So magst du mit der Schönen immer in
   Freuden leben."

Des schwuren sie sich Eide, die Ritter 15
   kühn und hehr.

Da schuf es ihnen beiden   viel Arbeit und
    Beschwer,
Eh sie die Wohlgetane   brachten an den
    Rhein.
Es mußten bald die Kühnen   darum in
    großen Sorgen sein.

16   Von wilden Gezwergen   hab' ich hören
    sagen,
Daß sie in hohlen Bergen   wohnen und
    Schirme tragen,
Die heißen Tarnkappen,   von wunder-
    barer Art;
Wer sie am Leibe trage,   der sei gar
    wohl darin bewahrt

17   Vor Schlägen und vor Stichen;   ihn
    mög' auch niemand sehn,
Solang er drin verweile;   hören doch und
    spähn
Mag er nach seinem Willen,   daß niemand
    ihn erschaut;
Ihm wachsen auch die Kräfte,   wie uns
    die Märe vertraut.

18   Die Tarnkappe führte   nun Siegfried mit
    hindann,
Die der kühne Degen   mit Sorgen einst
    gewann
Von einem Gezwerge   mit Namen
    Alberich.
Da schickten sich zur Reise   Recken kühn
    und ritterlich.

19   Wenn der starke Siegfried   die Tarnkappe
    trug,
So gewann er drinnen   der Kräfte genug,
Zwölf Männer Stärke,   so wird uns gesagt.
Er erwarb mit großen Listen   diese herr-
    liche Magd.

20   Auch war so beschaffen   die Nebelkappe
    gut,
Ein jeder mochte drinnen   tun nach
    seinem Mut,
Was er immer wollte,   daß ihn doch
    niemand sah.
Damit gewann er Brunhild,   durch die
    ihm bald viel Leid geschah.

*Elaborate preparations are made for the journey,
especially in the provision of rich clothing, and the*

*heroes make a fabulous sea voyage. The geographical
information about this voyage is very vague, in
marked contrast to the later precise description
of the journey to Etzel's court. Their arrival is
duly noted by the ladies, who greet them in proper
form. Brunhilde is told that one of the newcomers
looks like Siegfried, and that another is obviously
a great king.*

„Der dritte der Gesellen,   der hat gar
    grimmen Sinn,
Doch schönen Wuchs nicht minder,
    reiche Königin.
Die Blicke sind gewaltig,   deren so viel
    er tut:
Er trägt in seinem Sinne,   ich wähne,
    grimmigen Mut.

Der jüngste darunter,   gar löblich dünkt
    er mich:
Man sieht den reichen Degen   so recht
    minniglich
In jungfräulicher Sitte   und edler Haltung
    stehn:
Wir müßten alle fürchten,   wär' ihm ein
    Leid hier geschehn.

So freundlich er gebare,   so wohlgetan
    sein Leib,
Er brächte doch zum Weinen   manch
    weidliches Weib,
Wenn er zürnen sollte;   sein Wuchs ist
    wohl so gut,
Er ist an allen Tugenden   ein Degen
    kühn und wohlgemut."

Da sprach die Königstochter: „Nun
    bringt mir mein Gewand:
Und ist der starke Siegfried   gekommen in
    mein Land
Um meine Minne willen,   es geht ihm an
    den Leib:[7]

---

[7] The assumption on Brunhilde's part that it is
Siegfried who is coming to win her love seems to
argue that she already knows something about him
or that the author is recalling the tradition found in the
Norse versions that he had rescued her from the
ring of fire and later broke his troth to her and
married Guthrun (Kriemhilde in the German
version). To surmount the ring of fire was, of
course, a test as proof of manhood; the three con-
tests here described are intended to serve the same
purpose.

Ich fürcht' ihn nicht so heftig, daß ich
würde sein Weib."

29 Da trug die Königstochter bald erlesen
Kleid.
Es gab ihr Geleite manche schöne Maid,
Wohl hundert oder drüber; das war den
Gästen leid.
Aufstanden von den Sitzen die kühnen
Helden allbereit.

* * *

31 Als die Königstochter Siegfrieden sah,
Wohlgezogen sprach sie zu dem Gaste da:
„Seid willkommen, Siegfried, hier in
diesem Land.
Was meint eure Reise? Das macht mir,
bitt' ich, bekannt."

32 „Viel Dank muß ich euch sagen, Frau
Brunhild,
Daß ihr mich geruht zu grüßen, Fürs-
tentochter mild,
Vor diesem edeln Recken, der hier vor
mir steht:
Denn der ist mein Lehnsherr; der Ehre
Siegfried wohl enträt.

33 Er ist am Rheine König was soll ich
sagen mehr?
Dir nur zuliebe fuhren wir hierher.
Er will dich gerne minnen, was ihm geschehen mag.
Nun bedenke ich beizeiten: mein Herr
läßt nimmermehr nach.

34 Er ist geheißen Gunther, ein König
reich und hehr.
Erwirbt er deine Minne, nicht mehr ist
sein Begehr.
Mir gebot mit ihm zu fahren der Recke
wohlgetan;
Wenn er mein Herr nicht wäre, ich hätt'
es nimmer getan."

35 Sie sprach: „Wenn er dein Herr ist und
du in seinem Lehn,[8]

---

[8] When Brunhilde hears that Siegfried is merely
Gunther's liegeman she changes from the polite
plural to the familiar singular form of address.
(Siegfried has also used it to her.) This pretense on
Siegfried's part was to have dire consequences.

Will er, die ich erteile, meine Spiele dann
bestehn
Und bleibt darin der Meister, so werd'
ich sein Weib;
Gewinn' ich aber eines, es geht euch
allen an den Leib."

36 Da sprach von Tronje Hagen: „Nun
zeigt uns, Königin,
Was ihr für Spiel erteilet. Eh euch den
Gewinn
Mein Herr Gunther ließe, so müßt' es
übel sein:
Er mag wohl noch erwerben ein so
schönes Mägdelein."

37 „Den Stein soll er werfen und springen
danach,
Den Speer mit mir schießen: drum sei
euch zu jach.
Ihr verliert hier mit der Ehre Leben
leicht und Leib:
Drum mögt ihr euch bedenken", sprach
das minnigliche Weib.

*Gunther explains the reason for his coming, and
Brunhilde is eager to begin the contest. She arms
herself, and so do her attendants. Gunther's followers, who have had to relinquish their weapons
upon entering the queen's territory, are fearful
of the outcome; Gunther is even more afraid.
Siegfried fetches his cloak of invisibility and
stands beside Gunther to help him win.*

70 Da schoß mit großen Kräften die herr-
liche Maid
Den Speer nach einem neuen Schild, mäch-
tig und breit;
Den trug an seiner Linken Sieglindens
Kind.
Das Feuer sprang vom Stahle, als ob
es wehte der Wind.

71 Des starken Spießes Schneide so den
Schild durchdrang,
Daß das Feuer lohend aus den Ringen
sprang.
Von dem Schusse strauchelten die kraft-
vollen Degen:
War nicht die Tarnkappe, sie wären beide
da erlegen.

72   Siegfried dem kühnen   vom Munde brach
     das Blut.
     Bald sprang er auf die Füße: da nahm
     der Degen gut
     Den Speer, den sie geschossen   ihm hatte
     durch den Rand:
     Den warf ihr bald zurücke   Siegfried mit
     kraftvoller Hand.

73   Er dacht: „Ich will nicht schießen   das
     Mägdelein wonniglich."
     Des Spießes Schneide kehrt' er   hinter
     den Rücken sich;
     Mit der Speerstange   schoß er auf ihr
     Gewand,
     Daß es laut erhallte   von seiner kraft-
     reichen Hand.

74   Das Feuer stob vom Panzer,   als trieb'
     es der Wind.
     Es hatte wohl geschossen   der Sieglinde
     Kind:
     Sie vermochte mit den Kräften   dem
     Schusse nicht zu stehn;
     Das wär' von König Gunthern   in Wahr-
     heit nimmer geschehn.

75   Brunhild die Schöne   bald auf die Füße
     sprang:
     „Gunther, edler Ritter,   des Schusses habe
     Dank!"
     Sie wähnt', er selber hätt' es   mit seiner
     Kraft getan;
     Nein, geworfen hatte   sie ein viel stärkerer
     Mann.

76   Da ging sie hin geschwinde,   zornig war
     ihr Mut,
     Den Stein hoch erhub sie,   die edle
     Jungfrau gut;
     Sie schwang ihn mit Kräften   weithin
     von der Hand.
     Dann sprang sie nach dem Wurfe,   daß
     laut erklang ihr Gewand.

77   Der Stein war gefallen   zwölf Klafter von
     dem Schwung:
     Die Jungfrau wohlgeschaffen   erreicht'
     ihn doch im Sprung.

Hin ging der schnelle Siegfried   wo der
     Stein nun lag:
     Gunther mußt' ihn wägen,   des Wurfs
     der Verhohlne pflag.

Siegfried war verwogen,   kräftig und lang: 78
     Den Stein warf er ferner,   dazu er weiter
     sprang.
     Ein großes Wunder war es   und künstlich
     genug,
     Daß er in dem Sprunge   den König
     Gunther noch trug.

Der Sprung war ergangen,   am Boden lag   79
     der Stein,
     Gunther war's, der Degen,   den man sah
     allein.
     Brunhild die Schöne   ward vor Zorne
     rot;
     Gewendet hatte Siegfried   dem König
     Gunther den Tod.

Zu ihrem Ingesinde   sprach die Kön'gin   80
     da,
     Als sie gesund den Helden   an des
     Kreises Ende sah:
     „Ihr meine Freund' und Mannen,   tretet
     gleich heran:
     Ihr sollt dem König Gunther   alle werden
     untertan."

*Siegfried goes to the land where his treasure is
stored and after a struggle with the dwarfs who
guard it—a struggle he could have avoided had
he disclosed his identity—he returns with a large
retinue to accompany Brunhilde to the land of the
Burgundians. He rides on ahead to announce the
arrival of Gunther and Brunhilde and is well
received by Kriemhilde. At a great feast in honor
of the new queen, Kriemhilde and Siegfried are
betrothed. Brunhilde's suspicion is aroused because
a vassal, as Siegfried is supposed to be, is to become
Kriemhilde's husband. She wants to know the
reason for the match between Kriemhilde and
Siegfried, and when Gunther attempts to consummate their marriage, she ties him up and swears
that she will remain a virgin until she finds out.
Gunther complains to Siegfried of Brunhilde's
treatment of him, and again calls on Siegfried for
help. On the next night Siegfried, making use*

*of his cloak of invisibility, comes into the bedchamber
to break Brunhilde's resistance.*

94   Da er's nicht lassen wollte,   das Mägdlein
    aufsprang:
  „Euch ziemt nicht zu zerraufen   mein
    Hemd also blank.
  Ihr seid ungezogen: das wird euch noch
    leid.
  Des bring' ich euch wohl innen",   sprach
    die weidliche Maid.

95   Sie umschloß mit den Armen   den teuer-
    lichen Degen
  Und wollt' ihn auch in Bande   wie den
    König legen,
  Daß sie im Bette läge   mit Gemächlichkeit.
  Wie grimmig sie das rächte,   daß er zer-
    zerret ihr Kleid!

96   Was half ihm da die Stärke,   was seine
    große Kraft?
  Sie erwies dem Degen   ihres Leibes
    Meisterschaft.
  Sie trug ihn übermächtig,   das mußte nur
    so sein,
  Und drückt' ihn ungefüge   zwischen die
    Wand und einen Schrein.

97   „O weh", gedacht' er, „soll ich   Leben
    nun und Leib
  Von einer Maid verlieren,   so mag noch
    manches Weib
  In allen künft'gen Zeiten   tragen Fre-
    velmut
  Dem Manne gegenüber,   die sonst wohl
    nimmer es tut."

98   Der König hörte alles;   er bangte für den
    Mann.
  Da schämte sich Siegfried,   zu zürnen
    fing er an.
  Mit ungefügen Kräften   ihr widersetzt'
    er sich
  Und versuchte seine Stärke   an Brunhilden
    ängstiglich.

99   Wie sie ihn niederdrückte,   sein Zorn
    erzwang es doch

Und seine starken Kräfte,   daß ihr zum
    Trotz er noch
Sich aufrichten konnte;   seine Angst war
    groß.
Sie gaben in der Kammer   hin und her
    sich manchen Stoß.

100   Auch litt König Gunther   Sorgen und
    Beschwer:
  Er mußte manchmal flüchten   vor ihnen
    hin und her.
  Sie rangen so gewaltig,   daß es Wunder
    nahm
  Wie eines vor dem andern   mit dem Leben
    noch entkam.

101   Den König Gunther ängstigte   beider-
    seits die Not;
  Doch fürchtet' er am meisten   Siegfrie-
    dens Tod.
  Wohl hätte sie dem Degen   das Leben
    schier benommen;
  Durft' er nur, er wäre   ihm gern zu Hilfe
    gekommen.

102   Gar lange zwischen beiden   dauerte der
    Streit;
  Doch bracht' er an das Bette   endlich
    zurück die Maid:
  Wie sehr sie sich auch wehrte,   die Wehr
    zuletzt ward schwach.
  Gunther in seinen Sorgen   hing manchen
    Gedanken nach.

103   Dem König währt' es lange,   bis er sie
    bezwang.
  Sie drückte seine Hände,   daß aus den
    Nägeln sprang
  Das Blut von ihren Kräften;   das war
    dem Helden leid.
  Da zwang er zu verleugnen   diese herr-
    liche Maid

104   Den Ungestüm des Willens,   den sie
    ihm dargetan.
  Alles vernahm der König,   doch hört'
    er's schweigend an.
  Er drückte sie ans Bette,   daß sie aufschrie
    laut:

Des starken Siegfriedens Kräfte   schmerz-
      ten übel die Braut.

105   Da griff sie nach der Hüfte,   wo sie die
      Borte fand,
    Und dacht' ihn zu binden: doch wehrt' es
      seine Hand,
    Daß ihr die Glieder krachten,   dazu der
      ganze Leib.
    Da war der Streit zu Ende: da wurde
      sie Gunthers Weib.

106   Sie sprach: „Edler König,   laß mich
      leben doch;
    Was ich dir tat zuleide,   vergüt' ich dir
      wohl noch.
    Ich wehre mich nicht wieder   der edeln
      Minne dein:
    Nun hab' ich's wohl erfahren,   daß du
      magst Frauen Meister sein."

107   Aufstand da Siegfried,   liegen blieb die
      Maid,[9]
    Als dächt' er abzuwerfen   eben nur das
      Kleid.
    Er zog ihr vom Finger   ein Ringlein von
      Gold,
    Daß es nicht gewahrte   die edle Köni-
      gin hold.

108   Auch nahm er ihren Gürtel,   eine Borte
      gut.
    Ich weiß nicht, geschah es   aus hohem
      Übermut.
    Er gab ihn seinem Weibe: das ward ihm
      später leid,
    Da lagen beieinander   der König und die
      schöne Maid.

*Siegfried takes back with him to Xanten the girdle
and ring he has taken from Brunhilde and later
gives them to his wife—a fatal error. Siegfried
becomes the ruler of his father's kingdom. Nevertheless, Brunhilde continues to brood over the
thought that Kriemhilde is married to a vassal, and*

---

[9] In the more primitive versions of the story Siegfried did take Brunhilde's virginity. Here the
author substitutes scenes that come close to the
comic scenes in the *Spielmannsepen.*

*she complains that Siegfried is not performing
a liegeman's service to his lord. Later Gunther
invites Siegfried and Kriemhilde to a feast. At first
things go well, but then the two queens quarrel
over a question of precedence—who is to enter the
church first. In her anger, Kriemhilde produces the
ring and girdle Siegfried had given her, claiming
it as proof that it was Siegfried, not Gunther,
who had taken Brunhilde's virginity. Although
Siegfried swears that this is untrue and punishes
her for saying it, the damage is done.*

    *Gernot and Hagen are only too glad to be
provided with an excuse for avenging the supposed
insult to Gunther's honor, and they convince Gunther
that this can be done only by slaying Siegfried.
Kriemhilde naïvely reveals to Hagen the spot
between the shoulder blades where Siegfried is
vulnerable because a leaf had fallen there when
he bathed in the dragon's blood. A hunt is then
arranged and Hagen deliberately does not bring the
wine. When thirst overcomes them, he challenges
Siegfried to a footrace to a nearby spring, so that
when they get there Siegfried will be forced to
remove his armor in order to drink, laying bare
his vulnerable spot. Siegfried easily reaches the
spring first but courteously waits until Gunther has
drunk before bending down to quench his own thirst.*

Da entgalt er seiner höf'schen Zucht;   den   xv
      Bogen und das Schwert.
Trug beiseite Hagen   von dem Degen
      wert.
Dann sprang er zurücke,   wo den Speer
      er fand,
Und sah nach einem Zeichen   an des
      Kühnen Gewand.

Als der edle Siegfried   aus dem Brunnen
      trank,
Er schoß ihm durch das Kreuze,   daß
      aus der Wunde sprang
Das Blut von seinem Herzen   hoch an
      Hagens Kleid.
Kein Held begeht wohl wieder   solche
      Untat nach der Zeit.

Den Speerschaft im Herzen   ließ er ihm
      stecken tief.
Wie im Fliehen Hagen   da so grimmig
      lief,

So lief er wohl auf Erden   nie vor einem Mann![10]
Als da Siegfried Kunde   der schweren Wunde gewann,

69 Der Held in wildem Toben   von dem Brunnen sprang;
Ihm ragte von den Achseln   eine Speerstange lang.
Nun wähnt' er da zu finden   Bogen oder Schwert,
So hätt' er wohl Hagen   den verdienten Lohn gewährt.

70 Als der Todwunde   da sein Schwert nicht fand,
Da blieb ihm nichts weiter   als der Schildesrand.
Den rafft' er von dem Brunnen   und rannte Hagen an:
Da konnt' ihm nicht entrinnen   dieser ungetreue Mann.

71 Wie wund er war zum Tode,   so kräftig doch er schlug,
Daß von dem Schilde nieder   wirbelte genug
Des edeln Gesteines;   der Schild zerbrach auch fast:
So gern gerochen[11] hätte   sich der herrliche Gast.

72 Da mußte Hagen fallen   von seiner Hand zu Tal;
Der Anger von den Schlägen   erscholl im Widerhall.
Hätt' er sein Schwert in Händen,   so wär' es Hagens Tod.
Sehr zürnte der Verwundete,   es zwang ihn wahrhafte Not.

73 Seine Farbe war erblichen;   er konnte nicht mehr stehn.

Seines Leibes Stärke   mußte ganz zergehn,
Da er des Todes Zeichen   in lichter Farbe trug.
Er ward hernach betrauert   von schönen Frauen genug.

74 Da fiel in die Blumen   der Kriemhilde Mann.
Das Blut von seiner Wunde   stromweis nieder rann.
Da begann er die zu schelten,   ihn zwang die große Not,
Die da geraten hatten   mit Untreue seinen Tod.

75 Da sprach der Todwunde: „Weh, ihr bösen Zagen,
Was helfen meine Dienste,   da ihr mich habt erschlagen?
Ich war euch stets gewogen   und sterbe nun daran.
Ihr habt an euern Freunden   leider übel getan.

76 Die sind davon bescholten,   was ihrer auch geborn
Wird nach diesem Tage: ihr habt euern Zorn
Allzusehr gerochen   an dem Leben mein.
Mit Schanden geschieden   sollt ihr von guten Recken sein."

77 Hinliefen alle Leute,   wo er erschlagen lag.
Es war ihrer vielen   ein freudeloser Tag.
Wer Treue kannt' und Ehre,   der hat ihn beklagt:
Das verdient' auch wohl um alle   dieser Degen unverzagt.

78 Der König der Burgunden   klagt' auch seinen Tod.
Da sprach der Todwunde: „Das tut nimmer Not,
Daß der um Schaden weine,   von dem Mann ihn gewann:
Er verdient groß Schelten,   er hätt' es besser nicht getan."

---

[10] Hagen's apparently cowardly conduct is motivated by the logical argument that he needs to avenge his king's honor but knows he stands no chance against Siegfried in "fair fight." He has in fact been considerably humiliated by Siegfried's quite justified assumption of superiority ever since he arrived at the court of the Burgundians.

[11] **gerochen: gerächt.**

79 Da sprach der grimme Hagen: „Ich wieß
      nicht, was euch reut,
    Nun hat doch gar ein Ende,   was uns je
      gedräut.
    Es gibt nun nicht manchen,   der uns darf
      bestehn;
    Wohl mir, daß seiner Herrschaft   durch
      mich ein End' ist geschehn."

80 „Ihr mögt Euch leichtlich rühmen",
      sprach der von Niederland.
    „Hätt' ich die mörderische   Weis' an euch
      erkannt,
    Vor euch behütet hätt' ich   Leben wohl
      und Leib.
    Mich dauert nichts auf Erden   als Frau
      Kriemhild, mein Weib.

81 Auch mag es Gott erbarmen,   daß ich
      gewann den Sohn,
    Der nun auf alle Zeiten   den Vorwurf
      hat davon,
    Daß seine Freunde jemand   meuchlerisch
      erschlagen:
    Hätt' ich Zeit und Weile,   das müßt' ich
      billig beklagen.

82 Wohl nimmer hat begangen   so großen
      Mord ein Mann",
    Sprach er zu dem Könige,   „als ihr an mir
      getan.
    Ich erhielt euch unbescholten   in großer
      Angst und Not;
    Ihr habt mir schlimm vergolten,   daß
      ich so wohl es euch bot."

83 Da sprach im Jammer weiter   der tod-
      wunde Held;
    „Wollt ihr, edler König,   noch auf dieser
      Welt
    An jemand Treue pflegen,   so laßt befoh-
      len sein
    Doch auf eure Gnade   euch die liebe
      Traute mein.

84 Es komm' ihr zugute,   daß sie eure
      Schwester ist,
    Bei aller Fürsten Tugend,   helft ihr zu
      jeder Frist.

Mein mögen lange harren   mein Vater
      und mein Lehn:
    Es ist am lieben Freunde   noch keinem
      Weib so leid geschehn."

Er krümmte sich in Schmerzen,   wie ihm   85
      die Not gebot,
    Und sprach aus jammerndem Herzen:
      „Mein mördlicher Tod
    Mag euch noch gereuen   in der Zukunft
      Tagen;
    Glaubt mir in rechten Treuen,   daß ihr
      euch selber habt geschlagen."

Die Blumen allenthalben   waren vom   86
      Blute naß.
    Da rang er mit dem Tode,   nicht lange tat
      er das,
    Denn des Todes Waffe   schnitt ihn all-
      zusehr.
    Da mochte nicht mehr reden   dieser
      Degen kühn und hehr.

*Hagen makes no pretense at hiding his crime.
Siegfried's body is dumped unceremoniously outside
Kriemhilde's door where it is found by a servant.
Siegmund quickly comes to Worms when he hears
of Siegfried's death. It almost comes to a battle,
especially when the body starts to bleed when Hagen
approaches, a sure sign, by medieval standards,
that he was the murderer. Further bloodshed is
averted, and Kriemhilde elects to stay with Gunther
rather than go home to Xanten.*

*Siegfried's treasure is brought to Worms, and
when Kriemhilde, seeking to win a following,
starts to make liberal presents to various warriors,
Hagen persuades Gunther to take it from her,
in spite of the objections of Giselher. While the
brothers are away, Hagen sinks the treasure in the
Rhine.*

*Kriemhilde mourns for her husband for thirteen
years, and then a message arrives from Etzel,
seeking her hand in marriage. The bearer of the
message is Rüdiger, Margrave of Bechelaere, and
it is largely out of respect for him that all the
brothers agree to the marriage against the determined opposition of Hagen, who sees its dangers.
Kriemhilde at first refuses to consider the offer
and only after long persuasion by her brothers and
Rüdiger does she finally consent—after extorting*

a promise from Rüdiger that whatever wrong is done to her, he will avenge it.

There follows a long description of the journey to Etzel's court, of the reception by Rüdiger's family, the arrival, and marriage to Etzel. Kriemhilde is given a great deal of power, but although she is married to the king and bears him a son, she still mourns for Siegfried and blames her brothers that she is married to a heathen. After seven years she persuades Etzel to invite her brothers to his court. She makes sure that Hagen will be included in the party. He has strong misgivings about the purpose of the invitation, and when his advice to refuse it is disregarded, he collects a large band of heavily armed men to accompany the king and his brothers.

The Burgundians set out for Etzel's domain. When they reach the Danube, they find merwomen bathing. Hagen, who apparently knows of their power to foretell the future, steals their clothes to force them to make a prediction. While he has the clothes, they foretell a happy outcome for the journey but afterwards tell him that only the chaplain with the party will return alive. The ferryman who possesses the only means of crossing the river is a liegeman of King Gelpfrat and refuses to ferry possible enemies of his master across. He is tricked by Hagen, who says he is his brother, but on discovering the deceit he attacks Hagen with an oar. Hagen cuts off his head and ferries his companions over himself. While doing so he tests the merwomen's prophecy by throwing the chaplain into the water. He survives, even though he cannot swim. (At this point Hagen is convinced of the inevitable doom of his party.) On the other side of the river the Burgundians are attacked by the forces of King Gelpfrat but repel the assault. At Rüdiger's castle they are received with great joy.

X, 18 Die junge Markgräfin   nahm bei der Hand
Geiselher den jungen   von Burgundenland;[12]

---

[12] This whole idyllic scene at Rüdiger's court is so out of character that one wonders why it was put in. It certainly heightens the tragedy, particularly for Rüdiger, who seems to be the author's own invention and who is the most sympathetic of all the characters in the poem. He alone is motivated by unselfish considerations.

So nahm auch ihre Mutter   Gunthern, den kühnen Mann.
Sie gingen mit den Helden   beide fröhlich hindann.

Der Wirt ging mit Gernot   in einen weiten   19
Saal.
Die Ritter und die Frauen   setzten sich zumal.
Man ließ alsbald den Gästen   schenken guten Wein:
Gütlicher bewirtet   mochten Helden nimmer sein.

Mit zärtlichen Augen   sah da mancher an   20
Rüdigers Tochter,   die war so wohlgetan.
Wohl kost' in seinem Sinne   sie mancher Ritter gut;
Das mochte sie verdienen: sie trug gar hoch ihren Mut.

Sie gedachten, was sie wollten;   doch   21
konnt' es nicht geschehn.
Man sah die guten Ritter   hin und wieder spähn
Nach Mägdelein und Frauen;   deren saßen da genug.
Dem Wirt geneigten Willen   der edle Fiedeler trug.

Da wurden sie geschieden,   wie Sitte war   22
im Land:
Zu andern Zimmer gingen   Ritter und Fraun zur Hand.
Man richtete die Tische   in dem Saale weit
Und war den Fremden Gästen   zu allen Diensten bereit.

Den Gästen ging zuliebe   die edle Mark-   23
gräfin
Mit ihnen zu den Tischen: die Tochter ließ sie drin
Bei den Mägdlein weilen,   wo sie nach Sitte blieb.
Daß sie die nicht mehr sahen,   das war den Gästen nicht lieb.

Als sie getrunken hatten   und gegessen   24
überall,

Da führte man die Schöne   wieder in den Saal.
Anmut'ge Reden   wurden nicht gescheut:
Viel sprach deren Volker,   ein Degen kühn und allbereit.

25 Da sprach unverhohlen   derselbe Fiedel-mann:
„Vielreicher Markgraf,   Gott hat an euch getan
Nach allen seinen Gnaden,   da er euch hat gegeben
Ein Weib, ein so recht schönes,   dazu ein wonnigliches Leben.

26 Wenn ich ein König wäre",   sprach der Fiedelmann,
„Und sollte Krone tragen,   zum Weibe nähm' ich dann
Eure schöne Tochter: die wünschte sich mein Mut.
Sie ist minniglich zu schauen,   dazu edel und gut."

27 Da begann der Markgraf: „Wie möchte das wohl sein,
Daß ein König je begehrte   der lieben Tochter mein?
Wir sind hier fremde beide,   ich und auch mein Weib,
Und haben nichts zu geben: was hilft ihr dann der schöne Leib?"

28 Zur Antwort gab da Gernot,   der wohl-gezogne Mann:
„Sollt' ich nach meinem Herzen   ein Gemahl mir frein,
Ohne Gut zum Weibe   wär' ich der Schönen froh."
Da versetzte Hagen   mit höfischer Rede so:

29 „Nun soll sich doch beweiben   mein Herr Geiselher:
Es ist so hohen Stammes   die Markgräfin hehr,
Daß wir ihr gerne dienten,   ich und sein ganzes Lehn,
Wenn sie bei den Burgunden   unter Krone sollte gehn."

Diese Rede dauschte[13]   Rüdigern gut   30
Und auch Gotelinden;   wohl freute sich ihr Mut.
Da schufen es die Helden,   daß sie zum Weibe nahm
Geiselher der edle,   wie es durft' ohne Scham.

Soll ein Ding sich fügen,   wer mag ihm   31
widerstehn?
Man ließ die Jungfraue   hin zu Hofe gehn.
Da schwur man, ihm zu geben   das schöne Mägdelein,
Wogegen er gelobte,   ihr treu gewärtig zu sein.

The marriage takes place, and the journey continues. Dietrich, who is at Etzel's court, warns the king and his men of Kriemhilde's unrelenting grief and hatred, so that when she tells them to leave their weapons outside, they are prepared and refuse. The meeting with Kriemhilde is hostile. Only Giselher does she treat with affection. Kriemhilde's early attempts to bribe and incite her men against Hagen and Volker are unsuccessful, but at a tournament the first blood is drawn by Hagen.

There follows a series of individual combats and specific events, each of which is worked into the larger contest between the forces of Etzel, who are fighting under the urging of Kriemhilde, and the Burgundians, who are all eager for glory and who are inspired by Hagen. Dankwart the Burgundian kills Bloedelin and many others, but the real turning point is reached when Hagen, without provocation, cuts down Ortlieb, the son of Etzel and Kriemhilde. A general battle begins in which the Burgundians prove decidedly superior. Dietrich, who is holding himself aloof from the fighting, saves Etzel, Kriemhilde, and his own followers by arranging a short truce with Gunther, and Rüdiger and his men also obtain permission to leave the hall. Iring of Denmark challenges Hagen and wounds him, but is himself killed at their second encounter. After a great slaughter, Kriemhilde has the hall set on fire, but even this fails to dislodge the Burgundians. Rüdiger has up to now taken no part in the fighting and one of the Huns taunts him for it.

———————
[13] **dauschte: deuchte.**

He strikes the man dead with his fist, but it is not so easy to deal with Etzel's reproaches.

11 Da sprach zum Markgrafen Etzel der König hehr:
„Wie habt ihr uns geholfen, vieledler Rüdiger!
Wir hatten doch der Toten so viel in diesem Land,
Daß wir nicht mehr bedurften: mit Unrecht schlug ihn eure Hand."

12 Da sprach der edle Ritter: „Er beschwerte mir den Mut
Und hat mir bescholten die Ehre wie das Gut,
Des ich aus deinen Händen so große Gaben nahm,
Was nun dem Lügenbolde übel hier zustatten kam."

13 Da kam die Königstochter die hatt' es auch gesehn,
Was von des Helden Zorne dem Heunen war geschehn.
Sie beklagt' es ungefüge, ihre Augen wurden naß.
Sie sprach zu Rüdigeren: „Wie verdienten wir das,

14 Daß ihr mir und dem König noch mehrt unser Leid?
Nun habt ihr uns doch, Rüdiger, verheißen allezeit,
Ihr wolltet für uns wagen die Ehre wie das Leben;
Auch hört' ich viel der Recken den Preis des Mutes euch geben.

15 Ich mahn' euch nun der Treue, die mir schwur eure Hand,
Da Ihr mir zu Etzeln reitet, Ritter auserkannt,
Daß ihr mir dienen wolltet bis an unsern Tod.
Des war mir armen Weibe noch nie so bitterlich Not."

16 „Das leugn' ich mitnichten, ich schwur euch, Königin,
Die Ehre wie das Leben gäb' ich für euch dahin;
Die Seele zu verlieren hab' ich nicht geschworen.
Zu diesem Hofgelage bracht' ich die Fürsten wohlgeboren."

17 Sie sprach: „Gedenke, Rüdiger, der hohen Eide dein
Von deiner steten Treue, wie du den Schaden mein
Immer wolltest rächen und wenden all mein Leid."[14]
Der Markgraf entgegnete: „Ich war Euch stets zu Dienst bereit."

18 Etzel der reiche hub auch zu flehen an.
Da boten sie sich beide zu Füßen vor den Mann.
Den guten Markgrafen man da im Kummer sah;
Der vielgetreue Recke jammervoll begann er da:

19 „O weh, mir Gottverlaßnen, muß ich den Tag erleben!
Aller meiner Ehren soll ich mich nun begeben,
Aller Zucht und Treue, die Gott mir angebot;
O weh, Gott vom Himmel, daß mir's nicht wenden will der Tod!

20 Welches ich nun lasse, das andre zu begehn,
So ist doch immer böslich und arg von mir geschehn,
Und wenn ich beides lasse, so schilt mich alle Welt.
Nun möge mich erleuchten der mich dem Leben gesellt!"

21 Da baten ihn so lange der König und sein Weib,

---

[14]Kriemhilde is referring to the promise she extorted from Rüdiger when he fetched her from Worms. It was with exactly this sort of situation in mind that she had exacted the promise.

Daß bald viele Degen mußten   Leben
   und Leib
Von Rüd'gers Hand verlieren   und selbst
   der Held erstarb.
Nun mögt ihr bald vernehmen,   welchen
   Jammer er erwarb.

22 Er wußte, daß nur Schaden   und Unheil
     sein Gewinn.
    Er hätt' es auch dem König   und der
     Königin
    Gern versagen wollen: der Held besorgte
     sehr,
    Erschlug' er ihrer einen,   daß er der
     Welt ein Greuel wär'.

23 Da sprach zu dem Könige   Rüd'ger, der
     kühne Mann:
    „Herr Etzel, nehmt zurücke,   was ich von
     Euch gewann,
    Das Land mit den Burgen;   bei mir soll
     nichts bestehn:
    Ich will auf meinen Füßen   hinaus in das
     Elend gehn.

24 Alles Gutes ledig   räum' ich euch das
     Land,
    Mein Weib und meine Tochter   nehm'
     ich an die Hand,
    Eh' ich so ohne Treue   entgegen ging'
     dem Tod:
    Das hieß auf üble Weise   verdienen euer
     Gold so rot."[15]

25 Da sprach der König Etzel: „Wer aber
     hülfe mir?
    Mein Land und die Burgen,   das alles geb
     ich dir,
    Daß du mich rächest, Rüdiger,   an den
     Feinden mein:
    Du sollst neben Etzeln   ein gewalt'ger
     König sein."

---

[15] The author is at some pains to show that Rüdiger
is not motivated by material considerations. He is
prepared to give up all his wealth if he is *permitted*
to avoid fighting the Burgundians, who had been
his guests and to whom he had sworn friendship.
Unless Etzel grants this permission, he knows he
will be in the classic dilemma of choosing between
his personal affection and the honor of his lord—
and he will have to choose the latter.

„Wie darf ich ihnen schaden?"   sprach 26
   wieder Rüdiger;
„Heim zu meinem Hause   lud ich die
   Recken hehr;
Trinken und Speise   ich ihnen gütlich
   bot,
Dazu meine Gabe;   und soll ich sie nun
   schlagen tot?

Die Leute mögen wähnen,   ich sei zu 27
   verzagt:
Keiner meiner Dienste   war ihnen je
   versagt:
Sollt' ich sie nun bekämpfen,   das wär'
   nicht wohl getan.
So reute mich die Freundschaft,   die ich
   an ihnen gewann.

Geiselher, dem Degen,   gab ich die Toch- 28
   ter mein;
Sie konnt' auf Erden nimmer   besser
   verwendet sein,
Seh' ich auf Zucht und Ehre,   auf Treue
   oder Gut.
Nie ein so junger König   trug wohl
   tugendreichern Mut."

Da sprach wieder Kriemhild: „Vieledler 29
   Rüdiger,
Nun laß dich erbarmen   unsres Leids
   Beschwer,
Mein und auch des Königs;   gedenke
   wohl daran,
Daß nie ein Wirt auf Erden   so leide
   Gäste gewann."

Da begann der Markgraf   zu der Kön'gin 30
   hehr:
„Heut muß mit dem Leben   entgelten
   Rüdiger,
Was ihr und der König   mir Liebes hat
   getan:
Dafür muß ich nun sterben,   es steht
   nicht länger mehr an.

Ich weiß, daß noch heute   meine Burgen 31
   und mein Land
Euch ledig werden müssen   von dieser
   Helden Hand.

So befehl' ich Euch auf Gnade   mein
    Weib und mein Kind
Und all die Heimatlosen,   die da zu Bech-
    laren sind."

32 „Nun lohne Gott dir, Rüdiger!"   der
    König sprach da so;
Er und die Königin,   sie wurden beide
    froh.
„Uns sollen deine Leute   wohl befohlen
    sein;
Auch trau' ich meinem Heile,   du selber
    werdest glücklich sein."

*Rüdiger leads his men to the attack, and the
Burgundians can hardly believe that he is moving
against them. They remind him of their friendship,
but Rüdiger has to fight for his lord. In the melee
the Burgundians lose many men, and finally Rüdiger
and Gernot kill each other. Dietrich cannot believe
that Rüdiger is dead and sends Hildebrand to confirm it. His men persuade Hildebrand to go armed,
and they accompany him. A fight soon breaks
out—Volker is killed by Hildebrand, Dankwart
by Helpfrich, and Wolfhart and Giselher kill
each other. Hildebrand is gravely wounded by
Hagen, and when he leaves he has no men left. Of
the Burgundians only Gunther and Hagen survive.
Dietrich is horrified when told that his whole
company except Hildebrand has perished, but he
goes to Hagen and Gunther and asks them to
surrender.*

,1 Da suchte sich Herr Dietrich   selber
    sein Gewand;
Ihm half, daß er sich waffnete,   der alte
    Hildebrand.
Da klagte so gewaltig   der kraftvolle
    Mann,
Daß von seiner Stimme   das Haus zu
    schüttern begann.

2 Da gewann er aber wieder   rechten
    Heldenmut.
Im Grimme war gewaffnet   da der Degen
    gut.
Seinen Schild den festen,   den nahm er an
    die Hand:
Sie gingen bald von dannen,   er und Meis-
    ter Hildebrand.

Da sprach von Tronje Hagen: „Dort 3
    seh' ich zu uns gehn
Dietrich, den Herren: der will uns
    bestehn
Nach dem großen Leide,   das wir ihm
    angetan.
Nun soll man heute schauen,   wen man
    den Besten nennen kann.

Und dünkt sich denn von Berne   der 4
    Degen Dietrich
Gar so starkes Leibes   und so fürchterlich
Und will er an uns rächen,   was ihm ist
    geschehen",
Also sprach da Hagen,   „ich bin wohl
    Mann, ihn zu bestehn."

Die Rede hörte Dietrich   mit Meister 5
    Hildebrand.
Er kam wo er die Recken   beide stehen
    fand
Außen vor dem Hause,   gelehnt an den
    Saal.
Seinen Schild den guten,   den setzte
    Dietrich zu Tal.

In leidvollen Sorgen   sprach da Dietrich: 6
„Wie habt ihr so geworben,   Herr Gun-
    ther, wider mich,
Einen Heimatlosen?   Was tat ich euch
    wohl je,
Daß alles meines Trostes   ich nun verwai-
    set mich seh'?

Ihr fandet nicht Genüge   an der großen 7
    Not,
Als ihr uns Rüdigeren,   den Recken,
    schlüget tot:
Ihr mißgönntet sie mir alle,   die mir
    untertan.
Wohl hätt' ich solchen Leides   euch
    Degen nimmer getan.

Gedenkt an euch selber   und an euer 8
    Leid,
Eurer Freunde Sterben   und all die Not im
    Streit,
Ob es euch guten Degen   nicht beschwert
    den Mut.

O weh, wie so unsanft   mir der Tod
    Rüdigers tut!

9 So leid geschah auf Erden   niemanden je.
   Ihr gedachtet wenig   an mein und euer
       Weh.
   Was ich Freuden hatte,   das liegt von
       euch erschlagen:
   Wohl kann ich meine Freunde   nimmer
       genug beklagen."

10 „Wir sind wohl nicht so schuldig",   sprach
        Hagen entgegen.
    „Zu diesem Hause kamen   all eure Degen
    Mit vielem Fleiß gewaffnet   in einer
        breiten Schar.
    Man hat euch wohl die Märe   nicht so
        gesagt, wie sie war."

11 „Was soll ich anders glauben?   Mir sagt
        Hildebrand:
    Euch baten meine Recken   vom Ame-
        lungenland,
    Daß ihr ihnen Rüdigern   gäbet aus dem
        Haus:
    Da botet ihr Gespötte nur   meinen
        Recken heraus."

12 Da sprach der Vogt vom Rheine: „Sie
        wollten Rüd'gern tragen,
    Sagten sie, von hinnen: das ließ ich da
        versagen
    Etzeln zum Trotze,   nicht aber deinem
        Heer,
    Bis darob zu schelten   Wolfhart begann,
        der Degen hehr."

13 Da sprach der Held von Berne: „Es
        mußte nun so sein.
    Gunther, edler König,   bei aller Tugend
        dein
    Ersetze mir das Herzeleid,   das mir von dir
        geschehn;
    Versühn' es, kühner Ritter,   so lass' ich's
        ungerochen gehn.

14 Ergib dich mir zum Geisel   mit Hagen,
        deinem Mann:
    So will ich Euch behüten,   so gut ich
        immer kann,
    Daß euch bei den Heunen   hier niemand
        Leides tut.

Ihr sollt an mir erfahren,   daß ich getreu
    bin und gut."[16]

15 „Das verhüte Gott vom Himmel",   sprach
        Hagen entgegen,
    „Daß sich dir ergeben   sollten zwei Degen,
    Die noch in voller Wehre   dir entgegen
        stehn.
    Das wär' uns Unehre: d i e Feigheit
        soll nicht geschehn."

16 „Ihr solltet's nicht verweigern",   sprach
        wieder Dietrich.
    „Gunther und Hagen   ihr habt so bit-
        terlich
    Beide mir betrübet   das Herz und auch den
        Mut,
    Wollt ihr mir das vergüten,   daß ihr es
        billiglich tut.

17 Ich geb' euch meine Treue   und reich'
        Euch drauf die Hand,
    Daß ich mit euch reite   heim in euer
        Land.
    Ich geleit' euch wohl nach Ehren,   ich
        stürbe denn den Tod,
    Und will um Euch vergessen   all meiner
        schmerzhaften Not."

18 „Begehrt es nicht weiter",   sprach wieder
        Hagen;
    „Wie ziemt' es, wär' die Märe   von uns
        zu sagen,
    Daß zwei so kühne Degen   sich ergeben
        eurer Hand?
    Sieht man bei euch doch niemand   als
        alleine Hildebrand."

19 Da sprach Meister Hildebrand: „Ihr
        tätet wohl daran,
    Den Frieden meines Herren,   nähmet Ihr
        ihn an.
    Es kommt noch an die Stunde   vielleicht
        in kurzer Frist,
    Daß ihr ihn gerne nähmet,   und er nicht
        mehr zu haben ist."

---

16 Dietrich is the great hero of the southeastern
Germans and it is fitting that he should finish the
conflict without actually killing anyone. The historical Theoderic, the Ostrogoth king of Italy,
was never connected with the Huns and was not
the exile which Dietrich is always portrayed as
being.

20 „Auch nähm' ich eh die Sühne",   sprach
Hagen entgegen,
„Eh' ich mit Schimpf und Schande   so vor
einem Degen
Flöhe, Meister Hildebrand,   als ihr hier
habt getan:
Ich wähnt' auf meine Treue,   ihr stündet
besser euern Mann."

21 Da sprach Meister Hildebrand: „Was
verweiset ihr mir das?
Nun wer war's, der auf dem Schilde   vor
dem Wasgensteine saß,
Als ihm von Spanien Walter   so viel der
Freunde schlug?
Wohl habt ihr an euch selber   noch zu
rügen genug."

22 Da sprach der edle Dietrich: „Wie
geziemt solchen Degen
Sich mit Worten schelten,   wie alte
Weiber pflegen?
Ich verbiet' es, Meister Hildebrand,   spre-
chet hier nicht mehr.
Mich heimatlosen Recken   zwinget große
Beschwer."

23 „Laßt hören, Freund Hagen",   sprach da
Dietrich,
„Was sprachet ihr zusammen,   ihr Helden
tugendlich,
Als ihr mich gewaffnet   sahet zu Euch
gehn?
Ihr sagtet, ihr alleine   wolltet mich im
Streit bestehn."

24 „Das will euch niemand leugnen",   sprach
Hagen entgegen,
„Wohl will ich's hier versuchen   mit
kräftigen Schlägen,
Es sei denn, mir zerbreche   das Nibe-
lungenschwert:
Mich entrüstet, daß zu Geiseln   unser
beide ward begehrt."

25 Als Dietrich erhörte   Hagens grimmen
Mut,
Den Schild behende zuckte   der schnelle
Degen gut.
Wie rasch ihm von der Stiege   entgegen
Hagen sprang!
Niblungs Schwert das gute   auf Dietrichen
laut erklang.

26 Da wußte wohl Herr Dietrich,   daß der
kühne Mann
Grimmen Mutes fechte;   zu schirmen sich
begann
Der edle Vogt von Berne   vor ängstlichen
Schlägen.
Wohl erkannt' er Hagen,   er war ein auser-
wählter Degen.

27 Auch scheut' er Balmungen,   eine Waffe
stark genug:
Nur unterweilen Dietrich   mit Kunst
entgegenschlug,
Bis daß er Hagen   im Streite doch
bezwang.
Er schlug ihm eine Wunde,   die gar tief
war und lang.

28 Der edle Dietrich dachte: „Dich
schwächte lange Not;
Mir bräch' es wenig Ehre,   gäb' ich dir
den Tod.
So will ich nur versuchen,   ob ich dich
zwingen kann,
Als Geisel mir zu folgen."   Das ward mit
Sorgen getan.

29 Den Schild ließ er fallen: seine Stärke, die
war groß;
Hagen von Tronje   mit den Armen er umschloß.
So ward von ihm bezwungen   dieser
kühne Mann.
Gunther der edle   darob zu trauern
begann.[17]

30 Hagen band da Dietrich   und führt' ihn,
wo er fand

---

[17] It is worth noting that Gunther makes no move
to attack Dietrich while he is engaged with Hagen,
even though it would be clearly to his advantage
to do so. The rules of single combat are strictly
enforced. Kriemhilde's brutal behavior incenses
Hildebrand because she kills two defenseless warriors. We would find it hard to see the difference
between her action and that of Hagen in killing
Siegfried, but the author's sympathy is clearly
with Hildebrand, for he makes Kriemhilde cry out
in terror, while Gunther and Hagen die without
complaint. Kriemhilde did not, of course, need
the treasure. It had become to her a symbol of
revenge, a fact which Hagen fully appreciates in
denying it to her.

Kriemhild die edle,   und gab in ihre Hand
Den allerkühnsten Recken,   der je Gewaffen trug.
Nach ihrem starken Leide   ward sie da fröhlich genug.

31 Da neigte sich dem Degen   vor Freuden Etzels Weib:
„Nun sei dir immer selig   das Herz und auch der Leib.
Du hast mir wohl ergetzet   nach aller meiner Not:
Ich will dir's immer danken,   es verhindr' es denn der Tod."

32 Da sprach der edle Dietrich: „Nun laßt ihn am Leben,
Edle Königstochter: es mag sich wohl begeben,
Daß euch sein Dienst vergütet   das Leid, das er Euch tat:
Er soll es nicht entgelten,   daß ihr ihn gebunden saht."

33 Da ließ sie Hagen führen   in ein Haftgemach,
Wo niemand ihn erschaute   und er verschlossen lag.
Gunther, der edle König,   hub da zu rufen an:
„Wo blieb der Held von Berne?   Er hat mir Leides getan."

34 Da ging ihm hin entgegen   der Berner Dietrich.
Gunthers Kräfte waren   stark und ritterlich;
Er säumte da nicht länger,   er rannte vor den Saal.
Von ihrer beider Schwertern   erhob sich mächtiger Schall.

35 So großen Ruhm erworben   Dietrich seit alter Zeit,
In seinem Zorne tobte   Gunther so im Streit;
Er war nach seinem Leide   von Herzen feind dem Mann:
Ein Wunder mußt' es heißen,   daß da Herr Dietrich entrann.

36 Sie waren alle beide   so stark und mutesvoll,
Daß von ihren Schlägen   Palas und Turm erscholl,
Als sie mit Schwertern hieben   auf die Helme gut.
Da zeigte König Gunther   einen herrlichen Mut.

37 Doch zwang ihn der von Berne,   wie Hagen war geschehn.
Man mochte durch den Panzer   das Blut ihm fließen sehn
Von einem scharfen Schwerte: das trug Herr Dietrich.
Doch hatte sich Herr Gunther   gewehrt, der Müde, ritterlich.

38 Der König ward gebunden   von Dietrichens Hand,
Wie nimmer Könige sollten   leiden solch ein Band.
Er dachte, ließ er ledig   Gunthern und seinen Mann,
Wem sie begegnen möchten,   der müßte den Tod empfahn.

39 Dietrich von Berne   nahm ihn bei der Hand,
Er führt' ihn hin gebunden,   wo er Kriemhilden fand.
Ihr war mit seinem Leide   der Sorge viel benommen.
Sie sprach: „König Gunther,   nun seid mir höchlich willkommen."

40 Er sprach: „Ich müßt' euch danken,   viel edle Schwester mein,
Wenn euer Gruß in Gnaden   geschehen könnte sein.
Ich weiß euch aber Königin,   so zornigen Mut,
Daß ihr mir und Hagen   solchen Gruß im Spotte tut."

41 Da sprach der Held von Berne: „Königstochter hehr,
So gute Ritter sah man   als Geisel nimmermehr,

Als ich, edle Königin,   gebracht in eure
   Hut.
Nun komme meine Freundschaft   den
   Heimatlosen zugut."

42 Sie sprach, sie tät' es gerne.   Da ging Herr
   Dietrich
Mit weinenden Augen   von dem Helden
   tugendlich.
Da rächte sich entsetzlich   König Etzels
   Weib:
Den auserwählten Degen   nahm sie Leben
   und Leib.

43 Sie ließ sie gesondert   in Gefängnis legen,
Daß sich nie im Leben   wiedersahn die
   Degen;
Hatt' es gleich verschworen   zu tun das
   edle Weib,
Sie dacht': „Ich räche heute   meines lie-
   ben Mannes Leib."

44 Hin ging die Königstochter,   wo sie
   Hagen sah;
Wie feindselig sprach sie,   zu dem Recken
   da:
„Wollt ihr mir wiedergeben,   was ihr
   mir habt genommen,
So mögt ihr wohl noch lebend   heim zu
   den Burgunden kommen."

45 Da sprach der grimme Hagen: „Die Red'
   ist gar verloren,
Vieledle Königstochter.   Den Eid hab'
   ich geschworen,
Daß ich den Hort nicht zeige: solange
   noch am Leben
Blieb einer meiner Herren,   wird er
   niemand gegeben."

46 „Ich bring' es zu Ende", sprach das edle Weib.
Ihrem Bruder nehmen ließ sie   Leben da
   und Leib.
Man schlug das Haupt ihm nieder: bei
   den Haaren sie es trug
Vor den Held von Tronje: da gewann
   er Leids genug.

47 Als der Unmutvolle   seines Herren Haupt
   ersah,

Wider Kriemhilden   sprach der Recke da:
„Du hast's nach deinem Willen   zu Ende
   nun gebracht;
Es ist auch so ergangen,   wie ich mir
   hatte gedacht.

48 Nun ist von Burgunden   der edle König
   tot,
Geiselher der Junge,   dazu Herr Gernot.
Den Hort weiß nun niemand   als Gott und
   ich allein:
Der soll dir Teufelsweibe   immer
   wohl verhohlen sein."

49 Sie sprach: „So habt ihr üble   Vergeltung
   mir gewährt;
So will ich doch behalten   Siegfriedens
   Schwert.
Das trug mein holder Gatte,   als ich
   zuletzt ihn sah,
An dem mir Herzensjammer   vor allem
   Leide geschah."

50 Sie zog es aus der Scheide,   er konnt' es
   nicht wehren.
Da dachte sie dem Recken   das Leben zu
   versehren.
Sie schwang es mit den Händen,   das
   Haupt schlug sie ihm ab.
Das sah der König Etzel,   dem es großen
   Kummer gab.

51 „Weh!", rief der König,   „wie ist hier
   gefällt
Von eines Weibes Händen   der aller-
   besten Held,
Der je im Kampf gefochten   und seinen
   Schildrand trug!
So feind ich ihm gewesen bin,   mir ist leid
   um ihn genug."

52 Da sprach Meister Hildebrand: „Es
   kommt ihr nicht zugut,
Daß sie ihn schlagen durfte;   was man
   halt mir tut,
Ob er mich selber brachte   in Angst und
   große Not,
Jedennoch will ich rächen   dieses kühnen
   Tronjes Tod."

53 Hildebrand im Zorne   zu Kriemhilden sprang:
    Er schlug der Königstochter   einen Schwertesschwang.
    Wohl schmerzten solche Dienste   von dem Degen sie;
    Was konnt' es aber helfen,   daß sie so ängstlich schrie?

54 Die da sterben sollten,   die lagen all umher:
    Zu Stücken lag verhauen   die Königin hehr.
    Dietrich und Etzel   huben zu weinen an
    Und jämmerlich zu klagen   manchen Freund und Untertan.

55 Da war der Helden Herrlichkeit   erlegen all im Tod:
    Die Leute hatten alle   Jammer und Not.
    Mit Leid war beendet   des Königs Lustbarkeit,

Wie immer Leid die Freude   am letzten Ende verleiht.

56 Ich kann euch nicht bescheiden,   was seither geschah,
    Als daß man immer weinen   Christen und Heiden sah,
    Die Ritter und die Frauen   und manche schöne Maid:
    Sie hatten um die Freunde   das allergrößeste Leid.

57 Ich sag' euch nun nicht weiter   von der großen Not:
    Die da erschlagen waren,   die lasset liegen tot.
    Wie es im Heunenlande   dem Volk hernach geriet,
    Hie hat die Mär ein Ende: d a s   i s t   d a s   N i b e l u n g e n l i e d.

Konrad von Würzburg

(c. 1225/30–1287)

It will be noted that Konrad was born at a time when the great figures of the Middle High German classical period were ending their careers. This is significant, for his work is very closely modeled on the great romances yet is utterly different from them in spirit and execution.

Konrad was born in Würzburg, where Walther von der Vogelweide probably spent his last years and where he was buried. He did not stay there, however, nor did he find his patrons among nobles or bishops but among the bourgeoisie of Basel, Straßburg, and other areas of the upper Rhine. Again his career is typical of the new forces guiding literature. Konrad was a man of great talent. He wrote long romances, short verse narratives, and lyric poetry. He was a master of form, as his best lyrics show, but he was subject to the weakness of all writers who say things well but have little to say—he was best when he came closest to imitating the great classical writers, at his worst when he tried to be more sophisticated than they and to improve upon their techniques. Then the result was preciosity, exaggeration, and even absurdity. In his narrative work, Konrad was closer to Gottfried than to Wolfram and he delights in brilliant description. He chose his material from the French romances, as can be seen from the titles of his poems of thie type—*Partonopier* based on the work of Denis Piramus, and *Trojanerkrieg*, an unfinished version of the famous work of Benoit de Ste Maure —but needed a translator to help him with the language. His other long work, *Engelhard*, is based on a Latin story on the theme of faithful friends, one of whom sacrifices his children so that the other may be cured of leprosy by their blood; the children are miraculously restored to life. All these works have the common characteristics of the romance of adventure and show little of the human interest or psychological skill of a Wolfram or a Gottfried. Konrad is at his best where such skills would not be expected, namely in the short verse narrative. Here his technical abilities stood him in good stead. He could tell a story well, and there was no danger of his losing himself in overlong description. Three of these are saints' legends, Sylvester, Alexius, and Pantaleon, but the others fall into the category of the verse-novella, a new type in German literature. Most of them were probably written relatively early in his career. *Der Welt Lohn* tells of the temptation of Wirnt von Grafenberg, himself a poet, to devote himself to Frau Welt and his revulsion on learning her true character. *Otte mit dem Bart* is the story of a quarrel between Heinrich von Kempten and the emperor Otto and their subsequent reconciliation. *Schwanritter* is based on the widespread legendary history of the family of Godefroi de Bouillon.

The poem, of which a modernized version is given here, is based on a story which was told of several troubadours, as well as about Reinmar von Brennenberg. Konrad clearly intends to portray a love not unlike that of Tristan and Isolde, which goes beyond any earthly considerations. Each of the protagonists dies of love, each believes in a higher love. The eating of the heart is obviously a symbolic, almost religious gesture. Yet, as Konrad tells it, the story rarely rises above sentimentality. He is just not capable of depicting the passion of love as Gottfried does. Thus he tells a pleasant tale rather than a tragic love affair. One can be sorry for his lovers, but they are not tragic. It will be noted that a great deal of the work consists of speeches, an indication of Konrad's desire to probe into the feelings of his characters.

HERZMAERE

Ich mußte oft beklagen,
   Daß in den heutigen Tagen
Kaum einer noch der Liebe Preis,
Den hohen, recht zu deuten weiß!
5 Da schuf ich diese Märe,
Auf daß an ihrer Lehre
Die Ritter und die Frauen
Das Herze sich erbauen.
Denn Meister Gottfried hört' ich sagen,
10 Wer sich zu wahrer Minne schlagen,
Den Frauen redlich dienen will,
Der lausche mit Bedacht,
Und gebe treulich acht
Auf ferner Sagen fremdes Spiel,
15 Wo je zwei Menschen sich gefunden
Zu heißer Liebe sel'gen Stunden.
Das schien mir, traun, ein gutes Wort.
Zum Minnedienst sei hold belehrt,
Wer so der wahren Liebe Hort
20 Im Lied des Dichters klingen hört.
Drum will ich eifrig mich bemühn,
Von einer schönen Sagen
Die Kunde vorzutragen,
Damit nach edler Liebe glühn
25 Hinfort in Treuen, hell und rein,
Die Herzen euch mit lichtem Schein.
    So hört! Ein Weib war einst geliebt
Von einem Ritter; all ihr Denken
Täten sie in einander senken,
30 Und was den Busen ihr getrübt,
Das war auch seiner Seele gram.
Ach, daß ein bittres Ende nahm
Ihr Leben und ihr Lieben!
    Die Minne herrschte sieggewaltig
35 In beiden wohl vieltausendfaltig,
Sie pflanzte manche süße Pein
Dem Grunde ihrer Seele ein.
Ihr ganzes Wesen war durchflammt,
Von Feuergluten, liebenstammt,
40 So es die Worte dieser Erden
Umsonst zu deuten suchen werden.
Niemals ist rein'rer Treue
Von Mann und Weib gepflogen,
Als wie sie stets auf's neue
45 Die zwei sich zugewogen.
Nur mußten sie es meiden
Von Fug und Rechten sich zu sehn;
Den Liebespfad vereint zu gehn,

Das war versagt den beiden.
Denn, merkt es wohl, das süße Weib   50
War einem Mann zur Eh' gegeben,
Der wachte streng ob ihrem Leben
Und hütete den schönen Leib,
Daß nimmer der getreue Knecht
Der Herzenliebe heilig Recht   55
Mocht' sänftigen und stillen.
Das quälte seinen Willen,
Und schuf ihm Pein und viele Not,
Und deuchte schlimmer denn der Tod.
Nach ihrem Leibe minniglich   60
Sehnte der treue Ritter sich;
Er konnte nicht mehr hehlen
Des Herzens wildes Quälen;
Er trat bei der Geliebten ein
Und klagte von der Liebe sein,   65
Das schwer ihm auf der Seele lag.
    Da sah ihr Herr in solchen Taten
Zu kühn der Liebe sich verraten;
Daß von der Zauberin, der Minne,
Gebunden sei'n die beiden,   70
Des ward sein Herz da inne,
Das schuf ihm bittres Leiden.

*The husband decides to take his wife to the Holy
Land, but she persuades her lover to go and thus
save her from the journey. There he is seized by a
fever, and as he lies dying he orders his squire to
have his heart embalmed and to take it back to
his beloved.*

    An Freuden bar und arm an Luft,
Trug er vom heiligen Gestade
Das tote Kleinod in der Lade
Geschäftig nach der fernen Höh',
Allwo in ihrem Liebesweh'   5
Die Herrin sollte wohnen.
Die Veste sah er tronen
An stillem Felsen aufgebaut.
Da traf ihn auf dem Felde an
Von ohngefähr ein Rittersmann,   10
Der—so wie Mären uns besagen—
Nach edlem Wilde wollte jagen.
Das sollte unserm Knechte sein
Zu argem Schmerz bereitet sein.
Denn da der Ritter ihn erblickt,   15
Sprach es in seinem Herzen:
„Der ist von seinem Herren erschickt
In tausend Liebesschmerzen,
Auf daß er Kunde trage
Und meinem Weibe klage   20

Von seiner Minne Not!"
   Er sprengte zu ihm zornesrot,
Gewißheit zu erlangen,
Und sah am Gürtel prangen
25 Die goldgeschmückte Lade,
Darein der Fingerreif sich barg,
Die als des Herzens Liebessarg
Der Sterbende bedungen hatte.
   Den Jüngling grüßte er und fragte:
30 Das ihm so hell am Gürtel lachte,
Das schöne Kästchen, zier und klein,
Was drin beschlossen möchte sein.
   Und ihn beschied der junge Knabe:
„O Herr, wohl eine seltne Habe
35 Nahm ich aus fremdem Lande fort."
„Laß sehen, welchen teuren Hort
Du dorten dir geborgen",
Fiel flugs der Ritter ein.
„O Herr, das kann nicht sein,
40 Weil auf der ganzen weiten Erde
Nur eine lebt, der solches werde,
Vor der sich öffnen diese Schalen!"
   In wilden, eifersücht'gen Qualen
Flammten da auf des Ritters Worte:
45 „Nun wache, Schelm, ob deinem Horte,
Ich will ihn ha'n, ohn' deinen Dank!"
   Und siehe da, es währt nicht lang,
So hatte er den Schrein
Mit Gold und Edelstein

Geraubt dem waffenlosen Knaben.   50
Er brach das Schloß mit rauher Hand,
Und als er Herz mit Ringlein fand,
Mocht'er Gewißheit haben:
   „Der Liebste starb im heil'gen Land,
Und seiner Frauen dieses Pfand   55
Zu senden er den Knecht ermahnte,
Der sich die Pfade hierher bahnte."

The knight forces the squire to give up the heart.
He has it cooked and served to his lady. When she
inquires, he tells her what she has eaten.

„Ja", sprach sie unter tausend Schmerzen,
„Wenn ich genoß von seinem Herzen,
Der mir zu aller Frist
Holdesten Mut getragen,
Und der in Liebesklagen   5
Nach mir gestorben ist,
Soll länger keine Speise
Die Lebenskraft mir wahren,
Will ich nicht länger sparen
Des Todes letzte Reise.   10
Denn lieblos würd' ich seiner denken,
Wenn nach solchem Mahl noch schenken
Wollte an andres meine Lust.
Des einen bin ich mir bewußt,
Wie ich den Tod erlangen kann,   15
Zu brechen meines Lebens Bann."

𝔚ernher der Gartenaere

(fl. c. 1250–1280)

We know nothing of the author except what he tells us himself in the poem. The term *Der Gartenaere*, figuratively construed, is a worker in the garden of the Lord, and even if this does not apply to Wernher, there can be little doubt that the author was a cleric. He has considerable learning and is acquainted with the work of Wolfram von Eschenbach and other courtly writers. He also knows the society, including courtly society, of his own time, and the poem shows an intimate knowledge of the area of the Bavarian-Austrian Inn district in which the poem was written. The description of the area and of the events is so vivid that some critics have tried to show that Wernher was recounting an occurrence of which he had actual experience. This is unlikely in the narrow sense, but the poem undoubtedly reflects with fidelity the social mores of the time. In essence it is a sermon in verse, based on the parable of the prodigal son but with quite a different ending. It is a warning both to parents and children of the moral duty of a father to be ruthless in training his son in good conduct and of a son to follow dutifully the path his father prescribes and not to aspire to a rank in society which is unsuited for him. In the process, the poem criticizes sharply the decline in standards of conduct among the nobility and the increasing self-assertiveness of the peasants, shown in a desire for material display.

Although there are several passages of considerable comic power, in particular the one in which the young Helmbrecht shows off his newly acquired capabilities in courtly manners and foreign languages, the poem as a whole is deadly serious, and the doctrine it preaches, that Christian duty means stern punishment even of one's dearest kin, is graphically portrayed in the horrid fate meted out to the young Helmbrecht. The work shows Franciscan influence in its use of the *exemplum*, or story to teach a moral. If the amplification of the *exemplum* makes the work into an excellent poem, it nevertheless remains an *exemplum*. The work is written in the usual narrative form—rhyming four-beat lines. The brief prologue gives various reasons for writing poetry; the poet then speaks of the narrative he is going to tell: a personal experience, about a boy with blond hair and what happened to him. Wernher's description of the boy's cap is an obvious mockery of the elaborate descriptions found in courtly romances. The resemblance to Homer's portrayal of the shield of Achilles is almost certainly accidental. A more likely source is the description of the saddle in the Latin poem "Phyllis and Flora." The subjects depicted on the hood are first those of the romances of antiquity (*matière de Rome*), then those of the *chansons de geste* material (*matière de France*).

MEIER HELMBRECHT

Ein Meier[1] war genannt Helmbrecht,
  Und dessen Sohn war jener Knecht,
Von dem wir diese Märe haben.
Den Vater nannt' man wie den Knaben—
5 Und beider Name Helmbrecht war.
Mit kurzen Worten, schlicht und klar,
Sollt ihr die Märe jetzt erfahren,
Was ihm für Wunderdinge waren
Mit Kunst auf seine Haub' gefüget.
10 (Die Märe mein euch nicht belüget:
Was ich euch sag' ist wirklich wahr.)
Es war ihm über'm Nackenhaar,
Von seinem Scheitel bis zum Schopf
So ganz inmitten auf dem Kopf,
15 Der Kamm mit Vögeln überzogen,
Grad' so als wären sie geflogen
Dahin vom Spessartwalde[2] her.
Bei einem Bauern nimmermehr
Sah besser man das Haupt geschmückt
20 Als man's bei Helmbrecht hat erblickt.
Demselben rohen Bauerntor
War in der Näh' vom rechten Ohr
Ganz fein gestickt auf seiner Hauben
(Es ist die Wahrheit, ihr könnt's glauben),
25 Wie Troja schwer belagert ward,
Weil Paris in vermeßner Art
Dem Griechen König nahm sein Weib,
Ihm lieber als sein eig'ner Leib;
Und wie die Stadt genommen dann,
30 Und nur Aeneas d'raus entrann
Auf's weite Meer mit schnellen Kielen;
Und wie die hohen Türme fielen
Und manche feste Mauer.
O weh, daß je ein Bauer
35 Sollt' eine solche Haube tragen,
Von der so vieles ist zu sagen!
Seid ihr zu hören nun entbrannt,
Was auf der andern Seite stand
Aus Seiden sein gefüget?
40 Die Mär' euch nicht betrüget:
Es war gestickt da linker Hand
Der König Karl und Ruolant

Und Olivier mitsamt Turpin,[3]
Die in der Not nicht ließen ihn,
Und was durch ihre Riesenkraft   45
Sie wirkten bei der Heidenschaft;
Und von Provence und Arelat,[4]
Die König Karl bezwungen hat,
Mit klugem Sinn und Mannheit stark;
Er auch noch die span'sche Mark: 50
Da wohnten Heiden nur vorher.
Habt ihr zu hören nun Begehr,
Was hinten bei den Nesteln[5] steht—
Aus meinem Mund nicht Lüge geht—
Zwischen beiden Ohren sein?   55
Von Frau Helche's Söhnen fein,[6]
Wie beide sie vordem vor Raben[7]
Den jungen Leib verloren haben,
Da sie Herr Wittig hat gefällt,
Der kühne, ungestüme Held,   60
Zugleich mit Diether, dem von Berne.
Noch weiter mögt' ihr hören gerne,
Was da für Ding' dem Gauch und Narren
Gestickt auf seine Haube waren.
Es war dem dummen Bauersmann   65
Vorn, vor dem Haubenkamm daran,
Ringsum vom rechten Ohr hin
Bis zu dem linken, wie ich bin
Ganz richtig davon unterrichtet—
Nun hört, was man davon berichtet!—   70
Gestickt, was man mocht' gerne schauen:
Von Rittern und von Edelfrauen,[8]
Auch was man da nicht mochte meiden:
Von Burschen und von Bauermaiden
Stand vorn am Haubekamm ein Tanz   75
Genäht mit Seid' in vollem Glanz.
Und zwischen zweien Frauen nun,
Wie sie noch jetzt bei Tanze tun,

---

[3] Charles, Roland, and Oliver are the principal actors in the *Chanson de Roland* (c. 1100), of which there was a German version by Pfaffe Konrad. Turpin was the archbishop who was also in Roland's forces and to whom a Latin account of the fight at Roncesvalles was ascribed.

[4] **Arelat:** presumably the town of Arles.

[5] **Nesteln:** strings, lacing.

[6] The German stories referred to are the Dietrich poems, the *Rabenschlacht, Alpharts Tod,* and *Dietrichs Flucht.*

[7] Raben is Ravenna.

[8] The description of this scene, with its groups of dancing figures is a burlesque in two ways—mockery of the peasant who wears such finery and attempts thereby to associate himself with courtliness, and of the whole tradition of romance which purported to be able to depict scenes like this on cloaks, hoods, saddles, and the like.

---

[1] It will be noted that the protagonist of the poem is not Meier Helmbrecht but his son. *Meier* is an archaic word for "farmer."

[2] **Spessart:** a heavily wooded region near Aschaffenburg, city on the Main River.

Ein Ritter stand, der faßt' die Hände;
80 Und dorten an dem andern Ende,
Je zwischen zweien Maiden, ging
Ein Bursch, der ihre Hände fing.
Es standen Fiedler auch dabei.

There follows a description of how the cap was
made and of the kind of dress which the young
Helmbrecht wore. It is grossly overelaborate, with
decoration unsuited for a peasant's station. The
author wishes Neidhart von Reuental were still
alive to describe it.

Manch' Huhn verkauft' und manches Ei
Die Mutter, daß sie schaff' herbei
Ihm Hosen und den Gurt für's Geld.[9]
Nachdem er also wohl bestellt,
5 Trat stolz er vor den Vater hin.
„Nach Hofe ziehet mich mein Sinn",
Sprach er; „drum, lieber Vater mein,
Bedarf ich jetzt der Steuer dein.
Mir hat die Mutter mein gegeben,
10 Die Schwester auch, bei meinem Leben,
Auf daß ich alle meine Tage
Stets holden Sinn zu ihnen trage."
Dem Vater bracht' das Ungemach.
Zu seinem Sohn er also sprach:
15 „Ich will zu deiner Kleidung kaufen:
Noch einen Hengst, der schnell kann laufen
Und überspringen Zaun und Graben,
Den sollst du zu der Reise haben;
Und weite Strecke kann er laufen:
20 Von Herzen gern will ich ihn kaufen,
Wenn ich ihn käuflich finde . . ."

Although he is willing to help, the father attempts
to persuade his son to stay on the farm, but the boy
refuses to listen.

„O Vater, werde ich beritten,
So will ich in den höf'schen Sitten
Wahrhaftig stets so wohl gebaren
Wie die, die stets am Hofe waren.
5 Wer diese Haube wunderschön
Auf meinem Haupte hätt' gesehn,
Der würde tausendmal wohl schwören,
Ich müßt' zum Ritterstand gehören.

---

[9] Helmbrecht's female relations are largely responsible for his ambitions because of their determination to dress him above his station. The horse was
considered a sign of position or rank of the upper
classes, and by buying it the father also contributes
to his son's downfall.

Ob ich dein Vieh dir auch geweidet
Und lange deinen Pflug geleitet,   10
Wahrhaftig! wenn ich mich nur kleide
Mit dem Gewand, mit dem sie beide
Mich gestern ausgestattet fein,
Die Schwester und die Mutter mein,
So bin ich sicher allsogleich   15
Nicht einem Bauersmann mehr gleich—
Und wenn ich auch vor kurzer Zeit
Auf harte Tenne[10] noch Getreid'
Gedroschen und den Drischel[11] trug
Und Pfähle in die Erde schlug.   20
Wenn ich die Füße und die Bein'
Mit Hosen erst bekleidet fein
Und mit die Schuhn von Korduan,
So sieht's mir wahrlich keiner an,
Daß ich da früher Zäun und Mauern   25
Gezogen dir und andern Bauern.
Gibst du dazu den Hengst mir her,
So bin dem Ruprecht nimmermehr
Zu einem Eidam ich erschaffen:[12]
Nie will ich durch ein Weib erschlaffen!"   30
Der Vater sprach: „O schweige still
Und hör', was ich dir sagen will.
Wer folget guter Lehre,
Gewinnet Nutz und Ehre:
Das Kind, das seines Vaters Rat   35
Zu keiner Zeit befolget hat,
Das wird zuletzt mit Schmach und Schaden
Und großer Schande überladen.
Mein Sohn, wenn du willst sicherlich
Gleich sein und zugesellen dich   40
Dem echten Höfling hochgeboren—
Da ist dein ganzes Mühn verloren:
Er heget darum zu dir Haß."

The father sells some of his stock to buy the horse
(a very expensive item) but still attempts to con-
vince his son to stay. He is met by scorn, not only of
peasant life in general but of his own wisdom,
his "preaching," and his prophetic dreams. Young
Helmbrecht is thus guilty of pride and disobedience,
vices which his doting mother and his sister Gote-
linde have encouraged. He takes his horse and
fine clothing and leaves.

Er kam zu einer Burg geritten.
Der Burgherr war von wilden Sitten
Und liebte steten Kampf und Streit.

---

[10] **Tenne:** threshing floor.
[11] **Drischel** (*Bav.-Austr.*): flail.
[12] Ruprecht is a neighbor to whose daughter the
father wished to marry Helmbrecht.

Dort fanden Aufnahm' alle Zeit,
5 Die da verstanden kühn zu reiten
Und lustig mit den Feinden streiten.
Dem ward er Knappe als Gesinde.
Das Rauben lernt' er so geschwinde,[13]
Daß, was ein andrer liegen ließ,
10 In seinen Sack er eilig stieß.
Er stopfte alles da hinein:
Kein Beutestück war ihm zu klein
Und keines war ihm auch zu groß.
Ob es rauh war oder bloß,
15 Ob es krumm war oder recht—
Das raubte alles Helmbrecht,
Des alten Meier Helmbrecht Kind.
Er nahm das Roß, er nahm das Kind,
Er ließ dem Mann nicht Löffels Wert;
20 Er nahm das Wams mitsamt dem Schwert,
Er nahm den Mantel mit dem Rock,
Er nahm die Geiß, er nahm den Bock,
Den Widder mit dem Mutterschaf:
Dafür der Lohn ihn später traf.
25 Er zog den Rock dem Weibe
Und auch das Hemd vom Leibe,
Das Unter- und das Oberkleid.
Das hat er später schwer bereut,
Als ihm der Scherge machte zahm,
30 Daß je so viel den Frau'n er nahm;
Ja, das ist ganz gewißlich wahr!

After a year of successful plundering he decides to
visit his home. Although his family recognizes
him, he speaks to them in such tortured phrases
from many languages that they doubt the evidence
of their eyes and wonder whether it is indeed
Helmbrecht come home.

Sie sahen beid' einander an,
Der Mann das Weib, das Weib den Mann.
Die Hausfrau sprach zum Mann: „Herr Wirt,
Da haben beide wir geirrt:
5 Der Helmbrecht ist es nimmermehr;
Ein Wende oder Böhm' ist er.[14]

„Ein Wälscher[15] ist's", der Vater sprach
„Mein Sohn, den Gott behüten mag,
Der ist es wahrlich nimmermehr,
Und dennoch gleicht er ihm so sehr." 10
Da sprach die Schwester Gotelind:
„Er ist nicht euer beider Kind:
Er redete zu mir Latein;[16]
Ich glaub', es wird ein Pfaffe sein."
„Fürwahr", sprach da der freie Knecht, 15
„Verstand ich seine Rede recht,
So ist er in dem Sachsenland
Geboren oder in Brabant;
Sprach ‚säute Schwesterkindelein';
Für einen Sachsen halt' ich ihn." 20
Der Alte sprach da recht und schlecht:
„Bist du es denn, mein Sohn Helmbrecht?
Sogleich gewinnst du mich damit,
Sprichst du e i n Wort in deutscher Sitt',
Wie unsre Vordern es getan, 25
So daß ich dich erkennen kann.
Wenn ‚*dieu salue*'[17] man zu mir spricht—
Was das bedeutet, weiß ich nicht.
Deine Mutter ehr' und mich,
Wir verdienen's doch um dich, 30
Und sprich ein einz'ges deutsches Wort;
Ich s e l b s t will deinen Hengst sofort
Dir putzen auch, und nicht mein Knecht,
Mein lieber Sohn, mein Helmbrecht,
Ich wünsch' dir alles, was ich kann!" 35

The father cannot believe that such a person is his
son, but when Helmbrecht is able to give the names
of his cows, he is convinced and treats him like a
returning prodigal. Everything the farm can provide
is at his disposal. The father then tells what courts
were like in his youth.

Die Ritter kannten einer Art,
Wie man beliebt bei Frauen ward.
Da war ein Ding, Buhurd[18] genannt,

---

[13] At the time this poem was written there were
undoubtedly many so-called noblemen who robbed
and plundered in exactly the way described here.
A more "refined" form of plunder was to exact
tolls on goods passing through one's territory,
a practice that explains why there are so many
castles on the Rhine.

[14] The father and mother cannot understand Helmbrecht's words and conclude that the speaker
comes from one of the remote areas of the German-speaking territory, Bohemia in the southeast,
Saxony in the northeast, Brabant in the northwest.

The Wends were the Slavic inhabitants of the
Brandenburg area around Berlin.

[15] **Wälscher:** any person from a romance-speaking
area, usually France or Italy.

[16] Latin is mentioned because it is the first "incomprehensible" language that comes to mind.

[17] **Dieu salue:** French for "God save you."

[18] **buhurd** or **bohort:** a form of tournament in which
a large number of knights took the lists together,
divided into two sides, and fought until one side
was clearly beaten. The conditions approximated
those of actual combat much more than did the
formal joust between two individuals, which was
governed by an increasingly complex set of rules.

Das tat ein Hofmann mir bekannt,
5 Bei dem ich zu erkunden ging,
Wie man mit Namen hieß das Ding.
Sie sprengten an mit Schrein und Toben
(Und doch hört' ich sie deshalb loben),
Die Einen hin, die Andern her;
10 Da wollt' nun dieser, wollt' nun der
Den Andern stoßen in den Sand.
Bei Leuten, die von meinem Stand,
Ist nimmer solches Spiel geschehn,
Wie ich bei Hofe da gesehn.
15 Wenn sie nun das beendet hatten,
Zum Tanze sie zusammentraten,
Mit frischen, lustigen Gesängen,
Die lange Weile zu verdrängen.
Da schritt ein Spielmann schnell heran,
20 Und als zu geigen er begann,
Erhoben sich die Frauen,
Gar lieblich anzuschauen.
Der Ritter nun gegangen kam
Und an der Hand die Dame nahm.
25 Ei, da war Wonne viel zu sehn
An Rittern und an Frauen schön.

*The father adds to this somewhat idyllic picture
an account of the court's activities in singing and
hunting and then asks his son to tell him what the
courts are like now. He is told that they pass their
time mainly in heavy drinking and that good manners are now considered out of style. The cleverest
man is the one who can insult his fellows with most
effect. The father is horrified at the account, but
this does not prevent him from accepting the present
his son has brought nor from allowing his wife and
daughter, Gotelinde, to receive presents of a kind
quite unbecoming to their station in life.*

Der Vater sprach zu ihm das Wort:
„Mein Sohn, getraust du dich zu leben
Von dem, was wir dir können geben
So lange wir am Leben sind,
5 So bleib und iß mit uns, mein Kind;
Bleib' doch im Vater Hause hier
Und tu' die hof'sche Art von dir.
Sie ist ja bitter oft und sauer.
Ich bin viel lieber doch ein Bauer
10 Als so ein armer Rittersmann,
Der niemals sichers Gut gewann
Und durch die Land' zu allen Zeiten
Auf Lebensunterhalt muß reiten,
Am Abend spät und früh am Morgen,
15 Und immer schwebt in Angst und Sorgen,

Daß ihn der Feinde einer fängt
Und dann verstümmelt oder hängt."

*The offer is refused. Helmbrecht wishes to resume
his life of plunder and mentions the kind of people
he plans to attack and the reasons why. Helmbrecht
then gives the names of his associates—all are epithets
that reflect their greed—and tells his family that
his own name is Schlindasland. His father foretells
that they will all come to a bad end, and Helmbrecht
threatens to withdraw his "protection," which
has hitherto kept his father's goods intact. He also
says that his friend Lämmerschling wishes to
marry Gotelind and would make her a wonderful
husband. Gotelind secretly asks Helmbrecht to
take her to Lämmerschling, and, without the
knowledge of her parents, she leaves with him.*

*The passages that follow are a parody of exag-
gerated courtly love preceding the pair's marriage.
The character of the wedding feast is reminiscent
more of the peasants they are than of the nobles
they aspire to be. In the course of the festivities
Gotelinde is seized with a foreboding of evil that
quickly proves to be well-founded.*

Als sie nun nach dem Essen
Noch eine Weil' gesessen
Und vor der Braut der Spielleut' Schaar
Da sah man einen Richter kommen;
Vier Schergen waren sein Geleit.   5
Es dauerte nur kurze Zeit,
Bis Sieg er über sie gewann.
Der in den Ofen nicht entrann,
Der schlummert' unter einer Bank.
Der Eine vor den Andern drang.   10
Der sonst bestanden hatte vier,
Den zog des Schergen Knecht herfür
A l l e i n an seinem Haar.
Ja, es ist sicher wahr,
Ein rechter Dieb, wie kühn er sei,   15
Erschlüg' er auch des Tages drei,
Kann eines Schergen sicherlich
Doch nimmermehr erwehren sich.
So wurden nun gebunden
Die Zehn zu dieser Stunden   20
Mit Banden von des Schergen Hand;
Der Fessel keiner sich entwand.
Got'lind verlor ihr Brautgewand.
Bei einem Zaune man sie fand.
Da lag die Arme jämmerlich;   25
Sie konnte kaum die Blöße sich
Mit ihren beiden Händen decken.

So lag sie da, halb tot vor Schrecken.
Was ihr noch weiter ist geschehn,
30 Das künde einer, der's gesehn.

*The men in the company are haled off to judgment
and nine of them are hanged. Helmbrecht alone
escapes death because, as the tenth man, he is at
the disposition of the hangman.*

Was da geschehen s o l l, geschieht:
Gott selten durch die Finger sieht
Dem, der da tut, was doch nocht recht.
Das sieht man klar an Helmbrecht,
5 An dem man rächt den Vater sein.
Er büßte beide Augen ein.
Noch war der Rache nicht genug:
Man rächt' die Mutter, als man schlug
Die Hand ihm ab und einen Fuß.
10 Dafür, daß er so schlechten Gruß
Dem Vater und der Mutter bot,
Mußt' er erleiden Schand' und Not.
Weil er den Vater so sprach an:
„Wat seggst du, olle Buersmann?"[19]
15 Und „dummes Wief"[20] die Mutter sein
Genannt, drum mußt' er solche Pein
Erleiden und so große Not,
Daß lieber tausend Mal den Tod
Er sich erbeten hätte wohl,
20 Als solch ein Leben jammervoll.

*Helmbrecht makes his way back to his father's
house, but he is turned away in scorn.*

Der Vater höhnend zu ihm sprach,
Obschon ihm fast das Herze brach
(War's doch sein Sohn, sein leiblich Kind,
Das da vor ihm gestanden blind!):
„Ihr zogt herum die Kreuz und Quer,   5
Eur Hengst schritt langsam nicht daher,
Er konnte gut und schnell Euch tragen.
Durch Euch mußt' manches Herze klagen.
Ihr habet Schreckliches getan.
Manch Bauersweib, manch Bauermann   10
Ward arm durch Euch, Gott sei's geklagt!
Wie ist's mit den drei Träumen? Sagt,
Bewährten sie sich an Euch doch?
Glaubt mir, es kommt ganz anders noch.
Daß Euch noch schlimmer wird als weh.   15
Doch eh' den vierten wahr ich seh',
Hebt schnell Euch weg von meiner Tür'.
Geschwind, Knecht, stoß den Riegel für!
Ich brauche Ruh', will schlafen gehn.
Den Bettler, den ich nie gesehn,   20
Den pflegt' ich lieber bis zum Tod',
Eh' ich Euch gäb' ein halbes Brot."

*Helmbrecht thus leaves his house for the last time.
Wandering about the country, he is caught by some
peasants whom he had wronged and is summarily
hanged. His beautiful long locks hang in the mud.*

*The author ends his story with the moral: all
children should take warning not to behave like
Helmbrecht or they too will come to a bad end.*

---

[19] This line is a travesty of Low German.
[20] **Wief: Weib.**

Johannes von Tepl

(c. 1350–60–c. 1414)

The *Ackermann* has been given a great deal of attention by various scholars—attention perhaps out of proportion to the work's intrinsic value, although it is admittedly a very highly wrought piece of prose and its subject deserving of interest. The reasons for its popularity are several. Most important, it was "rediscovered" at a time when there was great interest in the Renaissance as a phenomenon and when most scholars thought of the Renaissance as a period sharply divided from the Middle Ages. Although the work was known to Gottsched, and an edition of it was published by Friedrich von der Hagen, real interest in it began to revive only in the late nineteenth century. Konrad Burdach devoted a lifetime of scholarship and twenty volumes to a detailed study of the work in an attempt to prove that it was the first humanistic work to be produced in German. Unfortunately his whole approach was one-sided, and in his anxiety to prove his point he neglected the medieval aspects of the work and advanced some untenable theses about the author. A great many of these errors were corrected by Arthur Hübner, but the controversy about how much the work owes to the medieval and how much to the Renaissance tradition continues, even though we no longer think of the two periods as sharply divided. Another reason for its popularity among scholars is the allusive nature of the style. Classical, biblical, medieval, and folklore references abound and these, with the legal aspects of the work, give an opportunity for an almost unlimited amount of footnotes.

This thorough research has disentangled from apparently conflicting evidence the name and to some degree the activities of the author. He is variously described in the manuscripts and other documents as Johannes von Tepl, Johannes von Saaz, and Johannes von Schüttwa. We now know that Johannes was born in Schüttwa, in Bohemia, between 1350 and 1360, that he studied at the University of Prague before becoming a schoolmaster in Tepl and later a headmaster and public official in Saaz. After 1411 he appears to have been an official in Prague. The most important document that pertains to him is a dedicatory epistle that he sent with a copy of the *Ackermann* to Peter Rothirsch of Prague, a letter that is unfortunately undated except for the notation "St. Bartholomew's Eve."

We do know that Johannes was married twice, and that his first wife died about 1400. Could he have written the dialogue in her memory? This is a matter for conjecture; we cannot assume it to be so. It bears many of the marks of a formal exercise.

The *Streitgedicht*, or *altercatio*, was a very popular form of writing in classical times and the Middle Ages. There are several such poems in the idylls of Theocritus and his imitators, and in the Middle Ages we find numerous discussions between Winter and Summer, the Body and the Soul, Water and Wine, etc. The arguments advanced tended to be formalized, and the whole genre is learned and usually rather uninspired. The *Ackermann* stands far above most examples of the type, since it is at one and the same time learned and lively and deals with a subject of more than routine interest. The author has deliberately made frequent use of legal forms and phraseology, so that the work appears as a serious charge against Death by an aggrieved person. With considerable skill he varies the attitudes of the two participants. The ploughman is at first emotional and personal and an easy mark for the sarcasm and apparent reasonableness of Death. But as the work progresses, his approach changes. The Ploughman ceases to think in terms of his own personal loss and argues against Death's alleged role as cleanser and purifier of the world. He sees Death as the enemy of mankind and of all true life, and as his arguments become less personal, Death appears to resent him more and plays into his hands by describing life itself as an unworthy business. Thus by the end of the dialogues the roles are reversed. The Ploughman has accepted his own loss but will not accept the fact that all the beauty in life must die, while Death sees the Ploughman's speeches as a personal attack on himself.

The highly polished rhetoric of the dialogue is apparent at a first reading. All the devices listed in the school books are there—repetition, metaphor, hyperbole, litotes, apostrophe, metonymy, and the rest. Proverbs are especially frequent at the beginning of the various speeches. On the other hand, there are relatively few references or quotations from the literature of classical antiquity, although reminiscences and indirect references are common. Less rhetorical are the numerous commonplace and even popular expressions which give the language a great deal of its force.

The rhythm of the work is closely related to the Latin prose rhythm of the *cursus*. In Cicero's time it had been customary for prose to have certain rhythmic *clausulae* or sentence endings which followed prescribed patterns of long and short syllables. During the Middle Ages the practice grew up, largely in the papal chancelleries, of using sentence endings of the same kind based on word stress. These were regularized into specific groupings for the ends of sentences (and sometimes even for the entire sentence) known as the *cursus velox* (x́xx x́x x́x), the *cursus planus* (x́xx x́x), and the *cursus tardus* (x́xx x́xx). So that the readers of this book may be able to follow the rhythm and also see what the language of southeastern Germany was like as it moved from the medieval to the modern period, the passages given in this anthology have been left in their original form, except for minor spelling changes and the capitalization of nouns. Note that there is no indication of umlaut in this dialect. The sound *ä* is represented by *e*, *ü* is either *u* or *ie*. Where modern German would have *u* we often find *w*, doubled consonants are still single, and some of the verb forms are unfamiliar. The text will be much easier to understand if it is read aloud. Words that may be unfamiliar to the student have been footnoted.

ACKERMANN AUS BÖHMEN

The work opens with an accusation in legal form of a certain "Ploughman" against Death for having deprived him of his joy; it becomes clear in later paragraphs that this refers to his wife.

Der Ackermann Grimmiger Tilger[1] aller Leute, schedlicher Echter[2] aller Werlte, freissamer[3] Morder aller Menschen, ir Tot, euch sei verfluchet![4] Gott, euer Tirmer,[5] hasse euch, unselden[6] Merunge[7] wone euch bei, Ungeluck hause gewaltiglich zu euch: zumale geschant[8] sei immer! Angst und Not und Jamer verlassen euch nicht, wo ir wandert; Leit, Betrubnuss und Kummer beleiten[9] euch allenthalben; leidige[10] Anfechtungen,[11] schentliche Zuversicht[12] und schemliche[13] Verserung[14] die betwingen[15] euch groblich[16] an aller State; Himel, Erde, Sunne, Mone, Gestirn, Mere, Wag, Berg, Gefilde, Tal, Awen, der Helle Abgrunt, auch alles das Leben und Wesen hat, sei euch unholt, ungustig und fluchen euch ewiglichen. In Bosheit versinket, in jamerigem Ellende verswindet und in der unwiderbringenden[17] swersten Echte[18] Gotes, aller Leute und jeglicher Schepfunge alle zukunftige Zeit

beleibet![19] Unverschamter Bosewicht, eur bose Gedechtnuss[20] lebe und tawre[21] hin on Ende; Grawe und Forchte scheiden von euch nicht ir wonet wo ir wonet: von mir und aller menneglich[22] sei uber euch ernstlich Zeter geschrin[23] mit gewunden[24] Henden!

Der Tot Hort, hort, horet newe Wunder! Grausam und ungehorte Teidinge[25] fechten uns an. Von wem die komen, das ist uns zumal fremde.[26] Doch drowens, fluchens, Zetergeschreies, hendewindens und allerlei Angeratungen[27] sei wir an allen Enden unz her wol genesen.[28] Dannoch, Sun, wer du bist, melde dich und lautmere,[29] was dir Leides von uns widerfaren sei, darum du uns so unzimlichen handelst,[30] des wir vormalen doch ungewonet sein, allein wir doch manigen kunstereichen, edeln, schonen, mechtigen und heftigen[31] Leuten sere uber den Rein gegraset,[32] davon Witwen und Weisen, Landen und Leuten Leides genugelich ist geschehen. Du tust dem geleich, als dir ernst sei und dich Not swerlich betwinge. Dein Clage ist one Reime;[33] da von wir prufen,[34] du wellest durch donens[35] und reimens willen deinem Sinn nicht entweichen. Bistu aber tobende, wutende, twalmig[36] oder anderswo

---

[1] **Tilger:** Zerstörer.

[2] **Echter:** Verfolger; as participle, **verbannt.**

[3] **freissam:** schrecklich.

[4] The opening speech is in due legal form, an emotional accusation for which no evidence is given or required. There is no specific mention of a crime but there is a demand that Death shall suffer the punishment of perpetual banishment. Note the careful rhythmic effects and the rhetorical sequences of words.

[5] **Tirmer:** Schöpfer.

[6] **unselde:** Unheil.

[7] **Merunge:** Zunahme.

[8] **geschant:** entehrt.

[9] **beleiten:** begleiten.

[10] **leidig:** bitter.

[11] **Anfechtung:** Anklage, Angriff.

[12] **Zuversicht:** Erwartung.

[13] **schemlich:** schmählich.

[14] **Verserung:** Feindschaft.

[15] **betwingen:** drücken.

[16] **groblich:** schwer, gräßlich.

[17] **unwiderbringend:** unaufhebbar, immerwährend.

[18] **Echt:** Bann.

---

[19] **beleiben:** bleiben.

[20] **Gedechtnuss:** Gedenken.

[21] **tawren:** dauern.

[22] **menneglich:** jedermann.

[23] **Zetergeschrei:** the formal call to all members of a parish to set out after a criminal—the hue and cry.

[24] **gewunden:** gerungen.

[25] **Teiding:** Anklage.

[26] **fremd:** unbekannt.

[27] **Angeratung:** Angriff.

[28] Death regards himself as unaffected by the accusation—indeed, he casts doubt on whether he can in fact be cited. He refers to himself by the honorific plural (as does the Ploughman), but he addresses his opponent with the familiar "du." Nevertheless he graciously consents to hear the accusation.

[29] **lautmeren:** bekannt geben.

[30] **handeln:** behandeln.

[31] **heftig:** hochstrebend.

[32] **uber den Rein grasen:** cut down; removed (the meaning is much disputed).

[33] **one Reime:** here the expression appears to mean "senseless," i.e., the accusation has no legal grounds.

[34] **prufen:** merken.

[35] **donen:** Lieder komponieren.

[36] **twalmig:** betrunken.

one Sinne, so verzeuch,[37] enthalt und bis[38] nicht zu snelle so swerlich zu fluchen, den Worten das du nicht bekumert werdest mit Afterrewe.[39] Wene[40] nicht, das du unser herliche und gewaltige Macht immer mugest geswechen.[41] Dannoch nenne dich und versweig nicht, welcherlei Sachen dir sei von uns so mit twenglicher[42] Gewalt begegent. Rechtfertig welle wir werden, rechtfertig ist unser Geferte.[43] Wir wissen nicht, wes du uns so frevellichen[44] zeihest.[45]

Der Ackermann Ich bins genant ein Ackerman: von Vogelwat[46] ist mein Pflug, und wone in Behemerlande.[47] Gehessig, widerwertig und widerstrebende sol ich euch immer wesen:[48] wann ir habt mir den zwelften Buchstaben,[49] meiner Freuden Hort,[50] aus dem Alphabet gar freissamlichen enzucket;[51] ir habet meiner Wunnen lichte Sumerblumen mir aus meines Herzen Anger jemerlich ausgereutet;[52] ir habt mir meiner Selden[53] Haft, mein auserwelte Turteltauben[54] arglistiglichen entfremdet;[55] ir habet unwider-

bringlichen[56] Raub an mir getan! Weget[57] es selber, ob ich nicht billichen zurne, wute und klage: von euch bin ich freudenreiches Wesens beraubet, tegelicher guter Lebetage entweret[58] und aller wunnebringender Rente[59] geeussert.[60] Frut[61] und fro was ich vormals zu aller Stunt; kurz und lustsam[62] was mir alle Weile Tag und Nacht, in gleicher Masse freudenreich geudenreich[63] sie beide; ein jeglichs Jar was mir ein gnadenreiches Jar. Nu wirt zu mir gesprochen: schab ab![64] bei trubem Getranke, auf durem Aste, betrubet, swarz und zerstroret beleib ich und heul on Underlass! Also treibet mich der Wint, ich swimme dahin durch des wilden Meres Flut, die Tunnen[65] haben Uberhant genomen, mein Anker haftet niergent. Hierumb ich on Ende schreien will: Ir Tot, euch sei verfluchet![66]

In answer to these accusations Death expresses surprise that they are made at all. He then gives a justification of his office: he is the reaper, the agent of God who must make room on earth for new growth. The Ploughman's complaint is at first markedly personal, on the ground that he has suffered irreparable loss. He relates in detail his wife's good qualities and speaks of the happiness she brought him. Gradually he shifts his ground, however, and accuses Death of destroying all good things in the world. He rejects the plea that Death is God's agent. Death now finds himself forced to attack life on earth as disgusting and uses many of the arguments of the ascetics to show that life is not worth living and that women in particular are a snare. He thus gives the Ploughman an advantage, for he is able to point out that Man is God's finest handiwork and cannot therefore be as useless and foul as Death claims.

---

[37] **verzeuch:** from **verziehen,** go away, get out.
[38] **bis : sei** (imperative).
[39] **Afterrewe: Reue.**
[40] **wenen: glauben.**
[41] **geswechen: vermindern.**
[42] **twenglich: gewaltsam.**
[43] **Geferte: Verfahren.**
[44] **frevellich: vermessen.**
[45] **Zeihen: bezichtigen; anklagen.**
[46] **Vogelwat: Federn.**
[47] Again in accordance with legal procedure, the Ploughman now identifies himself and sets out the formal charge. He is a "ploughman with the pen," a roundabout but not uncommon way of saying that he earned his living as a clerk. He is from Bohemia, and Death has robbed him of his wife. Note that here, as frequently, the charge against Death is not of having killed the Ploughman's wife but of having deprived him of something he had to which he was entitled.
[48] **wesen: sein.**
[49] In the Latin alphabet the twelfth letter is M, since J is not a separate letter. The ploughman's wife's name was Margareta, as he tells us later.
[50] **Hort: Schatz.**
[51] **enzucken: reißen.**
[52] **ausreuten: ausjäten.**
[53] **Selde: Glück.**
[54] **Turteltaube: turtledove.** Many of the expressions of endearment are derived from the tradition of the *Minnesang,* but they also have a long history in other literatures, e.g., turtledove from the *Song of Songs.*
[55] **entfremden: stehlen.**

[56] **unwiderbringlich: unersetzlich.**
[57] **wegen: bedenken.**
[58] **entweren: berauben; um etwas bringen.**
[59] **Rente: Besitz; Einkommen.**
[60] **geussern: bestehlen.**
[61] **frut: freudig.**
[62] **lustsam: fröhlich.**
[63] **geudenreich: freudevoll.**
[64] **schab ab!: hau' ab!**
[65] **Tunne: Woge.**
[66] The last sentences of his speech echo biblical languages and, incidentally, parodies of it are found in the Goliard poets.

Der Ackermann. (Holzschnitt aus dem Zyklus „Der Totentanz" von Hans Holbein dem Jüngeren.) *Courtesy of Columbia University Library.*

Der Ackermann Pfei euch boser Schandensack! Wie vernichtet,[67] ubel handelt[68] und uneret ir den werden Menschen, Gotes allerliebste Creature, da mit ir auch die Gotheit swechet! Aller erste prufe ich, das ir lugenhaftig seit und in dem Paradise nicht getirmet, als ir sprechet. Weret ir in dem Paradise gefallen,[69] so wesset ir, das Got den Menschen und alle Ding beschaffen hat, und hat sie allzumale gut beschaffen, und den Menschen uber sie alle gesetzet, im ir aller Herschaft befohlen[70] und seinen Fussen untertenig gemachet hat, also das der Mensche den Tieren des Erdreichs; den Vogeln des Himels, den Fischen des Meres und allen Fruchten der Erden herschen solte, als er auch tut. Solte dann der Mensche so snode,[71] bose und unrein sein, als ir sprechet, werlich do hette Got gar unreinlichen und gar unnutzlichen gewurket,[72] als ir schreibet —streflicher[73] und gemeilter[74] Wurker were er. So stunde auch das nicht, das Got alle Ding und den Menschen uber sie alle zumale gut hette beschaffen. Herre Tot, lasset euer unnutz Claffen! Ir schendet Gotes aller huberschestes Werk. Engel, Teufel, Schretlein,[75] Klagemuter,[76] das sint Geiste in Gotes Twang wesende: der Mensch ist der allerachtberest, das aller behendest[77] und das aller freieste Gotes Werkstuck. Im selber geleiche hat in Got gebildet, als er auch selber in der ersten Wurkunge der Werlte hat gesprochen. Wo hat je Werkman gewurket so behendes und reiches Werkstuck, einen so werkberlichen kleinen Kloss als eines Menschen Haubet? In dem ist kunstereiche Kunst, allen Gottern Ebenteuer,[78] verborgen. Da ist in dem Augenapfel das Gesichte, das aller gewissest[79] Gezeuge, meisterlich in Spiegels Weise verwurket;[80] bis an des Himels clare Zirkel wurket es. Da ist in den Oren das ferre[81] gewurkende Gehoren, gar durchnechtiglichen[82] mit einem dunnen Felle vergitert zu Prufunge und Merkung Underscheit[83] mancherlei susses Gedones. Da ist in der Nasen der Ruch[84] durch zwei Locher ein und aus geende, gar sinniglichen[85] verzimert[86] zu behegelicher Senftigkeit[87] alles lustsames und wunnesames riechens; da ist Narung der Sele. Da sint in dem Munde Zene, alles Leibfuters tegeliches malende Einsacker;[88] darzu der Zungen dunnes Blat den Leuten zu wissen bringet ganz der Leute Meinunge; auch ist da des Smackes allerlei Koste lustsame Prufunge. Da bei sint in dem Kopfe aus Herzengrunde geende Sinne,[89] mit den ein Mensche, wie ferre er will, gar snelle reichet; in die Gotheit und daruber gar klimmet der Mensche mit den Sinnen. Allein der Mensche ist empfahende[90] der Vernunft, des edelen Hortes; er ist allein der lieblich Kloss, dem geleichen niemant dann Gott gewurken kan, dar innen also behende Werk, alle Kunst und Meisterschaft mit Weisheit sint gewurket. Lat faren, Herre Tot! Ir seit des Menschen Feint: darumb ir kein gutes von im sprechet![91]

When the Ploughman requests advice on a second marriage, Death raises many familiar antifeminist arguments, to which his opponent replies by citing the honorable characteristics of women. He adds

---

[67] vernichten: zunichte machen.
[68] ubel handeln: beschimpfen.
[69] fallen: here, to be born (used of animals).
[70] befehlen: übergeben; anvertrauen.
[71] snode: schnöde; erbärmlich.
[72] gewurket: geschaffen.
[73] streflich: tadelswert.
[74] gemeilt: befleckt.
[75] Schretlein: Kobold.
[76] Klagemuter: Tod vorbedeutender Geist.
[77] behend: geschickt.
[78] Ebenteuer: gleich.
[79] gewiss: zuverlässig.
[80] verwurket: gebildet.

[81] ferre: fern.
[82] durchnechtlich: trefflich.
[83] Underscheit: Unterscheidung.
[84] Ruch: Geruch.
[85] sinniglich: sinnvoll.
[86] verzimert: eingerichtet.
[87] Senftigkeit: Süßigkeit.
[88] Einsacker: Verzehrer.
[89] Sinn: Gedanke.
[90] empfahend: in Besitz von.
[91] The language of this passage is deliberately reminiscent of Genesis, since the Ploughman's whole argument rests on the fact that Death was not created by God in Paradise but "dropped" there. Death came as a result of Man's fall from grace, so that the Ploughman's argument is tenable. The almost lyrical praise of Man as God's finest creation anticipates many similar passages in Renaissance literature, of which the most famous is the speech in *Hamlet* ("What a piece of work is Man"). Note the emphasis on the senses. In most medieval writing only the eye and the ear are thought worthy of praise.

that Death's power will cease when life on earth ceases and that from Death will come Life. Death's reply is the standard exhortation to prepare for the uncertainty of the time and place of death by living a pure life. At this point God gives his judgment.

Der Lenze,[92] der Sumer, der Herbest und der Winter, die vier Erquicker und Hanthaber[93] des Jares, die wurden zwitrechtig[94] mit grossen Kriegen.[95] Ir jeder rumpte sich[96] und wolte jeglicher in seiner wurkunge der best sein. Der Lenze sprach, er erquickte und machte guftig[97] alle Frucht; der Sumer sprach, er machte reif und zeitig alle Frucht; der Herbest sprach, er brechte und zuckte[98] ein beide in Stadel,[99] in Keller und in die Heuser alle Frucht; der Winter sprach, er verzerte und vernutzte[100] alle Frucht und vertribe alle gifttragende Wurme. Sie rump-

ten sich und kriegeten faste; sie hetten aber vergessen, das sie sich gewaltiger Herschaft berumpten. Ebengeleich tut ir beide. Der Klager klaget sein Verlust, als ob sie sein Erbrecht were; er wenet[101] nicht, das sie von Uns were verlihen. Der Tot berumpt sich gewaltiger Herschaft, die er doch allein von Uns zu lehen hat empfangen. Der klaget, das nicht sein ist, diser rumpt sich herschaft die er nicht von im selber hat. Jedoch der Krieg ist nicht gar one Sache:[102] ir habt beide wol gefochten; den twinget[103] Leit zu klagen, disen die Anfechtung des Klagers die Warheit zu sagen. Darumb, Klager, habt Ere! Tot, habe Sige! Sei je der Mensche dem Tode das Leben, der Erden den Leib, die Sele uns pflichtig ist zu geben.

The work ends with a series of prayers by the Ploughman for his wife's soul.

---

[92] **Lenze: Frühling.**
[93] **Hanthaber: Helfer.**
[94] **zwitrechtig sein: Meinungsverschiedenheiten haben.**
[95] It is appropriate that God should conclude the debate by reference to another famous *Streitgedicht,* the Conflict of the Seasons. Technically both the Ploughman and Death are guilty of the sin of pride, since they have claimed for themselves what really belongs to God. Death is granted the victory because in the nature of things he must win. He has a function to serve and natural law is on his side. The Ploughman gains honor because he has debated better.
[96] **sich rumpen: sich rühmen.**
[97] **guftig: üppig.**
[98] **zucken: wegnehmen.**
[99] **Stadel: Scheune.**
[100] **vernutzen: verbrauchen.**

[101] **wenen: verstehen, denken.**
[102] **one Sache: sinnlos, zwecklos.**
[103] **twingen: zwingen.**

Donaueschinger
Passion Play

The exact date of the Donaueschinger Passion play cannot be determined, but it may with virtual certainty be placed at the very end of the fifteenth century. Only one manuscript is extant and this is clearly the "playbook" used by the producers of the work. In all probability the play was produced on a stage divided into three parts to represent Heaven, Earth, and Hell, with fixed positions allocated to certain characters. Thus many persons would be on the stage throughout the performance, while others, particularly Christ and other important characters, would move from one place to another. It is likely that the audience sat around the stage rather than in front of it. The play calls for a considerable number of properties and scenic effects.

This is a Passion play in the true sense of the word. Although it was designed to take two days in performing, there are no events earlier than the ministry of Jesus, whereas in many so-called Passion plays, events of the Old Testament which prefigured the Christian revelation are included. After a prologue, the real drama begins with a depiction of the worldly life of Mary Magdalen and her conversion. Then follow the temptation of Jesus, several miracles, of which the most important is the raising of Lazarus, the cleansing of the Temple, the entry into Jerusalem, and the plots of the Jews against Christ's life. The second day begins with a short prologue followed by the Last Supper. After this, every detail of the biblical story of the Passion and Crucifixion is depicted. A great deal of attention is given to the stories of Christ's descent into Hell and the role of the soldiers who watch the sepulcher; these events are taken from the apocryphal *Evangelium Nicodemi*. On the other hand, there is no long "Quacksalber" scene, as there is in so many Easter plays.

Although many critics have stressed the crude realism of the play, especially in the crucifixion scenes, it is more remarkable for the way in which it follows the Bible, even to the extent of rendering many passages literally, and for the didactic content of many of the scenes. There is particular emphasis on the contrast between Mary Magdalen, who led an unregenerate life and was made whole by faith, and Judas, who was given every opportunity to be one of the elect and who threw away his chances because of his avarice and spiritual blindness. The scenes given here are good examples both of the didacticism and the comic vigor of the play. The horror of the fate of Judas and in particular of his inability to conceive that he could still be saved is tempered by the comic treatment of the devils.

The work is written in a modified Swabian dialect, modified, that is, by sporadic attempts by the author or copyist to write "Hochdeutsch." In the selection presented here, the language has been changed to modern German but wherever possible the word order in each line has been left unchanged, even when it sounds unnatural in modern speech. The result is that most, but not all the original rhymes have been retained and in general the rhythm of the poetry is that of the play as it has come down to us.

THE JUDAS SCENES

JUDAS

Ihr Herren, seht wieder euer Geld!
denn ich hab' sicherlich gefehlt;
ich hab' verraten gerechtes Blut,
was liegt mir schwer in meinem Mut.
5 Ich hab' ein großes Übel getan.
wenn ich es nur hätte nicht begangen,
das wäre mir armen Judas wohl.
Ich weiß nicht, wie ich mich halten soll.[1]

*Nun kommt Beelzebub, der Teufel, mit einem
Strick und geht um Judas herum.[2] Dann fängt
Urias[3] an und spricht zu Judas.*

URIAS

Judas, du sollst dein Geld behalten.
10 Uns geht die Sache nicht mehr an.
Ist deinem Meister Unrecht geschehen,
dasselbe sollst du empfinden und sehen.
Dies Geld ist befleckt; wir wollen es nicht.
Du hast es genommen für dein.
15 Es ziemt sich nicht zu gebrauchen für anders
    Gut,
weil wir haben es gegeben um das Blut.

JUDAS

*Hier soll Judas einen Baum und eine Leiter als
Gerüst haben, und ein Seil soll davon bis in die
Hölle gespannt sein mit Scheiben versorgt.[4] Und
auf diese Rede erschrickt Judas sehr, und der
Teufel geht vor ihm auf die Leiter hinauf und zieht*

---

[1] It will be noted that Judas repents of what he has
done. He goes to Hell not because of his betrayal
of Christ but because of the sin of despair, the
inability to believe that God's grace can save him.
[2] The devil is symbolic of the temptation to suicide.
[3] Urias was one of the money changers in the Temple.
He gave Judas the pieces of silver.
[4] The stage directions call for the necessary equip-
ment for the hanging of Judas and his transporta-
tion to Hell. The directions are not altogether
clear but probably there was a hook either on one
of the pulleys or concealed in Judas' clothing so
that he could be hung on the rope and pulled into
Hell by the devils.

*den Strick mit sich. Judas geht ihm nach und
spricht mit kläglicher Stimme.*

Ich muß darum des Teufels sein.
O Weh, o Weh der großen Schande,
wenn man das sagt in jedem Lande,
daß einer seinen Herrn verraten soll.   20
Es steht keinem Christenmenschen wohl.
Komm, Teufel, mit deiner höllischen Gewalt!
Nimm mich von diesem Jammer bald.
Nun bin ich doch böser als andere Diebe,
daß mir weltliches Gut so lieb   25
und lieber war als Seel' und Leib.
Verflucht seien die Brüste und das Weib,
die ich auf Erde gesogen habe.
O Meister, du gerechter Mann!
Verflucht müssen Vater und Mutter sein.   30
O Weh, des gerechten Herrn mein!
O Jesus, Meister mein und Herr,
Wär' ich gevolget deiner Lehr',
so wäre es dazu nicht gekommen.
Nun hilft kein weltliches Gut noch Bitte.   35
Unseliger Tag, da ich geboren.
Ich bin an weltlichem Gut verloren.
O weltliches Gut, wie hast du mich betrogen!
daß ich meinen Herrn hab' verleumdet
und verraten mit dem Kuß!   40
Komm, Teufel, mein Schwatzen ist umsonst.
Ich will mich selbst zum Tod erhängen
und dir hier Leib und Seel schenken.
O ihr Menschen, vernehmt meine Klage,
die ich an diesem heutigen Tage   45
vor aller Welt klagen muß.
O Weh, der schweren harten Buße,
die ich muß leiden mit Pein und Leid!
Das tut meine große Bosheit,
die ich an Gott begangen habe,   50
daß ich den seligen Mann verriet.
O Weh der harten elenden Fahrt,
da ich zu einem Verräter ward!
O Weh, daß ich je ward geboren!
Ich bin in Ewigkeit verloren.   55
Der Geiz hat mich dahinter gebracht.
Nur an Hoffart hab' ich gedacht.
Unrein bin ich je gewesen.
Völlerei war auch der Wille mein.
Neid und Haß hatt' ich im Herzen.   60
Durch Zorn so leid' ich große Schmerzen.
Ich war träge an Gottes Gebot:
Darum bin ich der Welt zum Spott.

Die sieben Todessünden haben mich verführt,[5]
65 wie man das alles an mir spürt.
O Weh des Tages und auch der Stunde,
da mir das Geld zuerst ward kund!
O Weh, daß ich um weltliches Gut
verraten habe' das unschuldige Blut.
70 O Weh Not über alle Not,
daß ich verkauft hab' in den Tod
Jesus, den treuen Herrn mein.
Komm bald, hilf mir aus der Not,
da ich so übel gesündet habe,
75 denn hier ist keine Erlösung mehr.
Weltliches Gut, du tust mir weh!

Mit dieser Rede legt Beelzebub Judas den Strick
an und befestigt ihn an dem Haken und setzt
sich hinter ihm auf ein Bänkchen und sagt:

Judas, lieber Geselle mein,
dir ist bereitet die höllische Pein
von Luzifer, der Hölle Fürst und Herr.
80 Wir wollen dich dein Geld zählen lehren.
Komm, du bist mir ein lieber Sohn.
Ich will nach deinen Begehren es tun
und dich zu einem Gesellen haben.
Wohlan, wir gehen mit einander daran.

Judas soll einen schwarzen Vogel und etwas
Darm vorne im Busen haben.[6] Beelzebub soll es

ihm so zurechtmachen, daß es herausfällt. Dann
fahren beide in die Hölle und Faderwusch[7] läuft
unter dem Seil zur Hölle und sagt:

Ihr Teufel, tut auf der Hölle Tor.   85
Gottes Verräter Judas steht davor,
der Jesus, seinen Herrn, hat verraten.
Wir haben einen guten, schmutzigen Braten.
Seel' und Leib sind unser eigen.
Er muß jetzt tanzen unseren Reigen,   90
denn er hat sich uns ergeben,
während er noch am Leben war.
Luzifer, lieber Herre mein,
empfang Judas, den Diener dein![8]

Nun läuft Luzifer voraus und nimmt Judas vom
Seil ab und sagt dabei:

Judas, du sollst nicht länger hangen.   95
Ich hatt' nach dir ein großes Verlangen,
bis daß du zu mir gekommen bist.
Jetzt freue ich mich zu dieser Frist.
Komm, dir ist ein Bad vorbereitet,
darin du badest in Ewigkeit,   100
mit Schwefel, Pech und heißem Feuer.
Dein verkaufter Betrug wird dir zu teuer.
Ihr werdet mir bald zu Teil,
denn um weltliches Gut sind feil
Seele und Leib, das sage ich dir.   105
Judas, komm, du mußt mit mir.

---

[5] Judas confesses to all of the seven deadly sins (pride, anger, envy, sloth, avarice, gluttony, and sensuality), but the greatest stress is laid on his greed. Traditionally, Judas was the treasurer of the apostles and was angered at receiving insufficient commission.

[6] The black bird represents Judas' wicked soul, the piece of intestine, his body, which were forfeit to the devils.

---

[7] **Faderwusch**: name of a minor devil.

[8] There is a deliberate play on the entrance of Judas into Hell in contrast with the harrowing of Hell by Christ which occurs later in the play.

Reineke Fuchs

The Low German version of the conflict between Isengrim the wolf and Reynard the fox is the last of the medieval beast epics. Stories about animals are, of course, common in all cultures, and the fables of Aesop were known, in Latin versions, to the Middle Ages. The beast epic, however, has certain qualities that set it apart. The conflict between the wolf and the fox is always the central issue but in many versions there are incidents in which neither appears. Although the fox may suffer an occasional setback, he is generally triumphant and this is due to his superior cunning, which defeats the wolf's greater physical strength. The court of king lion is the stage on and around which the various scenes are played.

The earliest beast epics centered on an incident that can be found in Aesop, the sickness of the lion who is cured by the prescription of the fox, a prescription that involves the flaying of the wolf and the use of his skin to keep the lion warm during his fever. Since this incident was used in a poem by Paulus Diaconus in the early ninth century, it is clear that it was known in western Europe, even though it does not appear in any of the Latin versions of Aesop. The early Latin beast epics, *Ecbasis captivi* (Escape of the Captive) of about 940 and the brilliant anticlerical satire *Ysengrimus,* of about 1150, both use this central incident but both add a large number of other incidents in which Reynard torments and, in the *Ysengrimus,* ultimately destroys the wolf.

The French *Roman de Renart* apparently began to appear about 1170, and there were constant accretions to the basic stories. Although it is possible to arrange the various incidents so that they form a continuous narrative, there is no evidence that the authors thought of them in this way. The French versions introduce a new "core" story—a trial scene in which Reynard is condemned for his numerous crimes against the other animals but succeeds in escaping by a trick.

The earliest German version of the beast epic is to be found in the fragments of a poem by Heinrich der Glichezaere (*c.* 1180). Although only 685 lines of this work survive, a reworking, dated about 1240, shows that the poem fell into three parts, the first a description of incidents in which Reynard was defeated, the second an account of the numerous defeats of Isengrim, and the third a version of the sick lion theme. This German version was not, as might be expected, the basis for the Low German versions of the fifteenth century. These are derived from several works in Middle Dutch which are based on incidents from the *Roman de Renart*. The earliest, *Van den vos Reynaerde,* written about 1269, describes the trial of Reynard, his acquittal because he revealed the whereabouts of a treasure (entirely imaginary), and his subsequent criminal behavior. This version was later expanded, principally by an account of a judicial combat between Isengrim and Reynard. This expanded form, often called *Reinaert II,* appeared in a prose version printed at Gouda in 1479 and in another printed version at Delft in 1485. (The Gouda version is the basis for Caxton's Middle English work.) In 1487 there appeared in Antwerp a rhyming verse version, of which only a fragment is extant, which formed the basis for the most famous of all works written in Low German, *Reinke Vos,* first printed in Lübeck in 1498 and reprinted in Rostock in 1517. These editions were reprinted again and again and were even used by the Protestant and Catholic churches as means of propaganda by the insertion of moralizing comment.

One of the more remarkable aspects of the development of the beast epic is that it was concentrated in northwestern Europe. This fact may well be responsible for the large amount of social criticism and satire to be found in it. The Latin *Ysengrimus,* written by Master Nivardus of Ghent, is bitterly anticlerical and particularly antimonastic. The later versions, especially those in Dutch and Low German, appear to reflect the total disillusionment of the bourgeoisie with the feudal system of justice to which their lords attempted to subject them. The principal actions of the later beast epic all call attention to the total lack of morality in feudal society and to the corrupt nature of the "justice" administered by feudal lords. This dissatisfaction is particularly evident in the perversion of justice when Reynard is able to corrupt the king by promises of wealth and in the mockery of judicial combat. It should be noted, however, that all the beast epics show medieval society in a very unfavorable light. No one is actuated by any but the basest motives and the only kind or even religious people are those who are too weak to be anything else. Isengrim is a monster of violence and lust, but Reynard who defeats him is utterly amoral. The beast epic is a very sound counterbalance to the romance.

REINEKE FUCHS

The lion, king of the beasts, issues a declaration of peace over his entire kingdom so that the animals can come to his court without fear of being attacked. There the wolf and several other animals launch an attack on Reynard the fox as a thief and adulterer. Reynard is not present, and his reputation is defended by Grimbart the badger, who, while admitting some of the deeds, says that they are no worse than those of Reynard's accusers. Just as he is making headway with his defense, the rooster appears and accuses Reynard of the murder of one of his numerous wives. A sad funeral procession confirms his allegations. The king takes council as to how he shall punish Reynard and sends Braun the bear with a letter summoning Reynard to court. Unfortunately the bear allows himself to be tempted by the promise of honey in a tree and is trapped; he manages to escape, losing a great deal of his skin. Hinze the cat is sent on a similar mission and suffers a similar fate. Grimbart the badger then persuades Reynard that he had better come to court. On the way Reynard confesses his sins and receives a light penance. His conduct during the journey to court indicates that his repentance will hardly be of long duration. In spite of a vigorous defense, Reynard is condemned to be hanged, and his enemies, with great glee, prepare to make an end of him. He asks to make a last confession and in the course of implicating the wolf in his misdeeds, introduces a new element:

„ ... Mir war die kleinste Rippe gelassen,
 Und die auch kriegte ich nicht zu
   fassen,
Eh' sie das Fleisch davon genagt.
Das litt ich alles unverzagt;
5 Denn, Gott sei Dank, ich hatt' es nicht Not,
Da mir mein Schatz noch Auskunft bot,
Ein gold- und silberreicher Hort,
Ein Wagen brächt' ihn schwerlich fort,
Und führ er siebenmal daran."
10 Zu horchen hub der König an,
Als er von dem Schatz vernommen;
Er sprach: „Wie seid Ihr daran gekommen?
Ich meine den Schatz—das tut mir kund."
Reineke sprach: „Aus welchem Grund
15 Sollt' ichs zu sagen mich nicht bequemen?
Ich kann ihn ja doch nicht mit mir nehmen.

Ich will's Euch sagen, macht es Euch Freude:
Niemand zu Lieb und niemand zu Leide.
Soll es länger bleiben verhohlen;
Wißt also, der Schatz war gestohlen.   20
Es war bestimmt, man sollt' Euch morden,
Wär' der Schatz nicht gestohlen worden;
Gnädiger Herr, das merkt in Huld,
Der vermaledeite Schatz war Schuld.
Daß so der Schatz gestohlen ward,   25
Dafür hat mein Vater die leidige Fahrt
Aus diesem Leben zu ewigem Schaden:
Doch zum Frommen gereicht' es Euern
   Gnaden."

There is immediate interest in the court when the treasure is mentioned, and in a short time Reynard is allowed to come down from the gallows to tell his story. In order to lend verisimilitude to his lies, he does not hesitate to implicate friends as well as enemies, and the chief villain in the plot he describes is his own father:

Er sprach: „Mein Vater hat gefunden
Den mächtigen Königs Ermenrich Schatz,
An einem abgelegenen Platz.
Da er nun hatte so großes Gut,
Ward er so stolz und voll Übermut,   5
Daß er alle Tiere fortan
Verachtete in seinem törichten Wahn,
Die früher seine Gesellen waren.
Da ließ er Hinze den Kater fahren
In die Ardennen, das wilde Land,   10
Wo sich Braun der Bär befand;
Er ließ ihm huldigen durch ihn
Und er möchte gleich gen Flandern ziehn,
Wenn er König zu werden begehre.
Da Braun den Brief hatte lesen hören,   15
Ward er fröhlich und unverzagt,
Denn es hätte ihm schon lange behagt.
Gen Flandern reist' er unverwandt,
Wo er meinen Herrn Vater fand.
Der empfing ihn wohl und schickte Gesandte   20
Zu Grimbart, dem weisen, unserm Ver-
   wandten
Und auch zu Isengrim alsofort.
Diese vier verhandelten lange dort;
Hinze der Kater war auch zugegen.
Ein Dorf, namens Iste ist da gelegen: 25
Zwischen Iste und Gent,
Hielten sie ihr Parlament
In einer düstern, langen Nacht.
Nicht mit Gott, durch des Teufels Macht,

30　Und durch meines Vaters List,
　　Dessen Geld sie zwang zu jener Frist,
　　Beschwuren sie da des Königs Tod.
　　Ein jeder dem andern seine Treue bot.
　　Sie schwuren alle fünf zu gleicher Zeit
35　Auf Isegrins Haupt einen teuren Eid:
　　Sie wollten den Bären zum König küren,
　　Ihn auf den Stuhl zu Aachen[1] führen
　　Und sein Haupt mit goldner Kron' umgeben.
　　Wolle dem jemand widerstreben,
40　Ein Verwandter des Königs oder ein Vasall,
　　Die solle Reineke verjagen all',
　　Mit seinem Schatz es hintertreiben,
　　Mit Bestechen, Bereden und Briefschreiben.
　　Hiervon bekam ich also Kunde:
45　Es geschah bei früher Morgenstunde,
　　Daß Grimbart, der den Wein nicht gespart,
　　Davon fröhlich und trunken ward.
　　Da vertraut' er es heimlich seinem Weibe
　　Und sprach, ‚Sieh zu, daß es bei dir bleibe.'
50　Sie schwieg so lange, versteht mich nur,
　　Bis es mein Weib von ihr erfuhr.
　　Sie schwur ihr, als sie zusammen kamen,
　　In der heiligen drei Könige Namen,
　　Bei ihrer Ehr' und Seligkeit,
55　Weder um Liebe noch um Leid
　　Wolle sie weiter davon sprechen."

Needless to say, the fox hears the story from his wife. He spies on his father, finds where the treasure is buried, and takes it away. Many nobles join the plot, but when they come to collect their share, the treasure cannot be found; Reineke's father hangs himself in fury, and the plot collapses. Reineke's story is full of detail; he has no qualms about incriminating relatives and friends, and he succeeds in arousing the cupidity of the royal couple.

　　Der König und die Königin
　　Hofften beide auf Gewinn.
　　Sie zogen Reineken bei Seit'
　　Und sprachen: „Gebt uns nun Bescheid,
5　Wohin der große Schatz gekommen!"
　　Reineke sprach: „Was sollt es mir frommen,
　　Wenn ich mein Gut dem König wiese,
　　Der mich zum Dank erhängen ließe?
　　Ihr glaubt den Mördern und den Dieben,
10　Die sich mit Lügen an mir üben,

Mir verräterisch nach dem Leben stehen."
„Nein", sprach die Königin, „das soll nicht
　　geschehn,
Der König soll Euch lassen leben
Und soll Euch freundlich vergeben
All seinen Zorn und übeln Mut,　　　　　　15
Wenn Ihr in Zukunft klüger tut,
Daß Euch der König stets vertraue."
Reineke sprach: „Meine liebe Fraue,
Wenn vor Euch der König mir
Das fest geloben will allhier,　　　　　　20
Daß er mir wieder schenkt die Huld
Und vergißt all meine Sünd' und Schuld,
Auch seinen Zorn beiseite stellt:
So ist kein König in der Welt
So reich, als ich ihn machen will;　　　　25
Denn des Schatzes ist unmäßig viel:
Ich will ihm zeigen diesen Hort."

Although the king is suspicious, he allows himself to be persuaded, but threatens that he will take grim revenge on all Reineke's family if he offends again. He then hears that the treasure is hidden at Krekelpütz, near Husterlo, and the exact spot is described. When the king protests that he has never heard of these two places, Reineke calls in Lampe the hare to confirm it. Lampe is far too frightened not to do so. The fox says that he cannot go with the king to find the treasure because he is excommunicate and has to make a pilgrimage to make peace with the Holy See. In spite of this obvious deception, the king formally forgives him, heaps honors upon him, and arrests his accusers. The male and female wolf have the skin torn from their paws to provide the fox with pilgrims shoes[2] —in other words, they are flayed like common criminals. Reineke then sets out on his "pilgrimage," accompanied by the hare and the ram. In fact, he takes them to his house, where he kills the hare and sends back his head to court in the ram's satchel. The ram is accused of murder, and he and his family are handed over to the beasts of prey. Isegrim and the bear are released from their prison now that it is evident that the fox has again deceived the king.

*　　The second part of the poem is in many ways a repetition of the first. There is another court*

---

[1] **Aachen:** city, the favorite residence of Charlemagne. The cathedral in which the coronation of the Holy Roman Emperor was supposed to be carried out was located there.

---

[2] In the original version of the sick lion story, which goes back to a fable of Aesop, the wolf's skin was flayed off and the king was wrapped in it. This motif is preserved in the provision of shoes of wolf's skin for Reineke.

scene, another trial scene, the fox again tells of his numerous misdeeds and again escapes punishment by telling of the magic mirror, comb, and ring. Into the description of the articles, embellishments, the author weaves numerous fables. Among these stories is an account of how Reineke's father once cured the king's father. This, the story of the sick lion, is the central theme of the earlier beast epics, such as the Latin Ysengrimus. *Here it is relegated to the previous generation of animals.*

„Der Winter war ingrimmig kalt,
Euer Vater lag in großen Plagen,
Man mußt' ihn auf eine Bahre tragen.
Alle Ärzte zwischen Rom und hier
5 Ließ er berufen: sie kamen schier
Und gaben ihn alle Gott befohlen.
Da ließ er zuletzt meinen Vater holen,
Er klagt' ihn jammernd seine Not,
Wie er krank sei bis in den Tod.
10 Das erbarmte meinen Vater sehr;
Er sprach: ‚Großmächtiger König hehr,
Möcht' ich Euch mit meinem Leben frommen,
Glaubt mir, ich ließ Euch nicht verkommen.
Macht Euer Wasser: hier ist ein Glas!'
15 Euer Vater, welcher gern genas,
Meines Vaters Räte befolgt er immer,
Doch klagt' er, es würde je länger je schlimmer.
Auf dem Spiegel stand das auch zu lesen,
Wie Euer Vater damals ist genesen.
20 Denn mein Vater sprach: ‚Wärt Ihr gern gesund,
Das einzige Mittel sei Euch kund:
Eines Wolfes Leber von sieben Jahren—
Ihr dürft die Kosten, Herr, nicht sparen—
Die sollt Ihr essen, sonst wird's nicht gut;
25 Denn Euer Wasser zeigt nur Blut,
Und Euer Leben ist der Preis.'
Der Wolf stand auch mit in dem Kreis;
Er vernahm es, doch gefiel's ihm nicht.
Ihr Vater sprach: ‚Ihr hört den Bericht,
30 Herr Wolf, soll ich am Leben sein,
So müßt Ihr mir Euer Leber leihn.'
Der Wolf sprach: ‚Herr, ich sag' Euch fürwahr,

Ich bin noch kaum im fünften Jahr.'
Da sprach mein Vater: ‚Ihr könnt nicht entgehen,
Ich will es wohl an der Leber sehn.'   35
Da mußte der Wolf zur Küche fort,
Die Leber schnitten sie ihm dort.
Sobald der König die Leber aß,
Fühlte er sich besser und genas.
Das dankte er meinem Vater sehr   40
Und gebot dem Hausgesind nachher,
Daß ihn ein jeder Doktor hieße,
Und das beileibe nicht unterließe. . . .‚"

The incident is typical of the utter selfishness of all the characters in the beast epic. Other stories are told of Reineke's exploits and, as before, he is able to persuade the king to let him go. Isegrim's only recourse is to challenge Reineke to a judicial combat. Reineke prepares for this by shaving off his coat and greasing himself but even so, in a travesty of a duel, he is almost beaten were it not for his foul tactics. The lion calls off the fight to save Isegrim from further punishment. Although he has won by unfair means, Reineke is surrounded by well-wishers and loaded with honors. Evil has triumphed—but not over good, which does not exist at the court of King Lion. The only way to succeed is to be utterly selfish and amoral, as the author observes in his sarcastic epilogue.

So ist nun Reineke hochgeehrt,
Wie Ihr hier kürzlich habt gehört.
Zur Weisheit wende sich Alter und Jugend,
Meide das Böse und lerne Tugend.
Darum ist dieses Buch gedichtet: 5
Auf diesen Sinn ist es gerichtet.
Fabeln und andere Gleichnisreden,
Dienen zur Lehre für all' und jeden,
Daß sie von Torheit sich entfernen,
Zu allen Zeiten Weisheit lernen.   10
Dies Buch verschmäht zu kaufen nicht:
Es gibt vom Lauf der Welt Bericht.
Willst du der Dinge Lauf erfahren,
So kauf dies Buch: du wirst noch sparen.
Also endigt Reinekens Historie.   15
Gott helf uns zu seiner ewigen Glorie!

The Age of the Reformation

If German literary developments were to be described in terms of an alternation between recurrent withdrawal from and renewed alliance with European poetic issues, the age of the Reformation would appear as a period of passionate introspection and self-absorbed tension within the nation itself. Germany had to resolve, within the soul of each individual believer, conflicts of far-reaching metaphysical relevance; inevitably it came to isolate itself, in the intensity and bitterness of the struggle, from the wider world of Renaissance poetry which insistently sought aesthetic rather than theological glories. The determined self-concern of a mind troubled by ultimate questions of grace and salvation, and the ensuing religious and political clashes, were not conducive to creating perfect artistic structures offering a disinterested aesthetic experience; and although the Muses were not entirely silent during the din of the violent disputes, German literature turned didactic, polemic, and decidedly partisan. Perhaps it is not entirely wrong to say that the metaphysical intensity of the Reformation substantially contributed toward the alienation of Germany from the artistic triumphs of the European Renaissance; it was only when the quarrels subsided and the new institutions were consolidated that Germany, in the age of the Baroque, fully, if belatedly, participated in the achievements of Petrarch, Ariosto, Tasso, the Pleiad, Spenser, and their resplendent kind.

In the sixteenth century Germany was, in area as well as in population, the largest country in Europe, but it was divided by almost 2500 local and regional authorities and had much less cohesion than its more powerful neighbors. The French and the Turks successfully attacked its border areas, and German princes, lawyers, and scholars agreed in theory that a constitutional reform was badly needed. There was great hope for a political change for the better when Maximilian of Habsburg (1493–1519) was elected emperor, and for a brief span his court in the cities of Vienna and Innsbruck (where he often lived) attracted some of the most important poets and scholars of the time; Maximilian took satisfaction in the role of a new Augustus or Charlemagne. But his death nearly coincided with Luther's fundamental writings against the Church hierarchy and papal authority and, during much of the reign of Maximilian's successor, Charles V, the disruptive forces again dominated the German scene. The imperial knights who had always claimed extreme independence rose against the emperor, the rich cities revolted against the territorial princes who coveted a share in commercial gains, and the revolutionary peasants marched against the castles of their lords. They failed to win decisive battles in the open field, however, and were butchered without mercy.

A divided country, a divided literature:—teachers and scholars wrote in Latin while different German dialects, shaped by region and the practices of the local printing press, nourished a popular literature oriented, in many of its interests and forms, toward the late Middle Ages. But not all Latin writing should be termed Humanist; the traditions of scholasticism continued to develop in monasteries, orders, and most of the German universities, while the Humanists (who were concerned with a philosophy of human affairs rather than with theological justifications) deliberately modeled their polished and urbane idiom on Cicero and the classical writers of pre-Christian Rome. One should not forget that at least part of the Humanist effort served German literature in its own way. Humanists were responsible for important attempts to translate Latin plays (Terence, Plautus), recent Italian poetry, and sophisticated prose (Petrarch, Boccaccio); at the court of Maximilian a new German version of Vergil's *Aeneid* appeared. The Humanist art of translation confronted the developing German language with classical eloquence and Renaissance finesse and sharpened the translators' as well as the readers' sensibilities, and although Luther differs from the Humanists in attending to the spoken rather than the elegantly written word, his return to the source texts of the Bible does conform to Humanist assumptions and practices. Sixteenth-century Humanism, in Germany, had a complex function: clearly, it strengthened the cosmopolitan orientation of important German scholars like Konrad Celtis and Heinrich Bebel and made them intellectual allies of the Italienate Dutch Anglophile Erasmus of Rotterdam (1466–1536), the most civilized and influential among the European Humanists; yet—at the same time—it compelled the German scholars to compare the intellectual (and political) achievements of their own nation with those of their Italian contemporaries who claimed to be the true heirs of the Romans, and, inevitably, gave rise to a scholarly feeling of national pride sustained by ideas, or rather wishful thinking, derived from Tacitus' *Germania,* which had been discovered by an Italian scholar in a German monastery in 1455. The study of the ancients paradoxically furthered nascent nationalism; voluminous histories demonstrated the proud

German past, and a sharpened sense of being German (still articulated in Latin) anticipated and later confirmed Protestant conflicts with the authority of Rome. After Luther had defined his essential arguments, it was the imperial knight Ulrich von Hutten who translated Humanist nationalism and Protestant aversions to Rome into concrete political terms, but his temperament was so fierce and his ideas so extreme that he shocked both Luther and his own fellow Humanists, and died in miserable loneliness.

Popular literature in the German vernacular developed at some distance from Humanist interests. Although it is sometimes difficult to draw a distinction between Humanists and specifically German writers in biographical terms, German writing was of a coarser grain and continued to use medieval forms related to the antiquated courtly tradition, or the ritual of the Church. German writing preferred tales from older epic materials, entertaining jokes and ribald stories, songs relating important historical events, moralizing satires, massive mystery plays, or *Predigtmärlein* of clearly didactic intent. With the advances of the printing press and new audiences, the chapbook, or *Volksbuch,* emerged as the most popular kind of literature. But it is important to note that in the *Singschulen,* which originated in the fourteenth century, middle-class amateurs and artisans gathered to develop poetic art by systematized respect for tradition, continued training, and supervised practice in the composition of stanzas and melodies; the sixteenth-century *Meistersinger* (who were as isolated from the Humanists as they were from the people) may have been less creative than Richard Wagner's opera suggests, but they certainly did sustain an awareness of the technical necessities of good writing. Their danger was an extreme traditionalism; only after 1500 did the *Meistersänger* Hans Folz demand that his colleagues should not merely imitate prescribed stanzas but invent new ones; and after he had left his native Worms and settled in rich Nuremberg, in an atmosphere more open to ingenious innovation, the *Meistersinger* in Nuremberg and elsewhere competed in inventiveness. Hans Sachs was the most prolific of the Nuremberg school, but his success as a popular playwright seems to have diverted the attention of many of his fellow singers to the more public attractions of the theater.

The events of the incipient Reformation did not necessarily reduce the distance between popular and Humanist literature but, after Luther had published his *An den christlichen Adel deutscher Nation* as well as his *Von der Freiheit eines Christenmenschen* and *Von der babylonischen Gefangenschaft der Kirche* (1520), the public disputes increased book production in German, new relationships and alliances crystallized, factions were formed, and didactic and polemical intent predominated for at least one generation. Luther did more for the artistic potential of the German language than for literary forms as such; although he did not create a German language uniting North and South, in his Bible translation as well as in his polemical writings, he integrated tendencies long inherent in German linguistic development and assured the final victory of the one standard language universal in the land.

The age of the Reformation directed its boundless energies to other than aesthetic questions but it contributed, in many important ways, to the developing potentialities of German writing. Religious and political conflicts provoked a host of pamphlets, allegories, and satires in which the German tongue was sharpened and refreshed; Luther and Hutten represented the new; Thomas Murner, in his *Vom großen lutherischen Narren,* defended Church traditions in equally belligerent German. It was the theater, however, that most eagerly responded to the challenges of the moment: being the most social of the arts, and of broadest appeal to the urban audiences, the theater could not avoid taking sides. Almost immediately, the *Fastnachtspiel* was adopted as a polemical weapon by Niklas Manuel in Berne and, since Luther himself had pointed to the dramatic usefulness of some Old Testament stories, many biblical plays, often retelling the stories of the Prodigal Son or Susannah, appeared in Latin and German. Only in the late sixties and the seventies, did the bitterness of the warring factions seem to relent, a modest interest in aesthetic issues reemerged, and important attempts were made to bridge the gap between Humanist and popular writing, to combine Latin art with native vigor. Johann Fischart tried to solve the problem by mobilizing an immense, not to say bizarre, richness in his German idiom; and Nikodemus Frischlin attempted to combine the traditions of the Humanist school play with the expansiveness of the German theatrical tradition. But these are beginnings; it is only fifty years later, in the age of Martin Opitz, that the cosmopolitan and the indigenous traditions are finally joined together.

𝕸artin Luther

(1483–1546)

It would be difficult to characterize Martin Luther in terms of German philological and literary developments alone—were we not accustomed to date a new age from Columbus' maritime discoveries, we would be justified in believing that modern German intellectual history begins with Luther's interpretation of the Pauline letters and his passionate polemics immediately preceding his break with traditional Church hierarchy (1520/21). As a popular and bold writer Luther did more for the German language than anyone before young Goethe and the Romantic generations. He both furthered and endangered literature as art; while vigorously contributing to the creation of an idiom of poetic energy and simplicity, he provoked religious and political conflicts which tended to transform contemporary literature into partisan propaganda and made more sensitive poets seek refuge in the protective shell of the unbroken continuity of Latin traditions.

In a restless age, Luther found himself, often against his will, the representative of many conflicting aspirations; the introspective and self-torturing monk and erudite professor of theology did not seek a place of revolutionary pre-eminence but was almost step by step forced to assume nearly all the burdens of his time. After he returned from hiding at the Thuringian Wartburg, he tried to steer a balanced course between his traditionalist enemies and the ruthless antitraditionalism of his anarchist allies; his metaphysical fervor, sustained by the most sensitive awareness of the moral responsibility of the individual, clashes strangely with his exhortation of the German nobility to kill the revolutionary peasants like mad dogs. The Old and the New are fused in his theology; although he defended a conservative idea of the true presence of Christ in the sacrament against symbolical interpretations, he conceived (centuries before the existentialists) an image of man, the lonely sinner, absorbed in his intimate encounter with a stern and infinitely forgiving God. The world, however, cried for active participation, intervention, and engagement, and the aging reformer was almost imprisoned by the petty quarrels among the princes whose protection he tried in vain to shed.

Luther's achievements as a German writer are intimately bound to his reconstituted image of man confronting, in a renewed solitude, a terrible and tender God; in a religious universe emptied of the consoling intermediaries of ritual and hierarchy, God's own word, the Bible, assumed an absolutely central place—the word itself was holy. Luther was not the first to translate the New and the Old Testaments for his contemporaries; before him at least eighteen attempts had been made to translate the Bible into the High or Low German vernacular. But Luther was the first who, in the tradition of Humanism, returned to the Hebrew and Greek sources rather than to the Vulgate, and, continuing the linguistic tendencies of his age, he completed the search for *eine gemeine teutsche Sprache* readily understandable both in the North and in the South; in practice, he relied on an East Central idiom (*ostmitteldeutsch*), as used by the Chancellery of the Saxon Prince Elector. Luther's famous defense of his technique of translation, his *Sendbrief vom Dolmetschen* (1530), reveals much of his forceful personality and the methodological assumptions of his work; it is (apart from its theological and biographical importance) an exemplary piece of polemical writing whose edge and dialectic power was not equaled in Germany until the ages of Lessing and Nietzsche.

Luther was far from considering himself a poet, and if, in the early twenties, he rewrote or created a number of songs and hymns he did so because he felt it was yet another way to strengthen a true community of believers as the ancient Psalms had done—*daß das Wort Gottes auch durch den Gesang unter den Leuten bleibe*. His *Geistliches Gesangbüchlein* (1524), partly prompted by his intent to counteract the spreading influence of the revolutionary, Thomas Münzer, gathered old songs of the prereform epoch, new versions of biblical Psalms, and some songs of his own; he thought to offer a beginning and instituted a tradition which, determined by his masculine grasp of language and emotion, continued to develop, visibly or as an undercurrent, throughout the centuries. Of the most modern poets even Bertolt Brecht gladly returned to Luther's poetic idiom.

Aus tiefer Not

Der 130. Psalm: *De profundis clamavi*

Aus tiefer Not schrei ich zu dir,
Herr Gott, erhör mein Rufen.
Dein gnädig Ohren kehr zu mir
Und meiner Bitt sie öffne.
Denn so du willst das sehen an,
Was Sünd und Unrecht ist getan,
Wer kann, Herr, vor dir bleiben?

Bei dir gilt nichts denn Gnad und Gonst,
Die Sünden zu vergeben.
Es ist doch unser Tun umsonst
Auch in dem besten Leben.
Vor dir niemand sich rühmen kann,
Des muß dich fürchten jedermann
Und deiner Gnaden leben.

Darum auf Gott will hoffen ich,
Auf mein Verdienst nicht bauen;
Auf ihn mein Herz soll lassen sich
Und seiner Güte trauen,
Die mir zusagt sein wertes Wort,
Das ist mein Trost und treuer Hort,
Des will ich allzeit harren.

Und ob es währt bis in die Nacht
Und wieder an den Morgen,
Doch soll mein Herz an Gottes Macht
Verzweifeln nicht noch sorgen.
So tu Israel rechter Art,
Der aus dem Geist erzeuget ward,
Und seines Gotts erharre.

Ob bei uns ist der Sünden viel,
Bei Gott ist viel mehr Gnaden;
Sein Hand zu helfen hat kein Ziel
Wie groß auch sei der Schaden.
Er ist allein der gute Hirt,
Der Israel erlösen wird
Aus seinen Sünden allen.

Ein' feste Burg

Der 46. Psalm: *Deus noster refugium et virtus*

Ein feste Burg ist unser Gott,
Ein gute Wehr und Waffen.
Er hilft uns frei aus aller Not,
Die uns jetzt hat betroffen.
Der alt böse Feind   5
Mit Ernst er's jetzt meint,
Groß Macht und viel List
Sein grausam Rüstung ist,
Auf Erd ist nicht seinsgleichen.

Mit unsrer Macht ist nichts getan,   10
Wir sind gar bald verloren,
Es streit für uns der Rechte Mann,
Den Gott hat selbst erkoren.
Fragst du, wer der ist?
Er heißt Jesu Christ,   15
Der Herr Zebaoth,
Und ist kein ander Gott,
Das Feld muß er behalten.

Und wenn die Welt voll Teufel wär
Und wollt uns gar verschlingen,   20
So fürchten wir uns nicht so sehr,
Es soll uns doch gelingen.
Der Fürst dieser Welt,
Wie saur er sich stellt,
Tut er uns doch nicht,   25
Das macht, er ist gericht,
Ein Wörtlein kann ihn fällen.

Das Wort sie sollen lassen stahn
Und kein Dank dazu haben,
Er ist bei uns wohl auf dem Plan   30
Mit seinem Geist und Gaben.
Nehmen sie den Leib,
Gut, Ehr, Kind und Weib,
Laß fahren dahin,
Sie habens kein Gewinn,   35
Das Reich muß uns doch bleiben.

EIN SENDBRIEF
VOM DOLMETSCHEN (1530)

Gnade und Friede in Christo. Ehrbarer, fürsichtiger,[1] lieber Herr und Freund![2] Ich habe Eure Schrift empfangen mit den zwei Quästionen oder Fragen, darin Ihr
5 meines Berichtes begehrt: Erstlich, warum ich zu den Römern[3] im dritten Kapitel die Worte S. Pauli: *Arbitramur, hominem justificari ex fide absque operibus* also verdeutscht habe: Wir halten, daß der Mensch gerecht
10 werde ohne des Gesetzes Werk allein durch den Glauben. Und zeigt daneben an, wie die Papisten sich über die Maßen unnütz machen, weil im Text Pauli nicht steht das Wort *sola,* „allein", und sei solcher Zusatz von mir
15 nicht zu leiden in Gottes Worten etc. Zum Andern, ob auch die verstorbenen Heiligen für uns bitten, weil wir lesen, daß ja die Engel für uns bitten etc. Auf die erste Frage, wo es euch gelüstet, mögt Ihr Euern Papisten
20 von meinetwegen antworten also: Zum Ersten, wenn ich, Doctor Luther, mich hätte des versehen mögen, daß die Papisten alle auf einen Haufen so geschickt wären, daß sie e i n Kapitel in der Schrift könnten recht
25 und wohl verdeutschen, so wollte ich fürwahr mich der Demut haben finden lassen[4] und sie um Hilfe und Beistand gebeten, das Neue Testament zu verdeutschen. Aber dieweil ich gewußt und noch vor Augen sehe,
30 daß ihrer keiner recht weiß, wie man dolmetschen oder deutsch reden soll, habe ich sie und mich solcher Mühe überhoben. Das merkt man aber wohl, daß sie aus meinem Dolmetschen und Deutsch lernen Deutsch
35 reden und schreiben, und stehlen mir also meine Sprache, davon sie zuvor wenig gewußt; danken mir aber nicht dafür, sondern brauchen sie viel lieber wider mich. Aber ich gönne es ihnen wohl; denn es tut mir doch
40 sanft,[5] daß ich auch meine undankbaren

Jünger, dazu meine Feinde, reden gelehrt habe.

Zum Andern mögt Ihr sagen, daß ich das Neue Testament verdeutscht habe auf mein bestes Vermögen[6] und auf mein Gewissen;
45 habe damit Niemand gezwungen, daß er's lese, sondern frei gelassen, und allein zu Dienst getan denen, die es nicht besser machen können. Ist Niemand verboten, ein Besseres zu machen. Wer's nicht lesen will,
50 der laß es liegen. Ich bitte und feiere Niemand darum. Es ist mein Testament und meine Dolmetschung und soll mein bleiben und sein. Habe ich drinnen etwa gefehlt (das mir doch nicht bewußt, und [ich] freilich
55 ungern einen Buchstaben mutwilliglich wollte unrecht verdolmetschen), darüber will ich die Papisten nicht zu Richter leiden. Denn sie haben noch zur Zeit zu lange Ohren dazu, und ihr Ika Ika[7] ist zu schwach, mein Ver-
60 dolmetschen zu beurteilen.

Ich weiß wohl, und sie wissen's weniger denn des Müllers Tier, was für Kunst, Fleiß, Vernunft, Verstand zum guten Dolmetscher gehört; denn sie haben's nicht versucht.
65 Es heißt: Wer am Wege baut, der hat viel Meister. Also geht mir's auch. Diejenigen, die noch nie haben recht reden können, geschweige denn dolmetschen, die sind allzumal meine Meister, und ich muß ihrer aller Jünger
70 sein. Und wenn ich sie hätte fragen sollen, wie man die ersten zwei Worte, Matth. 1,1: *Liber generationis,*[8] sollte verdeutschen, so hätte ihrer keiner gewußt Gack dazu zu sagen, und urteilen mir nun das ganze Werk,
75 die feinen Gesellen! Also ging es S. Hieronymus[9] auch, da er die Bibel verdolmetschte, da war alle Welt sein Meister, er allein war es, der nichts konnte, und verurteilten dem guten Mann sein Werk die-
80 jenigen, so[10] ihm nicht genug gewesen wären, daß sie ihm die Schuhe hätten wischen sollen. Darum gehört große Geduld dazu, so Jemand öffentlich Gutes tun will. Denn die Welt will Meister Klügling bleiben und muß
85 immer das Roß unter dem Schwanz zäumen, alles meistern und selbst nichts können.

---

[1] **fürsichtiger:** weiser.
[2] According to A. E. Berger, the letter was „an einen nicht genannten, wohl angenommenen Gönner gerichtet."
[3] **zu den Römern:** im Briefe an die Römer.
[4] **wollte ich … finden lassen:** I would have truly found the humility.
[5] **es tut mir sanft:** es tut mir wohl; schmeichelt mir.

---

[6] **Vermögen:** here, ability.
[7] **Ika Ika:** heehaw.
[8] **Liber generationis:** the book of the genealogy (of Jesus Christ).
[9] **Hieronymus:** translator of the Bible into Latin.
[10] **so:** die.

Das ist ihre Art, davon sie nicht lassen kann.

90 Ich wollte noch gern den Papisten ansehen, der sich hervor täte und etwa eine Epistel S. Pauli oder einen Propheten verdeutschte, so fern, daß er des Luthers Deutsch und Dolmetschen nicht dazu gebraucht: da sollte 95 man sehen ein feines, schönes, löbliches Deutsch oder Dolmetschen. Denn wir haben ja gesehen den Sudler[11] zu Dresden, der mein Neues Testament gemeistert hat (ich will seinen Namen in meinen Büchern nicht mehr 100 nennen; so hat er auch nun seinen Richter und ist sonst wohl bekannt). Der bekennt, daß mein Deutsch süß und gut sei und sah wohl, daß er's nicht besser machen könnte, und wollte es doch zu Schanden machen, 105 fuhr zu und nahm vor sich mein Neues Testament fast von Wort zu Wort, wie ich's gemacht habe, und tat meine Vorrede, Glosse und Namen davon, schrieb seinen Namen, Vorrede und Glosse dazu, verkaufte also 110 mein Neues Testament unter seinem Namen . . . .

Und daß ich wieder zur Sache komme, wenn euer Papist sich viel unnütze machen will mit dem Wort *sola*, allein, so sagt ihm 115 flugs also: Doctor Martinus Luther will's also haben und spricht: Papist und Esel sei ein Ding. *Sic volo, sic jubeo, sit pro ratione voluntas.*[12] Denn wir wollen nicht der Papisten Schüler noch Jünger, sondern ihre Meister 120 und Richter sein, wollen auch einmal stolziren und pochen mit den Eselsköpfen; und wie Paulus wider seine tollen Heiligen[13] sich rühmt, so will ich mich auch wider diese meine Esel rühmen. Sie sind Doctores? Ich 125 auch. Sie sind gelehrt? Ich auch. Sie sind Prediger? Ich auch. Sie sind Theologen? Ich auch. Sie sind Disputatores? Ich auch. Sie sind Philosophi? Ich auch. Sie sind Dialectici? Ich auch. Sie sind Legenten? Ich 130 auch. Sie schreiben Bücher? Ich auch.

Und will weiter rühmen: Ich kann Psalmen und Propheten auslegen; das können sie

nicht. Ich kann dolmetschen; das können sie nicht. Ich kann die heilige Schrift lesen; das können sie nicht. Ich kann beten; das können 135 sie nicht. Und daß ich herunter komme, ich kann ihre eigene Dialectica und Philosophie besser, denn sie selbst allesammt. Und weiß dazu fürwahr, daß ihrer keiner ihren Aristoteles versteht. Und ist einer 140 unter ihn allen, der ein *Prooemium* oder Kapitel im Aristoteles recht versteht, so will ich mich prellen[14] lassen. Ich rede jetzt nicht zu viel; denn ich bin durch alle ihre Kunst

Martin Luther. (Bildnis von Lucas Cranach dem Älteren.) *Courtesy of Yale University Library.*

erzogen und erfahren von Jugend auf, weiß 145 sehr wohl, wie tief und weit sie ist. So wissen sie auch wohl, daß ich's alles weiß und kann, was sie können; dennoch handeln die heillosen Leute gegen mich, als wäre ich ein Gast in ihrer Kunst, der allererst heut morgen 150 gekommen wäre und noch nie weder gesehen noch gehört hätte, was sie lehren oder können. . . .

---

[11] **Sudler:** sloven; a polemic allusion to Hieronymus Emser, one of Luther's philological rivals.
[12] **Sic volo ... voluntas:** This I wish, thus I command; be my will sufficient reason (Juvenal, *Satires* vi. 223).
[13] **tollen Heiligen:** reference to II Cor. 11:21 ff.; where Paul attacks the false prophets.

---

[14] **prellen:** toss (in a blanket).

Das sei auf Eure erste Frage geantwortet
155 und bitte Euch, wollt solchen Eseln ja nichts
anders noch mehr antworten auf ihr un-
nützes Geplärre vom Wort *sola*, denn also
viel: Luther will's so haben und spricht, er
sei ein Doctor über alle Doctoren im ganzen
160 Papsttum. Da soll's bei bleiben, ich will sie
hinfort schlecht verachten und verachtet
haben, so lange sie solche Leute (ich wollt
sagen: Esel) sind. Denn es sind solche un-
verschämte Tropfen[15] unter ihnen, die auch
165 ihre eigene, der Sophisten Kunst, nie gelernt
haben, wie Doctor Schmidt[16] und Doctor
Rotzlöffel[17] und seinesgleichen; und legen
sich gleichwohl wider mich in dieser Sache,
die nicht allein über die Sophisterei, sondern
170 auch, wie S. Paulus sagt, über aller Welt
Weisheit und Vernunft ist. Zwar es durfte ein
Esel nicht viel singen, man kennt ihn sonst
wohl bei den Ohren.

Euch aber und den Unsern will ich an-
175 zeigen, warum ich das Wort *sola* habe brauchen wollen, wiewohl Röm. 3,28 nicht *sola*,
sondern *solum* oder *tantum* von mir gebraucht
ist. Also fein sehen die Esel meinen Text an;
aber doch habe ich's sonst anderswo, *sola fide*,
180 gebraucht, und will auch beide, *solum* und *sola*,
haben. Ich habe mich des geflissen im Dolmetschen, daß ich reines und klares Deutsch
geben möchte. Und ist uns wohl oft begegnet,
daß wir vierzehn Tage, drei, vier Wochen
185 ein einziges Wort gesucht und gefragt haben,
haben's dennoch zuweilen nicht gefunden.

Im Hiob arbeiteten wir also, M. Philipps,[18]
Aurogallus[19] und ich, daß wir in vier Tagen
zuweilen kaum drei Zeilen fertigen konnten.
190 Lieber, nun es verdeutscht und bereit ist,
kann's ein Jeder lesen und meistern, läuft
einer jetzt mit den Augen durch drei, vier
Blätter und stößt nicht einmal an; wird aber
nicht gewahr, welche Wacken[20] und Klötze
195 da gelegen sind, da er jetzt überhin geht,

wie über ein gehobeltes Brett, da wir haben
schwitzen müssen und uns ängstigen, ehe
denn wir solche Wacken und Klötze aus dem
Wege räumten, auf daß man könnte so fein
daher gehen. Es ist gut pflügen, wenn der   200
Acker gereinigt ist; aber den Wald und die
Stöcke[21] ausrotten[22] und den Acker zurichten, da will Niemand an. Es ist bei der Welt
kein Dank zu verdienen. Kann doch Gott
selbst mit der Sonne, ja mit Himmel und   205
Erde, noch mit seines eigenen Sohnes Tod
keinen Dank verdienen; sie sei und bleibt
Welt in des Teufels Namen, weil sie ja nichts
anders will.

Ich habe hier Röm. 3,28 sehr wohl gewußt,   210
daß im lateinischen und griechischen Text
das Wort *solum* nicht steht, und hätten mich
solches die Papisten nicht dürfen lehren.[23]
Wahr ist's, diese vier Buchstaben *sola* stehen
nicht drinnen, welche Buchstaben die Esels-   215
köpfe ansehen, wie die Kuh ein neues Tor.
Sehen aber nicht, daß es gleichwohl die
Meinung des Textes in sich hat, und wo
man's will klar und gewaltiglich verdeutsch-
en, so gehört es hinein. Denn ich habe   220
deutsch, nicht lateinisch noch griechisch
reden wollen, da ich deutsch zu reden im
Dolmetschen vorgenommen hatte. Das ist
aber die Art unserer deutschen Sprache:
wenn sich eine Rede begiebt von zwei   225
Dingen, deren man eines bekennt und das
andere verneint, so braucht man des Wortes
„allein" neben dem Wort „nicht" oder
„kein". Als wenn man sagt: Der Bauer
bringt allein Korn und kein Geld. Nein, ich   230
habe wahrlich jetzt nicht Geld, sondern
allein Korn. Ich habe allein gegessen und
noch nicht getrunken. Hast du allein geschrieben und nicht übergelesen? Und
dergleichen unzählige Weise im täglichen   235
Brauch.

In diesen Reden allen, ob's gleich die
lateinische oder griechische Sprache nicht
tut, so tut's doch die deutsche, und ist ihre
Art, daß sie das Wort „allein" hinzusetzt, auf 240
daß das Wort „nicht" oder „kein" desto
völliger und deutlicher sei. Denn wiewohl
ich auch sage: Der Bauer bringt Korn und

---

15 **Tropfen (Tröpfe):** simpletons.
16 **Schmidt:** reference to Johannes Faber; later
   Bishop of Vienna (d. 1541).
17 **Rotzlöffel:** reference to Johannes Cochläus (d.
   1552). (**Cochlear:** *L.* spoon; **Rotzlöffel:** *lit.* a
   spoon of snot. Thus, snot nose, sniveling fellow.)
18 **M. Philipps:** Melanchthon (1497–1560); important
   Humanist.
19 **Aurogallus:** professor of Hebrew at the University
   of Wittenberg.
20 **Wacken:** heavy stones.

21 **Stöcke:** here, root stumps.
22 **ausrotten:** root out.
23 **hätten … lehren:** it was not necessary that the
   Papists teach me this.

kein Geld, so lautet doch das Wort „kein
Geld" nicht so völlig und deutlich, als wenn
ich sage: Der Bauer bringt allein Korn und
kein Geld; und hilft hier das Wort „allein"
dem Wort „kein" so viel, daß es eine völlige
deutsche klare Rede wird.

Denn man muß nicht die Buchstaben in
der lateinischen Sprache fragen, wie man
soll deutsch reden, wie diese Esel tun; sondern man muß die Mutter im Hause, die
Kinder auf der Gasse, den gemeinen Mann
auf dem Markt darum fragen und denselbigen
auf das Maul sehen, wie sie reden, und
darnach dolmetschen, so verstehen sie es
denn und merken, daß man deutsch mit
ihnen redet.

Als wenn Christus spricht Matth. 12,34:
Ex abundantia cordis os loquitur. Wenn ich den
Eseln soll folgen, die werden mir die Buchstaben vorlegen und also dolmetschen: Aus
dem Überfluß des Herzens redet der Mund.
Sage mir, ist das deutsch geredet? Welcher
Deutsche versteht solches? Was ist Überfluß
des Herzens für ein Ding? Das kann kein
Deutscher sagen, er wollte denn sagen, es
sei, daß einer ein allzu großes Herz habe oder
zu viel Herzen habe. Wiewohl das auch noch
nicht recht ist. Denn Überfluß des Herzens
ist kein Deutsch, so wenig als das Deutsch ist:
Überfluß des Hauses, Überfluß des Kachel-
ofens, Überfluß der Bank. Sondern also redet
die Mutter im Haus und der gemeine Mann:
Wes das Herz voll ist, des gehet der Mund
über. Das heißt gut deutsch geredet. Des ich
mich geflissen und leider nicht allwege
erreicht noch getroffen habe. Denn die
lateinischen Buchstaben hindern aus der
Maßen sehr, gut deutsch zu reden . . . .

Item, da der Engel Maria grüßt und
spricht: Gegrüßt seist du, Maria, voll Gnaden,
der Herr mit dir! Wohlan, so ist's bisher
schlecht, den lateinischen Buchstaben nach,
verdeutscht. Sage mir aber, ob solches auch
gut deutsch sei? Wo redet der deutsche
Mann also: Du bist voll Gnaden? Und
welcher Deutscher versteht, was gesagt sei
„voll Gnaden"? Er muß denken an ein Faß
voll Bier oder Beutel voll Geldes. Darum
habe ich's verdeutscht „du Holdselige";
damit doch ein Deutscher desto mehr hinzu-
denken kann, was der Engel mit seinem
Gruß meint. Aber hier wollen die Papisten
toll werden über mich, daß ich den enge-
lischen Gruß verderbt habe; wiewohl ich
dennoch damit nicht das beste Deutsch
getroffen habe. Und hätte ich das beste
Deutsch hier nehmen sollen und den Gruß
also verdeutschen: Gott grüße dich, du
liebe Maria (denn so viel will der Engel
sagen, und so würde er geredet haben, wann
er hätte wollen sie deutsch grüßen); ich halte,
sie sollten sich wohl selbst erhenkt haben
vor großer Andacht zu der lieben Maria, daß
ich den Gruß so zu nichte gemacht hätte.

Aber was frage ich darnach, sie toben oder
rasen? Ich will nicht wehren, daß sie verdeutschen, was sie wollen; ich will aber auch
verdeutschen, nicht wie sie wollen, sondern
wie ich will. Wer es nicht haben will, der laß
mir's stehen und halte seine Meisterschaft bei
sich; denn ich will ihrer weder sehen noch
hören. Sie dürfen für mein Dolmetschen
nicht Antwort geben noch Rechenschaft tun.
Das hörst du wohl, ich will sagen: du holdselige Maria, du liebe Maria; und laß sie
sagen: du voll Gnaden Maria. Wer deutsch
kann, der weiß wohl, welch ein herzlich
feines Wort das ist: die liebe Maria, der liebe
Gott, der liebe Kaiser, der liebe Fürst, der
liebe Mann, das liebe Kind. Und ich weiß
nicht, ob man das Wort „liebe" auch so
herzlich und genugsam in lateinischer oder
andern Sprachen reden möge, daß es also
dringe und klinge in's Herz durch alle Sinne,
wie es tut in unserer Sprache. . . .

Aus dem Neuen Testament (1522)

Matth. 1: 18–2: 12

¹⁸Die gepurt Chriſti war aber alſzo gethan,
Als Maria ſeyne muter dem Joſeph ver=
trawet war, ehe ſie mit eynander zu hauß
ſaſſen, erfand ſichs das ſie ſchwanger war, von
5 dem heyligen geyſt. ¹⁹Joſeph aber yhr man
war frum, vnd wolt ſie nit rugen, gedacht
aber ſie heymlich tzuuerlaſſen, ²⁰In dem er
aber alſzo gedacht, ſihe, da erſchyn yhm eyn
Engell des herrn ym trawm vnd ſprach,
10 Joſeph du ſon Dauid furcht dich nit Mariam
deyn weyb zu dyr zu nehmen, denn das yhn
yhr geporn iſt, das iſt von dem heyligen
geyſt, ²¹vnnd ſie wirt geperen eynen ſon, des
namen ſolltu heyſſen Jheſus, denn er wirt
15 ſeyn volck ſelig machen von yhren ſunden.
²²Das iſt aber alles geſchehen, auff das
erfullet wurd das der herr durch den pro=
pheten geſaget hatt, der do ſpricht. ²³Sihe,
eyne iunckfraw wirt entpfahen vnnd geperen
20 eynen ſon, vnd ſie werden ſeynen namen
heyſſen Emanuel, das iſt verdolmaſchet. Got
mit vns.
²⁴Do nu Joſeph vom ſchlaff erwachte, thet
er wie yhm des herrn Engell befolhen hatte,
25 vnnd nam ſeynn weyb zu ſich, ²⁵vnd er=
kennet ſie nicht, biß ſie yhren erſten ſon gepar,
vnd hieß ſeynen namen Jheſus.

Da Jheſus geporn war zu Bethlehem, yhm
Judiſchen land, tzur tzeyt des konigs Herodis,
30 ſihe, da kamen die weyſen vom morgenland
gen Hieruſalem, vnnd ſprachen. ²Wo iſt der
newgeborne konig der Juden? wyr haben
ſeynen ſtern geſehen ym morgen land, vnd
ſind komen, yhn antzubeten.
35 ³Do das der konig Herodes horte, erſchrack
er vnnd mit yhm das gantz Hieruſalem, ⁴vnd
ließ verſamlen alle hohe Prieſter vnd ſchrifft
gelertenn vntter dem volck, vnd erforſchete
von yhn, wo Chriſtus ſolt geporn werden?
40 ⁵vnnd ſie ſagten yhm, zu Bethlehem yhm
Judiſchen land. Denn alſo iſt geſchrieben
durch den propheten. ⁶Vnd du Bethlehem ym
Judiſchen land biſt mit nichte die kleynſt
vnter den furſten Juda, denn auß dyr ſoll
45 myr komen, der hertzog der vber meyn volck
von Jſrael eyn herr ſey.

Aus dem Neuen Testament (1911)

Das 1. Kapitel

¹⁸Die Geburt Christi war aber also getan.
Als Maria, seine Mutter, dem Joseph ver-
trauet war, fand sich's, ehe er sie heimholte,
daß sie schwanger war von dem heiligen
Geist. ¹⁹Joseph aber, ihr Mann, war fromm 5
und wollte sie nicht in Schande bringen,
gedachte aber, sie heimlich zu verlassen.
²⁰Indem er aber also gedachte, siehe, da
erschien ihm ein Engel des Herrn im Traum
und sprach: Joseph, du Sohn Davids, fürchte 10
dich nicht, Maria, dein Gemahl, zu dir zu
nehmen; denn das in ihr geboren ist, das ist
von dem heiligen Geist. ²¹Und sie wird einen
Sohn gebären, des Namen sollst du Jesus
heißen; denn er wird sein Volk selig machen 15
von ihren Sünden.
²²Das ist aber alles geschehen, auf daß
erfüllet würde, was der Herr durch den
Propheten gesagt hat, der da spricht: ²³Siehe,
eine Jungfrau wird schwanger sein und einen 20
Sohn gebären, und sie werden seinen Namen
Immanuel heißen, das ist verdolmetscht:
Gott mit uns.
²⁴Da nun Joseph vom Schlaf erwachte, tat
er, wie ihm des Herrn Engel befohlen hatte, 25
und nahm sein Gemahl zu sich. ²⁵Und er
erkannte sie nicht, bis sie ihren ersten Sohn
gebar; und hieß seinen Namen Jesus.

Das 2. Kapitel

¹Da Jesus geboren war zu Bethlehem im
jüdischen Lande, zur Zeit des Königs 30
Herodes, siehe, da kamen die Weisen vom
Morgenland nach Jerusalem und sprachen:
²Wo ist der neugeborne König der Juden?
Wir haben seinen Stern gesehen im Morgenland und sind gekommen, ihn anzubeten. 35
³Da das der König Herodes hörte, erschrak
er und mit ihm das ganze Jerusalem. ⁴Und
ließ versammeln alle Hohenpriester und
Schriftgelehrten unter dem Volk und erforschte von ihnen, wo Christus sollte geboren 40
werden. ⁵Und sie sagten ihm: Zu Bethlehem

⁷Da berieff Herodes die weysen heymlich, vnd erlernet mit vleyß von yhnen, wenn der stern erschynen were, ⁸vnd weyßet sie gen Bethlehem, vnnd sprach, ziehet hyn, vnd forsschet vleyssig nach dem kyndlin, vnnd wen yhrß findet, sagt myr widder, das ich auch kome vnd es anbete.

⁹Als sie nu den konig gehort hatten, zogen sie hyn, vnnd, sihe der stern, den sie ym morgen land gesehen hatten, gieng fur yhn hyn, biß das er kam, vnd stund oben vber, da das kyndlin war. ¹⁰Da sie den stern sahen, wurden sie hoch erfrawet, ¹¹vnd giengen ynn das hauß, vnd funden das kyndlin mit Maria seyner mutter, vnnd fielen nyder, vnnd betten es an, vnd theten yhre schetze auff, vnnd legten yhm geschenck fur, gollt, weyrack vnnd myrrhen. ¹²Vnnd gott befahl yhn ym trawm, das sie sich nitt sollten widder zu Herodes lencken, vnd zogen durch eynen andern weg wydder ynn yhr land.

im jüdischen Lande; denn also steht geschrieben durch den Propheten: ⁶Und du Bethlehem im jüdischen Lande bist mitnichten die kleinste unter den Fürsten Judas; denn aus dir soll mir kommen der Herzog, der über mein Volk Israel ein Herr sei. ⁷Da berief Herodes die Weisen heimlich und erlernte mit Fleiß von ihnen, wann der Stern erschienen wäre, ⁸und wies sie gen Bethlehem und sprach: Ziehet hin und forschet fleißig nach dem Kindlein; und wenn ihr's findet, so sagt mir's wieder, daß ich auch komme und es anbete.

⁹Als sie nun den König gehört hatten, zogen sie hin. Und siehe, der Stern, den sie im Morgenland gesehen hatten, ging vor ihnen hin, bis daß er kam und stand oben über, da das Kindlein war. ¹⁰Da sie den Stern sahen, wurden sie hoch erfreut ¹¹und gingen in das Haus und fanden das Kindlein mit Maria, seiner Mutter, und fielen nieder und beteten es an und taten ihre Schätze auf und schenkten ihm Gold, Weihrauch und Myrrhe. ¹²Und Gott befahl ihnen im Traum, daß sie sich nicht sollten wieder zu Herodes lenken; und sie zogen durch einen andern Weg wieder in ihr Land.

Das Volksbuch
von Doctor Faustus

The rapid development of the printing press in the mid-fifteenth century coincided with the growing concentration of populations in the cities and a renewed interest in learning, creating for the first time, in Europe and in Germany in particular, a literary mass-market as well as the means for supplying it; more people were able to read more printed chronicles, stories, and narratives. In the Romantic period it was assumed that the *Volksbücher* had their origin in the creative depth of the people; modern scholarship believes that the authors, as far as we know, were erudite amateurs (including noblewomen), clerics, and professors. The traditional term *Volksbücher* does have its sociological meaning; referring to the audience, it pertains to the most popular reading matter, the "best sellers," of the fifteenth, sixteenth, and seventeenth centuries; some of the stories, to be sure, survived among the less educated and in distant farm districts into the late nineteenth century. At the outset, the *Volksbücher* were still attractive to the erudite and scholarly and only later occupied a ground completely outside the sphere of the intellectual elite. Almost anything marketable served as raw material for the printers in Augsburg, Ulm, Straßburg, and Nuremberg: cosmographies, legends, oriental tales, simplified versions of knightly epics, chronicles, and collections of anecdotes. Although the production of these books was directed in the beginning at the well-to-do customer, their quality sharply deteriorated after 1550; cheaper paper, crude woodcuts, and a smaller format were used to satisfy the popular interest; thus the chapbook (the paperback of the fifteenth century) took the place of the "hard-cover" folio. Opposition against this kind of literature grew among the theologians; in the eighteenth century elegant writers and critics considered the *Volksbücher* worthless pulp, which in many cases they were. Only after the generation of Rousseau and Herder had made its claims for the collective gifts of the people, did poets and critics of the *Sturm und Drang* cherish the *Volksbücher* again, passing their enthusiasm on to the Romantics who delighted in and used the stories of Griseldis, Octavianus, and Faust. This is a peculiarly German development. If the generation of 1770 and the younger Romantics had not restored the chapbook to literary dignity and meaning, the *Volksbücher* would be nearly forgotten today as they are in France and England.

The chapbook of Doctor Faustus relates to the life and fate of a colorful mountebank of whose appearances in German taverns and fairs (from *c.* 1506 to 1536/39) we know from the letters and documents of some of his more staid compatriots. The historical Faust little resembled the figure in the *Volksbuch*, in Goethe's tragedy, or in Thomas Mann's novel. He was a "con man," homosexual, quack, vagabond, and purveyor of expensive horoscopes who deeply impressed the simpler minds only to astonish and disgust the more erudite and scholarly. Stories about his boasting, his promises, and his predictions accumulated and crystallized soon after his death. We first hear of his horrible end in 1548, and in the fifties a Latin story about his life was current among the Erfurt students who in turn elaborated upon his academic erudition and his pact with the Devil. In 1587, the first printed story of his life appeared at the shop of Johann Spieß (Frankfurt) and, as is borne out by contemporary business correspondence, was an immediate success; in an age in which people believed in the reality of the Devil, Faust was a deeply disturbing figure. But the story of the man who allied himself with God's adversary survived the time of its origins; the narration of his life and death was reedited, reprinted, transmuted and refined, turning out to be immensely adaptable through the centuries: Marlowe and the Elizabethan theater, Lessing and Goethe, Berlioz and Gounod, Stephen Vincent Benét and Paul Valéry were attracted by the richness of its implications. From the *Volksbuch* emerges, still in embryonic form, one of the mythical figures of our modern imagination.

DOCTOR FAUSTUS

Johannes Faustus, der weitberühmte Schwarzkünstler, ward geboren in der Grafschaft Anhalt,[1] und haben seine Eltern gewohnt in dem Markt oder Flecken Sond-
5 wedel: die waren arme fromme Bauersleute. Er hatte aber einen reichen Vetter zu Wittenberg, welcher seines Vaters Bruder war, derselbe hatte keine Leibeserben, darum er denn diesen jungen Faustus, welchen er
10 wegen seines fähigen Geistes herzlich lieb gewonnen hatte, an Kindes Statt auferzog und zur Schule fleißig anhielt; worauf dieser mit zunehmendem Alter von ihm auf die Hohe Schule zu Ingolstadt[2] geschickt worden.
15 Hier tat sich der junge Faustus in Künsten und Wissenschaften trefflich hervor, so daß er in der Prüfung elf andern Meistern der freien Künste vorangesetzt und selbst mit dem Magisterkäppchen geschmückt wurde.
20 Damals aber, da das alte päpstliche Wesen noch überall im Schwange ging, und man hin und wieder viel Segensprechen, Geisterbeschwören, Teufelsbannen und ander abergläubisches Tun trieb, beliebte auch
25 solches dem Faustus überaus. Weil er denn zu böser und gleichgesinnte Gesellschaft, ja unter solche Bursche geriet, welche mit dergleichen abergläubischen Zeichen-Schriften umgingen, die Studien aber auf die Seite
30 setzten, ward er gar bald und leicht verführt. Zu diesem kam noch, daß er sich zu den damals umschweifenden Zigeunern fleißig hielt, und von ihnen die Chiromantie, wie man nämlich aus den Händen wahrsagen
35 möge, erlernte: dazu in allerlei Zauberkünste, wo er nur Gelegenheit fand, sich einweihen ließ.
Als er nun in diese Dinge ganz versunken war, und sich also den Teufel gar einnehmen
40 ließ,[3] fiel er von der Theologie ab, legte sich mit Fleiß auf die Arzneikunst, erforschte den Himmelslauf, lernte den Leuten, was sie von ihrer Geburtzeit an für Glück und Unglück erleben sollen, verkündigen, und wußte mit Kalender- und Almanach-Rechnung wohl 45 umzugehen. Endlich kam er gar auf die Beschwörungen der Geister, welchen er dergestalt nachgrübelte und darin dermaßen zunahm, daß er zuletzt ein ausgemachter Teufelsbeschwörer wurde. 50

$$* \quad * \quad *$$

Als nun Doctor Faustus in seiner teuflischen Kunst erlernt und studieret, so viel ihm dienstlich sein würde, dasjenige zu überkommen, was er lang zuvor begehret hatte: siehe, da geht er einst an einem heitern 55 Tage aus der Stadt Wittenberg, um einen bequemen und gelegenen Ort zu finden, wo er füglich seine Teufelsbeschwörungen in's Werk setzen möchte, und findet auch endlich, ungefähr einer halben Meile Wegs von der 60 Stadt gelegen, einen Wegscheid,[4] welcher fünf Ausfahrten hatte, dabei auch groß und breit und also ein erwünschter Ort war. Hier verblieb er den ganzen Nachmittag, und nachdem der Abend herbeigekommen und 65 er gesehen, daß keine Fuhre mehr oder jemand anders durchging, nahm er einen Reif, wie die Küfer oder Büttner haben, machte daran viel wunderseltsame Charactere,[5] und setzte daneben noch zwei andere 70 Zirkel oder Kreise. Und da er solches alles nach Ausweisung der Nekromantie bestermaßen angestellt hatte, ging er in den Wald, der allernächst dabei gelegen war, der Spessart-Wald genannt, und erwartete mit Ver 75 langen die Mitternachtszeit, wo der Mond sein volles Licht haben würde: kaum aber ist die Zeit herbeigekommen, so beschwört er gleich zum Anfang, in den mittlern Reif tretend, unter Verlästerung des göttlichen 80 Namens, den Teufel zum ersten und andern und drittenmal.
Kaum waren die Worte recht ausgeredet, da sah er alsobald, während der Mond schon hell schien, eine feurige Kugel anher kom 85 men, die ging dem Kreise zu mit solchem

---

[1] **Anhalt:** region in central Germany.
[2] **Ingolstadt:** old university town in Bavaria. In 1802, the university was moved to Landshut and (later) to Munich: It is no coincidence that Mary Shelley's Frankenstein, following Faustus' example, also studied in Ingolstadt.
[3] **sich . . . liess:** let himself be completely taken in by the devil.

[4] **Wegscheid:** crossroad; since antiquity a place of special magical power.
[5] **Charactere:** i.e., letters, figures, symbols.

Knallen, gleich als ob eine Muskete wäre
losgebrannt worden, fuhr aber gleich darauf
mit einem feurigen Strahl in die Luft, ob
90 welchem allen denn der Doctor Faustus sehr
erschrak, so daß er auch aus dem Kreise
laufen wollte. Weil er jedoch, dem Reif
entwichen, nicht mehr lebendig heim zu
kommen hoffte, so faßte er sich wieder einen
95 Mut und beschwor den Teufel von Neuem
auf obige Weise; aber da wollte sich nichts
mehr regen, noch ein Teufel sehen lassen.
Er nahm derhalb eine härtere Beschwörung
zur Hand. Alsbald entstand im Wald ein
100 solcher ungestümer Wind und solches
Brausen, daß es das Ansehen hatte, als ob
Alles zu Grunde gehen wollte: kurz darauf
rannten etliche Wagen mit Rossen bespannt
bei dem Reif in Einem Rasen vorbei, und
105 machten einen solchen Staub, daß Faustus,
bei dem hellen Mondenschein, nichts sehen
konnte. Da endlich, obwohl Doctor Faust,
wie leicht zu glauben, so erschrocken und
verzagt war, daß er schier auf seinen Füßen
110 nicht mehr stehen konnte, und wohl mehr
als hundertmal wünschte, daß er hundert
Meilen Wegs von da wäre, sah er wider alles
Verhoffen, gleich als unter einem Schatten,
ein Gespenst oder einen Geist um den Kreis
115 herum wandern. Mutig beschwor er den
Geist: er sollte sich erklären, ob er ihm
dienen wollte, oder nicht? er sollte nur frei
reden. Der Geist gab bald zur Antwort:
„er wolle ihm dienen, jedoch mit diesem
120 Bedinge,[6] daß, so er anders etlichen Artikeln
nachkommen wolle, welche er ihm vorhalten
werde, er die Zeit seines Lebens nicht von
ihm scheiden werde." Doctor Faustus vergaß
auf dieses all seines vorigen Leides und
125 empfundenen Schreckens, und war in seinem
Gemüte recht fröhlich und zufrieden, daß
er endlich, nach so vielen Sorgen, dasjenige
überkommen[7] sollte, wornach[8] sein Herz so
lange Zeit verlanget hatte; daher sprach er
130 getrost zu dem Geist: „Wohlan, dieweil
Du mir dienen willst, so beschwöre ich Dich
nochmals zum ersten, andern und drittenmal,
daß Du morgen in meiner Behausung erscheinen sollest; allwo wir denn von allem

dem, was ich und Du zu tun haben, zur   135
Genüge reden und handeln wollen." Dieses
sagte der Geist dem Doctor Faustus zu:
alsobald zertrat dieser den Zirkel mit Füßen,
ging mit Freuden heraus, eilte der Stadtpforte
zu und erwartete mit sehnlichem Verlangen   140
den bald ankommenden Tag.
   Nun saß er unter tausenderlei verwirrten
Gedanken in seinem Stüblein. Eine, zwei
und mehr Stunden laufen vorbei, der Geist
will doch nicht erscheinen; hinter, vor und   145
neben sich forschet ohne Unterlaß Doctor
Faustus, ob er noch nichts erblicken möge;
aber Alles vergebens, so daß er sich schon
des Geistes und seiner Erscheinung verzeihen
wollte: endlich, da ersiehet er zur Mittagszeit 150
etwas nahe bei dem Ofen gleich als einen
Schatten hergehen, und dünkte ihm doch, es
wäre ein Mensch; bald aber sieht er denselben
auf eine andere Weise; daher er denn zur
Stunde seine Beschwörung auf's neue anfing, 155
und den Geist beschwor, er sollte sich recht
sehen lassen. Da ist alsobald der Geist hinter
den Ofen gewandert, und hat den Kopf als
ein Mensch hervorgesteckt, sich sichtbarlich
sehen lassen, und vor dem Doctor Faustus   160
sich wieder und wieder gebücket und seine
Reverenz gemacht. Nach einigem Bedenken
begehrte Faust, der Geist sollte hervorgehen
und ihm, seinem Versprechen nach, die
Punkte vorhalten, unter deren Beding er   165
ihm dienen wolle. Der Geist schlug ihm
solches anfangs ab, und meinte, er sei so gar
weit nicht von ihm, er könne dennoch mit
ihm von allerhand nötigen Dingen Unterredung pflegen. Da ereiferte sich Faustus,   170
und wollte auf's neue seine Verschwörung
anfangen, und ihm noch härter zusetzen;
das aber war dem Geist nicht gelegen und
so ging er hinter dem Ofen hervor. Da sah
nun Faust mehr, als ihm lieb war, denn die 175
Stube ward in einem Augenblick voller
Feuerflammen, die sich hin und wieder
ausbreiteten; der Geist hatte zwar einen
natürlichen Menschenkopf, aber sein ganzer
Leib war gar zottig, gleich als eines Bären, 180
und mit feurigen Augen blickte er Faustum
an, worüber dieser sehr erschrak und ihm
befahl, er sollte sich wieder hinter den Ofen
ducken, wie er auch tat. Darauf fragte ihn
Doctor Faustus, ob er sich nicht anders, denn 185
in einer so abscheulichen und greulichen

---

[6] **Bedinge:** Bedingung.
[7] **überkommen:** here, to obtain.
[8] **wornach:** wonach.

Gestalt zeigen könnte? Der Geist antwortete:
Nein; denn, sagte er, er wäre kein Diener,
sondern ein Fürst unter den Geistern; wenn
190 er ihm dasjenige leisten und halten wolle,
was er ihm vorhalten werde, so wolle er
ihm einen Geist zuschicken, der ihm bis an
sein Ende dienen werde, und nicht von ihm
weichen, ja in allem und jedem willfahren,
195 was nur seinem Herzen würde belieben zu
wünschen und zu begehren.

    Auf solchen Vorschlag des Satans ant-
wortete Faust, er solle ihm nur sein Verlangen
eröffnen und vorhalten. Der Teufel spricht:
200 „So schreibe sie denn von Wort zu Worten
auf, und gib alsdann richtigen Bescheid, es
wird Dich nicht gereuen! Ich will Dir hiermit fünf Artikel vorschreiben: nimmst Du
sie an, wohl und gut; wo aber nicht, sollst
205 Du mich hinfüro[9] nicht mehr zwingen zu
erscheinen, wenn Du auch gleich alle Deine
Kunst zu Rate ziehen würdest." Also nahm
Doctor Faustus seine Feder zur Hand und
verzeichnete, wie folgt:

210   1) Er soll Gott und allem himmlischen
        Heer absagen.
    2) Er soll aller Menschen Feind sein,
        und sonderlich derjenigen, so ihn
        seines bösen Lebens wegen würden
215   strafen wollen.
    3) Den Pfaffen und geistlichen Per-
        sonen soll er nicht gehorchen,
        sondern sie anfeinden.
    4) Zu keiner Kirche gehen, die
220   Predigten nicht besuchen, auch die
        Sakramente nicht gebrauchen.
    5) Den Ehestand hassen, sich in
        denselben nicht einlassen, nie
        verehelichen.

225 Wenn er diese fünf Artikel wolle annehmen, so solle er sie zur Bestätigung mit
seinem eigenen Blute bekräftigen, und ihm
einen Schuldbrief, von seiner eigenen Hand
geschrieben, übergeben, alsdann wolle er
230 ihn zu einem Mann machen, der nicht allein
alle erdenkliche Lust und Freude haben und
die Zeit seines Lebens über genießen solle,
sondern es sollte auch seines gleichen in der
Kunst nicht sein.
235 Doctor Faustus saß hierüber in sehr tiefen

---

[9] hinfüro: von nun an.

Gedanken, und je mehr und öfter er diese
greuliche und gottsvergessene Artikel
übersah und überlas, je schwerer sie ihm zu
halten fallen wollten: doch bedachte er sich
endlich und meinte, weil doch der Teufel 240
ein Lügner sei, und ihm schwerlich alles
dasjenige, wonach etwa sein Herz verlangen
würde, seiner Zusage nach, schaffen und
zuwege bringen würde, so wolle er auch
alsdann noch wohl andern Sinnes werden. 245
Und wenn es ja mit der Zeit dahin käme,
daß er ihn, als sein wahres Unterpfand, haben
und hinnehmen wollte, so könnte er wohl
bei Zeiten ausreißen und sich wiederum mit
der christlichen Kirche versöhnen; würde 250
ihm denn über alles Verhoffen Zeit und
Raum zu kurz, sich zu bekehren, so habe er
gleichwohl nach seines Herzens Lust und
Begierde in dieser Welt gelebt: halte der
Geist etwa in einem und anderm keinen 255
Glauben, trotz seiner Zusage, so sei er ihm
auch hinwiederum nicht Glauben zu halten
schuldig.

    So sagte er endlich in Leichtsinn und
Gottesvergessenheit zu einem Artikel um 260
den andern laut und unumwunden j a. Der
Geist aber, auf des Doctors deutliche Erklärung, wendete nichts weiter ein und sprach:
„So komm denn, so viel Dir immer möglich
ist, diesen Forderungen nach; aber Deine 265
eigene Handschrift mit Deinem Blut gezeich-
net wirst Du mir geben; stelle es also an, und
lege sie auf den Tisch, so will ich sie holen."
Doctor Faustus antwortete: „Wohlan, es ist
so gut: aber eines bitte ich Dich zum Letzten, 270
daß Du mir nicht mehr so greulich und in
Deiner jetzigen Gestalt erscheinen wollest,
sondern etwa in eines Mönchs oder eines
andern bekleideten Menschen Gestalt",
welches denn der Geist dem Faustus zusagte 275
und also verschwand.

    Nachdem nun der höllische Geist gewichen,
vielleicht die Zeit zu gewinnen, um die
versprochene Handschrift zu fertigen, hätte
Faust wohl noch Zeit gehabt, seinen Abfall 280
von Gott mit reuigem, bußfertigem Herzen
gut zu machen: allein er trachtete nur dahin,
wie er seine Wollust und sein Mütlein in
dieser Welt recht abkühlen möchte, und war
eben auch der Meinung, welcher jener 285
vornehme Herr gewesen, der unter andern auf

Dr. Faustus übergibt dem Teufel den Pakt.
(Aus einer spätromantischen Ausgabe des
Volksbuches.) *Courtesy of Yale University
Library*.

dem Reichstage[10] zu etlichen gesagt hat: Himmel hin, Himmel her, ich nehme hier das Meinige, mit dem ich mich auch erlustige, und lasse Himmel Himmel sein; wer weiß, ob die Auferstehung der Toten wahr sei?

So nahm denn Faustus ein spitziges Schreibmesser und öffnete sich an der linken Hand ein Äderlein; das ausfließende Blut faßte er in ein Glas, setzte sich nieder und schrieb mit seinem Blut und eigener Hand nachfolgenden Schuldbrief:

„Ich Johannes Faustus, Doctor, bekenne hier öffentlich am Tag, nachdem ich jederzeit zu Gemüt gefasset, wie diese Welt mit allerlei Weisheit, Geschicklichkeit, Hoheit begabet, und allezeit mit hochverständigen Leuten geblühet hat; dieweil ich denn von Gott dem Schöpfer nicht also erleuchtet, und doch der Magie fähig bin, auch dazu meine Natur himmlischen Einflüssen geneigt, zudem auch gewiß und am Tage ist, daß der irdische Gott, den die Welt den Teufel pflegt zu nennen, so erfahren, gewaltig und geschickt ist, daß ihm nichts unmöglich ist; so wende ich mich nun zu ihm, und nach seinem Versprechen soll er mir Alles leisten und erfüllen, was mein Herz, Gemüt und Sinn begehret und haben will, und soll an nichts ein Mangel sichtbar werden; und so denn dem also sein wird, so verschreibe ich mich hiermit mit meinem eigenen Blut, welches ich, obwohl ich bekennen muß, daß ich's von dem Gott des Himmels empfangen habe, samt Leib und Gliedmaßen, so mir durch meine Eltern gegeben sind, mit allem, was an mir ist, samt meiner Seele, hiemit diesem irdischen Gott zu Kaufe gebe, und verspreche mich ihm mit Leib und Seele.

Dagegen sage ich vermöge der mir vorgehaltenen Artikel ab allem himmlischen Heer, und Allem, was Gottes Freund sein mag. Zur Bekräftigung meiner Verheißung will ich diesem allen treulich nachkommen; und dieweil unser aufgerichtetes Bündnis vierundzwanzig Jahr währen soll, so soll denn der Satan, wenn diese Jahre verflossen sind, dieses sein Unterpfand, Leib und Seele, angreifen, und darüber zu schalten und zu walten Macht haben: soll auch kein Wort

Gottes, auch nicht die solches predigen und vortragen, hierin einige Verhinderung tun, ob sie mich schon bekehren wollten.

Zu Urkund dieser Handschrift habe ich solche mit meinem eigenen Blute bekräftiget und eigenhändig geschrieben.

FAUSTUS, DOCTOR.“

Als er nun solche gräßliche Verschreibung verfertiget hatte, erschien bald darauf der Teufel in eines grauen Mönchs Gestalt und trat zu ihm, da denn Doctor Faustus ihm seine Handschrift eingehändigt, darauf dieser gesagt: „Fauste, dieweil Du denn mir Dich also verschrieben hast, so sollst Du wissen, daß Dir auch soll treulich gedienet werden. Ich jedoch, als der Fürst dieser Welt, diene persönlich keinem Menschen; Alles, was unter dem Himmel ist, das ist mein, darum diene ich niemand: aber morgenden Tags will ich Dir einen gelehrten und erfahrenen Geist senden, der soll Dir die Zeit Deines Lebens dienen und gehorsam sein; sollst Dich auch vor ihm nicht fürchten noch entsetzen, er soll Dir in der Gestalt eines grauen Mönchs, wie ich anjetzo, erscheinen und dienen. Hiermit nehme ich diese Deine Handschrift; und gehabe Dich wohl!“ Also verschwand er.

Gleich Abends, als Doctor Faustus nun zu Nacht gegessen hatte und kaum in seine Studierstube gekommen war, siehe, da klopft jemand sittiglich an der Stubentüre, dessen Faustus sonst nicht gewohnt war, zumal die Haustüren allbereits verschlossen waren. Er merkte aber bald, was es bedeute, und öffnete die Tür: da stand ihm gegenüber eine lange in grauen Mönchshabit gekleidete Person, dem Ansehen nach eines ziemlichen Alters: denn der Fremde hatte ein ganz graues Bärtlein; den hieß er alsbald in die Stube gehen und sich zu ihm auf die Bank niedersitzen, welches der Geist auch getan. Auf das Befragen des Doctors, was denn des Geistes Geschäft sei, antwortete dieser: „O Fauste, wie hast Du mir meine Herrlichkeit genommen, daß ich nun eines Menschen Diener sein muß! Dieweil ich aber von unserm Obersten dazu gezwungen worden, muß ich es wohl lassen geschehen. Wenn aber das Ziel wird erreicht sein, so wird es mir iene kurze Zeit gewesen dünken, Dir aber

---

[10] **Reichstag:** here, assembly of the higher clergy and secular princes.

wird es ein Anfang sein einer unseligen, unendlichen Zeit! So will ich mich nun von jetzo Dir ganz unterwürfig machen, sollst 390 auch keinen Mangel bei mir haben, ich will Dir treulich dienen; so sollst Du Dich auch vor mir nicht entsetzen, denn ich bin kein scheußlicher Teufel, sondern ein *Spiritus familiaris,* d.i.,[11] ein vertraulicher Geist, der 395 gerne bei den Menschen wohnet."

„Wohlan denn", sagte hierauf Doctor Faustus, „so gelobe mir im Namen Deines Herrn Luzifer, daß Du allem fleißig nachkommen wollest, was ich Dir werde zumuten 400 und von Dir begehren." Der Geist beantwortete solches mit Ja. „Du sollst zugleich wissen", sagte er, „daß ich werde Mephistopheles genennet: und bei diesem Namen sollst Du mich hinfort jederzeit rufen, wenn 405 Du etwas von mir begehren willst, denn also heiße ich." Doctor Faustus erfreute sich hierüber in seinem Gemüthe, daß nun sein Begehren einmal zu einem erwünschten Ende gekommen sei, und sprach: „Nun, Mephis- 410 topheles, mein getreuer Diener, wie ich verhoffe, so wirst Du Dich allezeit gehorsamlich finden lassen, und in dieser Gestalt, wie Du jetzund erschienen bist. Ziehe nur für diesesmal wiederum hin, bis auf mein 415 ferneres Berufen." Auf diesen Bescheid bückte sich der Geist, und verschwand.

*   *   *

In Wahrheit hatte aber Faust auch ein herrliches Leben voll zeitlicher Macht und Wollust. In einem schönen, stattlichen Hause 420 bewohnte er zwei Säle, dort vernahm man mitten in der Winterszeit den Zusammenklang eines lieblichen Vogelgesanges; die Amsel, die Wachtel schlug fröhlich, die Nachtigall tirilirte unvergleichlich; der Papagei, ge- 425 genüber hängend, redete aufs Zierlichste: die Zimmer waren mit den schönsten Tapeten behangen, mit herrlichen Gemälden geziert, und mit Kostbarkeiten aller Art ausgestattet. Im Vorhofe des anstoßenden Zaubergartens 430 sah man mit Lust indianische Hähne und Hennen, Rebhühner und Haselhühner,

Kraniche, Reiher, Schwäne und Störche, ohne alle Scheu, lustwandeln. Der Garten selbst war nicht sonderlich groß, aber ausbündig herrlich, denn da, wiewohl sonst zur 435 Winterszeit in der Stadt Alles mit Schnee bedeckt war, sah man nie Winter, sondern immer nur lustigen, fröhlichen Sommer mit Gewächsen, Laub und Gras und den buntesten Blumen; dazu waren schöne Weinstöcke 440 zu sehen mit mancherlei Trauben behängt, alle schon reif; bunte Tulpen, gefüllte Josephsstäbe;[12] Narzissen und Rosen blühten und flammten dazwischen. An den Mauern des Gartens der Länge nach waren Granaten-, 445 Pomeranzen-, Limonien-, und Citronenbäume in schnurgeraden Reihen aufgestellt; Kirschen-, Birn-, und Apfelbäume standen bunt durcheinander, wie ein Wald, und alle hingen immer voll Früchte. Ja, da mochte 450 man erst Wunder sehen, denn da waren Birnbäume, die trugen Datteln, und junge Kirschbäume, daran hingen Feigen; und wiederum an dichten Apfelbäumen waren zeitige[13] schwarze Kastanien zu sehen. Zu 455 oberst im Hause, da stand ein schmuckes Taubenhaus, darin flogen Tauben aller Art und von den seltensten Farben, und nicht nur zahme, sondern auch wilde Feldtauben aus und ein. Unter aber im Hause, vor einem 460 Stall an der Einfahrt, lag des Doctor Faustus großer Zauberhund, der ihm, wenn er aus dem Hause ging, nicht von der Seite wich. Sein Name war Prästigiar,[14] oder Hexenmeister; der hatte Augen ganz feuerrot und 465 greulich, und schwarzes zottiges Haar; wenn ihm aber Faust über den Rücken fuhr, verwandelte sich seine Farbe und wurde bald grau, bald weiß, bald gelblich oder braun, und das Tier machte gar seltsame Sprünge 470 und Gaukeleien, wenn es mit seinem wunderlichen Herrn, der auch seinen eigenen Schritt hatte, dahinpudelte.

*   *   *

Doctor Faustus verbrachte ... ein rohes,

---

[11] **d.i.:** das ist.

[12] **Josephsstäbe:** Pseudo-Narcissus *L.* (common daffodil).

[13] **zeitige:** here, ripe.

[14] **Prästigiar:** prestidigitator.

475 sicheres und wüstes Leben, daß er das tägliche
Vollsaufen, Spielen und Buhlen für seine
höchste Ergötzlichkeit hielt. Er ersah aber
... in seiner Nachbarschaft eine schöne, doch
arme Dirne,[15] welche vom Land herein in
480 die Stadt gekommen, und sich in Dienste bei
einem Krämer begeben hatte; diese gefiel
nun Doctor Faust über die Maßen wohl,
daß er nach ihr auf allerlei Weise und Wege
trachtete und sie zu eigen haben wollte.
485 Die Jungfrau aber wollte niemals, was man
ihr auch versprechen mochte, in seinen
sündlichen Willen sich fügen, sondern sie
blieb ehrlich, und wollte nur von der Ehe
hören. Dazu rieten dem verliebten Faustus
490 denn endlich auch seine guten Brüder und
Freunde: der Geist Mephistopheles aber, als
er dieses vermerkte, sprach unverzüglich zu
Doctor Faust: was er nunmehr, da die ver-
sprochenen Jahre bald zu Ende sein würden,
495 aus sich selbst machen wolle? Er solle gedenken an seine Zusage und sein Versprechen,
zudem, so könne er sich in keinen Ehestand
einlassen, dieweil er nicht zwei Herren
zugleich dienen könne: „Denn der Ehestand
500 ist ein Werk des Höchsten, den wir Teufel
auf's Höchste hassen und verfolgen. Derohalben,[16] Fauste, siehe Dich vor: wirst Du
Dich versprechen zu verehelichen, so sollst
Du gewiß von uns zu kleinen Stücken zer-
505 rissen werden. Denke doch bei Dir selbst,
wie der Ehestand eine so große und schwere
Last auf sich hat, und was jederzeit für
Unlust daraus ist entstanden, Unruhe, Wider-
willen, Zorn, Neid, Uneinigkeit, Sorge,
510 Zerstörung der fröhlichen Herzen und
Gemüter, und was dessen mehr ist."
Dem allen gedachte zwar Doctor Faustus
eine Weile nach, er wollte aber doch auf
seiner Meinung verharren, wendete auch das
515 Rauhe heraus,[17] und sagte dem Geist:
„Kurzum, ich will mich verehelichen, es folge
gleich daraus was da wolle," gehet damit
hinweg und in seine obere Stube. Was folgte
aber hierauf? Alsbald gehet ein großer
520 Sturmwind seinem Hause zu, als wollte er's

zu Grunde werfen, es sprangen inwendig
alle Angel der Türen auf, und ward das
Haus voller Feuer. Doctor Faust lief die
Stiege hinab, wollte die Haustüre suchen und
davon laufen, da erhaschet ihn ein Mann, der 525
warf ihn zurück wie ein Ballen in die Stube
hinein, daß er weder Hände noch Füße regen
konnte; um ihn her ging allenthalben Feuer
auf, gleich als ob er jetzt verbrennen sollte;
er schrie in diesen Nöten zu seinem Geist um 530
Hilfe, er solle die Gefahr nur diesmal von
ihm abwenden; dann wolle er versprechen,
hinfort in Allem nach seinem Willen zu
leben.
Da erschien ihm der Fürst Luzifer ganz 535
schrecklich und leibhaftig, so grausam anzusehen, daß Faust auch seine Augen vor ihm
zuhielt, und seines elenden Endes gewärtig
war. Darauf ließ sich Luzifer also vernehmen:
„Sage nun an, wes Sinnes bist Du?" Doctor 540
Faustus, ganz kleinmütig und erschrocken,
auch mit zugetanen Augen, antwortet: „O Du
gewaltiger Fürst dieser Welt, verlängere mir
meine Tage, Du siehest, daß ich ein ver-
kehrtes, wankelmütiges Menschenherz habe, 545
daß ich auf andere Gedanken, welche Dir
zuwider sind, gefallen bin, hab' aber das
Werk noch nicht erfüllt; deswegen bitte ich
Dich, Du wollest noch zur Zeit nicht Hand
an mich legen, ich kann bald andern Sinnes 550
werden." Der Satan gab hierauf die Antwort
mit kurzen Worten: „Wohlan, siehe zu, daß
dem also sein möge, und beharre darauf, das
sage ich Dir bei meiner Gewalt"; und also
verschwand er samt dem Feuer. 555

* * *

Independent, affluent, of insatiable appetites,
Faustus, the one-time scholar, astonishes the
small university town with his provocative ut-
terances, practical jokes, and magic performances.
One night, he unfolds his coat in the garden, creates
a gust of wind, and flies three young barons to
Munich; on market day, he cheats a trader by
selling him a horse that changes into an old broom
as soon as it is touched by water; in Leipzig, he
rides a heavy wine barrel up the cellar stairs as
if it were a toy. He particularly likes to conjure
up the heroic figures of old epic poetry: one evening

---

[15] **Dirne:** here, a young girl of low social class.
[16] **derohalben:** deshalb.
[17] **wendete das Rauhe heraus:** schlug einen rauhen
Ton an.

he confronts his students with a procession of Homeric figures including the one-eyed giant Polyphemos; and, having been invited by the Emperor Maximilian to Innsbruck, he conjures up the great Alexander and his wife. But Faustus is not satisfied with these triumphs; he thinks of marrying a young girl and thereby displeases the Prince of Hell.

In order to satisfy Faustus' appetites while making him forget marriage, Mephistopheles inspires him to desire Helen of Troy, the most beautiful woman of the ancient world. Mephistopheles brings her forth from the realm of the dead; she has eine schöne längliche Gestalt, *and Faustus immediately falls in love; to the Devil's satisfaction, however, he does not intend to marry her. Helen becomes pregnant and gives birth to a son whom Faustus tenderly calls Justus Faustus. Unfortunately, Helen takes her son with her when she finally disappears, and Faustus is again left alone. He now realizes that the twenty-four years have passed and gathers his students and his assistant, Wagner, to distribute among them the riches he has accumulated; at first, he seems quite calm, but when the Devil appears and presents the signed agreement, he knows that the moment of reckoning has come.*

Das Stundenglas hatte sich nunmehr umgewendet, war ausgelaufen, die bestimmten vierundzwanzig Jahre Doctor Fausts oder die Endschaft seiner Verschreibung war
560 nun am nächsten, deswegen erschien ihm der Teufel abermal, und zwar in eben dieser Gestalt, wie er damals den verdammlichen Bund mit ihm aufgerichtet[18] hatte, zeigte ihm seine Handschrift, darin er ihm mit seinem
565 eigenen Blut seinen Leib und seine Seele verschrieben hatte, mit der Weisung, daß er auf folgende Nacht sein verschriebenes Unterpfand holen, und ihn hinweg führen wollte, dessen er sich denn gänzlich versehen
570 sollte: darauf der Teufel verschwand.
Wie dem Doctor Faust hierüber müsse zu Mut gewesen sein, läßt sich leichtlich denken; es kam das Bereuen, Zittern, Zagen und seines Herzens Bangigkeit mit aller Macht
575 an ihn, er wandte sich hin und wieder, klagte

sich selbst an ohne Unterlaß, wegen seines abscheulichen und greulichen Falls, weinte, zappelte, focht,[19] schrie und grämete sich die ganze Nacht über. In solchem erbärmlichem Zustand erschien ihm sein bisheriger Haus- 580 geist Mephistopheles zur Mitternachtszeit, sprach ihm freundlich zu, tröstete ihn und sprach: „Mein Fauste, sei doch nicht so kleinmütig, daß Du von hinnen fahren mußt, gedenke doch, ob Du gleich Deinen Leib 585 verlierest, ist's doch noch lang dahin, daß Du vor dem Gericht Gottes erscheinen wirst; Du mußt doch ohne das sterben, es sei über kurz oder über lang, obschon Du etliche hundert Jahr, so es möglich wäre, 590 lebtest: und ob Du schon als ein Verdammter stirbst, so bist Du es doch nicht allein, bist auch der Erste nicht; gedenke an die Heiden, Türken und alle Gottlosen, die in gleicher Verdammnis mit Dir sind und zu Dir kom- 595 men werden. Sei beherzt und unverzagt, denke doch an die Verheißung unsers Obersten, der Dir versprochen hat, daß Du nicht leiden sollest in der Hölle, wie die andern Verdammten." Mit solchen und 600 andern Worten wollte der Geist ihn beherzt machen und ihn etwas aufrichten.
Da nun Doctor Faustus sah, daß dem ja nicht anders sein konnte, und daß der Teufel sicher sein Unterpfand nicht würde dahinten 605 lassen, sondern auf die folgende Nacht es gewiß holen, stehet er früh Morgens auf, spaziert etwas vor die Stadt hinaus und nach Verfluß von etwa anderthalb Stunden, nachdem er wieder nach Haus gekommen, 610 befiehlt er seinem Famulus, daß er die Studenten, ehedessen[20] seine vertrauten Freunde, noch einmal zu ihm in das Haus berufen sollte, er hätte ihnen etwas Notwendiges anzukünden. 615
Weil nun diese vermeinten, Doctor Faust würde sich vollends bekehren, nahmen sie den Magister mit sich. Als sie aber angekommen, bat er sie, daß sie sich doch sämtlich wollten gefallen lassen, mit ihm 620 noch einmal in das Dorf Rimlich zu spazieren, denn daselbst wolle er sich mit ihnen lustig

---

[18] **aufgerichtet:** here, concluded.

[19] **focht:** argued against it.
[20] **ehedessen:** vormals.

erzeigen, welches er etliche Zeit bisher unterlassen hätte.

Der Geistliche verließ auf diese Worte die Behausung des Doctors, denn es hatte ihn ein Schauder bei seiner Rede ergriffen. Die Studenten aber waren dessen zufrieden, und spazierten mit einander dahin, hatten unterwegs allerlei Gespräche, und nachdem sie daselbst angelangt, ließ Doctor Faust ein gutes Mahl zurichten, und stellte sich auf das möglichste mit ihnen fröhlich, daß sie also beisammen recht lustig waren bis auf den Abend, da sie alle, ausgenommen Faustus, wieder nach Hause begehrten. Doctor Faustus aber bat sie gar freundlich, daß sie doch wollten nur noch dieses einzige Mal die Nacht über in dem Wirtshaus bei ihm verharren, es wäre doch schon die Zeit zur Heimkunft zu spät, er müsse ihnen nach dem Nachtessen etwas besonders vorhalten. Welches sie denn, weil es doch nicht anders sein können, ihm zusagten.

Als nun das Nachtmahl und der Schlaftrunk vorbei waren, bezahlte Doctor Faustus den Wirt, und bat die Gäste, sie sollten ein Kleines mit ihm in die nächste Stube gehen, er hätte ihnen etwas Wichtiges zu sagen, welches er bisher hätte verborgen gehalten, das betreffe sein Heil und seine Seligkeit; mit solcher Vorrede, ohne ferneren Umschweif, fing er an und sprach: „Wohlgelehrte, Ihr meine liebe, vertraute Herren, daß ich Euch heute Morgen durch meinen Famulus habe ersuchen lassen, einen Spaziergang hieher zu machen, und Ihr mit einer schlechten Mittagmahlzeit vorlieb genommen, auch auf mein Anhalten bei mir als auf die Nacht anjetzo²¹ verharret, dafür sage ich Euch schuldigen Dank; wisset aber zugleich, daß es um keiner andern Ursache willen geschehen, als Euch zu verkündigen, daß ich mich von meiner Jugend an, während ich von Gott mit einem guten Verstand bin begabt gewesen, jedoch mit solcher Gabe nicht zufrieden war, sondern viel höher steigen und über andere hinauskommen wollte, mit allem Fleiß und Ernst auf die Schwarzkunst

gelegt, in welcher ich mit der Zeit so hoch bin gekommen, daß ich einen unter den allergelehrtesten Geistern, Namens Mephistopheles, erlangt: jedoch solche Vermessenheit geriet mir bald zum Bösen und zu einem solchen Fall, wie er dem Luzifer selber widerfahren, da er aus Hoffart aus dem Himmel verstoßen worden. Denn als der Satan mir willig in allem meinem Vorhaben war, setzte er zuletzt mir zu, daß, so ich würde einen Bund mit ihm aufrichten, und mich mit meinem eigenen Blut verschreiben, ich, nach Verfluß von vier und zwanzig Jahren, sein wollte sein mit Leib und Seele, dazu Gott, der heiligen Dreifaltigkeit und allem himmlischen Heer absagen, denselben nimmermehr in Nöten und Anliegen anrufen, auch alle diejenigen anfeinden, so mich von meinem Vorhaben abwendig machen und bekehren wollten: daß ich alsdann nicht allein mit hohen trefflichen Künsten begabt sein, sondern auch Geister um und neben mir haben sollte, die mich in aller Gefährlichkeit schützen und meinen Widerwärtigen zuwider sein müßten; dazu, und welches eben das Meiste war, was ich auch in diesem Leben verlangte, Geld, gutes Essen und Trinken, und tägliches Wohlleben, das sollte mir nimmermehr mangeln, ja er wollte mich so hoch ergötzen nach allen meines Herzens Begierden, daß ich das Ewige nicht für das Zeitliche nehmen²² würde. . . .

„Es hat aber der Teufel, wie ich's bekennen muß, anfänglich mir eine geraume Zeit Glauben gehalten, mir alles dasjenige erfüllt und geleistet, was mein Herz begehret hat; doch aber hat er zuweilen gefehlt, und mich in etlichen Sachen stecken lassen, mit Vorwänden, ich sollte selbst durch meine Kunst mich fortbringen; und da ich mich darüber beklagte, so hat er nur ein Gespött mit mir getrieben: bin also aus Vermessenheit und Wollust in solchen Jammer geraten, zum ewigen Schaden meiner armen Seele, daraus mir nimmermehr kann geholfen werden. Nun aber sind solche Jahre auf diese Nacht aus und verlaufen; da wird denn der Teufel sein Unterpfand holen, und mit mir ganz

---

²¹ **anjetzo:** jetzt.

²² **nehmen:** here, exchange.

670
675
680
685
690
695
700
705
710
715

erschrecklich umgehen; das alles wollte ich doch gerne ausstehen, wenn nur die Seele
720 erhalten würde. Ich bitte Euch nun, günstige liebe Herren, Ihr wollet nach meinem Tod alle diejenigen, so mich geliebet, und wegen meiner Kunst im Wert gehalten haben, freundlich grüßen, und von meinetwegen
725 ihnen viel Gutes wünschen: was ich auch diese vier und zwanzig Jahr über für Abenteuer getrieben, und meine anderen Geschichten, die werdet Ihr in meiner Behausung aufgeschrieben finden, und mein Famulus
730 soll sie Euch nicht vorenthalten. Ihr wollet Euch anjetzt miteinander zur Ruhe begeben, sicher schlafen, und Euch nichts anfechten lassen, auch so Ihr ein Gepolter und ungestümes Wesen im Haus hören und vernehmen
735 werdet, wollet Ihr Euch darob nicht entsetzen, noch Euch fürchten, denn Euch soll kein Leid widerfahren, wollet auch vom Bette nicht aufstehen; allein dieses möchte ich zu guter Letzt von Euch erbeten haben, daß,
740 so Ihr meinen Leib findet, Ihr solchen zur Erde bestatten lasset. Gehabt Euch ewig wohl, Ihr Herren, und nehmet ein Exempel an meinem Verderben. Gute Nacht, es muß geschieden sein!"

745   Als nun die Mitternachtsstunde erschienen, da erhub sich plötzlich ein großer ungestümer Wind, der riß und tobte, als ob er das Haus zu Grund stoßen wollte. Wem war nun ängster und bänger als den Studenten? Sie wünsch-
750 ten zehn Meilen von da zu sein und sprangen aus den Betten mit großer Furcht, da sie denn kurz darauf in der Stube, in welcher Doctor Faustus liegen geblieben, ein greuliches Zischen und Pfeifen, als ob lauter
755 Schlangen und Nattern zugegen wären, vernommen: noch mehr aber wurden sie bestürzt, da sie das Stoßen und Herumwerfen in der Stube hörten, den armseligen Faust Zeter Mordio schreien, bald aber nichts
760 mehr. Und es verging der Wind, und legte sich und ward alles wieder ganz still. Kaum hatte es recht getagt und das Tageslicht in alle Gemächer des Hauses geleuchtet, da waren die Studenten auf, gingen mit einander
765 ganz erschrocken in die Stube, um zu sehen, wo Doctor Faustus wäre, und was es für eine Bewandtnis diese Nacht über mit ihm gehabt hätte. Sie kamen aber kaum dahin, so sahen sie bei Eröffnung der Stube, daß die Wände,

Tisch und Stühle voll Blutes waren; ja sie sahen mit Erstaunen, daß das Hirn Doctor Fausts an den Wänden anklebte, die Zähne lagen auf dem Boden; und also mußten sie augenscheinlich abnehmen,[23] wie ihn der Teufel von einer Wand zu der andern müsse geschleudert und daran zerschmettert haben. Den Körper suchten sie allenthalben im Hause, fanden ihn zuletzt außerhalb des Hauses auf einem nahe gelegenen Misthaufen liegen, er war aber ganz abscheulich anzusehen: denn es war kein Glied an dem Leichnam ganz, alles schlotterte und war ab; der Kopf war mitten von einander, und das Hirn war ausgeschüttet. Sie trugen also den Leichnam in aller Stille in das Haus, und beratschlagten sich, was ferner anzufangen sei.

Als die Studenten des Doctor Fausts Leichnam gefunden und beiseits gelegt hatten, gingen sie zu Rat, wie es nun anzugreifen wäre, daß seiner letzten Bitte ein Genügen getan und sein Leichnam zur Erde möchte bestattet werden, und beschlossen zuletzt, daß sie dem Wirt ein Geschenk machen wollten, damit er schwiege, und mit ihnen übereinstimmte, daß Doctor Faustus eines schnellen Todes wäre verstorben. Demnach nähten sie mit Beihilfe des Wirts den zerstümmelten Leichnam in ein Leintuch ein und meldeten dem Pfarrherrn des Orts, wie sie einem fremden Studenten hätten das Geleite gegeben, welchen diese Nacht ein schneller Schlagfluß getroffen, der ihn auf der Stelle seines Lebens beraubt; sie bäten den Herrn Pfarrer, er wolle es bei dem Schultheißen anbringen, und um die Erlaubnis bitten, solchen allhier zu begraben, sie wollten alle Unkosten auslegen: wie sie denn auch dem Pfarrherrn einen Goldgulden gaben, die Sache zu befördern, weil sie sich allda nicht lang aufzuhalten hätten. Dieses wurde denn auch am selbigen Nachmittag in's Werk gesetzt. Es hat aber der Wind damals, als man den Leichnam begrub, sich so ungestüm erzeigt, als ob er Alles zu Boden reißen wollte, da doch weder vor noch nach dergleichen verspüret worden. Woraus denn die Studenten schließen moch-

_____

[23] **abnehmen**: deduce.

ten, welch ein verzweifeltes Ende Doctor Faust müsse genommen haben.

Aber auch nachdem Doctor Faustus tot und begraben war, hatte seine arme Seele auf Erden noch keine Ruhe. Sein Geist regte sich, erschien zum öfteren seinem Diener Christoph Wagner, und hielt mancherlei Gespräche mit ihm. . . .

Die Nachbarn aber gewahrten den Geist des Doctor Faustus bei Nacht oftmals in seiner Behausung im Fenster liegend, sonderlich wenn der Mond schien. Da ging er in dem Hause herum, ganz leibhaftig, in Gestalt und Kleidung, wie er auf Erden gegangen war. Denn Doctor Faustus war ein höckeriges Männchen, von dürrer Gestalt, und hatte ein kleines, graues Bärtlein. Zu Zeiten fing sein Geist im Hause ganz ungestüm an zu poltern, was viele Nachbarn mit erschrockenem Herzen hörten. Sein Famulus Wagner aber beschwur den Geist und verhalf ihm auf Erden zu seiner Ruhe. Und ist es jetzt in dem Hause ganz friedlich und still.

Hans Sachs
(1494–1576)

In the Christian epoch, the echoes of the old fertility rites continued to
live on in the carnival (in Latin countries) and in the *Fastnacht* of the urban
centers of late medieval Germany, Austria, and Switzerland; to this day—in
Cologne, Munich, and Basel—they are as lively as ever. The glorious anticipation of the coming spring manifests itself in dances, rites, and unrestrained
processions in which colorful and grotesque masks have always dominated;
and as soon as the rites became articulate the "Shrovetide skit," or *Fastnachtspiel,*
made its appearance. Originally, it consisted of rhymed characterizations of
particular masks or figures (ridiculing a certain type or profession); later, it
used literary anecdotes or hardened into political satires determined by the
conflicts of the time (anti-Turkish or anti-Catholic skits). It was true popular
entertainment in its origins as well as in audience participation, and although
literary materials were used at times, the mode of presentation remained crude,
if not vulgar, and delighted in the physiological aspects of human life;
drunkards, gluttons, and betrayed husbands recur with a certain monotony.
There is little plot; a revue-like structure of repetitive motifs is preferred to
which the simple *Knittelvers* (rhymed couplets of eight or nine syllables, with
four stresses) corresponds. Shrovetide skits or plays were performed in private
houses, taverns, and public squares; and while in northern Germany, as for
example in Lübeck, the patriciate made attempts to insist on decent language
and moral messages, the famous Shrove skits of the rich city of Nuremberg
delighted in carnal and lusty jokes. In the mid-fifteenth century the *Fastnachtspiel*
provided a most popular form of entertainment; with Jacob Ayrer, it deteriorated again and was eclipsed by the more literary presentations of the schools,
the English players (who had more astonishing plots to offer), and the changed
demands of more refined audiences. Surviving as an element within literary
comedy, as in Gryphius, the Shrovetide play was rediscovered by the generation of the *Sturm und Drang* and transmitted to the Romantics who employed
it as a formal possibility for their literary satires. In the early twentieth century,
the German youth movement (*Jugendbewegung*) opposed what it termed the
middle-class ossification of the contemporary theater, resuscitated the popular
and "realistic" qualities of the Shrovetide skits once again, and staged the old
texts with a great deal of artless enthusiasm; the developing *Laienspielgruppen*
who stressed the collective participation of untrained actors in homespun
performances carried the heritage of the *Fastnachtspiel* into the youth groups
of both the radical Left and the Right. Brecht's *Lehrstücke* may owe as much
to these impulses as do the *Spielscharen* of the Hitler Youth.

The Nuremberg shoemaker Hans Sachs wrote at a time when his native town belonged to the most important commercial and intellectual centers of Europe; the Humanist Pirckheimer, the sculptors Kraft and Vischer, and the artist Albrecht Dürer were his contemporaries. Sachs received a good education, traveled as any apprentice would, married and settled to become a most respected citizen and prolific member of the *Meistersinger* who, in their guild organizations, came close to cultivate literature as a trade for tradesmen. When he made an inventory of his writings (1567), he counted thirty-four "Collections" including more than two hundred plays. Although his "Wittembergisch. nachtigall" (1523) seems to have been a most successful propaganda poem for Luther and the Protestant faction, his rhymed pieces as well as his tragedies are interesting as documents that reveal, however imperfectly, the social relationships of the time. Of all his works it was the *Fastnachtspiel* that most closely corresponded to his personal talents. *Der Bauer im Fegefeuer* aptly demonstrates how Sachs improves upon the traditions of his predecessors Folz and Rosenplüt. There is no lack of crudeness, but Sachs tries to arrange a play within a play, to imply his critical attitude towards the greedy and mundane monasteries, and to relate the farce about the jealous peasant in meaningful contrast to the Abbot's qualms about his loneliness and psychological frustration. We are almost able to observe the Shrovetide play in its potential development toward comedy.

DER BAUER IM FEGEFEUER[1]

(1552)

Ein Fastnachtspiel

Personen

Der Abt *von Zertal*
Herr Ulrich, *der Mönch*
Heinz Düppel,[2] *der eifersüchtige Bauer*
Els, seine Hausfrau, *eine Bäuerin*
Eberlein Grölzenbrei } *Bauern, seine*
Nickel Rübendunst } *Nachbarn*

Der Abt geht herein mit Herrn Ulrich und spricht:

Wie bist du, Glück, so wunderbar!
Gibst's keinem Menschen ganz und gar,
Daß er mit Wahrheit könnte sprechen:
Ich hab' es ganz ohn' all Gebrechen.

Herr Ulrich spricht:

Gnädiger Herr, Ihr seid betrübt
Und in des Glücks Anklag' Euch übt;
Hat es nicht reichlich Euch begabt,
Daß Ihr nun seid ein gefürst'ter Abt,[3]
Hat Euch das Glück nicht g'nug gegeben?

Der Abt spricht:

Doch hat's genommen mir darneben
Den heil'gen Ehestand gleicherzeit;
Dasselbe tut mir weh und leid,
Daß also hier mein guter Nam',
Auch mein Geschlecht und alter Stamm[4]
So ganz soll sterben ab mit mir.

Herr Ulrich spricht:

Gnädiger Herr, was klaget Ihr?
Wünscht Euch nicht in den Ehestand,
Darinnen stets doch gleich zur Hand
Ist Leid und Jammer vorn und hinten
An kleinen und an großen Kinden,[5]
Eins kränklich ist, eins ungeraten,
Sowohl mit Worten wie mit Taten;
Darob denn müsset Ihr Euch grämen,
Unehr' von ihnen und Schand' hinnehmen.
Bekommt Ihr gar ein zänkisch Weib,
Wird erst gepeinigt Euer Leib
Mit Keifen, Zank und andern Plagen,
Daß Ihr die Haut kaum könnt' ertragen;
Desgleichen habt mit Mägden und Knechten
Im Haus Ihr über Tag zu fechten.
Es ist nicht alles süß und gut,
Was in der Ehe gleißen tut;
Die Ehe hat viel heimlich Leid
Mit Haß und Eifersucht und Neid;
Dess seid Ihr hier entladen gar.[6]

Der Abt spricht:

Herr Ulrich, ja, es ist wohl wahr,
Von Sorgen ich wohl freier bin.
Nun woll'n wir's treiben denn forthin,
Wie wir getrieben es bisher.
Ich meinte, in der Ehe wär'
Nichts Saueres, nur Kuchen-Essen.

Herr Ulrich spricht:

Herr, Eure Gnad' kann wohl ermessen,
Daß sich gar viel Unrats[7] zutrage
Im Ehestande über Tage,
Weil Klag' viel vor Euch kommen tut
Von Eheleuten bös und gut.

Der Abt spricht:

Es kommt fürwahr stets über Tage
Vor mich manch wunderliche Klage,
Daß man es sich kaum träumen kann.
Hört, hört! Seht, wer da klopfet an
Im Kloster an der vordern Tür.

Herr Ulrich schaut hinaus und spricht:

Es steht 'ne Bäuerin darfür,
Heinz Düppels Weib von Milichtal,

---

[1] **Fegefeuer:** purgatory.
[2] **Düppel: Dummkopf.**
[3] **gefürsteter Abt:** abbot of princely rank.
[4] **alter Stamm:** old lineage; the abbot is apparently of noble birth.
[5] **Kinden: Kindern.**
[6] **Dess . . . gar:** you do not have to bear this burden.
[7] **Unrat:** *lit.*, rubbish; here, vexations.

Wird klagen Euch ihren Unfall.
Sie hat einen groben, tölpischen Mann,
Der weiter nichts als eifern[8] kann.

Der Abt spricht:

So gehet hin und laßt sie ein,
Laßt hören, was ihre Klag' wird sein.

Herr Ulrich bringt die Bäuerin;
sie spricht:

Ach, mein Herr Abt, ich arme Fraue
Komm', weil ich Eurem Rat vertraue.

Herr Ulrich spricht:

Sie ist einfältig überaus,
Fromm, schlecht und recht wie eine Maus.
Ihr werdet gute Schwänke hören;
Sie glaubet all's, ist leicht zu betören.

Der Abt spricht:

Sagt, liebe Frau, was liegt Euch an?

Die Bäuerin spricht:

Herr, ich hab' einen alten Mann,
Der eifert um mich Tag und Nacht,
Hat mir die Schwindsucht schier gebracht.
Er lauschet vorn mir nach und hinten,
Droht mich an eine Kett' zu binden,
Daß ich ihm bleiben muß im Haus,
Und hat mit mir gar manchen Strauß;[9]
Wenn einen andern ich seh' an,
Sag' ich auch nicht ein Wort dem Mann,
So heißt er einen Schleppsack[10] mich
Und schmäht und schlägt mich jämmerlich,
Daß ich es nicht mehr leiden mag.

Der Abt spricht:

Lieb' Tochter mein, aus deiner Klag'
Merk' ich, du bist vielleicht geneigt
Zur Buhlerei, hast's ihm erzeigt,
Daß er umsonst nicht eifersüchtig.

Die Bäuerin spricht:

Nein, mein Herr Abt, ehrbar und züchtig
Hab' ich mich stets bisher gehalten
Beim eifersücht'gen, groben Alten.
Drum ich zu Euch Vertrauen hab',
Daß Ihr helft diesem Eifern ab;
Wo nicht, so komme ich von Sinnen.

Der Abt spricht:

Keinen bessern Rat wüßt' ich darinnen,
Als daß den Alten man noch heuer
Einen Monat setzt' ins Fegefeuer,
Daß er sein Eifern darin büßte.

Die Bäuerin spricht:

Mein Alter aber sterben müßte.

Der Abt spricht:

Ja, doch wenn er ins Feg'feuer käme,
Des Eiferns Strafe er einnähme,
Und dann würd' wieder ihm gegeben
Auf mein Gebet sein natürlich Leben;
Dann wird er auf Erden der frömmste
        Mann
Und eifert um dich nicht mehr fortan.

Die Bäuerin spricht:

Ja, lieber Herr, so sei's getan.

Der Abt spricht:

Doch welchen Lohn soll ich empfahn,
Nehm' ich die Eifersucht ihm ab?

Die Bäuerin spricht:

Mein Herr, in meinem Kuhstall hab'
Ich einen Topf mit Pfenn'gen vergraben;
Denselben sollt zum Lohn Ihr haben,
Es sind, wie's mich bedünkt im Sinn,
Wohl an die sieben Pfund darin;
Doch kann ich ihn erst bringen dann,
Wenn im Feg'feuer ist mein Mann,
Da er zu tückisch[11] mir sieht drauf.

---

8 **eifern:** here, to be jealous.
9 **Strauß:** argument; fight.
10 **Schleppsack:** frump.

11 **tückisch:** cunningly.

Der Abt spricht:

Nun sei beschlossen dieser Kauf;[12]
Doch lass' es wissen nicht die Leute.
Schick' deinen Mann ins Kloster heute,
Daß er mir zum Geschenke bringe
Käs', Eier oder andre Dinge.
Dann soll es meiner Kunst schon glücken,
Ins Fegefeuer ihn zu schicken.

Die Bäuerin spricht:

Ja, lieber Herr, das will ich tun
Und heute Nacht ihn schicken nun.

     (Die Bäuerin geht ab.)

Herr Ulrich spricht:

Wie gefällt Euer Gnaden die Bäuerin?
Ist's nicht, wie ich Euch sagt' vorhin?

Der Abt spricht:

Es ist ein gar einfältig Tier,
Das paßt für mich fürtrefflich schier!
Sie hat mich treu um Rat gefragt,
Des Mannes Eifersucht beklagt.
Ich sollt' ihr helfen die vertreiben,
Sonst könnt' sie nicht mehr bei ihm bleiben.
Da riet ich, um mich zu ergötzen,
In's Fegefeuer ihn zu setzen,
Die Eifersucht darin zu büßen.
Rat', wie wir das angreifen müssen,
Daß uns die Sache mög' gelingen
Und wir den Geldtopf an uns bringen
Und also mit dem groben Alten
Auch so ein Fastnachtspiel noch halten.

Herr Ulrich spricht:

Die Kunst versteh' ich wahrlich schlecht,
Wie man in's Fegefeuer ihn brächt'.

Der Abt spricht:

Den Anfang will ich Euch wohl zeigen,
Doch tut bei Leib und Leben schweigen.
Die Bäuerin schickt von ungefähr
Den Bauern in das Kloster her;
Da will ich ihm denn geben ein

Mit einem Schlaftrunk süßen Wein.
Sobald der Schlaf ihn dann besiegt,
Daß wie ein Toter er daliegt,
Da wollen wir ihn legen ein
Im Chor in's Grab von Marmelstein;[13]
Wie es darnach soll weiter gehn,
Geb' ich hernach Euch zu verstehn.
Dies Tränklein steht in schönem Glas
In meinem Schrank: wenn ich Euch das
Heiß' holen, greifet mir dann recht.

Herr Ulrich spricht:

Dort kommt der dumme Bauerknecht.

Der Bauer bringt Birnen in einem Korbe und spricht:

Da komm' ich zu Euch, mein Herr Abt,
Mein Weib und ich haben Euch begabt
Mit Schlegelbirnen,[14] frisch und schön.
Bitt', laßt den Korb nicht verloren gehn:
Will ihn wohl an dem Bändlein kennen.

Der Abt spricht:

Du tust die Birnen nicht recht nennen,
Dieweil sie Regelbirnen heißen.
Sie sind noch viel zu hart zu beißen
Und taugen nicht zum Essen so.

Der Bauer spricht:

Herr Abt, legt sie nur auf das Stroh,
Sind zwischen hier dann und Lichtmessen[15]
Dreckweich, daß Ihr sie wohl könnt essen.

Der Abt spricht:

Von Birnen ist gered't genug!
Herr Ulrich, bringt ihm einen Trunk,
In der Abtei im Schrank er steht.

  (Der Abt gibt ihm einen Schlüssel, Herr Ulrich geht ab.)

---

[12] **Kauf:** bargain.

[13] **Marmelstein:** marble.
[14] **Schlegelbirnen:** a kind of pears. The peasant confuses one kind with the other (Schlegelbirnen/Regelbirnen).
[15] **Lichtmeß:** Candlemas; Church festival, celebrated Feb. 2.

Der Abt spricht:

Sagt, wie es Eurer Hausfrau geht?

Der Bauer spricht:

Sie sitzt daheim und spinnt und singt
Gar fröhlich, daß das Haus erklingt;
Ich weiß gar nicht, was sie sich freut,
Hab' sie doch dreimal geprügelt heut'.

*Herr Ulrich kommt, bringt das
Glas mit dem Schlaftrunk und
spricht:*

Draus sind zwei Bauern, die Euer Gnaden
Heut' haben vor sich her geladen.

Der Abt spricht:

Ja, heißt die Bauern alle zween[16]
Geschwind zu mir herauf nur gehn.

                    (Herr Ulrich geht ab.)

Der Abt spricht:

Du aber trink' und setz' dich nieder,
Darnach gehst du nach Hause wieder.

*Der Bauer trinkt aus, gibt dem
Abt das Glas wieder und spricht:*

Herr Abt, das Tränklein schmeckt mir
    wohl,
Wollt' Gott, das Glas wär' wieder voll!
        (Die beiden Bauern kommen.)

Der Abt spricht:

Was bringet ihr nicht Zins und Geld?
Wenn ich gleich schlage euch und schelt'
Und werf' euch in's Gefängnis schlecht,
Meint ihr, ich tät' euch da Unrecht?

Eberlein Grölzenbrei spricht:

Herr Abt, laßt Euer Zürnen sein!
Sobald wir's ausgedroschen rein,[17]
Woll'n wir das Zinskorn bringen an.

Der Abt spricht:

Doch kommet alle beide dann!
        (Heinz Düppel fällt auf der Bank nieder.)

Nickel Rübendunst spricht:

Schau, schau, wie fällt der Nachbar nieder!
Komm', laß uns ihm aufhelfen wieder.
        *(Heinz Düppel läßt Hände und Füße fallen,
        sie rütteln ihn.)*

Nickel Rübendunst spricht:

Ich sorg', ihn hat der Schlag getroffen.

Der Abt schaut nach ihm:

Ja, es ist anders nicht zu hoffen.
Seht ihr denn nicht, wie er erblichen?[18]
All seine Kraft ist ihm entwichen.
Seht, wie die Nase ihm erblich
Und seiner Augen Kraft entwich!
Sein Puls schlägt nicht, er ist schon tot.

Eberlein Grölzenbrei spricht:

Bist du denn hin in dieser Not?
Erst gestern wir zusammen saßen
Und Buttermilch mit einander aßen.
Wie bald ist's mit dem Menschen aus!

Nickel Rübendunst spricht:

Was sagt nun seine Frau zu Haus,
Wenn wir ihr bringen heim die Märe,[19]
Daß hier ihr Mann gestorben wäre?
Eberlein, willst du's ihr sagen?

Eberlein Grölzenbrei spricht:

Ja, sie wird nicht viel darnach fragen,
Weil er sie so geplaget hat
Mit seinem Eifern früh und spat,[20]
Wie das im Dorf weiß jedermann.

Der Abt spricht:

Ihr Bauern, greift den Toten an,
Tragt ihn zur Kirche in den Chor:

---

[16] **zween:** zwei.
[17] **Sobald ... rein:** as soon as we have completely
    finished the threshing.

[18] **erblichen,** *past part. of* **erbleichen:** to grow pale.
[19] **Märe:** news.
[20] **spat:** spät.

Gehauen ist ein Grab davor
Beim Sakrum[21] in einen Marmelstein:
Da woll'n wir legen ihn hinein,
Und morgen sei mit aller Pracht
Ihm eine Seelenmess' gebracht.
Das zeigt an seiner Frauen fromm,
Daß sie zum Opfer morgen komm'.

> (*Sie tragen den Toten weg, der Abt und Herr Ulrich kommen wieder.*)

Der Abt spricht:

Der Bauer ist in's Grab gebracht.
Nun gehet hin, sobald es Nacht,
Und nehmt ihn heimlich aus dem Grab,
Schleppt ins Gefängnis ihn hinab,
Laßt liegen ihn bis Mitternacht;
Wenn er vom Schlaftrunk dann erwacht,
So schreit ihn an ganz ungeheuer,
Tot sei er, sitz' im Fegefeuer;
Tut ihn mit Ruten weidlich hauen,
Weil er so eifert um seine Frauen;
Treibt mit ihm solches Affenspiel,
Wie ich Euch unterrichten will.
Doch daß es mir geheim geschieht,
Damit es niemand hört und sieht!

Herr Ulrich spricht:

Ich bring' ihn in das Fegefeuer
Und treib' mit ihm mein Abenteuer,
Lass' seine Eifersucht ihn büßen,
Daß er soll stets dran denken müssen.

> (*Herr Ulrich geht ab.*)

Der Abt spricht:

Nun möcht' ich gerne sehen zu,
Wie er sich da verhalten tu',
Wenn ihm Herr Ulrich saget frei,
Daß er im Fegefeuer sei.
Wie wird er klagen da und schrein:
Das wird ein Schwank zum Lachen sein!

> (*Der Abt geht ab.*)

Herr Ulrich bringt den Bauern, legt ihn nieder und spricht:

Wie ist Heinz Düppel doch so schwer!
Laß schauen, wenn erwachet er

Im Kerker, was er da wird sagen,
Nicht wissend, was sich zugetragen?

Der Bauer räuspert sich, steht auf, greift um sich nach allen vier Ecken und spricht:

Potz Lung', potz Leber, wo bin ich doch?
Was ist das für ein finstres Loch?
Ich seh' und hör' nichts an diesem Ende,
Greif' nichts als nur vier steinerne Wände!
Wie bin ich kommen hier herein?
Will rufen doch der Frauen mein:
Els, Els, tu' auf und laß mich aus!

Herr Ulrich spricht mit lauter Stimme:

Schweig', du bist jetzt im Feuerhaus,
Du wirst noch eine Weil' hier sitzen,
Mit andern armen Seelen schwitzen
Und wie sie leiden gleiche Pein.

Heinz Düppel spricht:

Potz Leichnam Angst! Wo mag ich sein?

Herr Ulrich spricht:

Du bist im Purgatorium.

Heinz Düppel spricht:

Ach, sag's mir Deutsch, ich bitt' dich drum!
Ich kann fürwahr kein Lagerdein.[22]

Herr Ulrich spricht:

Ach, Bauer, deine Freud' wird klein:
Du bist, ach, in dem Fegefeuer.

Heinz Düppel spricht.

O, da wird mir das Lachen teuer!
Doch sag' mir, bin ich denn gestorben?

Herr Ulrich spricht:

Ja, bist an einem Trunk verdorben;
Dein Leib ist schon begraben auf Erden.

---

[21] **Sakrum**: reliquary.

[22] **Lagerdein**: *mispronunciation of* **Latein**.

Heinz Düppel spricht:

Da will der Spaß zu toll doch werden!
So bin ich nur meine arme Seele?

*Herr Ulrich nimmt ihn bei dem
Hals, beugt ihn über die Bank
und spricht:*

Nun bücke dich, daß man dich quäle:
Mußt fühlen des Fegefeuers Pein;
Doch sollst du nur hinten geschlagen sein.

    *(Der Bauer beugt sich über die Bank, der
    Mönch haut ihn mit Ruten.)*

Der Bauer spricht:

Auweh, Auweh! tu' mich bescheiden,[23]
Warum ich diese Pein muß leiden.

Herr Ulrich, der Mönch, spricht:

Weil, voller Eifersucht, nicht trauen
Du wolltest deiner frommen Frauen,
So lang' du tätst auf Erden leben:
Drum leidest du die Strafe eben.

Heinz Düppel spricht:

War leider eifersüchtig sehr
Um meine Frau je länger, je mehr,
Weil ich das Weibsbild hatte lieb:
D a s zu der Eifersucht mich trieb.
Vom Mönche ward mir nie verkünd't,
Daß Eifersucht so große Sünd';
Sonst hätt' ich's wahrlich nicht getan.
Ich bitt' dich, woll' mir zeigen an,
Bist du ein Teufel, oder wer bist du,
Der also heftig mir setzt zu?

Herr Ulrich spricht:

Ich bin kein Teufel aus der Höll',
Bin gleich wie du auch eine Seel';
Muß auch im Fegefeuer leiden.

Heinz Düppel spricht:

Ach, Lieber, tu' mich noch bescheiden,
Ob wir zwei Seelen hier allein?

---

[23] tu'mich bescheiden: sage mir Bescheid.

Herr Ulrich spricht:

Jawohl, du arme Seel'! Nein, nein!
Sind ein'ge tausend Seelen hier,
Die braten müssen gleich wie wir;
Jedoch nicht sehn und hören können
Sich die, so hier im Feuer brennen.

        (Herr Ulrich geht ab.)

Heinz Düppel spricht:

Hör', sind wir unter dem Erdreich unten?
Hörst? Ach, die Seele ist verschwunden!
Ach wehe, weh' mir Armen, Armen!
Bin ich gestorben ohn' Erbarmen?
Wie schmerzt mein Weib mich und die
    Kinder,
Meine Äcker, Wiesen, Säu' und Rinder
Und auch mein eingegraben Geld,
Das ich hatt' oben in der Welt.
Nun muß ich sitzen hier verflucht;
Von wegen schnöder Eifersucht
Ist mir mein Leben abgebrochen.
Bin nur sechzig Jahr' auf der Welt gekrochen,
Hätt' noch acht Jahr' wohl können leben,
Wär' ich der Eifersucht nicht ergeben.

*Herr Ulrich kommt, bringt
Semmel und Wein und spricht:*

Da iß und trinke Brot und Wein,
Die dir heut' Nacht dein Weibelein
Geopfert zu den Seelenmessen.

Der Bauer spricht:

Dank ihr! hat mein noch nicht vergessen!
Sie hat mich doch ein bißchen lieb,
Wiewohl viel Zank ich mit ihr trieb.
Sag', essen denn die Seelen auch?

Herr Ulrich spricht:

O ja, es ist ihr alter Brauch.

Der Bauer spricht:

Warum sie mir nur opfern tät
Kein Licht, daß ich zu sehen hätt',
Weil's hier so finster wie im Grab?

Herr Ulrich spricht:

Sie opfert' eins, doch das brannt' ab,
Dieweil man dir die Messe sung.[24]

Der Bauer spricht:

Potz Lung' und Leber, dumm genug!
Das Licht mir wahrlich nöter[25] war
Als oben dem Münche[26] am Altar;
Der konnt' genug vom Tage sehen!

Herr Ulrich spricht:

Nun iß und trink' und laß es geschehen:
Kann im Fegefeuer nicht anders sein!

Der Bauer trinkt und spricht:

Ei, ei, was für ein saurer Wein'.
Den sauersten, den sie im Keller hat,
Hat mir geopfert der Unflat,
Mir armer Seel' die karge Gans!
Sag' wann hab' ich gebüßet ganz,
Daß ich dann kann gen Himmel fahren?

Herr Ulrich spricht:

Ja, Lieber, kaum in hundert Jahren,
Da du der Sünd' verfallen bist
Durch Eifersucht gar lange Frist;
Es wäre denn, daß dich begabte
Fürbitt' von deinem heil'gen Abte,
Daß deine Seele kommt zum Leib
Zurück und du zu deinem Weib.

*Der Bauer hebt die Hände auf und
spricht:*

O könnt' zurück ich zu der Erden,
So wollt' der frömmste Mann ich werden!
Wollt' nicht mehr eifern in meinem Leben
Und alles meinem Weib nachgeben,
Was sie nur wollte, groß und klein,
Daß ich zurück nicht käm' zur Pein.

*Der Abt kommt, bringt den
Schlaftrunk und spricht heimlich:*

Herr Ulrich, 's ist nun Scherz genug.
Gebt ihm nun wieder einen Trunk,

Daß er entschlaf'; bevor's dann tagt,
Ihn in sein Grab zurücke tragt,
Daß er vom Tode auferstehe
Und heim zu Weib und Kindern gehe.

*Herr Ulrich bringt ihm zu
trinken und spricht:*

So trink' auch diesen süßen Wein,
Den opfert' heut' die Fraue dein.

Der Bauer trinkt und spricht:

Ja wahrlich, dieser schmeckt mir baß:[27]
Bei der Mauer liegt das große Faß.

*Der Bauer fällt nieder, Herr
Ulrich trägt ihn fort und spricht:*

Jetzt ist Heinz Düppel nicht so schwer,
Ward in dem Fegefeuer leer,
Denn er hat schmale Kost gegessen,
Hab's teufelsknapp ihm zugemessen.

Der Abt kommt und spricht:

Nun hat er im Fegefeuer gelegen,
Die Eifersucht aus müssen fegen
Und hat darzu ganz fest geglaubt,
Daß er des Lebens sei beraubt.
Jetzt gleich wird wieder er erstehn
Und heim zu Weib und Kindern gehn:
Er und sein Weib sind alle beide
Ganz läppische und dumme Leute.

Der Bauer kommt und spricht:

Ach, mein Herr Abt, Dank habet Ihr,
Daß Eure Feistigkeit[28] hat mir
Erworben wiederum das Leben,
Wie mir das eine Seele eben
Hat angezeigt im Fegefeuer.

Der Abt spricht:

Nun treib' fortan so ungeheuer
Mit deinem Weib nicht Eifersucht,
Denn sie hält fest an Weibes Zucht.

---

[24] **sung**: sang.
[25] **nöter**: nötiger.
[26] **Münche**: Mönche.

[27] **baß** (*arch.*): besser.
[28] **Feistigkeit**: obesity. Note the play on words:
The proper form of address would be **Eure Heiligkeit**.

Der Bauer beut ihm die Hand und spricht:

Dran braucht Ihr nicht zu zweifeln, Herr!

Der Abt spricht:

Nun, dann zurück nach Hause kehr'!
Jetzund ich nach dem Frühamt[29] gehe,
Daß alles ordentlich geschehe.
Bis Sonntag komm' ins Kloster 'rein,
Sollst da bei mir zu Gaste sein:
Dann mußt du mir ausführlich sagen,
Was im Fegefeuer sich zugetragen.
> (*Der Abt geht ab. Indem kommen des Bauern Nachbarn.*)

Nickel Rübendunst spricht:

Uns ward gesagt von Kunz Rolanden,
Heinz Düppel sei vom Tod erstanden;
Wir sind geschickt von seiner Frauen
Hierher, die Wahrheit zu erschauen,
Wie er im Kloster geh' umher
Und sei lebendig wie vorher.
Ich kann es aber glauben nicht.

Eberlein Grölzenbrei spricht:

Schau, schau, trügt mich nicht mein Gesicht,
So steht im Kreuzgang dorten Heinz,
Sieht ernst und finster aus, so scheint's,
Als ob er totgebissen ein Kind
Oder der Wolf ihm geraubt ein Rind.

Nickel Rübendunst spricht:

Ja, wahrlich, 's ist nur seine Seel',
Heraufgefahren aus der Höll'.
Komm', laß uns eilends vor ihm fliehen!
> (*Die Beiden fliehen.*)

Heinz Düppel spricht:

Steht, steht, ihr Nachbarn, tut verzeihen!
Ich lebe wieder wahrhaftiglich:
Steht, steht, braucht nicht zu fürchten mich!
> (*Sie bleiben stehn.*)

---

[29] **Frühamt**: Frühmesse.

Eberlein Grölzenbrei spricht:

Bist, Lieber, wieder du genesen?
Wo ist dieweil deine Seel' gewesen?
Im Himmel oder in der Höll'?

Heinz Düppel spricht:

Es weilte meine arme Seel'
Vier Wochen lang im Fegefeuer,
Ward drin gepeinigt ungeheuer.

Nickel Rübendunst spricht:

Was littest du im Fegefeuer?

Heinz Düppel spricht:

Ach, Leiden groß und ungeheuer!
Man quält' mich auf verschiedne Weise
Mit hartem Lager, schlechter Speise;
Auch quälten mich darin die Mäuse,
Die Flöhe und die Haderläuse;
Auch schlug man böse mich mit Ruten,
Daß mir oft tät der Hintre bluten;
Auch war gestanden drin ein Pot,
Der stank nicht übel, schwere Not!
Auch war es drin pechrabendunkel,
Sah weder die Sonn' noch der Sterne Ge-
funkel,
Auch ward kein Licht mir angezünd't.

Eberlein Grölzenbrei spricht:

Doch, Heinz, sag' an, um welche Sünd'
Hat man mit Ruten dich gehauen?

Heinz Düppel spricht:

Daß ich geeifert um meine Frauen,
Das schafft' meiner Seele viel Beschwerden;
Es gibt nicht größre Sünd' auf Erden
Als Eifersucht. Drum, Nachbarn mein,
Laßt euch vor ihr gewarnet sein,
Weil man sie straft so ungeheuer
Mit Ruten unten im Fegefeuer.
Kommt heim mit mir zum Weibe mein,
Da woll'n wir frisch und fröhlich sein
Und neue Hochzeit mit ihr halten.
Will nicht mehr eifern mit meiner Alten,
Daß mir nicht Reue draus erwachs'
Im Fegefeuer—wünscht Hans Sachs.

The Age of the Baroque

There is hardly any other term in the modern theory and history of literature that has been more vigorously disputed than "baroque." Both its etymology and its field of reference are uncertain, and rather than to use the term in a dogmatic sense we are still inclined to employ it as a flexible instrument of preliminary exploration. For some time critics believed that "baroque" derived, as a term for a particularly farfetched kind of syllogism, from the technical vocabulary of logic; lately we rather assume that the Portuguese word *barroco* originally referred to an odd-shaped pearl which, precisely because of its irregularities of form, attracted by the charm of being almost ugly. It is in this sense that the term was used throughout the eighteenth and nineteenth centuries to denote particular forms of older architecture which were considered "bizarre" or in bad taste; only in the later nineteenth and early twentieth century was the meaning of the word extended to include certain qualities of the verbal arts. The German art historian Heinrich Wölfflin, in his *Renaissance und Barock* (1888) and *Kunstgeschicht-liche Grundbegriffe* (1915), tried to define norms of Baroque art as opposed to Renaissance style, and a number of German literary historians, among them Fritz Strich and Oskar Walzel, applied Wölfflin's terminology to particular forms and works of European literature. Baroque is among the youngest terms of literary history; although it has been accepted in Germany for more than a generation, it has not been taken up as readily in France and England. The most recent printing of the *Oxford English Dictionary* (1961) does not yet admit of any literary meaning of the term.

It has not necessarily furthered our knowledge of the German Baroque that early research was invigorated, and sometimes carried away, by the energies of the Expressionists (*c.* 1912–24); the temptation was great to interpret the writers of an earlier age as heralds of a twentieth-century style and to reduce Baroque complexity to a simplified image corre-

209

sponding to the wishful thinking of a later time. Every attempt to discover the *one* formula which would encompass all the characteristics of Baroque art has failed; it is not enough to reduce its riches to a fundamental tension of the spiritual and the sensual, of classical form and Christian spirit, or to say that Baroque art is above all dominated by certain rhetorical techniques, be it asyndeton, paradox, oxymoron, or conceit. The dissimilarities of Baroque art, in Germany and elsewhere, do not easily submit to reductive definitions: the courtly and the picaresque, the sensuous and the mystical, ode and romance, tragedy and farce, the refined and the rude unfold in such rich profusion that the historian trying to create order feels inclined to abdicate in favor of the admiring reader who may enjoy the individual work of art unconcerned with "styles" and "periods."

Yet it makes good sense to speak about a Baroque period. Clearly, new developments of German literature as art commence in the last decades of the sixteenth century; poetic energies emerge and coalesce, make substantial use of imported gifts and, finally, are refined to such a degree that, at the beginning of the eighteenth century, a renewed taste for greater sobriety and economy in art prepares the way for Gottsched and Lessing: Within these seventeenth-century developments, however, we should be ready to make a distinction between an earlier stage of Baroque literature close to an urbane Classicism, and the later stages characterized by a more difficult and "obscure" rhetoric. In the Baroque age, Germany reestablished its links with the European Renaissance; after the self-involvement of the Reformation, new attempts were made to reintegrate the country into the European artistic community, and, rather belatedly, to compete with the aesthetic achievements of the French, Dutch, English, Italians, and Spanish. If Germany seems to be a country endangered by a recurrent rhythm of withdrawal from and renewed participation in European intellectual and political affairs, the age of the Baroque marks a time of a violent desire to be European again.

However, Germany's late contributions to the splendors of the European Renaissance did not emerge from a prolonged period of peace but from a terrible war which lasted for an entire generation. Perhaps one should say that the Thirty Years' War (1618–48) really consisted of a cluster of related conflicts fought with differing intensity in different regions; although a few German territories escaped the worst and others had time to rebuild what had been destroyed, central Europe had never before suffered such devastation. The war began with a revolt of the Bohemian Protestants against the Catholic emperor and was fought, with a semblance of religious interest, in Bohemia, Bavaria, and central Germany, until the League of Catholic powers was close to victory over the Protestant Union (1622/23). At this moment the armies of the Protestant North intervened, first Denmark and later the mighty and efficient forces of

King Gustavus Adolphus of Sweden. But after the Swedish king had died on the battlefield (1632) and his hesitant enemy Wallenstein had been murdered with the full knowledge of the emperor (1634), the final phase of the war began; France exerted forceful military pressures, and battles were fought in distant Italy and Spain. When peace came (1648) Germany was a devastated and depopulated country; of 400,000 inhabitants of Württemberg, 48,000 survived; in the Palatinate, it is claimed, only 200 peasants were alive when the war was over. Terrible images of death emerge from contemporary chronicles: *Man wandert zehn Meilen, und siehet nicht einen Menschen . . . in allen Dörfern sind die Häuser voll toter Leichname und Äser gelegen, Mann, Weib, Kinder und Gesind, Pferde, Schweine, Kühe und Ochsen, neben und untereinander von Pest und Hunger erwürgt, voller Maden und Würmer, und von Wölfen, Hunden, Krähen und Raben gefressen.* To write, at such a time, a playful poem of love and desire or to discuss the niceties of a particular verse form required an extraordinary and fervent dedication to the arts—perhaps much of the tortured energies of German Baroque art derive from the artist's experiences in a world of discord and impermanence. Seen against the background of the Great War, many Baroque achievements have an almost heroic quality which does not necessarily appear on the printed page.

Many German territories and cities contributed to the intellectual life of the period. Heidelberg, a university town with substantial Humanist traditions, flourished briefly before war broke out, and in Leipzig, a rich musical tradition combined with the elegant and rough excitement of student life. Toward the middle of the century, Nuremberg, the old imperial city, as well as Hamburg, a rich republic of more recent fortune, dominated literary life; Straßburg retained some of its former importance but suffered grievously in the late years of the war. But it was in Silesia that a literary miracle happened; from a country of rolling hills and deep forests, a glorious constellation of highly talented poets emerged within a brief span of time who, from Opitz to Kuhlmann, essentially shaped many forms of poetry. There is no rational explanation for the sudden concentration of talent in Silesia. Although the country was not an island of peace in the seas of the war and, as Gryphius' poetry attests, suffered hardly less than central Germany, the famous Silesian schools, with their pedagogic traditions of literary instruction in Latin and German, continued to function. It is possible that the particular political situation of the country (under the Bohemian and Polish crown) as well as the uneasy balance between the Protestants and the Catholics created a tension on which scholars and poets continued to thrive. Here and elsewhere the Baroque tended toward the aristocratic, festive, and highly decorous; while during the Reformation scholars and theologians had predominated, during the seventeenth century well-bred diplomats, courtly administrators, noblemen, or erudite lawyers prevailed. Even though many of these writers may have been of middle-class or patrician origin they longed for and created a world in which the noble prince appears the mirror of elegance, nobility, and fortitude (many of them, indeed, were eventually ennobled or crowned laureate).

Modern scholarship agrees that, from a European point of view, German Baroque literature may have had its first beginnings in the songs of musicians and poets who imported the sophisticated poetic forms of the Italian Renaissance to some of the German courts after 1570 and substituted German for Italian texts for their new audiences; in the German versions of the Italian *canzoni* and *villanelle* a new artistic interest becomes apparent. These musician-poets, like Jacob Regnart, came to Germany from Flanders and Italy, and, in due course, German followers continued their efforts elsewhere. In Heidelberg, interest in good poetry in the vernacular was anticipated by Calvinist scholars who educated a new generation aware of the achievements of the Renaissance to which Germany had been responding with some delay. In the twenties of the seventeenth century, a Heidelberg group of younger men explored new possibilities in Latin and German; there Martin Opitz, a talented young student from Silesia, found friends eager to spread his fame all over Germany. Opitz wanted to elevate German literature to the excellence of the Dutch and the French; defending the richness and dignity of his German mother tongue (in a Latin pamphlet), he set out to create a canon of exemplary German poems. He gathered current ideas concerning good writing in his slim and influential *Buch von der deutschen Poeterey* (1624) in order to reestablish criteria enabling the German writer to compete successfully with his colleagues in Amsterdam, Florence, or Paris.

In the famous seventh chapter of his poetics, Opitz concerned himself with meter, rhyme, and stanza structure, and recommended, in some contrast to French practice, a rhythmic flow of alternating accented and unaccented syllables closely corresponding (as he believed) to the character of the German language itself; once his principles were widely accepted, German verse could no longer resist the more flexible charms of dactylic and anapestic elements. To further the integration of German literature in European traditions, Opitz recommended the Alexandrine as a meter both elegant and economic, adapted Greek and Dutch tragedies, translated courtly romances, and in his *Schäfereien* created a form of festive poetry in which he brilliantly combined the pastoral with the aristocratic world. In his preference for the clear, rational, and lean, he resembles Gottsched who set himself similar goals almost a hundred years later; Opitz was perhaps less pedantic than the Leipzig professor and had much more genuine talent. Even today, students of the period measure the achievements of individual poets in part by the extent to which they conform to and build upon Opitz' standards of pure language and structure and pursue his goal of elegant and urbane writing.

Opitz found his best friends and distinct adversaries among the diplomats, aristocrats, scholars, and students who gathered in the fashionable *Sprachgesellschaften* established in order to work toward the reform of German intellectual and literary life after the example of the most august academies abroad. The *Fruchtbringende Gesellschaft* (1617) was established as the first of its kind by the Prince of Anhalt-Köthen, who had come to admire the famous *Accademia della Crusca* in Florence; its members were mostly aristocrats concerned with the refinement of German manners. Other academies and clubs of literary importance were of predominantly middle-class character and attitude; in the *Königsberger Kürbishütte* poets and teachers continued the traditions of Protestant church music and moved close to popular tradition; in Nuremberg, diplomats, intellectuals, and students gathered as *Pegnitzschäfer* who preferred to cling to the artful convention of the pastoral world and extend the possibilities of poetic diction (among the Pegnitz shepherds, Georg Philip Harsdörffer has become famous as the author of *Poetischer Trichter, die deutsche Dicht- und Reimkunst . . . in sechs Stunden einzugiessen* [1647–53] rather than for his linguistic inventiveness). The substantial and serious patriciate prevailed in the Hamburg *Deutschgesinnte Genossenschaft* (1642) and the *Elbschwanenorden* (1660): Rist, the founder of the *Elbschwanenorden,* excelled in didactic poetry and oratorios, Philip von Zesen, his competitor in the *Genossenschaft,* wrote interesting novels anticipating later middle-class attitudes and a growing interest in the daily experiences of modern city life.

It is more difficult to account in historical terms for the massive achievement of Andreas Gryphius who dominates the German mid-seventeenth century. The language of his plays and poems builds upon the Opitzian reform and the work of the *Sprachgesellschaften.* Gryphius, like Opitz, learned much from the Dutch who transmitted many older aesthetic interests to their German disciples. Yet Gryphius' bitter sonnets and enraged plays are pervaded by such a tense and uncompromising feeling of the fatalities of human life, such a distinct awareness of the hidden incompatibilities of man's eternal and terrestrial destiny that they grow far beyond the sociable urbanity of early Baroque writing. There is both something vulcanic and cold in Gryphius' art, and although some of his later admirers have compared him to Shakespeare, his characters lack the Elizabethan flesh. Perhaps it was Gryphius' erudition which interfered with his talent for the living stage; there is hardly anything more instructive than to compare his terse, almost emblematic characters with those of his contemporary Grimmelshausen, who, in spite of his fragmentary education, created human beings who still provoke our modern sensibilities. Gryphius, the scholarly playwright, and Grimmelshausen, the innkeeper and storyteller, characterize the centrifugal tendencies of the century. They are both of an age in which refined poets think of the most elaborate metaphors while witches burn on many stakes.

Traditional literary scholarship sometimes speaks about a "First" (Opitzians) and a "Second Silesian School". Within the European context, the Second Silesian School, or rather the achievements of Hofmannswaldau and Lohenstein, demonstrate a prolonged attempt to open German poetic idiom to a difficult if not obscure style that had been fashionable in the South and West of Europe for a generation before it reached distant Silesia. Rather than to accuse the later Silesian poets of insincerity or lack of feeling, we should be grateful for their artistic passion—they enriched the German language (which before Opitz was thought unfit for a sonnet) with bold and surprising conceits, elaborate mythological allusions, and striking metaphors. However, we should have to admit that, as the age progressed, the continuity of literary developments seemed endangered by disparities and conflicts; the disciples of Marino and Góngora were divided by idiom and imagination from those who continued in the tradition of the Protestant hymn, and while mystics like Kuhlmann did not hesitate to overburden traditional language with unprecedented raptures and ecstasies, the opposition against obscurity, strained metaphors, and bold artfulness continued to grow and to seek examples of a simpler and more translucent style. The wheel had come full circle; while the age of the Baroque had begun with imitations of Italian songs and the return to the convention of the Petrarchan love poetry in the late sixties of the seventeenth century, the German disciples of the Italian poet Marino indulged in obscurities irritating to those who favored enlightened reason and common sense. After the "obscure" style, the enlightenment, in thought and poetry, was to prevail.

In competing with the sophisticated achievements of the European Renaissance, the German Baroque developed a refined awareness of formal questions and the technical problems of poetry; more intensively than ever before, poets and writers considered aspects of meter and metaphor and sought to crystallize their imagination within established genres. It would be difficult if not impossible to define the merits of the Baroque age in romantic terms of sincerity, true emotion, and personal experience; and although we immediately hear the voice of personal experience in Fleming, Grimmelshausen, Gryphius, or Angelus Silesius, most writers of the age still believed, as did their colleagues in Italy, France, and England, that it is the virtue of aesthetic form to hide and transmute the impure immediacy of intimate experience. Baroque poetry excels in an exquisite richness of forms which developed further in subsequent centuries. Italian stanza patterns, from the *villanelle* to the *ottava rime,* were explored by court musicians and *Sprachgesellschaften*; Weckherlin, Opitz, Fleming, and Gryphius explored the potentialities of the sonnet; the madrigal was introduced in midcentury; and the Alexandrine (destined to prevail for more than a hundred years) was perfected by belligerent satirists as well as meditating mystics. While the older tradition of the Lutheran hymn (as the popular elements it absorbed) did not completely disappear, poetry was, above all, dominated by the more complicated patterns imported from abroad. German poetry, more than any other mode of writing, owes a good deal to the experiments and explorations of the Baroque; indeed if one is willing to assume that in poetry the artful as well as the sincere has its legitimate place, the Baroque emerges as a central event which reconfirmed, in a forceful and unforgettable way, the virtues and the energies of the German lyric.

The Baroque novel seems of historical rather than critical interest; it has fulfilled its function within the continuous development of German prose, but very few works live on and form part of living German or European fiction. In the prose narrative, as well as on the stage, a fatal distance divided the elegant and scholarly from the popular (and sometimes vulgar)—while the fashionable world delighted in imports from France, Spain, and England, less privileged readers enjoyed artless narratives, picaresque stories, and crude jokebooks. Yet artless narrative has survived with greater tenacity than the refined romances. Baroque pastorals and bulky *Staatsromane* with their impossible if monotonous adventures of highborn travelers are remembered by literary historians; Grimmelshausen's forceful if homespun *Simplizissimus* and his *Die Landstörtzerin Courasche,* reeking with humanity, successfully compete with the novels of our own century.

Many conflicting forces shaped the German Baroque drama. During the last decades of the sixteenth century, troupes of English actors eager to find new audiences appeared in north German towns and princely courts; in 1592, the Duke of Brunswick-Wolfenbüttel hired English actors to train German apprentices at his court. It was a stage art of gesture and "show" rather than poetic idiom that the English carried to Germany; since the German audiences would not understand the text fully, melodramatic effects were more important than gentle verse. Throughout the seventeenth century, however, schools, universities, and orders continued to develop their own theater, imitate the tragedies of Seneca, and oppose the vulgarity of the traveling players; and on court stages elaborate musical festivities were arranged from which modern opera developed. In the Catholic South (where Balthasar Neumann built his magnificent churches) as well as in Silesia, the Jesuits used the stage in the service of their *propaganda fidei* and staged performances to impress religious messages on their fascinated audiences: While the texts were Latin for the most part, German plot descriptions were offered and, later, a few German plays made their appearance. In the comedies and tragedies of Gryphius, the most gifted of the Baroque playwrights, the popular and the artful elements were combined; rigidly constructing his tragedies in five acts, neatly observing the unities, and employing regular *Reyen* (choruses), Gryphius did not hesitate to employ melodramatic effects to demonstrate the immaculate virtues of his heroes; it is only in later Baroque drama that the effects endanger artistic integrity. Lessing wanted to do away with plays in which the characters were guided by unbelievable miracles; unfortunately he succeeded only too well in alienating the German stage from its splendid Baroque heritage. In contrast to France, the modern German stage has not lived up to the challenges of the seventeenth century; it is a rewarding task yet unfulfilled.

Angelus Silesius

(1624–1677)

An age disturbed by the brutal vicissitudes of a prolonged war had its own reasons to return to the mystics who fervently believed that the individual may find infinite happiness in his ecstatic union with God. In the thirteenth century, Meister Eckhart had created a German language of bold theological speculation, and the mystics of the Baroque era, from Angelus Silesius to the erratic Quirinus Kuhlmann, did not hesitate to explore the heritage of European mysticism to give expression to their new insights and raptures. It is curious to see how Angelus Silesius (Johannes Scheffler) alternates comprehensive ideas of mystic love with the most belligerent intolerance, and employs striking poetic formulations as well as deliberate imitations of the crudest folk style in the service of religious propaganda. Johannes Scheffler also belonged to those Breslau poets who seem to have dominated the scene of Baroque poetry. By profession, he was a physician who had studied at the universities of Straßburg, Leiden, and Padua, and was appointed *Hofmedicus* to the Silesian Duke Sylvius Nimrod von Württemberg-Oels. In his student years in Leiden, Scheffler had begun to read the mystical writings of his compatriot Jakob Böhme; after his return home he reestablished contact with friends of Daniel Czepko von Reigersfeld, another Silesian writer of mystical leanings, and met Abraham von Franckenberg, who encouraged his interest in Böhme, the Spanish mystics, and theosophic speculation. Scheffler found himself increasingly in conflict with the Lutheran orthodoxy; after Franckenberg's death, he decided to convert to Catholicism (1653), left his job at the Protestant court, and was immediately hailed by the Silesian Catholics allied to the interests of the imperial court in Vienna. One may dispute whether Scheffler became a Catholic because he embraced the beliefs of the Church or because he longed for powerful allies against his Lutheran enemies; after his conversion, the mystic tended to yield to the propagandist who heaped almost hysterical scorn upon his Protestant adversaries. At his death, the funeral oration preached by a famous Jesuit rightly praised his achievements as physician and writer but failed to mention his most important book of mystic verse for which he has been remembered throughout the centuries.

Scheffler kept the double strain of his personality neatly apart; he published more than fifty pamphlets and treatises under his real name but preferred to sign his poetry Angelus Silesius, i.e., the Silesian Angel. In 1657, he published his *Heilige Seelenlust,* a book of religious love songs directed by the soul toward Jesus, inspired, in part, by the imagery of the Song of Songs; in the same year appeared his *Geistreiche Sinn- und Schlussreime,* which he continued to expand and later reedited under the title of *Der Cherubinische Wandersmann* (1671). It is this book on which his achievement as a poet essentially rests, and although one might say that neither his form nor his ideas were strikingly original, he did succeed in combining traditional elements in formulations of incisive power and persuasive precision. Scheffler elaborated ideas inherited from Neoplatonism, Meister Eckhart, and Valentin Weigel, and stressed the unity of God, world, and man; the impossibility of circumscribing God, the Infinite, in finite terms; the necessity of changing one's life in the image of Christ. Employing a poetic structure already used by Daniel Czepko, Scheffler defines his mystical insights in skillfully handled Alexandrines; he develops a kind of mystical epigram which forces wide-ranging meditations into a fragile two-line construction of tight balance and tense paradox. Scheffler has explored and exhausted the possibilities of this particular form; there are later imitations but no one after him has used it with equal energy and imagination.

DER CHERUBINISCHE
WANDERSMANN

Gott kann allein vergnügen

Weg/weg/ihr Seraphim[1]/ihr könnt mich nicht
[erquicken!
Weg/weg/ihr Engel all' und was an euch tut
[blicken!
Ich will nun eurer nicht; ich werfe mich allein
Ins ungeschaffne Meer der bloßen Gottheit ein.

Gott lebt nicht ohne mich

Ich weiß/daß ohne mich Gott nicht ein Nu[2]
[kann leben/
Werd ich zu nicht/er muß von Not den Geist
[aufgeben.

Ich bin wie Gott und Gott wie ich

Ich bin so groß als Gott/er ist als ich so klein:
Er kann nicht über mich/ich unter ihm nicht sein.

Gott ist in mir und ich in ihm

Gott ist in mir das Feu'r und ich in ihm der
[Schein:
Sind wir einander nicht ganz inniglich gemein?

Die geistliche Maria

Ich muß Maria sein und Gott aus mir gebären/
Soll er mich ewiglich der Seligkeit gewähren.

Gott ergreift man nicht

Gott ist ein lauter Nichts/ihn rührt kein Nun
[noch Hier:

Je mehr du nach ihm greifst/je mehr entwird
[er dir.[3]

Das immerwährende Sterben

Ich sterb' und lebe Gott: will ich ihm ewig
[leben/
So muß ich ewig auch für ihm den Geist aufgeben.

Gott weiß ihm selbst kein Ende

Gott ist unendlich hoch (Mensch/glaube dies
[behende)/
Er selbst find't ewiglich nicht seiner Gottheit
[Ende.

In dir muß Gott geboren werden

Wird Christus tausendmal zu Bethlehem geboren
Und nicht in dir/du bleibst noch ewiglich ver-
[loren.

Die Rose

Die Rose/welche hier dein äußres Auge sieht/
Die hat von Ewigkeit in Gott also geblüht.

Es sind viel tausend Sonnen

Du sprichst /im Firmament sei eine Sonn' allein;
Ich aber sage/daß viel tausend Sonnen sein.

Gott außer Kreatur

Geh hin/wo du nicht kannst/sieh/wo du siehest
[nicht/
Hör'/wo nichts schallt und klingt/so bist du/
[wo Gott spricht.

---

[1] **Seraphim**: angels of the highest rank.
[2] **ein Nu**: einen Augenblick.

[3] **entwird er dir**: entzieht er sich dir.

Ohne warum

Die Ros' ist ohn' Warum/sie blühet/weil sie
[blühet/
Sie acht't nicht ihrer selbst/fragt nicht/ob man
[sie siehet.

Im Himmel ist kein Mann noch Weib

Im Himmel ist kein Mann noch Weib/was dan
[zu schauen?
Jungfräulich' Engel sind's und englische[5] Jung-
[frauen.

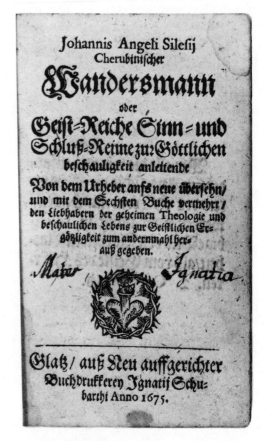

Schrift ohne Geist ist nichts

Die Schrift ist Schrift/sonst nichts. Mein Trost
[ist Wesenheit/
Und daß Gott in mir spricht das Wort der
[Ewigkeit.

Die Werke gelten gleich

Hab' keinen Unterscheid: heißt Gott den Mist
[verführen[4]/
Der Engel tut's so gern/als ruhn und musizieren.

Nichts Unreines kommt vor Gott

Ach/Mensch/werd' überformt: fürwahr/du mußt
[so fein
Vor Gottes Angesicht als Christi Seele sein.

Ein Seufzer

Man legte Gott auf's Stroh/als er ein Mensch
[ward/hin—
Ach/daß ich nicht das Heu und Stroh gewesen
[bin!

Johannes Angeli Silesii *Cherubinischer Wandersmann* (1675) Titelseite. (Aus der Sammlung Curt von Faber du Faur.) *Courtesy of Yale University Library.*

Die Gottheit

Die Gottheit ist ein Brunn'/aus ihr kommt alles
[her
Und läuft auch wieder hin/drum ist sie auch
[ein Meer.

Der Mensch

Das größte Wunderding ist doch der Mensch
[allein:
Er kann/nach dem er's macht/Gott oder Teufel
[sein.

---

[4] **verführen:** here, transport to another place.

[5] **englische:** engelgleiche.

Noch davon

Gott ist noch mehr in mir/als wann das ganze
[Meer
In einem kleinen Schwamm ganz und beisammen
[wär'.

Nichts kann ohne das Eins bestehen

Wie all' und jede Zahl'n ohn's Eines nicht
[bestehn/
So müssen die Geschöpf' ohn' Gott/das Eins/
[vergehn.

Dreierlei Schlaf

Der Schlaf ist dreierlei: der Sünder schläft im
[Tod/
Der Müd' in der Natur und der Verliebt' in Gott.

Erfahrung ist besser als Wissenschaft

Iß doch/was red'st du viel von Kraft der Wurzel
[Jesse:[6]
Mir schmecket nichts so gut/als was ich selber
[esse.

Der Larven-Mensch

Ein Mensch/der wie das Vieh in alle Lust
[ausbricht/
Ist nur ein Larven-Mensch: er scheint und ist's
[doch nicht.

Beschluß

Freund/es ist auch genug. Im Fall du mehr willst
[lesen/
So geh und werde selbst die Schrift und selbst
[das Wesen.

Zufall und Wesen

Mensch, werde wesentlich; denn wann die Welt
[vergeht,
So fällt der Zufall weg, das Wesen, das besteht.

---

[6] **Jesse:** father of David, forefather of Jesus.

꧁ndreas Gryphius

(1616–1664)

Although we know a good deal about his life, his artistic development, and his firm place in the German literary tradition, Gryphius remains a distant if not forbidding figure. After the two World Wars of our century, many of his poems were rediscovered because they articulate feelings shared by two generations who learned what it means to live among the fires and the dead; few, however, find any access to the plays of Gryphius, who was the first in his nation to transform the didactic stage of his epoch with scenic art and poetic language. It is unfortunate for the German theater that his plays (in language perhaps more remote to the modern audience than Shakespeare's idiom is to the twentieth-century spectator) are condemned to a silent life on the printed page.

In a time of war and upheaval (reflected in his long poem on the destruction of Freistadt) Gryphius never hesitated to pursue his researches; neither fateful changes of history nor continuing illness weakened his devotion to intellectual discipline. Gryphius was born and educated in the small Silesian town of Glogau. He continued his studies in Görlitz and Danzig where he was well known because of his scholarly inclinations and his philological interests (Chaldean was one of the languages he studied). In 1636, he was appointed tutor to the children of Georg Schönborn, an erudite administrator, who liked the young man so much that he officially bestowed the title *poeta laureatus* on him and left him money enough to finance a *grand tour*. Gryphius first proceeded to the University of Leiden where he studied and taught for nearly four years (lecturing on poetics, mathematics, history, and astronomy); later, he went to Paris where he seems to have spent his time reading in Richelieu's library rather than participating in fashionable entertainments; finally, he traveled to Italy and Straßburg where he wrote his first play in his native German. After returning to Silesia, Gryphius declined professorships at the universities of Heidelberg and Uppsala, and continued his private studies. Yet he could not isolate himself completely—in 1650 he accepted the post of a legal adviser, the highest honor that his native principality would bestow on a scholar of middle-class origin. He died, not quite 48 years old, while working on a report during one of the sessions of the Diet.

Gryphius is the last important polyhistorian of German letters: his poems and plays form but part of his wider intellectual pursuits, which include works on legal and historical problems as well as learned treatises on ghosts and mummies. Gryphius first wrote in Latin and only later decided to use his native tongue; however, as an epic poet delighting in traditional biblical themes he always remained loyal to scholarly Latin. In his poetry, Gryphius proceeded from translating Latin examples to odes and sonnets written in German; a critic as sensitive as Gundolf insisted that Gryphius was the first master of the German sonnet before Goethe. But Gryphius did not have a versatile temperament; he did not share the playful interests of his courtly colleagues and his satire often deteriorated into bitter clumsiness. In his *Kirchhofsgedanken* (1657) he is most convincing when he speaks in his manly, terse, and serious voice. Beleaguered by war, sickness, and death, he calmly examines the "condition of man" and forces the most oppressive experiences into the symmetries of a boldly calculated form open to the most realistic detail of contemporary life. The ubiquitous clash of opposites articulates in the bounty of oxymora, and the almost fatal rush of experience finds expression in the rhetorical figure of asyndeton often characteristic of his verse.

On his *grand tour,* Gryphius had a chance to note the achievements of Molière, Corneille, the Dutch poet Joost van den Vondel, and Monteverdi; on his way home, he set out to create a drama artful enough to compete with their great works. Writing in a society divided by politics and religion, and creating for a provincial stage without unified tradition, he single-handedly brought together the theatrical techniques of the wandering troupes (who often shocked their audiences with crude naturalism) as well as the high if didactic idiom of the plays produced by the schools and the Jesuits. For a decade literature and the theater were allied in his work, only to disintegrate after his death—it was not until the age of Gottsched and Lessing that artistic aims and the living theater were again united. Gryphius' comedies and farces are occasionally interesting for technical reasons; in his double play *Das Verliebte Gespenst/Die geliebte Dornrose* (1660) he tried to combine high comedy written in elegant Alexandrines with a popular farce in Silesian peasant dialect in order to demonstrate, in a final chorus, that the force of love closes the gap between high and low life. Clearly, Gryphius is much more impressive in his tragedies, which corresponded better to his temperament and his rhetoric. In his earliest attempt *Leo Arminius* (1646), he still seemed attracted by the theatrical possibilities of colorful palace intrigue, but in later plays (*Catharina von Georgien* [1647] and, in sympathy with the martyrdom of Charles I executed by Cromwell on January 30, 1649, *Carolus Stuardus* [1649]) he concentrated on the figure of the stoic hero, who, against all the temptations and dangers of the world, prefers a noble death to violation of the immutable laws of his religious and moral code. *Großmütiger Rechts-gelehrter oder sterbender Papinianus* (1659), Gryphius' last tragedy, again elaborates the theme of noble death; in creating the monumental figure of the conscientious lawyer who refuses to submit to the dictates of political power, Gryphius (who partly models his figure after the Dutch Protestant Oldenbarnevelt, executed on May 13, 1619) considers a question of fundamental importance. It is a play of ideas rather than developing characters, yet, among the theatrical production of the entire German seventeenth century, the only one that speaks directly to the political and ethical problems of our age.

TRÄNEN DES VATERLANDES

(ANNO 1636)

Wir sind doch nunmehr ganz, ja mehr denn
    ganz verheeret!
Der frechen Völker Schar, die rasende Posaun,
Das vom Blut fette Schwert, die donnernde
    Kartaun[1]
Hat aller Schweiß und Fleiß und Vorrat
    aufgezehret.

5 Die Türme stehn in Glut, die Kirch ist
    umgekehret,
Das Rathaus liegt im Graus, die Starken sind
    zerhaun,
Die Jungfern sind geschändt, und wo wir
    hin nur schaun,
Ist Feuer, Pest und Tod, der Herz und Geist
    durchfähret.

Hier durch die Schanz und Stadt rinnt allzeit
    frisches Blut.
10 Dreimal sind schon sechs Jahr, als[2] unser
    Ströme Flut,
Von Leichen fast verstopft, sich langsam
    fortgedrungen;[3]

Doch schweig ich noch von dem, was ärger
    als der Tod,
Was grimmer denn die Pest und Glut und
    Hungersnot,
Daß auch der Seelenschatz so vielen ab-
    gezwungen.

ES IST ALLES EITEL

Du siehst, wohin du siehst, nur Eitelkeit auf
    Erden.
Was dieser heute baut, reißt jener morgen
    ein;
Wo jetzund Städte stehn, wird eine Wiese
    sein,
Auf der ein Schäferskind wird spielen mit
    den Herden.

---

[1] **Kartaune:** short, thick cannon.
[2] **als: wie.**
[3] **sich fortdringen:** here, work one's way forward.

Was jetzund prächtig blüht, soll bald zer- 5
    treten werden.
Was jetzt so pocht und trotzt,[1] ist morgen
    Asch und Bein;[2]
Nichts ist, das ewig sei, kein Erz, kein
    Marmorstein.
Jetzt lacht das Glück uns an, bald donnern
    die Beschwerden.

Der hohen Taten Ruhm muß wie ein Traum
    vergehn.
Soll denn das Spiel der Zeit, der leichte 10
    Mensch, bestehn?
Ach, was ist alles dies, was wir vor köstlich
    achten,[3]

Als schlechte Nichtigkeit, als Schatten,
    Staub und Wind,
Als eine Wiesenblum, die man nicht wieder-
    findt.
Noch[4] will, was ewig ist, kein einig[5] Mensch
    betrachten.

MENSCHLICHES ELENDE

Was sind wir Menschen doch! Ein Wohn-
    haus grimmer Schmerzen,
Ein Ball des falschen Glücks, ein Irrlicht
    dieser Zeit,
Ein Schauplatz herber Angst, besetzt mit
    scharfem Leid,
Ein bald verschmelzter[1] Schnee und abge-
    brannte Kerzen.

Dies Leben fleucht[2] davon wie ein Ge- 5
    schwätz und Scherzen.
Die vor uns abgelegt des schwachen Leibes
    Kleid
Und in das Totenbuch der großen Ster-
    blichkeit
Längst eingeschrieben sind, sind uns aus
    Sinn und Herzen.

---

[1] **pochen und trotzen:** be vainglorious and bid
defiance.
[2] **Bein:** bone.
[3] **achten vor:** halten für.
[4] **noch:** dennoch.
[5] **einig:** einziger.
[1] **verschmelzt:** geschmolzen.
[2] **fleucht:** flieht.

Gleich wie ein eitel Traum leicht aus der
    Acht hinfällt[3]
10 Und wie ein Strom verscheußt,[4] den keine
    Macht aufhält,
So muß auch unser Nam, Lob, Ehr und
    Ruhm verschwinden.

Was itzund[5] Atem holt, muß mit der Luft
    entfliehn,
Was nach uns kommen wird, wird uns ins
    Grab nachziehn.
Was sag ich? Wir vergehn wie Rauch von
    starken Winden.

ABEND

Der schnelle Tag ist hin; die Nacht schwingt
    ihre Fahn
Und führt die Sternen auf. Der Menschen
    müde Scharen
Verlassen Feld und Werk; wo Tier und
    Vögel waren,
Trau'rt itzt[1] die Einsamkeit. Wie ist die
    Zeit vertan!

5 Der Port naht mehr und mehr sich zu der
    Glieder Kahn.
Gleich wie dies Licht verfiel, so wird in
    wenig Jahren
Ich, du und was man hat und was man sieht,
    hinfahren.
Dies Leben kömmt mir vor als eine Renne-
    Bahn.

Laß, höchster Gott! mich doch nicht auf
    dem Laufplatz[2] gleiten!
10 Laß mich nicht Ach, nicht Pracht, nicht
    Lust, nicht Angst verleiten!
Dein ewigheller Glanz sei vor und neben mir!

Laß, wenn der müde Leib entschläft, die
    Seele wachen,
Und wenn der letzte Tag wird mit mir Abend
    machen,

---

[3] aus der Acht hinfallen: vergessen werden.
[4] verscheußt (verschießt): here, flows on; surges
    forward.
[5] itzund: jetzt.
[1] itzt: jetzt.
[2] Laufplatz: Ort des Wettkampfes; Stadium.

So reiß mich aus dem Tal der Finsternis zu
    dir!

GRÖSSE UND ELEND DER SPRACHE

Das Wunder der Natur, das überweise Tier,
Hat nichts, das seiner Zungen sei zu gleichen.[1]
Ein wildes Vieh entdeckt mit stummen
    Zeichen
Des innern Herzens Sinn; durch Reden
    herrschen wir!
Der Türme Last, und was das Land be- 5
    schwert,
Der Schiffe Bau, und was die See durchfährt,
Der Sternen große Kraft,
Was Luft und Flamme schafft,
Was Chloris[2] läßt in ihren Gärten schauen,
Was das gesetzte Recht von allen Völkern 10
    will,
Was Gott der Welt ließ von sich selbst
    vertrauen,
Was in der Blüte steht, was durch die Zeit
    verfiel,
Wird durch dies Werkzeug nur entdecket.
Freundschaft, die Tod und Ende schrecket,
Die Macht, die wildes Volk zu Sitten hat 15
    gezwungen,
Der Menschen Leben selbst beruht auf
    seiner Zungen.

Doch nichts ist, das so scharf als eine Zunge
    sei!
Nichts, das so tief uns Arme stürzen könne!
O daß der Himmel stumm zu werden gönne
Dem, der mit Worten frech, mit Reden viel 20
    zu frei!
Der Städte Graus, das leichenvolle Feld,
Der Schiffe Brand, das Meer durch Blut
    verstellt,[3]
Die schwarze Zauberkunst,
Der eitlen Lehre Dunst,
Die Macht, durch Gift den Parzen[4] vor- 25
    zukommen,
Der Völker grimmer Haß, der ungeheure
    Krieg,

---

[1] gleichen: gleichstellen.
[2] Chloris: Greek goddess of flowers.
[3] verstellt: entstellt.
[4] Parzen: Parcae; the Fates in classical mythology.

Der Zank, der Kirch und Seelen eingenom-
men,
Der Tugend Untergang, der grimmen
Laster Sieg
Ist durch der Zungen Macht geboren,
30 Durch welche Lieb und Treu verloren.
Wie manchen hat die Zung in seine Gruft
verdrungen![5]
Der Menschen Tod beruht auf jedes Men-
schen Zungen!

GRABSCHRIFT MARIANAE GRYPHIAE,
SEINES BRUDERN PAULI TÖCHTERLEIN

Geboren in der Flucht, umringt mit Schwert
und Brand,
Schier in dem Rauch erstickt, der Mutter
herbes Pfand,
Des Vatern höchste Furcht, die an das Licht
gedrungen,
Als die ergrimmte Glut mein Vaterland
verschlungen:
5 Ich habe diese Welt beschaut und bald
gesegnet,
Weil mir auf einen Tag all Angst der Welt
begegnet.
Wo[1] ihr die Tage zählt, so bin ich jung
verschwunden,
Sehr alt, wofern ihr schätzt, was ich für
Angst empfunden.

ÜBER NICOLAI COPERNICI BILD

Du dreimal weiser Geist! Du mehr denn
großer Mann!
Dem nicht die Nacht der Zeit, die alles
pochen[1] kann,
Dem nicht der herbe Neid die Sinnen hat
gebunden,
Die Sinnen, die den Lauf der Erden neu
gefunden;

Der du der Alten Träum und Dünkel wider- 5
legt
Und recht uns dargetan, was lebt und was
sich regt:
Schau, itzund blüht dein Ruhm, den als auf
einem Wagen
Der Kreis, auf dem wir sind, muß um die
Sonnen tragen!
Wann dies, was irdisch ist, wird mit der
Zeit vergehn,
Soll dein Lob unbewegt mit seiner Sonnen 10
stehn.

GRABSCHRIFT, DIE ER IHM[1] SELBST
IN TÖDLICHER LEIBESSCHWACHHEIT
AUFGESETZET

Ich bin nicht mehr denn du, ich bin, was du
gewesen,
Bald wirst du sein, was ich. Mein Wissen,
Tun und Lesen,
Mein Name, meine Zeit, mein Leben, Ruhm
und Stand
Verschwunden als ein Rauch. Die leichte
Handvoll Sand
Verdeckt denselben Leib, den vorhin viel 5
geehret,
Den nächst der Fieber Glut itzt Fäul und
Stank[2] zerstöret.
Beweine, wer du bist, nicht mich, nur deine
Not:
Du gehst, indem du gehst und stehst und
ruhst, zum Tod.

ÜBER DEN UNTERGANG DER STADT
FREISTADT

Was soll ich mehr noch sehn? Nun grimme
Pestilenzen,

---

5 verdrungen: verdrängt.
1 wo: wenn.
1 pochen: batter; break.

1 ihm: sich.
2 Fäul und Stank (Fäulnis und Gestank): decay
and stench; putrefaction.

Nun bleiche Hungerangst verwüstet deine Grenzen,

Nun der Kartaunen Blitz, nun Hauptmann und Soldat

An unserm Gut und Blut sich satt gefressen hat,

5 Zeucht[1] eine Nacht noch auf voll tausendfacher Plagen,

Recht eine Nacht voll Nacht, voll Ach und Jammerklagen,

Und reißt, O Freistadt, was bisher noch von dir stund[2]

Gleich einem Zederbaum, mit Ast und Stumpf zugrund,

Eh jemand dies vermeint. Die Sonne war gewichen,

10 Der Himmel stund besternt, und Morpheus[3] kam geschlichen

Mit seiner Träume Schar; der Sorgen Feind, die Ruh,

Schloß der nun müden Schar die trägen Augen zu,

Als das Geschrei anging. O was für Donnerschläge

Empfind ich noch in mir, wenn ich den Blick erwäge,

15 Den ersten Jammerblick! Die schnelle Luft ersaust,

Der Mond, er fleucht bestürzt, der Winde Wüten braust,

Und Freistadt kracht im Brand. Es steigen Dampf und Flammen

Und Funken himmelan. Dort fällt ein Haus zusammen

Und schlägt das ander ein. Was nicht von diesem schmaucht,[4]

20 Ist schon Staub, Asch' und Graus; wo jener Haufen raucht,

War vor[5] der schönste Saal. Wo sind der Türme Spitzen,

Wo ist das Rathaus hin, und wo die Richter sitzen?

Die Kirchen prasselt auch! Soll denn kein Erz noch Stein,

O Freistadt, frei an dir von seinem Sterben sein?

Schützt keiner Mauren[6] Kraft? Sind keiner Retter Hände?   25

Ist alles Helfen aus, und gehn die kleinen Wände

Zusamt[7] den großen ein? O ja, dies ist der Schluß,

Der alles, was noch stund, zu Boden werfen muß. . . .

So wird die große Welt auf angesetzte Zeit,

Durch schwefelichte[8] Glut des Donners abgemeit,[9]   30

Verlodern und vergehn. Was seh ich dort für Haufen

Bestürzt und tränenvoll mit ihren Kindern laufen?

O Kinder, die ihr kaum das Vaterland erkannt,

Schaut, wie, was euch gebaut, noch eh ihr hin, verbrannt!

Wir sehen keine Stadt. Wie ist der Ort verworren   35

Mit dunkelroter Glut! Die Häuser sind verschorren[10]

In Asch und in sich selbst. Wird auch noch jemand sein,

Der aus den Kohlen sucht ein halbverbrannt Gebein

Von denen, die der Schlaf dem Feuer hat verraten?

Wir schauen derer Not, die in den Flammen braten,   40

Und schauen keinen Rat. Ihr Musen, ach umsunst,[11]

Auch euer Schatz vergeht! Es hat die tolle Brunst[12]

In dies, was heilig heißt, sich grimmig eingedrungen[13]

Und mit der Blätter Rest weit über Feld geschwungen;

Und was ein weiser Sinn erforschet und gedacht,   45

Wodurch ein sterblich Mensch sich ewig hat gemacht,

---

[1] **zeucht**: zieht.
[2] **stund**: stand.
[3] **Morpheus**: god of sleep in classical mythology.
[4] **schmauchen**: produce dense smoke.
[5] **vor**: vorher.

[6] **Mauren**: Mauern.
[7] **zusamt**: zusammen mit.
[8] **schwefelicht (schweflig)**: sulfurous.
[9] **abgemeit**: abgemäht.
[10] **verschorren**: verschüttet.
[11] **umsunst**: umsonst.
[12] **Brunst**: Brand.
[13] **hat sich eingedrungen**: ist eingedrungen.

Nimmt eine Stunde weg. Wir treten itzt
mit Füßen

Dies, was wir gestern Kunst und große
Weisheit hießen!

O daß mein Deutschland sich mit diesem
Zunder trägt,

50 In den der Wetter Macht mit schnellen
Funken schlägt,

Der uns zu Aschen brennt! Wenn Bosheit
wird verschwinden,

Denn[14] wird, was itzund hin, sich reicher
wiederfinden,

Denn wirst du, tote Stadt, aus deiner Kohlen-
gruft

Dein itzt verscharrtes Haupt aufheben in die
Luft,

55 Denn soll, wo Wolken jetzt von Rauch und
Flammen ziehen,

Dein aufgesetzte Zier gleich einer Rosen
blühen.

Denn wird, was jetzund bricht, durch Zutun
weiser Hand

Erlangen, was man wünscht, und in recht
neuem Stand

Sich breiten für und für. Es werden deine
Mauren

60 Nicht mehr voll Jammer stehn, und wo man
jetzund Trauren

Und Zeterrufen[15] hört, wo jetzt des Höchsten
Grimm

Ohn Maß und Ende tobt, da wird die Jubel-
stimm

Erschallen voll von Lust. Die neugebauten
Türme,

Des Hauses schöne Pracht wird Sicherheit
im Schirme[16]

65 Erhalten. Ja der Spieß, das halbverroste[17]
Schwert

Wird werden in ein Beil und einen Pflug
verkehrt;[18]

Auch wird die werte Treu, die Treu, die wir
verloren,

Von aller Redlichkeit stehn bei uns neuge-
boren.

GOTT VERLÄßT UNS NICHT

In meiner ersten Blüt, im Frühling zarter
Tage

Hat mich der grimme Tod verwaiset und
die Nacht

Der Traurigkeit umhüllt; mich hat die herbe
Macht

Der Seuchen ausgezehrt; ich schmacht in
steter Plage.

Ich teile meine Zeit in Seufzer, Not und   5
Klage,

Die Mittel, die ich oft für feste Pfeiler acht',

Die haben leider all gezittert und gekracht;

Ich trage nur allein den Jammer, den ich
trage.

Doch nein! Der treue Gott beut mir noch
Aug und Hand,

Sein Herz ist gegen mir[1] mit Vatertreu   10
entbrannt;

Er ist's, der jederzeit für mich, sein Kind,
muß sorgen.

Wenn man kein Mittel findt, sieht man sein
Wunderwerk,

Wenn unsre Kraft vergeht, beweist er seine
Stärk:

Man schaut ihn, wenn man meint, er habe
sich verborgen.

---

14 **denn: dann.**
15 **Zeterrufen:** loud cries of distress.
16 **Schirm:** here, protection.
17 **halbverrost: halbverrostet.**
18 **verkehrt:** transformed.

---

1 **gegen mir: mir gegenüber.**

GROSSMÜTIGER RECHTSGELEHRTER, ODER STERBENDER PAPINIANUS

Trauerspiel

Die erste Abhandlung

Aemilius Paulus Papinianus, renowned lawyer and chancellor of the Roman Empire under the dual government of Bassianus Caracalla and his stepbrother Antonius Geta, considers, in a revealing monologue, the dangers of his high position. He ponders the difficulties of administration because the hostility of the ruling brothers for one another threatens to plunge the state into civil war. He doubts the legality of the cruel persecution of the Christians, and admonishes himself to endure —with unswerving loyalty to the law—whatever vicissitudes the future may bring. It is the outstanding man rather than the ordinary citizen, he fears, who will first suffer in the coming disaster.

PAPINIANUS:

Wer über alle steigt und von der stolzen Höh
Der reichen Ehre schaut, wie schlecht[1] der
[Pöbel[2] geh,
Wie unter ihm ein Reich in lichten Flammen
[krache,
Wie dort der Wellen Schaum sich in die Felder
[mache[3]
Und hier der Himmel Zorn, mit Blitz und Knall
[vermischt,
In Türm' und Tempel fahr, und was die Nacht
[erfrischt,
Der heiße Tag verbrenn, und seine Siegeszeichen
Sieht hier und da verschränkt mit vielmal tausend
[Leichen,
Hat wohl (ich geb es nach[4]) viel über die Gemein.[5]
Ach! aber ach! wie leicht nimmt ihn der
[Schwindel ein

Und blendet unverhofft sein zitterndes Gesichte,
Daß er durch jähen Fall wird, eh man denkt,
[zunichte!
Wie leichte bricht der Fels, auf dem er stand
[gefaßt,
Und reißt ihn mit sich ab! Bald wird der Gipfel
[Last
Dem Abgrund selbst zu schwer, daß Berg und
[Tal erzittert
Und sich in Staub und Dampf in weite Brüche
[splittert;
Bald saust der rauhe Nord, und steht er dem
[zu fest,
So bringt der faule Süd die ungeheure Pest,
Die man Verleumdung heißt. Wen hat die nicht
[bekrieget![6]
Wen hat sie, wenn der Neid ihr beifällt, nicht
[besieget!
Was ists, Papinian! daß du die Spitz erreicht,
Daß keiner dir an Stand, noch Macht, noch
[Hoheit gleicht,
Daß Lager, Hof und Rat und Reich dir anver-
[trauet,
Daß Hauptmann und Soldat bloß auf dein
[Winken schauet,
Daß dich das röm'sche Volk der Länder Vater
[nennt,
Daß dich Süd, Ost und West und rauhe Scyth'[7]
[erkennt,[8]
Daß du mit Schwägerschaft den Kaisern nah
[verbunden,
Daß dich Sever[9] stets treu, du ihn stets Freund
[befunden,
Daß er, indem er schied, die Kinder dir befahl
Und baut auf deine Brust sein höchstes Ehrenmal,
Wenn eben dies, die Klipp, an der dein Schiff
[wird brechen,
Nun mich die Wahrheit nicht um Laster kann
[besprechen,
Ist Tugend mein Verweis,[10] die, als sie durch
[die Nacht
Mit hellen Strahlen drang und sich durchlauchtig
[macht,
Viel Nebel hat erweckt, die sich in Dünste teilen
Und um und neben mich als Donnerwolken eilen,

---

[1] **schlecht**: here, simple; insignificant; ordinary.
[2] **Pöbel**: the common people.
[3] **sich machen in**: eindringen; hineingehen.
[4] **nachgeben**: zugeben.
[5] **Gemein (Allgemeinheit)**: here, citizens; populace.

[6] **bekriegen**: make war upon.
[7] **Scythen**: Scythians; an ancient people at the borders of the Empire.
[8] **erkennen**: anerkennen.
[9] **Sever**: Severus; Roman emperor, former husband of Julia, and father of Antonius Geta.
[10] **Verweis**: here, shortcoming; fault.

Von harten Knallen schwer und schwanger mit
[der Not,
Erhitzt durch rote Glut, gestärkt mit Ach
[und Tod.
Welch Rasen steckt euch an, in Zank verwirrte
[Brüder?
Ists billig, daß ein Mensch selbst wüt in seine
[Glieder
Und eifer in sein Fleisch? Wie? oder mag das
[Reich
Das ersten Grund gelegt auf brüderliche Leich,
Nicht unter beiden stehn? Ist euch der Länder
[Menge,
Die große weite See, ja selbst die Welt zu enge?
Man teilte ja vorhin.[11] Wofern das Blutesband
Euch nicht mehr zwingen kann, so scheid euch
[Flut und Sand!
Nah dient es länger nicht, wofern nicht Rom
[soll zittern
Ob einem Jammerspiel. Mir ahnts, es will sich
[wittern.
Ich schau des Bruders Faust im brüderlichen
[Haar,
Die große Stadt in Not, die Länder in Gefahr,
Die Flott in lichtem Brand, den hohen Thron
[zerstücket
Und mich durch eines Fall (doch ohne Schuld)
[erdrücket.
Doch klag[12] ich Rom, nicht mich. Ich scheue
[keinen Tod,
Den mir von langer Hand die eisenfeste Not
An diese Seiten gab. Man ließ vor vielen Zeiten
Zu meinem Untergang das Werkzeug zubereiten;
Verleumdung schliff das Beil, das durch den Hals
[wird gehn,
Wenn mir der heiße Neid wird über Haupte
[stehn.
Und hierum hat man längst das Volk auf mich
[verhetzet
Und Lügen umgestreut und meinen Ruhm ver-
[letzet,
Der nach mir leben wird. Man murmelt hier
[und dar;
Man hält mich in Verdacht und schätzt für wahr
[und klar,
Was Argwohn von mir dicht. Die Lager sind
[beflecket,
Die Kirchen nicht zu rein, der Rat selbst ange-
[stecket.

Wer könnt es denn nicht sehn, daß meine Zeit
[ausrinnt,
Wenn jeder Tag für Tag mir[13] zu verderben
[spinnt.
Was hab ich denn verwirkt, unredliche Gemüter?
Kommt Kläger! tretet vor! entdeckt, wie herb
[und bitter
Auch eure Zunge sei! Ich fliehe die Gemein
(Sprecht ihr) und schließe mich vor Freund und
[Fremden ein.
Wahr ists, daß ich bisher den Umgang was
[beschnitten,
Seit dem, daß ich mich muß vor Freund und
[Fremden hüten,
Die, was mein offen Herz freimütig von sich gibt,
Das gar nicht schmeicheln kann und Falschheit
[nie geliebt,
Verkehrt und ganz vergällt dem Fürsten zuge-
[tragen.
Schämt ihr euch nicht, mein Wort verkehrt mir
[nachzusagen,
So stört mein Einsam-Sein durch eur Geräusche
[nicht.
Mein Hof ist dennoch frei, ich halte stets Gericht,
Geb öffentlich Verhör, auch wenn der lichte
[Morgen
Den Himmel noch nicht sieht und sich der Tag
[verborgen.
Ich fahre keine Witt'b[14] mit rauhen Worten an;
Ich helfe, wo ich mag;[15] den ich nicht retten kann,
Laß ich doch sonder[16] Trost nicht von dem
[Angesichte
Und klage, wenn ich nicht, was jemand wünscht,
[verrichte.
Man gibt mir ferner Schuld, daß ich der Götter
[Ehr
Als[17] aus den Augen setz und nicht der Christen
[Lehr
Mit Flamm und Schwert ausreut.[18] Ists aber wohl
[zu loben,
Daß man so grimmig will auf diese Leute toben
Und Leich auf Leichen häuft, da niemand recht
[erkennt
Was ihr Verbrechen sei? Wer itzund Christen
[nennt,

---

[11] **vorhin: früher schon.**
[12] **klag: beklage.**

[13] **mir: mich.**
[14] **Wittib (Witwe):** widow.
[15] **mag: vermag.**
[16] **sonder: ohne.**
[17] **als:** here, entirely; constantly.
[18] **ausreuten (ausrotten):** root out; destroy.

Will stracks,[19] daß man zur Qual auch ohn
[Erforschen eile,
Da doch das heilge Recht gesetzte Zeit und Weile
Beim Blutgericht erheischt. Man straft, ich weiß
[nicht was,
Und schier,[20] ich weiß nicht wie. Welch Recht
[spricht billig das,
Daß man ein ehrbar Weib der Unzucht übergebe
Und in ein offen Haus aus ihrem Zimmer hebe,
Um daß sie Christum liebt? Ist das die röm'sche
[Zucht?
Ist dies ein neues Recht, so sei dies Recht
[verflucht.
Man wirft mir weiter vor, daß ich der Fürsten
[Rasen
Und grimme Zwietracht stärk und Flammen helf
[aufblasen,
Die ich mit meinem Blut zu dämpfen willig bin.
Nimm, große Themis,[21] nimm den Schandfleck
[von mir hin!
Ich, der die ganze Zeit auch mit Gefahr des
[Lebens
Den Bassian[22] gehemmt, den Antonin[23] vergebens
Zu Freundschaft anermahnt, werd um ein Stück
[verdacht,
Drob sich mein Geist entsetzt! Wer hieß der
[Lager[24] Macht
Den Brüdern ingemein[25] den teuren Eid ablegen?
Noch gleichwohl wollt ich sie zu teilen nechst[26]
[bewegen.
Ihr Götter dieses Reichs! Wofern bei solchem
[Stand
Mein Rat aus Bosheit kam, so waffnet eure Hand
Mit Blitzen wider mich und laßt es nicht ge-
[schehen,
Daß ich mein eigen Haus muß außer Zwietracht
[sehen!
Noch ferner sprengt man aus, als ring ich nach
[dem Thron
Und sucht aus diesem Zwist der Antoninen Kron.
Fahrt, Rasende! fahrt fort, also mir nachzu-
[stellen,
So wird die Lügen selbst in eurem Mund
[erhellen![27]

Hat die Auflag[28] in mir wohl irgend einen
[Schein?[29]
Kommt mit dem Anschlag auch mein Leben
[überein?
Wen hab ich umgekauft,[30] das Werk mit mir
[zu wagen?
Wem die Verräterei, den Meineid vorgetragen?
Hab ich das Lager je zu meinem Dienst ersucht?
Kann dies mein Einsamkeit? Kann dies der
[Freunde Flucht?
Sind mir die fernen Reich und eingeteilten
[Waffen
Mit Pflichten zugetan, so kommt, Ergrimmte
[strafen,
Und fordert mich zur Pein! Ists denn ein eitel
[Wahn,
Warum bedenkt man nicht, was ich bisher getan?
Gilt ein vergifter Mund mehr als ein rein Gemüte,
So fege[31] Fremder Schuld mein unbefleckt
[Geblüte.
Und dies wird nun mein Lohn, daß ich so
[manche Nacht
Entfernt von süßer Ruh in Sorgen durchgebracht,
Daß ich so manchen Tag Staub, Sonn und Frost
[getragen,
Daß ich auf See und Land beherzt, den Leib
[zu wagen,
Mein und der Feinde Blut auf dieser Brust
[vermischt,
Durch meiner Glieder Schweiß der Länder
[Angst erfrischt,
Der Parthen[32] Macht gestützt, den Nil und
[Phrat[33] gezwungen,
Den stolzen Rhein umpfählt,[34] den Balth[35] ans
[Joch gedrungen,
Der Römer Recht erklärt, der Fürsten Schatz
[erfüllt,
Der Lager Trotz gezäumt, der Völker Sturm
[gestillt,
Die Stadt in Hungersnot mit Ostens Korn
[gespeiset,
Jetzt West, jetzt wüsten Süd und rauhen Nord
[durchreiset,
Dort Schanzen hingesetzt, hier Mauren aufgebaut,

---

[19] **stracks**: immediately; directly.
[20] **schier**: almost; nearly.
[21] **Themis**: goddess of law and order.
[22] **Bassian**: A. Bassianus Caracalla; Roman emperor.
[23] **Antonin**: Antonius Geta; stepbrother of Caracalla.
[24] **Lager**: here, army; legions.
[25] **ingemein**: zusammen; beiden zugleich.
[26] **nechst**: letzthin.
[27] **erhellen**: erschallen.

[28] **Auflag**: here, accusation.
[29] **Schein**: semblance (of justification).
[30] **umkaufen (erkaufen)**: bribe.
[31] **fegen**: here, torment.
[32] **Parthen**: Parthians; a people at the borders of the Empire.
[33] **Phrat**: Euphrates.
[34] **umpfählen**: palisade (fortify).
[35] **Balth**: the Baltic Sea.

Hier Damm und Wall gesenkt, und wo dem
[Frieden graut,
Der Briten rauhe Ström' und klippenreiche
[Wellen
Mit Brücken überlegt, nie vor[36] erkannte Quellen
Den Arabern entdeckt, mein Leben in Gefahr
Für Freiheit deines Rats, oh Rom, und dein Altar
Schier Tag für Tag gewagt, mir nichts zu schwer
[geschätzet,
Durch eignen Guts Verlust gemeines Best
[ergetzet,[37]
Der Feinde List entdeckt und Freund in Bündnis
[bracht,
Verjagt' ins Reich versetzt und die verschworne
[Macht
In erster Glut erstickt. Was könnt ich anders
[hoffen?
Ein schattenreicher Baum wird von dem Himmel
[troffen;
Ein Strauch steht unversehrt. Wer die gemeine
[Not
Zu lindern sich bemüht, sucht nichts als eignen
[Tod.
Wer sich für alle wagt, wird auch nicht einen
[finden,
Auf dessen rechte Treu er könn in Schiffbruch
[gründen.

*Laetus, Caracalla's evil adviser, continues to
provoke his imperial master against Antonius
Geta, and the brothers openly disagree on matters
of administrative policies. The enraged Caracalla
kills Geta in the presence of his mother Julia
(Emperor Severus' widow). As soon as the deed
is done Caracalla recognizes his crime and condemns Laetus to death. Only after he has heard
of Julia's melancholy (which conceals her personal
aspirations for power) does he permit her to determine Laetus' punishment and makes arrangements
for his brother's funeral.*

*Papinianus, the legal expert, is asked to prepare
an official speech of high political importance in
which Caracalla intends to defend his actions before
the senate and the army in order to reaffirm his
power. However, Papinianus refuses; he does not
want to sanction a murder. The emperor decides
to force him to agree: Papinianus is divested of
the signs of his high office, and his son is taken
from him. In the opinion of many, Caracalla, by
committing a crime, has deprived himself of any
legal sanction of his continued rule; delegates of the
army offer their support to Papinianus should he
decide to take power.*

*In the fifth act of the tragedy, Julia sends her
messenger with a similar offer to Papinianus
(she seems to conceive of Papinianus as her potential
husband and ruler of Rome), but he steadfastly
refuses all temptations and prefers, after he has
been confronted with the death of his son, to die
rather than to betray the principles of order and
legality. His wife, who is just on her way to mitigate
the wrath of the tyrant, encounters the servants
carrying the decapitated corpses of her husband and
her son in the corridors of the palace.*

Die fünfte Abhandlung

*DER KAISERIN KÄMMERER.
PAPINIANUS.*

KÄMMERER:

Mein Herr! Die enge Zeit vergönnt an diesem
[Ort
Bei so verwirrtem Lauf uns leider wenig Wort.
Er sieht, wohin sein Glanz (oh Licht der Welt!)
[verfalle.
Rom zittert über ihm und starrt; wir trauren alle;
Doch eine Seel allein sorgt standhaft noch vor
[ihn;
Wir sehen Julien in ihrem Sohn verblühn.
Sie hat der heiße Schmerz so heftig nicht
[gebunden,
Daß sie ohn Wehmut könnt empfinden seine
[Wunden.
Sie beut ihm ihre Recht', er reich' ihr seine Hand
Und rette sie und sich! Ihr beider Heil und Stand[38]
Besteh auf beider Treu! Ihm steht das Lager
[offen;
Sie hat durch ihn den Thron und er die Kron
[zu hoffen.
Nur mutig sich erklärt!

PAPINIANUS:

Fällt unter so viel Pein
Der großen Julien noch mein Gedächtnis[39] ein,
So überlege sie, wie ich vorhin gestanden,
Und glaube, daß ich noch (ob Pein und Tod
[verhanden[40]

---

[36] **vor:** zuvor; vorher.
[37] **ergetzen (ergötzen):** here, encourage; strengthen.

[38] **Stand:** here, a firm or unshaken position.
[39] **mein Gedächtnis:** der Gedanke an mich.
[40] **verhanden: (vorhanden):** at hand.

Und nach der Seelen Ziel) zu wanken nie gedacht!
Der Kaiser blitz' auf mich, mißbrauch' erhitzter
[Macht
Und suche meinen Fall, doch will ich treue
[sterben.
Ich suche keinen Thron durch Meuchelmord zu
[erben.

KÄMMERER:

Wer leider hier zu treu, hat Hals und Leib
[verscherzt.

PAPINIANUS:

Dem Fürsten ward das Pfand der Treu hierauf
[versetzt.

KÄMMERER:

Dem Fürsten, der nunmehr der Treusten nicht
[verschonet?
Man ist, wenns Kronen gilt, der Treu gar
[ungewohnet.

PAPINIANUS:

Mir wird, was ungewohnt, bei fremder Not
[anstehn.

KÄMMERER:

Läßt er, die so ihn acht, in ihrer Angst vergehn?

PAPINIANUS:

Sie wag ihr Schiff nicht mehr auf die ergrimmten
[Wellen!

KÄMMERER:

Sie sucht das sein' aus Sturm in sichren Port
[zu stellen.

PAPINIANUS:

Sie leide sich[41] und ruh' und meide die Gefahr!

KÄMMERER:

Sie ruft ihn auf den Stuhl[42] von schwarzer
[Totenbahr.

PAPINIANUS:

Die mir die Tugend selbst zum Ehrenbett
[aufsetzet,

---

[41] **sich leiden: geduldig sein; sich ergeben.**
[42] **Stuhl:** here, the emperor's chair; i.e., throne.

Die ich weit über Stühl und Lorbeerkranz
[geschätzet.
Man red uns nicht mehr ein![43] Und ob es wohl
[gemeint,
Taug doch die Meinung nichts. Wer meinen
[Fall beweint,
Sieht nicht, wie hoch ich sei durch diesen Fall
[gestiegen.

KÄMMERER:

Ach leider! Wenn sein Haupt wird vor dem
[Richtbeil liegen.

EUGENIA GRACILIS. PAPINIANUS
HOSTILIUS. PAPINIANUS.
EIN HAUPTMANN.

EUGENIA GRACILIS:

Ach was erwarten wir! Warum die grauen Haar
Auf diesen Tag verspart! Was sind die langen
[Jahr,
Als Staffeln[44] zu der Angst, die das gekränkte
[Leben
Nach so viel rauher Qual dem Abgrund
[übergeben,
In welchem Ehr und Ruhm und Stand und
[Glück versinkt
Und unser Hoffen selbst in tiefster Schmach
[ertrinkt!
Mein Sohn! Ach wenn du mir die Augen zuge-
[drücket,
Wenn du den kalten Leib zu letzter Gruft
[beschicket,
Eh dieses Licht anbrach, hätt ich nach höchster
[Lust
Das lieb Elyserfeld[45] mit freudenvoller Brust,
Umkränzt mit deiner Ehr und hohem Glanz
[besuchet.
Oh Wünschen sonder Frucht!

PAPINIANUS:

    Wer nur dem Wechsel fluchet
Und bloß die Hoheit liebt, die auf- und untergeht,
Nicht anders als Dian,[46] die itzt in Flammen steht,
Bald aber zankicht[47] wird und, ehe sie sich teilet,

---

[43] **einreden:** persuade; entreat.
[44] **Staffel:** step; rung.
[45] **Elyserfeld (Elysium):** abode of the good after death in classical mythology.
[46] **Diana:** moon goddess; here, the moon.
[47] **zankicht (zackig):** pointed; a reference to the crescent moon.

Schon vor der Sonn erblaßt und in ihr Dunkel
[eilet,
In dem sie ganz verschwindt, der kennt das
[strenge Recht
Des schnellen Lebens nicht. Was sterblich,
[schwebet schlecht
Auf lauter Ebb und Flut. Was uns pflag[48] groß
[zu machen,
Was vor der Welt uns ziert, das sind geborgte
[Sachen.
Was druckt[49] und was man druckt, ist nur der
[leere Tand.
Im Herzen steht der Schatz, den keiner Räuber
[Hand,
Im Herzen blüht der Ruhm, den keine Macht
[entführet.
Was, Mutter, mich und dich auf unvergänglich
zieret,
Nimmt uns kein Bassian. Heut ist der große Tag,
Den, wer uns treu und hold, mit Lust bejauchzen
[mag.
Der Tag ists, welcher dich zu einer Mutter
[machet
Des Sohnes, der den Trotz der rauhen Macht
[verlachet;
Des Sohnes, der vor Stand und Gold Gewissen
[schätzt
Und vor[50] das heil'ge Recht den reinen Leib
[aufsetzt.[51]
Dies ist der Tag, der mir die Ewigkeit bescheret,
Der mir, was Zeit noch Leid zutreten[52] kann,
[gewähret.
Auf Mutter! Trockne denn dies tränende Gesicht!
Mißgönne mir und dir die herrlichst' Ehre nicht!

HOSTILIUS:

Mein Sohn! Wen wollten nicht die hocherlauch-
[ten Sinnen,
Der unerschreckte Mut, der große Geist
[gewinnen?
Welch Vater sollte nicht ob einem solchen Sohn
Sich freuen, vielmal mehr denn über Stab und
[Kron?
Doch leide, daß ich noch mein schmachtend
[Herz ausgieße,
Das über deiner Not, die heiße Schmerzen risse,

Durchfoltert und zuzwickt! Man nennt dies
[Leiden schön;
Wahr ists, daß Socrates[53] mit Ruhm muß
[untergehn.
Callistenes[54] verfiel zu des Pellœers[55] Schande
Und immer neuen Schmach. Athen beseufzt die
[Bande
Des tapfern Phocions.[56] Die, die ihm Gift ge-
[mischt,
Hat die geschwinde Rach in höchstem Grimm
[erwischt.
Der große Seneca[57] hat, als er aufgerieben,
Des Fürsten grause Tat mit seinem Blut be-
[schrieben.
Des freien Pætus[58] Lob kann nimmermehr
[verblühn,
Und Burrhus[59] Redlichkeit wird keine Nacht
[beziehn.[60]
Schön ists, mit einem Wort, den Geist vors[61]
[Recht hingeben;
Doch schöner, Recht und Reich erretten durch
[sein Leben.
Wer vor die Tugend fällt tut wohl; der noch
[viel mehr,
Der vor die Tugend steht. Wenn Æolus[62] zu sehr
Sich gegen Segel setzt und die getrotzten Wellen

---

[53] **Socrates:** Greek philosopher (469–399 B.C.); accused of introducing strange deities and of corrupting youth. Sentenced to death, he could have escaped with the help of his friends, but chose instead to drink the draught of hemlock.

[54] **Callistenes:** Callisthenes (360?–?328 B.C.). Greek historian, nephew of Aristotle. He accompanied Alexander the Great on his expeditions, but lost favor with the king, was accused of a conspiracy, and is said to have died in prison.

[55] **Pellœer:** citizen of Pella, the capital of Macedonia. Here, the reference is to Alexander the Great.

[56] **Phocion:** Athenian general and statesman (402?–317 B.C.); highly esteemed by the state; later, falsely accused of treason and executed.

[57] **Seneca:** Roman philosopher (4 B.C.–A.D. 65). Tutor of Nero, who later accused him of participation in Piso's conspiracy. He was "allowed" to commit suicide, which he did with courage and dignity.

[58] **Pætus:** (Pætus Thrasea) (d. A.D. 66). Roman Stoic philosopher; known for his integrity and republican views. Condemned to death under Nero, he committed suicide.

[59] **Burrhus:** Burrus (d. A.D. 62); for many years tutor and advisor to Nero. He refused to approve certain assassinations ordered by the emperor, and died suddenly, possibly having been poisoned.

[60] **beziehen:** here, darken.

[61] **vors:** für das.

[62] **Æolus:** Greek god, keeper of the winds.

---

[48] **pflag: pflegte.**
[49] **drucken (drücken): grasp.**
[50] **vor: für.**
[51] **aufsetzen (einsetzen): risk; gamble.**
[52] **zutreten: zertreten.**

Mit Schlägen, Schaum und Sand das müde Schiff
[zuschellen,[63]
Gibt man den Winden nach und rudert, wie
[man kann,
Nimmt keine Strich' in acht, fährt rück- auch
[seitwärts an,
Bis sich der Sturm geschwächt; denn[64] eilt man
[einzubringen,
Was vor aus Not versäumt. So muß die Fahrt
[gelingen;
So bringt man Schiff und Gut an das gewünschte
[Land.
Wer hier sich widersetzt und durch das freche
[Band
Der tollen Klippen rennt, muß samt dem Mast
[versinken.
Es ist, ich geb es nach, schwer, grimmer Fürsten
[Winken
Stets zu Gebote stehn; doch kann ein großer
[Geist
Durch Sanftmut oft die Macht, die alles trotzt
[und reißt,
Entwehren,[65] daß sie sich als ein Gewitter lindert.
Man geb um etwas nach! Wenn man den Strom
[verhindert,
So reißt er strenger[66] durch. Oft hat geringe Zeit,
Oft ein gelinder Wort die scharfe Grausamkeit
Bezwungen und bepfählt.[67] Wenn die nun stillen
[Sinnen
Des heißen Zornes leer, denn[68] kann man viel
[gewinnen;
Denn pflanzt man Redlichkeit auch Wundertieren
[ein,
Zäumt Löwen, baut das Heil der sorgenden[69]
[Gemein;
Denn rettet man sich selbst, bringt Länder aus
[Verderben,
Schützt Völker, bauet Städt und zeucht[70] aus
[Fall und Sterben
Wonach der Tod schon griff.

PAPINIANUS:

Genug! Ich merk es schon,
Die väterliche Lieb und Neigung zu dem Sohn

---

[63] **zuschellen:** zerschellen.
[64] **denn:** dann.
[65] **entwehren:** here, disarm.
[66] **strenger:** here, stronger; more powerful.
[67] **bepfählen:** here, restrain.
[68] **denn:** dann.
[69] **sorgend:** troubled; apprehensive.
[70] **zeucht:** zieht.

Bringt diese Meinung vor. Papinian soll hören,
Was bei dem Unfall kann ein röm'scher Ratsherr
[lehren.
Hostilius versteht, daß sein Papinian
Wohl sterben, aber nicht dem Mörder schmei-
cheln kann.
Man muß je Fürsten was zuweilen übersehen,[71]
Nicht stets entgegen gehn, bemänteln, was
[geschehen,
Verdecken manchen Fehl, erinnern, wenn es
[Zeit,
Anzeigen, wo geirrt, und mit Bescheidenheit.
Wenn aber solch ein Stück, ob dem die Welt
[erzittert,
Ob dem, was nah und fern, bestürzt und höchst
[erbittert,
So sonder Scheu verübt, stehts keiner Seelen frei,
Daß sie so schnödes Werk vor schön und recht
[ausschrei.
Hier fordert mich der Fürst. Wie könnt ich doch
[entweichen?
Er steht nach meinem Ruhm. Eh muß die Sonn'
[erbleichen,
Als daß sie mich befleckt, verzagt und feig
[anschau!
Ich weiß, daß Antonin selbst ob der Mordtat
[grau;
Sollt ich denn solch ein Stück trotz Sinnen,
[trotz Gewissen
Ausstreichen und die Faust, die noch bluttriefend,
[küssen?
Nein! Nein! Es koste Stand, es koste was es will!
Mein Vater! Wer verliert, gewinnt auf diesem
[Spiel.

EUGENIA:

Ach was verlier ich nicht! Oh Stab der müden
[Jahre!

HOSTILIUS:

Oh letzter Trost! Oh Ruhm! Oh Schutz der
[grauen Haare!

PAPINIANUS:

Eur beider Lebensschiff eilt an das liebe Land
Und darf[72] nicht viel mehr Dienst. Vergönnt,
[daß ich die Hand
(Weil es des Himmels Schluß) dem Ruder was
[entziehe!

---

[71] **übersehen:** overlook; here, show indulgence.
[72] **darf:** bedarf.

Vergönnt, daß ich dem Sturm, der ankommt,
[schnell entfliehe!

HOSTILIUS:

Oh Dienst! Oh Schiff! Oh Sturm! Oh Schiff-
[bruch an dem Land!

EUGENIA:

Oh wer gibt meiner Asch' ein leichtes Häuflein
[Sand!

PAPINIANUS:

Geduld und Tugend kann ein ewig Grabmal
[stiften.

EUGENIA:

Wie wird mir? Irr ich schon in leichenvollen
[Grüften?

HOSTILIUS:

Ja freilich bin ich schon ein lebeloser Leib,
Der Freunde Furcht und Angst, der Feinde
[Zeitvertreib,
Des Kaisers Haß und Schimpf!

PAPINIANUS:

Nun Vater! Er betrachte,
Vor wen ihn Reich und Volk und Rom und
[Nachwelt achte!
Gebt, röm'scher Ratsherr! Gebt nicht zarten
[Schmerzen nach!
Ein steiler Felsen steht, ob schon die schnelle
[Bach[73]
Hell rauschend um ihn schießt. Eugenie! Be-
[denket,
Daß euch durch meine Schmach stets blühend
[Lob geschenket!
Entweicht! Man fordert uns! Verschmerzt, was
[euch betrübt!
Der zagt vor keiner Angst, der Recht und
[Götter liebt.
Was bringt der Hauptmann vor?

HAUPTMANN:

Der Kaiser hat befohlen,
Durchlauchter! alsobald ihn in den Rat zu holen.

PAPINIANUS:

Ich komm.

---

[73] **die Bach: der Bach.**

HAUPTMANN:

Ach, werter Held! Er nehme sich in acht!

PAPINIANUS:

Ich tu's und bin auf mein' und Kaisers Heil
[bedacht.

HAUPTMANN:

Man sagt, es sei sein Amt schon andern
[übergeben.

PAPINIANUS:

Es wird ein ander kaum nach meinen Sitten
[leben.
Mein Nachsaß[74] (glaubt es fest! Die Seele gibt
[mirs ein)
Wird töricht, oder bald mein ernster Rächer sein.

*BASSIANUS. PAPINIANUS. SEIN
SOHN. DIE AUFWÄRTER DES
KAISERS. PAPINIANI DIENER.
DIE SCHERGEN MIT DEN
WELLE-BEILEN*

BASSIANUS:

Wir sind, Papinian, auf die Geheimnis kommen.
Die Nebelkapp' entfällt, weil, was er vorge-
[nommen,
So hell als Phœbus[75] strahlt, vor aller Augen liegt.
Was ists, daß man uns stets mit Worten einge-
[wiegt,
Daß man so steif auf Recht und Heiligkeit kann
[pochen,
Wenn man verschworne Treu leichtsinnig hat
[gebrochen?

PAPINIANUS:

Mir kommt, was Antonin vor sonnenklar
[ausgibt,
Noch ziemlich dunkel vor. Wer reine Tugend
[liebt,
Bricht weder Treu noch Eid und achtet kein
[Verklagen,
Dafern[76] er hinterrücks wird giftig angetragen.[77]

BASSIANUS:

Was Not, daß man die Sach' als fremd' ins
[Ferne stößt,

---

[74] **Nachsaß: Nachfolger.**
[75] **Phœbus: epithet of Apollo as sun god.**
[76] **dafern: wofern.**
[77] **antragen: anklagen; angeben.**

Wenn der verdeckte Grund der Sinnen schon
[entblößt?
Kennt man die Häupter nicht, die sich auf uns
[verschworen
Und Getam[78] zu dem Thron durch unsern Tod
[erkoren?

PAPINIANUS:

Es sei auch, wie es sei, hier ist mir nichts bekannt.

BASSIANUS:

Bot nicht Papinian ihm selbst Rat, Hilf und Hand?
Wie steht er so verwirrt, so starrend, was zu
[schließen?
Schaut an! Ihn überweist[79] sein überzeugt
[Gewissen.

PAPINIANUS:

Ich starr und bin verwirrt ob dieser neuen List,
Frei aller Schand und Schuld. Komm, wer du
[Kläger bist!
Komm, wer du zeugen kannst! Entdecke mein
[Verbrechen!
Tritt vor, der du mich willst ob solcher Tat
[besprechen![80]
Wer ists, mit dem ich je auf solche Sprünge kam?
Den ich bereden konnt' und in den Bund
[annahm?
Mein Fürst! Ich bitt um Recht. Bin ich zu
[überweisen,
So fall ich willigst hin. Man brauche Stahl und
[Eisen,
Und was gerechtes Recht auf Erzverräter setzt!
Wofern Verleumdung sich mit dieser Schmach
[ergetzt,
So richt' auch, wer sich stets vor meinen Feind
[erkläret,
Und sprech ein Urteil aus! Was irr ich? Man
[beschweret
Mein' überreine Seel aus Neid mit dieser Schuld,
Damit man meinen Tod beschöne; nur Geduld!
Die Welt ist noch so blind, noch so verführter
[Sinnen,
Daß sie durch solche Träum' und Märchen zu
[gewinnen.
Glaubt es der Kaiser wohl (wie hoch er auch
[erhitzt),

Daß sich Papinian mit solcher Schmach be-
[schmitzt?[81]

BASSIANUS:

Die Sach' erlaubt uns nicht, ein lang Gericht
[zu hegen.
Papinian kann leicht die Klage widerlegen,
Wenn er mit erster Treu des Kaisers Schluß
[ausführt.
Was sind die Worte not, wo man die Werke
[spürt?
Fragt er, ob Antonin ihn ob der Tat verdenke,[82]
Wir fragen, ob er uns mit Ungehorsam kränke?
Doch glimmt die Liebe noch in seines Fürsten
[Brust.
Da ihm Papinian der schnöden Tat bewußt,
So glaub er, wir verzeihn. Er biet uns nur die
[Hände
Und bau auf erste Pflicht ein wohlgewünschtes
[Ende!
Dafern er sonder Schuld, warum sich widersetzt
Und durch Hartnäckigsein des Fürsten Macht
[verletzt?

PAPINIANUS:

Ihr Götter! Die ihr jetzt, und wenn wir nun
[entschlafen,
Die vorgesetzte Lust und wohlverdiente Strafen
Ohn Irren zuerkennt, die niemand trügen[83] kann,
Ich ruf euch auf dies Haupt zu Zeug- und
[Richtern an.
Gönnt, wo ich Ursach je zu diesen Wahn gegeben,
Mir nimmer Rast noch Ruh! es schwärme nach
[dem Leben
Mein hart beklemmter[84] Geist durch dicker
Nächte Luft
Und wimmer', seufz' und heul' um meine
[Totengruft!
Der Fürst verzeihe dem, der, was ich nie ver-
[richtet,
Der, was ich nie gedacht, mir gottlos angedichtet!
Mir seh er keine Schuld, List noch Verbrechen
[nach,
Weil wider ihn mein Herz mit Vorsatz nichts
[verbrach!
Ists tödlich, daß ich nichts tu wider mein
[Gewissen,

---

[78] **Getam**: Geta.
[79] **überweisen**: überführen.
[80] **besprechen**: here, accuse; defame.

[81] **beschmitzen (beschmutzen)**: defile.
[82] **verdenken**: in Verdacht haben; verdächtigen.
[83] **trügen**: betrügen.
[84] **beklemmt**: oppressed; anguished.

Daß der von Jugend auf der Rechte sich beflissen,
Auf den die große Welt mit vollen Augen sieht,
Der für des Fürsten Ehr unendlich sich bemüht,
Ein Stück, das Antonin in heißem Zorn begangen,
Nicht auszustreichen[85] weiß, so wünsch ich mit
    [Verlangen
Den höchst geliebten Tod. Ich bin des Lebens
    [satt,
Das so viel krummer Gäng und wenig rechter hat.

BASSIANUS:

Der geht sehr krumm, der stets die höchste
    [Macht will richten.

PAPINIANUS:

Krumm geht, wer Laster lobt und Tugend kann
    [vernichten.

BASSIANUS:

Hört den vergällten Mund, den falsch gesinnten
    [Geist!
Was hält uns länger auf? Die rasend Ehrfurcht
    [reißt
Den Mann auf fremde[86] Werk'. Jetzt, jetzt ists
    [Zeit zu dämmen
Und den geschwellten Mut durch letzten Zwang
    [zu hemmen.
Er sieht sein einig Kind und sieht es jetzt zuletzt,
Wo er mit einem Wort sich ferner widersetzt.
Stracks Diener! Stock und Beil!

PAPINIANI SOHN:

    Es ist ein Mensch geboren
Und als ein Mensch dem Tod in der Geburt
    [erkoren,
Geboren in die Welt, doch von Papinian!
Geboren, wo man nur durch Tugend leben kann,
Erkoren von dem Tod, als mich die Welt
    [empfangen,
Erkoren von dem Tod, der stets mir nachge-
    [gangen,
Noch an der Mutter Brust. Der Vater bebe nicht!
Mir wird der schöne Tod zu einem hellen Licht,
Das als ein schimmernd Stern wird durch die
    [Nachwelt strahlen,
So lang als Phœbe[87] soll die braunen Wolken
    [malen.
Mein Vater!

BASSIANUS:

    Reißt ihn fort!

PAPINIANUS:

    Warum? Der Kaiser hör!

BASSIANUS:

Warum? Um daß er sein

SOHN:

    Und teilhaft seiner Ehr.

PAPINIANUS:

Mein Kind! Mein wahres Blut! Du stirbst doch
    [sonder Schande
Vor mich, zu meiner Straf. Entschließt[88] die
    [ehrnen[89] Bande!
Ich habe nicht, mein Kind! des Kaisers Grimm
    [entsteckt;[90]
Mein steifer Vorsatz hat den harten Zorn erweckt.
Ich komm und bin bereit mit meinem Haupt
    [zu büßen.

BASSIANUS:

Der Kaiser will von dir nichts denn Gehorsam
    [wissen.

PAPINIANUS:

Wohl! Wohl! So stirb mein Kind! Weil es der
    [Kaiser heißt.
Wir sind gehorsam, Fürst! Ein unerschreckter
    [Geist
Tut willig, was uns nur das heil'ge Recht erlaubet.

SOHN:

Nun Vater, gute Nacht!

PAPINIANUS:

    Der grimme Zufall raubet,
Mein Sohn! dir Jahr und Stand, und was die
    [Erden schätzt;
Doch schenkt er, was kein Beil noch Sturm des
    [Glücks verletzt.
Mein Sohn, stirb unverzagt! Dies Leben ist ein
    [Kriegen
Voll Angst, ein solcher Tod das allerhöchste
    [Siegen.

---

[85] **ausstreichen**: here, extol; praise.
[86] **fremd**: here, odd; peculiar.
[87] **Phœbe**: moon goddess; here, the moon.

[88] **entschließen**: aufschließen.
[89] **ehrnen** (*contr. of* **ehernen**): eisernen.
[90] **entstecken** (**anstecken**): kindle; here, arouse.

BASSIANUS:

Der Sieg wird wahrlich dir gar nicht ersprießlich
[sein.

PAPINIANUS:

Dies ist der höchste Sieg, daß mein Gewissen
[rein.

BASSIANUS:

Schaut, Völker! Dieses heißt vor großer Weisheit
[rasen.

PAPINIANUS:

Solch Rasen hat mir nie die Geister angeblasen.

BASSIANUS:

Es bläset in den Wind, was dich so groß gemacht.

PAPINIANUS:

Wind, Schatten, Rauch und Spreu ist aller Men-
[schen Pracht.

BASSIANUS:

Das zeigt Papinian, der nichts aus allem worden.

PAPINIANUS:

Es stürmt heut aus dem Ost und morgen leicht
[aus Norden.

BASSIANUS:

Der Sturm riß deinen Stamm mit Ast und
[Wurzel aus.

PAPINIANUS:

Vor zweifelt ich, nun hab ich ein beständig Haus.

BASSIANUS:

Beständig, wenn dein Sohn in eignem Blute
[badet?

PAPINIANUS:

Dem weder Beil noch Grimm des Fürsten hat
[geschadet.

BASSIANUS:

Geschadet? Bringt hervor sein abgeschmissen
[Haupt!

PAPINIANUS:

Nun seh ich, oh mein Kind! was ich von dir
[geglaubt.
Ich schau den hohen Mut, die unverzagten
[Sinnen,
Die nicht durch Furcht, durch Angst, durch
[Dräuen[91] zu gewinnen,
Die in den frechen Tod sich unerschreckt gewagt,
Die, ob dem alles bebt und zittert, nicht verzagt,
Die standhaft, obwohl zart, vor Tränen Blut
[vergossen
Und engen Lebens Ziel mit weitem Ruhm
[beschlossen.
Rühmt, Eltern! eure Frucht, die um des Landes
[Heil
Für Wund und Sterben bot das edle Leben feil.
Mir bleib es unverwehrt, den Sohn recht auszu-
[streichen,
Der für Recht, Gott und Land und Vater wollt
[erbleichen,
Der meine blühend' Ehr ergetzt durch diesen
[Preis
Und seine fest gestellt. Wie großer Väter Fleiß
Und Glück und Ruhm ist nicht auf erstes Kind
[abkommen,
Durch das der Ahnen Licht beschwärzt und
[abgenommen,
Wie wenn Diane sich vor ihren Phœbus stellt[92]
Und den durchlauchten Glanz entzieht der trüben
[Welt!
Den grausen Kummer kann mir der Verlust
[benehmen;
Ich darf des meinen mich, weil Menschen sind,
[nicht schämen.

BASSIANUS:

(*redet allein, indessen treten die Hofleute, die dem
Kaiser aufwarten, zu Papiniano und reden in der
Stille mit ihm*)

Was Rat? Des teuren Manns standhafte Tap-
[ferkeit
Lockt aller Herzen an, uns zwingt die rauhe Zeit,
Auf Heil und Reich zu sehn. Soll unser Land
[denn sagen,
Wie steif Papinian sich gegen uns getragen,
Der, ob die Lippe schweigt, uns rauh und herb
[aufrückt,
(Entschuldigt ers nicht selbst?) was unser Herze
[drückt?

---

91 **Dräuen: Drohen.**
92 **Wie ... stellt:** an allusion to a solar eclipse.

Soll Rom und Lager denn stets auf uns beide
[sehen,
Und weil es jenen lobt, uns höchst empfindlich
[schmähen?
Oh Götter! Hätt er uns nicht tausendfach
[verpflicht?
Doch wenns ans Szepter geht, gilt Dienst und
[Freundschaft nicht.
Man muß! Wir haben schon sein Blut vergießen
[lassen;
Man gab ihm Anlaß sich zu rächen, uns zu
[hassen.
Sollt ihm, was wir verübt, nicht zu Gemüte gehn,
So muß in seiner Brust kein Vaterherze stehn.
Ach! Müssen wir die Faust in seinem Blute
[färben?
Wir müssen! Ach! Es sei! Papinian soll sterben.

PAPINIANUS:

Gar willig, großer Fürst! Dies kann, dies will
[ich tun.
Es müsse von nun an die lange Zanksucht ruhn,
Die Hof und Hof zerteilt und Freund auf Freund
[verhetzet!
Es falle, was bisher dir, Rom, sich widersetzet!
Laßt Götter mich vor Fürst, vor Rat, Volk und
[Gemein,
Vor Lager, Land und Reich ein rein Sühnopfer
[sein!
Ade geliebte Stadt! Beherrscherin der Erden!
Es müsse deine Macht um so viel größer werden,
Als ich mich vor dein Heil aufrichtig stets
[bemüht!
Ade, siegreicher Fürst! Der ins Verborgne sieht,
Sieht, daß sein Ruhm allein der Zweck sei meiner
[Taten.
Geht Götter! Die dem Thron so wohl und besser
[raten,
Als mir je möglich war. Kommt Diener! Kommt
[herzu!
Versichert Plautien,[93] daß ich in lange Ruh
Aus langer Not versetzt! Sie mäßig' ihre Zähren
(Die, wo was nach uns bleibt, die Geister mehr
[beschweren,
Als wohl der Pöbel meint)! Sie glaub, ob wir
[geschwind,
Doch durch der Parzen Schluß auf kurz getrennet
[sind!
Sie half ob dem, was uns kann nach dem End
[erheben!

Sie ehre meinen Tod und folge meinem Leben!
Erinnert die, die mich in dieses Licht gebracht,
Daß ein durchlauchter Tod uns reiß aus langer
[Nacht!
Nehmt Kleid und Mantel hin! Wenn sich das
[Schauspiel endet,
Wird der geborgte Schmuck, wohin er soll,
[gesendet.
Man halt in meinem Hof um mich kein Tod-
[Geschrei![94]
Wer noch leibeigen dient, sei los! Ich geb ihn frei.
Und hiermit gute Nacht! Bleibt, Freunde! bleibt
[gesegnet!
Bleibt, Helden! bleibt gegrüßt! Wer seiner Not
[begegnet,
Betödert[95] seine Lust und wird, wie klein er,
[groß.
Ihr, die den Spruch aufführt, kommt! Hals und
[Brust ist bloß.

Heilge Themis, die du Sitten
Ins Geblüt hast eingepflanzet,
Die der grimmen Völker Wüten
Durch gemeines[96] Recht umschanzet
Und durch dies, was du gesetzt,
Dein geliebtes Rom ergetzt,
Gönne, daß ich dir zu Ehren
Dir, die ich jetzt sterbend grüße,
Die ich annoch sterbend liebe,
Mein nicht schuldig Blut vergieße
Und (wo ich was bitten kann)
Schau dies Reich heilwärtig[97] an!

SCHERGE:

Geschehn, was mir der Fürst hat anbefehlen
[wollen.

BASSIANUS:

Du hättest unser Wort durchs Schwert ausführen
[sollen.
Wie wird uns? Ist er fort? Liegt nicht die Leich
[allhier?
Wir irren. Geta seufzt und winselt für und für.
Ach Vater! Ach Sever! Ach Bruder! Ach, wer
[springet
Mit Fackeln um uns um? Wer stößt uns? Ach!
[Wer schwinget

---

[93] **Plautia:** Papinianus' wife.

[94] **Tod-Geschrei:** traditional bewailing of the dead.
[95] **betödern** (betöbern [betäuben]): repress. The
spelling of **betödern** for **betöbern** is presumably
a slip of the pen.
[96] **gemein** (gemeinsam): common.
[97] **heilwärtig:** so, daß es zum Heil gereicht.

Das von Blut rote Schwert? Wie? Bricht der
[Grund entzwei?
Wer bläst das Streithorn? Ach! Wir spüren,
[was es sei.
Wie wir durch Beil und Stahl zu wüten sind
[geflissen,
So wütet in uns selbst ein rasend toll Gewissen.

PAPINIANUS HOSTILIUS.
EUGENIA GRACILIS. PLAUTIA.
DIE REIHEN[98] *DES RÖMISCHEN*
FRAUENZIMMERS.[99] *DER ERSTE*
DIENER PAPINIANI. DER
ANDERE DIENER. REIHEN DER
DIENER PAPINIANI. BEIDE
LEICHEN.

Hostilius:

Oh Seelen! Die ihr noch bei uns, nun alles fällt,
In wahrer Treue steht, die Rom der großen Welt
Als Lichter unser Zeit ruhmwürdigst vor wird
[stellen,
Ihr, die ihr uns, die wir verteuft[100] in Unglücks-
[wellen,
Noch Händ und Arme reicht und den entsteckten
[Grimm
Des Fürsten euch bemüht, durch Anmut eurer
[Stimm,
Durch Seufzen, durch Gewein und Vorbitt[101]
[aufzuheben,
Die ihr uns Sohn und Heil itzt wieder sucht zu
[geben,
Geht hin! Oh Sonnen! Geht, vertreibt die
[schwarze Nacht,
Die alles auf dem Hof bestürzt und dunkel macht!
Geht hin! Es ward wohl eh[102] ein reißend Löw
[beweget,
Daß er sich auf die Schoß der zarten Frauen leget
Und Raub und Zorn verließ. Geht! Was der
[Mund nicht spricht,
Bringt Stamm und Schönheit vor und eur
[betränt Gesicht!
Die Rosen, die der Tau der Zähren übergossen,
Der Zähren, die vor uns und unser Blut geflossen.
Geht! Ringt nach diesem Ruhm, daß ihr der
[Erden Licht,
Des Fürsten rechte Faust, Astreens[103] Zuversicht,

Nach der der Tod schon griff, durch euren Fleiß
[erhalten!
So müsse nimmermehr eur Haus und Lob
[veralten!
Geht! Und weil mir der Geist nur auf der
[Zungen hält,
Erlangt, daß mich die Lust entzück aus dieser
[Welt,
Daß ich die müden Jahr in Herzenswonne
[schließe
Und sterbe, wenn ich dich, mein Sohn! mein
[Leben! küsse!

Plautia:

Kommt, Mutter! Steurt[104] auf mich den abge-
[zehrten Leib!
Legt den verdorrten Arm um meinen Hals!
[Ich bleib,
Vor eure Schnur, itzt Stab.[105] Kommt, auser-
[korne Frauen!
Freundinnen, den nicht kann vor unserm Jammer
[grauen]
Umgebt dies vorhin hoch, itzt tief gestürzte
[Paar!
Kommt! Rettet neben mir so viel von einer Bahr!

Reihen:

Laßt uns zu allererst des Fürsten Mutter grüßen!
Sie komm' und knie mit uns zu des Erzürnten
[Füßen!
Kein großes Herz, das selbst ein rauher Unmut
[nagt,
Hat Beistand dem, der bat, in letzter Not versagt.

Papiniani erster Diener:

Reißt Erden! Himmel kracht! Rast Wirbelwind
[und sauset!
Ihr steile Klippen springt! Getrotzte Wellen
[brauset!
Führt, Süden! mich von hier, wo unerhörte Kält
Dem Nachruf Grenz und Ziel was auszubreiten
[stellt!
Jagt, Norden! jagt mich fort, wo ihm der Weg
[verriegelt
Und durch entsteckte Glut der Sonnen ganz
[versiegelt!

---

[98] **Reihen** (*pl.*): ranks; here, chorus.
[99] **Frauenzimmer**: women in general; the female sex.
[100] **verteufen**: versenken.
[101] **Vorbitt**: Fürbitte.
[102] **eh** (eher): sooner.
[103] **Astrea**: Astræa; goddess of justice. She lived among men during the Golden Age.

[104] **steuren**: stützen.
[105] **Ich bleib ... Stab**: Once I was (merely) your daughter-in-law (**Schnur**: obsolete meaning), now I am here to support you. (Possible double meaning: Once I was (merely) a "link" now I remain your staff of support.)

Doch ach! Wo wünsch ich hin? Der schrecken-
[volle Tag,
Die jammerschwangre Nacht bebt vor dem
[Donnerschlag.

PLAUTIA:

Ach Götter! Ach was ists? Ach Himmel ists
[geschehn?
Wo ist Papinian?

ERSTER DIENER:

Man wird ihn stracks hier sehen.

REIHEN:

Sag an! Was klagst du denn? Was bringst du
[Schrecklichs vor?

PLAUTIA:

Wo ist mein Herr und Kind?

ERSTER DIENER:

Nicht fern, nah an dem Tor.
Schaut an! Die treue Schar bringt sie hereinge-
[tragen.

*(Beide Leichen werden auf zwei Trauerbetten von
Papiniani Dienern auf den Schauplatz getragen
und einander gegenübergestellt. Plautia redet
nichts ferner, sondern geht höchst traurig von einer
Leiche zu der andern, küßt zuweilen die Häupter
und Hände, bis sie zuletzt auf Papiniani Leichnam
ohnmächtig sinkt und durch ihre Staatsjungfern*[106]
den Leichen nachgetragen wird.)

Doch beiden, leider! sind die Häupter abge-
[schlagen
Durch das verfluchte Beil! Oh Kaiser! Rom
[und Stand!
Oh Sohn! Oh Vater! Oh gestürztes Vaterland!

REIHEN DER DIENER:

Oh nunmehr, oh nun wir in deiner Burg
[erscheinen,
Ach, steh uns frei zu weinen!
Fließt Tränen, die vorhin der rauhe Hof verbot!
Ach, leider ach! Ach! Ach! Papinian ist tot!

REIHEN DER FRAUEN:

Oh schrecklich Anblick! Ach, die müde Mutter
[starret

---

[106] **Staatsjungfer (Hofdame):** lady-in-waiting.

Und weiß nicht, wie ihr wird! Der greise Vater
[harret
Den Atem einzuziehn und reißt die grauen Haar
Von dem schier kahlen Haupt und streut auf
[jede Bahr
Des hohen Alters Schnee. Schlag, Plautie, die
[Brüste!
Fall hin des Scheitels Pracht! Ja grüße, was dich
[küßte,
Wofern dein heißes Leid sich hierdurch lindern
[kann!
Hier liegt dein liebstes Kind, hier liegt dein
[werter Mann.

EUGENIA:

Ha! ha! ha! ha! ha! ha! ha! Sohn! ach! Sohn!
[ach Sonne!
Verdunkelt durch den Tod im Mittag deiner
[Wonne!
Und bin ich noch nicht hin! Oh hört mein
[Wünschen an!
Oh Götter! Oh wofern euch die erbitten kann,
Die nichts zu bitten weiß als ein geschwindes
[Ende,
Verwandelt, eh als ich mein Kind ins Grab
[versende,
Mich Mutter sonder Sohn in einen harten Stein!
Entzieht Verstand und Sinn dem schütternden
[Gebein!
Laßt mich wie Nioben[107] in einen Fels verarten![108]
Ich will den Donnerstrahl nun unerschrocken
[warten.[109]

REIHEN DER FRAUEN:

Ach überhäuftes Trauerspiel!
Ach höchster Seelen blutig Ziel!
Ach können die so schmählich untergehen,
Die vor das Reich, vor Fürst und Tugend stehen?

HOSTILIUS:

Ja schmählich dem, der sie zu diesem Beil
[verwies,

---

[107] **Niobe:** According to legend, the daughter of
Tantalus, and wife of Amphion. She had borne six
sons and six daughters and ventured to compare
herself to the goddess Leto, the wife of Zeus, who
had only two children. As a punishment for her
arrogance, Apollo and Artemis, Leto's children,
slew all Niobe's children. Niobe was changed into
stone by Zeus, but could not even in this form
forget her grief.
[108] **verarten: sich verwandeln: sich umwandeln.**
[109] **warten: erwarten.**

Euch rühmlich, Sohn und uns! Wer so die Welt
[verließ,
Besteigt der Himmel Burg. Ach aber! ach ich
[sterbe,
Indem ich euren Ruhm, mein Sohn und Sohns
[Sohn erbe.
Was steht die Ehre mich? Verwaister, alter Greis!
Was denkst, was gibst du an, Verlaßner? Ach,
[ich weiß,
Ich weiß nicht von mir selbst; ich bin in euch
[gestorben.
Oh hätt ich diese Gunst vor lange Dienst
[erworben,
Daß man das Richtbeil mir, das man auf euch
[gewetzt,
Mit ausgeholtem Streich hätt' an den Hals gesetzt!

REIHEN DER FRAUEN:

Der arme Vater kann der überhäuften Zähren
Sich, was er sich auch sucht zu zwingen, nicht
[erwehren.
Das Pfnutzen[110] dringt hervor; nur Plautien
[gebricht
Das Weinen mit der Red. Itzt schlägt sie das
[Gesicht
Auf ihres Liebsten Leich und starrt ob seinen
[Wangen
Und küßt sein blutig Haupt. Itzt eilt sie zu um-
[fangen
Des Sohns enthalsten Leib; ihr zweifelnd Geist
[erschrickt
Und streitet, wo die Lieb ein größer Leid erblickt.

EUGENIA:

Ach! ach! mein werter Sohn und du mein ander
[Leben!
Ach soll ich beider mich auf einen Tag begeben?
Euch ging das grimme Beil durch Nacken, mir
[durch Herz:
Euch tötete der Zorn des Fürsten, mich der
[Schmerz.

REIHEN DER FRAUEN:

Ach Schmerz! Ach Leiden!
Ach blutig Scheiden!

EUGENIA:

Ist dies Papinian? Ist dies das Angesicht,

Nach dem sich Rom und Welt als seinem Leit-
[stern richt?
Ist dies. die schöne Stirn, auf der der Tugend
[Wesen
In treu Aufrichtigkeit ausdrücklich war zu lesen?
Ist dies der weise Mund, ob dem die Erden
[starrt,
Auf dessen Ausspruch man als auf Weissagung
[harrt?
Ist dies die edle Faust, die Feind und Krieg
[vertrieben
Und Richtschnur und Gesetz der Nachwelt
[vorgeschrieben?
Ist dies Papinian? Ist dies sein blutig End?
Und kracht die Erden nicht, indem er in die Händ
Der Grausamkeit verfällt?

REIHEN:

Ach Ursach! ach, zu klagen!
Welch Höllendonner hat den Lorbeerbaum
[zuschlagen?[111]
Baum, unter dessen Zweig man Schutz und
[Ruhe fand?
Welch Räuber nimmt dich hin, höchst schätzbar
[Himmelspfand?
Wer wird, wer wird nunmehr die Unterdrückten
[schützen?
Der Witwen Beistand sein? Wer die Verwaisten
[stützen?

EUGENIA:

Und du mein Morgenstern! Oh Hoffnung von
[dem Staat!
Stirbst um des Vaters Schuld, der keine Schuld
[nicht hat!
Oh weh! Oh soll ich dir die Augen, leider!
[schließen
Und Zähren auf dein Blut (ich armes Weib!)
[vergießen?
Oh Rose, die der Sturm in erster Blüt abriß!
Wie, daß ich nicht noch nächst den müden Leib
[verließ,
Ja nicht vor Wonne starb, da Rom dich selig
[schätzte
Und sich ob deiner Ehr und Schauspiel höchst
[ergetzte?
Du hättest meinen Geist mit deiner Seel umfaßt;
Du hättest, was ich itzt soll tun, der Glieder Last
Der letzten Glut vertraut und die noch übrig
[Aschen

---

110 **pfnutzen** (niesen; schnauben); here, sob.

111 **zuschlagen**: zerschlagen.

Und dieser Knochen Rest mit Tränen abge-
[waschen,
Die mich vor[112] Balsam, Myhrr und Aloen
[erquickt!
Oh eitel Wünschen! Ach! ach! ach! Der Himmel
[schickt,
Was wider Recht der Zeit: die mich bestatten
[sollten,
Erfordern dies von mir! Heißt dies die Müh
[vergolten?
O Schluß der Götter! Ach! Ich, die nicht
[tüchtig[113] bin,
Leb und schwärm auf der Welt; die tüchtig sind,
[sind hin!
Schaut an mir, schaut und lernt, was wir zu
[hoffen haben!
Auf einmal soll ich Kind und Kindeskind
[vergraben.

HOSTILIUS:

Vergraben, Stamm und Haus und Hilf und
[Schutz und Ehr.
Doch nein, die Ehre blüht und wächst je mehr
[und mehr
Mein Sohn! aus deinem Blut. Doch liegt ihr auf
[der Bahre,
Verwaister Eltern Schmerz und Stab der letzten
[Jahre!
Oh Jahr! Oh Stab! Oh Angst! Mein krachend
[Herz erstickt,
Indem euch durch eur Blut gefärbte Purpur
[schmückt.

REIHEN DER FRAUEN UND DIENER
ZUSAMMEN:

Ach! wer wird, Rom! die Blutschuld dir
[abwischen,
Durch die die zwei ihr reines Blut vermischen?
Ach! ach! Oh Fluch! Oh Schmach! Ach Schmerz!
[Ach Leiden!
Ach kläglich Scheiden!

DER ZWEITE DIENER:

Betrübte, die ihr hier in lauter Tränen schwimmt,
Seht vor euch! Grimm auf Grimm und Trotz
[auf Trotz entglimmt.
Des Fürsten Zorn scheint ganz in Rasen sich
[zu wandeln.

Er heißt, was hier und da erwürgt, aufs heftigst
[handeln.[114]
Man schleift durch Gaß in Gaß in Hacken[115]
[Leich auf Leich.
Ach, daß Papinian der harten Schmach entweich!
Daß nicht sein Eingeweid beflecke Stein und
[Erden!
Eilt! Laßt die Tiber nicht des Greuels fähig
[werden!
Wo waschen wir uns wohl von dieser Untat rein,
Wenn der geweihte Fluß selbst wird entweihet
[sein?

HOSTILIUS:

Oh! Kann ein Schwefelpfeil auf schon Entleibte
[blitzen?
Kann sich die freche Glut auf toter Asch erhitzen?
Welch Nord reißt Wurzeln aus, wenn er den
[Stamm zubrach?[116]
Eilt! eilt! Tragt Bahr und Leich ins innerste
[Gemach!
Schafft schleunigst, was man darf[117] zu beider
[letzten Ehren!
Kommt Diener! Mich verlangt die Reden
[anzuhören,
Womit Papinian die schönen Taten schloß,
Mit welchen er sein Blut vor Fürst und Recht
[vergoß.

REIHEN DER FRAUEN:

Halt, Plautie, sie sinkt zu ihres Liebsten Füßen.
Bestürmte Plautie! Ob er dir schon entrissen,
Doch lebt sein hoher Geist in deiner keuschen
[Brust.
Sie liegt ganz atemlos!

EUGENIA:

Oh angenehme Lust!
Oh Sterben (wo du tot), das über alles Leben!
Oh Ruh (wo dich der Geist auf kurze Zeit be-
[geben)![118]
Tragt! tragt sie mit ihm hin! Kommt Jungfern
[helft uns nach!
Ich Lebend-Tote folg' euch Toten. Wo die Bach
Der Tränen sich verstopft, so soll mein Blut
[abrinnen

---

112 **vor: mehr als.**
113 **tüchtig:** capable; here, physically and mentally
sound.

---

114 **handeln: behandeln.**
115 **Hacken: mit Hacken.** With iron hooks; or pikes
(possible writing error: **in Hucken** = in baskets).
116 **zubrechen: zerbrechen.**
117 **was ... darf: wessen man bedarf.**
118 **begeben: verlassen.**

Und mit dem Geist den Gang durch jedes Glied
[gewinnen.

REIHEN DER FRAUEN:

Wir folgen, doch nicht dir, oh Held! zu deiner
[Gruft,
Nicht dir, den Ewigkeit in ihre Festen ruft.
Wir folgen, großer Mann! höchst klagend und
[gedenken,
Das Recht mit deiner Leich und Sohn ins Grab
[zu senken.

Andreas Gryphius „Aemilius
Papinianus" (1659) Textprobe.
(Aus der Sammlung Curt von
Faber du Faur.) *Courtesy of Yale
University Library.*

Hans Christoffel
von Grimmelshausen

(c. 1622–1676)

Many of the fashionable novels of the Baroque period no longer speak to modern readers, but Grimmelshausen's powerful images of suffering, vanity, and human tenacity in the epoch of the Thirty Years' War continue to appeal to our insecure age; his picaresque characters, trying to survive in a chaotic world, anticipate Thomas Mann's *Felix Krull,* Brecht's *Mother Courage,* and perhaps the dwarfish antihero in Günter Grass's *The Tin Drum.* Hans Christoffel von Grimmelshausen never enjoyed the advantages of a sustained education; when the town of Gelnhausen (east of Frankfurt, in Hessia), where he was born, was sacked by the Croatians, the young man decided to join the armies; drifting about, he fought on both sides and matured in a world of violence and deceit. When peace came (1648) his life changed completely: within a year, he married a soldier's daughter and settled as steward on one of the estates of his former commander. Sober and resourceful, an able horse trader and merchant, he made money enough to buy the local tavern Zum silbernen Stern; however, business was slow, and he decided to seek employment again. After he had administered the estates of a well-to-do Strassburg physician (who may have been helpful in furthering Grimmelshausen's contacts with the literary men of that city), he was appointed chief magistrate by the Bishop of Straßburg. His last years were overshadowed by war again; when he died, his village on the fringes of the Black Forest was once again exposed to plunder, fire, and the rapacity of victors and conquered alike.

Grimmelshausen wrote a number of religious and historical novels but when he seized upon the literary conventions of the picaresque novel (imported into Germany from Spain and France), he discovered the form most closely corresponding to his particular talent. In his *Abenteuerlicher Simplicissimus* (1669), he tells the story of a paradigmatic life in a period of brutality and vice; young Simplicissimus fights and travels all over Europe until he seems to find contentment in solitude and meditation; soon, however, he feels his recurrent desire to live in the world, sails around the globe and, when the reader last hears of him, settles as an unworldly hermit on a lonely island in the far seas. Simplicissimus shares his inventive energy and his quick wit with the unheroic vagabonds of the Spanish novels, but Grimmelshausen, who knew a prose version of *Parzival,* transcends the limits of the inherited form in his richness of erudite detail, his concern for the young man's development, and his closeness to the terrible experiences of the war. His essential virtues are not those of an historian; Grimmelshausen has such prolific imagination and creative energy that his characters, like those of Balzac, live beyond the individual novel. Most of Simplicissimus' friends and enemies reappear in narrative sequels in which they, in turn, become central figures, e.g., one of his companions in *Der seltsame Springinsfeld* (1670), and a lady of easy virtue well-known to him in *Die Landstörtzerin Courasche* (1670); they are figures of such independence and vitality that they constitute an epic universe of which each novel forms but a part.

In his *Ausführliche und wunderseltsame Lebensbeschreibung der Erzbetrügerin und Landstörtzerin Courasche,* Grimmelshausen combines the traditions of the picaresque novel and the epic effectiveness of a "true confession." An old and haggard sutler-woman who, in her prime, had a number of other professions, recounts her experiences not to amuse, but to take revenge upon her former lovers and to show how successfully she deceived them all. She is the young Czech girl Lebuschka (Libuška), born in the town of Bragoditz (Prachatitz) in Southern Bohemia; when the imperial army appears before the gates in the fall of 1620, she dresses like a boy to escape danger. As a boy, she enters the service of a handsome imperial officer to whom she is forced to reveal her true sex; the young officer marries her. In her account, she confesses that he was the only man she ever really loved; when he is killed in battle, her life is dominated by lust and greed; she marries again and again for money, and commences an adventurous life of deceit, prostitution, and many narrow escapes.

DIE LANDSTÖRTZERIN COURASCHE

Courasche schreitet zur dritten Ehe und wird aus einer Hauptmännin[1] eine Leutenantin,[2] trifft's aber nicht so wohl als vorher, schlägt sich mit ihrem Leutenant um die Hosen mit Prügeln und gewinnt solche[3] durch ihre tapfere Resolution[4] und Courage; darauf sich ihr Mann unsichtbar macht und sie sitzenläßt.[5]

Das VII. Kapitel

Mein Mann war kaum kalt und begraben, da hattte ich schon wiederum ein ganzes Dutzend Freier und die Wahl darunter, welchen ich aus ihnen nehmen wollte; denn
5 ich war nicht allein schön und jung, sondern hatte auch schöne Pferde und ziemlich viel altes Geld; und ob ich mich gleich[6] vernehmen ließ, daß ich meinem Hauptmann sel.[7] zu Ehren noch ein halbes Jahr trauern wollte, so
10 konnte ich jedoch die importunen[8] Hummeln, die um mich wie um einen fetten Honighafen,[9] der keinen Deckel hat, herumschwärmten, nicht abtreiben.[10] Der Obriste[11] versprach mir bei dem Regiment Unterhalt und Quartier,
15 bis ich meine Gelegenheit[12] anders anstellte;[13] hingegen ließ ich zwei von meinen Knechten Herrendienste[14] versehen; und wenn es Gelegenheit gab, bei der ich vor[15] meine Person vom Feind etwas zu erschnappen[16]
20 getraute, so sparte[17] ich meine Haut sowenig als[18] ein Soldat, allermaßen[19] ich in dem

anmutigen und fast lustigen Treffen bei Wimpfen[20] einen Leutenant und im Nachhauen[21] unweit Heilbrunn[22] einen Kornett samt[23] seiner Standart gefangen bekommen; 25 meine beiden Knechte aber haben bei Plünderung der Wägen ziemliche Beuten an barem Geld gemacht, welche sie unserem Akkord[24] gemäß mit mir teilen mußten. Nach dieser Schlacht bekam ich mehr Liebhaber als 30 zuvor, und demnach[25] ich bei meinem vorigen Mann mehr gute Tage als gute Nächte gehabt, zumalen[26] wider meinen Willen seit seinem Tod gefastet, siehe, so gedachte ich, durch meine Wahl alle solche Versäumnis wieder- 35 einzubringen, und versprach[27] mich einem Leutenant, der meinem Bedünken[28] nach alle seine Mitbuhler,[29] beides, an Schönheit, Jugend, Verstand und Tapferkeit, übertraf. Dieser war von Geburt ein Italiener, und 40 zwar schwarz von Haaren, aber weiß von Haut, und in meinen Augen so schön, daß ihn kein Maler hätte schöner malen können. Er bewies gegen mir fast eine Hundsdemut, bis er mich erlöffelt,[30] und da er das Jawort 45 hinweg hatte, stellte er sich so freudenvoll, als wenn Gott die ganze Welt beraubt und ihn allein beseligt hätte. Wir wurden in der Pfalz kopuliert[31] und hatten die Ehre, daß der Obriste selbst neben den meisten hohen 50 Offizieren des Regiments bei der Hochzeit erschienen, die uns alle vergeblich viel Glück in einer langwürigen[32] Ehe wünschten.

Dann nachdem wir nach der ersten Nacht bei Aufgang der Sonne beisammen lagen, 55 zu faulenzen, und uns mit allerhand liebrei-

---

[1] **Hauptmännin**: wife of a captain (**Hauptmann**).
[2] **Leutenantin**: wife of a lieutenant (**Leutnant**).
[3] **solche**: such; refers to the antecedent **Hosen**.
[4] **Resolution**: determination.
[5] **sitzen lassen**: desert.
[6] **ob ich mich gleich**: obgleich ich mich.
[7] **sel.** (*abbr. for* **selig**): deceased.
[8] **importun**: annoying; bothersome.
[9] **Honighafen**: Honigtopf.
[10] **abtreiben**: drive off.
[11] **Obriste (Oberst)**: colonel.
[12] **Gelegenheit (Angelegenheit)**: affairs; business.
[13] **anstellen**: arrange.
[14] **Herrendienste**: Soldatendienste.
[15] **vor**: für.
[16] **erschnappen**: snatch.
[17] **sparen**: here, give heed to; be mindful of.
[18] **als**: wie.
[19] **allermaßen**: nachdem.

[20] **Wimpfen**: town on the Neckar, where Tilly, commander in chief of the field forces of the Catholic League was victorious over Margrave George Frederick of Baden-Durlach (May 6, 1622). The latter was an adherent of the Protestant "Winter King," Frederick V.
[21] **Nachhauen**: pursuit of the enemy.
[22] **Heilbrunn**: present-day Heilbronn.
[23] **samt (mitsamt)**: together with.
[24] **Akkord**: contract.
[25] **demnach**: nachdem.
[26] **zumalen**: especially.
[27] **sich jemandem versprechen**: become engaged to someone.
[28] **Bedünken**: opinion.
[29] **Mitbuhler**: rival.
[30] **erlöffeln**: durch Schmeicheln und Werben gewinnen.
[31] **kopulieren**: join in marriage.
[32] **langwürig (langwierig)**: long-lasting.

chem und freundlichem Gespräch unter-
hielten, ich auch eben aufzustehen vermeinte,[33]
da rief mein Leutenant seinen Jungen zu sich
60 vors Bett und befahl ihm, daß er zwei starke
Prügel herbeibringen sollte. Er war gehorsam,
und ich bildete mir ein, der arme Schelm[34]
würde dieselben am allerersten versuchen
müssen; unterließ derowegen[35] nicht, vor[36]
65 den Jungen zu bitten, bis er beide Prügel
brachte und auf empfangenen Befehl auf den
Tisch zum Nachtzeug legte. Als nun der
Junge wieder hinweg war, sagte mein Hochzeiter zu mir: „Ja, Liebste, Ihr wißt, daß
70 jedermann davorgehalten[37] und geglaubt, Ihr
hättet bei Eures vorigen Mannes Lebzeiten
die Hosen getragen, welches ihm dann bei
ehrlichen Gesellschaften zu nicht geringerer
Beschimpfung nachgeredet worden; weil
75 ich dann nicht unbillig[38] zu besorgen[39] habe,
Ihr möchtet in solcher Gewohnheit verharren
und auch die meinigen tragen wollen, welches
mir aber zu leiden unmöglich oder doch sonst
schwerfallen würde; seht, so liegen sie dort
80 auf dem Tische und jene zwei Prügel zu dem
Ende[40] dabei, damit wir beide uns, wenn Ihr
sie etwa wie vor diesem[41] Euch zuschreiben
und behaupten wolltet, zuvor darum schlagen
könnten, sintemal[42] mein Schatz selbst erach-
85 ten kann, daß es besser getan ist, sie fallen
gleich jetzt im Anfang dem einen oder
andern Teil zu, als wenn wir hernach in
stehender[43] Ehe täglich darum kriegen.[44]“ Ich
antwortete: „Mein Liebster!“ und damit gab
90 ich ihm gar einen herzlichen Kuß, „ich hätte
vermeint gehabt, diejenige Schlacht, so[45] wir
einander diesmal zu liefern, sei allbereit[46]
gehalten; so hab ich auch niemals in Sinn
genommen,[47] Euere Hosen zu prätendieren,[48]

sondern, gleich wie ich wohl weiß, daß das   95
Weib nicht aus des Mannes Haupt, aber wohl
aus seiner Seite genommen worden, also habe
ich gehofft, meinem Herzliebsten werde solches
auch bekannt sein und er werde derowegen
sich meines Herkommens erinnern und mich   100
nicht, als wenn ich von seinen Fußsohlen genommen worden wäre, vor[49] sein Fußtuch, sondern vor[50] sein Ehegemahl halten, vornehmlich,[51] wenn ich mich auch nicht unterstünde,
ihm auf dem Kopf zu sitzen, sondern mich an   105
seiner Seite behülfe mit demütiger Bitte, er
wollte diese abenteuerliche Fechtschule einstellen.“—„Ha ha!“ sagte er, „das sind die rechten
Weibergriffe, die Herrschaft zu sich reißen ehe
mans[52] gewahr wird; aber es muß zuvor darum   110
gefochten sein, damit ich wisse, wer dem
anderen künftig zu gehorsamen[53] schuldig.“
Und damit warf er sich aus meinen Armen
wie ein anderer Narr; ich aber sprang
aus dem Bett und legte mein Hemd und   115
Schlafhosen an, erwischte den kürzesten, aber
doch den stärksten Prügel und sagte: „Weil Ihr
mir je zu fechten befehlt und dem obsiegen-
den[54] Teil die Oberherrlichkeit (an die ich
doch keine Ansprache[55] zu haben begehrt)   120
über den Überwundenen zusprecht, so wäre ich
wohl närrisch, wenn ich eine Gelegenheit aus
den Händen ließe, etwas zu erhalten, daran
ich sonst nicht gedenken[56] dürfte.“ Er hingegen auch nicht faul: dann nachdem ich also   125
seiner wartete und er seine Hosen auch angelegt, ertappte[57] er den andern Prügel und
gedachte, mich beim Kopf zu fassen, um mir
alsdann den Buckel[58] fein mit guter Muße
abzuraumen.[59] Aber ich war ihm viel zu   130
geschwind, denn ehe er sichs versah, hatte
er eins am Kopf, davon er hinaustürmelte[60]
wie ein Ochs, dem ein Streich worden. Ich
raffte die zwei Stecken[61] zusammen, sie zur Tür

---

[33] **vermeinen**: here, intend.
[34] **Schelm**: here, chap; fellow.
[35] **derowegen: deswegen.**
[36] **vor: für.**
[37] **davorhalten (dafürhalten)**: be of the opinion.
[38] **unbillig**: unreasonable; here, needless.
[39] **besorgen**: here, fear; be apprehensive.
[40] **zu dem Ende**: to that end; for that purpose.
[41] **vor diesem: vorher.**
[42] **sintemal** (*arch.*): since; inasmuch as.
[43] **stehend: bestehend.**
[44] **kriegen**: fight.
[45] **so: die.**
[46] **allbereit(s): already.**
[47] **ich . . . genommen**: it never occurred to me.
[48] **prätendieren: claim.**

[49] **vor: für.**
[50] **vor: für.**
[51] **vornehmlich: besonders.**
[52] **mans: man es.**
[53] **gehorsamen: obey.**
[54] **obsiegend: siegend.**
[55] **Ansprache (Anspruch)**: demand; claim.
[56] **gedenken: denken.**
[57] **ertappte: ergriff.**
[58] **Buckel** (*vulgar*): hump; here, back.
[59] **abraumen: verprügeln.**
[60] **hinaustürmeln (hinaustaumeln)**: stagger out.
[61] **Stecken**: stick; here, cudgel.

hinauszuwerfen, und da ich solche öffnete, standen etliche Offiziere davor, die unserem Handel[62] zugehört und zum Teil durch einen Spalt zugesehen hatten; diese ließ ich lachen, solang sie mochten, schlug die Tür vor ihnen wieder zu, warf meinen Rock um mich und brachte meinen Tropfen,[63] meinen Hochzeiter wollte ich sagen, mit Wasser aus einem Lavor[64] wieder zu sich selbst; und da ich ihn zum Tisch gesetzt und mich ein wenig angekleidet hatte, ließ ich die Offiziere vor der Tür auch zu uns ins Zimmer kommen.

Wie wir einander allerseits angesehen, mag jeder bei sich selbst erachten.[65] Ich merkte wohl, daß mein Hochzeiter diese Offiziere veranlaßt, daß sie sich um diese Zeit vorm Zimmer einstellen und seiner Torheit Zeugen sein sollten; dann als sie den Hegel[66] gefoppt,[67] er würde mir die Hosen lassen müssen, hatte er sich gegen ihnen gerühmt, daß er einen sonderbaren[68] Vorteil[69] wisse, welchen er den ersten Morgen ins Werk setzen und mich dadurch so geschmeidig[70] machen wollte, daß ich zittern würde, wenn er mich nur scheel[71] ansähe; aber der gute Mensch hätte es gegen eine andere als die Courasche probieren mögen.[72] Gegen mir hat er soviel ausgerichtet, daß er jedermanns Gespött worden, und ich hätte nicht mit ihm gehaust,[73] wenn mirs nicht von Höheren befohlen und auferlegt worden wäre. Wie wir aber miteinander gelebt, kann sich jeder leicht einbilden,[74] nämlich wie Hund und Katze. Als er sich nun anderergestalt[75] an mir nicht revanchieren und auch das Gespött der Leute nicht mehr gedulden konnte, rappelte er einmal alle meine Barschaft zusammen[76]

---

und ging mit den drei besten Pferden und einem Knecht zum Gegenteil.[77]

Courasche hält sich in einer Okkasion[78] trefflich frisch,[79] haut einem Soldaten den Kopf ab, bekommt einen Major gefangen und erfährt, daß ihr Leutenant als ein meineidiger Überläufer gefangen und gehenkt worden.

Das VIII. Kapitel

Also wurde ich nun zu einer Halbwittib,[80] welcher Stand viel elender ist, als wenn eine gar keinen Mann hat. Etliche argwohnten, ich würde ihm folgen und wir hätten unsere Flucht also miteinander angelegt;[81] da ich aber den Obristen um Rat und Befehl fragte, wie ich mich verhalten sollte, sagte er, ich möchte bei dem Regiment verbleiben, so wollte er mich, solang ich mich ehrlich hielte, wie andere Wittweiber[82] verpflegen lassen; und damit benahm ich jedermann den gedachten Argwohn. Ich mußte mich ziemlich schmal behelfen, weil meine Barschaft ausgeflogen[83] und meine stattlichen Soldatenpferde fort waren, auf denen ich auch manche stattliche Beute gemacht; doch ließ ich meine Armut nicht merken, damit mir keine Verachtung zuwüchse. Meine beiden Knechte, die Herrendienste versahen, hatte ich noch samt einem Jungen und noch etlichen Schindmähren[84] oder Bagagepferden;[85] davon und von meiner Männer Bagage versilberte[86] ich, was Geld galt, und machte mich wieder trefflich beritten. Ich durfte zwar als Weib auf keine Partei reiten,[87] aber unter den Fouragieren[88] fand sich nicht meinesgleichen. Ich wünschte mir oft wieder eine Battalia[89] wie vor Wimpfen; aber was halfs? ich mußte die Zeit erwarten, weil man mir zu Gefallen

---

[62] **Handel**: here, quarrel; brawl.
[63] **Tropfen: Tölpel.**
[64] **Lavor: Waschbecken.**
[65] **bei ... erachten**: sich selbst vorstellen.
[66] **Hegel (Zuchtstier)**: bull kept for breeding.
[67] **foppen**: tease; taunt.
[68] **sonderbar**: singular; unusual.
[69] **Vorteil**: here, scheme; trick.
[70] **geschmeidig**: docile; yielding.
[71] **scheel**: cross-eyed; here, malevolently.
[72] **mögen: sollen.**
[73] **hausen (mit)**: live with.
[74] **sich einbilden**: sich vorstellen.
[75] **anderergestalt**: auf andere Weise.
[76] **zusammenrappeln (zusammenraffen)**: snatch up.

[77] **Gegenteil (Gegner)**: here, the enemy.
[78] **Okkasion (Gefecht; Scharmützel)**: battle; skirmish.
[79] **frisch**: here, spirited; courageous.
[80] **Halbwittib**: "half-widow."
[81] **anlegen**: plot; contrive.
[82] **Wittweib (Witwe)**: widow.
[83] **ausgeflogen**: fort (-geflogen).
[84] **Schindmähre**: sorry-looking nag.
[85] **Bagagepferd**: packhorse.
[86] **versilbern**: here, sell; turn into cash.
[87] **auf Partei reiten**: participate (ride) in a raid.
[88] **Fouragier (Furagier)**: soldier in search of spoils.
[89] **Battalia: Schlacht.**

doch keine Schlacht gehalten, wenn ichs
gleich begehrt hätte. Damit ich aber gleich-
205 wohl auch wiederum zu Geld kommen
möchte, dessen es auf dem Fouragieren
selten setzte,[90] ließ ich (beides, um solches
zu verdienen und meinen Auseißer um seine
Untreu zu bezahlen) mich von denen treffen,
210 die spendierten; und also brachte ich mich
durch und dingte mir noch einen starken
Jungen zum Knecht, der mir mußte helfen
stehlen, wann[91] die anderen beiden mußten
wachen. Das trieb ich so fort, bis wir den
215 Braunschweiger über den Main jagten und
viele der Seinigen darin ersäuften, in welchem
Treffen ich mich unter die Unserigen mischte
und in meines Obristen Gegenwart dergestalt[92] erzeigte, daß er solche Tapferkeit von
220 keinem Mannsbild[93] geglaubt hätte; dann ich
nahm in der Caracolle[94] einen Major vom
Gegenteil vor seiner Truppe hinweg, als er
die Charge reduplieren[95] wollte; und als ihn
einer von den Seinigen zu erretten gedachte
225 und mir zu solchem Ende eine Pistole an den
Kopf losbrannte, daß mir Hut und Federn
davonstoben, bezahlte ich ihn dergestalt mit
meinem Säbel, daß er noch etliche Schritte
ohne Kopf mit mir ritte, welches beides,
230 verwunderlich und abscheulich, anzusehen
war. Nachdem nun dieselbe Eskadron getrennt und in die Flucht gewendet worden,
mir auch der Major einen ziemlichen Stumpen[96] Goldsorten samt einer goldenen Kette
235 und kostbarlichem[97] Ring vor[98] sein Leben
gegeben hatte, ließ ich meinen Jungen das
Pferd mit ihm vertauschen und lieferte ihn
den Unserigen in Sicherheit, begab mich
darauf an die zerbrochene Brücke, allwo es
240 in dem Wasser an ein erbärmliches Ersaufen
und auf dem Land an ein grausames Nieder-
machen ging: und alldieweil[99] noch ein
jeder bei seiner Truppe bleiben mußte, soviel
immer möglich, packte ich eine Kutsche mit
245 sechs schönen Braunen an, auf welcher weder

Geld noch lebendige Personen, aber wohl
zwei Kisten mit kostbaren Kleidern und
weißem Zeug[100] sich befanden. Ich brachte
sie mit meines Knechtes oder Jungen Hilfe
dahin, wo ich den Major gelassen hatte, 250
welcher sich schier zu Tod kränkte, daß er
von einem solchen jungen Weib gefangen
worden; da er aber sah, daß sowohl in meinen
Hosensäcken[101] als in den Halftern Pistolen
steckten, die ich samt meinem Karbiner[102] 255
dort wieder lud und fertig machte, auch
hörte, was ich hiervor bei Wimpfen ausgerichtet, gab er sich wiederum etwas zufrieden
und sagte: „Der Teufel möchte mit so einer
Hexe etwas zu schaffen haben!" Ich ging 260
mit meinem Jungen (den ich ebenso fest als
mich und mein Pferd gemacht hatte) hin, noch
mehr Beuten zu erschnappen,[103] fand aber
den Obristleutenant von unserem Regiment
dort unter seinem Pferde liegen, der mich 265
kannte und um Hilfe anschrie. Ich packte
ihn auf meines Jungen Pferd und führte ihn
zu den Unserigen in meine erst eroberte
Kutsche, allda[104] er meinem gefangenen
Major Gesellschaft leisten mußte. Es ist nicht 270
zu glauben, wie ich nach dieser Schlacht
sowohl von meinen Neidern als meinen
Gönnern gelobt wurde; beide Teile sagten, ich
wäre der Teufel selber; und eben damals
war mein höchster Wunsch, daß ich nur kein 275
Weibsbild[105] wäre; aber was wars drum? es
war Null und verhimpelt.[106] Ich gedachte oft,
mich vor[107] einen Hermaphroditen auszuge-
ben, ob ich vielleicht dadurch erlangen
möchte, öffentlich Hosen zu tragen und 280
vor einen jungen Kerl zu passieren; hergegen[108] hatte ich aber durch meine unmäßige
Begierde so viel Kerle empfinden lassen, wer
ich wäre, daß ich das Herz nicht hatte, ins
Werk zu setzen, was ich gerne gewollt; 285
dann so viel Zeugen würden sonst ein anderes
von mir gesagt und verursacht[109] haben, daß

---

[90] **setzte: gab.**
[91] **wann: während.**
[92] **dergestalt (derart): in such a way.**
[93] **Mannsbild: Mann.**
[94] **Caracolle: Getümmel.**
[95] **die Charge reduplieren: repeat the attack.**
[96] **Stumpen (Haufen): heap; pile (of money).**
[97] **kostbarlich (kostbar): valuable.**
[98] **vor: für.**
[99] **alldieweil: weil.**

[100] **weißes Zeug (Weißzeug): linen.**
[101] **Hosensack (Hosentasche): trouser pocket.**
[102] **Karbiner (Karabiner): firearm of the cavalry.**
[103] **erschnappen: snatch; lay hold of.**
[104] **allda: (wo): where.**
[105] **Weibsbild: Weib; Frau.**
[106] **verhimpelt (verpfuscht): botched; bungled.**
[107] **vor: für.**
[108] **hergegen (dagegen): on the other hand.**
[109] **verursachen: testify, produce (conflicting) testi-
mony.**

es dahin kommen wäre, daß mich beide,
Medici und Hebammen, beschauen müßten;
290 behalf mich derowegen, wie ich konnte; und
wenn man mir viel verweisen wollte, antwortete ich, es wären wohl ehe[110] Amazonen
gewesen, die so ritterlich als die Männer
gegen ihre Feinde gefochten hätten. Damit ich
295 nun des Obristen Gnade erhalten und von ihm
wider meine Mißgünstigen[111] beschützt werden möchte, präsentierte ich ihm neben dem
Gefangenen auch meine Kutsche mitsamt den
Pferden, davor[112] er mir 200 Reichstaler
300 verehrte, welches Geld ich samt dem, was ich
sonst auf ein Neues erschnappt und sonst
verdient hatte, abermal in einer namhaften
Stadt verwahrte.

Indem wir nun Mannheim eingenommen
305 und Frankenthal noch belagert hielten und
also den Meister in der Pfalz spielten, siehe,
da schlugen Corduba und der von Anhalt
abermal den Braunschweiger und Mansfelder
bei Floreack, in welchem Treffen mein aus-
310 gerissener Mann, der Leutenant, gefangen,
von den Unserigen erkannt und als ein meineidiger Überlaufer mit seinem allerbesten Hals
an einen Baum geknüpft worden; wodurch
ich zwar wieder von meinem Mann erlöst
315 und zu einer Wittib ward; ich bekam aber so
einen Haufen Feinde, die da sagten: „Die
Strahl-Hexe hat den armen Teufel ums Leben
gebracht!“, daß ich ihm das Leben gern
länger gönnen und mich noch eine Weile
320 mit ihm gedulden mögen, bis er gleichwohl
anderwärts[113] ins Gras gebissen[114] und einen
ehrlicheren Tod genommen, wenn es nur
hätte sein können.

Courasche quittiert[115] *den Krieg, nachdem ihr
kein Stern mehr leuchten will und sie fast von
jedermann vor einen Spott gehalten wird.*[116]

Das IX. Kapitel

Also kam es nach und nach dahin, daß ich
325 mich je länger je mehr leiden mußte.[117] Meine

Knechte wurden mir verführt,[118] weil zu ihnen
gesagt wurde: „Pfui Teufel, wie möchtet ihr
Kerle einer solchen Vettel[119] dienen?“ Ich
hoffte, wieder einen Mann zu bekommen, aber
ein jeder sagte: „Nimm du sie, ich begehre 330
ihrer nicht!“ Was ehrlich gesinnt war, schüt-
telte den Kopf über mich, und also taten
auch beinahe alle Offiziere; was aber geringe
Leute und schlechte Potentaten[120] waren, die
durften sich nicht bei mir anmelden; so hätte 335
ich ohnedas auch keinen aus denselbigen
angesehen. Ich empfand zwar nicht am Hals
wie mein Mann, was unser närrisches Fechten
ausgerichtet; aber doch hatte ich länger daran,
als er am Henken,[121] zu verdauen. Ich wäre 340
gerne in eine andere Haut geschloffen, aber
beides, die Gewohnheit und meine täglichen
Gesellschaften, wollte mir keine Besserung
zulassen, wie denn die allermeisten Leute im
Krieg viel eher ärger als frömmer zu werden 345
pflegen. Ich putzte mich[122] wieder und
richtete dem einen und andern allerhand
Netze und Stricke, ob ich etwa diesen oder
jenen anseilen und ins Garn bringen möchte;[123] aber es half nichts; ich war schon 350
allbereit viel zu tief im Geschrei;[124] man
kannte die Courasche schon allerdings bei
der ganzen Armee, und wo ich bei den
Regimentern vorüberritt, wurde mir meine
Ehre durch viele tausend Stimmen öffentlich 355
ausgerufen, also daß ich mich schier[125] wie
eine Nachteule bei Tage nicht mehr durfte
sehen lassen. Im Marschieren äußerten[126] mich
ehrliche Weiber; das Lumpengesindel beim
Troß schurrigelte[127] mich sonst,[128] und was 360
etwa vor ledige Offiziere wegen ihrer Nacht-
weide mich gern geschützt hätten, mußten
bei den Regimentern bleiben, bei welchen
mir aber durch ihr schändliches Geschrei mit
der allerschärfsten Lauge aufgegossen[129] ward, 365

---

110 **ehe**: here, previously.
111 **Mißgünstige**: envious persons.
112 **davor (wofür)**: for which.
113 **anderwärts**: anderswo.
114 **ins Gras beißen**: sterben.
115 **quittieren**: leave; withdraw from.
116 **vor einen Spott halten**: verspotten.
117 **sich leiden müssen**: Verdruß haben.

118 **verführen**: here, lure away.
119 **Vettel**: old woman; hag; witch.
120 **schlechte Potentaten**: unbedeutende Kerle.
121 **Henken**: hanging; here, the state of being hung.
122 **sich putzen**: "doll up"; adorn oneself.
123 **möchte**: könnte.
124 **im Geschrei**: in schlechtem Ruf.
125 **schier**: very nearly; almost.
126 **äussern**: here, shun; steer clear of.
127 **schurrigeln (schurigeln)**: vex; worry; plague.
128 **sonst**: ohnedies; sowieso.
129 **mit der allerschärfsten Lauge aufgiessen**: *lit.*,
    throw extremely caustic lye upon someone; *fig.*,
    jeer at; insult.

also daß ich wohl sah, daß meine Sache so in
die Länge kein gut mehr tun werde. Etliche
Offiziere hatte ich noch zu Freunden, die aber
nicht meinen, sondern ihren Nutzen suchten;
370 teils suchten ihre Wollüste, teils mein Geld,
andere meine schönen Pferde; sie alle aber
machten mir Ungelegenheit und Schmarotzen,[130] und war doch keiner, der mich zu
heiraten begehrte, entweder daß sie sich
375 meiner schämten oder daß sie mir eine un-

ja ich kann mich auch nicht überreden lassen
zu glauben, daß sich unter andern ehrlichen
Leuten viele gefunden haben, die um meine
Hinfahrt viel geweint, es seien denn etliche
wenige junge Schnapper ledigen Standes   390
unter den mittelmäßigen Offizieren gewesen,
denen ich zu Zeiten etwa ein Paar Schlafhosen gewaschen. Der Obriste hatte den Ruhm
nicht gern, daß seine schöne Kutsche durch
die Courasche vom Feind erobert und ihm   395

„Die Ertzbetrügerin und Land-
störtzerin Courasche" (1670):
Illustrierte Titelseite (Aus der
Sammlung Curt von Faber du
Faur.) *Courtesy of Yale University
Library.*

glückliche Eigenschaft zuschrieben, die allen
meinen Männern schädlich wäre, oder aber
daß sie sich sonst, ich weiß nicht warum, vor
mir fürchteten.
380   Derowegen beschloß ich mit mir selbsten,
nicht nur dies Regiment, sondern auch die
Armada, ja den ganzen Krieg zu quittieren,
und konnte es auch um soviel desto leichter
ins Werk setzen, weil die hohen Offiziere
385 meiner vorlängst[131] gern losgewesen wären;

verehrt worden sein sollte. Daß ich den verwundeten Obristleutnant aus der Battalia
und Todesgefahr errettet und zu den Unserigen geführt, davon schrieb er ihm so wenig
Ehre zu, daß er mir meiner Mühe[132] nicht   400
allein mit „Potz Velten!"[133] dankte, sondern
auch, wenn er mich sah, mit griesgramen-
den[134] Mienen errötete und mir, wie leicht
zu gedenken, lauter Glück und Heil an den
Hals wünschte. Das Frauenzimmer oder die   405

---

130 **schmarotzen:** live at other people's expense;
  sponge (upon people).
131 **vorlängst: längst.**

132 **meiner Mühe: für meine Mühe.**
133 **Potz Velten:** an oath.
134 **griesgramend (griesgrämig):** surly; sullen.

Offiziersweiber haßten mich, weil ich weit schöner war als eine unter dem ganzen Regiment, zumalen teils ihren Männern auch besser gefiel; und beides, hohe und niedere Soldaten, waren mir feind, um daß ich trotz einem unter ihnen allen das Herz hatte, etwas zu unterstehen[135] und ins Werk zu setzen, das die größte Tapferkeit und verwegenste Hazarde erforderte und darüber sonst manchem das kalte Wehe angestoßen[136] hätte.

Gleichwie ich nun leicht merkte, daß ich viel mehr Feinde als Freunde hatte, also konnte ich mir auch wohl einbilden, es würde ein jedweder von meiner widerwärtigen Gattung[137] gar nicht unterlassen, mir auf ihre sonderbare Manier eins anzumachen,[138] wenn sich nur die Gelegenheit dazu ereignet. „O Courasche", sagte ich zu mir selbst, „wie willst du so vielen unterschiedlichen Feinden entgehen können, von denen vielleicht ein jeder seinen besondern Anschlag auf dich hat? Wenn du sonst nichts hättest als deine schönen Pferde, deine schönen Kleider, dein schönes Gewehr und den Glauben, daß du viel Geld bei dir habest, so wären es Feinde genug, einige Kerle anzuhetzen,[139] dich heimlich hinzurichten. Wie? wenn dich dergleichen Kerle ermordeten oder in einer Okkasion niedermachten? was würde wohl für ein Hahn danach krähen?[140] wer würde deinen Tod rächen? Was? solltest du auch wohl deinen eigenen Knechten trauen dürfen?" Mit dergleichen Sorgen quälte ich mich selbst und fragte mich auch selbst, was Rats? weil ich sonst niemand hatte, ders treulich mit mir meinte; und eben deswegen mußte ich mir auch selbst folgen.

Demnach sprach ich den Obristen um einen Paß an in die nächste Reichsstadt, die mir eben an der Hand stand[141] und wohl gelegen war, mich von dem Kriegsvolk zu retirieren; den erlangte ich nicht allein ohne große Mühe, sondern noch anstatt eines Abschieds eine Urkunde, daß ich einem Hauptmann vom Regiment (denn von meinem letzten Mann begehrte ich keinen Ruhm zu haben) ehrlich verheiratet gewesen und, als ich solchen vorm Feind verloren, mich eine Zeitlang bei dem Regiment aufgehalten und in solcher währenden Zeit also wohl, fromm und ehrlich gehalten, wie einer rechtschaffenen ehr- und tugendliebenden Dame gebühre und wohlanständig sei, mich derowegen jedermänniglichen[142] um solchen meines untadelhaften tugendlichen Wandels willen bestens rekommendierend. Und solche fetten Lügen wurden mit eigenhändiger Subskription[143] und beigedrucktem Sigill[144] in bester Form bekräftigt. Solches lasse sich aber niemand wundern;[145] denn je schlimmer sich einer hält und je lieber man einen gerne los wäre, je trefflicher wird der Abschied sein, den man einem solchen mit auf den Weg gibt; sonderlich[146] wenn derselbe zugleich sein Lohn sein muß. Einen Knecht und ein Pferd ließ ich dem Obristen unter seiner Kompanie, welcher trutz einem Offizier mundiert war,[147] um meine Dankbarkeit damit zu bezeugen; hingegen brachte ich einen Knecht, einen Jungen, eine Magd, sechs schöne Pferde (darunter das eine 100 Dukaten wert gewesen) samt einem wohlgespickten[148] Wagen davon; und kann ich bei meinem großen Gewissen (etliche nennen es ein weites Gewissen) nicht sagen, mit welcher Faust ich alle diese Sachen erobert und zuwege gebracht habe.

Da ich nun mich und das Meinige in bemeldete[149] Stadt in Sicherheit gebracht hatte, versilberte ich meine Pferde und gab sonst alles hinweg, was Geld galt und ich nicht gar nötig brauchte; mein Gesinde schaffte ich auch miteinander ab, einen geringen Kosten[150] zu haben. Gleichwie mirs aber zu Wien war

---

135 **etwas unterstehen: etwas wagen.**

136 **das ... angestoßen: in Todesgefahr gebracht.**

137 **widerwärtige Gattung:** hateful sort; here, Courasche's enemies, collectively.

138 **jemandem eins anmachen (jemandem etwas antun; etwas "anhängen"):** "pin" the blame for something on someone.

139 **anhetzen (aufhetzen):** incite; stir up.

140 **was ... krähen?:** *lit.*, what rooster would crow about it? i.e., who would care?

141 **an der Hand stehen:** be nearby.

142 **jedermänniglichen: jedermann.**

143 **Subskription:** here, signature.

144 **Sigill (Siegel):** seal.

145 **Solches ... wundern: darüber soll sich aber niemand wundern.**

146 **sonderlich (insbesondere):** in particular.

147 **trutz ... war:** equipped like an officer, although he was only a poor imitation of one.

148 **wohlgespickt: gut gefüllt.**

149 **bemeldet: erwähnt; besagt.**

150 **einen geringen Kosten: geringe Kosten.**

490 gegangen, also ging mirs auch hier: Ich
konnte abermal des Namens Courasche nicht
los werden, wiewohl ich ihn unter allen meinen Sachen am allerwohlfeilsten[151] hinweg-
gegeben hätte; denn meine alten oder viel-
495 mehr die jungen Kunden von der Armee
ritten mir zu Gefallen in die Stadt und fragten
mir mit solchem Namen nach, welchen auch
die Kinder auf der Gasse eher als das Vater-
unser lernten; und eben darum wies ich
500 meinen Galanen die Feigen.[152] Als aber
hingegen diese den Stadtleuten erzählten, was
ich vor[153] ein Tauß-Es[154] wäre, so erwies ich
hinwiederum[155] denselben ein anderes mit
Brief und Siegel und beredete sie, die Offiziere
505 gäben keiner anderen Ursache halber solche
losen Stücke von mir aus,[156] als weil ich nicht
beschaffen sein wollte, wie sie mich gerne
hätten. Und dergestalt biß ich mich ziemlich
heraus und brachte vermittelst meiner guten
510 schriftlichen Zeugnisse zuwege, daß mich die
Stadt, bis ich meine Gelegenheit anders
machen konnte, um ein geringes Schirmgeld[157] in ihren Schutz nahm; allwo ich mich
dann wider meinen Willen gar ehrbarlich,
515 fromm, still und eingezogen[158] hielt und meiner Schönheit, die je länger je mehr zunahm,
aufs beste pflegte, der Hoffnung, mit der
Zeit wiederum einen wackern Mann zu
bekommen.

Courasche erfährt, wer ihre Eltern gewesen, und
bekommt wieder einen andern Mann.

Das X. Kapitel

520   Aber ich hätte lang harren müssen, bis mir
etwas Rechtes angebissen;[159] denn die guten
Geschlechter[160] verblieben bei ihresgleichen,
und was sonst reich war, konnte auch

sonst reiche und schöne und vornehmlich
(welches man damals noch in etwas beobach- 525
tete) auch ehrliche Jungfrauen zu Weibern
haben, also daß sie nicht bedurften, sich an
eine verlassene Soldatenhure zu hängen.
Hingegen waren etliche, die entweder Banke-
rott gemacht oder bald zu machen gedachten; 530
die wollten zwar mein Geld, ich wollte aber
darum sie nicht; die Handwerksleute waren
mir ohnedas zu schlecht. Und damit blieb
ich ein ganzes Jahr sitzen,[161] welches mir,
länger zu gedulden, gar schwer und ganz 535
wider die Natur war, sintemal ich von der
guten Sache, die ich genoß, ganz kützelig[162]
wurde; denn ich brauchte[163] mein Geld, so
ich hie und dort in den großen Städten
hatte, den Kauf- und Wechselherren zuzeiten 540
beizuschießen,[164] daraus ich so ein ehrliches
Gewinnchen erhielt, daß ich ziemlich gute
Tage davon haben konnte und nichts von
der Hauptsumme verzehren durfte.[165] Weil
es mir denn an einem andern Ort mangelte 545
und meine schwachen Beine diese gute Sache
nicht mehr ertragen konnten oder wollten,
machte ich mein Geld per Wechsel auf[166]
Prag, mich selbst aber mit etlichen Kaufher-
ren hernach[167] und suchte Zuflucht bei 550
meiner Kostfrau zu Bragoditz, ob mir vielleicht alldorten ein besser Glück anstehen[168]
möchte.

Dieselbe fand ich gar arm, weder ich sie
verlassen;[169] denn der Krieg hatte sie nicht 555
allein sehr verderbt,[170] sondern sie hatte auch
allbereit vor dem Krieg mit mir und ich nicht
mit ihr gezehrt.[171] Sie freute sich meiner
Ankunft gar sehr, vornehmlich als sie sah, daß
ich nicht mit leerer Hand angestochen kam.[172] 560
Ihr erstes Willkommheißen aber war doch

---

151 **am allerwohlfeilsten:** am allerbilligsten.
152 **wies . . . Feigen:** wies ich meine Galane mit
   Hohn ab.
153 **vor:** für.
154 **Tauß-Es** (Tausendsassa? [*colloq.*]: rascal.
155 **hinwiederum:** dagegen.
156 **etwas von jemand ausgeben** (etwas von jemand
   erzählen): tell tales about someone.
157 **Schirmgeld:** sum levied by a city for the right
   to live there.
158 **eingezogen:** here, withdrawn; reserved.
159 **anbeißen:** rise to the bait.
160 **die guten Geschlechter:** families of good lineage;
   patricians.

161 **sitzen bleiben:** remain on the shelf.
162 **kützelig (kitzelig):** filled with desire (for sensual
   gratification).
163 **brauchen:** benutzen.
164 **beischießen** (zuschießen; dazugeben): here,
   lend.
165 **dürfte:** brauchte.
166 **machen auf:** schicken nach.
167 **hernach:** hinterher; hinterdrein.
168 **anstehen:** bevorstehen.
169 **arm . . . verlassen:** ärmer als ich sie verlassen.
170 **verderben:** here, ruin (economically).
171 **mit jemandem zehren** (von jemandem zehren):
   eat someone's food; i.e., live off someone.
172 **daß . . . kam:** that I did not "blow in" empty-
   handed.

lauter Weinen, und indem sie mich küßte, nannte sie mich zugleich ein unglückseliges Fräulein, welches seinem Herkommen gemäß schwerlich würde sein Leben und Stand führen mögen, mit fernerem Anhang,[173] daß sie mir fürderhin[174] nicht mehr wie vor diesem zu helfen, zu raten und vorzustehen wisse, weil meine besten Freunde und Verwandten entweder verjagt oder gar tot wären; und überdas, sagte sie, würde ich mich schwerlich vor den Kaiserlichen dürfen sehen lassen, wenn sie meinen Ursprung wissen wollten. Und damit heulte sie immer fort, also daß ich mich in ihre Rede nicht richten noch begreifen konnte, ob es gehauen oder gestochen, gebrannt oder gebohrt wäre. Da ich sie aber mit Essen und Trinken (denn die gute Tröpfin[175] mußte den jämmerlichen Schmalhansen[176] in ihrem Quartier herbergen) wiederum gelabt und also zurechtgebracht, daß sie schier ein Tummel[177] hatte, erzählte sie mir mein Herkommen gar offenherzig und sagte, daß mein natürlicher Vater ein Graf und vor wenig Jahren der gewaltigste Herr im ganzen Königreich gewesen, nunmehr aber wegen seiner Rebellion wider den Kaiser des Landes vertrieben worden und, wie die Zeitungen mitgebracht, jetzunder an der türkischen Porten[178] sei; allda er auch sogar seine christliche Religion in die türkische verändert haben solle. Meine Mutter, sagt sie, sei zwar von ehrlichem Geschlecht geboren, aber ebenso arm als schön gewesen; sie hätte sich bei des gedachten Grafen Gemahlin vor[179] eine Staatsjungfer aufgehalten, und indem sie der Gräfin aufgewartet, wäre der Graf selbst ihr Leibeigener geworden und hätte solche Dienste getrieben, bis er sie auf einen adeligen Sitz verschafft,[180] da sie mit mir niedergekommen; und weil eben damals sie, meine Kostfrau, auch einen jungen Sohn entwöhnt,[181] den sie mit des-

selbigen Schlosses Edelmann erzeugt, hätte sie meine Säugamme werden und mich folgends[182] zu Bragoditz adelig auferziehen müssen, wozu dann beide, Vater und Mutter, genugsame Mittel und Unterhaltung[183] hergegeben. „Ihr seid zwar, liebes Fräulein", sagte sie ferner, „einem tapferen Edelmann von Euerem Vater versprochen worden; derselbe ist aber bei Eroberung Pilsens gefangen und als ein Meineidiger neben andern mehr durch die Kaiserlichen aufgehängt worden."

Also erfuhr ich, was ich vorlängst[184] zu wissen gewünscht, und wünschte doch nunmehr, daß ichs niemals erfahren hätte, sintemal ich so schlechten Nutzen von meiner hohen Geburt zu hoffen; und weil ich keinen andern und bessern Rat wußte, so machte ich einen Akkord mit meiner Säugamme, daß sie hinfort meine Mutter und ich ihre Tochter sein sollte. Sie war viel schlauer als ich, derowegen zog ich auf ihren Rat mit ihr von Bragoditz auf Prag; nicht allein zwar, daß wir den Bekannten aus den Augen kämen, sondern zu sehen, ob uns vielleicht alldorten ein anderes Glück anscheinen möchte. Im übrigen so waren wir recht vor[185] einander. Nicht, daß sie hätte kuppeln und ich huren sollen, sondern weile sie einer Ernährerin, ich aber einer getreuen Person bedurfte (gleich wie diese eine gewesen), der ich beides, Ehr und Gut, vertrauen konnte. Ich hatte ohne Kleider und Geschmuck[186] bei 3000 Reichstaler bar Geld beieinander und dannenhero[187] damals keine Ursache, durch schändlichen Gewinn meine Nahrung zu suchen. Meine Mutter kleidete ich wie eine ehrbare alte Matrone, hielt sie selbst in großen Ehren und erzeigte ihr vor den Leuten allen Gehorsam; wir gaben uns vor[188] Leute aus, die auf der deutschen Grenze durch den Krieg vertrieben worden wären, suchten unseren Gewinn mit Nähen, auch Gold-, Silber- und Seidensticken, und hielten uns im übrigen gar still und eingezogen, meine Batzen[189] genau zusammenhal-

---

173 **mit fernerem Anhang (mit dem weiteren Zusatz)**: with the additional comment.
174 **fürderhin**: künftig.
175 **Tröpfin**: poor woman; miserable wretch.
176 **Schmalhans** (*colloq.*): Hunger personified.
177 **Tummel** (*colloq. for* **Rausch**): giddiness; intoxication.
178 **an . . . Porten**: reference to the Turkish court.
179 **vor**: für.
180 **verschaffen**: move to another place.
181 **entwöhnen**: wean.

182 **folgends**: dann; daraufhin.
183 **Unterhalt(ung)**: support.
184 **vorlängst**: längst.
185 **vor**: für.
186 **Geschmuck (Schmuck)**: jewelry.
187 **dannenhero**: von da an.
188 **vor**: für.
189 **Batzen**: coins.

650 tend, weil man solche zu vertun pflegt, ehe
mans vermeint, und deren keine anderen
kann gewinnen, wenn man gern wollte.

Nun, dies wäre ein feines Leben gewesen,
das wir führten, ja gleichsam ein klösterliches,
655 wäre. Ich bekam bald Buhler:[190] etliche
suchten mich wie das Frauenzimmer im
Bordel, und andere Tropfen, die mir meine
Ehre nicht zu bezahlen getrauten, sagten mir
viel vom Heiraten; beide Teile aber wollten
660 mich bereden, sie würden durch die grausame
Liebe, die sie zu mir trügen, zu ihren Begierden
angespornt. Ich hätte aber keinem geglaubt,
wenn ich selbst eine keusche Ader in mir
gehabt; es ging halt nach dem alten Sprich-
665 wort: Gleich und gleich gesellt sich gern.
Denn gleich wie man sagt: Das Stroh in den
Schuhen, eine Spindel im Sack und eine Hure
im Haus läßt sich nicht verbergen, also wurde
ich auch gleich bekannt und wegen meiner
670 Schönheit überall berühmt. Dannenhero
bekamen wir viel zu stricken, und unter
anderem einem Hauptmann ein Wehrgehenk,[191] welcher vorgab, daß er vor Liebe
in den letzten Zügen läge. Hingegen wußte
675 ich ihm von der Keuschheit so einen Haufen
aufzuschneiden,[192] daß er sich stellte, als
wollte er gar verzweifeln; denn ich ermaß
die Beschaffenheit und das Vermögen meiner
Kunden nach der Regel meines Wirts „Zum
680 goldenen Löwen" zu N. Dieser sagte: „Wenn
mir ein Gast kommt und gar zu unmäßig
viel höflicher Komplimente macht, so ist
eine gewisse Anzeigung,[193] daß er entweder
nicht viel zum besten oder sonst nicht im
685 Sinn hat, viel zu vergeben;[194] kommt aber
einer mit Trutzen[195] und nimmt die Einkehr
bei mir gleichsam mit Pochen[196] und einer
herrischen Botmäßigkeit,[197] so gedenke ich:
Holla, diesem Kerl ist der Beutel ge-
690 schwollen,[198] den mußt du schröpfen.[199] Also
traktiere ich die Höflichen mit Gegenhöf-

lichkeit, damit sie mich und meine Herberge
anderwärts loben, die Schnarcher[200] aber mit
allem, das sie begehren, damit ich Ursache
habe, ihren Beutel rechtschaffen zu aktio-
695 nieren."[201] Indem ich nun diesen meinen
Hauptmann hielt wie dieser Wirt seine höflichen Gäste, als hielt er mich hingegen wo
nicht gar vor einen halben Engel, jedoch
700 wenigst vor ein Muster und Ebenbild der
Keuschheit, ja schier vor die Frömmigkeit
selbsten. In Summa, er kam so weit, daß er
von der Verehelichung mit mir anfing zu
schwätzen,[202] und ließ auch nicht nach, bis
705 er das Jawort erhielt. Die Heiratspunkte[203]
waren diese, daß ich ihm 1000 Reichstaler
Bargeld zubringen, er aber hingegen mich in
Deutschland zu seiner Heimat um dieselbi-
gen versichern sollte, damit, wenn er vor mir
710 ohne Erben sterben sollte, ich deren wieder
habhaft werden könnte; die übrigen 2000
Reichstaler, die ich noch hatte, sollten an
einem gewissen Ort auf Zins gelegt und in
stehender[204] Ehe die Zinsen von meinem
715 Hauptmann genossen werden, das Kapital
aber unverändert bleiben, bis wir Erben
hätten; auch sollte ich Macht haben, wenn
ich ohne Erben sterben sollte, mein ganzes
Vermögen, darunter auch die 1000 Reichs-
720 taler verstanden, die ich ihm zugebracht, hin
zu vertestieren,[205] wohin ich wollte usw.[206]
Demnach wurde die Hochzeit gehalten;
und als wir vermeinten, zu Prag beieinander,
solang der Krieg währte, in der Garnison
725 gleich wie im Frieden in Ruhe zu leben,
siehe, da kam Ordre, daß wir nach Holstein in
den dänemärkischen Krieg marschieren
müßten.

*Her fourth husband is soon killed too, and
Frau Courasche finds herself in dire straits. She
tries to continue her old way of life, joins one of
Simplicissimus' friends, marries again, and
meets Simplicissimus himself. Her charms begin
to fade; once adored by many officers, she now
has to be content with poor soldiers. Finally, she*

---

[190] **Buhler:** suitor.
[191] **Wehrgehenk:** sword belt.
[192] **aufschneiden:** exaggerate; tell lies.
[193] **Anzeigung (Anzeichen):** indication.
[194] **vergeben (ausgeben):** spend.
[195] **Trutzen (Trotzen):** haughty bearing.
[196] **Pochen:** arrogance.
[197] **Botmäßigkeit: Auftreten.**
[198] **ist . . . geschwollen: hat viel Geld in der Tasche.**
[199] **schröpfen:** *lit.,* bleed; fleece.

[200] **Schnarcher:** here, braggart.
[201] **ihren . . . aktionieren:** ihre Geldbörse ordentlich
plündern.
[202] **schwätzen:** talk.
[203] **Heiratspunkte:** marriage stipulations.
[204] **stehender: währender.**
[205] **vertestieren:** dispose of by will.
[206] **usw.: und so weiter.**

falls in with a band of Gypsies, and becomes one of them; unlike Defoe's heroine, Moll Flanders, she does not repent her life in middle-class respectability but stubbornly clings to crime, vice, and pride.

In our own century, Brecht picked up the tough figure of the camp follower and transformed her into a suffering mother but retained her greed and made it the central issue of his successful play.

Paul Fleming

(1609–1640)

In many of his personal experiences and artistic achievements Paul Fleming profoundly differs from his German contemporaries; one of the critics to whom we owe an informed assessment of his efforts suggests that Fleming was not a "Baroque" poet in the accepted meaning of the word. Steeped in traditions older than those of the Baroque, Fleming, in the course of his wide travels far outside the German sphere, developed a poetic idiom which at times distinctly anticipates the expressive poetic confessions of J. C. Günther and perhaps even young Goethe.

Paul Fleming, like Lessing of Saxon origin, pursued his first studies at the famous Thomasschule in Leipzig and intended to conclude his medical courses at Leipzig University when the approaching imperial army and the plague, which was devastating the country, changed all his plans. In Leipzig he belonged to a group of young students who admired the new imaginative flights of contemporary German poetry; only after he had been introduced by his friend Gloger to the work of Martin Opitz did Fleming add literary exercises in German to his early poetry written exclusively in Latin. The great adventure of his life began when it was suggested to him that he take part in an expedition organized by the Duke of Holstein; he was to join the Duke's ambassadors and to see the Baltic, Russia, and Persia. Young Fleming tried to interpret the undertaking in terms of the Crusades but its commercial aspect was hard to ignore; with the North German trade sadly lagging, the Duke (advised by the Hamburg merchant Brüggemann) had conceived the bold idea of rerouting the Oriental silk trade, by land, via Russia to Holstein where the imports were to be distributed by his agents. Fleming signed up as *Hoff-Juncker* (one of his duties presumably being the ceremonial carving of the roast) but turned into the poet of the expedition; while his friend Olearius wrote a fascinating reportage of the trip (translated subsequently into many languages), Fleming celebrated the Kremlin, the Volga, and the Caspian Sea in elegant sonnets. In August 1634 the ambassadors reached Moscow and after only one week were permitted to move freely within the city; "a miracle," one of the group remarked, "that did not happen to any other ambassadors before." After a delay of almost a year (which the young men spent in Reval drinking and flirting) the expedition set out once again, and after many dangers reached Astrakhan, the Caspian Sea, and Persia. Unfortunately, the joy of having finally arrived at the court of the Shah was tempered by the presence of a competing Dutch ambassadorial expedition which had just arrived by sea. On the return journey, the group stopped again at Reval, and Paul Fleming wooed and won Anna Niehusen (whose older sister Elsabe he had loved when he set out for Persia).

But before marrying Anna, he wanted to receive his M.D. degree; he traveled to Leiden where he completed his dissertation within six months. Fleming was never to see Reval and Anna again; on the return trip he fell ill and died, after a few days, in Hamburg where he was buried in St. Catherine's Church. His old friend Olearius and Anna's father collected his writings and arranged their publication: a selection first (1641), and later his complete works (1646) on which our knowledge of his achievement rests.

In his early Latin poems Fleming demonstrated that he knew how to use the accumulated imagery and motifs of Renaissance poetry; when he branched out into German translations and literary exercises he continued to rely on traditions developed by the many disciples of Petrarch. Fleming also wrote the prescribed love poetry cultivated for at least two centuries by court poets as well as pedants in Latin, French, Dutch, and German: intense suffering caused by the cruelty of the distant (and married) lady of the poet's infatuation; dark passion which neither knows nor wants fulfillment (inspiration would suffer, the critic Heinsius believed); the instinctive yearning to renounce all love and to seek salvation in the stoic resolution of a personality asserting nothing but itself. Yet the language of Petrarch and his imitators offered to Fleming merely a starting point from which he came to develop different modes and feelings; often, a single stanza within a traditional poem betrays something of his personal attitude. His meditations on death and time, written in sinuous Alexandrines, remind one of Gryphius (although Fleming excels in elegance rather than in massive substance), but on his journeys through regions distant in time and space from European literary traditions, he may have matured to a more direct handling of the inherited themes; and many of the Petrarchan clichés may have assumed new meaning when he had to ponder his personal inclinations wavering between Elsabe and Anna. He had never cultivated the eccentricities of the Petrarchans; in his later poems, a new self-discipline urges him to divest his poems of the inherited mythological allusions, overdone antitheses, and the literary pessimism of traditional despair. Instead, he prefers a relaxed tone, an almost conversational simplicity of diction or, elsewhere, a high seriousness which cherishes loyalty and manly endurance. It will remain a difficult task to define Fleming's achievement within and beyond literary tradition; reading his "Nachwehen" or his "Grabschrift" (perhaps the best of his poems) one feels indeed that Fleming does not entirely belong in the mainstream of Baroque rhetoric. He comes close to voicing an unmediated feeling that will triumphantly reemerge, in German poetry, long after the rhetorical fury of the conceit has spent itself.

GEDANKEN ÜBER DER ZEIT

Ihr lebet in der Zeit und kennt doch keine
    Zeit;
So wißt ihr Menschen nicht, von und in was
    ihr seid.
Dies wißt ihr, daß ihr seid in einer Zeit geboren
Und daß ihr werdet auch in einer Zeit ver-
    loren.
5 Was aber war die Zeit, die euch in sich
    gebracht?
Und was wird diese sein, die euch zu nichts
    mehr macht?
Die Zeit ist was und nichts, der Mensch in
    gleichem Falle,
Doch was dasselbe Was und Nichts sei,
    zweifeln alle.
Die Zeit, die stirbt in sich und zeugt sich auch
    aus sich.
10 Dies kömmt aus mir und dir, von dem du
    bist und ich.
Der Mensch ist in der Zeit, sie ist in ihm
    ingleichen,[1]
Doch aber muß der Mensch, wenn sie noch
    bleibet, weichen.
Die Zeit ist, was ihr seid, und ihr seid, was
    die Zeit,
Nur daß ihr wen'ger noch, als was die Zeit
    ist, seid.
15 Ach daß doch jene Zeit, die ohne Zeit ist, käme
Und uns aus dieser Zeit in ihre Zeiten
    nähme
Und aus uns selbsten uns, daß wir gleich
    könnten sein
Wie d e r itzt jener Zeit, die keine Zeit geht
    ein!

WIDERSTREIT IN SICH SELBST

Umsonst ist's, was ich tu, und tu ich noch
    so sehr,
Denn mein Verhängnis will's. Was darf ich
    wollen mehr?

---

[1] **ingleichen**: likewise; in the same way.

So lieg ich stets mit mir und wider mich zu
    Felde,
Verkaufe mich mir selbst mit meinem eignen
    Gelde,
Bestreite mich durch mich. Der zweifelhafte   5
    Krieg
Spricht meinem Feinde bald, bald mir zu sei-
    nen Sieg.
Ich bin mir Freund und Feind. So streitet
    Streit mit Friede,
So schlagen sie sich selbst stets aneinander
    müde,
Bis sich mein matter Leib nicht länger
    regen kann.
Da fängt der muntre Geist erst seinen   10
    Lärmen an,
Wacht, wenn sein Gastwirt schläft. Und weil
    ich mich verwirre,
So macht er selbsten sich in seinem Wesen
    irre,
Spielt oft das Widerspiel, und da er weinen
    soll,
So läuft, so springet er und jauchzet Lachens
    voll.

WAS BIN ICH DOCH BEMÜHT

Was bin ich doch bemüht, um alles zu erler-
    nen,
Was nahe bei uns ist und was uns kommt von
    fernen,
Was hier und da und dort und überall
    geschieht,
Danach ein geizig's Aug aus Herzenshunger
    sieht?
Könnt ich einst jede Kunst, wär aller Reich-   5
    tum meine,
Hätt ich der Ehren Thron zu eigen ganz
    alleine,
Ging alles mir nach Lust und wüßt ich keine
    Zeit,
Die mich von Jugend auf nicht herzlich
    hätt erfreut—
Ja, wüßt ich (welches doch noch keinem ist
    gegeben),
Daß ich auch keinen Tod auf Erden sollt   10
    erleben,

Mein Name reichte hin bis in die neue Welt,
An mir wär alles das, was man für alles hält,
Ganz alles hätt ich ganz—was wäre dieses
      alles?
Ein Alles auf den Schein. Ein Konterfei[1] des
      Schalles.
15 Des Schattens lieblich Bild, Verblendung des
      Gesichts.[2]
Ein Schlauch an Leere voll. Mit einem Worte:
      nichts.

WIE ER WOLLE GEKÜSSET SEIN

Nirgends hin, als auf den Mund,
Da sinkt's in des Herzens Grund.
Nicht zu frei, nicht zu gezwungen,
Nicht mit gar zu fauler Zungen.

5 Nicht zu wenig, nicht zu viel,
Beides wird sonst Kinderspiel.
Nicht zu laut, und nicht zu leise:
Bei der Maß ist rechte Weise.

Nicht zu nahe, nicht zu weit,
10 Dies macht Kummer, jenes Leid.
Nicht zu trocken, nicht zu feuchte;
Wie Adonis[1] Venus reichte.

Nicht zu harte, nicht zu weich;
Bald zugleich, bald nicht zugleich.
15 Nicht zu langsam, nicht zu schnelle,
Nicht ohn' Unterschied der Stelle.

Halb gebissen, halb gehaucht,
Halb die Lippen eingetaucht.
Nicht ohn' Unterschied der Zeiten,
20 Mehr alleine, denn bei Leuten.

Küsse nun ein Jedermann,
Wie er weiß, will, soll, und kann:
Ich nur, und die Liebste wissen,
Wie wir uns recht sollen küssen!

---

[1] **Konterfei** (*M. Lat., contrefactum*): copy; reflection.
[2] **Gesicht**: sight; view; range of vision.
[1] **Adonis**: in Greek mythology, a youth of extraordinary beauty.

NACHWEHEN

Ist dieses nun das süße Wesen,
Nach dem mich so verlanget hat?
Ist dieses der gesunde Rat,
Ohn' den ich konnte nicht genesen?
Und ist dies meiner Wehmut Frucht,   5
Die ich so emsig aufgesucht?

O Feind, o Falscher, o Tyranne,
Cupido,[1] das ist deine List!
Der bist du, der du allzeit bist!
Du hast mich nun in deinem Banne!   10
Der Dienst der falschen Ledigkeit[2]
Hat meiner Freiheit mich entfreit.

Wie unverwirrt ist doch ein Herze,
Das nicht mehr als sich selbsten kennt,
Von keiner fremden Flamme brennt,   15
Selbst seine Lust, und selbst sein Schmerze.
Seit, daß ich nicht mehr meine bin,
So ist mein ganzes Glücke hin.

Ich schlaf, ich träume bei dem Wachen,
Ich ruh und habe keine Ruh.   20
Ich tu, und weiß nicht, was ich tu,
Ich weine mitten in dem Lachen;
Ich denk. Ich mache dies und das,
Ich schweig, ich red, und weiß nicht, was?

Die Sonne scheint für mich nicht helle,   25
Mich kühlt die Glut, mich brennt das Eis.
Ich weiß, und weiß nicht, was ich weiß,
Die Nacht tritt an des Tages Stelle.
Itzt bin ich dort, itzt da, itzt hier,
Ich folg, und fliehe selbst für mir.   30

Bald billig ich mir meinen Handel,
Bald drauf verklag ich mich bei mir.
Ich bin verändert für und für,
Und standhaft nur in stetem Wandel.
Ich selbst bin mit mir selbst nicht eins: 35
Bald will ich Alles, bald gar Keins.

Wie wird mir's doch noch endlich gehen?
Ich wohne nunmehr nicht in mir.
Mein Schein nur ist es, den ihr hier

---

[1] **Cupido**: Cupid (Amor), Roman name for the Greek god Eros, god of love.
[2] **Ledigkeit**: single state; according to Grimm, "in older usage, veiled language for concubinage."

40 In meinem Bilde sehet stehen.
Ich bin nun nicht mehr selber Ich.
Ach, Liebe, wozu bringst du mich?

BEKENNTNIS

Mehr böse noch als bös' hab ich bisher gelebet,
Bei kalter Gottesfurcht mich brennend
angestellt,
Den Himmel oft getäuscht, mehr mein Freund
und der Welt;
Bin selten über mich, und Wolken-an ge-
schwebet;

5 Der schnöden Eitelkeit der Erden angeklebet;
Ich habe das getan, was mir selbst nicht
gefällt,
Ein Schuldner alles deß, was Moses Rechnung[1] hält,
Der ich mit Eifer auch hab oftmals wider-
strebet.

Ich muß, will ich schon nicht, bekennen wider
mich,
10 Mein Urteil, meine Straf und Todesart sprech
ich:
Ich hab es so und so, und ärger noch
getrieben.

Und, was erzähl ich viel die ungezählte Zahl
Von meinen Schulden her? Gott liest sie
allzumal
Von meiner Stirnen ab, auf der sie sind
geschrieben.

AN SICH

Sei dennoch unverzagt! Gib dennoch
unverloren!
Weich keinem Glücke nicht; steh höher als
der Neid;

Vergnüge dich an dir, und acht es für kein
Leid,
Hat sich gleich wider dich Glück, Ort und
Zeit verschworen.

Was dich betrübt und labt, halt Alles für 5
erkoren,[1]
Nimm dein Verhängnis an. Laß Alles un-
bereut.
Tu, was getan muß sein, und eh man dir's
gebeut.[2]
Was du noch hoffen kannst, das wird noch
stets geboren.

Was klagt, was lobt man doch? Sein Un-
glück und sein Glücke
Ist sich ein Jeder selbst. Schau alle Sachen 10
an:
Dies Alles ist i n   d i r! Laß deinen eitlen
Wahn,

Und eh du fürder gehst, so geh in dich
zurücke.
Wer sein selbst Meister ist, und sich beherr-
schen kann,
Dem ist die ganze Welt und Alles untertan!

ER VERWUNDERT SICH
SEINER GLÜCKSELIGKEIT

Wie mir es gestern ging, und wie ich ward
empfangen
In meiner Freundin Schoß, weiß sie nur und
nur ich,
Das allerliebste Kind das herzt' und küßte
mich,
Sie hielt so feste mich, wie ich sie hart umfangen.

Auf meinem lag ihr Mund, auf ihren meine 5
Wangen,
Oft sagte sie mir auch, was nicht läßt sagen
sich,

---

[1] **Moses Rechnung**: the Ten Commandments (?).

[1] **erkoren**: chosen; ordained by God.
[2] **gebeut**: gebietet.

Darum du, Momus,[1] nicht hast zu bekümmern
    dich!
Bei ihr ist noch mein Sinn, bei mir noch ihr
    Verlangen.

O wohl mir, der ich weiß, was nur die Götter
    wissen,
10 Die sich auch, wie wir uns, in reiner Keusch-
    heit küssen.
O wohl mir, der ich weiß, was kein Verliebter
    weiß.

Wird meiner Seelen Trost mich allzeit also
    laben,
Mir allzeit also tun, so werd' ich an ihr haben
Ein weltlich Himmelreich, ein sterblich
    Paradeis.

PAUL FLEMINGS GRABSCHRIFT,

*die er sich selbst gemacht in Hamburg, den
28. März 1640, auf seinem Totenbette,
drei Tage vor seinem Absterben.*

Ich war an Kunst und Gut und Stande groß
    und reich.
Des Glückes lieber Sohn. Von Eltern guter
    Ehren.
Frei. Meine.[1] Konnte mich aus meinen
    Mitteln nähren.
Mein Schall floh überweit. Kein Landsmann
    sang mir gleich.

Von Reisen hochgepreist, für keiner Mühe   5
    bleich,[2]
Jung, wachsam, unbesorgt. Man wird mich
    nennen hören,
Bis daß die letzte Glut dies Alles wird ver-
    stören.
Dies, deutsche Klarien![3] dies Ganze dank'
    ich euch.

Verzeiht mir, bin ich's wert, Gott, Vater,
    Liebste, Freunde!
Ich sag' euch gute Nacht, und trete willig ab.   10
Sonst Alles ist getan bis an das schwarze
    Grab.

Was frei dem Tode steht, das tu er seinem
    Feinde.
Was bin ich viel besorgt den Atem aufzu-
    geben?
An mir ist minder nichts, das lebet, als mein
    Leben!

---

[1] **Meine** : independent.
[2] **für . . . bleich**: ich verbleichte vor keiner Mühe;
nahm alle Mühen auf mich.
[3] **Klarien**: the Muses.

---

[1] **Momus**: Greek god, personification of scorn and
stinging criticism.

Christian Hofmann
von Hofmannswaldau
(1617–1679)

To his contemporaries, Christian Hofmann von Hofmannswaldau was a poet of dominating excellence, and after having been disregarded by a century of romantic scholarship, he is assuming increasing importance to twentieth-century sensibilities. It is now evident that he refined the German poetic language; in his effort to compete with the brilliant Italian literature of his age, he combined the traditional and the new possibilities of European Baroque rhetoric. His biography reflects a career similar to that of several other Silesian poets of the time (Gryphius, Lohenstein). Hofmann von Hofmannswaldau was born in Breslau, attended school there and in Danzig, and in 1637 went to the famous Dutch university of Leiden to study law—following in his father's footsteps, he was to prepare for a distinguished career in the civil service. On his *grand tour,* he visited London and Oxford, met Hugo Grotius, the outstanding legal mind of the age, in Paris, and spent considerable time in Italy—only after six years of study and travel did he again return to Breslau. At thirty-three he was appointed a member of the city government and entrusted with important political missions to the Diet of Regensburg and the imperial court in Vienna to represent the interests of the Breslau community; late in life, he was made president of the city government and thus attained the highest office Breslau had to offer.

In his later work, Hofmann von Hofmannswaldau seems to have repudiated the poetry he had written in his younger years, but when he died his colleague and fellow poet Daniel Casper von Lohenstein pronounced a funeral oration in which he praised the comprehensive talents of the diplomat, lawyer, and fertile artist: *Der große Pan ist tot. . . . Wundere sich niemand, daß ich diesen großen Mann einen Pan nenne, welchen das heidnische Altertum vergöttert, zu einem Bilde der ganzen Natur gemacht und mit einem Namen verehrt, der so viel als alles heißt."*

In his youth, Hofmann von Hofmannswaldau was a scholarly reader of older literature; he seems to have been one of the few men of the century familiar with the works of Otfried von Weißenburg, Wolfram von Eschenbach, and Walter von der Vogelweide. Nevertheless he did not burden his poetry with cumbersome erudition; in his translations of contemporary Italian literature he demonstrated a lightness of touch rare among his German provincial compatriots. It may be characteristic of his attitude that he destroyed his unfinished Latin epic *De bello Germanico* and left no grand tragedy; apparently he knew the particular quality of his talents and concentrated on epigrams, songs, sonnets, and the occasional poem. Readers of his own time were impressed, above all, with his *Heldenbriefe,* a collection of twenty-eight poetic love letters ascribed to heroic personages of history and structured according to Ovid's *Heroica.* It was Hofmann von Hofmannswaldau's historical task to lighten the majestic language of Gryphius by learning from the playful and bolder imagery of the Italian poet Giambattista Marino. Hofmann von Hofmannswaldau illuminates the dark and somber element which dominates the world of Gryphius by his characteristic interest in *kräftige Beiwörter* (i.e., strong adjectives charged with meaning), fashionable conceits, and antithetical constructions. The stately syntax of the earlier German Baroque poets yields to grace, elegance, and a new wealth of elaborate stanza patterns which Hofmann von Hofmannswaldau handles with impeccable precision. It is a poetry of transition and combination which employs the entire repertoire of Baroque techniques: there is the symptomatic obsession with death and decay—counteracted by a belief in the enduring loyalty of the heart ("Vergänglichkeit der Schönheit")—the concern with the vicissitudes of the heroic life compressed into subtle Alexandrines ("Grabschrift General Wallensteins") and, increasingly, exquisite poems in praise of worldly pleasure. The inevitable stoicism of the generation of the Great War seems to belong to the past, and an almost pagan and epicurean desire for a joyous life emerges in rich colors and an abundance of artistic forms.

AUF DEN MUND

Mund! der die Seelen kann durch Lust zusam-
  menhetzen,
Mund! der viel süßer ist als starker Himmels-
  wein,
Mund! der du Alikant[1] des Lebens schenkest
  ein,
Mund! den ich vorziehn muß der Juden
  reichen Schätzen,
5 Mund! dessen Balsam uns kann stärken und
  verletzen,
Mund! der vergnügter blüht, als aller Rosen
  Schein,
Mund! welchem kein Rubin kann gleich
  und ähnlich sein,
Mund! den die Grazien[2] mit ihren Quellen
  netzen;
Mund! Ach Korallen-Mund, mein einziges
  Ergötzen!
10 Mund! laß mich einen Kuß auf deinen Purpur setzen.

VERGÄNGLICHKEIT
DER SCHÖNHEIT

Es wird der bleiche Tod mit seiner kalten
  Hand
  Dir endlich mit der Zeit um Deine Brüste
  streichen,
Der liebliche Korall der Lippen wird ver-
  bleichen;
  Der Schultern warmer Schnee wird werden
  kalter Sand,
5 Der Augen süßer Blitz, die Kräfte deiner
  Hand,
Für welchen solches fällt, die werden zeitlich[1]
  weichen,
Das Haar, das itzund kann des Goldes Glanz
  erreichen,

Tilgt endlich Tag und Jahr als[2] ein gemeines
  Band.
Der wohlgesetzte Fuß, die lieblichen Ge-
  bärden,
Die werden teils zu Staub, teils nichts und 10
  nichtig werden;
  Denn[3] opfert keiner mehr der Gottheit
  deiner Pracht,
Dies und noch mehr als dies muß endlich
  untergehen,
Dein Herze kann allein zu aller Zeit bestehen,
  Dieweil[4] es die Natur aus Diamant gemacht.

AN AMARANTHEN, ÜBER SEIN AN
SIE GESCHICKTES BILDNIS

Mein Bildnis hast du hier auf dünnes Glas
  geleget,
  Es scheint, daß zwischen Mensch und Glas
  Verwandnis[1] sei,
Denn die Gebrechlichkeit ist beiden einge-
  präget,
  Sie sein[2] von dem Verderb[3] fast keine
  Stunde frei.
So bald[4] ein Glas zerbricht, kann auch ein 5
  Mensch vergehen,
  Das Glas zerbricht der Mensch, den Men-
  schen Gottes Hand;
Es können beide nicht die Länge[5] recht
  bestehen,
  Ihr End und Anfang ist fast nichts als
  Asch und Sand.
Zerbricht das Glas nicht ganz, so kriegt es
  schnöde[6] Flecken,
  Läuft von dem Wetter an, und wird sehr 10
  ungestalt:

---

[1] **Alikant:** sweet wine from the vicinity of Alicante,
  Spain.
[2] **die Grazien:** the Graces, goddesses of grace and
  spiritual beauty.
[1] **zeitlich:** beizeiten.

---

[2] **als:** wie.
[3] **denn:** dann.
[4] **dieweil:** weil.
[1] **Verwandnis (Verwandtschaft):** relationship;
  here, analogy.
[2] **sie sein:** sie sind.
[3] **Verderb:** destruction.
[4] **so bald:** so schnell, wie.
[5] **(auf) die Länge:** for some (length of) time.
[6] **schnöde:** ugly; despicable.

So will die Krankheit oft uns allen Schein[7]
    verdecken,
  Und macht Gemüt und Leib verdrießlich,
    schwach und kalt.
Zerfällt das schönste Glas, wer achtet dessen
    Stücke?
  Man stößt es schändlich hin, als[8] schlechten
    Ziegel-Graus:[9]
15 Die Menschen sparen[10] nicht den Menschen
    ihre Tücke,
  Man hat uns kaum verscharrt, so ist die
    Freundschaft aus.
Ruhm, Name und Gestalt ist alsobald ver-
    schwunden,
  Wenn man uns nach Gebrauch[11] das letzte
    Hemde gibt.
Wo hat man dieser Zeit[12] wohl einen Freund
    gefunden,
20 So[13] an das Grab gedenkt, und nach dem
    Tode liebt.
Hier ist das dünne Glas, willst du es bald
    zerbrechen,
  So nehm ich es von dir vor[14] keine Feind-
    schaft an;

Denn Amaranthen weiß ich nicht zu wider-
    sprechen,
  Indem mich ihre Hand in nichts verletzen
    kann.

GRABSCHRIFT
GENERAL WALLENSTEINS

Hier liegt das große Haupt, so[1] itzt wird
    ausgelacht;
Viel[2] wissen mehr von mir, als ich jemals
    gedacht.
Doch wußt ich, daß ein Stein nicht leicht
    ein Stern kann werden,
Ein Stein, wie hoch er steigt, fällt endlich
    zu der Erden.

---

[7] **Schein:** luster (beauty).
[8] **als: wie.**
[9] **Graus:** rubble.
[10] **sparen:** withhold from; spare.
[11] **nach Gebrauch:** according to custom.
[12] **dieser Zeit: zu dieser Zeit.**
[13] **so: der.**
[14] **vor: für.**

---

[1] **so: das.**
[2] **viel: viele.**

STREIT DER SCHWARZEN AUGEN, ROTEN LIPPEN UND WEIßEN BRÜSTE

SCHWARZE AUGEN:

Wir schwarzen Wolken wir, mit Sonnen
    angefüllet,
Wir schöne Finsternis, da Venus Wache
    hält:
Wir dunklen Brunnen wir, da Blitz und
    Feuer quillet,
Wir sind Besiegerin der Freiheit dieser
    Welt.
5 Das Eis zerschmilzt für uns, das Eisen muß
    uns weichen,
Die Felsen geben nach, es bricht der
    Diamant;
Den Purpur heißen wir durch unsre Macht
    erbleichen,
Und manches Herz zerfließt durch diesen
    süßen Brand.

ROTE LIPPEN:

Ihr Augen tut gemach,[1] kann euer Blitz ent-
    zünden,
10 So denkt, daß auch der Mund voll Glut
    und Feuer steckt;
Das Rote, was sich will in diesen Lippen
    finden,
Ist Brand von reiner Art mit Rosen
    überdeckt.
Der Atem, so itzund aus diesem Tale fähret,
Läuft Jagens halber[2] aus, und rennet durch
    die Welt.
15 Ich schwöre, daß er nicht von dort zurücke
    kehret,
Bis daß er einen Geist hat in das Garn
    gefällt[3]

WEIßE BRÜSTE:

Wenn alles reden will, wie können wir denn[4]
    schweigen?
Es will zwar nicht der Schnee von unsern
    Hügeln gehn;

Doch wollen Flammen sich auch auf den
    Spitzen zeigen,
Die rüstig[5] Tag und Nacht in vollem 20
    Brande stehn.
Wer einen leichten[6] Blick in diesen Zirkel[7]
    schicket,
Der wird alsbald bestrickt durch süße
    Zauberei,
Das Netze, so[8] mit Lust den leichten Geist
    bestricket,
Reißt keine Helden-Hand und harter
    Stahl entzwei.

SCHWARZE AUGEN:

Rühmt, Schwestern! was ihr wollt, den 25
    Ruhm von unsern Flammen
Hat keine Zeit verletzt, kein Winter
    abgetan;[9]
Hier steht die Lieblichkeit und auch die
    Kraft beisammen,
Und denken auf[10] ein Band, das Herzen
    fangen kann.
Die Schlüssel hängen hier zu tausend Männer
    Herzen,
Die Liebe hat bei uns das Zeughaus[11] 30
    ihrer Macht;
Cupido holet hier das Feuer zu den Kerzen;
Ja, Lieben haben wir auf diese Welt
    gebracht.

ROTE LIPPEN:

Ein wohlgeschärfter Spruch von unserm
    roten Throne
Tut und verrichtet mehr als euer stolzes
    Licht;
Was seid ihr bei der Nacht? Ich red es euch 35
    zu Hohne,
Wann[12] nicht die Sonne scheint, so sieht
    das Auge nicht.
Wir aber herrschen auch, wenn Phöbus
    von uns weichet,
Ja, wenn ihr Sternenheer von Wolken
    wird bedeckt,

---

[1] **gemach:** gently; softly.
[2] **Jagens halber: wegen des Jagens; im Hinblick auf das Jagen.**
[3] **bis ... gefällt:** until a soul falls into the net (of love); analogy to the trapping of birds.
[4] **denn: dann.**

[5] **rüstig: kriegsbereit.**
[6] **leicht: leichtfertig.**
[7] **Zirkel:** circle; "target."
[8] **so: das.**
[9] **abtun: entkräften.**
[10] **auf etwas denken: auf etwas hinarbeiten.**
[11] **Zeughaus:** armory; arsenal.
[12] **wann: wenn.**

So hat manch kluges Wort, so[13] durch die Rosen streichet,

40 Die Löwen eingeschläfft[14] und harte Stein' erweckt.

WEIßE BRÜSTE:

Wenn unsre Kugeln nicht mit süßem Triebe scherzen,

Und dieser weiße Schild der Männer Freiheit legt,[15]

So stellt die Venus ja vergebens auf[16] die Herzen,

Und selten wird ein Brand ohn unsre Kraft erregt.

45 Das Heben, so man stets um unsre Grenzen spüret,

Bläst tausend Flammen auf, und leget Feuer an,

Ja dieses, was bei uns verborgen wird geführet,

Hat oftmals mehr, als das, was sich gezeigt, getan.

SCHWARZE AUGEN:

Wenn keine Brust sich zeigt, wenn Lippen schweigen müssen,

50 So reden wir alsdenn[17] durch unsern klaren Schein,

Wir fügen oftermals[18] durch einen Blick zu wissen,

Daß Adern, Blut und Mark voll Glut und Flammen sein.[19]

Lust, Hoffnung, Liebe, Zorn, kann jeder in uns lesen,

Wir reden ohne Wort, und sprechen ohne Mund;

55 Dies, was noch kommen soll, und allezeit gewesen,

Dies macht das Augenlid durch kluge Blicke kund.

ROTE LIPPEN:

Der reinen Lieblichkeit, so unser Blut durchstreichet,

Vergleichet sich der Trank der Götter selber nicht;

Die Rosen, deren Glanz kein Purpur hat erreichet,

Sind als ein Meisterstück im Himmel 60 zugericht.

Der wunderstarke Saft, der süße Tau der Seelen,

So um Rubinen fließt, und hier auf Perlen steht.

Gibt deutlich zu verstehn, daß in der Augen Höhlen

Die Reizung[20] öfters schläft, hier niemals untergeht.

WEIßE BRÜSTE:

Was euer Strahl bezwingt, was eure Wort 65 verrichten,

Ist uns genug bekannt, ist uns genug bewußt.

Doch lassen wir uns auch nicht ganz und gar vernichten,

Wir sind, bedenkt es wohl, der Garten voller Lust.

Die Äpfel, so[21] allhier auf diesem Stocke schweben,

Sind süßer noch als die, so Abels Mutter 70 aß:

Ja besser, weil sie nicht verletzen an dem Leben,

Und keine Schlange nicht auf ihren Blättern saß.

SCHWARZE AUGEN:

Je kleiner unser Reich, je größer unsre Stärke,

Wir schrecken manche Brust, und stopfen[23] manchen Mund;

Die Federn werden stumpf in Rühmung 75 unsrer Werke,

Und manch verbrochnes Wort[24] tut unsre Kräfte kund.

Das Herze klopft für uns, die Glieder lernen zittern,

Und wer dies wahre Wort für nichts und nichtig hält,

---

[13] **so**: das.
[14] **eingeschläfft (eingeschläfert)**: lulled to sleep.
[15] **legen (erlegen)**: here, conquer.
[16] **auf etwas stellen**: nach etwas jagen.
[17] **alsdenn**: alsdann.
[18] **oftermals**: oftmals; oft.
[19] **sein**: sind.

[20] **Reizung**: allurement; enticement.
[21] **So**: die.
[22] **keine Schlange nicht**: keine Schlange.
[23] **stopfen**: here, silence.
[24] **verbroch(e)nes Wort**: blunted, spoiled (by lesser writers).

Denselben soll der Strahl von unserm
  Blitz erschüttern,
Zum Zeugnis unsrer Macht, zur Warnung
  dieser Welt.

ROTE LIPPEN:

Die Seelen pflegen hier Zusammenkunft
  zu haben,
Und speisen sich mit Lust durch süßen
  Honigseim:
Hier pflanzet die Natur den Reichtum ihrer
  Gaben,
Und Venus kocht allhier den allerbesten
  Leim,
Ein Tropfen recht gebraucht, leimt Geist
  und Geist zusammen;
Tut nun der Leim zu schlecht des Mundes
  Kräfte kund,
Und zeiget nicht genug die Funken meiner
  Flammen,

So küsse man alsbald doch einen schönen
  Mund.

WEISSE BRÜSTE:

Dies, was ihr itzt gerühmt, das findt ihr hier
  begraben;
Des Himmels rundes Bild, der Rosen   90
  Lieblichkeit,
Des Frühlings bunte Lust, des Sommers
  süße Gaben,
Die sind mit reicher Hand hier kräftig
  eingestreut.
Der brandbefreite Schnee kann Felsen
  selbst entzünden,
Und unsre Blumen tilgt kein heißer Sonnen-
  schein;
Cupido wird sich uns zu loben unter-   95
  winden.[25]
Die Feder wird sein Pfeil, wir werden Blätter
  sein.

---

[25] sich unterwinden: auf sich nehmen.

Daniel Casper von Lohenstein

(1635–1683)

Daniel Casper von Lohenstein belongs to those Baroque poets who were misjudged for centuries by puritanical scholars and Romantic critics who, believing that the artist should express himself with sincerity, were unable to appreciate the precise craftsmanship and bold metaphors of an earlier age. The rediscovery of English metaphysical poetry and the brilliant achievements of the Italian and Spanish sixteenth-century writers have helped us to evaluate the poetry of the German High Baroque on its own terms. Nothing would be more misleading than to identify Casper von Lohenstein as a man and honest citizen with his ecstasies of language and his shocking metaphors; he and his like anticipated the modern belief that to be artificial was not a perversion but a virtue of the arts. Lohenstein (born Daniel Casper and ennobled later because of diplomatic services rendered by his father) was a very successful lawyer and diplomat. He spent his childhood in a small town in the Silesian principality of Brieg, moved to Breslau to receive his early education at the renowned Magdalenengymnasium, and studied law at the universities of Jena and Tübingen. Like many other fashionable men of the day, he concluded his studies with a *grand tour,* visited Holland (where he was very much impressed with the Dutch theater), Hamburg, Switzerland, Austria, and Hungary, where he found himself at the frontiers of the mighty Turkish empire; he also wanted to go to Italy but the spreading plague stopped him on his way. He was in his early twenties when he settled down, married, and became a highly successful lawyer and magistrate; when the central government in Vienna threatened to abrogate the financial privileges of Breslau, he was dispatched as an envoy to the court and pleased the Austrian emperor and the Breslau city government so well that he received high honors from both. He was a man of an almost Roman sense of duty, untiringly industrious and active in public and literary affairs; when he died in his forty-eighth year he seemed to have spent infinite resources of energy.

Lohenstein's tragedies continue to follow the example of Seneca, the authors of classical French tragedy, and Gryphius, but often indulge in naturalistic effects that Gryphius had fastidiously avoided. Whether Lohenstein's heroes are Turkish (*Ibrahim Bassa,* 1653), Greek, or Roman (*Agrippina,* 1665), their dramatic world tends to explode in scenes of inhuman cruelty and endless remorse. His novel *Großmächtiger Feldherr Arminius,* in eighteen volumes, offers astonishing compilations from his historical readings but none of the noble characters come to life; it concludes an interesting if abortive stage in the development of the German novel. After *Arminius,* prose narratives become more compact and begin to reflect the common sense of the expanding middle classes.

Lohenstein's massive poem "Venus," a hymn on the all-powerful goddess of love, moves with the stately grace and the brilliant pomp of a court celebration. The poet tries to evolve a language as remote as possible from daily and relaxed communication, takes pride in creating a garland of obscure mythological allusions, and delights in his personal love for precious stones and rare plants; conjuring up their magnificence, he coins bold adjectives and compound nouns charged with difficult metaphoric meaning. But Lohenstein's boldness extends far beyond his linguistic refinement; in an age tired of the strife between competing Christian religions he resolutely renews a pagan view of the universe held together by the pleasures of sensuous love, timeless, vital, and pervasive.

VENUS

...**S**chön sein ist eine Gabe,
Die die Natur uns schenkt, daß man ein Vorrecht habe
  Für[1] andern in der Welt. Es ist der Sinnen Frau,
  Der Geister Geist und Herr. Der äußerliche Bau
5 Der Glieder, und der Glanz des rötenden Geblütes[2]
Gibt Zeugnis von der Glut und Tugend des Gemütes,
  Die in den Herzen brennt. So wenig als ein Kreis
  Ist ohne Mittel-Punkt, so wenig Schnee und Eis
Kann ohne Kälte sein, die Sonne sonder[3] Leuchten,
10 Der Himmel ohne Stern, der Regen ohne Feuchten.
  Das Feuer ohne Brand, der Mittag ohne Licht,
  So wenig kann ein schön und wohlgestalt Gesicht
Auch ohne Tugend blüh'n. Denn wer hat jemals pflegen[4]
In Schalen aus Smaragd geringen Kot zu legen?
15 Man schließt die Perl in Gold, den Bisam[5] in Damast,
  Den Amber in Saphir. Kein marmorner Palast
Hegt ein Corydon.[6] Kein Prinz pflegt zu bewohnen
Ein rauchig Hirten-Haus. Man setzet Gold und Kronen
  Den Eulen selten auf. Wie sollte die Natur,
20   Die kluge Mutter, denn so unrecht die Natur,
An Göttern messen aus? Die hurtigen Gelenke

Der Glieder Artigkeit[7] sind der Gemüts-Geschenke
Bedeutungen an ihr. Hingegen spürt man bald
  Des Herzens Niedrigkeit aus häßlicher Gestalt.
Zudem so ist sie auch nicht nur für sich 25 alleine
Die Göttin so sehr schön. Kein Mensch ist, der verneine,
  Du Quell' der Freundlichkeit, daß du der Wollust Haus,
  Der Brunn' der Schönheit bist. Du teilest beides aus.
Die stolze Juno[8] muß von deiner Hand empfangen
Die Perlen auf die Brust, die Rosen auf 30 die Wangen,
  Den Purpur auf den Mund. Du mußt den Hals beziehn
  Mit Schnee, das Haar mit Gold, die Lippen mit Rubin,
Die Schoß[9] mit Elfenbein. Noch mehres: du kannst stiften,
Daß frische Schönheit wächst aus harten Stein und Grüften,
  Das ein Thersites[10] oft und hinkender 35 Vulcan,[11]
  Ein schön' Achilles[12] wird. Wer denket nicht daran,
Der jemals deine Gunst und Huld hat wahrgenommen,
Von wannen Phaon[13] hat die Schönheit her bekommen,
  Der alle Sterblichen, ja Götter selber fast
  An Schönheit übertraf. Wer weiß nicht, 40 daß du hast
In Alabaster ihm ein Balsam-Öl verehret,
An statt des Schiffer-Lohns, mit Salben ihn gelehret
  Die Haut zu streichen an, davon sein ganzer Leib

---

[1] **für**: vor.
[2] **Geblüte**: Blut.
[3] **sonder**: ohne.
[4] **wer … pflegen** (hat gepflogen): who was ever in the habit.
[5] **Bisam**: perfume (*lit.*, musk).
[6] **Corydon**: a shepherd (Virgil, *Eclogues* vii).

---

[7] **Artigkeit**: gracefulness.
[8] **Juno**: being the wife of Jupiter, she was regarded as the queen (*Juno Regina*), the highest goddess.
[9] **die Schoß**: der Schoß.
[10] **Thersites**: the ugliest man in the Greek army at Troy; hated for his insolent remarks. He was severely beaten by Odysseus for speaking evil of Agamemnon (Homer, *Iliad* II, 212–277).
[11] **Vulcan**: Roman god of fire.
[12] **Achilles**: hero of the *Iliad*.
[13] **Phaon**: legendary boatman of Lesbos.

Zu lauter Schönheit ward. In Lesbos
wohnt kein Weib,
45 Das nicht durch Phaons Zier und Anmut
angezündet,
Und Sappho bevoraus wird rasende für
Brunst,[14]
Daß sie sich selbst nicht kennt. Zwar
manche lern' die Kunst
Der Schmink' und Malerei. Es borgt das
Frauenzimmer
Zu lieblicher Gestalt noch jetzo Glanz und
Schimmer:
50 Die Haare bisamt Staub,[15] den Atem zim-
met ein,[16]
Und Blum' und Purpur muß der Wangen
Farbe sein,
Geklärter Morgen-Tau den Glanz der Haut
erheben;
Die Venus aber kann noch mehr als Schönheit
geben,
Den Kalten gießt sie Glut, den Frischen
pflanzt sie Pein,
55 Den Kranken rege Lust, den Toten Seelen
ein.
Sie kann selbst der Natur gestellte Richtschnur meistern,
Ein unbeseeltes Herz, ein Marmor-Bild
begeistern.
Hier ist Pygmalion,[17] der ihr es Zeugnis
gibt,
Der in sein eigen' Werk sich einmal so verliebt,
60 Daß er durch dumme Brunst gezwungen war
zu wüten,
Durch Wahnwitz angefrischt die Gnidie[18]
zu bitten
Um so ein schönes Weib, als sein ge-
schnitztes Bild,
Sein eigen' Abgott war: der Wunsch war
ihm erfüllt,
Der Marmor ward beseelt durch Erycinens[19]
Güte,
65 Der Adern Türkis[20] war erfüllet mit Geblüte,

Er rötete sich an der Wangen Elfenbein,
Der Glieder Eis war Glut, und kurz: der
tote Schein
Ward ein vernünftig Mensch, der Kinder hat
gezeuget,
Die mit der Mutter-Milch des Paphus Mund
gesäuget.
Lernt nun ihr Sterblichen, und stimmt 70
mir jeder bei,
Daß unsre Paphie[21] der Brunn' der Schön-
heit sei,
Die Wurzel süßer Lust, der Stamm der meis-
ten Gaben,
Der Quell' der Regungen, die Feuer in sich
haben,
Das Meer, aus welchen rinnt der Sanftmut
milder Saft,
Der wahre Lebens-Quell', der Klugen 75
Wissenschaft.
[v. 803–877]
Man kann nicht, was man will,
Und will nicht was man kann. Dies ist der
Liebe Spiel:
Den Alten neue Glut, den Sterbenden das
Leben,
Dem was beseelt nicht ist, kann Geist und
Seele geben.
Luft, Erde, See und Feuer, ja diese ganze 80
Welt
Wird durch der Liebe Geist begeistert
und erhellt.
Gib Achtung, wenn die Nacht so viel Gestirne
malen,
Was meinst du, daß sie sind, die feuerlichten[22]
Strahlen?
Was will ihr Glimmen wohl? Bild es dir
kühnlich[23] ein,
Daß sie von Liebes-Glut also erhitzet 85
sein.[24]
Schau an das blaue Dach der schimmernden
Gewölber:[25]
Der Himmel, glaub' es, fühlt die Liebes-
Flammen selber,
Daß er die Erde nur genüglich[26] schauen
kann,
So blickt er sie die Nacht mit tausend
Augen an.

---

[14] **für Brunst:** vor Liebe.
[15] **Staub:** here, powder.
[16] **einzimmen:** wohlriechend machen.
[17] **Pygmalion:** legendary king of Cyprus, who fell
in love with the statue of a maiden he himself had
carved in ivory and implored Aphrodite to give
it life. His wish was granted, and the maiden bore
him a son named Paphos.
[18] **die Gnidie:** Aphrodite; i.e., Venus.
[19] **Erycine: Aphrodite.**
[20] **Türkis:** turquoise (semiprecious stone, usually
blue).

---

[21] **Paphie = Paphia:** Aphrodite.
[22] **feuerlicht (feurig):** fiery.
[23] **kühnlich (kühn):** boldly.
[24] **sein: sind.**
[25] **Gewölber (Gewölbe):** arch; vault.
[26] **genüglich:** sufficiently.

90 Es mangelt ihm auch nicht an reichem Liebes-
Segen:
Er schwängert ihren Bauch mit fruchtbar-
reichem Regen,
Davon sie dann auch Gras, Laub, Bäume,
Blumen, Kraut,
Und sonst noch viel gebärt. Sie selbst, die
grüne Braut,
Die große Tellus,²⁷ liebt den Himmel gleich-
falls wieder,
95 Der hohlen Grüfte Schall, das Beben ihrer
Glieder,
Sind Zeichen ihrer Gunst, und Zeugen
ihrer Pein;
Ins grüne Haar flicht sie vielfärbig Blum-
Werk ein.
Die Schoß beperlet sie mit Gold und Edel-
steinen,
Dem Liebsten desto schön- und holder zu
erscheinen:
100 Der, daß er gleichfalls ihr nicht minder
wohlgefällt,
Mit Demant und Rubin sein türkisblaues
Zelt,
Gleich als mit Rosen, stickt. Man spüret an
Gewächsen,
Daß sie die Liebe rührt't. Die Tannen-Bäume
lechsen,²⁸
Die lange Zeder seufzt. Meinst du verge-
bens? Nein,
105 Aus heißer Liebes-Brunst, die sie so sehr
nimmt ein,
Die macht, daß Myrten sich mit andern
Myrten küssen,
Daß jenen Ulmen-Baum die Reben rings
umschließen,
Daß Eppich²⁹ überall sich um die Erlen
flicht,
Und um die Dornen schränkt, und wenn sie
wer³⁰ zerbricht,
110 So weinen sie vor Leid, daß sich ein Teil
entfernen
Von Liebes-Ästen soll. Die goldnen Wiesen-
Sternen,
Der Erden gelbes Haar, die edlen Blumen
fühl'n

Der Liebe Zauberwerk in ihren Wurzeln
spiel'n,
Die Perlen ihres Taus sind bittre Liebes-
Tränen;
Der kräftige Geruch ist ihr verliebtes Sehnen, 115
Und ihrer Seufzen Hauch: der Farbe
Purpur-Blut
Auf ihren Knospen ist die lichte Liebes-
Glut.
Die Liebes-Blume kann für Liebe nicht
verwelken,
Ihr Feuer färbet an die scharlach-roten
Nelken,
Und macht die Veilchen blaß. Das flücht'ge 120
Lenzen-Kind,
Zuvor des Phöbus Wunsch, der schwar-
ze Hyacinth³¹
Ist jetzt, und war auch vor³² von Liebes-
Brunst entzündet,
Eh' er zur Blume ward. Dieweil man Brun-
nen findet,
Brennt der Narzissen³³ Schnee vor lauter
Liebes-Glut,
Verliebt so sehr, als vor, wie die kristallene 125
Flut
Sein Schönheits-Spiegel war. Daß sich die
Sonnen-Wende
Stets zu der Sonnen kehrt, das tun die Liebes-
Brände,
Weil sie des Cynthius³⁴ noch nicht verges-
sen kann,
Den sie, die Clythie,³⁵ vor auch so starr sah
an,
Weil sie beim Leben war.³⁶ 130

[v. 1407–1461]
Betrachte nur, wie schön

---

²⁷ **Tellus**: Roman goddess of the earth; here, the
earth itself.
²⁸ **lechsen (lechzen)**: gape or split from drought;
lechzen also means "yearn for," so that it can be
interpreted in two ways.
²⁹ **Eppich (Efeu)**: ivy.
³⁰ **wer**: jemand.

³¹ **Hyacinth**: Hyacinthus; beautiful youth, beloved
of Apollo. When the god accidentally killed him
with a discus, the flower of the same name grew
from his blood.
³² **vor**: zuvor schon; zuerst.
³³ **Narzissen** (*pl.*): narcissus. According to legend,
Narcissus rejected the love of the nymph Echo,
and Aphrodite punished him by inspiring him with
a passion for his own reflection in the water. He
pined away and was changed into a flower of the
same name.
³⁴ **Cynthius**: epithet for Apollo as brother of Cynthia
(Diana).
³⁵ **Clythie**: Clytia; in Greek mythology a water
nymph in love with Apollo who eventually deserted her. She was changed into the heliotrope,
a flower which always turns its head in the direction
of the sun's movement.
³⁶ **Weil ... war**: solange sie am Leben war.

Die Garten-Sonnen dort, die Tulipanen[37]
blühen,
Die Röte deutet an, wie sie für Liebe glühen,
  Daß manche dort ihr Haupt so auf die
  Seite bückt,
135   Geschieht vielleicht, daß sie was Liebes wo
  erblickt.
Schau wie die Lilie dort zu silber-klaren
Flüssen
Die milchern[38] Wangen senkt! Sie will den
Buhler küssen,
  Den lieben Fluß, der sich durch manch
  unfeistes[39] Tal,
  Um sie zu finden, krümmt. O heißer
  Liebes-Strahl!
140 Der auch die Kälte warm, das Eis kann bren-
  nend machen,
  Daß Brunnen, Quell' und Bach in lichten
  Flammen krachen;
    In Flammen, die der Brand der Lüste
    zündet an,
    Die weder See noch Schnee, noch Wasser
    löschen kann,
Als nur die Liebe selbst . . . .

                                        [v. 1476–1489]
145 O große Kaiserin der stern-beblümten
  Zinnen,
  Beherrscherin der Welt, Besüßerin[40] der
  Sinnen,
    Du Sorgen-Töterin, du Brunn' der Freund-
    lichkeit,
    Du Mutter süßer Pein, Verkürzerin der
    Zeit,
  Gebärerin der Lust, Vermehrerin der Dinge,
150 Vergib mir, daß ich dir nur leere Worte
  bringe,

So schlechtes Ding, das nicht den Göttern
  zugehört,
Und dir, die alle Welt mit tausend Opfern
  ehrt.
Ja weil ein menschlich Fuß die hohen Götter-
  Throne
Doch nicht besteigen kann, soll meine Philo-
  mene[41]
    Mein Abgott, meine Lust, mein Engel,   155
    meine Pein,
    Mein Leben, meine Qual, und meine
    Venus sein.
Dafern[42] ich denn nun ihr, als schönsten auf
  der Erde,
Mein Herze, mein ganz Ich zu eigen geben
  werde,
    So nimm, o Venus! Doch solch Opfer an
    von mir,
    Nicht anders, als es selbst gewidmet wäre   160
    dir.
So lang ich werd ihr Knecht, sie meine
  Göttin bleiben,
So lange mich zu ihr wird mein Verhängnis
  treiben,
    So lang ihr Schön-Sein wird mein himm-
    lisches Altar,
    Ihr Mund mein Lippen-Zweck, ihr gold-
    durchmengtes Haar
Mein Seelen-Netze sein, ihr Leben meine   165
  Wonne,
Ihr Augen-Licht mein Tag, ihr Antlitz meine
  Sonne.
    So lange wird dein Preis mein Atem, deine
    Pein
    Mein Singen, deine Brust mein Liebes-
    Tempel sein.

                                        [v. 1864–1887]

---

[37] **Tulipanen (Tulpen):** tulips.
[38] **milchern (milchig):** like milk; i.e., white.
[39] **unfeist:** not luxuriant.
[40] **Besüßerin (Versüßerin):** giver of blessings;
    benefactress.

---

[41] **Philomene:** the poet's beloved.
[42] **dafern: wofern; wenn anders.**

Quirinus Kuhlmann
(1651–1689)

Only during the last fifty years has Quirinus Kuhlmann been rediscovered as one of the most fascinating figures of the late Baroque period. Kuhlmann came from Breslau where he excelled early as a student in the famous Magdalenengymnasium; in 1670, he went to Jena to study law and later to Leiden where he began to read the mystical writings of his compatriot Jakob Böhme. A week of overwhelming religious experiences and ecstasies, his *Wunderwoche* (January 20–28, 1674), radically transformed his life and made the talented student a proud man of prophetic visions, messianic claims, and adventurous political and literary projects. He saw himself as a new instrument of mankind's salvation and, as a son of Christ, ruler of the coming fifth realm of utopian happiness for all; with astonishing energy, he set out to make converts, high and low, to his intolerant beliefs. He married one of his first admirers, an aging widow with three children, settled in London where he enjoyed the support of John Bathurst, and prepared to set out for his expeditions to conquer the world for his new paradise. While his friend Bathurst went to the West Indies, Kuhlmann traveled to Constantinople and failed miserably in his quest; in vain he tried to present his writings to the Sultan and finally left again for England. The failure may have induced him to undertake his next voyage—to Jerusalem— only as a *Geistreise,* studying the writings of the Spanish mystic Juan de la Cruz, writing poetry, and sketching his political program in an interesting pamphlet *De Monarchia Jesuelitica* (Geneva, 1682). In 1689, he went to Russia to apprise the Orthodox Church of his plans but, on the order of the Czarina and the Patriarch, he was seized, tried, and burned as a politically dangerous heretic. His ashes were buried in Russian soil; and it seems that his tombstone was rescued by a Russian freethinker who (like many others in the secret societies of Europe) continued to cherish Kuhlmann's memory.

As a student, Quirinus Kuhlmann wrote poetry in the predominant fashion of the day until his mystic experiences changed his literary efforts into a vehicle of religious polemics and bold self-expression. Kuhlmann's poetic world derives its vitality from an inherited mystical imagery enhanced (as is the later poetry of William Blake) by a consistent private mythology. Kuhlmann was fascinated by a curious passage in the *Acta Apostolorum* where, *tempora refrigerii* (3: 19–20), times of coolness and virtue, are promised to mankind; he related his own name (Kuhlmann = Kühlmann) to the biblical prophecy and saw himself as the central figure of the approaching *Kühlzeit,* the long expected age of final salvation. He wrote forty works, mostly polemics and treatises, in German, Latin, Dutch, and English but he concentrated his true energy in his *Kühlpsalter* (1684/86) in which he gathered poems from more than fifteen years of his life.

Here, the rich materials of a spiritual diary are forced—Kuhlmann uses strict patterns of occult alphabets and number schemes—into highly complicated sequences; bitter incantations, intense prayers, jubilant hymns alternate with the most sincere confessions of a thirsting soul. Kuhlmann's poetry relies on the elements of baroque rhetoric; above all, on techniques of enhancement and antithetical construction. Often, however, his fervor tends to modify and destroy the self-imposed discipline: jarring images, strange compounds, un-heard-of verbs emerge; and one is tempted to say that his poetic achievement resides in his sinewy verbs and explosive nouns rather than in the usual splendor of the illustrative and precious adjectives. The *Kühlpsalm* of the fifth book belongs to the most personal poems of the collection; in its abrupt shifts and metaphysical passion it distinctly anticipates many of the more violent poems of the German expressionists of the twentieth century.

DER 4 (64) KÜHLPSALM

(1)

*A*us tiefster Not schrei abgemergelt'[1]
Herz!
Laß mich noch einst[2] die matte Hand aufheben!
Es harnischt mich und panzert recht der Schmerz!
Die Zunge klebt! Angst hat mich rings umgeben!
5 Mein Gott, mein Gott! Du zentnerst[3] stete Last!
Hör auf, hör auf, eh' ich bin ganz verdrücket.[4]
Gib endlich gib um Jesu Kreuz mir Rast!
Wie lange soll dein Werk sein ganz entschmücket?[5]
Was ist der Mensch, der ewigst wird gepreßt?
10 Halt' innen halt', eh' Geist und Seel' ausbläst.

(2)

Beschwerst[6] du mich als[7] deinen ärgsten Feind?
Es hat mich Schmach nach aller Wunsch getroffen.
Sie schaun mehr Lust als sie zu schau'n vermeint:[8]
Verloren wird mehr täglich mir mein Hoffen.
15 Dein Wort scheint nichts als nur ein leerer Traum:
Dein Führen wird ein lauteres[9] Verführen.
Sie zweigen sich[10] gleich einem Eichenbaum:
Du aber läßt mich mehr und mehr verlieren.
Du mästest[11] sie und nimmst mir A.L.L.E.S. hin:
20 Verirrest mich,[12] gibst Schaden zum Gewinn.

---

[1] **abmergeln**: exhaust.
[2] **noch einst: noch einmal.**
[3] **zentnern**: *fig.*, weigh down with a heavy burden.
[4] **verdrücken**: crush; oppress.
[5] **entschmücket: des Schmucks beraubt.**
[6] **beschweren**: burden.
[7] **als: wie.**
[8] **vermeinen**: believe; hope.
[9] **lauter**: here, sheer.
[10] **sich zweigen**: branch forth; i.e., thrive.
[11] **mästen**: fatten.
[12] **jemanden verirren (jemanden irreführen)**: mislead someone.

(3)

Christ Gott und Mensch! Schau her, ich bin dein Glied!
Soll Harmung,[13] Frost und Armut mich aufzehren!
Ich liege hier, stimm' an dies Trauerlied,
Voll Elend, ach, und tausender Beschweren![14]
25 Voll Kummer, Sorg' und was mein Stand[15] erweckt!
Muß Herzenleid unhörlich[16] in mich fressen!
Bin höchstbedrängt und über A.L.L. befleckt
Als hättest du schon deines Knechts vergessen!
Mein Gaumen klebt vor Durst an meine Lipp'
30 Und werde ich lebendig zum Geripp.

(4)

Die Jugend fleucht![17] verging als wie das Laub!
Ihr Süß'tes ist mir bitter weggeflossen.
Ich träne[18] hier: heut' etwas, morgen Staub.
Die Tage sind mit Jammern mir entschossen.[19]
35 Bin ich, mein Gott, zu lauter Schand gemacht?
Sollt' ich allein unendlich mich abquälen?
Mein Leben war nur eine Trauernacht:
Es ist zu viel mein Elend zu erzählen.
Doch traue ich, mein Gott, dir felsenstark:
40 Hilf gnädigst, eh' vertrocknet Blut und Mark.

(5)

Erscheinst du, Gott, mit einem Gnadenblick?
Ach willst du, Gott, mein Gott, mich noch erlaben?[20]

---

[13] **Harmung (Harm)**: grief; affliction.
[14] **Beschwer**: trouble.
[15] **Stand: Zustand.**
[16] **unhörlich (ungehört)**: unheard (by God).
[17] **fleuchen: fliehen.**
[18] **tränen**: be filled with tears; here, cry.
[19] **entschießen: enteilen.**
[20] **erlaben**: refresh; restore.

Du spielst mit mir im vollen Wunderschick:²¹
Noch Habakuk²² muß Danieln erdraben.²³
45 Das Löwenmaul²⁴ verlieret seine Art:
Sie können nicht, ob sie schon woll'n, zermalmen.
Dein Rat wird selbst dir, Babel, zugepaart:
Sie werden bald statt unser dich aushalmen.²⁵
Ob alles A.U.S. auf unser' Seite ruft:
50 Doch ist es nur, O Babel, deine Gruft.

Er wohnt in ihr als seiner festen Höhl',
Daß tausend Gütt³² sie täglich sich erwirbet.
Der Vater hält sie nun vor³³ seinen Sitz,   65
Darin sein Wort von ihm aus ihm geboren:
Der Heil'ge Geist geht aus in sanfter Hitz',³⁴
Weil zum Palast Jehovens sie erkoren.
Jemehr zerknirscht, jemehr vom Eignem leer:
Jemehr wohnt Gott in Uns mit seinem Heer.   70

(6)

Furcht schreckt Uns wohl, weil alles Rechte krumm,
Und unser End' ist nach gottloser Weise:
Doch sieht Gott vor, daß wir nicht kommen um,
Und alles eilt zu seinem höchsten Preise.
55 Gott jobisiert Uns²⁶ bis zur letzten Prob';
Bis Isaac meist und David sind verschwunden:
Dann reißt er aus²⁷ zu seinem Ehrenlob,
Und ist der Port²⁸ so plötzlich fort empfunden.
Soviel vor²⁹ Angst, so viel erfolget Lust;
60 Weil Gott in Uns nur stärker wird bewußt.

(8)

Höchstkläglich ist durch Gottesruf aufsteh'n,
Und scheinen doch gleich als im Eignen laufen:
Mit Abraham durch Gott von Ur³⁵ ausgehen,
Und soviel Jahr' nur leeren Wind einkaufen.
Der Geist und Fleisch sind stets im schwersten Kampf: 75
Wo einer siegt, da muß das andre fliehen.
Was himmlisch ist, das ist der Erde Dampf:
Was irdisch, mag nicht in den Himmel ziehen.
Wo die Vernunft zur Richterin gesetzt,
Was Wunder, daß Pilatus neu verletzt?   80

(7)

Gott ist sehr groß in der zerknirschten Seel',
Die ganz zermahlt,³⁰ nicht bloß nur durchgemürbet:³¹

(9)

Im Fische trägt doch Jonas Christi Bild,
Ob³⁶ ihn die Straf' um seine Schuld ergriffen:
Zwar David fleucht, weil Gott die Straf' erfüllt,
Doch Kidrons Bach³⁷ muß ihm von Christo triffen.³⁸
So straft oft Gott, die er ihm auserwählt,   85
Uns ist die Straf' ein segenreich' Geheimnis:
Gott schlägt den Feind, der sie in Nöten quält,

²¹ **im Wunderschick**: in der Form, in der Gestalt **von Wundern**.
²² **Habakuk**: Habakkuk; the prophet who, according to the Book of Daniel in the O.T., was miraculously brought to Babylonia by an angel to bring nourishment to Daniel in the lions' den.
²³ **erdraben**: ertraben (erreichen?).
²⁴ **Löwenmaul**: lion's mouth; (pars pro toto: the lions).
²⁵ **aushalmen** (wie Getreide schneiden): to cut as wheat; to mow down.
²⁶ **Gott jobisiert uns**: Gott behandelt uns wie **Hiob** (Job).
²⁷ **ausreißen**: ausholen.
²⁸ **Port**: haven.
²⁹ **vor**: vorher.
³⁰ **zermahlt**: ground; crushed (as between millstones).
³¹ **durchgemürb(e)t** broken, battered.

³² **Gütt**: Güter (?).
³³ **vor**: für (als; wie).
³⁴ **Hitze**: here, love; fervor.
³⁵ **Ur**: city of ancient Sumer; traditionally, Abraham's birthplace.
³⁶ **ob** (obgleich): although.
³⁷ **Kidrons Bach**: Probably a reference to II Sam. 16: 5–14. David, put to flight by Absalom, is taunted by Shimei, son of Gera from Saul's kinship; but he prays God to forgive the one who has insulted him. He anticipates Christ's prayer for his enemies.
³⁸ **triffen** (triefen): drip, flow.

Ihr Fallen wird zum Wachsen neue Käumnis.[39]
Wann Petrus fällt, so steht er tränend auf:
90 Bekehrt dadurch den allergrößten Hauf.

(10)

Kommt Samson um, so stirbt er mächtig
   teuer.
Wirkt Wunderwerk in seinem Unterliegen:
Er ruft zu Gott, und rächt sich ungeheur,
Vorfiguriert[40] alsdann recht Christi Siegen.
95 Die Gott gesalbt, eh' sie die Mutter kennt,
Läßt Gott im Fall'n nicht weltgebor'ne
   Schmerzen:
Sie haben Gott, nicht Menschen, sich ver-
   rennt;[41]
Gott will in Ernst die Feind' und Spötter
   stürzen.
Wer Gottes Kraft in Gotteshelden höhnt,
100 Höhnt Gott, nicht sie, wie man sich auch
   beschönt.[42]

(11)

Läuft ab von Gott, den Gott zum König
   sandt,
Josias[43] wird zur rechten Stund' doch
   kommen.
Ist Bileam[44] in schnöden Geiz[45] entbrannt:
Doch Gott bleibt Gott, der einst aus ihm
   vernommen.
105 Die lästern Gott und seinen Heil'gen Geist,
Die Gottes Wort und Menschen-Worte
   gleichen[46]

---

[39] **Käumnis (das Keimen; der Keim):** germ, seed-
bud.
[40] **vorfigurieren:** vorgestalten; vorbilden.
[41] **sich verrennen (sich versperren):** shut oneself
away from something.
[42] **beschönen:** justify; palliate.
[43] **Josias:** Josiah; king of Judah (reigned 638?–?608
B.C.). He began a religious reform, barring pagan
cults from the Temple.
[44] **Bileam:** Balaam; pagan soothsayer *and* prophet
of Jahweh; ordered by the Moabite king Balak
to curse the Israelites in the name of their God.
The story of his journey, of his being rebuked by
his ass, and of Balaam's blessing instead of cursing
the Israelites, is found in Num. 22–24.
[45] **Geiz:** avarice.
[46] **gleichen:** gleichsetzen.

Mut willig wird der Staub vor[47] Gold ge-
   preist,[48]
Weil[49] jeder kann den Unterschied erreichen.
Der Satan hält bei falschem Urteil Haus:
Er herrscht in ihm, und spricht es selbsten 110
   aus.

(12)

Muß der Prophet erfüllen mit dem Tun,
Nicht nur mit Mund und Schrift dem Volk
   weissagen,
Schwer ist sein Amt, unruhbar (Ah!) sein
   Ruh'n:
Untragbar all's was er muß täglich tragen.
Das Volk wird blind, wann A.L.L.E.S. sich 115
   verkehrt,
Und erst an ihm das Vorspiel[50] muß gesche-
   hen:
Es urteilt sich, jemehr sie ihn bewährt,[51]
Wie endlich lehrt ein Danielsches Flehen.[52]
Es ist zu spät bei schon verzehrtem Stamm
Zu retten erst die Äst' aus lichter Flamm.' 120

(13)

Noch schwerer ist, wann Gott im Rätsel
   spielt,
Und offenbart, was er sehr tief verbirget:
Setzt nah, was fern, und fern, was nah gefühlt,
Erhöhet heut', die morgen sind erwürget
Die Welt wird stolz, ein jeder aufgebläht, 125
Vernarret sind, die Gottes Weisheit küsset:
Der ist ein Spott, der voller Glauben sät,
Bis sie den Hohn in Kindeskindern büßet.
Daß hörbar ist des Innern äußer' Hall:
Was innen fiel, wird auch des Äußern Fall. 130

(14)

O schwerste Schwer, entzünd't im Gottes
   Grimm,

---

[47] **vor:** über.
[48] **gepreist (gepriesen):** praised; extolled.
[49] **weil:** da doch.
[50] **Vorspiel (Vorbild):** example.
[51] **bewähren (erproben):** put to the test.
[52] **ein Danielsches Flehen:** allusion to Daniel's
prayers, which brought him divine deliverance.

Wann der Prophet des Volks falsch' Wesen
   träget![53]
Gott redet falsch durch des Propheten
   Stimm':
Belohnt das Volk, wie es sein Wort ge-
   pfleget.[54]
135 Gott zürnt mit Recht, gibt Satan Haupt-
   gewalt,
Um Gottes Feind durch den Prophet zu
   sichten[55]
Verstockt[56] das Volk nach eig'ner Sinngestalt,[57]
Dann narrt[58] Christin, wie man zuvor
   wollt richten.[59]
Wann Micha[60] red't dem A.H.A.B.[61] plötzlich
   wohl,
140 Ist da die Zeit, da er verderben soll.

(15)

Prüft Gott mich nicht zur Prob', Verächter,
   euch?
Läßt er's nicht zu, daß ihr euch sollt ver-
   greifen.
Eur' Maß ist voll! Ihr sodomitet[62] reich!
Je heller Sonn': je schnelleres Ausreifen.
145 Mich feurt[63] die Not, die sechste Probungs-
   glut;

---

[53] **Wann . . . träget**: if the prophet takes on the false
   ways of the people (instead of teaching God's ways).
[54] **pflegen**: here, deal with, care for. God rewards
   the people in the same way in which it cared for
   his word (he revenges neglect by falsehood).
[55] **sichten (sichtbar machen)**: to make visible, to
   sift. One sees who follows the false prophet, and
   thus the false believers are separated from the truly
   faithful.
[56] **verstocken**: to harden. The false prophet (subject
   of the sentence) hardens the hearts of the people.
[57] **Sinngestalt**: desire; wish.
[58] **narren: ein Narr sein.**
[59] **Christin** = Kristina Poniatowska, a Polish
   "prophetess", much admired by Kuhlmann
   (. . . when this happens even the inspired Kristina
   Poniatowska will be considered a fool). **Wie man
   zuvor wollt richten**: as people did in 1628 when
   she prophesied.
[60] **Micha**: Micah, a prophet; raised his voice against
   the injustices of the kings.
[61] **Ahab**: king of Israel (*c.* 875–852 B.C.); his policies
   conflicted with those of the prophets.
[62] **sodomiten** (*neologism*): live a godless life (like the
   people of Sodom before the destruction).
[63] **feuren (feuern)**: temper; make stronger, more
   resilient (through hardship [**Not**]).

Sie tönet[64] mich mit allerhöchster Tönung:[65]
Sie kühlt und frischt mit himmelweiterm
   Mut;
Ihr Notfeuer schenkt der Überwindung
   Krönung.
Loths[66] Spott[67] ist klein, groß Sodoms Unter-
   gang:
Das Kreuz dauert kurz, der Bosheit Strafe 150
   lang.

(16)

Quellt A.L.L.E.S. nicht aus Jesu Kreuzes
   Quell'?
Die Jünger selbst die haben ihn verlassen.
Kein Witz[68] vermocht (als dunkel, was nun
   hell,
Verborgen, was nun offen) Jesum fassen.
Er ärgert' all und sprach, was jeden stieß;[69] 155
Red't mit der Tat, und ward fast nicht
   gehöret:
Schien gänzlich falsch, als er den Geist aus-
   blies,
Bis er entschloß,[70] was er zuvor gelehret.
Wen Christus schickt, dem muß, wie Christo,
   gehn:
Die Welt wird ihn, wie Christum vor,[71] 160
   verstehn.

(17)

Recht auf, Vernunft! Lieg auch an Jesu
   Schoß,
Wo du begehrst sein Reich in dir zu lernen!
Komm, tische mit![72] Laß deine Ichheit los!
Er ist die Kost: Kein Stern wird mehr dich
   fernen.[73]

---

[64] **tönen**: shade; color (allusion to potter's workshop?
   [**Ton**: clay].
[65] **Tönung (Farbenabstufung)**: laying on of colors.
[66] **Loth**: Lot; the only God-fearing man to be saved
   from Sodom's destruction.
[67] **Spott**: mockery; derision.
[68] **Witz**: here, mind; brain.
[69] **stoßen (anstoßen)**: here, anger.
[70] **entschließen (aufschließen)**: here, reveal.
[71] **vor: vorher.**
[72] **tischen (speisen)**: partake of food (allusion to the
   Last Supper).
[73] **fernen (fernhalten)**: keep at a distance.

A. Z.

Der

KÜHLPSALTER

Oder

Di Funffzehngesænge.

AMSTERDAM,
Im Jahre Jesu Christi, 1684.
im October.

Quirinus Kuhlmanns „Kühlpsalter" (1684): Titelblatt. (Aus der Sammlung Curt von Faber du Faur.) *Courtesy of Yale University Library.*

Quirinus Kuhlmanns „Kühlpsalter" (1684) Textprobe. (Aus der Sammlung Curt von Faber du Faur.) *Courtesy of Yale University Library.*

Oben, unten, nah und fern.
2. 8. Gros und klein ist ausgeflossen,
VVi sein schœpffer es beschlossen,
Nach der eignen Ordnung art:
Eines-zehen-hundert-tausend
Aus der Ewikeit herbrausend
VVird vom Schœpffer gleichgepaart,
Gleich gehalten, gleich bewahrt.
Lobt Gott gleich, was gleich bequemet,   9410
Di ihr gleichen Anfang nehmet,
Brodmet lobvoll Gott den Herrn,
Oben, unten, nah und fern.
3. 9. Gros und kleines, hoch und nidrig
Scheint Geschœpffen in sich widrig
Nach gewichte, mas und zahl:
Doch bei Gott ist gantz kein wählen,
Kein gewichte, mas und zæhlen;
Nur ein einig Allzumahl;
Gleich im Ewikeiten strahl.   9410
Rühmt Gott alle gleichverlesen,
Di da werden, sind, gewesen,
Hauchet lobvoll Gott den Herrn,
Oben, unten, nah und fern.
    Zweiter Gegensatz.   15 Febr.
1. 10. Gott ist heiligheilig heilig,
Eine Dreiheit unvertheilig,
Da di Einheit unverletzt.
Gott der Vater itts begehren,
Cott der Sohn sein Lustverklæhren,
Gott der heilge Geist ergetzt,   9430
VVeil er würklich alls darsœtzt.
Aller admen ist verschieden:
Drei und einig, doch im friden.
Ides admen singt den Herrn;
Oben, unten, nah und fern.
2. 11. Gott ist gros in Cherubinen,
Grœsser in den Seraphinen,
Allergrœst in ihrem Haupt:
Heilig durch di Christvorlauffer,
Heiliger im Christustauffer,   9440
Allerheiligst, da geglaubt,
VVas di Erde neugoldlaubt.
Alle brodmen nach vermœgen,
Drei und einigt, sich nicht gegen.
Ides brodmen hallt den Herrn;
Oben, unten, nah und fern.
3. 12. Gott ist Allen ALLES worden,
Voller und auch sonder Orden,
Allesaller Creatur;
Læsst sich gros und grœsser zeigen;   9450
Sich ausreden, sich ausschweigen;   Alles

Aller Aller Allescur,
Auch nach aller zahlen spur.
Alle hauchen nur das Eines,
Das von Allen ewigt Keines.
Ides hauchen dankt dem Herrn;
Oben, unten, nah und fern.

    Der 4 (64) Kühlpsalm,
Als er nun bei 7 Monden das Josephverkauffen wegen des Gottlichen Verkes erfahren, und endlich durch den Brekling-Felinschen Scheingeist um der Kühlpropheten, an der verfallenen Anthosetten Sterl tag, unter so vilem Ungemach auch leiblich erlag, bei entsetzung des falschen Gesichtscentrum und vilen Verfallen verdrükket, und erquikkt angestimmt zu Amsterdam den 16. 19 Nov und 25. 27. Dec. 1680.

1. Aus tiffster Noth schrei abgemergelt Hertz!
Las mich noch einst di matte hand aufheben!
Es harnischt mich und pantzert recht der schmertz!   9460
Di zunge klebt! Angst hat mich rings umgeben!
Mein Gott, mein Gott! Du zentverst stete last!
Hœhr auf, hœhr auf, eh ich bin gantz verdrükket.
Gib endlich gib um Jesu Kreutz mir rast!
VVi lange sol dein VVerk sein gantz entschmükket?
VVas ist der Mensch, der ewigt wird gepresst?
Halt innen halt, eh Geist und Seel ausblæst.
2. Befehrst du mich als deinen ærgsten Feind?
Es hat mich schmach nach aller wunsch getroffen.
Si schaunmehr lust als si zuschaun vermeint: 9470
Verlohren wird mehr taglich mir mein hoffen.
Dein Wort scheint nichts als nur ein leerer traum:
Dein führen wird ein lauteres verführen.
Si zweigen sich gleich einem Eichen baum:
Du aber læst mich mehr und mehr verführen.
Du mastest si und nimmt mir A. L. L. E. S. hin:
Verirrest mich, gibst schaden zum gewin.
3. Christ Gott und Mensch! Schau her, ich bin dein Glid!
Sol harmung, frost und armut mich aufzehren!   9480
Ich lige hir, stimm an di dis Trauerlid,
Voll Elend, Ach, und tausender beschweren!
Voll Kummer, sorg und was mein stand erwekkt!
Mus hertzenleid unnœchlich-n mich fressen!
Bin hœchstbedrængt und über A. L. L. beslekkt
Als bœttest du schon deines Knechts vergessen!
Mein gaumen klebt vor durst an meine lipp
Und werde ich lebendig zum geripp.
4. Di Jugend fleucht! verging als wi das laub!   9490
Ihr Süsses ist mir bitter weggeflossen.
Ich trahne hir, heut etwas, morgen Staub.
Di Tage sind mit jammern mir ent t chossen.
Bin ich, mein Gott, zu lauter schand gemacht?   Solt

165 Sieh Adam recht, Wie, Wem und wo er fiel!
Du wirst nicht mehr in trüben Lachen[74]
    angeln.
Erkenne dich, und deines Schöpfers Ziel:
Die Wahrheit wird von oben nirgends
    mangeln.
Der Schöpfer schuf Geschöpf' im Freiheits-
    kranz,
170 Daß sie ihr Herz ihm widerstrahlten ganz.

(18)

Such ernst, Vernunft, im Bleikleid erstes
    Gold!
Der Lebensbaum schwimmt noch in dir
    bearchet.[75]
Durchperle dich mit der Sophien[76] hold:
Die Fleischvernunft wird stracks in dir
    versarchet.[77]
175 Die Morgenröt' durchrosenliljet[78] hoch:
Der König zeucht[79] zum Hochzeitfeste
    prächtig.
Das Paradeis entjocht das Erdenjoch:
Die Zeit wird gleich der ersten Kühlzeit[80]
    mächtig.
Wir ernten ein nun aller Heil'gen Müh.
180 Eilt, Schnitter, eilt! Genießt der Perlen früh.

(19)

Trutz, Nimrod,[81] trutz, der du ein kleins[82]
    noch trutzst!
Dein Urreich sinkt! Das Jesuelsche[83] glänzet!
Du putzest[84] Uns, wann du dich nur ent-
    putzest.
Der Frost ist weg. Die erste Kühlung lenzet.[85]

Der Heil'gen Blut, mit dem du dich gefärbt,   185
Christähnlichet:[86] es hat dein Reich verrissen.
Dein Adler wird mit seinem Zehn[87] gesterbt:[88]
Er muß sein Blut, wie er's vergoß, vergießen.
Das Christusreich nimmt aller Reiche Würd'
Ausgittelt[89] A.L.L.S. und gibt dem Feur die   190
    Bürd'.

(20)

Unmögend[90] Volk, das du hochmögend[91]
    prangst
Und Christo nicht auftorest[92] deine Länder!
Nimrodisierst![93] Ja bis du Rom erlangst![94]
Sein Schwert und Feur und eisenharte Bänder.
Was bild'st du mir im Osten Caiphas[95] vor?   195
Dein DAMM ist schwach, ob du dich noch so
    dämmest.
Ach DÄMME nicht! Der Christrock ist
    empor!
Du klemmst und hemmst, jemehr du klemmst
    und hemmest.
Was Christo wird im Kleinsten zugefügt,
Das hat ihn selbst, nicht nur sein Glied,   200
    gerügt.[96]

(21)

Wohlan, du Löw'![97] Als du den Siebenpfeil
Zu ehren Gott nach dem Euphrat geschossen,
War Gott mit dir; Sein Segen ward dein Teil!
Du bist geschwind hochästig aufgesprossen.
Welch Undank, Ach! Was Mißbrauch Gottes   205
    Güt'?

---

[74] **Lache**: puddle.
[75] **bearchet**: as in the ark (Noah's Ark is the pro-
    totype).
[76] **Sophie**: Sophia; symbolic figure of divine wisdom.
[77] **versarchen (in einen Sarg tun)**: put into a coffin.
[78] **durchrosenliljen** (*neologism*): "radiate" with roses
    and lilies.
[79] **zeucht**: zieht.
[80] **Kühlzeit**: time of coolness and virtue. See p. 281.
[81] **Nimrod**: legendary biblical character (Gen. X:
    8–12). Reputed to be the first ruler on earth; the
    prototype of the powerful overlord.
[82] **ein kleins**: für eine kurze Zeit.
[83] **Jesuelsche (Reich)**: Reich Jesu.
[84] **putzen**: adorn.
[85] **lenzet**: beginnt frühlingsgleich.

[86] **christähnlichen**: Christus ähnlich sein.
[87] **der Zehn (die Zehe)**: here, claw.
[88] **gesterbt (sterben)**: slain.
[89] **ausgitteln**: (allem Verlangen) ein Ende bereiten.
[90] **unmögend**: schwach.
[91] **hochmögend**: stark.
[92] **auftoren**: öffnen.
[93] **nimrodisieren** (*neologism*): conduct oneself like
    a "Nimrod."
[94] **erlangen**: attain; come up to (the level of).
[95] **Caiphas**: Caiaphas; high priest at Jerusalem during
    the time of Christ's death. Last one of four high
    priests called to perform this office by the procurator
    Valerius Gratus, who had been sent to Judea by
    Tiberius.
[96] **rügen**: here, revile; vilify.
[97] **Löw'**: reference to Nimrod (?).

Soll Gottes Werk nun hier erst Schiffbruch
leiden?
Bewegt nicht Krieg, Sturm, Wasser dein
Gemüt?
Wohlan, du Löw'. Es ist hoch Zeit zu
scheiden.
Ein Loth verbleibt bis auf der Strafe Uhr,[98]
210 Weil er sie hielt, daß sie nicht widerfuhr.[99]

(22)

Xerxire[100] du, du große Völker-Meng'!
Du Sand und Staub! vorn Waffen ohne
Waffen!
Komm, komm zum Streit mit mächtigem
Gepräng!
Komm, rüste dich! Wir woll'n in Gott
einschlafen!
215 Wann du dich nahst, mit Millionen dräust,[101]
Erwacht in Uns, der dich aus sich verlodert.[102]
Dann ist's zu spät, ob du dies ewigst reust:[103]
Du fürchtest dich, und hast doch aus-
gefordert.[104]
Der Weltkreis ist dem heil' gen Volk erlöst:
220 Nun jagt Gott aus, die den aufs neu
verböst.[105]

(23)

Ypslonisir,[106] Besitze beiden Weg:
Sei rechts und links, bediene Gott und
Mammon.

Schallt das Geschrei des Bräutigams, sei reg:
Auf, einige voll Klugheit Christ und Ham-
mon.[107]
Doch wisse, daß der Glauben innen werkt,[108]   225
Und dich belampt[109] das Öl der Fünf Jung-
frauen:
Du kommst nicht ein, wo nicht neu Öl dich
stärkt,
Wo du nicht kannst ganz deinem Gott ver-
trauen.
Der Gott und Welt nach seinem Vorteil
sucht,
Verscherzet beid': ist beiden gleich verflucht.   230

(24)

Zerbrochen ist, Gott dank, durch deine
Kraft,
O Gottes Lamm, das sechst' im siebnen
Siegel![110]
Zerbrich nun bald des Sieb'nen Sieben-
schaft,[111]
Daß alle Welt sich seh' im Henochsspiegel.[112]
Zerbrich in mir, was noch ist ohne Bruch,   235
Bis siebenfach das Siebendrei[113] gebrochen!
Eröffne mich und lies mich als dein Buch,
Das Ros' und Lilje in aller Welt gerochen.
Ich bin nur dein, nicht mein, dein Eigentum:
Was du gabest, kann ich einzig geben: 240
Laß mich ewigst an dir kleben.

---

[98] **Uhr:** Stunde.

[99] **weil ... widerfuhr:** weil er glaubte, sie (die Strafe) könnte nicht über ihn verhängt werden.

[100] **xerxieren** (*neologism*): feel like the mighty Xerxes; Persian king, reigned 486–465 B.C..

[101] **dräuen:** drohen.

[102] **verlodern:** be consumed by fire.

[103] **reuen:** repent; rue.

[104] **ausfordern (herausfordern):** challenge (to battle).

[105] **verbösen (erbosen):** make angry.

[106] **Ypslonisieren** (*neologism*): branch out like a "Y"; i.e, serve two masters.

[107] **Hammon:** a place name in the Old Testament, sometimes etymologically related to the Egyptian God *amanu*.

[108] **werken (wirken):** act; work.

[109] **belampen:** wie eine Lampe zum Leuchten bringen.

[110] **sechst' ... Siegel:** the sixth among the seven seals. Reference to Rev. 5:1 ff. When the sixth seal is opened, the world will come to an end and the Day of Judgment will have arrived. The saints will enter Heaven (Rev. 6:12–17); when the seventh seal is opened, the godless will be destroyed (Rev. 8;9;10).

[111] **Siebenschaft:** the term stands for "godlessness."

[112] **Henochsspiegel:** *lit.*, mirror of Enoch. Enoch, one of the patriarchs in the O.T., was carried off to heaven at the age of 365 years by God because of his piety. Enoch was considered an apocalyptic seer; it is possible that the metaphor "*Henochsspiegel*" refers to this.

[113] **siebenfach das Siebendrei:** hyperbole combining mystical numbers.

The Age of Enlightenment

We have become used to characterizing the early and middle years of the eighteenth century as the Age of Enlightenment, and although we are certain that Gottsched and Lessing, each in his own way, outstandingly represent the issues of their particular decades, we are far less certain where the period begins and ends—it is an age of loose fringes. Perhaps we should be aware that the traditional term *Aufklärung* stems from philosophical tradition and tends to create difficulties if applied to poetic and literary developments; although a fable may closely correspond to one of the systematic assumptions of a rational philosophy, it might be much harder to say in what way a tragedy or an ode crystallizes philosophical reason. The term *Aufklärung* at best indicates something of the characteristic ideological interests of the age, but does not necessarily suffice to enlighten us about literary developments.

In the eighteenth century, Germany fully participated in the European efforts to arrive at a world view independent of inherited authorities, to make reason an instrument of analysis, and boldly to examine the traditional values of religion and ethics. Descartes and the French Encyclopedists; Leibnitz, Locke, Hume, and the English freethinkers provided the systematic statements and, in his famous essay *Was ist Aufklärung?* (1784) Kant proudly declared: *Aufklärung ist der Ausgang der Menschen aus ihrer selbstverschuldeten Unmündigkeit,* and demanded that the individual should make public use of his reason. German literature, however, often derived its enlightened orientations from diligent popularizers like Thomasius and Christian Wolff who transmitted to the middle classes the new spirit of tolerance, optimism, and sober scrutiny. From a philosophical point of view, the German Enlightenment does not rest on monolithic attitudes; at the beginning of the century, Wolff turned German attention toward the systematic and possibly rigid rationalism of the French, but as time progressed intellectuals became increasingly interested in British empiricism and studied the new intro-

spective psychology of sensation and sensibilities. After the middle of
the century, many strands from the various sources combined to prepare
the unusual richness of developing German philosophy, but it may be
fair to say that with the year 1781, when Lessing died, and Kant's *Kritik
der reinen Vernunft* as well as Schiller's *Die Räuber* appeared, the concentrated unity of enlightened interests, in thought and literature, rapidly
disintegrated.

Politically, the German scene changed considerably, and the military
conflicts of Prussia and Austria that dominated the midcentury really
were a part of global wars; the Seven Years' War (1756–63) was fought
not only on the battlefields of Silesia but also in India and the American
colonies of Great Britain. Constitutional life in most of the German
territorial states ossified; only in some of the important cities, in the
territories of Hannover, and in the Southwest did the underprivileged
middle classes begin to exert oblique pressures, but they were on the
whole far from ready to compete with the importance of the British
merchants or the French bourgeoisie. Yet within the apparent stability
of constitutional life the second advance of the middle classes began to
gather momentum after the catastrophe of the Thirty Years' War; the
sociological changes affected literary life, and independent middle-class
tastes emerged. The old imperial and free cities that flourished from the
fifteenth and seventeenth centuries lost much of their importance. The
shift of commerce to the Atlantic seaboard, the decrease in trade with
the Orient, which had sustained older communications over the Alps
and to the Rhineland, as well as the destruction caused by the Thirty
Years' War, threatened, if not destroyed, the functions of cities like Ulm,
Nuremberg, Augsburg, and Cologne. With the noticeable shift in trade
routes—in the modest beginnings of a modern industry often established
and furthered by the government itself—new centers of commercial
interests assumed cultural importance: Leipzig, the organizing center of
German trade with the East; Hamburg, the old *Hansestadt* long invigorated by the Atlantic trade; Zurich, the independent patrician republic;
and, last but not least, Berlin, the frontier town developed for strategic
reasons by the Hohenzollern dynasty out of a fishing village. For some
time court patronage was suspended or ineffective; in Berlin where
King Frederick II preferred Voltaire to young Goethe, the German
literati were unable to impress their king by their achievements, and young
Klopstock was obliged to accept Danish support. Frederick went on
writing in French and continued to believe that German literature was
a rather rude and impolite affair.

In contrast to the philosophical ferment and the psychological trans-
formations, literature at least until the late forties of the century surprises
one by its strong conservatism. Writers wanted to preserve rather than
demolish, and the critical dialogues were dominated by concepts elabo-

rated during the Renaissance or ultimately derived from the successive European interpretations of Horace and Aristotle. Even the later *Sturm-und-Drang* generation did not, as nineteenth-century German scholarship asserted, completely part ways with tradition but rather preferred a different set of norms than their immediate predecessors. In literature and the arts philosophical Enlightenment corresponds to an age of classicism. As a technical term, *classicism* closely corresponds to the intentions and forms of literature and indicates (if we use it flexibly enough) that most writers of the time still believed that new achievements in literature should live up to the great examples of classical antiquity, represent nature, create characters of dignity and beauty who reconcile inclinations and duties, distinguish between high, middle, and low levels of subject and style, consciously construct works of art that are to be lucid and luminous wholes, and respect the technical patterns and useful tactics employed in the well-defined genres from tragedy to the epigram. If anybody insisted on the rules he did so because he believed that the rules or rather laws inherent in great art were to be discovered in and derived from the achievements of tradition, above all Homer, Horace, Theocritus, Vergil, and Pindar. The individual writer still thought of himself as an integrated member of a wide and cosmopolitan community of the erudite and, when judging or writing a work of art, continued to appeal to ideas valid beyond national boundaries. Lacking the modern and sharpened sense of history, the critical sensibility of the time still confronted Aristotle and the ancients as if they were contemporaries to whose authority one might appeal for legitimate support.

Classicists of course prefer certain genres of literature and have some difficulty in coming to terms with others (above all the Elizabethan theater, which is intimately related to popular tradition). Although people did not yet speak about *Lyrik* (the Abbé Batteux reintroduced the concept in 1747), there was a tendency to cherish a standard cluster of poetic forms confirmed by tradition: playful Anacreontic poetry recommended by the French Renaissance, the didactic poem concerning the nature of things, the entertaining fable which does not fail to teach a moral lesson, the belligerent satire attacking the vices of petty court and small town, and, as the august epic of the older civilizations seemed more and more incompatible with the new way of life, the mock epic which parodies the old form and yet demonstrates the living knowledge of its conventions. It is the question of the epic and of the traditional ode that tended to divide the minds and pointed to future developments; older classicists preferred the mock epic and the Horatian poem whereas the younger enthusiasts renewed the grand epic and the passionate ode inherited from Pindar.

German playwrights, like most of their colleagues, continued to distinguish between tragedy and comedy and often to interpret the inherited

ideas in a narrow moralistic way. Tragedy is to explicate a moral truth
by treating noble characters in high places; comedy, permitted to stoop
to middling figures, ridicules deficiencies of human character and tries
to teach polite manners undisturbed by vice and deformation. We have
to admit that after the impressive flowering of the Baroque novel, earlier
eighteenth-century Germany does not have any book to offer that would
be enjoyed by the modern reader. Cervantes, Defoe, Fielding, Smollett,
and Sterne were imitated with a good deal of success, but it is difficult
to speak of any important novel before Wieland's *Agathon* (1766/67),
which was theoretically justified in Blankenburg's highly interesting
Versuch über den Roman (1774).

It would be misleading to sketch a static portrait of the age and to
ignore the tensions and the bitter conflicts among groups and factions.
In the thirties, Gottsched firmly dominated the scene as arbiter in matters
of theory and taste. Although his image has been disfigured by generations
of adversaries, we should admit that he was a highly erudite, if somewhat pedantic scholar, who, for the last time as it were, attempted to
consolidate for the Germans the European norms of a disciplined classicism and, as Boileau had done centuries earlier in France, to reconsti-
tute literary taste within the confines of an elegant language untainted
by local dialect. His was a classicism of Latin and French examples; he
preferred Vergil to Homer, and Molière to the undisciplined English.
If he was accused of having "Frenchified" the German theater, it was
only because, in his patriotic fervor, he wanted the uncultured German
stage to emulate the supreme achievements of French art. It would be
highly unfair to misjudge Gottsched's many efforts to make German
literature again part of the civilized European constellation—his frequent
attempts to publish moral weeklies in order to educate the new middle-
class readers; to reunite high literature and the stage, which had parted
ways after Gryphius and Lohenstein; to edit and preserve the most important documents of the German literary and theatrical past in order
to define standards. Gottsched suffered from the limitations of his particular virtues; with many other European critics he shared a dogmatic
belief in the didactic function of the arts and, gazing fixedly at the excellence of the Latin and French traditions, was unable to cope with the
greatness of Homer, Milton, and Shakespeare. He defined the poet as
a skillful imitator of all natural things—it was his fate that he excluded
from his idea of nature most of man's imaginative, metaphysical, and
religious desires. Gottsched was most at home with an art gracefully
reflecting middle-class experience and closed his eyes to the wider realms
of the imagination.

In the early forties, important signs of change in literary and political
life emerged. Frederick II succeeded to the Prussian throne, and Maria
Theresia to the Austrian, and Austro-Prussian tension immediately grew;

not less important for German literature, the first of Shakespeare's plays to be translated into German, *Julius Caesar,* appeared in 1741. After Gottsched had dominated the German scene for almost a decade, opposition gathered and articulated, and the Swiss professors Bodmer and Breitinger who both taught and published in Zurich began to define aesthetic preferences that ran counter to Gottsched's orthodoxy. Yet it would be wrong to construct a melodramatic antithesis between the ideas of Gottsched and those of the Swiss. There is much the warring parties shared; both the *Leipziger* and the *Schweizer* subscribed to classicist assumptions, and the noise of the conflict dividing literary Germany into two camps should not hide the fact that a shift of talents and tastes rather than a total opposition of two worlds was involved. The *Leipziger* and the *Schweizer* believed in the ancients as the final authorities to whom educated judgment should appeal; both assumed that art constitutes an imitation of nature; both continued to believe that poetry should fulfill above all a moral and didactic function to be worthy of the attention of the civilized reader. Within these assumptions interests perceptibly shifted. The Swiss again preferred a language strengthened by regional and local elements rather than Gottsched's cosmopolitan if somewhat abstract German; and if Gottsched was concerned with the character of the work of art itself, the Swiss were very much interested in the psychological and emotional responses of the reader. Whereas Gottsched stressed the reasonable and disciplined, the Swiss were inclined to claim the marvelous and the new as the mainspring of art; Gottsched preferred the probable, seasoned with a grain of the marvelous; the Swiss insisted on the marvelous which should, of course, be checked by probability—but their "probability" included the realm of religious imagination and was far from being identical with Gottsched's almost mathematical concept. Increasingly, a change of tastes emerged from the literary battle. Gottsched (who represents a reaction against the aesthetic excesses of the Baroque) remained committed to an enlightened and scholarly universe, but the Swiss, for many reasons close to the fervor of the English Puritans, imagined a world radiant with religious meaning; Gottsched kept his universe neat and closed, the Swiss opened it again to imagination and myth. In literary taste, the Swiss turned away from the French, spoke of "Saspar" (as they found Shakespeare spelled in their Italian sources), and explicated Milton's rich and expansive epic poem as the exemplary achievement of European poetry. The dispute did not have immediate effects on literary life; in Leipzig, the Saxon comedy clearly fulfilling Gottsched's demands achieved remarkable success, and the most sophisticated Anacreontic poetry emerged from this decade. But the Swiss faction more and more attracted the support of the younger generation which was dissatisfied with the inflexibility of the aging Gottsched. In Halle a group of young poets cultivated the enthusiastic ode and asserted in its own pamphlets that the Gottsched "sect" harmed German taste. In the later years of the decade another group gathered around an influential journal called the *Bremer Beiträge* and tended to support Swiss ideas; it is in this journal that the first three cantos of Klopstock's *Messias* were published (1748) and thus a young German poet made his appearance who seemed to fulfill all the desires of the Swiss theoreticians. Only from a later point of view did these symptoms of dissatisfaction with and opposition to the dictates of Leipzig appear as the first substantial signs of a whole movement which was finally articulated in the belligerence of the Storm-and-Stress generation.

In the fifties, the battle between Leipzig and Zurich was over and literary Germany settled for a fruitful and lively coexistence of ideas whose continuing ferment was intensified by the political and military conflicts of the time. The renewed war between Austria and Prussia and the worldwide collision of their mighty allies awakened the Germans to the necessities of political involvement and commitment. Although not everybody sided with Prussia (as some older German literary historians want us to believe), many younger people in the territories and principalities distant from world politics fervently admired the young Prussian king who by winning battles and suffering catastrophic defeats reoriented the imagination of the age. Even if unable or unwilling to embrace Prussia's political cause, some of the talented younger people were at least ready to be *fritzisch gesinnt,* and a wide literature of popular ballads on recent events, patriotic odes, and poetic meditations on death and immortality began to counteract the conventional niceties of Anacreontic poetry; fervent patriotism strengthened the reawakening metaphysical imagination. These were years of rapid development, suddenly emerging new genres, and ingenious theoretical attempts to define the overwhelming innovations in the light of the ancients; the time had not yet come to break completely with tradition and to proclaim the triumph of radical individuality. Gotthold Ephraim Lessing tried to achieve a subtle compromise between the traditional and the new, the substance of which he recognized with little hesitation; and although we may deplore that he was unfair to Gottsched and discouraged the Germans from relishing their Baroque theater, he was successful in his attempt to defend new poets and forms by appealing to Aristotle. Shakespeare emerged, in Lessing's interpretation, as truly "Aristotelian" and was absorbed into German contemporary taste with far less difficulty than was the case in France. In his theories, Lessing (who said of himself that he was neither an actor nor a poet) tended to the conservative side; in his literary practice, he was among the experimenters and innovators who, like Diderot in France, explored the middle ground between high tragedy and low comedy in search of a theater that would reflect the more modest and mixed realities of the midcentury. In his discussions concerning the *weinerliches oder rührendes Lustspiel* (1754) he comes close to anticipate nineteenth-century arguments in favor of the realistic novel. "His enthusiasm for Shakespeare did not prevent Lessing from imitating Diderot," the Austrian playwright Grillparzer once noted in his diary, and it would be difficult to characterize the ambivalence of Lessing and his age with more precision and insight.

Johann Christoph Gottsched

(1700–1766)

Johann Christoph Gottsched, an academic ally of Voltaire, Addison, and Pope, wanted German art to be lucid, elegant, and well-ordered; inevitably, he was opposed and ignored by those who preferred poetry to be closer to unbridled imagination. He has been misjudged for two centuries: between him and the modern reader stand reckless young Lessing (who disliked Gottsched's French taste), the chaotic minds of the Storm-and-Stress movement, as well as the Romantic generations who in Germany were responsible for the dominant idea of the poet as the lonely visionary. Only a few Germans, among them the learned, liberal Dünzer, have had the courage to rediscover, in opposition to growing irrationalism, Gottsched's vital if professorial concern for a civilized literature of international relevance.

Gottsched was born in Judittenkirchen near Königsberg. He began to study theology when he was fourteen but found himself more attracted by the enlightened philosophers and the pedestrian poetry of his teacher Pietsch whom he imitated in his first literary exercises. Gottsched was untiringly industrious: at eighteen, he wrote scholarly essays on the monads and on the omnipresence of God, and was well on his way to establishing himself as a successful teacher at the University of Königsberg. One day, however, he heard that there were Prussian officers in town who wanted to conscript tall men into King Frederick's élite regiment, the *lange Kerle*, based in Potsdam. Since he was over six feet tall, he fled and went via Poland to Saxon territory where he continued his academic work at the University of Leipzig. Here he rose quickly through the ranks: in 1724, he received permission to teach; hardly nine years later he was appointed full professor to teach logic, metaphysics, poetry, and poetics. His wife Adelgunde, née Kulmus (1713–1762), a gifted playwright and translator, joined him in his literary projects, and the Gottscheds were soon a famous team of supreme arbiters in matters of literary taste. Gottsched was an erudite but rather inflexible man; when the Swiss critics began to voice their opposition to his ideas, he retorted by stubborn and dogmatic statements and increasingly lost the sympathy of his former students who joined the literary opposition. When he died, he had far outlived his time.

In the thirties and forties, Gottsched was a famous professor whose lectures attracted audiences from many countries. Unlike many of his colleagues, however, he did not consider it below his academic dignity to edit popular journals, collaborate with Frau Neuber, the most interesting actress and stage producer of the day, and to compile many useful collections of older poetry. In 1725–26, he edited *Die vernünftigen Tadlerinnen,* a "moral" periodical in imitation of the London *Tatler* and *Spectator,* in order to elevate the tastes of his female readers; if he introduced French ideas and examples he did so to refine provincial German sensibilities. As a reformer of the contemporary stage, Gottsched wanted to reunite the theater and elegant literature; he rightly suspected the popular stage of pandering to vulgarity, but he was unwilling to realize that even the refined stage worthy of the interest of the educated could not cease to rely on its sensuous charms. His "regular" tragedy *Sterbender Cato* (compiled from English and French predecessors) was considered the epitome of the new noble drama, yet after some time it disappeared from the German stage never to return. Perhaps Gottsched did more to serve the theater by compiling much needed anthologies of older plays for actors and producers (e.g., *Deutsche Schaubühne, nach den Regeln und Exempeln der Alten*, 1742–45); the popular stage which then relied on mimics and textual improvisation (*Stegreif*) needed printed texts, and Gottsched, supported by his Adelgunde, provided an entire repertoire.

J. Ch. Gottscheds „Critische Dichtkunst" (1730): Titelblatt. (Aus der Sammlung Curt von Faber du Faur.) *Courtesy of Yale University Library.*

Gottsched's *Versuch einer kritischen Dichtkunst für die Deutschen* (1730) demonstrates his erudition as well as his strict adherence to the theoretical assumptions of European neoclassicism. His book has many virtues: by drawing on the work of distinguished minds like Boileau, Fontenelle, Dacier, Addison, and Maffei, he made the German reader aware of the critical norms prevalent in contemporary France, England, and Italy. Resolutely critical, the *Dichtkunst* never escaped the responsibility of evaluating works of art; and, most important in the thirties, Gottsched tried to relate judgments of taste to a consistent philosophy of the arts and to develop literary insights *aus ersten Gründen;* in this way, he prepared the ground for the systematic aesthetics of Immanuel Kant. The entire first part of the *Dichtkunst* defines and elaborates general concepts; Gottsched discusses the historical development of the verbal arts, sketches the image of the ideal poet, and comments upon the principles of probability and the marvelous (of course, he prefers the former). Only the second part comes close to what one may term the "rules" of art: here, Gottsched defines traditional genres and poetic forms (the ode, the epic, the tragedy, etc.) as well as formal innovations (the madrigal, the sonnet, etc.); yet it is quite clear that he likes to speak of setting examples rather than of giving rules that have to be mechanically followed. Of course, the *Dichtkunst* does have a number of blind spots: Gottsched's moral theory of tragedy was more than pedestrian (his rational mind could not come to terms with the disturbing quality of tragedy). Preferring the old Latins and the modern French, he seems too ready to ignore the achievements of Homer, the Renaissance epic, and, above all, Milton, whom he considered the very example of poetry exaggerated—tasteless, conceited, and improbable; only in his attacks against the opera, in anticipation of Brecht, is he fiercer and more unfair.

The second chapter of the *Kritische Dichtkunst* unites wide learning, sober prose, and a serious concern for the civilized, knowledgeable, and disciplined mind to create the ideal image of the enlightened poet. Gottsched defines him as a "skillful imitator of things *natural*." Hardly anywhere else in German criticism does the poet emerge as a figure more at ease with history and society; it is not difficult to see why the following romantic generations had little sympathy for Gottsched and his commonsense demands.

VERSUCH
EINER CRITISCHEN
DICHTKUNST

Das II. Hauptstück:
Von dem Charaktere eines Poeten

Nachdem wir den Ursprung und das allmählige Wachstum der Poesie kürzlich erwogen haben: so ist es nicht undienlich, von einem wahren Poeten einen
5 Abriß zu machen, und ihn nach allen seinen Eigenschaften zu beschreiben. Man ist mit diesem Namen zu allen Zeiten gar zu freigebig gewesen; weil man nicht sattsam eingesehen, was für eine große Fähigkeit
10 der Gemütskräfte, wieviel Gelehrsamkeit, Erfahrung, Übung und Fleiß zu einem rechtschaffenen Dichter gehören. Und das ist kein Wunder gewesen. Gemeiniglich haben sich's diejenigen angemaßt, den
15 Titel eines Poeten auszuteilen, die einen viel zu seichten Verstand, und eine viel zu blöde[1] Einsicht in das Wesen der wahren Dichtkunst gehabt. Der Pöbel[2] hat sich allezeit ein Recht zueignen wollen, von poetischen Scribenten[3]
20 zu urteilen: und dieses ist desto lächerlicher, da ihm die Beurteilung prosaischer Schriften niemals zugestanden worden. Kann er nun hierinnen keinen gültigen Ausspruch tun, und die Verfasser derselben, weder für
25 gute Historienschreiber, noch für Redner, Philosophen, Arzneiverständige oder Rechtsgelehrte erklären: wie wird er vermögend sein, von Gedichten zu urteilen, deren Einrichtung und Ausarbeitung desto schwerer
30 zu prüfen ist; je mehr sie unter so vielen äußerlichen Schönheiten und Zieraten, dadurch auch kritische Augen zuweilen verblendet werden, verhüllt ist, ja tief verborgen liegt. Plinius[4] schreibt an einem
35 Orte; von Künstlern könne nur ein Künstler urteilen. Man wird also mit der Poesie wohl nicht unbilliger umgehen wollen, als

mit der Musik, Malerei, Baukunst und dem Bildschnitzen. Wer beruft sich aber in allen diesen Künsten auf das Urteil des großen Haufens? Das würden schlechte Meister
5 darinnen werden, die ihren Ruhm in dem Beifalle eines eigensinnigen Volkes suchen wollten, welches ohne Verstand und ohne Regeln von ihren Sachen urteilt; und dessen Geschmack die unbeständigste Sache von der
10 Welt ist.
Es trifft freilich zuweilen zu, daß ein ganzes Land oder eine große Stadt sich an lauter regelmäßige Sachen gewöhnt, und so zu reden, eine zeitlang Geschmack daran findet.
15 Aber dieser gute Geschmack kann nicht lange Zeit erhalten werden; wenn es nicht Kunstverständige darunter gibt, die dasjenige, was der gemeine Mann nach der sinnlichen Empfindung liebt, nach richtigen Grund-
20 regeln für gut und schön erkennen. Ohne solche Meister geht der gute Geschmack bald wieder verloren, wie wir an Beispielen der Griechen und Römer, ja der neueren Wälschen[5] und Franzosen gesehen haben.
25 Die Leichtsinnigkeit der menschlichen Gemüter sucht allezeit eine Veränderung: und wie leicht geschieht es da, daß Leute von keiner Einsicht, anstatt der wahren Schönheiten, die aus wirklichen Vollkommenheiten
30 entstehen, auf scheinbare verfallen; die oft die bloße Sinnlichkeit eben so sehr belustigen, als die ersten. Alsdann verfällt alles in Verachtung, was vorhin mit gutem Grunde war hochgeschätzt worden. Der allgemeine
35 Beifall einer Nation kann also nicht eher von der Geschicklichkeit eines Meisters in freien Künsten[6] ein gültiges Urteil fällen, als bis man vorher den guten Geschmack derselben erwiesen hat. Dieses aber geschieht nicht
40 anders, als wenn man zeigt: daß derselbe mit den Regeln der Kunst übereinstimmt, die aus der Vernunft und Natur hergeleitet worden. Ich habe hiermit beiläufig meinen Begriff von dem guten Geschmack entdeckt;
45 einer Sache, davon zu jetziger Zeit überall so viel Redens und Schreibens ist. Weiter unten wird mehr davon vorkommen; denn zu einem guten Poeten gehört auch ein guter Geschmack. Aus dem vorhergehenden

---

[1] **blöde:** stupid; dull (of intellect).
[2] **Pöbel:** the common people.
[3] **Scribenten (Schriftsteller):** writers; authors.
[4] **Plinius:** Pliny the Younger (*c.* A.D. 61–113). Roman author.

[5] **Wälschen:** Southern Europeans; here, Italians.
[6] **die freien Künste:** *lit.,* the liberal arts; the arts and attainments worthy of a free man.

aber schließe ich, daß wir die zu einem
wahren Dichter gehörigen Eigenschaften
von denen lernen müssen, die das innere
Wesen der Poesie eingesehen; die Regeln
5 der Vollkommenheit, daraus ihre Schönheiten entstehen, erforscht haben, und also
von allem, was sie an einem Gedichte loben
und schelten, den gehörigen Grund
anzuzeigen wissen.

10   Wenn man nun ein gründliches Erkenntnis[7]
aller Dinge Philosophie nennt: so sieht ein
jeder, daß niemand den rechten Charakter
von einem Poeten wird geben können, als
ein Philosoph; aber ein solcher Philosoph,
15 der von der Poesie philosophieren kann,
welches sich nicht bei allen findet, die jenen
Namen sonst gar wohl verdienen. Nicht ein
jeder hat Zeit und Gelegenheit gehabt, sich
mit seinen philosophischen Untersuchungen
20 zu den freien Künsten zu wenden, und da
nachzugrübeln: woher es komme, daß
dieses schön und jenes häßlich ist; dieses
wohl, jenes aber übel gefällt? Wer dieses
aber weiß, der bekömmt[8] einen besonderen
25 Namen, und heißt ein Kriticus. Dadurch
verstehe ich nämlich nichts anders, als einen
Gelehrten, der von freien Künsten philosophieren, oder Grund anzeigen kann.
Diesen Begriff hat niemand besser ins Licht
30 gestellt, als der berühmte Graf Shaftsbury,[9]
in seinem gelehrten Werke: *Characteristics*
of Men, Manners and Times, im II. Teile des
I. Bandes, *Advice to an Author;* welches
Werk neulich von einer geschickten Feder
35 ins Deutsche übersetzt worden. Was uns
nun dergleichen Kunstrichter, solche
philosophy Poeten, oder poesieverständige
Philosophen sagen werden, das wird wohl
ohne Zweifel weit gründlicher sein, und
40 einen richtigern Begriff von einem wahren
Dichter bei uns erwecken; als was der große
Haufe, nach einer betrüglichen[10] Empfindung seines unbeständigen Geschmacks,
zu loben oder zu tadeln pflegt. Denn ich
45 bin hier gar nicht der Meinung des sonst so

scharfsinnigen Cicerons[11] zugetan, der in
seinem anderen Buche vom Redner schreibt:
Omnes tacito quodam sensu, sine ulla arte aut
ratione, quae sint in artibus ac rationibus recta ac
prava, dijudicant.[12] Vielmehr halte ich's mit   5
dem Seneca,[13] der an einem Orte seiner Schriften das Gegenteil behauptet: *Non tam bene*
cum rebus mortalium agitur, ut meliora pluribus
placeant. Argumentum pessimi, turba est.[14]

    Unter den Griechen ist ohne Zweifel 10
Aristoteles[15] der beste Kriticus gewesen,
was nämlich die Redekunst und Poesie
anlangt. Es ist ein Glück, daß seine Schriften
von beiden Künsten nicht ganz verloren
gegangen; denn von der Dichtkunst haben 15
wir freilich nur einen Teil übrig behalten.
Indessen zeugen doch beide Bücher, eben
so wohl von dem durchdringenden Verstande dieses großen Weltweisen, als seine
übrige Schriften. Er hat das innere Wesen 20
der Beredsamkeit und Poeterei aufs gründ-
lichste eingesehen, und alle Regeln, die er
vorschreibt, gründen sich auf die unverän-
derliche Natur der Menschen, und auf die
gesunde Vernunft. Haben gleich einige 25
andere Kunstrichter und poetische Freigeister
sein Joch abzuschütteln gesucht, und uns
entweder von allen Regeln befreien, oder
ganz neue und willkürliche einführen wollen:
so haben sie doch bei keinem Vernünftigen 30
Beifall gefunden. Nichts würde also für
mich erwünschter sein, als wenn dieser
tiefsinnige Mann auch den ausführlichen
Charakter eines wahren Poeten gemacht
hätte: denn so dürfte man sich nur daran 35
halten, und könnte so wohl sich selbst, als
andere, nach Anleitung desselben, gehörig

---

[7] **Erkenntnis:** knowledge; cognition.
[8] **bekömmt:** bekommt.
[9] **Shaftsbury:** Anthony Ashley Cooper Earl of
Shaftesbury (1671–1713). English philosopher and
politician. The work mentioned here is his most
significant one.
[10] **betrüglich:** fallacious; doubtful.

[11] **Cicero:** Marcus Tullius Cicero (106–43 B.C.).
Roman orator, statesman, and writer on rhetoric,
statesmanship, and philosophy.
[12] **Omnes tacito ... dijudicant:** Everybody is able
to discriminate between what is right and wrong
in matters of art and proportion by a sort of sub-
conscious instinct, without having any theory of
art or proportion of his own.
[13] **Seneca:** Lucius Annæus Seneca (4 B.C.–A.D. 65).
Roman philosopher, writer, and poet.
[14] **Non tam bene ... turba est:** Human affairs are
not so happily ordered that the majority prefer
the better things; a proof of the worst choice is the
crowd.
[15] **Aristoteles:** Aristotle (384–322 B.C.). Greek philosopher. Gottsched here refers to the treatises
Rhetoric and *Poetics.*

prüfen. Allein wir finden in seiner Poetik im I. II. und III. Kapitel nur etwas weniges, das uns auf die rechte Spur helfen kann. Er lehrt nämlich gleich im Anfange derselben, daß die ganze Poesie nichts anders sei, als eine Nachahmung menschlicher Handlungen; und daß also der Unterschied verschiedener Gedichte, bloß auf die mancherlei Arten der Nachahmung ankomme. Man könne aber die Handlungen der Menschen in gute und böse einteilen; und die Sitten der Welt wären nur durch diese beiden Eigenschaften unterschieden. Wer also Menschen abbilden wolle, der könne sie sich entweder besser, oder schlechter vorstellen, als sie sind; oder dieselben ganz ähnlich schildern. Dieses erläutert er durch das Exempel der Maler, und zieht es hernach auf verschiedene Arten der Poesie. Dieses gibt, meines Erachtens, Anleitung genug, wie man einen Poeten zu charakterisieren habe.

Ich sage also erstlich: ein Poet sei ein geschickter Nachahmer aller natürlichen Dinge: und dieses hat er mit den Malern, Bildhauern, Musikverständigen u.a.m.[16] gemein. Er ist aber zum anderen, auch von ihnen unterschieden; und zwar durch die Art seiner Nachahmung, und durch die Mittel, wodurch er sie vollzieht. Der Maler ahmt sie durch Pinsel und Farben nach; der Bildschnitzer durch Holz und Stein, oder auch durch den Guß in Gips und allerhand Metallen; der Tanzmeister durch den Schritt und die Bewegungen des ganzen Leibes; der Tonkünstler durch den Takt und die Harmonie: der Poet aber tut es durch eine taktmäßig abgemessene, oder sonst wohl eingerichtete Rede; oder, welches gleich viel ist, durch eine harmonische und wohlklingende Schrift, die wir ein Gedicht nennen. Eben das hat uns Horaz[17] oben zu verstehen gegeben, da er schrieb:

Respicere exemplar vitae morumque, jubebo
Doctum imitatorem, et veras hinc ducere voces.[18]

Imgleichen:

Ficta voluptatis causa sint proxima veris.[19]
Oder auch:

Aut famam sequere, aut sibi convenientia finge.[20]

So fremd vielen diese Beschreibung eines Dichters vorkömmt,[21] so vollständig und fruchtbar ist sie in der Tat. Ein Poet wird dadurch nicht nur von den Meistern obgedachter freien Künste; sondern auch von den Liebhabern aller anderen Teile der Gelehrsamkeit unterschieden. Ein Geschichtschreiber soll nicht nachahmen, was wir Menschen zu tun pflegen, oder wahrscheinlicher Weise getan haben könnten, tun sollten, oder tun würden, wenn wir in solchen Umständen befindlich wären: sondern man fodert[22] von ihm, daß er getreulich dasjenige erzählen solle, was sich hier oder da, für Begebenheiten zugetragen haben. Ein Redner soll nicht nachahmen, was andere Leute tun; sondern die Leute überreden, etwas für wahr oder falsch zu halten, und sie bewegen, etwas zu tun oder zu lassen. Ein Weltweiser[23] ist gleichfalls von der Nachahmung entfernt, indem er uns die Gründe von der Möglichkeit aller Dinge untersuchen lehrt. Wie die Rechtsgelehrsamkeit, Arzneikunst und andere Wissenschaften mehr, von der Poesie unterschieden sind, das wird ein jeder leicht abnehmen[24] können. Der Dichter ganz allein, hat dieses zu einer Haupteigenschaft, daß er der Natur nachahmt,[25] und sie in allen seinen Beschreibungen, Fabeln und Gedanken, sein einziges Muster sein läßt.

Es ist wahr; man macht hier verschiedene Einwürfe. Der Geschichtschreiber, sagt man, schildert ja auch diejenigen Personen, Sachen und Örter ab; von welchen er uns Erzählungen macht. Er führt seine Helden wohl gar redend ein, und läßt sie oft Dinge sagen, die sie zwar hätten sagen können, aber in der Tat niemals gesagt haben: wie wir in griechischen und lateinischen Scribenten häufige

---

[16] **u. a. m.:** und andere mehr.
[17] **Horaz:** Quintus Horatius Flaccus (65–8 B.C.). Roman poet.
[18] **Respicere ... voces:** I would advise one who has learned the imitative art to look for life and manners for a model, and draw from thence living words.
[19] **Ficta ... veris:** Fictions meant to please should be close to the real.
[20] **Aut famam ... finge:** Either follow tradition or invent what is self-consistent.
[21] **vorkömmt:** vorkomme.
[22] **fodert:** fordert.
[23] **ein Weltweiser:** a philosopher.
[24] **abnehmen:** here, deduce.
[25] **daß er der Natur nachahmt:** *modern usage,* **daß er die Natur nachahmt.**

Exempel davon vor Augen haben. Dieser Zweifel ist es schon wert, daß er beantwortet werde. Ich sage also fürs erste: nicht alles, was ein Geschichtschreiber tut; das tut er als ein Geschichtschreiber. Z.E.[26] Er schreibt ja auch nach den Regeln der Sprachkunst: wer glaubt es deswegen, daß die richtige Schreibart zum Wesen der Historie gehöre, und nicht vielmehr der Grammatik eigen sei? Ein Geschichtschreiber kann freilich wohl auch moralisieren, und politische Anmerkungen in seine Erzählungen mischen, wie Tacitus[27] und andere getan haben: gehört das aber eigentlich zur Historie? Und ist dieses deswegen nicht für eines Sittenlehrers und Staatskundigen eigentliche Pflicht zu halten? Eben so geht's mit den vielen Bildern, Charakteren und erdichteten Reden, die in Geschichtbüchern vorkommen. Sie sind poetische Kunststücke, die ein Geschichtschreiber nur entlehnt, um seine trockene Erzählungen dadurch ein wenig anmutiger zu machen. Er ist gleichsam, wie ein Bildschnitzer beschaffen, der die Gesichter und Kleidungen seiner Kunststücke, auch noch mit Pinsel und Farben übermalt: nicht, als wenn das Malen eigentlich sein Werk wäre; sondern weil er einer anderen Kunst Hilfe braucht, seine Arbeit zur Vollkommenheit zu bringen.

Für's andere haben's auch die Kunstrichter an einigen Geschichtschreibern vorlängst gemißbilligt,[28] daß sie die Regeln der historischen Schreibart gar zu sehr aus den Augen gesetzt. Man lese nur nach, was einige von dem Florus,[29] und le Clerc[30] vom Curtius,[31] wegen seiner gekünstelten Beschreibungen geurteilt haben. Man hat kein Bedenken getragen, diesen Scribenten eine poetische Schreibart zuzueignen: welches sattsam zeigt, daß die lebhaften Beschreibungen eigentlich in der Dichtkunst zu Hause gehören; sonderlich, wenn sie, wie des Curtius seine, nur aus dem bloßen Witze des Scribenten herkommen. Und was soll ich von den Reden eines Thucydides,[32] Xenophons,[33] Livius,[34] Sallustius,[35] u.a.m. sagen? Man hat es längst erkannt, daß sie Proben von der dichtenden Einbildungskraft dieser Scribenten wären; dazu sie, als Geschichtschreiber, nicht wären verbunden gewesen. Sie haben aber hierin lieber dem Homer, dessen Schriften einen allgemeinen Beifall hatten, nachahmen, als ihre eigene Pflichten in Betrachtung ziehen wollen. Und man hat sie deswegen mit Recht getadelt; weil es einem aufrichtigen Verfasser historischer Nachrichten nicht zusteht; das geringste in den wahren Begebenheiten zu ändern, auszulassen oder hinzu zu setzen. Wie haben aber gedachte Scribenten diese Pflicht in solchen Reden beobachten können, die sie berühmten Leuten viele Jahrhunderte nach ihrem Tode gedichtet? Zum wenigsten hat Curtius dem scythischen[36] Gesandten eine Anrede an Alexandern[37] in den Mund gelegt; die derselbe, allem Ansehen nach, unmöglich so schön und künstlich hätte halten können. Was ich hier von der Historie zur Antwort gegeben habe, das läßt sich mit leichter Mühe, auf alle übrige Einwürfe, die man von andern Wissenschaften hernimmt, deuten, und gehörigermaßen anwenden.

Aristoteles hat es schon ausgeführt, wie natürlich es dem Menschen sei, alles was er sieht und hört, nachzuahmen. In unserer zärtesten[38] Jugend geht dieses schon an. Man sagt, die Kinder sind wie Affen; weil sie alles nachmachen, was die Erwachsenen tun. Man möchte aber mit besserem Rechte sprechen, die Affen sind wie Kinder: denn diesen gebührt sonder Zweifel im Nachahmen der Vorzug. Alles, was wir lernen und

---

[26] **z. E.**: zum Exempel; zum Beispiel.

[27] **Tacitus**: Cornelius Tacitus (*c.* 55-*after* A.D. 117). Roman historian.

[28] **gemißbilligt (mißbilligt)**: disapproved; criticized.

[29] **Florus**: probable reference to Lucius Annæus Florus (*c.* A.D. 120); compiled a short history of Rome.

[30] **Le Clerc**: François Le Clerc du Tremblay (1577–1638). French Capuchin monk and diplomat.

[31] **Curtius**: Quintus Curtius Rufus (1st cent. A.D.). Roman historian.

[32] **Thucydides**: Greek historian (471?–?400 B.C.).

[33] **Xenophon**: Greek historian and essayist (434?–?355 B.C.).

[34] **Livius**: Titus Livius (59 B.C.–A.D. 17). Roman historian.

[35] **Sallustius**: Gaius Sallustius Crispus (86–35 B.C.). Roman historian.

[36] **scythisch**: Scythian. The Scythians; an ancient nomadic people in southern Russia.

[37] **Alexander**: Alexander the Great.

[38] **zärtesten**: most tender; i.e., earliest.

fassen, das fassen und lernen wir durch die Nachahmung. Das Gehen und Stehen, Reden und Singen, das. Essen und Trinken, ja Lesen und Schreiben, entsteht bei uns aus
5 keiner anderen Quelle.

Von ander'n Tieren zwar, kennt jedes
[seine Kraft,
Und weiß auch von Natur von seiner
[Eigenschaft;
Der Mensch allein, ihr Haupt, der Herr so
[vieler Sachen,
Muß alles, was er tut, von ander'n lernen
[machen:
10 Und daß er ißt und trinkt, red't, sitzt,
[steht, geht und liegt,
Kömmt nur durch Unterricht, schläft auch
[nicht ungewiegt.

Opitz[39] im II. Buch der *Trostgedichte*.

Daraus leitet nun der tiefsinnige Weltweise[40] den Ursprung der Poesie her. So viel ist
15 gewiß, daß diejenigen Knaben, welche die größte Geschicklichkeit zum Nachahmen an sich blicken lassen, auch die größte Fähigkeit zur Poesie besitzen. Zeigt sich aber jene sonderlich im Schreiben, in der Malerei und
20 Musik, imgleichen im Tanzen u.s.f.:[41] so sieht man wohl, daß Kinder, die zu dergleichen Übungen viel Naturell und Lust haben, auch zur Dichtkunst selbst, eine treffliche Geschicklichkeit erlangen können; wenn nur
25 auch die Auferziehung sonst darnach eingerichtet ist.

Weil nun diese natürliche Geschicklichkeit im Nachahmen bei verschiedenen Leuten auch sehr verschieden ist; so daß einige fast
30 ohne alle Mühe eine große Fertigkeit darinnen erlangen, andere hergegen bei vieler Qual und Arbeit dennoch hinten bleiben: so hat man angefangen zu sagen, daß die Poeten nicht gemacht; sondern geboren
35 würden, daß sie den heimlichen Einfluß des Himmels fühlen, und durch ein Gestirn in der Geburt zu Poeten gemacht sein müßten: das heißt in ungebundener Schreibart nichts anders, als ein gutes und zum Nachahmen
40 geschicktes Naturell bekommen haben. Opitz schreibt:

Es ist hier nicht genug, die arme Rede
[zwingen,
Die Silben über Hals und Kopf in Reime
[bringen,
Der Wörter Henker sein: wer nicht den
[Himmel fühlt,
Nicht scharf und geistig ist, nicht auf die
[Alten zielt,
5 Nicht ihre Schriften kennt, der Griechen
[und Lateiner,
Als seine Finger selbst, und schaut, daß
[ihm kaum einer
Von allen außen bleibt; wer die gemeine
[Bahn
Nicht zu verlassen weiß, ist zwar ein guter
[Mann,
Doch nicht gleich ein Poet.

Opitz im I. Buch der *Poetischen Wälder*. 10

Unser Poet fodert also von einem Dichter, er solle den Himmel bei sich fühlen, ja scharf und geistig sein. Das zielt ebenfalls auf das gute Naturell oder den fähigen Kopf eines Dichters. Rachel[42] stimmt diesem bei: 15

Denn wer nicht von Natur hierzu ist wie
[geboren,
Bei dem ist Kunst und Fleiß und Übung
[auch verloren.
Hör, was der Römer spricht: Die Stadt
[gibt jährlich zwar
Der Bürgermeister zwei: jedoch nicht alle
[Jahr
Kömmt ein Poet hervor. So viel hat das 20
[zu sagen,
Wenn jemand will mit Recht das Lorbeer-
[kränzlein tragen.

Das ist nun, meines Erachtens, die beste Erklärung, die man von dem Göttlichen in der Poesie geben kann; davon so viel Streitens unter den Gelehrten ist. Ein glücklicher 25 munterer Kopf ist es, wie man insgemein[43] redet; oder ein lebhafter Witz, wie ein Weltweiser sprechen möchte: das ist, was oben beim Horaz, *Ingenium et mens divinior*[44] hieß. Dieser Witz ist eine Gemütskraft, 30 welche die Ähnlichkeiten der Dinge leicht wahrnehmen, und also eine Vergleichung zwischen ihnen anstellen kann. Er setzt die

---

[39] **Opitz:** Martin Opitz (1597–1639). Poet, critic, and metrical reformer.
[40] **der tiefsinnige Weltweise:** Aristotle.
[41] **u.s.f.: und so fort.**

[42] **Rachel:** Joachim Rachel (1619–69). Satirist.
[43] **insgemein (allgemein):** generally.
[44] **Ingenium et mens divinior:** gifts inborn and soul divine.

Scharfsinnigkeit zum Grunde, welche ein Vermögen der Seelen anzeigt, viel an einem Dinge wahrzunehmen, welches ein anderer, der gleichsam einen stumpfen Sinn, oder blöden Verstand hat, nicht würde beobachtet haben. Je größer nun die Scharfsinnigkeit bei einem jungen Menschen ist; je aufgeweckter sein Kopf ist, wie man zu reden pflegt: desto größer kann auch sein Witz werden, desto sinnreicher werden seine Gedanken sein. Denn wo man viele Eigenschaften der Dinge angemerkt, und auf alle Kleinigkeiten bei einer Person, Handlung, Begebenheit u.s.w. Acht gegeben hat: da kann man desto leichter die Ähnlichkeit einer solchen Person, Handlung, Begebenheit oder Sache mit anderen dergleichen Dingen wahrnehmen. Die Einbildungskraft nämlich bringt, bei den gegenwärtigen Empfindungen, sehr leicht wiederum die Begriffe hervor, die wir sonst schon gehabt; wenn sie nur die geringste Ähnlichkeit damit haben. Alle diese Gemütskräfte nun, gehören nicht in gemeinem, sondern in sehr hohem Grade für denjenigen, der geschickt nachahmen soll: und ein Poet muß dergestalt, sowohl als ein Maler, Bildschnitzer u.s.w. eine starke Einbildungskraft, viel Scharfsinnigkeit und einen großen Witz schon von Natur besitzen, wenn er den Namen eines Dichters mit Recht führen will.

Doch alle diese natürliche Gaben sind an und für sich selbst noch roh und unvollkommen, wenn sie nicht aufgeweckt, und von der ihnen anklebenden Unrichtigkeit gesäubert werden. Viele witzige Köpfe verrosten gleichsam bei ihrer guten Fähigkeit, aus Mangel der Anführung. Kinder, denen es an Unterrichte fehlt, bleiben bei aller ihrer natürlichen Geschicklichkeit dennoch stekken: und wenn sie sich gleich unter andern ihres gleichen, durch ein lebhafteres Wesen hervortun; so ist doch all ihr Witz gleichsam ein ungebautes Feld, das nur wilde Pflanzen hervortreibt; ein selbst wachsender Baum, der nur ungestalte Äste und Reiser hervorsprosset. Geraten solche Leute in anwachsenden Jahren aufs Reimen, so werden sie Possenreißer,[45] Pritschmeister,[46] und alber-

ne Reimenschmiede;[47] die allerhand abgeschmackte Einfälle zusammen häufen, sich alles für erlaubt halten, und nur den Beifall des Pöbels suchen. Sie folgen schlechterdings ihrer Phantasie, und dichten Quodlibete,[48] Lieder, Romane, Pickelheringspossen,[49] und andere phantastische Erfindungen in theatralischen Sachen, die weder Art noch Geschick haben. Man kann aber junge Knaben beizeiten aufwecken, und ihren Witz, so zu reden, in die Falten rücken,[50] wenn man ihnen bald allerlei gute sinnreiche Schriften zu lesen gibt; wenn man sie auf die trefflichsten Stellen derselben aufmerksam macht; ihnen die Schönheit derselben recht vor Augen stellt, und durch ein vernünftiges Lob ihrer Verfasser, sie anspornt, nach gleicher Ehre zu streben.

Dieses tut man, wenn die Jugend ihren Verstand schon einigermaßen brauchen kann: der Grund aber kann noch früher dazu gelegt werden, wenn man sie beizeiten im Zeichnen und Reißen[51] unterweisen lässt. Es glaubt niemand, was diese Übung jungen Leuten für Vorteil schafft; als wer sie mit philosophischen Augen ansieht. Wer einen vor Augen liegenden Riß[52] nachmalen will, der muß sehr genau auf alle gerade und krumme Linien, Verhältnisse, Größen, Stellungen, Entfernungen, Erhebungen, Schattierungen und Strichlein, ja auf die allerkleinsten Punkte Achtung geben. Durch dergleichen Übung und Bemühung erlangt man also einen hohen Grad der Aufmerksamkeit, auf jede vorfallende Sache;[53] welche endlich zu einer Fertigkeit gedeiht, in großer Geschwindigkeit, und fast im Augenblicke viel an einer Sache wahrzunehmen; welche Fertigkeit wir vorhin die Scharfsinnigkeit genannt haben. Indem aber ein solcher Knabe sich ferner

---

[45] **Possenreißer:** one who writes, or acts in, a farce.

[46] **Pritschmeister:** epithet for a poet, who, in the 16th and 17th cent., recited a poem written for a spe-

cial occasion, and who accompanied his recital with claps of a wooden paddle to attract attention.

[47] **Reimenschmiede:** rhymesters.

[48] **Quodlibete** (*pl.*): *quodlibet*; arbitrary combination of familiar melodies or texts.

[49] **Pickelheringspossen:** lowest form of theatrical entertainment, farces in which the main part was played by **Pickelhering,** a buffoon.

[50] **in die Falten rücken: schulen; disziplinieren.**

[51] **Reißen:** geometric drawing.

[52] **Riß:** drawing.

[53] **jede vorfallende Sache: jede Sache, die in das Feld der Erfahrung tritt.**

bemüht, seinen Riß, dem vorgelegten Mus-
terbilde ähnlich zu machen: so muß er die
Ähnlichkeiten zwischen beiden wahrnehmen
lernen, das ist, seinen Witz üben. Fängt er
endlich gar an, wirkliche Personen abzuschildern,[54] oder Gegenden und Landschaften zu
malen, die er wirklich vor sich sieht: so wird
er noch fertiger.[55] Am höchsten bringt er's
endlich, wann er aus seiner eigenen Erfindung
ganze Historien wohl zu entwerfen, und auf
eine sehr lebhafte, natürliche und folglich
anmutige Art auszumalen geschickt wird.
Dergleichen Übungen nun bilden unver-
merkt poetische Geister. Denn dafern durch
das Studieren, solchen jungen Leuten zugleich die Fertigkeit in der Sprache, die
Kenntnis vieler Sachen, nebst den Regeln
der gebundenen Schreibart beigebracht wird:
so werden sie hernach eben so geschickt, mit
der Feder, als mit Pinsel und Farben, die
Nachahmung natürlicher Dinge zu voll-
ziehen wissen.

Denn das muß man notwendig wissen,
daß es mit Einbildungskraft, Scharfsinnigkeit und Witz bei einem Poeten noch
nicht ausgerichtet ist. Dies ist zwar der
Grund von seiner Geschicklichkeit, den die
Natur legt: aber es gehört zu dem Naturelle
auch die Kunst und Gelehrsamkeit. Muß
doch ein Maler, der was rechtes tun will, in
der Meßkunst, Perspectiv, Anatomie, Mytho-
logie, Historie, Baukunst, ja Logik und
Moral was getan haben; wenn er's zu einiger
Vollkommenheit bringen will. So wird denn
ein Poet, der auch die unsichtbaren Gedanken
und Neigungen menschlicher Gemüter nachzuahmen hat, sich nicht ohne eine weitläufige
Gelehrsamkeit behelfen können. Es ist keine
Wissenschaft von seinem Bezirke ganz ausgeschlossen. Er muß zum wenigsten von
allem etwas wissen, in allen Teilen der unter
uns blühenden Gelehrtheit sich ziemlicher
maßen[56] umgesehen haben. Ein Poet hat ja
Gelegenheit, von allerlei Dingen zu schreiben.
Begeht er nun Fehler, die von seiner Unwissenheit in Künsten und Wissenschaften
zeugen, so verliert er sein Ansehen. Ein
einzig Wort gibt oft seine Einsicht, oder

auch seine Unerfahrenheit in einer Sache zu
verstehen. Ein einzig Wort kann ihn also in
Hochachtung oder in Verachtung setzen;
nachdem es entweder seine Gelehrsamkeit,
oder Unwissenheit an den Tag legt. Daraus
folgt nun unfehlbar, daß ein Poet keine
Wissenschaft so gar verabsäumen müsse, als
ob sie ihn nichts anginge. Er muß sich
vielmehr bemühen, von allen, zum wenigsten
einen kurzen Begriff zu fassen; damit er sich,
wo nicht in allen geschickt erweisen, doch
mindstens in keiner einzigen auf eine lächerliche Art verstoßen möge.

Vielleicht wendet man mir ein: Ich machte
den Begriff von einem Poeten zu groß und
zu vollkommen; dergleichen Leute von
allgemeiner Gelehrsamkeit hätte es wohl
noch nie gegeben; inskünftige[57] aber, würde
man sie noch weniger zu gewarten haben, da
die Anzahl der Wissenschaften und Künste
fast täglich größer würde. Hierauf will ich
zur Antwort geben: daß man nicht übel tue,
wenn man eine Sache nach ihrer größesten
Vollkommenheit abschildert. So haben die
Stoiker[58] ihren Weisen, die Lehrer der
Redekunst ihren vollkommenen Redner, und
die heutigen Weltweisen einen vollkommenen Philosophen beschrieben. Es ist gut,
wenn man ein Ziel vor Augen hat, darnach
man streben kann, wenn es gleich noch
niemand erreicht hätte. Je näher man ihm
ankömmt, desto vollkommener ist man:
und der am wenigsten davon entfernt
bleibt, der ist am lobwürdigsten. Gesteht
aber Seneca von dem stoischen Weisen,
Cicero von einem vollkommenen Redner,
und Herr Wolff[59] von einem vollkommenen
Philosophen, daß dergleichen noch niemals
in der Welt zu finden gewesen: so wollen wir
auch bekennen, daß noch kein Poet den
höchsten Gipfel in seiner Kunst erreicht habe.
Die Erfahrung hat es gewiesen. An den
berühmtesten alten und neuen Dichtern
haben scharfe Kunstrichter mit gutem Grunde so viel auszusetzen gefunden; daß man
auch hier die menschliche Unvollkommen-
heit nur gar zu deutlich hat wahrnehmen

---

[54] **abzuschildern (abschildern)**: portray.
[55] **fertig**: here, skillful.
[56] **ziemlicher maßen (einigermassen)**: to some
    extent.

[57] **inskünftige**: in the time to come.
[58] **Stoiker**: Stoics; members of a Greek school of
    philosophy.
[59] **Wolff**: Christian Wolff (1697–1754). Philosopher;
    champion of the Enlightenment.

können. Wie aber deswegen, weder die
Stoiker nach Weisheit, noch die Redner nach
Beredsamkeit, noch die Philosophen nach
der philosophischen Erkenntnis zu streben
5 aufgehört haben: also darf auch kein Liebhaber der Dichtkunst den Mut sinken lassen.

Denn dies gilt dahin nicht, daß diese Schwie-
[rigkeit
Dich lässig machen soll. Der Gaben Unter-
[scheid
Der hebt nicht alles auf. Kannst du dem
[Überreichen,
10 An seinem großen Schatz und Vorrat, nicht
[wohl gleichen:
So ist dir wenig g'nug. Spann alle Sinnen an,
Wer weiß, was nicht dein Fleiß dir mehr
[erwerben kann?
Schreib wenig, wo nicht viel; doch das nach
[Arbeit schmecket:
Ein kleines Werklein hat oft großen Ruhm
[erwecket.
15 Zwo Zeilen oder drei, von Buchnern[60] auf-
[gesetzt,[61]
Sind billig mehr als dies mein ganzes Buch
[geschätzt.
Nur eine Fliege, wohl und nach der Kunst
[gemalet,
Ist ihres Lobes wert, und wird so wohl
[bezahlet,
Als nach des Lebens Maß ein großer Ele-
[phant,
20 Den nur ein Sudler hat geschmieret von der
[Hand.
Kannst du kein Opitz sein, kein teurer
[Fleming[62] werden:
O! es ist Raum genug vom Himmel bis zur
[Erden

                                   Rachel Sat. der Poet.

Vor allen Dingen aber ist einem wahren
Dichter eine gründliche Erkenntnis des
25 Menschen nötig, ja ganz unentbehrlich. Ein
Poet ahmt hauptsächlich die Handlungen der
Menschen nach, die von ihrem freien Willen
herrühren, und vielmals aus den verschiedenen Neigungen des Gemüts und heftigen
30 Affekten ihren Ursprung haben. Denn wenn

gleich einige, wie Tasso,[63] Milton,[64] und
seine Nachahmer unter uns, auch Engeln
und Teufel nachzuahmen gesucht: so ist
dieses so zu reden, aus ihrer Sphäre ausgeschweift. Wie kann eine Abschilderung gelin- 5
gen, deren Originale man wenig, oder gar
nicht kennt? Strabo[65] setzt also mit Recht
den Menschen zum Gegenstande der Dichtkunst. Daher muß derselbe ja die Natur und
Beschaffenheit des Willens, der sinnlichen 10
Begierde, und des sinnlichen Abscheues in
allen ihren mannigfaltigen Gestalten gründlich einsehen lernen. Wie würde es ihm sonst
möglich sein, einen Geizigen, Stolzen, Ver-
schwenderischen, Zänkischen, Verliebten, 15
Traurigen, Verzagten, u.s.w. recht zu charakterisieren? Alle Bewegungen des Willens
entstehen aus den Meinungen und Urteilen
des Verstands, so wie diese in den verschiedenen Vorstellungen der Sinne ihren Grund 20
haben. Der Poet muß also auch die Gemütskräfte der vernünftigen Seele, und ihren verschiedenen, sowohl bösen als guten Gebrauch
kennen; damit er törichte Leute töricht,
und so ferner Abergläubische, Leichtgläu- 25
bige, Ungläubige, Vernünftler, Grübler,
Zweifler, Einfältige, Spitzfündige,[66] Ver-
schlagene, Dumme und Kluge nach ihrer
gehörigen Art abzuschildern und nachzuahmen im Stande sei. Sind ferner die 30
Handlungen der Menschen gut oder böse: so
wird er nicht im Stande sein, dieselben
recht zu beurteilen, wenn er nicht das Recht
der Natur, die Sittenlehre und Staatskunst
gründlich versteht. Das ist nun diejenige 35
Wissenschaft von den Charaktern und
Pflichten der Menschen, die Horaz in seiner
obstehenden Dichtkunst so eifrig von einem
Poeten fodert, und ihm zu wiederholten
malen einschärft. 40

Qui didicit Patriae quid debeat, et quid Amicis,
Quo fit amore parens, quo frater amandus, et
    hospes,
Quid fit conscripti, quod judicis officium, quae

---

[60] **Buchner:** August Buchner (1591–1661). Poet; as
    professor of poetry, he spread Opitz' theories.
[61] **aufgesetzt:** put down in writing.
[62] **Fleming:** Paul Fleming (1609–40). Lyric poet.

[63] **Tasso:** Torquato Tasso (1544–95). Italian poet.
[64] **Milton:** John Milton (1608–74). English poet.
[65] **Strabo:** Greek historian and geographer (63 B.C.?–
    after A.D. 20).
[66] **Spitzfündige (Spitzfindige):** cunning, shrewd
    persons.

Partes in bellum missi ducis, ille profecto.
Reddere personae scit convenientia, cuique.[67]

So notwendig nun einem Poeten die Philosophie ist: so stark muß auch seine Beurteilungskraft sein. Es würde nicht helfen, witzig und scharfsinnig zu sein, wenn der Witz übel angebracht würde, oder gar nicht rechter Art wäre. Eine gar zu hitzige Einbildungskraft macht unsinnige Dichter: dafern das Feuer der Phantasie nicht durch eine gesunde Vernunft gemäßigt wird. Nicht alle Einfälle sind gleich schön, gleich wohlgegründet, gleich natürlich und wahrscheinlich. Das Urteil des Verstandes muß Richter darüber sein. Es wird nirgends leichter ausgeschweift, als in der Poesie. Wer seinen regellosen Trieben den Zügel schießen läßt, dem geht es wie dem jungen Phaeton.[68] Er hat wilde Pferde zu regieren; aber sehr wenig Verstand und Kräfte sie zu bändigen, und auf der rechten Bahn zu halten: sie reißen ihn fort, und er muß folgen wohin sie wollen, bis er sich in den Abgrund stürzt. So ist es mit einem gar zu feurigen poetischen Geiste auch bewandt. Er reißt sich leicht aus den Schranken der Vernunft: und es entstehen lauter Fehler aus seiner Hitze, wenn sie nicht durch ein reifes Urteil gezähmt wird. Statius,[69] Claudian,[70] Lucan[71] und der tragische Seneca können uns unter den Lateinern zu Warnung dienen. St. Evremont[72] hält den Brebeuf,[73] der Lucans Pharsale[74] übersetzt hat, seinem Originale nicht nur gleich; sondern sagt gar, daß er denselben

noch, an wildem Feuer der Einbildung, übertroffen habe. Von den Italienern und Spaniern hat uns Bouhours,[75] in hundert Exempeln die Früchte gar zu hitziger Geister gewiesen, die keine Prüfung der Vernunft aushalten. Unter den Engländern aber, die überhaupt sehr stark zu den Ausschweifungen der Phantasie geneigt sind, hat Milton, alles was man dadurch schwärmendes aushecken[76] kann, in seinem verlorenen Paradiese gewiesen. Von unsern Landesleuten mag ich kein Exempel anführen. Es ist bekannt, daß Hofmannswaldau[77] und Lohenstein[78] nebst einigen Neuern, dem verderbten italienischen Geschmacke gefolgt sind, und ihr Feuer nicht allemal zu mäßigen gewußt haben. Viele von ihren Anbetern sind noch weiter gegangen, als sie: aber ich weiß nur einen einzigen Neukirch,[79] der beizeiten umgekehrt, und wieder der Vernunft und Natur nachzugehen angefangen: wie bereits auf der 8.9. S. des Vorb. aus dem sechsten Teile der Hofm. W. Ged. 101. S. angeführt worden.[80] Man lese auch des Herrn von Brück[81] Gedanken, von der Dichtkunst, im I. B.[82] der deutschen Gesellschaft[83] eigenen Schriften und Übersetzungen, hin und wieder.

Außer allen diesen Eigenschaften des Verstands, die ein wahrer Poet besitzen und wohl anwenden muß, soll er auch von rechtswegen ein ehrliches und tugendliebendes Gemüt haben. Der Beweis davon ist leicht. Ein Dichter ahmt die Handlungen der Menschen nach; die entweder gut oder

---

[67] **Qui didicit... convenientia, cuique:** He who has learned what he owes his country and his friends, what love is due a parent, a brother, and a guest, what is imposed on senator and judge, what is the function of a general sent to war, he surely knows how to give each character his fitting part.

[68] **Phaeton:** Phaëton; in Greek mythology, the son of Helios, the sungod.

[69] **Statius:** Publius Papinius Statius (1st cent. A.D.). Roman poet.

[70] **Claudian:** Claudius Claudianus (*c.* A.D. 375–404). The last of the Latin classic poets.

[71] **Lucan:** Marcus Annaeus Lucanus (A.D. 39–65). Roman poet.

[72] **St. Evremont:** Charles Seigneur de Saint Evremont (1613–1703). French author and critic.

[73] **Brebeuf:** Georges de Brébeuf (1618–1661). French poet.

[74] **Pharsale:** *Pharsalia*; Lucanus' major work.

[75] **Bouhours:** Dominique Bouhours (1628–1702). Influential French critic and philologist.

[76] **aushecken:** devise; concoct.

[77] **Hofmannswaldau:** Christian Hofmann von Hofmannswaldau (1617–79). German poet.

[78] **Lohenstein:** Daniel Casper von Lohenstein (1635–83). Silesian poet.

[79] **Neukirch:** Benjamin Neukirch (1665–1729). Poet.

[80] **wie bereits ... angeführt worden: wie bereits auf Seite 8 und 9 des Vorberichts aus dem sechsten Teil der Hofmannswaldauschen Werke: „Gedichte" S. 101 angeführt worden ist.**

[81] **Herr von Brück:** publisher of the papers of the „Deutschen Gesellschaft."

[82] **B.** (*abbr. for* **Band**): volume.

[83] **Deutsche Gesellschaft:** literary society founded at the end of the 17th cent. in Leipzig, and dedicated to the advancement of poetry and language. For a time headed by Gottsched.

böse sind. Er muß also in seinen Schildereien
die guten als gut, das ist schön, rühmlich
und reizend; die bösen aber als böse, das ist
häßlich, schändlich und abscheulich abmalen.
5　Täte er dieses nicht, und unterstünde er sich
die Tugend als verächtlich, schädlich und
lächerlich, das Laster hergegen als angenehm,
vorteilhaft und lobwürdig zu bilden: so
würde er die Ähnlichkeit ganz aus den Augen
10　setzen, und die Natur derselben sehr übel
ausdrücken. Molière[84] verdient in diesem
Stücke viel Tadel, weil er in seinem Spotten
nicht allezeit dieser Regel gefolgt ist: wie
Riccoboni[85] in seinen Réflexions sur Molière[86]
15　bemerkt hat. Ich schweige noch, daß ein so
schädlicher Scribent in einer wohlbestellten
Republik nicht zu dulden wäre: worauf
denn Plato gesehen haben mag, wenn er in
der seinigen, wie man insgemein vorgibt,
20　gar keine Dichter hat leiden wollen. Es hat
nämlich zu allen Zeiten auch solche verderbte
Versmacher gegeben, die, weil sie selbst
übel gesittet gewesen, und gottlos gelebt,

auch andere durch ihre Gedichte zu allerhand
Schande und Lastern gereizt haben. Sonderlich ist die Geilheit unzüchtigen Gemütern
allezeit ein Stein des Anstoßes geworden.
Ein Ovid[87] und Catull[88] sind wegen ihrer　5
unzüchtigen Gedichte, bei allen ihren Schönheiten, schädlich zu lesen. Selbst Horaz ist
nicht überall so keusch in seinen Ausdrük-
kungen[89] als er wohl hätte sein können; wenn
er sich den züchtigen Virgil hätte zum Mei-　10
ster nehmen wollen. Gleichwohl rühmt er
in einem Schreiben an den Kaiser August,[90]
daß ein wahrer Poet, das Ohr eines Knaben,
dessen Auferziehung er zu besorgen hat, von
schändlichen Zoten abwende; und ihm viel-　15
mehr gute Sitten beizubringen bemüht sei.

Os tenerum pueri balbumque Poëta figurat,
Torquet ab obscoenis iam nunc sermonibus aurem;
Mox etiam pectus praeceptis format amicis;
Asperitatis et invidiae corrector et irae,　20
Recte facta refert.[91]

　　　　　　　　　　　　　　　　Lib. II. Ep. i

---

[87] **Ovid:** Publius Ovidius Naso (43 B.C.–A.D. 17).
Roman poet. Gottsched means mainly the *Amores*
(love poems) and *Ars amandi,* or *amatoria* (*The Art
of Love*).
[88] **Catull:** Gaius Valerius Catullus (84?–54B.C.).
Roman lyric poet.
[89] **Ausdrückungen:** descriptions; forms of expression.
[90] **August:** Augustus (63 B.C.–A.D. 14). Roman
emperor.
[91] **Os tenerum ... facta refert:** The poet fashions
the tender, lisping lips of childhood; even then he
turns the ear from unseemly words; presently, too,
he molds the heart by kindly precepts, correcting
roughness and envy and anger. He tells of noble
deeds.

---

[84] **Molière:** pseudonym of Jean Baptiste Poquelin
(1622–73). Great French playwright, noted for his
comedies.
[85] **Riccoboni:** Luigi Riccoboni (1676–1753). Italian
writer and actor.
[86] **„Réflexions sur Molière":** „Gedanken über
Molière."

𝕴ohann Jakob Bodmer   &   𝕴ohann Jakob Breitinger

𝕴ohann Jakob Bodmer
(1698–1783)

&

𝕴ohann Jakob Breitinger
(1701–1776)

The opposition against Gottsched's dogmatism first crystallized in Zurich where J.J. Bodmer and J.J. Breitinger, friends and colleagues, boldly defined new approaches to contemporary literature. Bodmer, merchant, magistrate, and professor of Swiss history, was a man of many interests and little self-criticism; he translated Milton's *Paradise Lost* into prose and verse, wrote biblical epics and plays, and tried to attract young talent who would continue to fight for his ideas. Breitinger, a professor of Hebrew and Greek, knew the limits of his philological talents; he wrote less, but whatever he published was concise and well-organized. As patriotic citizens of Zurich, Bodmer and Breitinger were almost destined to develop views different from those of Gottsched: Italy was near (Bodmer spent a few years there), and the republican spirit as well as the Protestantism of the Swiss had fruitful affinities to Puritan England; unlike Gottsched who lived in a country dominated by the aristocracy and a Catholic dynasty, the Swiss were very much interested in English political and literary developments.

Bodmer and Breitinger met in a literary club and published the gist of the club's discussions in a periodical entitled *Diskurse der Mahlern* (1721–23); the title refers to the decision of the contributors to speak in the guise of famous painters. The conflict with Gottsched erupted when the Swiss insisted on defending Milton and continued publishing theoretical treatises (*Von dem Einfluß und Gebrauch der Einbildungskraft*, 1727, or Bodmer's *Kritische Abhandlung von dem Wunderbaren in der Poesie*, 1740), disputing a dogmatic point of view; in the late thirties, factions were formed, and pamphlets and mock epics were penned by the supporters of the Swiss and the Leipzig group. Although the warring factions held some of the basic beliefs of classicism in common, the conflict revolved around marked shifts in theoretical accents and substantial differences in taste. The Swiss were apt to stress the marvelous more than the probable; they seemed to cherish genius more than artistic discipline; they definitely preferred Milton's religious poetry to Voltaire and his German imitators.

In the sixth part of his *Kritische Dichtkunst* (1740) Breitinger develops the ideas of the new (*das Neue*) and the marvelous (*das Wunderbare*) in defiance of the more rigorous beliefs of European neoclassicism. Breitinger praises *das Neue* as the ultimate source of poetic beauty; if it moves away from accepted conventions, it changes into the marvelous which causes "a pleasant confusion to the senses." To be sure, Breitinger is careful not to separate the marvelous from the probable, but he substantially weakens the links between them; the marvelous, he stresses, may rest on both the real *and* potential truth, and thus poetry may, at least by implication, eagerly transcend the limits of the merely "natural" as postulated by the commonsense philosophy of Gottsched. The road to Romanticism may still have been a long one but Breitinger had made an irrevocable step along the way.

J. J. Breitinger

VON DEM WUNDERBAREN
UND
DEM WAHRSCHEINLICHEN
(1740)

Wer meine gegebene Erklärung von dem
Neuen, als der Urquelle aller poetischen
Schönheit, vor Augen hat, wird leicht gedenken[1] können, daß auch dieses Neue seine
verschiedenen Grade und Staffeln[2] haben
müsse, je nachdem es mehr oder weniger von
unsren Sitten abgeht und sich entfernt.
Nach dem Grade dieser Entfernung wächst
und verstärkt sich die Verwunderung, die
durch das Gefühl dieser Neuheit in uns
entsteht; wenn denn[3] die Entfernung so weit
fortgeht, bis eine Vorstellung unsern gewöhnlichen Begriffen, die wir von dem
ordentlichen Laufe der Dinge haben, entgegen zu stehen scheint, so verliert sie den
Namen des Neuen, und erhält an dessen
Statt den Namen des Wunderbaren. Sobald
ein Ding, das das Zeugnis der Wahrheit oder
Möglichkeit hat, mit unsren gewöhnlichen
Begriffen zu streiten scheint, so kann es uns
nicht bloß als neu und ungewohnt vorkommen, sondern es wird das Gemüt in eine
angenehme und verwundernsvolle Verwirrung hinreißen, welche daher entspringt, weil
wir mit unserm Verstand durch den reizenden
Schein der Falschheit durchgedrungen, und
in dem vermeinten Widerspruch ein geschicktes Bild der Wahrheit und eine ergötzende
Übereinstimmung gefunden haben.

Demnach ist das Wunderbare in der
Poesie die äußerste Staffel des Neuen, da die
Entfernung von dem Wahren und Möglichen
sich in einen Widerspruch zu verwandeln
scheint. Das Neue geht zwar von dem
gewöhnlichen Laufe und der Ordnung der
Dinge auch ab, doch entfernt es sich niemals
über die Grenzen des Wahrscheinlichen, es
mag uns in Vergleichung mit unsern Gewohnheiten und Meinungen noch so fremd und
seltsam vorkommen, so behält es doch immer
den Schein des Wahren und Möglichen.
Hingegen legt das Wunderbare den Schein
der Wahrheit und Möglichkeit ab, und
nimmt einen unbetrüglichen[4] Schein des
Falschen und Widersprechenden an sich; es
verkleidet die Wahrheit in eine ganz fremde
aber durchsichtige Maske, sie den achtlosen
Menschen desto beliebter und angenehmer
zu machen. In dem Neuen herrscht dem
Scheine nach das Wahre über das Falsche; in
dem Wunderbaren hat hingegen der Schein
des Falschen die Oberhand über das Wahre.

Ich begreife demnach unter dem Namen
des Wunderbaren alles, was von einem
andern widerwärtigen[5] Bildnis oder für wahr
angenommenen Satze ausgeschlossen wird;
was uns, dem ersten Anscheine nach, unsren
gewöhnlichen Begriffen von dem Wesen der
Dinge, von den Kräften, Gesetzen und dem
Laufe der Natur, und allen vormals erkannten Wahrheiten in dem Licht zu stehen,
und dieselben zu bestreiten dünkt. Folglich
hat das Wunderbare für den Verstand immer
einen Schein der Falschheit; weil es mit den
angenommenen Sätzen desselben in einem
offenbaren Widerspruch zu stehen scheint:
Allein dieses ist nur ein Schein, und zwar
ein unbetrüglicher Schein der Falschheit;
das Wunderbare muß immer auf die wirkliche oder die mögliche Wahrheit gegründet
sein, wenn es von der Lüge unterschieden
sein und uns ergötzen soll. Denn wofern der
Widerspruch zwischen einer Vorstellung und
unsren Gedanken eigentlich und begründet
wäre, so könnte eine solche keine Verwunderung in uns gebären, ebensowenig, als
eine offenbare Lüge oder die Erzählung von
lediglich unmöglichen und unglaublichen
Dingen den Geist des Menschen rühren und
belustigen kann; und falls das Wunderbare
aller Wahrheit beraubt sein würde, so wäre
der gröbste Lügner der beste Poet, und die
Poesie wäre eine verderbliche Kunst. Die
Poeten sind dem Junius Brutus[6] gleich, der

---

[1] **gedenken (denken):** here, realize; recognize.
[2] **Staffeln (Stufen):** steps; rungs.
[3] **wenn denn: wenn aber.**

[4] **unbetrüglich (untrüglich):** undeniable.
[5] **widerwärtig:** here, contradictory; opposing.
[6] **Junius Brutus:** Lucius Junius Brutus; led the Romans in revolt against the Roman king Tarquinius Superbus (534–510 B.C.). According to legend, he feigned insanity in order to hide his plans.

witzig und gescheit war, ob er gleich dem
König Tarquinius, dem Stolzen, als wahn-
witzig vorkam, weil er sich mit Fleiß angestellt,[7] als ob er im Hirn verrückt wäre, damit
5 er seine Anschläge und Anstalten, der Tyran-
nie dieses Fürsten ein Ende zu machen, unter
dieser Verstellung desto sicherer verbergen
möchte.[8] Also sind auch die vermeinten
Deliria[9] und Ausschweifungen der poetischen
10 Phantasie mit einer verwundersamen Urteils-
Kraft begleitet, und ein bequemes Mittel, die
Aufmerksamkeit der Menschen zu erhalten
und ihre Besserung zu befördern. Das
Wunderbare ist demnach nichts anderes,
15 als ein vermummtes[10] Wahrscheinliches. Der
Mensch wird nur durch dasjenige gerührt,
was er glaubt; darum muß ihm ein Poet nur
solche Sachen vorlegen, die er glauben kann,
welche zum wenigsten den Schein der
20 Wahrheit haben. Der Mensch verwundert
sich nur über dasjenige, was er für etwas
Außerordentliches hält; darum muß der Poet
ihm nur solche Sachen vorlegen, die außer
der Ordnung des gemeinen Laufes sind; und
25 diese beiden Grund-Regeln, die einander so
sehr entgegenzulaufen scheinen, mit einander
zu vergleichen, muß er dem Wunderbaren
die Farbe der Wahrheit anstreichen, und das
Wahrscheinliche in die Farbe des Wunder-
30 baren einkleiden. Auf einer Seite sind die
Begebenheiten, die aufhören wahrscheinlich
zu sein, weil sie allzu wunderbar sind, nicht
fähig, die Menschen zu rühren; auf der
andern Seite, machen die Begebenheiten, die
35 so wahrscheinlich sind, daß sie aufhören
wunderbar zu sein, die Leute nicht aufmerksam genug. Mit den Meinungen[11] hat es
eben die Bewandtnis, wie mit den Begebenheiten. Die Meinungen, die nichts Wunder-
40 bares in sich haben, dieses mag in der Groß-
mütigkeit oder in der Zueignung[12] der Meinung, oder in der Nettigkeit[13] des Gedankens,
oder in der Richtigkeit des Ausdrucks bestehen, scheinen glatt. Jedermann, heißt es,

hätte dieses gedenken können. Hingegen
scheinen allzu wunderbare Meinungen falsch,
und über die Schnur getrieben.[14] In den
Romanen von Amadis, von Lancelot[15] und
andern irrenden Rittern, fehlt es fürwahr an 5
Wunderbarem nicht, im Gegenteil sind sie
damit angefüllt, aber ihre Erdichtungen ohne
Wahrscheinlichkeit und ihre allzu wunder-
tätigen Begebenheiten verursachen bei Lesern
von gesetztem Urteil, die an Virgil und 10
seines gleichen einen Geschmack finden,
lauter Ekel. Kurz, das Wunderbare kann
einem richtigen Kopf[16] weder gefallen, noch
Ergötzen bringen, wenn es nicht mit dem
Wahrscheinlichen künstlich vereinigt, und 15
auf dasselbe gegründet ist.

Weil nun in dieser Verbindung des
Wunderbaren mit dem Wahrscheinlichen die
vornehmste Schönheit und Kraft der Poesie
besteht, so würde ich auf halbem Wege 20
stehen bleiben, wenn ich nicht jetzt die
Natur des poetischen Wahrscheinlichen er-
klärte, nachdem ich die Natur des Wunderbaren erklärt habe. Nach diesem wird ein
Leichtes sein, ein jedes von diesen beiden 25
Stücken in seine gehörigen Grenzen einzu-
schließen.

Ich verstehe durch das Wahrscheinliche in
der Poesie alles, was nicht von einem andern
widerwärtigen Begriff oder für wahr ange- 30
nommenen Satz ausgeschlossen wird, was
nach unsren Begriffen eingerichtet zu sein,
mit unsrer Erkenntnis und dem Wesen der
Dinge und dem Laufe der Natur überein-
zukommen[17] scheint; hiemit alles, was in 35
gewissen Umständen und unter gewissen
Bedingungen nach dem Urteil der Verständi-
gen möglich ist und keinen Widerspruch in
sich hat. Dieses Wahrscheinliche gründet
sich demnach auf eine Vergleichung mit 40
unsren Meinungen, Erfahrungen, und angenommenen Sätzen, nach welchen wir unsren
Beifall[18] einzurichten und die Glaubwürdig-
keit einer Vorstellung zu beurteilen pflegen,
und es besteht in einer Übereinstimmung 45

---

[7] **mit Fleiß angestellt:** absichtlich verstellt.
[8] **möchte:** könnte; vermochte.
[9] **Deliria:** Wahnsinnszustände.
[10] **vermummtes:** masked.
[11] **Meinungen:** views; ideas.
[12] **Zueignung (Anwendung):** application; attribu-
tion.
[13] **Nettigkeit:** elegance; clarity.

---

[14] **über die Schnur getrieben:** das rechte Maß
überschreitend.
[15] **Amadis; Lancelot:** typical novels about knights.
[16] **einem richtigen Kopf:** einem gebildeten Leser.
[17] **übereinkommen (übereinstimmen):** agree; conform.
[18] **Beifall (Zustimmung):** approval; consent.

mit denselben. Hiemit ist es nicht dem lediglich Unmöglichen, wie das Wahre, sondern dem Wunderbaren, welches nur einen Schein der Falschheit hat, entgegen gesetzt. Ich habe an einem andern Orte angemerkt, daß in dem weitläufigsten Verstande alles kann wahrscheinlich genannt werden, was durch die unendliche Kraft des Schöpfers der Natur möglich ist, hiemit alles, was mit den ersten und allgemeinen Grundsätzen, auf welchen alle Erkenntnis der Wahrheit beruht, in keinem Widerspruch steht. Das Unmögliche und sich selbst Widersprechende hat auch in der Macht des Schöpfers keinen Grund der Wahrheit, und der menschliche Verstand kann solches keineswegs begreifen. Also ist unmöglich, daß etwas zugleich sein und nicht sein, so und anders sein könne; daß etwas ohne einen zureichenden Grund seiner Wirklichkeit sein könne; daß ein Teil so groß sei, als sein Ganzes; daß zwei grade Zahlen mit einander verbunden eine ungrade Zahl ausmachen, und so fort. Was mit diesen und andern dergleichen sich selbst beweisenden Grundsätzen streitet, das ist eine offenbare Lüge, und hat in keinen Umständen und unter keiner Bedingung einige Möglichkeit; angesehen es auch lediglich unmöglich ist, daß durch die göttliche Kraft selbst etwas von dieser Art sein könne. Das Unwahrscheinliche in der Poesie hat allemal eine Möglichkeit, schlechterdings zu reden,[19] die in der Macht des Schöpfers der Natur gegründet ist; es ist unwahrscheinlich und unmöglich alleine in Absicht auf gewisse ausgesetzte[20] Bedingungen und Umstände, mit und in welchen es vorkommt, wenn es mit denselben in einem Widerspruch steht, ob es gleich unter andern Bedingungen und in andern Umständen nicht unmöglich wäre. Der Schöpfer der Natur hat allen erschaffenen Dingen ein ausgesetztes Wesen, Kraft und Vermögen mitgeteilt, er hat ihnen gewisse Gesetze vorgeschrieben, nach welchen sie ihre Handlungen einrichten müssen, er hat sie auch der Zeit und des Ortes halber nach gewissen Absichten mit einander verknüpft. Was nun durch die Kraft dieser erschaffenen Wesen nach den bestimmten

Gesetzen der Bewegung und dem Laufe der Natur in gewissen Umständen möglich ist, das ist wahrscheinlich, weil es mit unsern gewöhnlichen Begriffen übereinstimmt; und dieses Wahrscheinliche ist von dem Wahren alleine darin unterschieden, daß es kein genügsames Zeugnis der Wirklichkeit hat. Weil aber die gegenwärtige Einrichtung der Welt der wirklichen Dinge nicht schlechterdings notwendig ist, so hätte der Schöpfer bei andern Absichten Wesen von einer ganz andern Natur erschaffen, selbige[21] in eine andere Ordnung zusammen verbinden, und ihnen ganz andere Gesetze vorschreiben können. Da nun die Poesie eine Nachahmung der Schöpfung und der Natur nicht nur in dem Wirklichen, sondern auch in dem Möglichen ist, so muß ihre Dichtung, die eine Art der Schöpfung ist, ihre Wahrscheinlichkeit entweder in der Übereinstimmung mit den gegenwärtiger Zeit[22] eingeführten Gesetzen und dem Laufe der Natur gründen, oder in den Kräften der Natur, welche sie bei andern Absichten nach unsern Begriffen hätte ausüben können. Beidemal besteht die Wahrscheinlichkeit darin, daß die Umstände mit der Absicht übereinstimmen, daß sie selber in einander gegründet sein,[23] und sich zwischen denselben kein Widerspruch erzeige. Was die Erdichtung und Aufstellung[24] ganz neuer Wesen und neuer Gesetze anbelangt, so hat der Poet diesfalls eine große Vorsicht und Behutsamkeit zu gebrauchen, daß das Wunderbare nicht unglaublich werde und allen Schein der Wahrheit verliere. Er muß darum seine Freiheit zu erdichten wenigstens nach dem Wahne[25] des größten Haufens der Menschen einschränken, und nichts vorbringen, als was er weiß, daß es schon einigermaßen in demselben gegründet ist. Wenn Aristoteles in seiner Poetik von der poetischen Materie handelt, so eignet er derselben zu, was entweder war, oder jetzt ist, oder was zu sein scheint, und was laut der Sage ist, oder was sein soll. Damit lehrt er zugleich, was der Grundstein und das Band der Vereinigung des Wunder-

---

[19] **schlechterdings zu reden: offen gesagt.**
[20] **ausgesetzte:** fixed; determined.

[21] **selbige:** diese.
[22] **gegenwärtiger Zeit:** in der gegenwärtigen Zeit.
[23] **sein:** sind.
[24] **Aufstellung:** here, creation.
[25] **Wahn:** here, belief.

baren mit dem Wahrscheinlichen sei. Nämlich, die Wahrscheinlichkeit und die Möglichkeit auch der seltsamsten und wunder-
barsten Vorstellungen muß in einem von
folgenden Stücken gegründet sein: entweder
in dem Zeugnis der Historie, oder der Sage
und eines angenommenen Wahnes, oder in
einer Vermehrung oder Verminderung der
wirklichen Vollkommenheiten. Das Wahrscheinliche muß demnach von der Einbildung
beurteilt werden, und die Grundsätze, auf
welche diese ihr Urteil gründet, sind folgende:
I. Was durch glaubwürdige Zeugen bestätigt
wird, das kann man annehmen. II. Den
Vorstellungen der Sinnen darf man trauen.
III. Was bei einem großen Haufen der
Menschen Glauben gefunden hat, und eine
Zeitlang von einem Geschlechte zu dem andern fortgepflanzt worden, das ist nicht zu
verwerfen. IV. Was nach gewissen Graden
eingeschränkt ist, das kann vollkommener
oder unvollkommener sein. V. Was einmal
geschehen ist, das kann wieder geschehen.
Was nun mit diesen und andern dergleichen
Grundsätzen des Wahnes übereinstimmt, es
mag dem reinen Verstande noch so wunderbar und widersinnig vorkommen, das ist
für die Einbildung glaublich und wahrscheinlich. Man muß also das Wahre des Verstandes
und das Wahre der Einbildung wohl unterscheiden; es kann dem Verstande etwas
falsch zu sein dünken, das die Einbildung

für wahr annimmt: hingegen kann der Verstand etwas für wahr erkennen, welches der
Phantasie als unglaublich vorkommt; und
darum ist gewiß, daß das Falsche bisweilen
wahrscheinlicher ist, als das Wahre. Das
Wahre des Verstandes gehört für die Welt-
weisheit, hingegen eignet der Poet sich das
Wahre der Einbildung zu; daher hat Aristoteles im 25. Kapitel der Poetik gesagt: „Der
Poet muß die unmöglichen Dinge, wenn
solche nur wahrscheinlich sind, den möglichen, die bei ihrer Möglichkeit unglaublich
sind, vorziehen." Er hat nicht nötig seine
Vorstellungen für wahr zu verkaufen; wenn
sie nur nicht unglaublich sind, so eröffnen sie
ihm schon den Zugang zu dem menschlichen
Herzen, so daß er dadurch die erforderliche
Wirkung auf dasselbe tun kann. Die eigen-
tümliche Kunst des Poeten besteht demnach
darin, daß er die Sachen, die er durch seine
Vorstellung angenehm machen will, von
dem Ansehen der Wahrheit bis auf einen
gewissen Grad künstlich entferne, jedoch
allezeit in dem Maße, daß man den Schein
der Wahrheit auch in ihrer weitesten Entfernung nicht gänzlich aus dem Gesicht
verliert. Folglich muß der Poet das Wahre als
wahrscheinlich, und das Wahrscheinliche
als wunderbar vorstellen, und hiemit hat das
poetische Wahrscheinliche immer die Wahrheit, gleichwie das Wunderbare in der
Poesie die Wahrscheinlichkeit zum Grunde.

Anacreontic Poetry

Anacreontic poetry excels in a skillful and witty treatment of literary conventions which were imported into Germany from France and, to a lesser degree, from England. Themes and forms are traditional; the individual writer is not concerned with creating a radically new kind of poem but rather intends to vary and refine the efforts of his predecessors and contemporaries—he endeavors to achieve a particular nuance rather than power or originality. It is a poetry of well-defined interests and attitudes. The poet and his audience are delighted by friendships, wine, and gay flirtations, but they prefer a delight undisturbed by destructive passions, high seriousness, or romantic involvement; they carouse mildly without ever becoming intoxicated; to the ecstasies of love they prefer the erudite play of allusions, an unquestioning adherence to a fashionable code of behavior, and a light and lucid tone. Inevitably, the structures and rhythms of their poems are uncomplicated: short pieces of a few stanzas, and a brief line of a few syllables. There is little interest in complex rhyme schemes, and the entire vocabulary remains close to the conversational language of the elegant and educated, a level of style equidistant from the serious and the comic. Within these confines the poet moves with considerable freedom. He may elaborate his poetic program ("An die Dichtkunst"), address the great goddess of love (Venus/Cythere) and her son Cupid, pretend to confess charming dreams, tell an anecdote culminating in a revealing punchline ("Die Namen"), or sing the praise of the laziness that prevents him from writing the poem ("Lob der Faulheit"). Sometimes, however, the poem may suggest something of the new feeling for nature and a surprising sincerity of feeling; if this happens, as in "Die Nacht," the conventions are transmuted by a new sensibility that anticipates later developments of German literature.

European Anacreontic writers liked to believe that they created their poetry in imitation of the Greek Anacreon of Teos (sixth century B.C.), but it was an imitation of his poetry that they imitated. In 1554, the philologist Henri Estienne edited a collection of sixty Greek poems; he called these poems *Anacreontea,* and his contemporary readers (with the notable exception of the Italian critic Robortello) believed that he had discovered very ancient songs of wine and love. The French Renaissance poets were particularly enchanted by the courtly manner and the wit of these poems. For more than two centuries, from Ronsard to Voltaire, French poets liked to cultivate *ces riens naïfs et pleins de grace* (these little nothings full of grace); from France, the fashion spread to England, and finally to eighteenth-century Germany where it was taken up by middle-class civil servants, students, lawyers, and clergymen. Friedrich von Hagedorn introduced the new style (1729), and beginning about 1740 Gleim,

Uz, and Götz, three young men who had met in Halle, combined their talents to translate the Estienne collection again and to emulate the Greek examples in their own poetry. Gleim's *Versuch in scherzhaften Liedern* (1744) and Uz's *Lyrische Gedichte* (1749) set the tone for their German contemporaries, and they were immediately followed by many young poets including Lessing in his early period and later the youthful Goethe—it was the period of elegant rococo furniture and Mozart's minuets. Only in the early 1770's did a new generation, obsessed with their belief in passion, untrammeled expression, and sincerity, turn resolutely away from the Anacreontics and follow Klopstock and his enthusiastic odes.

Friedrich von Hagedorn
(1708–1754)

AN DIE DICHTKUNST

Gespielin meiner Nebenstunden,
Bei der ein Teil der Zeit verschwunden,
Die mir, nicht andern, zugehört:
O Dichtkunst, die das Leben lindert!
5 Wie manchen Gram hast du vermindert,
Wie manche Fröhlichkeit vermehrt!

Die Kraft, der Helden Trefflichkeiten
Mit tapfern Worten auszubreiten,
Verdankt Homer und Maro[1] dir.
10 Die Fähigkeit, von hohen Dingen
Den Ewigkeiten vorzusingen,
Verliehst du ihnen und nicht mir.

Die Lust, vom Wahn mich zu entfernen,
Und deinem Flaccus[2] abzulernen,
15 Wie man durch echten Witz gefällt;
Die Lust, den Alten[3] nachzustreben,
Ist mir im Zorn von dir gegeben,
Wenn nicht mein Wunsch das Ziel erhält.

Zu eitel ist das Lob der Freunde:
20 Uns drohen in der Nachwelt Feinde,
Die finden unsre Größe klein.
Den itzt an Liedern reichen Zeiten
Empfehl' ich diese Kleinigkeiten:
Sie wollen nicht unsterblich sein.

DER WUNSCH

Du holder Gott der süß'sten Lust auf Erden,
Der schönsten Göttin schöner Sohn![1]
Komm, lehre mich die Kunst, geliebt zu
werden;
Die leichte Kunst zu lieben weiß ich schon.

Komm' ebenfalls und bilde Phyllis'[2] Lachen,   5
Cythere![3] gieb ihr Unterricht;
Denn Phyllis weiß die Kunst, verliebt zu
machen;
Die leichte Kunst zu lieben weiß sie
nicht.

Johann Wilhelm Ludwig Gleim
(1719–1803)

ANAKREON

Anakreon, mein Lehrer,
Singt nur von Wein und Liebe;
Er salbt den Bart mit Salben,
Und singt von Wein und Liebe;
Er krönt sein Haupt mit Rosen,   5
Und singt von Wein und Liebe;
Er paaret sich im Garten,
Und singt von Wein und Liebe;
Er wird beim Trunk ein König,
Und singt von Wein und Liebe;   10
Er spielt mit seinen Göttern,
Er lacht mit seinen Freunden,
Vertreibt sich Gram und Sorgen,
Verschmäht den reichen Pöbel,
Verwirft das Lob der Helden,   15
Und singt von Wein und Liebe:
Soll denn sein treuer Schüler
Von Haß und Wasser singen?

GESCHÄFTE

Mir deucht,[1] so oft ich schlafe,
Schlaf' ich bei lauter[2] Mädchen;

---

[1] **Maro:** Vergil.
[2] **Flaccus:** Horace.
[3] **die Alten:** the ancients (poets).
[1] **der schönsten ... Sohn:** Cupid, son of Venus.

[2] **Phyllis:** characteristic name for a country girl
(from Vergil's *Eclogues*).
[3] **Cythere:** Venus.
[1] **deucht:** dünkt.
[2] **lauter** (*indecl. adj.*): here, nothing but.

Und immer, wenn ich träume,
Träum' ich von nichts als Mädchen;
5 Und wenn ich wieder wache,
Denk' ich an nichts als Mädchen;
Im Schlaf, im Traum, im Wachen
Spiel' ich mit lauter Mädchen.

Doch, ich will mein bestes tun,   5
Nach der Arbeit ist gut ruhn.

Höchstes Gut! wer dich nur hat,
Dessen ungestörtes Leben —
Ach! — ich — gähn' — ich — werde matt —
Nun — so — magst du — mirs vergeben,   10
Daß ich dich nicht singen kann;
Du verhinderst mich ja dran.

Gotthold Ephraim Lessing
(1729–1781)

DIE NAMEN

Ich fragte meine Schöne:
Wie soll mein Lied dich nennen?
Soll Dich als Dorimene,
Als Galathee, als Chloris,
5 Als Lesbia, als Doris,[1]
Die Welt der Enkel kennen?
Ach! Namen sind nur Töne:
Sprach meine holde Schöne.
Wähl' selbst. Du kannst mich Doris,
10 Und Galathee und Chloris,
Und—wie du willst mich nennen;
Nur nenne mich die Deine.

LOB DER FAULHEIT

Faulheit, jetzo will ich dir
Auch ein kleines Loblied bringen.—
O — wie — sau — er[1] — wird es mir —
Dich — nach Würden — zu besingen!

Johann Peter Uz
(1720–1796)

DIE NACHT

Du verstörst uns nicht, o Nacht!
Sieh! wir trinken im Gebüsche;
Und ein kühler Wind erwacht,
Daß er unsern Wein erfrische.

Mutter holder Dunkelheit,   5
Nacht, Vertraute süßer Sorgen,
Die betrogner Wachsamkeit
Viele Küsse schon verborgen!

Dir allein sei mitbewußt,
Welch Vergnügen mich berausche,   10
Wann ich an geliebter Brust
Unter Tau und Blumen lausche!

Murmelt ihr, wann alles ruht,
Murmelt, sanftbewegte Bäume,
Bei dem Sprudeln heischrer[1] Flut   15
Mich in wollustvolle Träume!

---

[1] **Dorimene, Galathee, Chloris, Lesbia, Doris:**
names of Greek girls; found in conventional bucolic
poetry since Theocritus.
[1] **sauer:** here, troublesome; laborious.

---

[1] **heischrer = heiser:** husky.

Friedrich Gottlieb Klopstock

(1724–1803)

Alone among the enlightened writers of the mid-eighteenth century, Friedrich Gottlieb Klopstock revived the forgotten image of the poet as seer, prophet, and saintly visionary. In a world of imitation and wit, he proclaimed the demands of the passionately feeling individual in his intimacy with God, nature, and love; by breaking through the hardening conventions of neoclassicism and drawing upon the hidden sources of a fervent personal religion, Klopstock gave to the figure of the poet renewed dignity, and to the German language new boldness and intensity. Goethe, Hölderlin, and the later Rilke continued his work.

Klopstock's unwillingness to share in the fashions of the day may be partly explained by his birth in provincial Quedlinburg in northern Germany, and his conservative education at the famous pedagogical institute at Schulpforta. He conceived the central idea of his life—to be Germany's foremost Christian epic poet—while in school reading Vergil, Tasso, Milton, and Bodmer. When he left Schulpforta he pronounced an oration in which he enthusiastically praised the great epics of the past as the true guides to the future glories of German poetry. In 1745, he went to Jena to study theology; there, he began to write his *Messias,* a Christian epic designed to compete with Milton's *Paradise Lost;* and upon the advice of Bodmer, the first three cantos were printed in the *Bremer Beiträge* (1748). For a time Klopstock, like many young students of his era, was employed as a tutor, but Bodmer, who was always happy to see young talent follow his ideas, invited him to Zurich. Young Klopstock's behavior seems to have been less than angelic in Zurich and the encounter ended in mutual disappointment. In the meantime, King Frederick V of Denmark, unlike Frederick of Prussia, a friend of contemporary German literature, asked Klopstock to come to Copenhagen where, supported by the king himself, he was to finish his epic poem. In Copenhagen, then, Klopstock lived for twenty years working loyally on his *Messias,* until a change in the political climate of the Danish court forced him to move to Hamburg where he was closer to his German readers. There he died and was buried with honors never before bestowed on any German writer.

Klopstock's *Messias* follows Christ's suffering for mankind until his moment of supreme triumph. Although the poem lacks Milton's majestic awareness of a glorious universe, it often convinces by the intensity of an introverted feeling nourished by the long traditions of Pietism and its sustained metallic rhythm:

> *Sing, unsterbliche Seele, der sündigen Menschen Erlösung,*
> *Die der Messias auf Erden in seiner Menschheit vollendet,*

Und durch die er Adams Geschlechte die Liebe der Gottheit
Mit dem Blute des heiligen Bundes von neuem geschenkt hat.

As in Milton, the figure of the lonely and hellish apostate (Abadonna) seems more alive than the overpowering if impersonal figure of God; unlike Milton, however, Klopstock did not dare to condemn his Abadonna completely and had him pardoned on the day of the Last Judgment. Biblical interests also dominate Klopstock's plays *Der Tod Adams, Salomo,* and *David;* on the other hand, inspired, as many others were, by the supposed Celtic songs of Ossian and the increasing enthusiasm for folk poetry, Klopstock wrote a trilogy about the heroes of the Germanic past and, responding to a growing feeling of German patriotism, tried to replace Latin and Greek myths by introducing Germanic mythology to literature; he was a man of many inspirations and a few whims. Fundamentally, Klopstock's talents were of the lyric rather than of the epic or dramatic kind; although his plays are forgotten, his *Messias* belongs to literary history and his poems (odes) continue to appeal to modern readers and have contributed essentially to new developments in German writing.

Klopstock's odes are poetic gestures of liberation. They may, at times, allude to values dear to the Anacreontics (friendship, wine, and love), but the context, the attitude of the poet, and the language have radically changed. The poetic ego unfolds its own universe of feeling; the horizon expands magnificently, and what had been a literary convention assumes religious and metaphysical meaning. Language and rhythms correspond to the expansive movement; Klopstock uses metrical forms derived from Horace (the Asclepiadean in "Der Zürchersee," the Alcaic in "An Gott") and, for the first time in the development of German poetry, moves toward free verse ("Die Genesung"). Bold adjectives and compound nouns emerge; the syntactical construction, often jagged and harsh, echoes the discontinuity of emotion rather than logical sequences; a proud and self-conscious individuality again elevates writing poetry, in imitation of God's work, to an act of creation.

DER ZÜRCHERSEE

Schön ist, Mutter Natur, deiner Erfindung
    Pracht
Auf die Fluren verstreut, schöner ein froh
    Gesicht,
Das den großen Gedanken
Deiner Schöpfung noch einmal denkt.

5 Von des schimmernden Sees Traubenge-
    staden her,
Oder, flohest du schon wieder zum Himmel
    auf,
Komm' in rötendem Strahle
Auf dem Flügel der Abendluft,

Komm', und lehre mein Lied jugendlich
    heiter sein.
10 Süße Freude, wie du! gleich dem beseel-
    teren
Schnellen Jauchzen des Jünglings,
Sanft, der fühlenden Fanny[1] gleich.

Schon lag hinter uns weit Uto,[2] an dessen
    Fuß
Zür'ch in ruhigem Tal freie Bewohner nährt;
15 Schon war manches Gebirge
Voll von Reben vorbeigefloh'n.

Jetzt entwölkte sich fern silberner Alpen
    Höh',
Und der Jünglinge Herz schlug schon
    empfindender,
Schon verriet es beredter
20 Sich der schönen Begleiterin.
„Hallers Doris",[3] die sang, selber des Liedes
    wert,

Hirzels Daphne,[4] den Kleist[5] innig wie
    Gleimen[6] liebt;
Und wir Jünglinge sangen,
Und empfanden, wie Hagedorn.[7]

Jetzo nahm uns die Au[8] in die beschat- 25
    tenden
Kühlen Arme des Walds, welcher die Insel
    krönt;
Da, da kamest du, Freude!
Vollen Maßes auf uns herab!

Göttin Freude, du selbst! dich, wir emp-
    fanden dich!
Ja, du warest es selbst, Schwester der 30
    Menschlichkeit,
Deiner Unschuld Gespielin,
Die sich über uns ganz ergoß!

Süß ist, fröhlicher Lenz, deiner Begeist'rung
    Hauch,
Wenn die Flur dich gebiert, wenn sich dein
    Odem[9] sanft
In der Jünglinge Herzen, 35
Und die Herzen der Mädchen gießt.

Ach du machst das Gefühl siegend, es steigt
    durch dich
Jede blühende Brust schöner, und bebender,
Lauter redet der Liebe
Nun entzauberter Mund durch dich! 40

Lieblich winket der Wein, wenn er Emp-
    findungen,
Beßre sanftere Lust, wenn er Gedanken
    winkt,
Im sokratischen Becher[10]
Von der tauenden Ros' umkränzt;

---

[1] **Fanny:** In the first version of the poem "der fühlenden Schinzinn gleich" (Miss Schinz and her brother were present during this journey on the lake of Zurich). However, the name Fanny tends to relate the stanza to Maria Josepha Schmidt (1731–1799), Klopstock's cousin and beloved, whom he had celebrated as "Fanny" (a name derived from his English readings) in his odes prior to his trip to Zurich.
[2] **Uto:** Ütliberg, mountain near Zurich affording a good view.
[3] **Hallers Doris:** Doris Marianne von Haller, née Wyss, wife of Albrecht von Haller (1708–77), Swiss poet, physician, and naturalist. The song referred to is the poem "Doris," which the poet dedicated to her.

---

[4] **Hirzels Daphne:** Johanna Maria Hirzel, wife of Hans Kaspar Hirzel (1725–1803), writer and alderman of Zurich. He was the guide for the journey Klopstock immortalized in song.
[5] **Kleist:** Ewald Christian von Kleist (1715–59). Poet, Prussian officer.
[6] **Gleim:** Johann Wilhelm Ludwig Gleim (1719–1803). Anacreontic poet.
[7] **Hagedorn:** Friedrich von Hagedorn (1708–54). Anacreontic poet, writer of fables.
[8] **die Au:** a wooded island on the Lake of Zurich.
[9] **Odem: Atem.**
[10] **im sokratischen Becher:** alludes to serene philosophical joys rather than to undisciplined intoxication (cf. line 46, **Säufer**).

45 Wenn er dringt bis ins Herz, und zu Ent-
   schließungen,
   Die der Säufer verkennt, jeden Gedanken
   weckt,
   Wenn er lehret verachten,
   Was nicht würdig des Weisen ist.

   Reizvoll klinget des Ruhms lockender Sil-
   berton
50 In das schlagende Herz, und die Unsterblichkeit
   Ist ein großer Gedanke,
   Ist des Schweißes der Edlen wert!

   Durch der Lieder Gewalt, bei der Urenkelin
   Sohn und Tochter noch sein; mit der Ent-
   zückung Ton
55 Oft beim Namen genennet,[11]
   Oft gerufen vom Grabe her,

   Dann ihr sanfteres Herz bilden, und, Liebe,
   dich,
   Fromme Tugend, dich auch gießen ins
   sanfte Herz,
   Ist, beim Himmel! nicht wenig!
60 Ist des Schweißes der Edlen wert!

   Aber süßer ist noch, schöner und reizender,
   In dem Arme des Freunds wissen ein Freund
   zu sein!
   So das Leben genießen,
   Nicht unwürdig der Ewigkeit!

65 Treuer Zärtlichkeit voll, in den Umschat-
   tungen,
   In den Lüften des Walds, und mit gesenktem
   Blick
   Auf die silberne Welle,
   Tat ich schweigend den frommen Wunsch:

   Wäret ihr auch bei uns, die ihr mich ferne
   liebt,
70 In des Vaterlands Schoß einsam von mir
   verstreut,
   Die in seligen Stunden
   Meine suchende Seele fand;

   O so bauten wir hier Hütten der Freundschaft uns!
   Ewig wohnten wir hier, ewig! Der Schat-
   tenwald

Wandelt' uns sich in Tempe,[12]   75
Jenes Tal in Elysium!

DIE GENESUNG

Genesung, Tochter der Schöpfung auch,
Aber auch du der Unsterblichkeit nicht ge-
   boren,
Dich hat mir der Herr des Lebens und des
   Todes
Von dem Himmel gesandt!

Hätt' ich deinen sanften Gang nicht vernom-   5
   men,
Nicht deiner Lispel[1] Stimme gehört;
So hätt' auf des Liegenden kalten Stirn
Gestanden mit dem eisernen Fuße der Tod!

Zwar wär ich auch dahin gewallet,
Wo Erden wandeln um Sonnen,   10
Hätte die Bahn betreten, auf der der be-
   schweifte Komet
Sich selbst dem doppelten Auge verliert;

Hätte mit dem ersten entzückenden Gruße
Die Bewohner gegrüßt der Erden und der
   Sonnen,
Gegrüßt des hohen Kometen   15
Zahllose Bevölkerung;

Kühne Jünglingsfragen gefragt,
Antworten vollen Maßes bekommen,[2]
Mehr in Stunden gelernt, als der Jahrhunderte
Lange Reihen hier enträtseln.   20
Aber ich hätt' auch hier das nicht vollendet,
Was schon in den Blütenjahren des Lebens
Mit lauter süßer Stimme
Mein Beruf zu beginnen mich rief.

Genesung, Tochter der Schöpfung auch,   25

---

[11] genennet: genannt.

[12] Tempe: Vale of Tempe, valley in Greece with
a sanctuary dedicated to Apollo, who here is
regarded as god of poetry. The earthly landscape
of Lake Zurich would (if the friends were there)
change into an ideal pastoral haven where the gods
dwell.
[1] Lispel: whisper; murmuring.
[2] Antworten ... bekommen: ausführliche Antworten bekommen.

Aber auch du der Unsterblichkeit nicht
    geboren,
Dich hat mir der Herr des Lebens und des
    Todes
Von dem Himmel gesandt!

WEIHTRUNK
AN DIE TOTEN FREUNDE

Daß euer stilles Gebein, und was ihr mehr
    noch wart
Als vermodernd Gebein, diesen geweihten
    Wunsch
In dem Schoße der Erde
Und Elysiums Tal vernehm!

5 Daß wir weise, wie ihr, und der Erinnerung
Eures Todes getreu, leben, zwar fröhlich
    sein;
Doch als stündet ihr alle
Mit den glücklichern Freunden hier.

AN GOTT

Ein stiller Schauer deiner Allgegenwart
Erschüttert, Gott! mich. Sanfter erbebt
    mein Herz,
Und mein Gebein. Ich fühl', ich fühl' es,
Daß du auch hier, wo ich weine, Gott! bist.

5 Von deinem Antlitz wandelt, Unendlicher,
Dein Blick, der Seher, durch mein eröffnet
    Herz.
Sei vor ihm heilig, Herz, sei heilig,
Seele, vom ewigen Hauch entsprungen!

Verirrt mich Täuschung?[1] oder ist wirklich
    wahr,
10 Was ein Gedanke leise dem andern sagt?
Empfindung, bist du wahr, als dürft' ich
Frei mit dem Schöpfer der Seele reden?

---

[1] **Verirrt mich Täuschung?**: Macht mich die
    Täuschung irren?

Gedanken Gottes, welche der Ewige,
Der Weis' itzt denket! wenn ihr den mensch-
    lichen
Gedanken zürnet: o wo sollen   15
Sie vor euch, Gottes Gedanken! hinfliehn?

Flöhn[2] sie zum Abgrund; siehe, so seid ihr
    da!
Und wenn sie bebend in das Unendliche
Hineilten; auch im Unbegrenzten,
Wärt ihr, Allwissende! sie zu schauen!   20

Friedrich Gottlieb Klopstock.
(Bildnis von J. M. Bernigeroth.)
*Courtesy of Yale University
Library.*

Und wenn sie Flügel nähmen der Seraphim,
Und aufwärts flögen, in die Versammlungen,
Hoch ins Getön, ins Halleluja,
In die Gesänge der Harfenspieler;

Auch da vernähmt[3] ihr, göttliche Hörer! sie. 25
Flieht denn nicht länger, seid ihr auch
    menschlicher,
Flieht nicht; der ewig ist, der weiß es,
Daß er in engen Bezirk euch einschloß.

Des frohen Zutrauns! auch der Beruhigung,

---

[2] **flöhn (flöh'n)**: *arch. subj. of* **fliehen.**
[3] **vernähmt (vernähm't)**: *arch. subj. of* **vernehmen.**

30 Daß meine Seele, Gott! mit dir reden darf!
Daß sich mein Mund vor dir darf öffnen,
Töne des Menschen herabzustammeln!

Ich wag's, und rede! Aber du weißt es ja,
Schon lange weißt du, was mein Gebein
verzehrt,
35 Was, in mein Herz tief hingegossen,
Meinen Gedanken ein ewig Bild ist!

Nicht heut erst sahst du meine mir lange
Zeit,
Die Augenblicke, weinend vorübergehn!
Du bist es, der du warst; Jehova
40 Heißest du! aber ich Staub von Staube!

Staub, und auch ewig! denn die Unsterb-
liche,
Die du mir, Gott! gabst, gabst du zur
Ewigkeit!
Ihr hauchtest du, dein Bild zu schaffen,
Hohe Begierden nach Ruh und Glück ein!

45 Ein drängend Heer! Doch Eine ward herr-
licher
Vor allen andern! Eine ward Königin
Der andern alle, deines Bildes
Letzter und göttlichster Zug, die Liebe!

Die fühlst du selber, doch als der Ewige;
50 Es fühlen jauchzend, welche du himmlisch
schufst,
Die hohen Engel deines Bildes
Letzten und göttlichsten Zug, die Liebe!

Die grubst du Adam tief in sein Herz hinein!
Nach seinem Denken von der Vollkommenheit,
55 Ganz ausgeschaffen, ihm geschaffen,
Brachtest du, Gott! ihm der Menschen Mutter!

Die grubst du mir auch tief in mein Herz
hinein!
Nach meinem Denken von der Vollkommenheit,
Ganz ausgeschaffen, mir geschaffen,
60 Führst du sie weg, die mein ganzes Herz
liebt!
Mit allen Tränen, welche sie weinen kann,

Der meine Seele ganz sich entgegen gießt!

Die volle Seele ganz zuströmet!
Führst du sie mir, die ich liebe, Gott, weg!

Weg, durch dein Schicksal, welches, unsicht- 65
bar sich
Dem Auge, fortwebt, immer ins Dunklre
webt!
Fern weg den ausgestreckten Armen!
Aber nicht weg aus dem bangen Herzen!

Und dennoch weißt du, welch ein Gedank' es
war,
Als du ihn dachtest, und zu der Wirklichkeit 70
Erschaffend riefst, der, daß du Seelen
Fühlender, und für einander schufest!

Das weißt du, Schöpfer! Aber dein Schicksal
trennt
Die Seelen, die du so für einander schufst,
Dein hohes, unerforschtes Schicksal, 75
Dunkel für uns, doch anbetungswürdig!

Das Leben gleichet, gegen die Ewigkeit,
Dem schnellen Hauche, welcher dem Ster-
benden
Entfließt; mit ihm entfloß die Seele,
Die der Unendlichkeit ewig nachströmt! 80

Einst löst des Schicksals Vater in Klarheit auf,
Was Labyrinth war; Schicksal ist dann nicht
mehr!
Ach dann, bei trunknem Wiedersehen,
Gibst du die Seelen einander wieder!

Gedanke, wert der Seel' und der Ewigkeit! 85
Wert, auch den bängsten Schmerz zu be-
sänftigen!
Dich denkt mein Geist in deiner Größe;
Aber ich fühle zu sehr das Leben,

Das hier ich lebe! Gleich der Unsterblichkeit,
Dehnt, was ein Hauch war, fürchterlich mir 90
sich aus!
Ich seh', ich sehe meine Schmerzen,
Grenzenlos dunkel, vor mir verbreitet!

Laß, Gott, dies' Leben, leicht wie den Hauch
entfliehn!
Nein, das nicht! gib mir, die du mir gleich
erschufst!
Ach, gib sie mir, dir leicht zu geben! 95

Gib sie dem bebenden, bangen Herzen!

Dem süßen Schauer, der ihr entgegen wallt!
Dem stillen Stammeln der, die unsterblich ist,
Und, sprachlos ihr Gefühl zu sagen,
Nur, wenn sie weinet, nicht ganz verstummet.

Gib sie den Armen, die ich voll Unschuld oft,
In meiner Kindheit, dir zu dem Himmel hub,[4]
Wenn ich, mit heißer Stirn voll Andacht,
Dir[5] um die ewige Ruhe flehte.

Mit einem Winke gibst du, und nimmst du ja
Dem Wurm, dem Stunden sind wie Jahr-
    hunderte,
Sein kurzes Glück; dem Wurm, der Mensch
    heißt,
Jähriget,[6] blühet, verblüht, und abfällt.

Von ihr geliebet, will ich die Tugend schön
Und selig nennen! Will ich ihr himmlisch
    Bild
Mit unverwandten Augen anschaun,

Ruhe nur das, und nur Glück das nennen,

Was sie mir zuwinkt! Aber o frömmere,
Dich auch, o die du ferner und höher wohnst,
Als uns're Tugend, will ich reiner,   115
Unbekannt, Gott nur bemerket, ehren!

Von ihr geliebet, will ich dir feuriger
Entgegenjauchzen! will ich mein voller Herz,
In heißer'n Hallelujaliedern,
Ewiger Vater, vor dir ergießen!   120

Dann, wenn sie mit mir deinen erhabnen
    Ruhm
Gen Himmel weinet, betend, mit schwim-
    mendem
Entzücktem Auge;[7] will ich mit ihr
Hier schon das höhere Leben fühlen!

Das Lied vom Mittler, trunken in ihrem Arm 125
Von reiner Wollust sing' ich erhabner dann
Den Guten, welche gleich uns lieben,
Christen wie wir sind, wie wir empfinden.

---

[4] hub: hob.
[5] dir: dich.
[6] jähriget: einige Jahre lebt.

---

[7] mit schwimmendem Auge: mit tränenerfülltem
Auge.

Gotthold Ephraim Lessing
(1729–1781)

Gotthold Ephraim Lessing incarnates the intricate richness and admirable energy of German literature in the mid-eighteenth century. He was as erudite as Gottsched but did not share his petty pedantry. Not only was he well-trained in the classics, but he also studied Shakespeare, Voltaire, and Diderot in order to separate the wheat from the chaff of his day. Critics from Friedrich Schlegel to Hannah Arendt have continued to admire his incisive mind and his lean prose. Lessing, who was born in Kamenz, Saxony, came from one of those pastors' families that have given so many brilliant talents to Germany. He was destined for the Church but quickly abandoned his studies of theology (as well as medicine) and chose to become a free-lance writer with a view to being independent of kings and the favors of the nobility. Within seven years (1749–56) he established himself as a critic whom many feared and a playwright whom many admired. After a rather erratic career in Leipzig and Breslau he was appointed advisor and "press officer" to the newly established *Hamburg Nationaltheater* (1767–68). Unfortunately, this pioneering institution could not muster enough support and failed; Lessing was forced to seek employment in the service of the duke of Brunswick. At the time of his death Lessing was the duke's librarian at Wölfenbüttel. He died a bitter, disappointed, and lonely man who, by his love for rational truth, had made many enemies and few friends.

Lessing's writings range from rococo poetry in the Anacreontic mode to deeply probing essays on the correct interpretation of Aristotle's theory of tragedy and the essence of religious revelation. In his early student years in Leipzig, he wanted to emulate Molière and wrote a spate of comedies of character which should have appealed, in their strict adherence to convention, to Gottsched himself. In the fifties and sixties, Lessing was concerned with broadening and refining the theoretical and practical fundamentals of the German stage. He experimented with the traditional Alexandrine form as well as a new prose style in writing a "bourgeois" tragedy in the English vein (*Miss Sara Sampson*, 1755), and followed Diderot's suggestion of a mixed genre of serious and comic elements in his *Minna von Barnhelm* (1767), one of the few almost impeccable comedies still alive on the German stage. But the problems of tragedy attracted him again and again; he studied Aristotle and his commentators, and tried, in *Emilia Galotti* (1772), to create the character of a sensitive and proud young woman, who, to escape disgrace, coolly induces her father to kill her in a moment of provoked rage; it is a disturbing play rendered fascinating by the paradoxical character of the heroine as well as by the almost mathematical astringency of construction. In his later *Nathan der Weise* (1779) Lessing used the stage as his pulpit, as he himself admitted, and articulated his ideas about an enlightened ethic; by reworking an age-old parable he pleaded for tolerance, rationality, and benevolence among men of differing races and creeds.

Lessing's theoretical writings mark a turning point in the history of taste; in his *Laokoon* (1766) he skillfully separated the artistic possibilities of the visual and the verbal arts and for the first time in Germany discussed the artistic treatment of the ugly which, a few generations later, became one of the central concerns of realism and naturalism. His *Hamburgische Dramaturgie,* designed as a running commentary on the performances of the *Nationaltheater,* grew into a meandering, elaborate, and passionate document of Lessing's effort to reinterpret, in a pragmatic way corresponding to his enlightened image of man, the meaning of the unities of plot, time, and place as well as the traditional idea of the audience's purgation by the tragic experience. His is a relaxed classicism that tries to hold the narrow ground between the ossified dogmatism of the older generation and the rejection of all aesthetic discipline popular with the angry young men of the late sixties and seventies (*Sturm und Drang*).

Philotas (1759) belongs to Lessing's years of bold experimentation with conventions and forms. Long dissatisfied with Alexandrine tragedy and its majestic plot remote from contemporary experience, he chose a bare if muscular prose and a story which (although "located" in the time of Alexander the Great) clearly appealed to an audience concerned about the vicissitudes of the Prussian war against Austria, the Saxons, and their mighty allies. The allusion to an effeminate prince who might mature into a severe king points to the personal problems of Frederick of Prussia himself, and Philotas' and Aridäus' discussion of the alleged virtues and vices of preventive war refers to Frederick's attack on Saxony (1756) to weaken Austria by destroying one of her major allies. Yet it would be misleading to read *Philotas,* as has been done by the Prussian interpreters of the Wilhelminian age, as a simple statement of enthusiastic patriotism; it is, of course, a play about war and heroism, but it is easy to underestimate the ambivalence of its message and the unusual brilliance of its artistic structure.

Noble simplicity, effective symmetry, and neat balance dominate its dramatic world. There are no episodes to distract our interest, no intrigues of love (usual in French tragedy), no colorful proliferation of characters; female charm seems infinitely remote from this realm of soldiers, generals, and kings. The few characters appearing on the stage are complemented by those of whom we hear indirectly: Aridäus by the enemy-king, once his friend; Philotas by Polytimet; General Strabo by Aristodem, whom Philotas greatly admires; fatherly Parmenio by the bold soldier of Aridäus' army. It is a well-ordered universe in which translucent relationships triumph. The arrangement of the scenic sequence is in equally strict balance: eight scenes, of which the first four analytically reestablish the past, and the remaining four scenes aim at the future—the desire to gain time, the necessary sword, the heroic death; and, in the very center of the play, Philotas' sudden idea, half inspiration, half choice, to kill himself and to deprive Aridäus of all possible political and military advantages.

Philotas remains the central figure and the crucial character in any adequate reading of Lessing's message. Undoubtedly, Lessing admires his youth in the first fires of manhood, his enthusiasm, his burning devotion to his particular

concept of kingship. But it is difficult to ignore the many warnings voiced by
Strabo and Aridäus, as well as Parmenio; enemies as well as friends are disturbed by Philotas' all too abstract disregard of humanity, his wild dedication
to the war aims, and his almost solipsistic attitude which ignores the well-being
of his subjects and the blessings of peace. Lessing had his particular reasons to
contrast the young "demon" with the wiser King Aridäus who knows what
it is to be a human being, laughing and weeping. Aridäus may, in a moment
of rage, relapse into barbarism, but he quickly regains control and adheres
to rational decorum, to more civilized rules of behavior, and to an idea of life
that puts the desires of the individual above the unfeeling necessities of the
state. One is almost tempted to believe that Lessing, in contrasting Philotas
with Aridäus, anticipated a conflict of forces which, for centuries, were to shape
the fortunes of his compatriots.

AUS DEN BRIEFEN, DIE NEUESTE LITERATUR BETREFFEND

Siebzehnter Brief
(16. Februar 1759)

„Niemand", sagen die Verfasser der „Bibliothek",[1] „wird leugnen, daß die deutsche Schaubühne einen großen Teil ihrer ersten Verbesserung dem Herrn Professor Gott-
5 sched zu danken habe."

Ich bin dieser Niemand; ich leugne es gerade zu. Es wäre zu wünschen, daß sich Herr Gottsched niemals mit dem Theater vermengt hätte. Seine vermeinten Verbes-
10 serungen betreffen entweder entbehrliche Kleinigkeiten, oder sind wahre Verschlimmerungen.

Als die Neuberin[2] blühte, und so mancher den Beruf fühlte, sich um sie und die Bühne
15 verdient zu machen, sahe es freilich mit unserer dramatischen Poesie sehr elend aus. Man kannte keine Regeln; man bekümmerte sich um keine Muster. Unsre Staats- und Heldenaktionen waren voller Unsinn, Bom-
20 bast, Schmutz und Pöbelwitz. Unsre Lustspiele bestanden in Verkleidungen und Zaubereien; und Prügel waren die witzigsten Einfälle derselben. Dieses Verderbnis einzusehen, brauchte man eben nicht der
25 feinste und größte Geist zu sein. Auch war Herr Gottsched nicht der erste, der es einsahe; er war nur der erste, der sich Kräfte genug zutraute, ihm abzuhelfen. Und wie ging er damit zu Werke? Er verstand ein
30 wenig Französisch und fing an zu übersetzen; er ermunterte alles, was reimen und „Oui Monsieur" verstehen konnte, gleichfalls zu übersetzen; er verfertigte, wie ein schweizerischer Kunstrichter[3] sagt, mit Kleister und
35 Schere seinen Cato;[4] er ließ den Darius und die Austern, die Elise und den Bock im Prozesse, den Aurelius und den Witzling, die Banise und den Hypochondristen,[5] ohne Kleister und Schere machen; er legte seinen Fluch auf das Extemporieren; er ließ den
40 Harlekin feierlich vom Theater vertreiben, welches selbst die größte Harlekinade war, die jemals gespielt worden; kurz, er wollte nicht sowohl unser altes Theater verbessern, als der Schöpfer eines ganz neuen sein. Und
45 was für eines neuen? Eines französierenden; ohne zu untersuchen, ob dieses französierende Theater der deutschen Denkungsart angemessen sei, oder nicht.

Er hätte aus unsern alten dramatischen
50 Stücken, welche er vertrieb, hinlänglich abmerken können, daß wir mehr in den Geschmack der Engländer, als der Franzosen einschlagen; daß wir in unsern Trauerspielen mehr sehen und denken wollen, als
55 uns das furchtsame französische Trauerspiel zu sehen und zu denken gibt; daß das Große, das Schreckliche, das Melancholische, besser auf uns wirkt als das Artige, das Zärtliche, das Verliebte; daß uns die zu große Einfalt
60 mehr ermüde, als die zu große Verwicklung etc. Er hätte also auf dieser Spur bleiben sollen, und sie würde ihn geraden Weges auf das englische Theater geführet haben.—Sagen Sie ja nicht, daß er auch dieses zu
65 nutzen gesucht; wie sein Cato es beweise. Denn eben dieses, daß er den Addisonschen Cato[6] für das beste englische Trauerspiel hält, zeiget deutlich, daß er hier nur mit den Augen der Franzosen gesehen, und damals
70 keinen Shakespeare, keinen Jonson,[7] keinen Beaumont[8] und Fletcher[9] etc. gekannt hat, die er hernach aus Stolz auch nicht hat wollen kennen lernen.

---

1 **Bibliothek:** a pro-Gottsched oriented publication.
2 **die Neuberin** Friederike Karoline Neuber, née Weißenborn (1697–1760); most famous actress of her epoch. She also wrote occasional.
3 **ein schweizerischer Kunstrichter:** reference to Johann Jakob Bodmer (1698–1783). See p. 315.
4 **Cato:** Gottsched's tragedy *Sterbender Cato* (1732).

5 **Darius ... Hypochondristen:** the works mentioned are those of Gottsched's adherents and were published by him in his *Deutsche Schaubühne. Darius* (tragedy); *Aurelius* (tragedy); *Die Austern, Der Bock im Prozesse, Der Hypochondrist* (comedies); *Elisie* (pastoral play); *Der Witzling* (comedy written by Gottsched's wife); *Banise* (dramatic adaptation of a famous baroque novel).
6 **der Addisonsche Cato:** Cato, tragedy by Joseph Addison (1672–1719), English essayist, poet, and statesman.
7 **Jonson:** Ben Jonson (1573–1637). English dramatist.
8 **Beaumont:** Francis Beaumont (1584–1616). English dramatist.
9 **Fletcher:** John Fletcher (1579–1625). English dramatist.

Wenn man die Meisterstücke des Shakespeare, mit einigen bescheidenen Veränderungen, unsern Deutschen übersetzt hätte, ich weiß gewiß, es würde von bessern Folgen gewesen sein, als daß man sie mit dem Corneille[10] und Racine[11] so bekannt gemacht hat. Erstlich würde das Volk an jenem weit mehr Geschmack gefunden haben, als es an diesen nicht finden kann; und zweitens würde jener ganz andere Köpfe unter uns erweckt haben, als man von diesen zu rühmen weiß. Denn ein Genie kann nur von einem Genie entzündet werden; und am leichtesten von so einem, das alles bloß der Natur zu danken zu haben scheinet, und durch die mühsamen Vollkommenheiten der Kunst nicht abschrecket.

G. E. Lessing. (Bildnis von J. H. W. Tischbein.) *Courtesy of Yale University Library.*

Auch nach den Mustern der Alten die Sache zu entscheiden, ist Shakespeare ein weit größerer tragischer Dichter als Corneille; obgleich dieser die Alten sehr wohl, und jener fast gar nicht gekannt hat. Corneille kömmt ihnen in der mechanischen Einrichtung, und Shakespeare in dem Wesentlichen näher. Der Engländer erreicht den Zweck der Tragödie[12] fast immer, so sonderbare und ihm eigene Wege er auch wählet; und der Franzose erreicht ihn fast niemals, ob er gleich die gebahnten Wege der Alten betritt. Nach dem Ödipus des Sophokles muß in der Welt kein Stück mehr Gewalt über unsere Leidenschaften haben, als Othello, als König Lear, als Hamlet etc. Hat Corneille ein einziges Trauerspiel, das Sie nur halb so gerührt hätte, als die Zaïre[13] des Voltaire? Und die Zaïre des Voltaire, wie weit ist sie unter dem Mohren von Venedig, dessen schwache Kopie sie ist, und von welchem der ganze Charakter des Orosmans entlehnet worden?

Daß aber unsre alten Stücke wirklich sehr viel Englisches gehabt haben, könnte ich Ihnen mit geringer Mühe weitläuftig beweisen. Nur das bekannteste derselben zu nennen; Doktor Faust hat eine Menge Szenen, die nur ein Shakespearesches Genie zu denken vermögend gewesen. Und wie verliebt war Deutschland, und ist es zum Teil noch, in seinen Doktor Faust![14]

AUS DEN ABHANDLUNGEN VON DEM WEINERLICHEN ODER RÜHRENDEN LUSTSPIELE (1754)

Neuerungen machen, kann sowohl der Charakter eines großen Geistes, als eines kleinen sein. Jener verläßt das alte, weil es unzulänglich, oder gar falsch ist; dieser, weil es alt ist. Was bei jenem die Einsicht veranlaßt, veranlaßt bei diesem der Eckel.[1] Das G e n i e will mehr thun als sein Vorgänger; der A f f e des Genies nur etwas anders.

Beide lassen sich nicht immer auf den ersten Blick von einander unterscheiden.

---

[10] **Corneille:** Pierre Corneille (1606–84). French playwright.

[11] **Racine:** Jean Baptiste Racine (1639–99). French dramatic poet.

[12] **der Zweck der Tragödie:** the cleansing (*Gr.*, *katharsis*) of tragedy.

[13] **Zaïre:** *Zaïre* (1732), drama by Voltaire (1694–1778), French writer.

[14] In the conclusion of the 17th letter, Lessing communicates, to his readers, the "old" fragment of a Faust play. Needless to say, it was written by him.

[1] **Eckel (Ekel):** disgust.

Bald macht die flatterhafte Liebe zu Veränderungen, daß man aus Gefälligkeit diesen für jenes gelten läßt; und bald die hartnäckige Pedanterei, daß man, voll unwissenden
15 Stolzes, jenes zu diesem erniedriget. Genaue Beurtheilung muß mit der lautersten Unpartheilichkeit verbunden sein, wenn der aufgeworfene[2] Kunstrichter weder aus wollüstiger Nachsicht, noch aus neidischem
20 Eigendünkel fehlen soll.

Diese allgemeine Betrachtung findet hier ganz natürlich ihren Platz, da ich von den Neuerungen reden will, welche zu unsern Zeiten in der dramatischen Dichtkunst sind
25 gemacht worden. Weder das Lustspiel, noch das Trauerspiel, ist davon verschont geblieben. Das erstere hat man um einige Staffeln erhöhet, und das andre um einige herabgesetzt. Dort glaubte man, daß die Welt lange
30 genug in dem Lustspiele gelacht und abgeschmackte Laster ausgezischt habe; man kam also auf den Einfall, die Welt endlich einmal auch darinne weinen und an stillen Tugenden ein edles Vergnügen finden zu lassen. Hier
35 hielt man es für unbillig, daß nur Regenten und hohe Standespersonen in uns Schrecken und Mitleiden erwecken sollten; man suchte sich also aus dem Mittelstande Helden, und schnallte ihnen den tragischen Stiefel an, in
40 dem man sie sonst, nur ihn lächerlich zu machen, gesehen hatte.

Die erste Veränderung brachte dasjenige hervor, was seine Anhänger das r ü h r e n d e L u s t s p i e l, und seine Widersacher das
45 w e i n e r l i c h e nennen.

Aus der zweiten Veränderung entstand das b ü r g e r l i c h e T r a u e r s p i e l.

Jene ist von den F r a n z o s e n und diese von den E n g l ä n d e r n gemacht worden.
50 Ich wollte fast sagen, daß sie beide aus dem besondern Naturelle dieser Völker entsprungen zu sein scheinen. Der Franzose ist ein Geschöpf, das immer größer scheinen will, als es ist. Der Engländer ist ein anders, welches alles große zu sich hernieder ziehen will.
55 ches alles große zu sich hernieder ziehen will. Dem einen ward es verdrüßlich, sich immer auf der lächerlichen Seite vorgestellt zu sehen; ein heimlicher Ehrgeitz[3] trieb ihn, seines gleichen aus einem edeln Gesichts-
60 punkte zu zeigen. Dem andern war es

ärgerlich, gekrönten Häuptern viel voraus zu lassen;[4] er glaubte bei sich zu fühlen, daß gewaltsame Leidenschaften und erhabne Gedanken nicht mehr für sie, als für einen aus seinen Mitteln wären.
65 aus seinen Mitteln wären.

Dieses ist vielleicht nur ein leerer Gedanke; aber genug, daß es doch wenigstens ein Gedanke ist.—Ich will für diesesmal nur die erste Veränderung zu dem Gegenstande
70 meiner Betrachtungen machen, und die Beurtheilung der zweiten auf einen andern Ort sparen.

Ich habe schon gesagt, daß man ihr einen doppelten Namen beilegt, welchen ich auch
75 so gar in der Überschrift gebraucht habe, um mich nicht durch die bloße Anwendung des einen, so schlecht weg gegen den Begriff des andern zu erklären. Das w e i n e r l i c h e L u s t s p i e l ist die Benennung derjenigen, welche wider diese neue Gattung eingenom-
80 men sind. Ich glaube, ob schon nicht hier, sondern anderwärts, das Wort w e i n e r - l i c h, um das Französische *larmoyant* auszudrücken, am ersten gebraucht zu haben. Und ich wüßte es noch jetzt nicht besser zu
85 übersetzen, wenn anders der spöttische Nebenbegriff, den man damit hat verbinden wollen, nicht verloren gehen sollte. Man sieht dieses an der zweiten Benennung, wo ihre Vertheidiger ihre Rechnung dabei
90 gefunden haben, ihn gänzlich wegzulassen. Ein r ü h r e n d e s L u s t s p i e l läßt uns an ein sehr schönes Werk denken, da ein w e i n e r l i c h e s, ich weiß nicht was für ein kleines Ungeheuer zu versprechen schei-
95 net.

Aus diesen verschiedenen Benennungen ist genugsam, glaube ich, zu schließen, daß die Sache selbst eine doppelte Seite haben müsse, wo man ihr bald zu viel, und bald
100 zu wenig thun könne. Sie muß eine gute Seite haben, sonst würden sich nicht so viel schöne und scharfsinnige Geister für sie erklären: sie muß aber auch eine schlechte haben, sonst würden sich andre, die eben so
105 schön und scharfsinnig sind, ihr nicht widersetzen. . . .

Anfangs muß man über die Erklärung der rührenden oder weinerlichen Komödie einig werden. Will man eine solche darunter ver-
110

---

[2] *aufgeworfen:* supercilious.
[3] *Ehrgeitz* (*Ehrgeiz*): ambition.

[4] *gekrönte ... lassen:* gekrönte Häupter so ausgezeichnet zu sehen.

standen haben, welche hier und da rührende
und Thränen auspressende Scenen hat; oder
eine solche, welche aus nichts als dergleichen
Scenen besteht? Meinet man eine, wo man
115 nicht immer lacht, oder wo man gar nicht
lacht? Eine, wo edle Charaktere mit unge-
reimten verbunden sind, oder eine, wo
nichts als edle Charaktere vorkommen?

Wider die erste Gattung, in welcher
120 Lachen und Rührung, Scherz und Ernst
abwechseln, ist offenbar nichts einzuwenden.
Ich erinnere mich auch nicht, daß man
jemals darwieder etwas habe einwenden
wollen. Vernunft und Beispiele der alten
125 Dichter vertheidigen sie. Er, der an Scherz
und Einfällen der reichste ist, und Lachen
zu erregen nicht selten Witz und Anständig-
keit, wie man sagt, bei Seite gesetzt hat,
P l a u t u s[5] hat die G e f a n g n e n gemacht
130 und, was noch mehr ist, dem P h i l e m o n[6]
seinen S c h a t z, unter der Aufschrift[7]
T r i n u m m u s abgeborgt. In beiden Stük-
ken, und auch in andern, kommen Auftritte
vor, die einer zärtlichen Seele Thränen
135 kosten müssen . . . .

Worauf kömmt es also nun noch weiter
an? Darauf, sollte ich meinen, daß man den
Grad der Nützlichkeit des neuen Schau-
spiels, gegen die Nützlichkeit der alten
140 Komödie bestimme, und nach Maßgebung
dieser Bestimmung entscheide, ob man
beiden einerlei Vorzüge einräumen müsse
oder nicht? Ich habe schon gesagt, daß
man niemals diejenigen Stücke getadelt habe,
145 welche Lachen und Rührung verbinden; ich
kann mich dieserwegen unter andern darauf
berufen, daß man den D e s t o u c h e s[8]
niemals mit dem l a C h a u s s e e[9] in eine
Klasse gesetzt hat, und daß die hartnäckig-
150 sten Feinde des letztern, niemals dem
erstern den Ruhm eines vortrefflichen komi-
schen Dichters abgesprochen haben, so viel
edle Charaktere und zärtliche Scenen in
seinem Stücke auch vorkommen. Ja, ich
155 getraue mir zu behaupten, daß nur dieses

----

⁵ **Plautus**: Titus Maccius Plautus (254?–184 B.C.).
Roman comic poet.
⁶ **Philemon**: Greek poet (*c.* 363–*c.* 264 B.C.).
⁷ **Aufschrift**: title.
⁸ **Destouches**: Philippe Destouches (1680–1754).
French playwright.
⁹ **la Chaussee**: Pierre-Claude Nivelle de la Chaussée
(1692–1754). French dramatist.

allein wahre Komödien sind, welche so
wohl Tugenden als Laster, so wohl Anstän-
digkeit als Ungereimtheit schildern, weil sie
eben durch diese Vermischung ihrem Originale, dem menschlichen Leben, am nächsten 160
kommen. Die Klugen und Thoren sind in
der Welt untermengt, und ob es gleich
gewiß ist, daß die erstern von den letztern an
der Zahl übertroffen werden, so ist doch eine
Gesellschaft von lauter Thoren beinahe eben 165
so unwahrscheinlich, als eine Gesellschaft von
lauter Klugen. Diese Erscheinung ahmet das
Lustspiel nach, und nur durch die Nachahmung derselben ist es fähig, dem Volke
nicht allein das, was es vermeiden muß, 170
auch nicht allein das, was es beobachten
muß, sondern beides zugleich in einem
Lichte vorzustellen, in welchem das eine das
andre erhebt. Man sieht leicht, daß man von
diesem wahren und einigen Wege auf eine 175
doppelte Art abweichen kann. Der einen
Abweichung hat man schon längst den Namen
des P o s s e n s p i e l s gegeben, dessen cha-
rakteristische Eigenschaft darinne besteht,
daß es nichts als Laster und Ungereimtheiten, 180
mit keinen andern als solchen Zügen schildert, welche zum Lachen bewegen, es mag
dieses Lachen nun ein nützliches oder ein
sinnloses Lachen sein. Edle Gesinnungen,
ernsthafte Leidenschaften, Stellungen, wo 185
sich die schöne Natur in ihrer Stärke zeigen
kann, bleiben aus demselben ganz und gar
weg; und wenn es außerdem auch noch so
regelmäßig ist, so wird es doch in den
Augen strenger Kunstrichter dadurch noch 190
lange nicht zu einer Komödie. Worinne
wird also die andre Abweichung bestehen?
Ohnfehlbar darinne, wenn man nichts als
Tugenden und anständige Sitten, mit keinen
andern als solchen Zügen schildert, welche 195
Bewunderung und Mitleid erwecken, beides
mag nun einen Einfluß auf die Beßrung der
Zuhörer haben können, oder nicht. Lebhafte
Satyre, lächerliche Ausschweifungen, Stellungen, die den Narren in seiner Blöße 200
zeigen, sind gänzlich aus einem solchen
Stücke verbannt. Und wie wird man ein
solches Stück nennen? Jedermann wird mir
zurufen: das eben ist die weinerliche Komödie! Noch einmal also mit einem Worte: das 205
P o s s e n s p i e l will nur zum Lachen
bewegen: das w e i n e r l i c h e L u s t-

s p i e l will nur rühren; die wahre
K o m ö d i e will beides. Man glaube nicht,
daß ich dadurch die beiden erstern in eine
Klasse setzen will; es ist noch immer der
Unterschied zwischen beiden, der zwischen
dem Pöbel und Leuten von Stande ist. Der
Pöbel wird ewig der Beschützer der Pos-
senspiele bleiben, und unter Leuten von
Stande wird es immer gezwungne Zärtlinge
geben, die den Ruhm empfindlicher Seelen
auch da zu behaupten suchen, wo andre
ehrliche Leute gähnen. Die wahre Komödie
allein ist für das Volk, und allein fähig einen
allgemeinen Beifall zu erlangen, und folglich
auch einen allgemeinen Nutzen zu stiften.
Was sie bei dem einen nicht durch die Scham
erlangt, das erlangt sie durch die Bewunderung; und wer sich gegen diese verhärtet,
dem macht sie jene fühlbar. Hieraus scheinet
die Regel des C o n t r a s t s , oder der
A b s t e c h u n g , geflossen zu sein, vermöge
welcher man nicht gerne eine Untugend
aufführt, ohne ihr Gegentheil mit anzubrin-
gen; ob ich gleich gerne zugebe, daß sie
auch darinne gegründet ist, daß ohne sie der
Dichter seine Charaktere nicht wirksam
genug vorstellen könnte.

Dieses nun, sollte ich meinen, bestimme
den Nutzen der weinerlichen Komödie genau
genug. Er ist nehmlich nur die Hälfte von
dem Nutzen, den sich die wahre Komödie

vorstellet; und auch von dieser Hälfte geht
nur allzuoft nicht wenig ab. Ihre Zuschauer
wollen ausgesucht sein, und sie werden
schwerlich den zwanzigsten Theil der gewöhnlichen Komödiengänger ausmachen. Doch
gesetzt sie machten die Hälfte derselben aus.
Die Aufmerksamkeit, mit der sie zuhören,
ist, wie es der Herr Prof. G e l l e r t[10]
selbst an die Hand giebt, doch nur ein
Kompliment, welches sie ihrer Eigenliebe
machen; eine Nahrung ihres Stolzes. Wie
aber hieraus eine Beßrung erfolgen könne,
sehe ich nicht ein. Jeder von ihnen glaubt
der edlen Gesinnungen, und der groß-
müthigen Thaten, die er siehet und höret,
desto eher fähig zu sein, je weniger er an
das Gegentheil zu denken, und sich mit
demselben zu vergleichen Gelegenheit findet.
Er bleibt was er ist, und bekömmt von den
guten Eigenschaften weiter nichts, als die
Einbildung, daß er sie schon besitze.

Wie steht es aber mit dem Namen? Der
Name ist etwas sehr willkührliches, und man
könnte unserer neuen Gattung gar wohl
die Benennung einer Komödie geben, wenn
sie ihr auch nicht zukäme. Sie kömmt ihr
aber mit völligem Recht zu, weil sie ganz
und gar nicht etwas anders als eine Komödie,
sondern bloß eine Untergattung der Komödie
ist.

---

[10] **Prof. Gellert:** Christian Fürchtegott Gellert (1715–
69). Author, popular during the Age of Enlightenment.

PHILOTAS

Ein Trauerspiel

Personen :

Aridäus, König

Strato, Feldherr des Aridäus

Philotas, gefangen

Parmenio, Soldat

Die Szene ist ein Zelt in dem Lager des Aridäus

Erster Auftritt

PHILOTAS

So bin ich wirklich gefangen? — Gefangen!
— Ein würdiger Anfang meiner kriegeri-
schen Lehrjahre! — O ihr Götter! O mein
Vater! — Wie gern überredte ich mich, daß
alles ein Traum sei! Meine früheste Kindheit
hat nie etwas anders als Waffen und Läger und
Schlachten und Stürme geträumet. Könnte
der Jüngling nicht von Verlust und Entwaff-
nung träumen? — Schmeichle dir nur,
Philotas! Wenn ich sie nicht sähe, nicht
fühlte, die Wunde, durch die der erstarrten
Hand das Schwert entsank! — Man hat sie
mir wider Willen verbunden. O der grausa-
men Barmherzigkeit eines listigen Feindes!
Sie ist nicht tödlich, sagte der Arzt und glaubte mich zu trösten. — Nichtswürdiger, sie
sollte tödlich sein! — Und nur eine Wunde,
nur eine! — Wüßte ich, daß ich sie tödlich
machte, wenn ich sie wieder aufriß und wieder verbinden ließ und wieder aufriß — Ich
rase, ich Unglücklicher! — Und was für
ein höhnisches Gesicht — itzt fällt mir es
ein — mir der alte Krieger machte, der
mich vom Pferde riß! Er nannte mich:
Kind! — Auch sein König muß mich für ein
Kind, für ein verzärteltes Kind halten. In
was für ein Zelt hat er mich bringen lassen!
Aufgeputzt,[1] mit allen Bequemlichkeiten
versehen! Es muß einer von seinen Beischlä-
ferinnen[2] gehören. Ein ekler Aufenthalt
für einen Soldaten! Und anstatt bewacht zu
werden, werde ich bedienet. Hohn-
sprechende Höflichkeit! —

Zweiter Auftritt

STRATO. PHILOTAS

STRATO. Prinz —

PHILOTAS. Schon wieder ein Besuch?
Alter, ich bin gern allein.

STRATO. Prinz, ich komme auf Befehl des
Königs —

PHILOTAS. Ich verstehe dich! Es ist wahr,
ich bin deines Königs Gefangener und es
stehet bei ihm, wie er mir will begegnen
lassen[3] — Aber höre, wenn du der bist,
dessen Miene du trägst — bist du ein alter
ehrlicher Kriegsmann, so nimm dich meiner
an und bitte den König, daß er mir als einem
Soldaten und nicht als einem Weibe begegnen lasse.

STRATO. Er wird gleich bei dir sein; ich
komme, ihn zu melden.

PHILOTAS. Der König bei mir? und du
kömmst, ihn zu melden? — Ich will nicht,
daß er mir eine von den Erniedrigungen
erspare, die sich ein Gefangener muß gefallen
lassen. — Komm, führe mich zu ihm! Nach
dem Schimpfe,[4] entwaffnet zu sein, ist mir
nichts mehr schimpflich.

STRATO. Prinz, deine Bildung,[5] voll
jugendlicher Anmut, verspricht ein sanftres
Gemüt.

PHILOTAS. Laß meine Bildung unverspot-
tet! Dein Gesicht voll Narben ist freilich
ein schöners Gesicht — —

STRATO. Bei den Göttern! eine große
Antwort! Ich muß dich bewundern und
lieben.

---

[1] **aufgeputzt:** here, beautifully appointed.
[2] **Beischläferin:** concubine.
[3] **es stehet . . . lassen: er hat die Wahl wie man
mich behandeln soll.**
[4] **Schimpf:** disgrace.
[5] **Bildung:** here, build (physique).

PHILOTAS. Möchtest du doch, wenn du mich nur erst gefürchtet hättest.

STRATO. Immer heldenmütiger! Wir haben den schrecklichsten Feind vor uns, wenn unter seiner Jugend der Philotas viel sind.

PHILOTAS. Schmeichle mir nicht! — Euch schrecklich zu werden, müssen sie mit meinen Gesinnungen größre Taten verbinden. — Darf ich deinen Namen wissen?

STRATO. Strato.

PHILOTAS. Strato? Der tapfre Strato, der meinen Vater am Lykus schlug? —

STRATO. Gedenke mir dieses zweideutigen Sieges nicht![6] Und wie blutig rächte sich dein Vater in der Ebene Methymna! So ein Vater muß so einen Sohn haben.

PHILOTAS. O dir darf ich es klagen, du würdigster der Feinde meines Vaters, dir darf ich mein Schicksal klagen. — Nur du kannst mich ganz verstehen; denn auch dich, auch dich hat das herrschende Feuer der Ehre, der Ehre fürs Vaterland zu bluten, in deiner Jugend verzehrt. Wärst du sonst, was du bist? — Wie habe ich ihn nicht, meinen Vater, seit sieben Tagen — denn erst sieben Tage kleidet mich die männliche Toga[7] — wie habe ich ihn nicht gebeten, gefleht, beschworen, siebenmal alle sieben Tage auf den Knieen beschworen, zu verstatten,[8] daß ich nicht umsonst der Kindheit entwachsen sei, und mich mit seinen Streitern ausziehen zu lassen, die mir schon längst so manche Träne der Nacheiferung gekostet. Gestern bewegte ich ihn, den besten Vater, denn Aristodem half mir bitten. — Du kennst ihn, den Aristodem; er ist meines Vaters Strato. — „Gib mir, König, den Jüngling morgen mit", sprach Aristodem; „ich will das Gebirge durchstreifen, um den Weg nach Cäsena offen zu halten." — „Wenn ich euch nur begleiten könnte!" seufzte mein Vater. — Er liegt noch an seinen Wunden krank. — „Doch es sei!" Und hiermit umarmte mich mein Vater. O was fühlte der glückliche Sohn in dieser Umarmung! — Und die Nacht, die darauf folgte! Ich schloß kein Auge; doch verweilten mich

Träume[9] der Ehre und des Sieges bis zur zweiten Nachtwache auf dem Lager. — Da sprang ich auf, warf mich in den neuen Panzer, strich die ungelockten Haare unter den Helm, wählte unter den Schwertern meines Vaters, dem ich gewachsen zu sein glaubte, stieg zu Pferde und hatte ein Roß schon müde gespornt, noch ehe die silberne Trommete[10] die befohlne Mannschaft weckte. Sie kamen, und ich sprach mit jedem meiner Begleiter, und da drückte mich mancher wackere Krieger an seine narbigte Brust! Nur mit meinem Vater sprach ich nicht; denn ich zitterte, wenn er mich noch einmal sähe, er möchte sein Wort widerrufen. — Nun zogen wir aus! An der Seite der unsterblichen Götter kann man nicht glücklicher sein, als ich an der Seite Aristodems mich fühlte! Auf jeden seiner anfeuernden Blicke hätte ich, ich allein, ein Heer angegriffen und mich in der feindlichen Eisen gewissesten Tod gestürzet. In stiller Entschlossenheit freute ich mich auf jeden Hügel, von dem ich in der Ebene Feinde zu entdecken hoffte; auf jede Krümmung des Tals, hinter der ich auf sie zu stoßen mir schmeichelte. Und da ich sie endlich von der waldigten Höhe auf uns stürzen sahe,[11] sie mit der Spitze des Schwerts meinen Gefährten zeigte, ihnen bergan entgegenflog — rufe dir, ruhmvoller Greis, die seligste deiner jugendlichen Entzükkungen zurück — du konntest nie entzückter sein! — Aber nun, nun sieh mich, Strato, sieh mich von dem Gipfel meiner hohen Erwartungen schimpflich herabstürzen! O wie schaudert mich, diesen Fall in Gedanken noch einmal zu stürzen! — Ich war zu weit voraus geeilt; ich ward verwundet und — gefangen! Armseliger Jüngling, nur auf Wunden hieltest du dich, nur auf den Tod gefaßt — und wirst gefangen. So schicken die strengen Götter, unsere Fassung[12] zu vereiteln, nur immer unvorgesehenes Übel? — Ich weine; ich muß weinen, ob ich mich schon, von dir darum verachtet zu werden, scheue. Aber verachte mich nicht! — Du wendest dich weg?

---

[6] gedenke mir ... nicht!: erinnere mich an den zweideutigen Sieg nicht!

[7] die männliche Toga: *toga virilis,* garment, worn by young men on coming of age.

[8] verstatten (gestatten): allow; admit.

[9] doch ... Träume: doch brachte ich die Zeit mit Träumen (auf dem Lager) zu.

[10] Trommete: Trompete.

[11] sahe: sah.

[12] Fassung: here, purpose; determination.

STRATO. Ich bin unwillig; du hättest mich nicht so bewegen sollen. — Ich werde mit dir zum Kinde —

PHILOTAS. Nein; höre, warum ich weine! Es ist kein kindisches Weinen, das du mit deiner männlichen Träne zu begleiten würdigest — Was ich für mein größtes Glück hielt, die zärtliche Liebe, mit der mich mein Vater liebt, wird mein größtes Unglück. Ich fürchte, ich fürchte, er liebt mich mehr, als er sein Reich liebt! Wozu wird er sich nicht verstehen,[13] was wird ihm dein König nicht abdringen,[14] mich aus der Gefangenschaft zu retten! Durch mich Elenden wird er an einem Tage mehr verlieren, als er in drei langen mühsamen Jahren durch das Blut seiner Edeln, durch sein eignes Blut gewonnen hat. Mit was für einem Angesichte soll ich wieder vor ihm erscheinen; ich, sein schlimmster Feind? Und meines Vaters Untertanen — künftig einmal die meinigen, wenn ich sie zu regieren mich würdig gemacht hätte — wie werden sie den ausgelösten Prinzen ohne die spöttischste Verachtung unter sich dulden können? Wann ich denn vor Scham sterbe und unbetauert[15] hinab zu den Schatten schleiche, wie finster und stolz werden die Seelen der Helden bei mir vorbeiziehen, die dem Könige die Vorteile mit ihrem Leben erkaufen mußten, deren er sich als Vater für einen unwürdigen Sohn begibt![16] — O das ist mehr, als eine fühlende Seele ertragen kann!

STRATO. Fasse dich, lieber Prinz! Es ist der Fehler des Jünglings, sich immer für glücklicher oder unglücklicher zu halten, als er ist. Dein Schicksal ist so grausam noch nicht; der König nähert sich, und du wirst aus seinem Munde mehr Trost hören.

Dritter Auftritt

KÖNIG ARIDÄUS. PHILOTAS. STRATO

ARIDÄUS. Kriege, die Könige unter sich zu führen gezwungen werden, sind keine persönliche Feindschaften. — Laß dich umarmen, mein Prinz! O welcher glücklichen Tage erinnert mich deine blühende Jugend! So blühte die Jugend deines Vaters! Dies war sein offenes, sprechendes Auge; dies seine ernste, redliche Miene; dies sein edler Anstand! — Noch einmal laß dich umarmen; ich umarme deinen jüngern Vater in dir. — Hast du es nie von ihm gehört, Prinz, wie vertraute Freunde wir in deinem Alter waren? Das war das selige Alter, da wir uns noch ganz unserm Herzen überlassen durften. Bald aber wurden wir beide zum Throne gerufen, und der sorgende König, der eifersüchtige Nachbar unterdrückte, leider! den gefälligen Freund. —

PHILOTAS. Verzeih, o König, wenn du mich in Erwiderung so süßer Worte zu kalt findest. Man hat meine Jugend denken, aber nicht reden gelehrt. — Was kann es mir itzt helfen, daß du und mein Vater einst Freunde waren? Waren: so sagst du selbst. Der Haß, den man auf verloschne Freundschaft pfropfet,[17] muß unter allen die tödlichsten Früchte bringen; — oder ich kenne das menschliche Herz noch zu wenig. — Verzögere daher, König, verzögere meine Verzweiflung nur nicht. Du hast als der höfliche Staatsmann gesprochen; sprich nun als der Monarch, der den Nebenbuhler seiner Größe ganz in seiner Gewalt hat.

STRATO. O laß ihn, König, die Ungewißheit seines Schicksals nicht länger peinigen.—

PHILOTAS. Ich danke, Strato! — Ja, laß mich es nur gleich hören, wie verabscheuungswürdig du einen unglücklichen Sohn seinem Vater machen willst. Mit welchem schimpflichen Frieden, mit wie viel Ländern soll er ihn erkaufen? Wie klein und verächtlich soll er werden, um nicht verwaist zu bleiben? — O mein Vater! —

ARIDÄUS. Auch diese frühe, männliche Sprache, Prinz, war deines Vaters! So höre ich dich gern! Und möchte, meiner nicht minder würdig, auch mein Sohn itzt vor deinem Vater so sprechen! —

PHILOTAS. Wie meinst du das? —

ARIDÄUS. Die Götter — ich bin es überzeugt — wachen für unsere Tugend, wie sie für unser Leben wachen. Die so lang als

---

[13] **verstehen (sich zu etwas verstehen):** agree (to something).

[14] **was wird ... abdringen:** was wird dein König von ihm fordern.

[15] **unbetauert (unbedauert):** unlamented.

[16] **deren er sich als Vater ... begibt:** die er als Vater eines unwürdigen Sohns verliert.

[17] **pfropfen:** here, graft (*hort.*).

mögliche Erhaltung beider ist ihr geheimes, ewiges Geschäft. Wo weiß ein Sterblicher, wie böse er im Grunde ist, wie schlecht er handeln würde, ließen sie jeden verführerischen Anlaß, sich durch kleine Taten zu beschimpfen, ganz auf ihn wirken? — Ja, Prinz, vielleicht wäre ich der, den du mich glaubst; vielleicht hätte ich nicht edel genug gedacht, das wunderliche Kriegesglück, das dich mir in die Hände liefert, bescheiden zu nützen; vielleicht würde ich durch dich ertrotzt haben, was ich zu erfechten nicht länger wagen mögen; vielleicht — Doch fürchte nichts; allen diesen Vielleicht hat eine höhere Macht vorgebauet; ich kann deinen Vater seinen Sohn nicht teurer erkaufen lassen, als — durch den meinigen.

PHILOTAS. Ich erstaune! Du gibst mir zu verstehen —

ARIDÄUS. Daß mein Sohn deines Vaters Gefangener ist wie du meiner. —

PHILOTAS. Dein Sohn meines Vaters? Dein Polytimet? — Seit wenn?[18] Wie? Wo?

ARIDÄUS. So wollt es das Schicksal! Aus gleichen Wagschalen nahm es auf einmal gleiche Gewichte, und die Schalen blieben noch gleich.

STRATO. Du willst nähere Umstände wissen. — Eben dasselbe Geschwader,[19] dem du zu hitzig entgegeneiltest, führte Polytimet; und als dich die Deinigen verloren erblickten, erhob sie Wut und Verzweiflung über alle menschliche Stärke. Sie brachen ein, und alle stürmten sie auf den einen, in welchem sie ihres Verlustes Ersetzung sahen. Das Ende weißt du. — Nun nimm noch von einem alten Soldaten die Lehre an: Der Angriff ist kein Wettrennen; nicht der, welcher zuerst, sondern welcher zum sichersten auf den Feind trifft, hat sich dem Siege genähert. Das merke dir, zu feuriger Prinz; sonst möchte der werdende Held im ersten Keime ersticken.

ARIDÄUS. Strato, du machst den Prinzen durch deine zwar freundschaftliche Warnung verdrüßlich.[20] Wie finster er da steht! —

PHILOTAS. Nicht das! Aber laßt mich; in tiefe Anbetung der Vorsicht[21] verloren —

ARIDÄUS. Die beste Anbetung, Prinz, ist dankende Freude. Ermuntere dich! Wir Väter wollen uns unsere Söhne nicht lange vorenthalten. Mein Herold hält sich bereits fertig; er soll gehen und die Auswechselung beschleunigen. Aber du weißt wohl, freudige Nachrichten, die wir allein vom Feinde erfahren, scheinen Fallstricke. Man könnte argwohnen, du seist vielleicht an deiner Wunde gestorben. Es wird daher nötig sein, daß du selbst mit dem Herolde einen unverdächtigen Boten an deinen Vater sendest. Komm mit mir! Suche dir einen unter den Gefangenen, den du deines Vertrauens würdigen kannst. —

PHILOTAS. So willst du, daß ich mich vervielfältiget[22] verabscheuen soll? In jedem der Gefangenen werde ich mich selbst erblicken. — Schenke mir[23] diese Verwirrung! —

ARIDÄUS. Aber —

PHILOTAS. Unter den Gefangenen muß sich Parmenio befinden. Den schicke mir her; ich will ihn abfertigen.[24]

ARIDÄUS. Wohl; auch so! Komm, Strato! Prinz, wir sehen uns bald wieder.

Vierter Auftritt

PHILOTAS

Götter! Näher konnte der Blitz, ohne mich ganz zu zerschmettern, nicht vor mir niederschlagen. Wunderbare Götter! Die Flamme kehrt zurück; der Dampf verfliegt, und ich war nur betäubt. — So war das mein ganzes Elend, zu sehen, wie elend ich hätte werden können? Wie elend mein Vater durch mich? — Nun darf ich wieder vor dir erscheinen, mein Vater! Zwar noch mit niedergeschlagenen Augen; doch nur die Scham wird sie niederschlagen, nicht das brennende Bewußtsein, dich mit mir ins Verderben gerissen zu haben. Nun darf ich nichts von dir fürchten als einen Verweis mit Lächeln, kein stummes Trauren;[25] keine durch die stärkere Gewalt der väterlichen Liebe erstikkte Verwünschungen. —

---

[18] **wenn : wann.**

[19] **Geschwader:** troop; squad.

[20] **verdrüßlich (verdrießlich):** cross; ill-tempered.

[21] **Vorsicht (die Vorsehung):** providence.

[22] **vervielfältiget** (*adv.*): **auf vielfältige Art und Weise.**

[23] **schenke mir : erlasse mir.**

[24] **abfertigen:** dispatch; i.e., send off with the message.

[25] **Trauren : Trauern.**

Aber — ja bei dem Himmel! ich bin zu gütig gegen mich. Darf ich mir alle Fehler vergeben, die mir die Vorsicht zu vergeben scheint? Soll ich mich nicht strenger richten, als sie und mein Vater mich richten? Die allzugütigen! — Sonst jede der traurigen Folgen meiner Gefangenschaft konnten die Götter vernichten; nur eine konnten sie nicht: die Schande! Zwar jene leicht verfliegende wohl, die von der Zunge des Pöbels strömt; aber nicht die wahre daurende Schande, die hier der innere Richter, mein unparteiisches Selbst, über mich ausspricht!—

Und wie leicht ich mich verblende! Verlieret mein Vater durch mich nichts? Der Ausschlag,[26] den der gefangene Polytimet — wenn ich nicht gefangen wäre — auf seine Seite brächte, der ist nichts? — Nur durch mich wird er nichts! — Das Glück hätte sich erkläret, für wen es sich erklären sollte; das Recht meines Vaters triumphierte, wäre Polytimet, nicht Philotas und Polytimet, gefangen! —

Und nun — welcher Gedanke war es, den ich itzt dachte? Nein, den ein Gott in mir dachte — Ich muß ihm nachhängen! Laß dich fesseln, flüchtiger Gedanke! — Itzt denke ich ihn wieder! Wie weit er sich verbreitet, und immer weiter; und nun durchstrahlt er meine ganze Seele! —

Was sagte der König? Warum wollte er, daß ich zugleich selbst einen unverdächtigen Boten an meinen Vater schicken sollte? Damit mein Vater nicht argwohne — so waren ja seine eigne Worte — ich sei bereits an meiner Wunde gestorben. — Also meint er doch, wenn ich bereits an meiner Wunde gestorben wäre, so würde die Sache ein ganz anders Ansehen gewinnen? Würde sie das? Tausend Dank für diese Nachricht! Tausend Dank! — Und freilich! Denn mein Vater hätte alsdann einen gefangenen Prinzen, für den er sich alles bedingen[27] könnte; und der König, sein Feind, hätte — den Leichnam eines gefangenen Prinzen, für den er nichts fordern könnte; den er — müßte begraben oder verbrennen lassen, wenn er ihm nicht zum Abscheu werden sollte.

Gut! Das begreif ich! Folglich, wenn ich, ich elender Gefangener, meinem Vater den Sieg noch in die Hände spielen will, worauf kömmt es an? Aufs Sterben. Auf weiter nichts? — O fürwahr, der Mensch ist mächtiger, als er glaubt, der Mensch, der zu sterben weiß!

Aber ich? Ich, der Keim, die Knospe eines Menschen, weiß ich zu sterben? Nicht der Mensch, der vollendete Mensch allein muß es wissen; auch der Jüngling, auch der Knabe; oder er weiß gar nichts. Wer zehn Jahr gelebt hat, hat zehn Jahr Zeit gehabt, sterben zu lernen; und was man in zehn Jahren nicht lernt, das lernt man auch in zwanzig, in dreißig und mehrern nicht.

Alles, was ich werden können, muß ich durch das zeigen, was ich schon bin. Und was könnte ich, was wollte ich werden? Ein Held. — Wer ist ein Held? — O mein abwesender vortrefflicher Vater, itzt sei ganz in meiner Seele gegenwärtig! — Hast du mich nicht gelehrt, ein Held sei ein Mann, der höhere Güter kenne als das Leben? Ein Mann, der sein Leben dem Wohle des Staats geweihet; sich, den Einzeln, dem Wohle vieler? Ein Held sei ein Mann — Ein Mann? Also kein Jüngling, mein Vater? — Seltsame Frage! Gut, daß sie mein Vater nicht gehöret hat! Er müßte glauben, ich sähe es gern, wenn er N e i n darauf antwortete. — Wie alt muß die Fichte sein, die zum Maste dienen soll? Wie alt? Sie muß hoch genug und muß stark genug sein.

Jedes Ding, sagte der Weltweise, der mich erzog, ist vollkommen, wenn es seinen Zweck erfüllen kann. Ich kann meinen Zweck erfüllen, ich kann zum Besten des Staats sterben: ich bin vollkommen also, ich bin ein Mann. Ein Mann, ob ich gleich noch vor wenig Tagen ein Knabe war.

Welch Feuer tobt in meinen Adern? Welche Begeisterung befällt mich? Die Brust wird dem Herzen zu eng! — Geduld, mein Herz! Bald will ich dir Luft machen![28] Bald will ich dich deines einförmigen langweiligen Dienstes erlassen! Bald sollst du ruhen und lange ruhen —

Wer kömmt? Es ist Parmenio. — Geschwind entschlossen! — Was muß ich zu

---

[26] **Ausschlag:** here, *fig.*, favorable turn of events. Cf. **Ausschlag (Neigung) der Waage:** turn(ing) of the scale.

[27] **alles bedingen: alle möglichen Bedingungen stellen.**

[28] **Luft machen:** set free.

ihm sagen? Was muß ich durch ihn meinem Vater sagen lassen? — Recht! das muß ich sagen, das muß ich sagen lassen.

Fünfter Auftritt

PARMENIO. PHILOTAS

PHILOTAS. Tritt näher, Parmenio. — Nun? warum so schüchtern? So voller Scham? Wessen schämst du dich? Deiner oder meiner?

PARMENIO. Unser beider, Prinz.

PHILOTAS. Immer sprich, wie du denkst. Freilich, Parmenio, müssen wir beide nicht viel taugen, weil wir uns hier befinden. Hast du meine Geschichte bereits gehöret?

PARMENIO. Leider!

PHILOTAS. Und als du sie hörtest?

PARMENIO. Ich betaurete dich, ich bewunderte dich, ich verwünschte dich, ich weiß selbst nicht, was ich alles tat.

PHILOTAS. Ja, ja! Nun aber, da du doch wohl auch erfahren, daß das Unglück so groß nicht ist, weil gleich darauf Polytimet von den Unserigen — —

PARMENIO. Ja nun; nun möchte ich fast lachen. Ich finde, daß das Glück zu einem kleinen Schlage, den es uns versetzen will, oft erschrecklich weit ausholt. Man sollte glauben, es wolle uns zerschmettern, und hat uns am Ende nichts als eine Mücke auf der Stirne totgeschlagen.

PHILOTAS. Zur Sache! — Ich soll dich mit dem Herolde des Königs zu meinem Vater schicken.

PARMENIO. Gut! So wird deine Gefangenschaft der meinigen das Wort sprechen. Ohne die gute Nachricht, die ich ihm von dir bringen werde, und die eine freundliche Miene wohl wert ist, hätte ich mir eine ziemlich frostige von ihm versprechen müssen.

PHILOTAS. Nein, ehrlicher Parmenio; nun im Ernst! Mein Vater weiß es, daß dich der Feind verblutet und schon halb erstarrt von der Walstatt[29] aufgehoben. Laß prahlen, wer prahlen will; der ist leicht gefangen zu

nehmen, den der nahende Tod schon entwaffnet hat. — Wieviel Wunden hast du nun, alter Knecht? —

PARMENIO. O, davon konnte ich sonst eine lange Liste hersagen. Jetzt aber habe ich sie um ein gut Teil verkürzt.

PHILOTAS. Wie das?

PARMENIO. Ha! ich rechne nun nicht mehr die Glieder, an welchen ich verwundet bin; Zeit und Atem zu ersparen, zähle ich die, an welchen ich es nicht bin. — Kleinigkeiten bei dem allem! Wozu hat man die Knochen anders, als daß sich die feindlichen Eisen darauf schartig hauen sollen?

PHILOTAS. Das ist wacker! — Aber nun — was willst du meinem Vater sagen?

PARMENIO. Was ich sehe; daß du dich wohl befindest. Denn deine Wunde, wenn man mir anders die Wahrheit gesagt hat, —

PHILOTAS. Ist so gut als keine.

PARMENIO. Ein kleines liebes Andenken. Dergleichen uns ein inbrünstiges Mädchen in die Lippe beißt. Nicht wahr, Prinz?

PHILOTAS. Was weiß ich davon?

PARMENIO. Nu nu; kömmt Zeit, kömmt Erfahrung. — Ferner will ich deinem Vater sagen, was ich glaube, daß du wünschest — —

PHILOTAS. Und was ist das?

PARMENIO. Je eher, je lieber wieder bei ihm zu sein. Deine kindliche Sehnsucht, deine bange Ungeduld —

PHILOTAS. Mein Heimweh lieber gar! Schalk! warte, ich will dich anders denken lehren!

PARMENIO. Bei dem Himmel, das mußt du nicht! Mein lieber frühzeitiger Held, laß dir das sagen: Du bist noch Kind! Gib nicht zu, daß der rauhe Soldat das zärtliche Kind so bald in dir ersticke. Man möchte sonst von deinem Herzen nicht zum besten denken; man möchte deine Tapferkeit für angeborne Wildheit halten. Ich bin auch Vater, Vater eines einzigen Sohnes, der nur wenig älter als du, mit gleicher Hitze — du kennst ihn ja.

PHILOTAS. Ich kenne ihn. Er verspricht alles, was sein Vater geleistet hat.

PARMENIO. Aber wüßte ich, daß sich der junge Wildfang[30] nicht in allen Augenblicken, die ihm der Dienst frei läßt, nach seinem Vater sehnte und sich nicht so nach

---

[29] **Walstatt:** battlefield.

[30] **Wildfang:** headstrong person.

ihm sehnte, wie sich ein Lamm nach seiner Mutter sehnt, so möchte ich ihn gleich — siehst du! — nicht erzeugt haben. Itzt muß er mich noch mehr lieben als ehren. Mit dem Ehren werde ich mich so Zeit genug müssen begnügen lassen; wenn nämlich die Natur den Strom seiner Zärtlichkeit einen andern Weg leitet; wenn er selbst Vater wird. — Werde nicht ungehalten, Prinz.

PHILOTAS. Wer kann auf dich ungehalten werden? — Du hast recht! Sage meinem Vater alles, was du glaubest, daß ihm ein zärtlicher Sohn bei dieser Gelegenheit muß sagen lassen. Entschuldige meine jugendliche Unbedachtsamkeit, die ihn und sein Reich fast ins Verderben gestürzt hätte. Bitte ihn, mir meinen Fehler zu vergeben. Versichere ihn, daß ich ihn nie durch einen ähnlichen Fehler wieder daran erinnern will; daß ich alles tun will, damit er ihn auch vergessen kann. Beschwöre ihn —

PARMENIO. Laß mich nur machen! So etwas können wir Soldaten recht gut sagen. — Und besser als ein gelehrter Schwätzer; denn wir sagen es treuherziger. — Laß mich nur machen! Ich weiß schon alles. — Lebe wohl, Prinz, ich eile —

PHILOTAS. Verzieh![31]

PARMENIO. Nun? — Und welch feierliches Ansehen gibst du dir auf einmal?

PHILOTAS. Der Sohn hat dich abgefertigt, aber noch nicht der Prinz. — Jener mußte fühlen; dieser muß überlegen. Wie gern wollte der Sohn gleich itzt, wie gern wollte er noch eher als möglich wieder um seinen Vater, um seinen geliebten Vater sein; aber der Prinz — der Prinz kann nicht. — Höre!

PARMENIO. Der Prinz kann nicht?

PHILOTAS. Und will nicht.

PARMENIO. Will nicht?

PHILOTAS. Höre!

PARMENIO. Ich erstaune — —

PHILOTAS. Ich sage, du sollst hören und nicht erstaunen. Höre!

PARMENIO. Ich erstaune, weil ich höre! Es hat geblitzt, und ich erwarte den Schlag.[32] — Rede! — Aber, junger Prinz, keine zweite Übereilung! —

PHILOTAS. Aber, Soldat, kein Vernünfteln! — Höre! Ich habe meine Ursachen, nicht

eher ausgelöset zu sein als morgen. Nicht eher als morgen! Hörst du? — Sage also unserm Könige, daß er sich an die Eilfertigkeit des feindlichen Herolds nicht kehre.[33] Eine gewisse Bedenklichkeit, ein gewisser Anschlag[34] nötige den Philotas zu dieser Verzögerung. — Hast du mich verstanden?

PARMENIO. Nein!

PHILOTAS. Nicht? Verräter! —

PARMENIO. Sachte, Prinz! Ein Papagei versteht nicht, aber er behält, was man ihm vorsagt. Sei unbesorgt. Ich will deinem Vater alles wieder herplappern, was ich von dir höre.

PHILOTAS. Ha! ich untersagte dir, zu vernünfteln; und das verdreußt[35] dich. Aber wie bist denn du so verwöhnt? Haben dir alle deine Befehlshaber Gründe gesagt? —

PARMENIO. Alle, Prinz; ausgenommen die jungen.

PHILOTAS. Vortrefflich! Parmenio, wenn ich so empfindlich wäre als du — —

PARMENIO. Und doch kann nur derjenige meinen blinden Gehorsam heischen, dem die Erfahrung doppelte Augen gegeben.

PHILOTAS. Bald werde ich dich also um Verzeihung bitten müssen. — Nun wohl, ich bitte dich um Verzeihung, Parmenio. Murre nicht, Alter! Sei wieder gut, alter Vater! — Du bist freilich klüger als ich. Aber nicht die Klügsten allein haben die besten Einfälle. Gute Einfälle sind Geschenke des Glückes; und das Glück, weißt du wohl, beschenkt den Jüngling oft lieber als den Greis. Denn das Glück ist blind. Blind, Parmenio; stockblind gegen alles Verdienst. Wenn es das nicht wäre, müßtest du nicht schon lange Feldherr sein?

PARMENIO. Sieh, wie du zu schmeicheln weißt, Prinz — Aber im Vertrauen, lieber Prinz! Willst du mich nicht etwa bestechen? mit Schmeicheleien bestechen?

PHILOTAS. Ich schmeicheln! Und dich bestechen! Du bist der Mann, der sich bestechen läßt!

PARMENIO. Wenn du so fortfährest, so kann ich es werden. Schon traue ich mir selbst nicht mehr recht!

---

[31] **verzieh!:** wait!
[32] **Schlag (Donnerschlag):** thunderclap.
[33] **sich an etwas kehren:** sich um etwas kümmern.
[34] **Anschlag:** scheme; plan.
[35] **verdreußt:** verdrießt.

PHILOTAS. Was wollte ich also sagen? —
So einen guten Einfall nun, wollte ich sagen,
als das Glück oft in das albernste Gehirn
wirft, so einen habe auch ich itzo ertappt.
Bloß ertappt; von dem Meinigen ist nicht
das geringste dazu gekommen. Denn hätte
mein Verstand, meine Erfindungskraft einigen Anteil daran, würde ich ihn nicht gern
mit dir überlegen wollen? Aber so kann ich
ihn nicht mit dir überlegen; er verschwin-
det, wenn ich ihn mitteile; so zärtlich, so
fein ist er, ich getraue mir ihn nicht in
Worte zu kleiden; ich denke ihn nur, wie
mich der Philosoph Gott zu denken gelehrt
hat, und aufs höchste könnte ich dir nur
sagen, was er nicht ist. — Möglich zwar
genug, daß es im Grunde ein kindischer
Einfall ist; ein Einfall, den ich für einen
glücklichen Einfall halte, weil ich noch
keinen glücklichern gehabt habe. Aber mag
er doch; kann er nichts nützen, so kann er
doch auch nichts schaden. Das weiß ich
gewiß; es ist der unschädlichste Einfall von
der Welt; so unschädlich als — als ein
Gebet. Wirst du deswegen zu beten unterlassen, weil du nicht ganz gewiß weißt, ob
dir das Gebet helfen wird? — Verdirb mir
immer also meine Freude nicht, Parmenio,
ehrlicher Parmenio! Ich bitte dich, ich
umarme dich — Wenn du mich nur ein
klein wenig lieb hast — Willst du? Kann
ich mich darauf verlassen? Willst du machen,
daß ich erst morgen ausgewechselt werde?
Willst du?

PARMENIO. Ob ich will? Muß ich nicht?
muß ich nicht? — Höre, Prinz, wenn du
einmal König wirst, gib dich nicht mit dem
Befehlen ab. Befehlen ist ein unsicheres
Mittel, befolgt zu werden. Wem du etwas
recht Schweres aufzulegen hast, mit dem
mache es, wie du es itzt mit mir gemacht
hast, und wenn er dir alsdenn seinen Gehorsam verweigert — Unmöglich! Er kann dir
ihn nicht verweigern! Ich muß auch wissen,
was ein Mann verweigern kann.

PHILOTAS. Was Gehorsam? Was hat die
Freundschaft, die du mir erweisest, mit dem
Gehorsame zu tun? Willst du, mein Freund? —

PARMENIO. Hör auf! hör auf! Du hast
mich schon ganz. Ja doch, ich will alles. Ich
will es, ich will es deinem Vater sagen, daß er
dich erst morgen auslösen soll. Warum zwar
erst morgen, — das weiß ich nicht! Das

brauch ich nicht zu wissen! Das braucht auch
er nicht zu wissen. Genug, ich weiß, daß du
es willst. Und ich will alles, was du willst.
Willst du sonst nichts? Soll ich sonst nichts
tun? Soll ich für dich durchs Feuer rennen?
Mich für dich vom Felsen herabstürzen?
Befiehl nur, mein lieber kleiner Freund,
befiehl! Itzt tu ich dir alles! Sogar — sage
ein Wort, und ich will für dich ein Verbrechen, ein Bubenstück[36] begehen! Die Haut
schaudert mir zwar; aber doch, Prinz, wenn
du willst, ich will, ich will —

PHILOTAS. O mein bester, feuriger Freund!
O du — wie soll ich dich nennen? — du
Schöpfer meines künftigen Ruhmes! Dir
schwöre ich bei allem, was mir am heiligsten
ist, bei der Ehre meines Vaters, bei dem
Glücke seiner Waffen, bei der Wohlfahrt
seines Landes schwöre ich dir, nie in meinem
Leben diese deine Bereitwilligkeit, deinen
Eifer zu vergessen! Möchte ich ihn auch
würdig genug belohnen können! — Höret,
ihr Götter, meinen Schwur! — Und nun,
Parmenio, schwöre auch du! Schwöre mir,
dein Wort treulich zu halten. —

PARMENIO. Ich schwören? Ich bin zu alt
zum Schwören.

PHILOTAS. Und ich bin zu jung, dir ohne
Schwur zu trauen. Schwöre mir! Ich habe dir
bei meinem Vater geschworen, schwöre du
mir bei deinem Sohne. Du liebst ihn doch,
deinen Sohn? Du liebst ihn doch recht
herzlich?

PARMENIO. So herzlich wie dich! — Du
willst es, und ich schwöre. Ich schwöre dir
bei meinem einzigen Sohne, bei meinem
Blute, das in seinen Adern wallet, bei dem
Blute, das ich gern für deinen Vater geblutet,
das auch er gern für dich einst bluten wird,
bei diesem Blute schwöre ich dir, mein
Wort zu halten! Und wenn ich es nicht
halte, so falle mein Sohn in seiner ersten
Schlacht und erlebe sie nicht, die glorreichen
Tage deiner Regierung! — Höret, ihr
Götter, meinen Schwur —

PHILOTAS. Höret ihn noch nicht, ihr Götter! — Du hast mich zum besten, Alter. In
der ersten Schlacht fallen; meine Regierung
nicht erleben; ist das ein Unglück? Ist früh
sterben ein Unglück?

PARMENIO. Das sag ich nicht. Doch nur

---

[36] **Bubenstück:** Streich, Schandtat

deswegen, um dich auf dem Throne zu sehen, um dir zu dienen, möchte ich — was ich sonst durchaus nicht möchte — noch einmal jung werden. — Dein Vater ist gut; aber du wirst besser als er.

PHILOTAS. Kein Lob zum Nachteile meines Vaters! — Ändere deinen Schwur! Komm, ändere ihn so: Wenn du dein Wort nicht hältst, so möge dein Sohn ein Feiger, ein Nichtswürdiger werden; er möge, wenn er zwischen Tod und Schande zu wählen hat, die Schande wählen; er möge neunzig Jahr ein Spott der Weiber leben und noch im neunzigsten Jahre ungern sterben.

PARMENIO. Ich entsetze mich — doch schwöre ich: Das mög er! — Höret den gräßlichsten der Schwüre, ihr Götter!

PHILOTAS. Höret ihn! — Nun gut, nun kannst du gehen, Parmenio. Wir haben einander lange genug aufgehalten und fast zu viel Umstände über eine Kleinigkeit gemacht. Denn ist es nicht eine wahre Kleinigkeit, meinem Vater zu sagen, ihn zu überreden, daß er mich nicht eher als morgen auswechsle? Und wenn er ja die Ursache wissen will; wohl, so erdenke dir unter Weges eine Ursache.

PARMENIO. Das will ich auch! Ich habe zwar, so alt ich geworden bin, noch nie auf eine Unwahrheit gesonnen. Aber doch, dir zuliebe, Prinz — Laß mich nur; das Böse lernt sich auch noch im Alter. — Lebe wohl!

PHILOTAS. Umarme mich! — Geh!

Sechster Auftritt

PHILOTAS

Es soll so viele Betrieger[37] in der Welt geben, und das Betriegen ist doch so schwer, wenn es auch in der besten Absicht geschieht. — Habe ich mich nicht wenden und winden müssen! — Mache nur, guter Parmenio, daß mich mein Vater erst morgen auslöset, und er soll mich gar nicht auszulösen brauchen. — Nun habe ich Zeit genug gewonnen! — Zeit genug, mich in meinem Vorsatze zu bestärken — Zeit genug, die sichersten Mittel

zu wählen. — Mich in meinem Vorsatze zu bestärken? — Wehe mir, wenn ich dessen bedarf! — Standhaftigkeit des Alters, wenn du mein Teil nicht bist, o so stehe du mir bei, Hartnäckigkeit des Jünglings!

Ja, es bleibt dabei! es bleibt fest dabei! — Ich fühl es, ich werde ruhig, — ich bin ruhig! — Der du itzt dastehest, Philotas — (*indem er sich selbst betrachtet*) — Ha! es muß ein trefflicher, ein großer Anblick sein: ein Jüngling gestreckt auf den Boden, das Schwert in der Brust!

Das Schwert? Götter! o ich Elender! ich Ärmster! — Und itzt erst werde ich es gewahr? Ich habe kein Schwert; ich habe nichts! Es ward die Beute des Kriegers, der mich gefangen nahm. — Vielleicht hätte er es mir gelassen, aber Gold war der Heft.[38] — Unseliges Gold, bist du denn immer das Verderben der Tugend?

Kein Schwert? Ich kein Schwert? — Götter, barmherzige Götter, dies einzige schenket mir! Mächtige Götter, die ihr Erde und Himmel erschaffen, ihr könntet mir kein Schwert schaffen — wenn ihr wolltet? — Was ist nun mein großer, schimmernder Entschluß? Ich werde mir selbst ein bitteres Gelächter —

Und da kömmt er auch schon wieder, der König. — Still! Wenn ich das Kind spielte? — Dieser Gedanke verspricht etwas. — Ja! Vielleicht bin ich glücklich —

Siebenter Auftritt

ARIDÄUS. PHILOTAS

ARIDÄUS. Nun sind die Boten fort, mein Prinz. Sie sind auf den schnellsten Pferden abgegangen, und das Hauptlager deines Vaters ist so nahe, daß wir in wenig Stunden Antwort erhalten können.

PHILOTAS. Du bist also, König, wohl sehr ungeduldig, deinen Sohn wieder zu umarmen?

ARIDÄUS. Wird es dein Vater weniger sein, dich wieder an seine Brust zu drücken? — Laß mich aber, liebster Prinz, deine Gesellschaft genießen. In ihr wird mir die Zeit

---

[37] **Betrieger**: Betrüger.

[38] **der Heft** (**das Heft**): haft; handle.

schneller verschwinden, und vielleicht, daß es auch sonst glückliche Folgen hat, wenn wir uns näher kennen. Liebenswürdige Kinder sind schon oft die Mittelspersonen zwischen veruneinigten Vätern gewesen. Folge mir also in mein Zelt, wo die besten meiner Befehlshaber deiner warten. Sie brennen vor Begierde, dich zu sehen und zu bewundern.

PHILOTAS. Männer, König, müssen kein Kind bewundern. Laß mich also nur immer hier. Scham und Ärgernis würden mich eine sehr einfältige Person spielen lassen. Und was deine Unterredung mit mir anbelangt — da seh ich vollends nicht, was daraus kommen könnte. Ich weiß weiter nichts, als daß du und mein Vater in Krieg verwickelt sind; und das Recht — das Recht, glaub ich, ist auf seiten meines Vaters. Das glaub ich, König, und will es nun einmal glauben — wenn du mir auch das Gegenteil unwidersprechlich zeigen könntest. Ich bin Sohn und Soldat und habe weiter keine Einsicht als die Einsicht meines Vaters und meines Feldherrn.

ARIDÄUS. Prinz, es zeiget einen großen Verstand, seinen Verstand so zu verleugnen. Doch tut es mir leid, daß ich mich also auch vor dir nicht soll rechtfertigen können. — Unseliger Krieg! —

PHILOTAS. Jawohl, unseliger Krieg! — Und wehe seinem Urheber!

ARIDÄUS. Prinz! Prinz! Erinnere dich, daß dein Vater das Schwert zuerst gezogen. Ich mag in deine Verwünschung nicht einstimmen. Er hatte sich übereilt, er war zu argwöhnisch —

PHILOTAS. Nun ja; mein Vater hat das Schwert zuerst gezogen. Aber entsteht die Feuersbrunst erst dann, wenn die lichte Flamme durch das Dach schlägt? Wo ist das geduldige, gallose,[39] unempfindliche Geschöpf,[40] das durch unaufhörliches Nekken[41] nicht zu erbittern wäre? — Bedenke, — denn du zwingst mich mit aller Gewalt von Dingen zu reden, die mir nicht zukommen — bedenke, welch eine stolze, verächtliche Antwort du ihm erteiltest, als er — Doch

du sollst mich nicht zwingen; ich will nicht davon sprechen! Unsere Schuld und Unschuld sind unendlicher Mißdeutungen, unendlicher Beschönigungen fähig. Nur dem untrieglichen[42] Auge der Götter erscheinen wir, wie wir sind; nur das kann uns richten. Die Götter aber, du weißt es König, sprechen ihr Urteil durch das Schwert des Tapfersten. Laß uns den blutigen Spruch aushören![43] Warum wollen wir uns kleinmütig von diesem höchsten Gerichte wieder zu den niedrigern wenden? Sind unsere Fäuste schon so müde, daß die geschmeidige Zunge sie ablösen müsse?

ARIDÄUS. Prinz, ich höre dich mit Erstaunen —

PHILOTAS. Ach! — Auch ein Weib kann man mit Erstaunen hören!

ARIDÄUS. Mit Erstaunen, Prinz, und nicht ohne Jammer! — Dich hat das Schicksal zur Krone bestimmt, dich! — Dir will es die Glückseligkeit eines ganzen mächtigen, edeln Volkes anvertrauen, dir! — Welch eine schreckliche Zukunft enthüllt sich mir! Du wirst dein Volk mit Lorbeern und mit Elend überhäufen. Du wirst mehr Siege als glückliche Untertanen zählen. — Wohl mir, daß meine Tage in die deinigen nicht reichen werden! Aber wehe meinem Sohne, meinem redlichen Sohne! Du wirst es ihm schwerlich vergönnen, den Harnisch abzulegen —

PHILOTAS. Beruhige den Vater, o König! Ich werde deinem Sohne weit mehr vergönnen! weit mehr!

ARIDÄUS. Weit mehr? Erkläre dich —

PHILOTAS. Habe ich ein Rätsel gesprochen? — O verlange nicht, König, daß ein Jüngling, wie ich, alles mit Bedachte und Absichten sprechen soll. — Ich wollte nur sagen: Die Frucht ist oft ganz anders, als die Blüte sie verspricht. Ein weibischer Prinz, hat mich die Geschichte gelehret, ward oft ein kriegerischer König. Könnte mit mir sich nicht das Gegenteil zutragen? — Oder vielleicht war auch dieses meine Meinung, daß ich noch einen weiten und gefährlichen Weg zum Throne habe. Wer weiß, ob die Götter mich ihn vollenden lassen? — Und laß mich ihn nicht vollenden, Vater der

---

[39] **gallos (gallenlos):** without gall; i.e., without rancor.
[40] **Geschöpf:** creature.
[41] **Necken:** provocation.

[42] **untrieglich (untrüglich):** infallible.
[43] **aushören: abwarten.**

Götter und Menschen, wenn du in der Zukunft mich als einen Verschwender des Kostbarsten, was du mir anvertrauet, des Blutes meiner Untertanen, siehest!

ARIDÄUS. Ja, Prinz; was ist ein König, wenn er kein Vater ist! Was ist ein Held ohne Menschenliebe! Nun erkenne ich auch diese in dir und bin wieder ganz dein Freund! — Aber komm, komm; wir müssen hier nicht allein bleiben. Wir sind einer dem andern zu ernsthaft. Folge mir!

PHILOTAS. Verzeih, König —

ARIDÄUS. Weigere dich nicht!

PHILOTAS. So wie ich bin, mich vor vielen sehen zu lassen? — —

ARIDÄUS. Warum nicht?

PHILOTAS. Ich kann nicht, König; ich kann nicht.

ARIDÄUS. Und die Ursache?

PHILOTAS. O die Ursache! — Sie würde dich zum Lachen bewegen.

ARIDÄUS. Um so viel lieber laß sie mich hören. Ich bin ein Mensch und weine und lache gern.

PHILOTAS. Nun, so lache denn! — Sieh, König, ich habe kein Schwert, und ich möchte nicht gern ohne dieses Kennzeichen des Soldaten unter Soldaten erscheinen.

ARIDÄUS. Mein Lachen wird zur Freude. Ich habe in voraus hierauf gedacht, und du wirst sogleich befriediget werden. Strato hat Befehl, dir dein Schwert wieder zu schaffen.

PHILOTAS. Also laß uns ihn hier erwarten.

ARIDÄUS. Und alsdenn begleitest du mich doch? —

PHILOTAS. Alsdenn werde ich dir auf dem Fuße nachfolgen.

ARIDÄUS. Gewünscht! da kömmt er! Nun, Strato —

Achter Auftritt

STRATO mit einem Schwert in der Hand.
ARIDÄUS. PHILOTAS

STRATO. König, ich kam zu dem Soldaten, der den Prinzen gefangen genommen, und forderte des Prinzen Schwert in deinem Namen von ihm zurück. Aber höre, wie edel sich der Soldat weigerte. „Der König", sprach er, „muß mir das Schwert nicht nehmen. Es ist ein gutes Schwert, und ich werde es für ihn brauchen. Auch muß ich ein Andenken von dieser meiner Tat behalten. Bei den Göttern, sie war keine von meinen geringsten! Der Prinz ist ein kleiner Dämon. Vielleicht aber ist es euch nur um den kostbaren Heft zu tun" — Und hiermit, ehe ich es verhindern konnte, hatte seine starke Hand den Heft abgewunden und warf mir ihn verächtlich zu Füßen. — „Da ist er!" fuhr er fort. „Was kümmert mich euer Gold?"

ARIDÄUS. O Strato, mache mir den Mann wieder gut! —

STRATO. Ich tat es. Und hier ist eines von deinen Schwertern!

ARIDÄUS. Gib her! — Willst du es, Prinz, für das deinige annehmen?

PHILOTAS. Laß sehen! — Ha! (*Beiseite*) Habet Dank, ihr Götter! (*Indem er es lange und ernsthaft betrachtet*) — Ein Schwert!

STRATO. Habe ich nicht gut gewählet, Prinz?

ARIDÄUS. Was findest du deiner tiefsinnigen Aufmerksamkeit so wert daran?

PHILOTAS. Daß es ein Schwert ist! — (*Indem er wieder zu sich kömmt*) Und ein schönes Schwert! Ich werde bei diesem Tausche nichts verlieren. — Ein Schwert!

ARIDÄUS. Du zitterst, Prinz.

PHILOTAS. Vor Freuden! — Ein wenig zu kurz scheinet es mir bei alledem. Aber was zu kurz? Ein Schritt näher auf den Feind ersetzt, was ihm an Eisen abgehet. — Liebes Schwert! Welch eine schöne Sache ist ein Schwert, zum Spiele und zum Gebrauche! Ich habe nie mit etwas andern gespielt. —

ARIDÄUS (*zum Strato*). O der wunderbaren Vermischung von Kind und Held!

PHILOTAS (*beiseite*). Liebes Schwert! Wer doch bald mit dir allein wäre! — Aber, gewagt!

ARIDÄUS. Nun lege das Schwert an, Prinz, und folge mir!

PHILOTAS. Sogleich! — Doch seinen Freund und sein Schwert muß man nicht bloß von außen kennen. (*Er zieht es, und Strato tritt zwischen ihn und den König*)

STRATO. Ich verstehe mich mehr auf den Stahl als auf die Arbeit. Glaube mir, Prinz, der Stahl ist gut. Der König hat in seinen männlichen Jahren mehr als einen Helm damit gespalten.

PHILOTAS. So stark werde ich nicht werden! Immerhin! — Tritt mir nicht so nahe, Strato.

STRATO. Warum nicht?

PHILOTAS. So! (*Indem er zurückspringt und mit dem Schwerte einen Streich durch die Luft tut*) Es hat den Zug, wie es ihn haben muß.

ARIDÄUS. Prinz, schone deines verwundeten Armes! Du wirst dich erhitzen! —

PHILOTAS. Woran erinnerst du mich, König? — An mein Unglück; nein, an meine Schande! Ich ward verwundet und gefangen! Ja! Aber ich will es nie wieder werden! Bei diesem meinem Schwerte, ich will es nie wieder werden! Nein, mein Vater, nein! Heut sparet dir ein Wunder das schimpfliche Lösegeld für deinen Sohn; künftig spar es dir sein Tod! Sein gewisser Tod, wenn er sich wieder umringt siehet! — Wieder umringt? — Entsetzen! Ich bin es! Ich bin umringt! Was nun? Gefährte! Freunde! Brüder! Wo seid ihr? Alle tot? Überall Feinde? — Überall! — Hier durch, Philotas! Ha! Nimm das, Verwegner! — Und du das! — Und du das! (*Um sich hauend*)

STRATO. Prinz, was geschieht dir? Fasse dich! (*Geht auf ihn zu*)

PHILOTAS (*sich von ihm entfernend*). Auch du, Strato? auch du? — O Feind, sei großmütig! Töte mich! Nimm mich nicht gefangen! — Nein, ich gebe mich nicht gefangen! Und wenn ihr alle Stratos wäret, die ihr mich umringet! Doch will ich mich gegen euch alle, gegen eine Welt will ich mich wehren! Tut euer Bestes, Feinde! — Aber ihr wollt nicht? Ihr wollt mich nicht töten, Grausame? Ihr wollt mich mit Gewalt lebendig? — Ich lache nur! Mich lebendig gefangen? Mich? — Eher will ich dieses mein Schwert, will ich — in diese meine Brust — eher — (*Er durchsticht sich*)

ARIDÄUS. Götter! Strato!

STRATO. König!

PHILOTAS. Das wollt ich! (*Zurücksinkend*)

ARIDÄUS. Halt ihn, Strato! — Hülfe, dem Prinzen zur Hülfe! — Prinz, welche wütende Schwermut —

PHILOTAS. Vergib mir, König! ich habe dir einen tödlichern Streich versetzt als mir!

— Ich sterbe; und bald werden beruhigte Länder die Frucht meines Todes genießen. — Dein Sohn, König, ist gefangen; und der Sohn meines Vaters ist frei —

ARIDÄUS. Was hör ich?

STRATO. So war es Vorsatz, Prinz? — Aber als unser Gefangener hattest du kein Recht über dich selbst.

PHILOTAS. Sage das nicht, Strato! — Sollte die Freiheit zu sterben, die uns die Götter in allen Umständen des Lebens gelassen haben, sollte diese ein Mensch dem andern verkümmern[44] können? —

STRATO. O König! — Das Schrecken hat ihn versteinert! — König!

ARIDÄUS. Wer ruft?

STRATO. König!

ARIDÄUS. Schweig!

STRATO. Der Krieg ist aus, König!

ARIDÄUS. Aus? Das leugst[45] du, Strato! — Der Krieg ist nicht aus, Prinz! — Stirb nur! stirb! Aber nimm das mit, nimm den quälenden Gedanken mit: Als ein wahrer unerfahrner Knabe hast du geglaubt, daß die Väter alle von einer Art, alle von der weichlichen, weibischen Art deines Vaters sind. — Sie sind es nicht alle! Ich bin es nicht! Was liegt mir an meinem Sohne? Und denkst du, daß er nicht ebensowohl zum Besten seines Vaters sterben kann, als du zum Besten des deinigen? — Er sterbe! Auch sein Tod erspare mir das schimpfliche Lösegeld! — Strato! ich bin nun verwaiset, ich armer Mann! — Du hast einen Sohn; er sei der meinige! — Denn einen Sohn muß man doch haben. — Glücklicher Strato!

PHILOTAS. Noch lebt auch dein Sohn, König! Und wird leben! Ich hör es!

ARIDÄUS. Lebt er noch? — So muß ich ihn wiederhaben. Stirb du nur! Ich will ihn doch wiederhaben! Und für dich! — Oder ich will deinem toten Körper so viel Unehre, so viel Schmach erzeigen lassen! — Ich will ihn —

PHILOTAS. Den toten Körper! — Wenn du dich rächen willst, König, so erwecke ihn wieder! —

ARIDÄUS. Ach! — Wo gerat ich hin!

PHILOTAS. Du taurest[46] mich! — Lebe

---

[44] **verkümmern:** here, forbid; curtail.

[45] **das leugst (lügst) du:** you lie about this.

[46] **du taurest (dauerst) mich:** I pity you.

wohl, Strato! Dort, wo alle tugendhafte Freunde, und alle tapfere Glieder e i n e s seligen Staates sind, im Elysium sehen wir uns wieder! — Auch wir, König, sehen uns wieder —

ARIDÄUS. Und versöhnt! — Prinz! —

PHILOTAS. O, so empfanget meine triumphierende Seele, ihr Götter; und dein Opfer, Göttin des Friedens! —

ARIDÄUS. Höre mich, Prinz! —

STRATO. Er stirbt! — Bin ich ein Verräter, König, wenn ich deinen Feind beweine? Ich kann mich nicht halten. Ein wunderbarer Jüngling!

ARIDÄUS. Beweine ihn nur! — Auch ich! — Komm! Ich muß meinen Sohn wiederhaben! Aber rede mir nicht ein, wenn ich ihn zu teuer erkaufe! — Umsonst haben wir Ströme Bluts vergossen; umsonst Länder erobert. Da zieht er mit unserer Beute davon, der größere Sieger! — Komm! Schaffe mir meinen Sohn! Und wenn ich ihn habe, will ich nicht mehr König sein. Glaubt ihr Menschen, daß man es nicht satt wird? —

(*Gehen ab*)

Bibliography

Texts and Translations

"Hildebrandslied," ed. Georg Baesecke in *Das Hildebrandslied: Eine geschichtliche Einführung für Laien* (1948), with facsimiles and notes on the text;
> trans. Gotthold Bötticher and Karl Kinzel, *Denkmäler der älteren deutschen Literatur,* Vol. I (1903).

Heliand, ed. Otto Behagel, rev. W. Mitzka (1958), trans. Karl Simrock (latest ed., 1959): Reproduces alliterative verse form of original.

Otfried von Weißenburg, *Evangelienbuch,* ed. Otto Erdman, rev. E. Schröder and L. Wolff (1962), trans. Johannes Seidler in Gotthold Bötticher and Karl Kinzel, *Denkmäler der älteren deutschen Literatur,* Vol. II, Part iii (1900).

Ludwigslied, ed. Wilhelm Braune, *Althochdeutsches Lesebuch* (1st ed., 1875, frequently reprinted). Has excellent notes.

Hartmann von Aue, *Gregorius,* ed. Hermann Paul, rev. L. Wolff (9th ed., 1959).
> *Iwein,* ed. Karl Lachmann, rev. L. Wolff (6th ed., 1959), trans. Wolff Graf von Baudissin (1845). Retains verse form of original.

Wolfram von Eschenbach, *Parzival,* ed. Karl Lachmann, rev. E. Hartl (1952), trans. Wilhelm Hertz (1898). In verse form of original but frequently paraphrased rather than translated. More accurate prose translation by Wilhelm Stapel (1950).

Gottfried von Straßburg, *Tristan und Isot,* ed. Friedrich Ranke (1930, latest reprint 1964), trans. Wilhelm Hertz (1877). In verse of original but has numerous omissions and paraphrases.

Minnesang (Friedrich von Hausen, Heinrich von Morungen, Reinmar der alte) in *Des Minnesangs Frühling,* ed. Karl Lachmann, latest revision by Carl von Kraus (1953). Contains texts of all lyric poetry earlier than that of Walther von der Vogelweide.

Heinrich von Morungen, ed. Carl von Kraus (1925). Useful notes.

Walther von der Vogelweide, ed. Carl von Kraus (12th ed., 1959);
> ed. Wilhelms Wilmanns, rev. V. Michels, 2 vols. (1916, 1924). Has excellent notes.

Die Lieder Walthers von der Vogelweide unter Beifügung erhaltener und erschlossener Melodien, ed. Friedrich Maurer, 2 vols. (1955, 1956). Divides poems by types, arranges in (editor's) chronological order, gives music when available.

Walther von der Vogelweide, ed. Peter Wapnewski (2nd ed., 1966). Selection, facing translation, good notes.

Neidhart von Reuental, ed. Eduard Wießner (1955).

Nibelungenlied, ed. Karl Bartsch, rev. H. de Boor (1959), trans. Karl Simrock (1827, frequently reprinted). A minor classic. Most spirited if not most accurate translation.

Konrad von Würzburg, *Herzmaere,* ed. Eduard Schröder in *Konrad von Würzburg, Kleinere Dichtungen* (2nd ed., 1930).

Wernher der Gartenaere, *Meier Helmbrecht,* ed. Friedrich Panzer, rev. K. Ruh (1960), trans. Karl Pannier (1876).

Johann von Tepl, *Der Ackermann aus Böhmen,* ed. Keith Spalding (1950), M. O'C. Walshe (1951), Willi Krogmann (1954).

Das Donaueschinger Passionsspiel, ed. Eduard Hartl in *Deutsche Literatur in Entwicklungsreihen,* Drama des Mittelalters, Vol. IV (1935).

Reinecke Fuchs, ed. Friedrich Prien (1887), trans. Karl Simrock (1845).

Further Suggestions for Reading and Study

Blackall, E.A., *The Emergence of German as a Literary Language* (1959).

Cantor, Norman F., *Medieval History* (1963). Good general account.

De Boor, Helmut, *Geschichte der deutschen Literatur,* Vol. I (1949, reprinted 1955), Vol II (1953, 7th ed., 1964), Vol. III, Part i (1962). Excellent objective presentation of history of literature to 1350.

Deutsche Literaturgeschichte in Grundzügen, ed. B. Boesch (1946). By a group of Swiss scholars; compact and sober.

Ehrismann, Gustav, *Geschichte der deutschen Literatur bis zum Ausgang des Mittelalters,* 2 vols., the second in three parts (1918–1935). Indispensable for details of content of works and for bibliography to date of publication. Critical judgments outdated.

Fisher, John H., ed., *The Medieval Literature of Western Europe,* (1966). Present state of research in all medieval literatures with titles of important secondary literature since 1930.

Haskins, Charles H., *The Renaissance of the Twelfth Century* (1927).

Jackson, William T. H., *The Literature of the Middle Ages* (1960). Study of major works and cultural background. Bibliographical suggestions.

Robertson, J.G., *A History of German Literature,* rev. Edna Purdie (1959).

Rose, Ernst, *A History of German Literature* (1960). Compact account by an American scholar.

Schwietering, *Die deutsche Dichtung des Mittelalters* (1940). Sensitive interpretation.

Stammler, Wolfgang, and Karl Langosch, *Die deutsche Literatur des Mittelalters: Verfasserlexikon,* 5 vols. (1933–55). Basic information on all authors and works. Brief bibliographies.

———, *Von der Mystik zum Barock* (2nd ed., 1952). Excellent account of late medieval and Renaissance literature. Detailed bibliographical notes.

Old High German Period

General

Bostock, J. Knight, *A Handbook on Old High German Literature* (1955). Factual. Good summary of research.

Fuchs, A., *Les Débuts de la littérature allemande du VIIIe au XIIe siècle* (1952).

Klein, Karl Kurt, *Die Anfänge der deutschen Literatur* (1954).

Wolff, Ludwig, *Das deutsche Schrifttum bis zum Ausgang des Mittelalters: Von der germanischen Welt bis zum christlich-deutschen Mittelalter,* Vol. I (to 1158; 2nd ed., 1951).

Hildebrandslied

Baesecke, Georg, *Das Hildebrandslied: Eine geschichtliche Einleitung für Laien* (1945). Text, facsimiles, attempt to show that language is Langobardic.

Braune, Wilhelm, *Althochdeutsches Lesebuch* (1st ed., 1875, frequently reprinted). Excellent notes on the language of the poem.

Rosenfeld, Hellmut, "Das Hildebrandslied, die Indogermanischen Vater-Sohn-Kampf-Dichtungen und das Problem ihrer Verwandschaft," *DVLG* (1952).

Heliand

Baesecke, Georg, "Fulda und die altsächsischen Bibelepen," *Niederdeutsche Mitteilungen* (1948).

Drögereit, Richard, *Werden und der Heliand* (1951). Poem written in Werden.

Grosch, Elisabeth, "Das Gottes- und Menschenbild im Heliand," *BGDSL* (1950). Stresses formal theological elements.

Rupp, Heinz, "Leid und Sünde im *Heliand* und in Otfrieds *Evangelienbuch,*" (1957).

Otfrieds Evangelienbuch

Gössler, Hulda, "Das Christusbild in Otfrieds *Evangelienbuch* und im *Heliand,*" *ZDP* (1935).

Neumann, Friedrich, "Otfrieds Auffassung vom Versbau," *BGDSL* (1957).

Rupp, Heinz, "Otfried von Weissenburg und die spätantike Bibeldichtung," *Wirkendes Wort* (1957).

Ludwigslied

Naumann, Hans, *Das Ludwigslied und die verwandten lateinischen Gedichte,* diss. (1932).

High Middle Ages

General

Curtius, Ernst Robert, *Europäische Literatur und lateinisches Mittelater* (1st ed., 1948). One of the most influential of all books on medieval literary study.

Glunz, H., *Die Literarästhetik des Mittelalters* (1937). Large part on *Parzival.*

Kuhn, Hugo, "Zum neuen Bild vom Mittelalter," *DVLG* (1950).

Naumann, Hans, *Deutsche Kultur im Zeitalter des Rittertums* (1938). Largely artistic. Old fashioned in judgments.

Neumann, H., "Der Streit um das ritterliche Tugendsystem," *Festschrift für Karl Helm* (1951). Excellent critique of various views.

Ranke, Friedrich, *Gott, Welt und Humanität in der*

deutschen Dichtung des Mittelalters (1953). Relation between secular and religious aspects.

Hartmann von Aue

Eggers, Hans J., *Symmetrie und Proportionen epischen Erzählens: Studien zur Kunstform Hartmanns von Aue* (1956). Most significant structural study.

Kuhn, Hugo, "Hartmann von Aue als Dichter," *Deutschunterricht* (1952). Excellent evaluation of poetical qualities.

Nobel, Hildegard, "Schuld und Sühne in Hartmanns *Gregorius* und in der frühscholastischen Theologie," *ZDP* (1957).

Sacker, Hugh, "An Interpretation of Hartmann's *Iwein*," *GR* (1961). Original in its assessment of "courtly values."

Schieb, Gabriele, "Schuld und Sühne in Hartmanns *Gregorius*," *BGDSL* (1950).

Sparnaay, Hendrik, *Hartmann von Aue: Studien zu einer Biographie*, 2 vols. (1933, 1938).

———, "Hartmann von Aue," in *Arthurian Literature in the Middle Ages* ed. R.S. Loomis (1959).

Wapnewski, Peter, *Hartmann von Aue*, Sammlung Metzler (1962). Best introduction with useful bibliography.

Wolfram von Eschenbach

Adolf, Helen, "New Light on Oriental Sources for Wolfram's *Parzival* and other Grail Romances," *PMLA* (1947).

Bumke, Joachim, *Wolfram von Eschenbach*, Sammlung Metzler (1964). Best introduction.

Eggers, Hans J., "Strukturprobleme mittelalterlicher Epik, dargestellt am *Parzival* Wolframs von Eschenbach," *Euphorion* (1953).

Fourquet, Jean, *Wolfram von Eschenbach et le Conte del Graal* (1938). Establishes Chrétien de Troyes as Wolfram's main source.

Kahane, Henry and Renée, *The Krater and the Grail* (1965). Argues Byzantine and Arab influences.

Katann, Oskar, "Einflüsse des Katharentums auf Wolframs Parzival," *Wirkendes Wort* (1957/8).

Klein, Karl Kurt, "Wolframs Selbstverteidigung," *ZDA* (1954). Contrasts knight (Wolfram) with writer (Gottfried).

Maurer, Friedrich, "Parzivals Sünden," *DVLG* (1950). Distinguishes theological from human lapses.

Ringbom, Lars Ivar, *Graltempel und Gralparadies* (1951). Finds Grail as pearl in temple in Iran.

Sacker, Hugh, *An Introduction to Wolfram's Parzival* (1963). Summarizes interpretations and problems.

Schröder, Wilhelm J., "Vindaere wilder maere: Zum Literaturstreit zwischen Gottfried und Wolfram," *BGDSL* (1958). Stylistic dispute only.

Schwietering, Julius, "Parzivals Schuld," *ZDA* (1944).

Springer, Otto, "Wolfram von Eschenbach" in *Arthurian Literature in the Middle Ages*, ed. R.S. Loomis (1959). Excellent study.

Wapnewski, Peter, *Wolframs Parzival: Studien zu Religiosität und Form* (1955). Patristic influences.

Gottfried von Straßburg

Bindschedler, Maria, "Gottfried von Straßburg und die höfische Ethik," *BGDSL* (1954). Importance of chivalric standards.

De Boor, Helmut, "Die Grundauffassung von Gottfrieds *Tristan*," *DVLG* (1940). Sees lovers as martyrs.

Gruenter, Rainer, "Das wunnecliche Tal," *Euphorion* (1962). Best study of ideal landscape in the poem.

Jackson, William T.H., "Tristan the Artist in Gottfried's Poem," *PMLA* (1962). Intellectual aspects of the poem.

———, "Gottfried von Straßburg" in *Arthurian Literature in the Middle Ages*, ed. R.S. Loomis (1959).

Schwietering, Julius, *Der Tristan Gottfrieds von Straßburg und die Bernhardinische Mystik* (1943). Basic study of influences of mysticism.

Speckenbach, Klaus, *Studien zum Begriff "edelez herze" im Tristan Gottfrieds von Straßburg* (1965). Summarizes earlier opinions and offers thesis that term is connected with mysticism.

Tax, Petrus, *Wort, Sinnbild, Zahl im Tristanroman* (1961). Useful stylistic and interpretative study.

Weber, Gottfried, *Gottfrieds von Straßburg Tristan und die Krise des hochmittelalterlichen Weltbildes um 1200*, 2 vols. (1953). Detailed study of theological influences. Views summarized in *ZDA* (1948/50). Poem is seen as essentially anti-religious.

Minnesang

Gennrich, Friedrich, *Grundriß einer Formlehre des mittelalterlichen Liedes* (1932).

———, *Troubadours, trouvères, Minne- und Meistergesang* (1951). Studies of structure and music.

Hatto, A.T., and R.J. Taylor, "Recent Work on the Arithmetical Principle in Medieval Poetry," *MLR* (1951).

Jungbluth, Günther, "'Min herze und min lip diu wellent scheiden': zu Friedrich von Hausen, 47,9," *Euphorion* (1953).

Kolb, Herbert, *Der Begriff der Minne und das Entstehen der höfischen Lyrik* (1958). Best examination of theoretical principles but weighted for theological influence, against Arabic theory.

Kraus, Carl von, *Untersuchungen zum Minnesangs Frühling* (1939). Notes on text criticism and interpretation.

Moret, André, *Les Débuts du lyrisme en Allemagne des origines à 1350* (1951). Best summary of theories of origins, lives of poets.

Schwietering, Julius, "Der Liederzyklus Heinrichs von Morungen," *ZDA* (1948/50). Poems are arranged in a specific order, showing progress of love.

Walther von der Vogelweide

Böhm, Hans, *Walther von der Vogelweide. Minne, Reich, Gott* (2nd ed., 1949). Popular study.

Halbach, Kurt, *Walther von der Vogelweide,* Sammlung Metzler (1965). Unusually detailed for this series.

Huisman, Johannes H., *Neue Wege zur dichterischen und musikalischen Technik Walthers von der Vogelweide* (1950). Arithmetical principles.

Kralik, Dietrich, *Die Elegie Walthers von der Vogelweide* (1952).

Kraus, Carl von, *Walther von der Vogelweide. Untersuchungen* (1935). Notes on text criticism and interpretation.

Maurer, Friedrich, *Die politischen Lieder Walthers von der Vogelweide* (1954). Sees political *Sprüche* as strophes of political *Lieder.*

Schirmer, Karl-Heinz, *Die Strophik Walthers von der Vogelweide* (1956).

Zitzmann, Rudolf, "Der Ordo-Gedanke des mittelalterlichen Weltbildes und Walthers Sprüche im ersten Reichston," *DVLG* (1951). Sees political views based on contemporary theology.

Neidhart von Reuental

Hatto, A.T., and R.J. Taylor, *The Songs of Neidhart von Reuental* (1958). Selections of the melodies and study of their importance for meter.

Schröder, Friedrich R., "Die tanzlustige Alte," *GRM* (1951). Antecedents of a common character in the poems.

Wießner, Edmund, *Kommentar zu Neidharts Liedern* (1954).

——, *Wörterbuch zu Neidharts Liedern* (1954). Indispensable.

Winkler, Karl, *Neidhart von Reuental. Leben, Liebe, Lieder* (1956). Stresses evidence of local topography in poems.

Nibelungenlied

Beyschlag, Siegfried, "Die Funktion der epischen Vorausdeutung im Aufbau des Nibelungenliedes," *BGDSL* (1954).

De Boor, Helmut, *Das Attilabild in Geschichte, Legende und heroischer Dichtung* (1932). East and West have different pictures of Attila.

Dürrenmatt, Nelly, *Das Nibelungenlied im Kreis der höfischen Dichtung* (1945).

Heusler, Andreas, *Nibelungensage und Nibelungenlied* (3rd ed., 1929). Most widely accepted theory of origins of poem.

Kuhn, Hugo, "Kriemhilts Hort und Rache," in *Festschrift P. Kluckhohn und H. Schneider* (1948). Condemns demand for treasure at end of poem as inartistic.

Panzer, Friedrich, *Das Nibelungenlied* (1955). Strong on sources and analogs, weak on literary aspects.

——, "Der Weg der Nibelungen," *Festschrift K. Helm* (1951). On author's knowledge of topography.

Stroheker, K.F., "Studien zu den historisch-geographischen Grundlagen der Nibelungendichtung," *DVLG* (1958).

Thorp, Mary, *The Study of the Nibelungenlied* (1940). Thorough account of scholarship 1795–1937.

Tonnelat, Ernest, *La Chanson des Nibelungen. Etude sur la composition et la formation du poème épique* (1926). Early attempt to show non-Germanic influences.

Weber, Gottfried, *Das Nibelungenlied* (1963). First real attempt at evaluation of character, motivation, moral background.

——, and Werner Hoffmann, *Das Nibelungenlied,* Sammlung Metzler (1961). Sound introduction.

Konrad von Würzburg

Moret, André, *Un Artiste méconnu: Conrad de Wurzebourg* (1932). Only full study.

Later Medieval Literature

General

Fischer, H., "Neue Forschungen zur Dichtung des Spätmittelalters, 1250–1500," *DVLG* (1957).

———, "Probleme und Aufgaben deutscher Literaturforschung zum deutschen Spätmittelalter," *GRM* (1959).

Huizinga, Johan, *The Waning of the Middle Ages* (1924). Brilliant study of cultural forces.

Rosenfeld, H., "Die Literatur des ausgehenden Mittelalters in soziologischer Sicht," *Wirkendes Wort* (1955).

———, "Die Entwicklung der Standessatire im Mittelalter," *ZDP* (1951).

Wernher der Gartenaere

Fischer, Hans, "Gestaltungsschichten in *Meier Helmbrecht*," *BGDSL* (1957). Story essentially that of Prodigal Son.

Gough, C.E., "The Homeland of Wernher der Gartenaere," *Proceedings of the Leeds Philosophical Society* (1953).

Jackson, William T.H., "The Composition of *Meier Helmbrecht*," *MLQ* (1957).

Martini, Fritz, "Der *Meier Helmbrecht* des Wernher der Gartenaere und das mittelalterliche Bauerntum," *Zeitschrift für Deutschkunde* (1937). Basic study of realistic elements.

Nordmeyer, George, "Structure and Design in Wernher's *Meier Helmbrecht*," *PMLA* (1952). Stresses comic elements.

Schiffmann, Konrad, "Die Heimat des Helmbrecht," *BGDSL* (1940).

Wirtz, Erika, "Meier Helmbrecht's Cap," *MLR* (1954/5). Detailed study of motifs on cap.

Johannes von Tepl

Bäuml, Franz H., "*Der Ackermann aus Böhmen* and the Destiny of Man," *GR* (1958). Useful summary of views on relation of God to man in work.

———, *Rhetorical Devices and Structure in the "Ackermann aus Böhmen"* (1960). Detailed study of structure and interpretation.

Burdach, Konrad, and Alois Bernt, *Vom Mittelalter zur Reformation* (1917). Contains the text and massive, often confusing annotation.

Hübner, Arthur, "Deutsches Mittelalter und italienische Renaissance im *Ackermann aus Böhmen*," *Zeitschrift für Deutschkunde* (1937). Arguments whether it is a medieval or Renaissance work.

Schirokauer, Arno, "Der Ackermann aus Böhmen und das Renaissanceproblem," *MDU* (1949).

Donaueschinger Passionsspiel

Creizenach, Wilhelm, *Geschichte des neueren Dramas* (1911). Still standard for factual information.

Hartl, Eduard, *Drama des Mittelalters*, Vol. IV (1942) in *Deutsche Literatur in Entwicklungsreihen*. Best text. Good introduction.

Kindermann, Heinz, *Theatergeschichte Europas*, Vol. II (1959). On staging and presentation.

Michael, Wolfgang, "Die Bedeutung des Wortes 'Figur' im geistlichen Drama Deutschlands," *GR* (1946). Interpretation as allegory.

Prosser, Eleanor, *Drama and Religion in the English Mystery Plays* (1961). Importance of religious elements, equally valid for German plays.

Tashiro, Tom, "The Donaueschinger Passion Play: A Study of the Theme and Structure of Spiritual Blindness," *GR* (1962).

Reinecke Fuchs

Flinn, John, *Le Roman de Renart dans la littérature française et dans les littératures étrangères du moyen âge*, 2 vols. (1963). Attempts to show connections with contemporary events and people.

Jackson, William T.H., *The Literature of the Middle Ages* (1960). Summary of development of beast epic.

Jauss, Hans R., *Untersuchungen zur mittelalterlichen Tierdichtung* (1959). Shows that there is a central theme in each work.

The Age of the Reformation

General

Holborn, H., *A History of Modern Germany: The Reformation* (1959). Indispensable.

Lortz, J. *Die Reformation in Deutschland*, 2 vols. (1962[4]). Luther and his age, seen by an erudite Roman Catholic historian.

Luther

Bainton, R., *Here I Stand: A Life of Martin Luther* (1950). Valuable introduction.

Berger, A.E., *Martin Luther in kulturgeschichtlicher Darstellung*, 3 vols. (1895–1921).

Bluhm, Heinz S., *Martin Luther, Creative Translator* (1966). Translation as a work of art. Impact on the English Bible.

Holl, K., *Luther* (1928[3]). Initiated the Luther research of the 20th century.

Lilje, H., *Martin Luther: eine Bildmonographie* (1964).

Ritter, G., *Luther, His Life and Work* (1963). Essential short account by leading German historian.

Sachs

Geiger, E., *Hans Sachs als Dichter in seinen Fast-nachtspielen* (1903).
Geiger, E., *Der Meistergesang des Hans Sachs* (1956).
Genée, R., *Hans Sachs und seine Zeit* (1894).
Strich F., "Hans Sachs und die Renaissance" in *Festschrift für Hans R. Hahnloser,* ed. E.J. Beer (1961), 361–72.

Volksbücher/Faust

Benz, R., *Geschichte und Aesthetik des deutschen Volksbuchs* (1924²). Romantic defense of the chap book.
Puknat, S.B., "The Volksbuch and the Intellectual Temper of the Fifteenth and Sixteenth Centuries," *JEGP* (1948), pp. 357–64. Important.
Szövérffy, J., "Das Volksbuch: Geschichte und Problematik," *Deutschunterricht* (1962), 5–28.
———, "Volkserzählung und Volksbuch," *Fabula* (1957/8), 3–18. Essential distinctions.
Butler, E.M., *The Fortunes of Faust* (1952). From the Volksbuch to Valéry. Witty and extremely erudite.
Jantz, H., "An Elizabethan Statement on the Origin of the German Faust Book, with a Note on Marlowe's Sources," *JEGP* (1952), 137–53.
The Sources of the Faust Tradition from Simon Magus to Lessing, eds. P.M. Palmer and R.P. More (1936).

The Age of the Baroque

The Concept

Hatzfeld, H. "Use and Misuse of 'Baroque' as a Critical Term in Literary History," *Univ. of Toronto Quarterly* (1962), 180–200.
Wellek, R., "The Concept of Baroque in Literary Scholarship," in *Concepts of Criticism* (1963), 69–127.

General

Aus der Welt des Barock, eds. A. Druckenmüller and Hermann Leins (1957). On cultural features of the age.
Faber du Faur, C. von, *German Baroque Literature* (1958). Catalogue of a great collection. A literary history and a work of art.
Hankamer, P., *Deutsche Gegenreformation und deutsches Barock* (1964³). Rather traditional in ideas and language.

Müller, Günther, *Deutsche Dichtung von der Renaissance bis zum Ausgang des Barock* (1927). Thorough and richly illustrated.
Newald, R., "Die deutsche Literatur vom Späthumanismus zur Empfindsamkeit 1570–1750," in *Geschichte der deutschen Literatur*, Vol. 5 (1951). Rich materials but descriptive rather than critical.

Forms and Problems

Alewyn, R., *Vorbarocker Klassizismus und griechische Tragödie* (1962²). Important study on stages of development.
Benjamin, Walter, *Ursprung des deutschen Trauerspiels* (1963). Rather difficult reading but philosophically productive.
Kayser, Wolfgang, *Die Klangmalerei bei Harsdörffer* (1932).
Lunding, E., *Das schlesische Kunstdrama* (1940). Important.
Spahr, Blake L., *The Archives of the Pegnesischer Blumenorden* (1960).
Waterhouse, G., *The Literary Relations of England and Germany in the Seventeenth Century* (1914).

Silesius

Ellinger, G., *Angelus Silesius, Ein Lebensbild* (1927). Standard monograph.
Sammons, J.L., *Angelus Silesius* (1968). Thorough introduction by young American scholar.

Gryphius

Faber du Faur, C. von, "Andreas Gryphius, der Rebell," *PMLA* (1959), 14–27.
Gundolf, F., *Andreas Gryphius* (1927).
Heckmann, H., *Elemente des barocken Trauerspiels: Am Beispiel des 'Papinian' von Andreas Gryphius* (1959).
Ryder, F.G., "Individualization in Baroque Dramatic Verse: a Suggestion Based on Gryphius' 'Papinianus,'" *JEGP* (1962), 604–15.
Szyrocki, Marian, *Andreas Gryphius: sein Leben und Werk* (1964).

Grimmelshausen

Hayens, K.C., *Grimmelshausen* (1932). Introductory.
Hiller, Robert L., "The Sutler's Cart and the Lump of Gold," *GR* (1964), 137–44.
Rohrbach, Günter, *Figur und Charakter: Strukturuntersuchungen zu Grimmelshausens Simplicissimus* (1959).

Scholte, J.H., *Der Simplicissimus und sein Dichter* (1950). Considerations of biographical and documentary materials.

Fleming

Pyritz, H.W., *Paul Flemings Liebeslyrik: Zur Geschichte des Petrarkismus* (1963). Fundamental study.

Hofmann von Hofmannswaldau

Ibel, R., *Hofmann von Hofmannswaldau* (1928).

Ryder, F.G., "The Design of Hofmannswaldau's 'Vergänglichkeit der Schönheit,'" *Monatshefte* (1959), 97–102.

Casper v. Lohenstein

Gillespie, G.E.P., *Daniel Casper von Lohenstein's Historical Tragedies* (1965).

Katz, M.O., *Zur Weltanschauung D. Caspers v. Lohensteins* (1933).

Kuhlmann

Beare, R.L., "Quirinus Kuhlmann: The Religious Apprenticeship," *PMLA* (1953), 828–62.

Bock, C.V., *Quirinus Kuhlmann als Dichter* (1957).

Dietze, W., *Quirinus Kuhlmann: Ketzer und Poet* (1963). More informative on sociological than on aesthetic aspects.

Faber du Faur, C. von, "Die Keimzelle des 'Kühlpsalter,'" *JEGP* (1947), 150–63.

Spahr, Blake L., "Quirin Kuhlmann: The Jena Years," *MLN* (1957), 605–10.

Vordtriede, W. (ed.), *Quirinus Kuhlmann: Aus dem Kühlpsalter*. Selected readings, with an epilogue 1966.

The Age of the Enlightenment

General

Hettner, H.J.T., *Geschichte der deutschen Literatur im 18. Jahrhundert,* ed. E. Boucke (Leipzig 1929, Berlin 1961/62). A work of classical importance.

Newald, R., "Von Klopstock bis zu Goethes Tod: 1750–1832," in *Geschichte der deutschen Literatur,* Vol. 6/1 (1957). On Klopstock and Lessing, pp. 15–76.

Schneider, F.J., "Die deutsche Dichtung vom Ausgang des Barocks bis zum Beginn des Klassizismus: 1700–1785," in *Epochen der deutschen Literatur,* Vol. 3 (1924). Concrete and unusually well written.

Wolff, H.M., *Die Weltanschauung der deutschen Aufklärung* (1949).

Gottsched and the Swiss

Arlt, G.O., *Acquaintance with Older German Literature in the 18th Century,* (1931).

Bräker, J., *Der erzieherische Gehalt in J.J. Breitingers "Critischer Dichtkunst"* (1950).

Braitmaier, F., *Geschichte der poetischen Theorie und Kritik von den Diskursen der Maler bis auf Lessing* (1888/9). Dry but useful.

Danzel, T.W., *Gottsched und seine Zeit* (1855[2]). Extensive excerpts from contemporary correspondence.

Pelz, A., *Die vier Auflagen von Gottscheds 'Critischer Dichtkunst' in vergleichender Betrachtung,* Diss. Breslau (1929).

Reichel, E., *Gottsched* (1908/12). A solemn defense of the learned professor.

Schöffler, H., *Das literarische Zürich 1700–1750* (1925). Admirable sociological view of intellectual life.

Servaes, F., *Die Poetik Gottscheds und der Schweizer* (1887).

Wehrli, M., *Johann Jakob Bodmer und die Geschichte der Literatur* (1936). A first-rate critical study.

Anacreontic Poetry

Merker, E., "Anakreontik," in *Reallexikon der deutschen Literaturgeschichte,* ed. W. Kohlschmidt and W. Mohr, Vol. 1 (1958[2]). Instructive.

Anger, A., "Landschaftsstil des Rokoko," *Euphorion* (1957), 151–91. Sophisticated and highly useful.

Anger, A., "Literarisches Rokoko," in *Realienbücher für Germanisten, Reihe D* (1962). Essential research tool.

Ansfeld, F., *Die deutsche anakreontische Dichtung des 18. Jahrhunderts* (1907). Themes and motifs.

Klemperer, V., "Der Begriff Rokoko," *Jahrbuch für Philologie* (1925), 444–67.

Lees, J., *The Anacreontic Poetry of Germany in the 18th Century* (1911).

Stamm, I.S., "German Literary Rococo," *GR* (1961), 230–41. Relation to the fine arts and music.

Klopstock

Beissner, F., *Klopstocks Ode 'Der Zürchersee'* (1949).

Betteridge, H.T., "Young Klopstock," *Orbis Litterarum* (1960), 3–35.

Kaiser, G., *Klopstock, Religion und Dichtung* (1963). Important recent study.

Langen, A., *Der Wortschatz des deutschen Pietismus* (1954).

Muncker, F., *Friedrich Klopstock: Geschichte seines Lebens und seiner Schriften* (1888). A monument of positivist scholarship.

Ritschl, A., *Geschichte des Pietismus* (1880/86). Fundamental study of religious developments.

Rychner, M., "Zum 150. Todestage Klopstocks," in *Bedachte und bezeugte Welt* (1962). Thoughts of the late Swiss critic.

Schleiden, K.A., *Klopstocks Dichtungstheorie als Beitrag zur Geschichte der deutschen Poetik* (1954).

Vietor, K., *Geschichte der deutschen Ode* (1923). Essential view of formal problems and achievements.

Lessing

Garland, H.B., *Lessing, the Founder of Modern German Literature* (1937). Useful introduction.

Jolles, Matthijs, "Lessing's Conception of History," *MPh* (1945/6), 175–91.

Kettner, Gustav, *Lessings Dramen im Lichte ihrer und unserer Zeit* (1904). Detailed explication. Highly useful.

Kommerell, M., *Lessing und Aristoteles* (1940). Best study of Lessing's theoretical thought.

Leeuwe, H.H.J. de, "Lessings 'Philotas' eine Deutung," *Neophilologus* (1963), 34–40.

Mann, O., *Lessing: Sein und Leistung* (1949). A recent conservative view.

Mehring, F., *Die Lessing-Legende: eine Rettung* (1893). The first Marxist critic attacks the patriotic university professors of his time. Some relevance to Philotas discussion.

Nolte, O.F., "Lessing and the Bourgeois Drama," *JEGP* (1932), 66–83.

Rilla, Paul, *Lessing und sein Zeitalter* (1960). An intelligent view from East Berlin.

Schmidt, Erich, *Lessing: Geschichte seines Lebens und seiner Schriften,* 2 vols. (1884/92). Fundamental historical study.

Ulmer, B., "Another Look at Lessing's Philotas," *Studies in Germanic Languages and Literatures* (1963), 35–42.